D1348610

THE WORKS OF
THOMAS MANTON

The Works of
THOMAS MANTON

VOLUME 1

THE BANNER OF TRUTH TRUST

THE BANNER OF TRUTH TRUST
3 Murrayfield Road, Edinburgh EH12 6EL
P.O. Box 621, Carlisle, Pennsylvania 17013, USA

*

This edition first published by James Nisbet & Co 1870
First Banner of Truth Trust reprint 1993
ISBN 0 85151 648 3

*

Printed in Great Britain by
The Bath Press, Avon

THE COMPLETE WORKS

OF

THOMAS MANTON, D.D.

With Memoir of the Author
BY THE REV. WILLIAM HARRIS, D.D.

And an Essay
BY THE REV. J. C. RYLE, B.A.,
VICAR OF STRADBROKE, SUFFOLK.

VOLUME I.

CONTAINING

MEMOIR BY REV. DR HARRIS.
A PRACTICAL EXPOSITION OF THE LORD'S PRAYER.
ON CHRIST'S TEMPTATION AND TRANSFIGURATION.
ON REDEMPTION BY CHRIST AND HIS ETERNAL EXISTENCE.

LONDON:
JAMES NISBET & CO., 21 BERNERS STREET.
1870.

Mr Ryle's Essay will form the Prefatory matter to Vol. II.—Ed.

CONTENTS.

SOME MEMOIRS OF THE LIFE AND CHARACTER

OF THE

REVEREND AND LEARNED

THOMAS MANTON, D.D.

By WILLIAM HARRIS, D.D.[1]

THOUGH the lives of great and excellent persons have been always reckoned a useful piece of history, and scarce anything is read with greater entertainment, yet it has often happened that they have been undertaken with great disadvantage, and not till the best means of collecting proper materials, either by the neglect of their friends, or the distant publication of their works, have been in a great measure lost. So it was in the Life of the famous Mr Richard Hooker, which was not undertaken by Dr Walton till near seventy years after his death. By this means there is reason to fear some memorable passages were past recovery, after all inquiry, in the lately-published account of that extraordinary person, Mr John Howe, by Dr Calamy. And thus it has proved in the present case. One cannot but wonder that the life of a person of so great worth and general esteem, and who bore so great a part in the public affairs of his own time, was never attempted while his most intimate friends, and they who were best acquainted with the most remarkable passages concerning him, were yet alive. It has been thought, however, not improper upon this occasion to retrieve that error as far as may be, and lay together in one view what can be now gathered from some of his relations yet living, from his own writings, and the memoirs of those who published his works and were contemporary with him. And it is to be hoped that this short and imperfect account, drawn up under disadvantage indeed, but with strict regard to truth, may do some justice to the memory of so excellent a person and the interest he espoused, and give some entertainment and instruction to the world.

Dr THOMAS MANTON was born in the year 1620, at Lawrence-Lydiat, in the county of Somerset. His father and both his grandfathers were ministers. He had his school-learning at the free school of Tiverton,

---

[1] This Memoir was originally prefixed to a second edition of Manton's works, of which only the first volume appears to have been published.—ED.

in Devonshire. He run through his grammatical studies, and was qualified to enter upon academical learning at the age of fourteen, which was very unusual in those days, when the methods of school-learning were more difficult and tedious, and youth designed for the university were commonly detained to eighteen or nineteen years of age. But his parents, either judging him too young, or loth to part with him so soon, kept him some time longer before he was sent to Oxford. He was placed in Wadham College in the year 1635; and, after preparatory studies, he applied himself to divinity, which was the work his heart was chiefly set upon, and which he designed to make the business of his life.[1] By a course of unwearied diligence, joined with great intellectual endowments, he was early qualified for the work of the ministry, and took orders much sooner than was usual, and than he himself approved upon maturer thoughts and after he had more experience. There is a remarkable passage to this purpose in his Exposition of James, in which he expresses the humble acknowledgment of his fault, and which has proved monitory and affecting to others. He delivered it with tears in his eyes. It is on the 19th verse of the first chapter, ' Be slow to speak.' ' I remember,' says he, ' my faults this day; I cannot excuse myself from much of crime and sin in it. I have been in the ministry these ten years, and yet not fully completed the thirtieth year of my age—the Lord forgive my rash intrusion.' He was ordained by the excellent Joseph Hall, then Bishop of Exeter, afterwards removed to Norwich, who took particular notice of him upon that occasion, and expressed his apprehensions ' that he would prove an extraordinary person.'[2] The times when he first entered into the ministry were full of trouble, the king and parliament being at open variance, and hostilities breaking out on both sides. He was confined to Exeter when it was besieged by the king's forces. After its surrender he went to Lime. He preached his first sermon at Sowton, near Exeter, on those words, ' Judge not, that ye be not judged,' a copy of which is now in the hands of a relation. It was some time before he had any fixed place for the exercise of his ministry. He first began at Culliton, in Devonshire, where he preached a weekly lecture, and was much attended and respected. There he had an occasion of reforming the disorderly practice of those who, after the example of a leading gentleman, fell to their private devotion in the congregation after the public worship was begun. At his coming to London, he was soon taken notice of as a young man of excellent

---

[1] Anthony Wood ('Athenæ Oxon.,' p. 600) says he was accounted in his college a hot-headed person—which is as remote from what was known to be the true character of Dr Manton as it is agreeable to his own. If he had not been a hot-headed writer, he would not everywhere appear so full of prejudice and spite, nor have thrown out so many rash and injudicious reflections upon the best men of the Established Church who had any degree of temper and moderation, as well as upon the Nonconformists, and reserved his kindness and tenderness to the Popishly-affected and Nonjurors.

[2] Mr Wood, *ubi supra*, says he became a preacher, though not in holy orders, at Culliton, in Devonshire; and afterwards, that he took orders at Westminster, from Thomas, Bishop of Galloway, in the beginning of 1660. He seems to suppose that he had preached without orders all that time, when he was certainly ordained by Bishop Hall before he was twenty. And though he was ordained only to Deacon's orders, he never would submit to any other ordination. His judgment was, that he was properly ordained to the ministerial office, and that no power on earth had any right to divide and parcel it out.

parts and growing hopes. Here he neither wanted work, nor will to perform it, for he was in the vigour of his youth, and applied himself to it with great diligence and pleasure, for which he was remarkable all his life. About this time he married Mrs Morgan, who was a daughter of a genteel family of Manston, in Sidbury, Devon, and not Mr Obadiah Sedgwick's daughter, whom he succeeded in Covent Garden, as Mr Wood mistakes it. She was a meek and pious woman, and though of a weak and tender constitution, outlived the doctor twenty years, who was naturally hale and strong.

He had not been above three years in the ministry, before he had his first settlement, which was at Stoke Newington, in Middlesex, near London. He was presented to this living by the Honourable Colonel Popham, in whom he had a most worthy and kind patron;[1] and was highly honoured and esteemed by him and his religious lady. It was here he began and finished his excellent exposition of the Epistle of James on his week-day lectures, which he carried on without an assistant, besides his constant preaching both parts of the Lord's-day. This exposition has been thought by good judges to be one of the best models of expounding Scripture, and to have joined together with the greatest judgment the critical explication and practical observations upon the several parts. Some time after, he went through the Epistle of Jude. This, though excellent in its kind, is not so strictly expository, but more in a sermon way, which he says was more in compliance with the desires of others than with his own judgment. This was almost finished while he continued at Newington, and was dedicated to the Lady Popham. It is worth observing with what respect and sense of obligation he treats the colonel and his lady, and—so contrary to the modern modish way of address—with what faithfulness at the same time he warns them of their temptations and danger. I shall only give the reader a taste of his spirit and expression in his younger years. 'By this inscription,' says he to the colonel, 'the book is become not only mine, but yours. You own the truths to which I have witnessed; and it will be sad for our account in the day of the Lord, if, after such solemn professions, you and I should be found in a carnal and unregenerate state. Make it your work to honour him who has advanced you. The differences of high and low, rich and poor, are only calculated for the present world, and cannot outlive time. The grave takes away the civil differences; skulls wear no wreaths and marks of honour; the small and great are there; the servant is free from his master. So at the day of judgment I saw the dead, both great and small, stand before the Lord. None can be exempt from standing before the bar of Christ. When the civil difference ceases, the moral takes place; the distinction then is, good and bad, not great and small. Then you will see that there is no birth like that to be born again of the Spirit, no tenure like an interest in the covenant, no estate like the inheritance of the saints, no magistracy like that whereby we sit at Christ's right hand judging angels and men. How will the faces of great men gather blackness, who now flourish in the pomp and splendour of an outward estate, but then shall become the scorn of God, and of saints and angels—

[1] See 'Dedication to the Epistle of James.'

and these holy ones shall come forth and say, " Lo, this is the man who made not God his strength, but trusted in the abundance of his riches, and strengthened himself in his wickedness!" Wealth and power are of no use in that day, unless it be to aggravate and increase the judgment. Many who are now so despicable and obscure that they are lost in the tale and count of the world, shall then be taken into the arms of Christ; he will not be ashamed to confess them before men and before his Father—" Father, this is one of mine." So also in heaven there are none poor; all the vessels of glory are filled up. If there is any difference in degree, the foundation of it is laid in grace, not in greatness. Greatness hath nothing greater than a heart to be willing, and a power to be able, to do good. Then it is a fair resemblance of that perfection which is in God, who differs from man in nothing so much as in the eternity of his being, the infiniteness of his power, and the unweariedness of his love and goodness. It is a fond ambition of men to sever these things. We all affect to be great, but not good; and would be as gods, not in holiness, but in power. Nothing has cost the creature dearer : it turned angels into devils, and Adam out of Paradise. You will bear with my plainness and freedom—other addresses would neither be comely in me nor pleasing to you. Our work is not to flatter greatness, but, in the Scripture sense, not in the humour of the age, to level mountains.'

In his epistle to Lady Popham he tells her, ' It is a lovely conjunction when goodness and greatness meet together. Persons of estate and respect have more temptations and hindrances than others, but greater obligations to own God. The great Landlord of the world expects rent from every cottage, but a larger revenue from great houses. Now usually it falls out so, that they who hold the greatest farms pay the least rent. Never is God more neglected and dishonoured than in great men's houses, and in the very face of all his bounty. If religion chance to get in there, it is soon worn out again. Though vice lives long in families, and runs in the blood from father to son, it is a rare case to see strictness of religion carried on for three or four descents. It was the honour of Abraham's house, that from father to son, for a long while, they were heirs of the same promise. But where is there such a succession in the families of our gentry? The causes of which he reduces to " plenty, ill-governed," which disposes to vice, as a rank soil is apt to breed weeds, and to a certain " false bravery of spirit," which thinks strictness inglorious, and the power of religion a mean thing; and to " the marriage of children into carnal families," wherein they consult rather with the greatness of their houses than the continuance of Christ's interest in their line and posterity. How careful are they that they match in their own rank for blood and estate ! Should they not be as careful for religion also ? All this is spoken, madam, to quicken you to greater care in your relation, and that you may settle a standing interest for Christ, so hopefully already begun in your house and family. Though your course of life be more private and confined, yet you have your service. The Scripture speaks of women gaining upon their husbands, seasoning the children, encouraging servants in the ways of godliness, especially of their own sex. It is said of Esther (chap. iv. 16), " I also and my maidens will fast like-

wise." These maidens were either Jews (and then it shows what servants should be taken into a nearer attendance, such as savour of
religion), or else, which is more probable, such as she had instructed
in the true religion; for they were appointed her by the eunuch, and
were before instructed in the court fashions (chap. ii. 9). But that
did not satisfy. She takes them to instruct them in the knowledge of
the true God; and, it seems, in her apartments had opportunity of
religious commerce with them in the worship of God.'

He continued seven years at Newington, and possessed the general
respect of his parishioners, though there were several persons of different sentiments from himself. Being generally esteemed an excellent preacher, he was often employed in that work in London on the
week-days; and other weighty affairs sometimes called for his attendance there. The custom of preaching to the sons of the clergy began
in his time. Dr Hall (afterwards Bishop of Chester, and son of the
famous Bishop Hall of Norwich) preached the first sermon to them,
as Mr Manton did the second. The sermon is printed at the end of
the third volume, in folio, upon Ps. cii. 28. He was several times,
though not so often as some others, called to preach before the Parliament, and received their order in course for printing his sermons;
though, I think, he never published but two of them himself. Some
of them are printed among his posthumous works. In all of them the
wisdom and judgment of Dr Manton, in the suitableness of the subject
to the circumstances of the times, and the prudent management of it
to the best advantage, are very visible; particularly after he had given
his testimony among the London ministers against the death of the
king, he was appointed to preach before the Parliament. His text was,
Deut. xxxiii. 4, 5, 'Moses commanded us a law, even the inheritance
of the congregation of Jacob; and he was king in Jeshurun, when the
heads of the people and the tribes of Israel were gathered together.'
When they were highly offended at this sermon, some of his friends
advised him to withdraw, for some in the House talked of sending him
to the Tower, but he never flinched, and their heat abated.

His removal from Newington to Covent Garden was occasioned by
the great age of Mr Obadiah Sedgwick, who was now disabled for his
work. The people growing uneasy, several worthy persons were proposed for the place, but Mr Sedgwick would not be prevailed with to
resign till Mr Manton was mentioned, and to that he readily yielded.
He was presented to the living, with great respect and satisfaction, by
his noble and generous patron, the Earl, afterwards Duke, of Bedford,
who greatly esteemed him to his dying day, and sent him, as a mark
of his respect, a key of the garden which then belonged to Bedford
House, either to walk in it at his leisure, or as a convenient passage
to the Strand. He had in this place a numerous congregation of persons of great note and rank, of which number was oftentimes the
excellent Archbishop Usher, who used to say of him, that he was one
of the 'best preachers in England,' and that he was a 'voluminous
preacher;' not that he was ever long and tedious, but because he had
the art of reducing the substance of whole volumes into a narrow compass, and representing it to great advantage. Mr Charnock used to
say of him, that he was the 'best collector of sense of the age.'

Dr Manton had a great respect for Mr Christopher Love, who was beheaded in the year 1651, by the then Parliament, for being concerned with some others in sending remittances abroad to support the royal family in their distress. I am informed that he attended him on the scaffold at Tower Hill, and that Mr Love, as a token of his respect, gave him his cloak. The doctor was resolved to preach his funeral sermon, which the Government understanding, signified their displeasure, and the soldiers threatened to shoot him; but that did not daunt him, for he preached at St Lawrence Jury, where Mr Love had been minister, to a numerous congregation, though not graced with the pulpit cloth, or having the convenience of a cushion. He was too wise to lay himself open to the rage of his enemies; but the sermon was printed afterwards, under the title of 'The Saint's Triumph over Death.' Lord Clarendon [1] speaks of Mr Love in terms of great disrespect, upon the report of a sermon he preached when he was a young man, at Uxbridge, at the time of the treaty. How far he might fail in his prudence in so nice a circumstance, I am not able to say; but it appears, from the accounts of them who well knew him, and by the resentment his death generally met with at that time, as well as by several volumes of sermons printed after his death, that he was a person of worth and esteem. It was certainly a rash and ungenerous censure in the noble author, of one he knew so little at that time, and who afterwards lost his life for serving the royal family.

The Government afterwards, for what reason it was best known to themselves, seemed at least to have an esteem for him, though he was far from courting their favour. When Cromwell took on him the Protectorship, in the year 1653, the very morning the ceremony was to be performed, a messenger came to Dr Manton, to acquaint him that he must immediately come to Whitehall. The doctor asked him the occasion: he told him he should know that when he came there. The Protector himself, without any previous notice, told him what he was to do, that is, to pray upon that occasion.[2] The doctor laboured all he could to be excused, and told him it was a work of that nature which required some time to consider and prepare for it. The Protector replied that he knew he was not at a loss to perform the service he expected from him; and opening his study-door, he put him in with his hand, and bid him consider there, which was not above half an hour. The doctor employed that time in looking over his books, which, he said, was a noble collection. It was at this time, as I am informed, that the worthy Judge Rookesby had the misfortune, by the fall of a scaffold, to break his thigh, by which he always went lame, and was obliged to have one constantly to lead him. He was an upright judge, and a wise and religious person; he was constant to his principles, and always attended the preaching of good old Mr Stretton to his dying day.

About this time the doctor was made one of the chaplains to the Protector; and appointed one of the committee to examine persons

---

[1] History, in folio, vol. ii., pp. 445, 446 ; vol. iii., pp. 337, 338.
[2] Whitlock, who was present, says, 'He recommended His Highness, the Parliament, the Council, and forces, and the whole Government and people of the three nations, to the blessing and protection of God.'—*Memorials*, p. 661.

who were to be admitted to the ministry, or inducted into livings; as
he was afterwards appointed one in 1659, by an act of that Parliament in which the secluded members were restored. And though
this proved troublesome to him, considering his constant employment
in preaching, yet he has been heard to say, that he very seldom
absented himself from that service, that he might, to his power, keep
matters from running into extremes; for there were many in those
days, as well as in these, who were forward to run into the ministry,
and had more zeal than knowledge; and perhaps sometimes persons
of worth liable to be discouraged. There is a pretty remarkable
instance of his kind respect to a grave and sober person, who appeared
before them (cap in hand, no doubt), and was little taken notice of,
but by himself: he, seeing him stand, called for a chair, in respect to
his years and appearance; at which some of the commissioners were
displeased. This person appeared to be of a Christian and ingenuous
temper; for, after the Restoration, he was preferred to an Irish
bishopric, perhaps an archbishopric; for he used to give in charge
to Bishop Worth, whose occasions often called him over to England,
that on his first coming to London he should visit Dr Manton, and
give his service to him, and let him know, that if he was molested in
his preaching in England, he should be welcome in Ireland, and have
liberty to preach in any part of his diocese undisturbed. What
interest he had in the Protector he never employed for any sordid
ends of his own, who might have had anything from him, but purely
to do what service he could to others: he never refused to apply to
him for anything in which he could serve another, though it was not
always with success. He was once desired by some of the principal
Royalists to use his interest in him for sparing Dr Hewit's life, who
was condemned for being in a plot against the then Government;
which he did accordingly. The Protector told him, if Dr Hewit had
shown himself an ingenuous person, and would have owned what he
knew was his share in the design against him, he would have spared
his life; but he was, he said, of so obstinate a temper, that he resolved
he should die. The Protector convinced Dr Manton before he parted
that he knew how far he was engaged in that plot.

While he was minister at Covent Garden, he was invited to preach
before the Lord Mayor and Court of Aldermen, and the Companies
of the city, upon some public occasion, at St Paul's. The doctor
chose some difficult subject, in which he had opportunity of displaying
his judgment and learning, and appearing to the best advantage. He
was heard with the admiration and applause of the more intelligent
part of the audience; and was invited to dine with my Lord Mayor,
and received public thanks for his performance. But upon his return
in the evening to Covent Garden, a poor man following him, gently
plucked him by the sleeve of his gown, and asked him if he were the
gentleman who had preached that day before my Lord Mayor. He
replied, he was. 'Sir,' says he, 'I came with earnest desires after
the word of God, and hopes of getting some good to my soul, but I
was greatly disappointed; for I could not understand a great deal of
what you said; you were quite above me.' The doctor replied, with
tears in his eyes, 'Friend, if I did not give you a sermon, you have

given me one; and, by the grace of God, I will never play the fool to preach before my Lord Mayor in such a manner again.' Upon a public fast at Covent Garden church, for the persecuted Protestants in the valleys of Piedmont, Dr Manton had got Mr Baxter, who happened to be then in London, and Dr Wilkins, who was afterwards Bishop of Chester, to assist him. Mr Baxter opened the day, and preached upon the words of the prophet Amos, chap. vi. 6: 'But they are not grieved for the afflictions of Joseph.' He, after his manner, took a great compass, and grasped the whole subject. Dr Manton succeeded him, and had chosen the same text: he was obliged often to refer to the former discourse, and to say, every now and then, 'As it has been observed by my reverend brother.' Dr Wilkins sat cruelly uneasy, and reckoned that between them both he should have nothing left to say; for he had got the same text too. He insisted upon being excused, but Dr Manton obliged him to go up into the pulpit; and by an ingenious artifice, he succeeded admirably. Before he named his text, he prepared the audience by expressing the fears of their narrow-spiritedness, and little concern for the interest of God in the world: 'For,' says he, 'without any knowledge or design of our own, we have all three been directed to the same words.' Which, spoken with the majesty and authority peculiar to the presence and spirit of that excellent person, so awakened the attention, and disposed the minds of the people, that he was heard with more regard, and was thought to do more good than both the former, though he had scarce a single thought throughout the sermon distinct from the other two.

In the year 1660 he was very instrumental, with many other Presbyterian divines, in the restoration of King Charles II. It must be owned, by impartial judges, that the Presbyterian party, who had the greatest influence in the nation at that time, had the greatest share in that change; nor could all the Episcopal party in the three kingdoms have once put it into motion, or brought it to any effect, without them, though they had all the favour and preferment bestowed upon them afterwards; which, whether it were more just or politic, more agreeable to the laws of equity or the rules of prudence, I leave to the reader to determine.[1] Perhaps, if the king had been brought in upon the conditions the noble Earl of Southampton would have proposed, and which were approved by the Earl of Clarendon, when it was too late, it had prevented a great deal of the arbitrary and violent proceedings of that loose and luxurious reign, and contributed to the safety and happiness of the prince, and people too. He was one of the divines appointed to wait upon the king at Breda, where they were well received, and for some time after greatly caressed. The doctor was sworn one of the king's chaplains by the Earl of Manchester, Lord Chamberlain, who truly honoured him. He was one of the commissioners at the Savoy Conference, and used his utmost endeavours in that unsuccessful affair. Dr Reynolds, afterwards Bishop of Norwich, joined with those divines who were for alterations in ecclesiastical affairs. He was the first who received the commission from the Bishop of London, of which he immediately acquainted

---

[1] See Bishop Burnet's 'History of his Own Times,' p. 89.

Dr Manton. The original letter is now in my hands, and expresses the candour and goodness of that excellent person, and his great respect for Dr Manton. It is in these words:—

'SIR,—This morning the Bishop of London sent me the commission about revising the Liturgy under the great seal, to take notice of; with direction to give notice to the commissioners who are not bishops. I went to Mr Calamy, and it is desired that we meet to-morrow morning at nine o'clock, at his house, in regard of his lameness, to advise together, and send a joint letter to those who are out of this town. He and I desire you not to fail; and withal to call upon Dr Bates and Dr Jacomb in your way, to desire their company. So, with my best respects,
'I remain your most loving brother,
'EDWARD REYNOLDS, B.N.
'LONDON, *April* 1, 1660.'

He was offered at this time the deanery of Rochester, which Dr Harding was in great fear he would accept, and plied him with letters to come to some resolution; having reason to hope that, upon his refusal, he should obtain it, as he afterwards did. The doctor kept it some time in suspense, being willing to see whether the king's declaration could be got to pass into a law, which they had great encouragements given them to expect, and which would have gone a great way towards uniting the principal parties in the nation, and laying the foundation of a lasting peace. [1] Many persons who had, in the former times, purchased bishops' and deans' lands, earnestly pressed him to accept the deanery, with hopes they might find better usage from him in renewing their leases, and offered their money for new ones, which he might have taken with the deanery, and quitted again in 1662, there being then no assent and consent imposed; but he was above such underhand dealings, and scorned to enrich himself with the spoils of others. When he saw the most prudent and condescending endeavours, through the violence and ambition of some leading men, availed nothing to the peace of the church and the happiness of the nation, he sat down under the melancholy prospect of what he lived to see come to pass, namely, the decay of serious religion, with a flood of profaneness and a violent spirit of persecution. The greatest worth and the best pretensions met with no regard where there were any scruples in point of ceremony and subscription.

In the interval between the Restoration and his ejectment, he was greatly esteemed by persons of the first quality at court. Sir John Baber used to tell him, that the king had a singular respect for him. Lord Chancellor Hyde was always highly civil and obliging to him. He had free access to him upon all occasions, which he always im-

---

[1] The declaration was drawn up by Lord Chancellor Hyde, and contained, among other things, the following concessions:—That no bishops should ordain or exercise any part of jurisdiction, which appertaineth to the censures of the church, without the advice and assistance of the presbyters: that chancellors, commissaries, and officials should be excluded from acts of jurisdiction; and the power of pastors in their several congregations restored; and that liberty should be granted to all ministers to assemble monthly for the exercise of their pastoral persuasive power, and the promoting of knowledge and godliness in their flocks; that ministers should be free from the subscription required by the canon, and from the oath of canonical obedience; and that the use of the ceremonies should be dispensed with, where they were scrupled.

proved, not for himself, but for the service of others. I shall only give a single instance. Mr James, of Berkshire, who was afterwards known by the name of Black James, an honest and worthy person, was at the point of being cast out of his living, which was a sequestration. He came to London to make friends to the Lord Chancellor, but could find none proper for his purpose. He was at length advised to go to Dr Manton, to whom he was yet a stranger, as the most likely to serve him in this distress. He came to him late in the evening, and when he was in bed. He told his case to Mrs Manton, who advised him to come again in the morning, and did not doubt but the doctor would go with him. He answered, with great concern, that it would be too late; and that if he could not put a stop to it that night, he and his family must be ruined. On so pressing a case the doctor rose, and, because it rained, went with him in a coach to the Lord Chancellor, at York House; who spying the doctor in the crowd, where many persons were attending, called to him to know what business he had there at that time of night. When he acquainted him with his errand, my lord called to the person who stamped the orders upon such occasions, and asked him what he was doing? He answered, 'that he was just going to put the stamp to an order for passing away such a living.' Upon which he bid him stop; and upon hearing further of the matter, bid the doctor not trouble himself, his friend should not be molested. He enjoyed it to the time of his ejectment, in 1662, which was a great support to a pretty numerous family. Upon his refusing the deanery, he fell under Lord Clarendon's displeasure, so fickle is the favour of the great; and he once accused him to the king for dropping some treasonable expressions in a sermon. The king was so just and kind as to send for him, and ordered him to bring his notes. When he read them, the king asked, whether upon his word this was all that was delivered; and upon the doctor's assurance that it was so, without a syllable added to it, the king said, 'Doctor, I am satisfied, and you may be assured of my favour; but look to yourself, or else Hyde will be too hard for you.'

In whatsoever company he was, he had courage, as became a faithful minister of Christ, to oppose sin; and upon proper occasions, to reprove sinners. Duke Lauderdale, who pretended to carry it with great respect to him, in some company where the doctor was present, behaved himself very indecently: the doctor modestly reproved him, but the duke never loved him afterward. He was once at dinner at Lord Manchester's in Whitehall, when several persons of great note began to drink the king's health, a custom which then began to be much in vogue, and was commonly abused to great disorders. When it came to him, he refused to comply with it, apprehending it beneath the dignity of a minister to give any countenance to the sinful excess it so often occasioned in those times. It put a stop to it at that time, and Prince Rupert, who was present, inquired who he was. Many of the Scotch nobility greatly respected him, particularly the Duchess of Hamilton, who attended his ministry. Notwithstanding the great and weighty affairs then on foot, which took up a great part of his time, he never omitted his beloved work of constant preaching, to the time of his ejection, in 1662. He then usually resorted to his own church, where he was succeeded by Dr Patrick, the late Bishop of Ely. It happened cross, that Dr Patrick receiving a scurrilous letter from an unknown person, full of reflections upon himself, had so little wisdom at that time as to charge it upon Dr Manton, in a letter to him, with very unbecoming reflections. This occasioned his not attending any more his preaching ; for no man living more abhorred a base and unworthy action. Having this occasion of speaking a little to his disadvantage, I shall take the opportunity of doing a piece of justice to the memory of that learned person, who has since, by many books of devotion, and excellent paraphrases and commentaries on the scripture, as well as by his exemplary life, done so much good to the world, and deserved so well of the Christian church. It has been generally allowed, that Dr Patrick wrote the first volumes of the 'Friendly Debate,' in the heat of his youth, and in the midst of his expectations ; which by aggravating some weak and uncautious expressions, in a few particular writers, designed to expose the Nonconformist ministry to contempt and ridicule. The design was afterwards carried on by a worse hand, and with a more virulent spirit,[1] a method altogether unreasonable and unworthy, because it will be always easy to gather rash and unadvised expressions from the weaker persons of any party of men, and only serves to expose religion to the scorn and contempt of the profane. But Bishop Patrick in his advanced age, and in a public debate in the House of Lords, about the 'Occasional Bill,' took the opportunity to declare himself to this purpose : ' That he had been known to write against the Dissenters with some warmth, in his younger years ; but that he had lived long enough to see reason to alter his opinion of that people, and that way of writing; and that he was verily persuaded there were some who were honest men and good Christians, who would be neither, if they did not ordinarily go to church, and sometimes to the meeting ; and on the other hand, some were honest men and good Christians, who would be neither, if they did not ordinarily go to the meetings and sometimes to church.' A rare instance this of retractation and moderation ; which I think redounds greatly to his honour, and is worthy of imitation.

But to return to the history. After he ceased to attend upon Dr Patrick's ministry, he used to preach on the Lord's-day evenings in his own house to his family, and some few of his neighbours; and some time after, on Wednesday mornings, when the violence of the times would allow it. Upon the increase of his hearers, he was obliged to lay two rooms into one ; which yet, by reason of the number of the people, and the straitness of the place, proved very inconvenient to him, especially in hot weather, and prejudicial to his health. He had lived in that respect and good-will in the parish, that his neighbours were generally civil to him, and gave him no trouble. Only a little before his ejectment, one Bird, a tailor, a zealous stickler for the Common Prayer, complained to Dr Sheldon, then Bishop of London, that Dr Manton deprived him of the means of his salvation ; meaning the use of the Common Prayer. ' Well,' says the bishop, ' all in good time ; but you may go to heaven without the Common Prayer.' There was one Justice Ball, within a few doors of him, who often threatened him,

[1] Dr Samuel Parker, afterwards Bishop of Oxford.

and was at last as good as his word.   He was sometimes in danger
from the churchwardens, of which number there were always three.
The Duke of Bedford having always the choice of one, took care to
have him a friend to the doctor ; and his well-known respect to him
gave him countenance and protection from the malice of the meaner
people.   His meeting afterwards adjoined to Lord Wharton's house in
St Giles's, which he allowed him the convenience of, whether he was
in town or not.   The good-natured Earl of Berkshire lived next door,
who was himself a Jansenist Papist, and offered him the liberty, when
he was in trouble, to come to his house ; which it was easy to do, by
only passing over a low wall which parted the gardens.

Not long after the Act of Ejectment, when the Government was
forming a plot for the Presbyterians, for they had none of their own,
in a debate in the House of Lords, Dr Ward, bishop of Salisbury,
said, ' It was time to look after them, when such men as Dr Manton
refused to take the oaths ;' which slander was soon contradicted by
Lord Chamberlain Manchester, who assured the House of the falseness
of the charge ; and that he himself had administered the oath to him
when he was sworn one of His Majesty's chaplains.   The doctor took
notice of this as very disingenuous, because, not long before, the bishop
and he had met at Astrop Wells ; and the bishop had treated him with
great civility, and entered into particular freedoms with him.   The
doctor, indeed, was in his judgment utterly against taking the Oxford
oath, viz., ' That it is not lawful, upon any pretence whatsoever, to
take up arms against the king ; and, that we will not at any time
endeavour any alteration of the government in Church or State.'   And
when some few of his brethren were satisfied to take it upon an explication allowed them by the Lord Keeper Bridgman, that is, that the oath
meant only unlawful endeavours, the famous Mr Gouge came from
Hammersmith with a design to take it ; but calling upon Dr Manton
to know his opinion of it, he was so well satisfied with the reasons of
his judgment, that he was perfectly easy in his mind, and never took
it afterwards.

In the year 1670, the meetings seemed for some time to be connived
at, and were much attended.   I remember to have heard some of the
worthy ejected ministers speak of this period with particular pleasure ;
they observed that, after the looseness and excess which followed the
Restoration, the reproaches and persecutions of the Nonconformists,
for several years, and the late terrible judgments of plague and fire,
multitudes everywhere frequented the opened meetings, some from
curiosity, and some upon better motives ; and many were delivered
from the prejudices they had entertained, and received the first serious
impressions upon their minds.   God remarkably owned their ministry
at that time, and crowned it, under all their disadvantages, with an
extraordinary success.   Soon after this indulgence expired, the doctor
was taken prisoner, on a Lord's-day, in the afternoon, just after he had
done his sermon.   The door happened to be opened to let a gentleman
out, at the very time the Justice and his attendants were at the door ;
who immediately rushed in, and went up-stairs ; but finding the doctor
in his prayer, they stayed till he had done, and then took the names of
the principal persons.   The doctor being warm with preaching, they

were so civil to take his word to come to them after some convenient time. He went to them to a house in the Piazzas, where many persons of note were gathered together ; among whom was the then Duke of Richmond. After some discourse, they tendered him the Oxford oath. Upon his refusing to take it, they threatened to send him to prison. It was thought they questioned their own skill to draw up a warrant which would be sufficient to hold him ; and that it was afterward drawn up by the Lord Chief-Justice Vaughan. They dismissed him, however, at that time, upon his promise to come to them within two or three days ; and then gave the warrant to a constable, and committed him to the Gatehouse ; only allowing him a day's respite, till his room could be got ready. This imprisonment, by the kind providence of God, was more favourable and commodious than could have been thought, or than his enemies designed, or than he expected. The keeper of the prison at that time was the Lady Broughton, who was noted for her strictness and severity in her office, though she carried it quite otherwise towards the doctor ; for she allowed him a large handsome room joining to the Gatehouse, with a small one sufficient to hold a bed. For some time it was not thought prudent to admit any to come to him, but his wife and servant who attended him. It is worth notice here, that the doctor could not omit his delightful work of preaching, though to so small a congregation ; which he did, according to his former custom, both parts of the Lord's-day and once on a week-day. After some time his children, and some few friends, to the number of twelve or fifteen, were admitted to hear him preach. The Lady Broughton was highly civil and obliging, and placed a great confidence in him. When she designed to go for a little time into the country, she would have ordered the keys of the common jail to be brought to him every night ; the doctor, smiling, told her that he, being a prisoner himself, could not think it proper to be the keeper or jailer to others. However, no person had the opening and shutting of the door of the house where he was but his own servant, so that he might have gone out of prison when he pleased, for any restraint he was under. When the town was pretty empty, he ventured, once with his keeper and once without, to visit his worthy friend Mr Gunston of Newington, who was agreeably surprised to see him, as he had a very high and hearty respect for him. Thus like Joseph,[1] 'he found favour in the sight of the keeper of the prison ;' and the ' keeper of the prison' would have ' committed to his hands all the prisoners who were in the prison.' This, it must be owned, was a milder confinement and gentler usage than many others met with in those days, who lay under long and close confinements, and suffered confiscation of goods, and banishment, and death. This Protestant persecution fell short indeed of dragooning and dungeons and galleys in France, and of the racks and tortures of the Inquisition in Spain ; but that a person of Dr Manton's worth and merit should be thought to deserve such treatment from a Government which he helped to lay the foundations of, and which he not only never injured, but had served in circumstances of danger and importance, when others of less desert and pretensions had all the opportunities of public service, and all the

[1] Gen. xxxix. 21, 22.

favour and preferment, I believe will appear shocking, at this distance, to all impartial lovers of liberty and of their country, and fix a brand for ever upon the gratitude and politics of those times.

Some time after his imprisonment, when the indulgence was renewed, he preached in a large room taken for him in Whitehart Yard, not far from his house; but there also he was at length disturbed. A band of rabble came on the Lord's-day morning to seize him; but the doctor, having notice of it overnight, escaped their fury. Mr James Bedford was got to preach for him, who had taken the Oxford oath. When they found themselves disappointed, they were in a great rage, and took the names of several; but did not detain the minister, for their malice was levelled against the doctor. The good Lord Wharton was there, whom they pretended not to know; and upon his refusing to tell them his name, they threatened to send him to prison; but they thought better of it. The place was fined forty pounds, and the minister twenty, which was paid by Lord Wharton.

Sir John Baber, his near neighbour, and who owed all his preferment at court to the doctor's interest there, continued his hearty friend, though a great courtier. He often visited the doctor, by which means he had opportunity of greater intelligence than most others. About this time there happened some difference among the ministers of the city, about the manner of addressing the king for his indulgence. Some contended earnestly to have it expressed more largely, and others opposed it; for though they always thought they had a right to their liberty, they feared giving any countenance to the dispensing power, or advantage to the Papists; which were things well known to be in view, and much at heart at that time. The difference came to be known at court, and there were apprehensions of ill consequences. Sir John Baber carried Dr Manton and Dr Bates to Lord Arlington's, at Whitehall, who was then Secretary of State, it was supposed, by his order. When they were together, the king, to their great surprise, came into the room—it was thought by design. Dr Bates pressed Dr Manton to address the king for his indulgence; which he did in a few words, and with great caution; but it was kindly accepted by the king, and well approved by the ministers, when it was communicated to them; and put a happy end to their contentions about it.[1] It was by the means of Sir John Baber that Dr Manton and Mr Baxter were invited to confer with the Lord Keeper Bridgman, about a comprehension and toleration, in the year 1668. They afterwards met with Dr Wilkins and Dr Burton. Proposals were drawn up and corrected by mutual consent; in pursuance of which the excellent Judge Hale prepared a bill to be laid before the next session of Parliament; but it was rejected upon the first motion by the High Church party.[2] In the year 1674, Dr Manton and Mr Baxter, with Dr Bates and Mr Pool, met with Dr Tillotson and Dr Stillingfleet, to consider of an accommodation, by the encouragement of several Lords, spiritual and temporal. They canvassed several

---

[1] Dr Manton gives a particular account of this interview, in a letter to Mr Baxter.—*Life*, Part III., p. 37.

[2] Dr Calamy's Abridgment, vol. i., pp. 317, 342.

draughts, and at length all agreed in one; but when it came to be communicated to the bishops, several things in which they had agreed could not be obtained, and the whole design miscarried. So easy a thing it has ever been found for wise and sober men to adjust matters of difference, and agree upon terms of accommodation; when nothing will satisfy unreasonable prejudice, and where the lust of power, and the bias of interest, strongly lead men the other way.

When the indulgence was more fully fixed in 1672, the merchants, and other citizens of London, set up a lecture at Pinner's Hall. Dr Manton was one of the six first chosen, and opened the lecture. He was much concerned at the little bickerings which began there in his time, and afterward broke out into scandalous contentions, and an open division at last. Mr Baxter was often censured for his preaching there; and once published a sheet upon that occasion, which he called, 'An Appeal to the Light.' His preaching upon these words, 'And ye will not come unto me, that you might have life,' in which he fully justified the great God, and laid the blame of men's destruction upon themselves, though it was followed by another upon these words, 'Without me you can do nothing,' occasioned a great clamour against him among some people of which he complained to Dr Manton. The doctor, on his next turn, in the close of his sermon, pretty sharply rebuked them for their rash mistakes, and unbecoming reflections upon so worthy and useful a person. It was observed, that his reproof was managed with so much decency and wisdom, that he was not by any reflected upon for his freedom therein. He has been heard to express his esteem of Mr Baxter in the highest terms; namely, that he thought him one of the most extraordinary persons the Christian church had produced since the apostles' days; and that he did not look upon himself as worthy to carry his books after him. This was the opinion of one who knew him with the greatest intimacy for many years, and was a great judge of true worth.

When he first began to grow into ill health, he could not be persuaded by his friends and physicians to forbear preaching for any considerable time; which had been the delightful work of his life. He was at length prevailed with to spend some time at Woburn, with Lord Wharton, for the benefit of the air. But finding little good by it, he returned to town on the beginning of the week, in order to administer the Lord's Supper the next Lord's-day, of which he gave notice to his people; but he did not live to accomplish it. The day before he took his bed, he was in his study, of which he took a solemn leave, with hands and eyes lift up to heaven, blessing God for the many comfortable and serious hours he had spent there, and waiting in joyful hope of a state of clearer knowledge and higher enjoyments of God. At night he prayed with his family under great indisposition, and recommended himself to God's wise disposal; desiring, 'If he had no further work for him to do in this world, he would take him to himself;' which he expressed with great serenity of mind, and an unreserved resignation to the divine good pleasure. When he went to bed he was suddenly seized with a kind of lethargy, by which he was deprived of his senses, to the great grief and loss of his friends who came to visit him. He died October 18th, 1677, in the fifty-seventh year of his age, and lies interred in the chancel of the church of Stoke Newington.

Dr Bates preached his funeral sermon, who had a most affectionate esteem for him, very frequently visited him, always advised with him in matters of moment, and, for some years after his death, would weep when he spoke of him. He says of him:—[1] 'His name is worthy of precious and eternal memory. God had furnished him with a rare union of those parts which are requisite to form an eminent minister of his word. A clear judgment, a rich fancy, a strong memory, and happy elocution met in him; and were excellently improved by his diligent study. In preaching the word he was of conspicuous eminence; and none could detract from him, but from ignorance or envy. He was endowed with an extraordinary knowledge of the scripture; and in his preaching, gave such perspicuous accounts of the order and dependence of divine truths, and with that felicity applied the scripture to confirm them, that every subject, by his management, was cultivated and improved. His discourses were so clear and convincing, that none, without offering violence to conscience, could resist their evidence; and from hence they were effectual, not only to inspire a sudden flame, and raise a short commotion in the affections, but to make a lasting change in the life. His doctrine was uncorrupt and pure; the truth according to godliness. He was far from the guilty, vile intention to prostitute the sacred ordinances for acquiring any private secular advantage; neither did he entertain his hearers with impertinent subleties, empty notions, intricate disputes, dry and barren, without productive virtue; but as one who always had in his eye the great end of his ministry, the glory of God, and the salvation of men. His sermons were directed to open their eyes, that they might see their wretched condition as sinners, to hasten their flight from the wrath to come, and make them humbly, and thankfully, and entirely receive Christ as their Prince and all-sufficient Saviour; and to build up the converted in their holy faith, and more excellent love, which is the "fulfilling of the law:" in short, to make true Christians eminent in knowledge and universal obedience.

'And as the matter of his sermons was designed for the good of souls, so his way of expression was proper for that end. His style was not exquisitely studied, not consisting of harmonious periods, but far distant from vulgar meanness. His expression was natural and free, clear and eloquent, quick and powerful; without any spice of folly; and always suitable to the simplicity and majesty of divine truth. His sermons afforded substantial food with delight, so that a fastidious mind could not disrelish them. He abhorred a vain ostentation of wit in handling sacred truths, so venerable and grave, and of eternal consequence. His fervour and earnestness in preaching was such as might soften and make pliant the most stubborn and obstinate spirit. I am not speaking of one whose talent was only voice, who laboured in the pulpit as if the end of preaching were the exercise of the body, and not for the profit of souls. But this man of God was inflamed with holy zeal, and from thence such expressions broke forth as were capable of procuring attention and consent in his hearers. He spake

[1] Dr Bates's Works, p. 771.

as one who had a living faith within him of divine truth. From this union of zeal with his knowledge, he was excellently qualified to convince and convert souls. His unparalleled assiduity in preaching declared him very sensible of those dear and strong obligations which lie upon ministers to be very diligent in that blessed work. This faithful minister abounded in the work of the Lord; and, which is truly admirable, though so frequent in preaching, yet was always superior to others, and equal to himself. He was no fomentor of faction, but studious of the public tranquillity; he knew what a blessing peace is, and wisely foresaw the pernicious consequences which attend divisions.

'Consider him as a Christian, his life was answerable to his doctrine. This servant of God was like a fruitful tree, which produces in the branches what it contains in the root. His inward grace was made visible in a conversation becoming the gospel. His resolute contempt of the world secured him from being wrought upon by those motives which tempt low spirits from their duty. He would not rashly throw himself into troubles, nor, *spreta conscientia*, avoid them. His generous constancy of mind in resisting the current of popular humour, declared his loyalty to his divine Master. His charity was eminent in procuring supplies for others, when in mean circumstances himself. But he had great experience of God's fatherly provision, to which his filial confidence was correspondent. I shall finish my character of him by observing his humility. He was deeply affected with the sense of his frailty and unworthiness. He considered the infinite purity of God, and the perfection of his law, the rule of duty; and by that humbling light discovered his manifold defects. He expressed his thoughts to me a little before his death. "If the holy prophets were under strong impressions of fear upon extraordinary discoveries of the divine presence, how shall we poor creatures appear before the holy and dreadful Majesty? It is infinitely terrible to appear before God, the Judge of all, without the protection of the blood of sprinkling, which speaketh better things than that of Abel." This alone relieved him, and supported his hopes. Though his labours were abundant, yet he knew that the work of God, passing through our hands is so blemished, that without appealing to pardoning mercy and grace, we cannot stand in judgment.' This was the subject of his last public sermon, upon 2 Tim. i. 18, which was published from his notes, with the second edition of his funeral sermon.

Mr Collins, a man of a most sweet and obliging temper, as well as of great abilities and worth, on his turn to preach at the merchants' lecture, after the doctor's death, took great notice of it, and was much affected with the loss of so valuable a person. Good old Mr Case used to say, long before his death, that he should live to preach his funeral sermon; and he did preach upon that occasion, when he was almost dead himself, for he was above eighty years of age. His text was, 2 Kings x. 32; 'In those days the Lord began to cut Israel short.' After he had considered the text, he came to speak of several worthy ministers cut off by death about that time, as well as others cut off by the laws which forbade their preaching. The last he named was Dr

Manton. At the mention of his name he stopped, and wept for some time before he could proceed ; and then said, ' If I had mentioned no other but Dr Manton, I might well say, that God began to cut England short ;' with other expressions of his love and esteem. He had always a high opinion of the doctor's preaching, and would often urge him to print. When the doctor answered him that he had not time, in the midst of such constant employments, to prepare anything, with due care, for the public view ; he would reply, ' You need only send your notes to the press, when you come out of the pulpit.' Dr Manton wrote a very ingenious and serious preface to Mr Case's Meditations, drawn up when he was prisoner in the Tower, and published under the title of ' Correction, Instruction ;' which is a very useful practical book upon the subject of afflictions. He also wrote a preface to the second edition of ' Smectymnus ;' to Mr Clifford's ' Book of the Covenant ;' to ' Ignatius Jourdain's Life ;' Mr Strong's ' Sermons of the Certainty and Eternity of Hell Torments ;' and to the second edition, in quarto, of the Assembly's ' Confession of Faith,' &c.

His works were published by several principal ministers of that time, and it will entertain the reader to see the high apprehensions they had of him, and the beautiful variety in which they represent them. They have indeed drawn their own character, as well as his, in the different turn of their mind and manner of expression. The first which came out was ' Twenty Sermons,' in quarto, in the year 1678. Dr Bates gives this fine and beautiful account of them : ' The main design of them is to represent the inseparable connexion between Christian duties and privileges, wherein the essence of our religion consists. The gospel is not a naked, unconditionate offer of pardon and eternal life in favour of sinners, but upon the most convenient terms for the glory of God and the good of men, enforced by the strongest obligations upon them to receive humbly and thankfully those benefits. The promises are attended with commands to repent and believe, and persevere in a uniform practice of obedience. The Son of God came into the world, not to make God less holy, but to make us holy ; and not to vacate our duty, and free us from the law as a rule of obedience, for that is both impossible, and would be most infamous and reproachful to our Saviour. To challenge such an exemption in point of right is to make ourselves gods ; to usurp it in point of fact is to make ourselves devils. But his end was to enable and induce us to return to God as our rightful Lord and proper felicity, from whom we rebelliously and miserably fell, in seeking for happiness out of him. Accordingly, the gospel is called the law of faith, as it commands those duties upon motives of eternal hopes and fears, and as it will justify or condemn men with respect to their obedience or disobedience, which is the proper character of a law. These things are managed in the following sermons in that convincing, persuasive manner as makes them very necessary for these times, when some who aspire to extraordinary heights in religion, and esteem themselves favourites of heaven, yet wofully neglect the duties of the lower hemisphere, as righteousness, truth, and honesty ; and when carnal Christians are so numerous, who despise serious godliness as a solemn hypocrisy, and live in open violation of Christ's precepts, and yet presume to be saved by him.

'I shall only add further, they commend to our ardent affections and endeavours true holiness, as distinguished from the most refined unregenerate morality. The doctor saw the absolute necessity of this, and spake with great jealousy of those who seemed in their discourses to make it their highest aim to improve and cultivate some moral virtues, as justice, temperance, benignity, &c., by philosophical helps, representing them as becoming the dignity of our nature, agreeable to reason, and beneficial to society, and but transiently speaking of the operations of the Holy Spirit, which are as requisite to free the soul from the chains of sin as to release the body at last from the bands of death ; who seldom preach of evangelical graces, faith in the Redeemer, the love of God for his admirable wisdom in our salvation, zeal for his glory, humility in ascribing all we can return in grateful obedience to the most free and powerful grace of God in Christ, which are the vital principles of good works, and derive the noblest forms to all virtues. Indeed, men may be composed and considerate in their words and actions, may abstain from gross enormities, and do many praiseworthy actions, by the rules of moral prudence, yet without the infusion of divine grace to cleanse their stained nature, to renew them according to the image of God shining in the gospel, to act them from motives superior to all that moral wisdom propounds,—all their virtues, of what elevation soever, though in a heroic degree, cannot make them real saints. As the plant-animal has a faint resemblance of the sensitive life, but remains in the lower rank of vegetables, so these have a shadow and appearance of the life of God, but continue in the corrupt state of nature. The difference is greater between sanctifying saving grace, wrought by the special power of the Spirit, with the holy operations flowing from them, and the virtuous habits and actions which are the effect of moral counsel and constancy, than between true pearls produced by the celestial beams of the sun, and counterfeit ones formed by the smoky heat of the fire.' No doubt the proper Christian graces require the influence of the Divine Spirit, and are the effect of nobler motives than mere pagan morality.

In 1679 was published, in octavo, ' Eighteen Sermons on the Second Chapter of the Second Epistle to the Thessalonians, containing the Description, Rise, Growth, and Fall of Antichrist ; with divers Cautions and Arguments to establish Christians against the Apostasy of the Church of Rome.' This was well fitted for common use, and very seasonable at that time. In the preface to this volume, Mr Baxter says of him, ' How sound he was in judgment against extremes in the controversies of these times ; how great a lamenter of the scandalous and dividing mistakes of some self-conceited men ; how earnestly desirous of healing our present breaches, and not unacquainted with the proper means and terms ; how hard and successful a student ; how frequent and laborious a preacher ; and how highly and deservedly esteemed, is commonly known here. The small distaste which some few had of him, I took for a part of his honour, who would not win reputation with any by flattering them in their mistakes, or unwarrantable ways. He used not to serve God with that which cost him nothing; nor was of their mind who cannot expect or extol God's grace without denying those endeavours of men to which his necessary grace exciteth them. He knew that, "without Christ we can do nothing;" and yet that, "by Christ strengthening us, we can do all things" which God hath made necessary to be done by us. He was not of their mind who think it derogatory to the honour of Christ to praise his works in the souls and lives of any of his servants; and that it is to the honour of his grace that his justified ones are graceless, and that their Judge should dishonour his own righteousness, if he make his disciples more righteous personally than the scribes and pharisees; and will say to them, "Well done, good and faithful servant; thou hast been faithful over a few things, enter thou into the joy of thy Lord." He knew how to regard the righteousness and intercession of Christ, with pardon of sin and divine acceptance, instead of legal personal perfection, without denying either the necessity or assigned office of our faith and repentance, and evangelical sincerity in obeying Him who redeemed and justifies us. He knew the difference between man's being justified from the charge of being liable to damnation as Christless, impenitent, unbelieving, and ungodly; and being liable to damnation for mere sin as sin, against the law of innocence, which required of us no less than personal, perfect, and perpetual obedience. He greatly lamented the wrong which truth and the church underwent from those who neither know such difference, nor have humility enough to suspect their judgment, nor to forbear reviling those who have not as confused and unsound apprehensions and expressions as themselves.'

In the year 1684 Dr Bates published his 'Exposition of the Lord's Prayer,' in octavo. In 1685 Mr Hurst published, in octavo, 'Several Discourses tending to promote Peace and Holiness among Christians;' and dedicated them to Arthur, Earl of Anglesea, to whom he was chaplain. In the same year was published, 'Christ's Temptations and Transfiguration explained and improved; and Christ's Eternal Existence and the Dignity of his Person asserted and proved, in opposition to the Socinians,' in octavo. Dr Jacomb, who published this volume, says of him, 'That he did not so much concern himself in what is polemical and controversial; but chose rather, in a plain way, as best suiting with sermon-work, to assert and prove the truth by scripture testimony and argument; and that he has done to the full.' In 1703 was published, 'A Practical Exposition of Isaiah liii.' This, though published last, was earlier written than any of the other; for so he speaks in the preface to the Exposition of James, 'I have the rather chosen this scripture, that it might be an allay to those comforts, which, in another exercise, I have endeavoured to draw out of Isaiah liii. I would, at the same time, carry on the doctrine of faith and manners, and show you your duty, together with your encouragement; lest, with Ephraim, you should only love to tread out the corn, and refuse to break the clods. We are all apt to divorce comfort from duty, and content ourselves with a barren, unfruitful, knowledge of Christ; as if all He required of the world were only a few naked, cold, unactive apprehensions of his merit, and all things were so done for us, that nothing remained to be done by us. This is the wretched conceit of many in the present age; and, therefore, they abuse the sweetness of grace to looseness, and the power of it to laziness. Christ's merits, and the Spirit's efficacy, are the common places from whence they draw all the defence and excuse of their own wantonness and idleness.'

Besides these lesser volumes, there are five large volumes in folio. The first was, ' Sermons upon the 119th Psalm,' published in the year 1681. Dr Bates says, ' They were preached by him in his usual course of three times a week; which I do not mention to lessen their worth, but to show how diligent and exact he was in performing his duty. I cannot but admire the fecundity and variety of his thoughts; that though the same things so often occur in the verses of this psalm, yet, by a judicious observing the different arguments and motives whereby the psalmist enforces the same request, or some other cir- cumstance, every sermon contains new conceptions, and proper to the text.' Mr Alsop says of them, ' The matter of them is spiritual, and speaks the author one intimately acquainted with the secrets of wis- dom. He writes like one who knew the psalmist's heart, and felt in his own soul the sanctifying power of what he wrote. Their design is practical, beginning with the understanding, dealing with the affections, but still driving on the design of practical holiness. The manner of handling is not inferior to the dignity of the matter; so plain, as to accommodate the most sublime truths to the meanest spiritual capacity; and yet so elevated, as to approve itself to the most refined understanding; which knows how to be succinct without obscurity; and, where the weight of the argument requires it, to enlarge without nauseous prolixity. He studied more to profit than please; and yet an honest heart will be then best pleased when most profited. He chose rather to speak appositely than elegantly, and yet the judicious account propriety the greatest elegance. He laboured more industriously to conceal his learning than others to ostentate theirs; and yet, when he would most veil it, the discerning reader cannot but discover it, and rejoice to find such a mass and treasure of useful learning couched under a well-studied and artificial plainness. I have admired, and must recommend to the observation of the reader, the fruitfulness of the author's holy invention, accompanied with solid judgment, in that whereas the coincidence of the matter in this psalm might have superseded his labours in very many verses; yet, without force, or offering violence to the sacred text, he has, either from the connexion of one verse with its predecessor, or the harmony between the parts of the same verse, found out new matter to entertain his own meditations, and the reader's expectations.'

The second volume was published in 1684, and contains sermons on the whole of the 25th of Matthew and 17th of John, and the 6th and 8th of the Romans, and the 5th of the Second Epistle to the Corinthians. Dr Collings, who seems to have written the preface to this volume, says, ' In all his writings one finds a quick and fertile invention, governed with a solid judgment; and the issue of both expressed in a grave and decent style. He had a heart full of love and zeal for God and his glory; and out of the abundance of his heart his mouth continually spake. So frequent, and yet so learned and solid, preaching by the same person was little less than miraculous. He was a good and learned, a grave and judicious, person; and his auditory never failed, though he laboured more than most preachers, to hear from him a pious, learned, and judicious discourse. He is one of those authors upon the credit of whose name not only private and less intelligent people, but even scholars, may venture to buy any book which was his.' The third volume was published in 1689, and contains sermons upon the 11th chapter of the Epistle to the Hebrews; with a treatise of the Life of Faith, and another of Self-denial; and some preparatory sermons for the Lord's Supper, and sermons before the Parliament. It was dedicated to King William, soon after the Revolution, by Mr Howe, in as noble and masterly a preface as is, perhaps, anywhere to be met with. The fourth volume was published in 1693, and contains sermons upon several texts of scripture. It is directed to the Lord Philip Wharton, by Mr William Taylor, who was many years my lord's chaplain, and transcribed a great part of the doctor's notes for the press, and was himself a person of great integrity and wisdom. He tells my lord, ' Though his preaching was so constant, yet in all his sermons may be observed a solidity of judgment, exactness of method, fulness of matter, strength of argument, persuasive elegance, together with a serious vein of piety running through the whole, as few have come near him, but none have exceeded him.' Mr Alsop says of this volume:—'Acquired learning humbly waits upon divine revelation; great ministerial gifts were managed by greater grace. A warm zeal, guided by solid judgment; a fervent love to saints and sinners, kindled by a burning zeal for the interest of a Saviour; and a plain elegance of style adapted to the meanest capacity, and yet far above the contempt of the highest pretender.' The fifth volume was published in 1701, and contains sermons on the 5th chapter to the Ephesians, on the 3d of the Philippians, on the 1st chapter of the Second Epistle to the Thessalonians, and on the 3d chapter of the First Epistle of John, with one hundred and forty sermons on particular texts. This volume, though it appeared last, and after so many others, is so far from running dregs, that, in my opinion, it contains some of his ripest and most digested thoughts; and is preferable, both for the subject and management, to any one of the former. This was directed to the excellent Sir Thomas Abney, then Lord Mayor of London, and to the Lady Abney, by Mr Howe; in which he expresses his sense of Dr Manton in this remarkable paragraph: 'And that an eminent servant of Christ, who, through a tract of so many years, hath been so great and public a teacher and example of the ancient seriousness, piety, righteousness, sobriety, strictness of manners, with most diffusive charity (for which London has been renowned, for some ages, beyond most cities in the world), should have his memory revived by such a testimony from persons under your character, and who hold so public a station as you do in it, can never be thought unbecoming, as long as clearly explained and exemplified religion, solid useful learning, and good sense, are in any credit in the world.'

There are some sermons of his in the several volumes of the ' Morning Exercises;' for Dr Manton was too considerable to be missed in any design which was set on foot for the public good. There is one in that at St Giles's, on 'Man's Impotency to Help himself out of the Misery he is in by Nature;' another in that at Cripplegate, about 'Strictness in Holy Duties;' a third in the Supplement, concerning 'The Improvement of our Baptism;' and a fourth in that against Popery, upon 'The Sufficiency of the Scripture.' There is also a funeral sermon for Mrs Jane Blackwel, upon 'The Blessed Estate of them who Die in the Lord,' in the year 1656. These sermons, with the two before the House of Commons,[1] and one on the death of Mr Love, including the Exposition on James and Jude, were all he published himself;[2] and are written with a correct judgment and beautiful simplicity. His other works were all printed from his sermon-notes, prepared for the pulpit; and whosoever shall consider the greatness of the number and variety of the subjects, the natural order in which they are disposed, and the skilful management; the constant frequency of his preaching, and the affairs of business in which he was often engaged, will easily be able to make a judgment of his great abilities and vast application, and to make the requisite allowances for posthumous works; especially when he tells us that he was 'humbled with the constant burden of four times a week preaching;'[3] and to the last, three times; and that where 'the style seems too curt and abrupt, know that I sometimes reserved myself for sudden inculcations and enlargement.' And though, as they now appear, they have been well received, and very useful to younger ministers and Christian families, yet I believe I might safely venture to say, that if he had had the same leisure to compose and polish, he was capable of equalling any performances of that kind of the celebrated writers of the age; and that hardly any, under his disadvantage, and so constantly employed, would have exceeded his. As no man of the age had a greater number of his sermons published after his death, perhaps it will not displease the reader to see his own judgment of posthumous writings. 'Let it not stumble thee,' says he, 'that the piece is posthumous, and comes out so long after the author's death; it were to be wished that they who excel in public gifts would during life publish their own works, to prevent spurious obtrusions upon the world, and to give them their last hand and polishing, as the apostle Peter was careful to write before his decease (2 Pet. i. 12). But usually the Church's treasure is most increased by legacies. As Elijah let fall his mantle when he was taken up into heaven, so God's eminent servants, when their persons could no longer remain in this world, have left behind them some worthy pieces, as monuments of their graces, and zeal for the public welfare. Whether it be out of a modest sense of their own endeavours, as being loth, upon choice and of their own accord, to venture abroad into the world; or whether it be that being occupied and taken up with other labours; or whether

[1] One is 'Meat for the Eater; or, Hopes of Unity in and by Divided and Distracted Times,' on Zech. xiv. 10. The other is 'England's Spiritual Languishing, with the Causes and Cure,' on Rev. ii. 3.
[2] Anthony Wood mentions 'Smectymnus Redivivus,' in answer to 'The Humble Remonstrance,' Lond. 1653, which I have never seen.
[3] See Preface to the Exposition on James.

it be in conformity to Christ, who would not leave his Spirit till his departure; or whether it be out of hope that their works would find a more kindly reception after their death, the living being more liable to envy and reproach, but when the author is in heaven, the work is more esteemed upon earth; whether for this or that cause, usual it is that not only the life, but the death of God's servants have been profitable to the Church. By that means many useful treatises have been freed from that privacy and obscurity to which, by the modesty of their authors, they had formerly been confined.'[1]

He was a person of general learning, and had a fine collection of books, which sold for a considerable sum after his death; among which was the noble 'Paris edition of the Councils,' in thirty volumes, in folio, which the bookseller offered him for sixty pounds, or his Sermons on the One Hundred and Nineteenth Psalm. He began to transcribe them fair, but finding it too great an interruption in the frequent returns of his stated work, he chose rather to pay him in money. His great delight was in his study, and he was scarce ever seen without a book in his hand, if he was not engaged in company. He had diligently read the Fathers, and the principal schoolmen, which was a fashionable piece of learning in those times. And though he greatly preferred the plainness and simplicity of the former to the art and subtilty of the latter, yet he thought that we were more properly the Fathers, who stood on their shoulders, and have the advantage of seeing farther, in several respects, than they did. Perhaps scarce any man of the age had more diligently studied the scripture, or was a greater master of it. He had digested the best critics and commentators, and made a vast collection of judicious observations of his own, which appears in the pertinent and surprising use of the scripture upon all occasions, and the excellent glosses which are everywhere to be found in his writings. As he had a great reverence for the scripture himself, so he was observed to show a great zeal against using scripture phrases lightly in common conversation, or without a due regard to the sense and meaning of them, as a profanation of the scripture and a great dishonour to God. Dr Bates used to say, 'that he had heard the greatest men of those times sometimes preach a mean sermon, but never heard Dr Manton do so upon any occasion.' This will appear the less surprising, if we consider the great care he took about them. He generally writ the heads and principal branches first, and often writ them over twice afterwards, some copies of which are now in being. When his sermon did not please him, nor the matter open kindly, he would lay it aside for that time, though it were Saturday night, and sit up all night to prepare a sermon upon an easier subject, and more to his satisfaction. If a good thought came into his mind in the night, he would light his candle, and put on his gown, and write sometimes for an hour together at a table by his bedside, though the weather was ever so cold. He was well read in all the ancient and modern history, which he made his diversion, and in which he took a particular pleasure. This, by the advantage of an excellent judgment and strong memory,

[1] Epistle to Dr Sibb's Comment on the First Chapter of the Second Epistle to the Corinthians.

made his conversation very instructing and entertaining, and recommended him particularly to young gentlemen, who used to visit him after their travels. He would discourse with them as if he had been with them upon the spot, and bring things to their remembrance which they had forgot; and sometimes, to their great surprise, show a greater acquaintance with things abroad, attained by reading, than they had got by all the labour and expense of travelling. The celebrated Mr Edmund Waller, who first refined the English poetry, and brought it to the ease and correctness in which it now appears, used to say of him, upon this account, that 'he never discoursed with such a man as Dr Manton in all his life.' By this means he became a great judge of men and things; and was often resorted to by persons of the greatest note and figure in the world. He took his degree of Bachelor of Arts in the year 1639, and was created Bachelor of Divinity in 1654, and by virtue of His Majesty's letters was created Doctor of Divinity at the same time with Dr Bates, and several of the Royalists, in 1660.[1] It was pleasantly said upon this latter occasion, that none could say of him that *Creatio fit ex nihilo*, having both learning and a degree before.

He was a strict observer of family religion. His method was this: he began morning and evening with a short prayer, then read a chapter, his children and servants were obliged to remember some part of it, which he made easy and pleasant to them by a familiar exposition; then he concluded with a longer prayer. Notwithstanding the labours of the Lord's-day, he never omitted, after an hour's respite, to repeat the heads of both his sermons to his family, usually walking, and then concluded the day with prayer and singing a psalm. His great acquaintance with the scriptures, and deep seriousness of mind, furnished him with great pertinency and variety of expression upon all occasions, and preserved a great solemnity and reverence in all his addresses to God. His prayer after sermon usually contained the heads of his sermon. He was noted for a lively and affectionate manner of administering the Lord's Supper. He consecrated the elements of bread and wine apart; and whilst they were delivering, he was always full of heavenly discourse. He would often utter, with great fervour, those words: 'Who is a God like unto thee, pardoning iniquity, transgression, and sin?' and illustrate, in an affecting manner, the glory of the divine mercy to the lost world, in the death of Christ; and pathetically represent the danger of those who neglect and slight their baptismal covenant, and how terrible a witness it would be against them at the day of judgment.

Monday was his chief day of rest, in which he used to attend his visitors. On his Wednesday lecture several persons of considerable quality and distinction, who went to the Established Church on the Lord's-day, would come to hear him. One observing to him that there were many coaches at his doors on those days, he answered, smiling, 'I have coach-hearers, but foot-payers;' and yet he was far from the love of filthy lucre; for when it was proposed to him to bring his hearers to a subscription, he would not yield to it, but said his house should be free for all, as long as he could pay the rent of it.

[1] Anthony Wood's Fasti Oxon.

Some of his parishioners, and others who attended his ministry, used to present him, about Christmas, with what they collected among themselves, which was seldom above twelve or thirteen pounds. He had several persons of the first rank who belonged to his congregation, as the Countesses of Bedford, Manchester, Clare; the Ladies Baker, Trevor, the present Lord Trevor's mother; the Lord and Lady Wharton, and most of their children, &c. By this means he had always a considerable collection for the poor at the sacrament, which was a great pleasure to him. He used to say sometimes, pleasantly, that he had money in the poor's bag when he had little in his own. This he sometimes distributed among poor ministers, who were, many of them, at that time, in strait circumstances, as well as the poor of the congregation. Though he was a man of great gravity, and of a regular unaffected piety, yet he was extremely cheerful and pleasant among his friends, and upon every proper occasion. His religion sat easy, and well became him, and appeared amiable and lovely to others. He greatly disliked the forbidding rigours of some good people, and the rapturous pretensions of others; and used to say he had found it, by long observation, that they who would be over-godly at one time, would be under-godly at another.

I shall conclude with this summary account of his person and character. He was of a middle stature, and of a fair and fresh complexion, with a great mixture of majesty and sweetness in his countenance. In his younger years he was very slender, but grew corpulent in his advanced age; not by idleness or excess,[1] for he was remarkably temperate and unweariedly diligent. He had naturally a little appetite, and generally declined all manner of feasts; but by a sedentary life, and the long confinement of the five-mile-act, which, he used to complain, first broke his constitution. In short, perhaps few men of the age in which he lived had more virtues and fewer failings, or were more remarkable for general knowledge, fearless integrity, great candour and wisdom, sound judgment, and natural eloquence, copious invention, and incredible industry, zeal for the glory of God, and good-will to men; for acceptance and usefulness in the world, and a clear and unspotted reputation, through a course of many years, among all parties of men.

---

[1] Anthony Wood ('Athenæ Oxon.,' p. 600), says, 'When he took his degree at Oxford, he looked like a person rather fatted for the slaughter, than an apostle; being a round, plump, jolly man; but the Royalists resembled apostles by their macerated bodies and countenances.' Which, besides the injurious falsehood of the insinuation, is a coarse and butcherly comparison. I doubt it would not be safe to make that the standing measure of apostolical men.

A PRACTICAL EXPOSITION

OF

THE LORD'S PRAYER.

PREFACE.

Such is the divine matter and admirable order of the Lord's Prayer, as became the eternal wisdom of God, that composed and dictated it to his disciples. In it are opened the fountains of all our regular petitions, and the arguments contained to encourage our hopes for obtaining them. In our addresses to men, our study is to conciliate their favourable audience; but God is most graciously inclined and ready to grant our requests, therefore we are directed to call upon him by the title of 'Our Father in heaven,' to assure us of his love and power, and thereby to excite our reverent attention, to raise our affections, to confirm our confidence in prayer. The supreme end of our desires is the glory of God, in conjunction with our own happiness: this is expressed in the two first petitions, that 'his name may be hallowed,' and 'his kingdom come,' that we may partake of its felicity. In order to this, our desires are directed for the means that are proper and effectual to accomplish it. And those are of two kinds—the good things that conduct us, and the removal of those evils that obstruct our happiness. The good things are either, the spiritual and principal means to prepare us for glory, an entire, cordial, and constant obedience to the divine commands, expressed in the third petition, 'Thy will be done on earth, as it is in heaven;' or, natural and subservient, the supports and comforts of this life, which are contained in the fourth petition, 'Give us this day our daily bread.' The removal of evils is disposed according to the order of the good things we are to seek: we pray that our sins may be forgiven, the guilt of which directly excludes from his glorious kingdom; that we may be preserved from temptations, that withdraw us from observing the divine commands; and to be delivered from all afflicting evils, that hinder our arrival at our blessed end. The conclusion is to strengthen our faith, by ascribing to our heavenly Father, the kingdom, power, and glory, and to express our ardent desires of his blessing, by saying, Amen.

This divine comprehensive prayer is the subject of the following sermons, wherein the characters of Dr Manton's spirit are so conspicuous, as sufficiently discover them to be his; and the reader is assured they have been diligently compared with his own copy.

William Bates.

INTRODUCTION.

But thou, when thou prayest, enter into thy closet; and when thou hast shut the door, pray to thy Father, &c.—MAT. VI. 6–8.

I INTEND to go over the Lord's Prayer ; and, to make way for it, I shall speak a little of these foregoing verses, wherein our Lord treats of the duty of prayer, and the necessity of being much therein.

In the beginning of this chapter our Lord taxeth the hypocrisy of the Pharisees, which was plainly to be seen in all their duties—their alms, their prayers, and their fasting.

I. For their alms: Christ deals with that in the first four verses. It seems it was their fashion, when they gave alms, to sound a trumpet ; and their pretence was to call all the poor within hearing, or to give notice that such a rabbi giveth alms to-day. Now, our Lord showeth that though this were the fair pretence to call the poor, yet their heart was merely upon their own glory, their own esteem with men ; and therefore he persuades his disciples to greater secrecy in this work, and to content themselves with God's approbation, which will be open, and manifest, and honourable enough in due time, when the archangel shall blow the trumpet to call all the world together, 1 Thes. iv. 16, and Christ shall publish their good works in the hearing of men and angels : Mat. xxv. 34–36. Thus he deals with them upon the point of alms.

II. For their prayers : Christ taxeth their affectation of applause, because they sought out places of the greatest resort,—the synagogues and corners of the streets,—and there did put themselves into a praying posture, that they might be seen of men, and appear to be persons of great devotion, and so might the better accomplish their own ends, their public designs upon the stage (for the Pharisees were great sticklers at that time), and also their private designs upon widows' houses, that they might be trusted with the management of widows' and orphans' estates, as being devout men, and of great sanctity and holiness.

In which practice there was a double failing :—

1. As to the circumstance of place, performing a personal and solitary prayer in a public place, which was a great indecorum, and argued the action to be scenical, or brought upon the stage merely for

public applause. And certainly that private praying which is used by men in churches doth justly come under our Lord's reproof.

2. Their next failing was as to their end: 'Verily they do it to be seen of men.'

Object. But what fault was there in this? Doth not Christ himself direct us, in his Sermon, Mat. v. 16, 'Let your light so shine before men, that they may see your good works, and glorify your Father which is in heaven'? And yet the Pharisees are here taxed for praying, fasting, and giving alms, that they might be seen of men; how can these places stand together?

By way of answer:—

1. We must distinguish of the different scope and intention of Christ in these two places. *There,* Christ's scope is to commend and enjoin good works to be seen of men, *ad edificationem,* for their edification; *here,* his scope is to forbid us to do good works to be seen of men, *ad ostentationem,* for our own ostentation: *There,* Christian charity to the souls of men is commended; and *here,* vainglory is forbidden.

2. Again, good works are to be distinguished. Some are so truly and indeed; others only in outward show and appearance. Good works, that are truly so and indeed, Christ enjoins there; hypocritical and feigned acts, that are only so in outward show and semblance, are forbidden here. To pray is a good work, take inward and outward acts of it together, and so it is enjoined. But hypocritical and superstitious prayer, which hath only the face and show of goodness, this is forbidden.

3. We must distinguish of the ends of good works; principal and subordinate; adequate and inadequate. First, the principal and primary end of good works must not be that we may be seen of men, but the glory of God; but now the subordinate, or less principal end, may be to be seen of men. Again, it must not be our adequate end, that is, our whole and main intention and scope; but a collateral and side end it may be. It is one thing to do good works, only that they may be seen; it is another thing to do good works, that they may not only be seen, but also be imitated, to win others by them to give glory to God. It is one thing to do good works for the glory of God, another thing to do them for the glory of ourselves. We may do good works to be seen in the first respect, but not in the last. We may not pray with the Pharisees merely to be seen of men, yet we may let our light shine before men, to draw them to duty, and give more glory to God.

4. Again, *there* Christ speaks of the general bent of our conversation, and *here* only of particular and private duties. It would argue too much hypocrisy to do these in public, though the whole frame and course of our carriage before men must be religious in their sight. And that is agreeable to what the apostle saith, 2 Cor. viii. 21, 'We should provide for honest things, not only in the sight of the Lord, but also in the sight of men.' And, Phil. ii. 15, Christians are advised there to be 'blameless and harmless, the sons of God, without rebuke, in the midst of a crooked and perverse generation, shining among them as lights in the world.' That which

is obvious to the sight and observance of men, must be such as will become our holy calling. But our private and particular duties, which are to pass between God and us, these must be out of sight. I hope another man may approve himself to be honest and religious to me, though he doth not fall down and make his personal and private prayers before me. But to leave no scruple, if possible ;

5. We must distinguish of the diverse significations of that phrase which is used here, ὅπως, *that we may be seen*. There is a twofold sense of ὅπως, or *that*. It may be taken two ways, as they speak, either causally or eventually. Causally, and then it implies and imports the end and scope why we do such a thing, namely, for this very purpose, that we may obtain it. And thus the Pharisees here did pray, ὅπως, *that they might be seen of men*, that is, this was their main end and scope. Thus *that* is taken causally. Secondly, *that* sometimes is taken eventually, and then it doth not import the end and scope, but only the event that will fall out and follow upon such a thing. Thus *that* is often taken in scripture. John ix. 39 : Christ saith there, ' For judgment I am come into the world, that they which see not, might see ; and that they which see, might be made blind.' It was not Christ's scope to do so, but Christ foresaw that this would be the event of his coming into the world, and, therefore, he saith, *that*, &c. So Luke xiv. 10 : Christ tells them there, ' But when thou art bidden to a feast, go and sit down in the lowest room, that when he that bade thee comes, he may say unto thee, Friend, go up higher : then shalt thou have worship in the presence of them that sit at meat with thee.' *That* is taken eventually, not causally ; for Christ doth not bid them there to set themselves at the lower end of the table, for this very end, or to make this their scope : that is the thing he forbids—affectation of precedency ; but *that, hoc est*, then it will follow, that is, this is likely to be the event ; then the master of the house will come to you if you do this. Not that it should be your scope to feign humility, that you may obtain the highest place at the table. And so may Christ's words be taken, ' Let your light so shine,' &c. This will fall out upon it then—men will be conscious to your Christian carriage and gracious behaviour, and by that means God will be much honoured and glorified. There it is taken eventually, but here it is taken causally. The Pharisees did it that they might be seen of men ; that is, this was their scope and principal intention. And thus may you reconcile these two places of scripture.

Well, now, Christ having taxed them for these two faults : for their undue *place*, the synagogue and corners of the streets being unfit for a private and personal act of worship ; and for their end, that they might be seen of men,—he saith, ' They have their reward.' That is, the whole debt is paid, they can challenge nothing at God's hands. God will be behindhand with none of his creatures. As they have what they looked for, so they must expect no more, they must be content with their penny. The phrase is borrowed from matters of contract between man and man, and is a word proper to those which give a discharge for a debt. As creditors and money-lenders, when they are paid home the full sum which is due to them, then they can exact no more; so here they must be contented with the empty, windy puffs of vainglory, and to feed upon the unsavoury breath of the people: they can expect no more from God, for the bond is cancelled, and they have received their full reward already. Briefly, here is the difference in the several rewards that the hypocrites and the children of God have: the hypocrites, they are all for the present, and have their reward, and much good may it do them; there is not a jot behind, it will be in vain to expect any more: but now, for the children of God, your Father will reward you; they must expect and wait for the future. And yet in scripture we read oftentimes that the children of God have their reward in this life; but then the word in the original is ἔχουσι, which signifieth they have but in part; not the word which is used here, ἀπέχουσι, which signifies they have what is due, it is fulfilled, paid them. So those expressions in scripture are to be taken: 'Ye have eternal life,' 'and he hath,' 'and that ye may have.' It is often spoken in scripture of the children of God, so that they seem to have their reward too. They have their reward, but it is partially, not totally: there is something, the best things, yet behind. A child of God, he hath promises, first-fruits, some beginnings of communion with God here, but he looks for greater things to come.

Well, then, Christ, having disproved the practice of the Pharisees, seeks to set his own disciples right in the management of their prayers, as well as in their alms. Pharisaism is very natural in the best. We are apt to be haunted with a carnal spirit in the best duties; not only in alms, where we have to do with men, but in prayer, where our business lieth wholly with God; especially in public prayer; even there much of man will creep in. The devil is like a fly, which, if driven from one place, pitcheth upon another; so drive him out of alms, and he will seek to taint your prayers.

Therefore Christ, to rectify his disciples in their personal and solitary prayers, instructs them to withdraw into some place of recess and retirement, and to be content with God for witness, approver, and judge. 'But thou, when thou prayest, enter into thy closet; and when thou hast shut thy doors, pray to thy Father which is in secret,' &c.

In which words you may observe:—

I. A supposition concerning solitary prayer: 'But thou, when thou prayest.'

II. A direction about it: 'Enter into thy closet, and shut thy door, and pray to thy Father which is in secret.'

III. Encouragement to perform it: 'And thy Father, which seeth in secret, shall reward thee openly.' Where two things are asserted:—

1. God's sight: He is conscious to thy prayers when others are not.

2. God's reward: 'He will reward thee openly.'

To open the circumstances of the text:—

In the supposition, 'But thou, when thou prayest,' observe:—

1. Christ takes it for granted that his disciples will pray to God. He doth not say, *if* thou prayest, but *when* thou prayest, as supposing them to be sufficiently convinced of this duty of being often with God in private.

2. I observe, again, Christ speaks of solitary prayer, when a man alone, and without company, pours out his heart to God. Therefore Christ speaks in the singular number: ' When thou prayest;' not plurally and collectively, when *ye* pray, or meet together in prayer. Therefore he doth not forbid public praying in the assemblies of the saints, or family-worship; both are elsewhere required in scripture. God hath made promises to public and church prayer, praying with men or before men: Mat. xviii. 19, 'When two or three are met together, and shall agree on earth as touching anything that they shall ask, it shall be done for them of my Father which is in heaven.' And when they shall agree in one public prayer, it seems to have a greater efficacy put upon it—when more are interested in the same prayer—when, with a combined force, they do as it were besiege the God of heaven, and will not let him go unless he leaves a blessing. Look, as the petition of a shire and county to authority is more than a private man's supplication, so when we meet as a church to pray, and as a family, there is combined strength. And in this sense, that saying of the schoolmen is orthodox enough—viz., that prayer made in the church hath a more easy audience with God. Why? Because of the concurrence of many which are met there to worship God. Christ doth not intend in this any way to jostle out that which he seeks to establish elsewhere. Let your intentions be secret, though your prayers be public and open in the family or assemblies of the saints.

II. Let us open the direction our Lord gives about solitary prayer. The direction is suited so as to avoid the double error of the Pharisees; their offence as to place, and as to the aim and end.

1. Their offence as to the place: 'Enter into thy closet, and shut thy door.' These words are not to be taken metaphorically, nor yet pressed too literally. Not metaphorically, as some would carry them. Descend into thy heart, be serious and devout with God in the closet of thy soul, which is the most inward recess and retiring-place of man. This were to be wanton with scripture. The literal sense is not to be left without necessity, nor yet pressed too literally, as if prayer should be confined to a chamber and closet. Christ prayed in the mountain, Mat. xiv. 23; and Gen. xxiv. 63, Isaac went into the field to meditate. The meaning is, private prayer must be performed in a private place, retired from company and the sight of men as much as may be.

2. Christ rectifieth them as to the end: ' Pray to thy Father which is in secret;' that is, pray to God, who is in that private place, though he cannot be seen with bodily eyes; wherein Christ seems secretly to tax the hypocrisy of the Pharisees, who did rather pray to men than to God, who was invisible; because all their aim was to be approved of men, and to be cried up by them as devout persons. So that what the Lord saith concerning fasting, Zech. vii. 5, 6, 'When ye fasted and mourned in the fifth and seventh month, even those seventy years, did ye at all fast unto me, even to me? and when ye did eat, and when ye did drink, did not ye eat for yourselves, and drink for yourselves?' So here, was this unto God? No, though the force and sound of the words carried it for God, yet they were directed to men. When God is not made both the object and aim, it is not to him;

when you seek another paymaster, you decline God, yea, you make him your footstool, a step to some other thing.

III. Here are the encouragements to this personal, private, and solitary prayer; and they are taken from God's sight, and God's reward.

1. From God's sight: 'Thy Father seeth in secret;' that is, observeth thy carriage. The posture and frame of thy spirit, the fervour and uprightness of heart which thou manifestest in prayer, is all known to him. Mark, that which is the hypocrite's fear, and binds condemnation upon the heart of a wicked man, is here made to be the saints' support and ground of comfort—that they pray to an all-seeing God: 1 John iii. 20, 'If our hearts condemn us, God is greater than our hearts, and knoweth all things.' Their heavenly Father seeth in secret; he can interpret their groans, and read the language of their sighs. Though they fail as to the outside of a duty, and there be much brokenness of speech, yet God seeth brokenness of heart there, and it is that he looks after. God seeth. What is that? He seeth whether thou prayest or no, and how thou prayest. (1.) He seeth whether thou prayest or no: mark that passage, Acts ix. 11, 'The Lord said to Ananias, Arise, and go into the street which is called Straight, and inquire in the house of Judas for one called Saul of Tarsus; for behold, he prayeth.' Go into such a city, such a street, such a house, such a part, in such a chamber, behold he prayeth. The Lord knew all these circumstances. It is known unto him whether we toil or loiter away our time, or whether we pray in secret; he knows what house, in what corner of the house, what we are doing there. (2.) He seeth *how* you pray: Rom. viii. 27. It is propounded as the comfort of the saints, 'And he that searcheth the heart knoweth what is the mind of the spirit.' God knoweth you thoroughly, and can distinguish of your prayers, whether they be customary and formal, or serious acts of love to God, and communion with him.

2. The other thing which is propounded here is God's reward: 'And he will reward them openly.' How doth God reward our prayers? Not for any worth or dignity which is in them. What merit can there be in begging? What doth a beggar deserve in asking alms? But it is out of his own grace and mercy, having by promise made himself as it were a debtor to a poor, faithful, and believing supplicant. But 'he will reward thee openly.' How is that? Either by a sensible answer to thy prayers, as he doth often to his children, by granting what they pray for; as when Daniel was praying in secret, God sent an angel to him, Dan. ix. 20; or by an evident blessing upon their prayers in this world, for the conscionable performance of this duty. Abraham, Isaac, and Jacob, that were men of much communion with God, were eminently and sensibly blessed; they were rewarded openly for their secret converse with him; or it may be, by giving them respect externally in the eyes of others. A praying people dart conviction into the consciences of men. It is notable that Pharaoh in his distress sent for Moses and Aaron, and not for the magicians. The consciences of wicked men are open at such a time, and they know God's children have special favour and

great audience with him; and he having the hearts of all men in his hands, can manage and dispose respect according as he pleaseth. And when they are in distress, this honour God hath put upon you, they shall send for you to pray with them; and those which honour him, though but in secret, God will openly put honour upon them: 1 Sam. ii. 30. But chiefly this is meant at the day of judgment; then those which pray in secret their heavenly Father will reward them openly. When thou relievest the poor, and showest comfort to the needy, they cannot recompense thee; but then thou shalt be recompensed at the resurrection of the just, Luke xiv. 14. There is the great and most public reward of Christians: 1 Cor. iv. 5, 'Then he will bring to light the hidden things of darkness, and will make manifest the counsels of the heart; and then shall every man have praise with God;' that is, every man that is praiseworthy, however he be mistaken and judged of the world; for the apostle speaks it to comfort them against the censures of men. And mark, this is opposed to the reward which the Pharisees pleased themselves with: it was much with them to be well thought of in such a synagogue, or before such a company of men; ' but your Father, which seeth in secret, will reward you openly;' that is, not only in the eyes of such a city or town, but before all the world.

The point is this :—

Doct. That private, solitary, and closet-prayer is a duty very necessary and profitable.

It is a necessary duty; for Christ supposeth it of his disciples, to whom he speaks: ' But thou, when thou prayest,' &c. And it is profitable, for unto it God makes promises: You have a Father which seeth in secret, and one day shall be owned before all the world.

First, It is a duty necessary; and that will appear :—

1. From God's precept. That precept which requireth prayer, requireth secret and closet-prayer; for God's command to pray first falls upon single persons, before it falls upon families and churches, which are made up of single persons. Therefore where God hath bidden thee to pray, you must take that precept as belonging to you in particular. I shall give some of the precepts: Col. iv. 2, ' Continue in prayer, and watch in the same with thanksgiving;' and 1 Thes. v. 17, 'Pray without ceasing.' These are principally meant of our personal addresses to God, every man for himself; for in joining with others, the work is rather imposed upon us than taken up upon choice. And that can only be at stated times, when they can conveniently meet together; but we ourselves are called upon to continue to pray, and that without ceasing; that is, to be often with God, and to keep up not only a praying frame, but a constant correspondence with him. Surely every man which acknowledgeth a God, a Providence, and that depends upon him for blessings, much more every one that pretends he hath a Father in heaven, in whose hands are the guidance of all the things of the world, is bound to pray personally and alone, by himself to converse with God.

2. I shall argue it from the example of Christ, which bindeth us, and hath the force of a law in things moral. As Christ's word is our rule, so his practice is our copy. This is true religion, to imitate him whom we worship. In this you must do as Christ did. Now we often read

that Christ prayed alone—he went aside to pray to God; therefore, if we be Christians, so it should be with us: Mark i. 35, ' And in the morning, rising up a great while before day, he went out and departed into a solitary place, and there prayed.' He left the company of his disciples, with whom he often joined, that he might be alone with God betimes in the morning. And again you have it: Mat. xiv. 23, ' And when he had sent the multitude away, he went up into a mountain apart to pray; and when the evening was come, he was there alone.' And, Luke vi. 12, it is said, ' He went out into a mountain to pray, and continued all night in prayer to God.' You see Christ takes all occasions in retiring and going apart to God. Now the pattern of Christ is both engaging and encouraging.

It is very engaging. Shall we think ourselves not to need that help which Christ would submit unto? There are many proud persons which think themselves above prayer. Christ had no need to pray as we have ; he had the fulness of the Godhead dwelling in him bodily; yet he was not above prayer. And if he had need of prayer, he had no need of retirement to go and pray alone; his affections always served, and he was not pestered with any distraction, and all places and companies were alike to him; and yet he would depart into a solitary place that he might be private with God.

Then the pattern of Christ is very encouraging ; for whatever Christ did, he sanctified in that respect—his steps in every duty leave a blessing. Look, as Christ sanctified baptism by being baptized himself, and made the water of baptism to be saving and comfortable for us; and the Lord's supper, by being a guest himself, and eating himself at his own table, so he sanctified private prayer: when he prayed, a virtue went out from him, he left a strength to enable us to pray. And it is encouraging in this respect, because he hath experimented this duty. He knows how soon human strength is spent and put to it, for he himself hath been wrestling with God in prayer with all his might. His submitting to these duties gave him sympathy ; he knows the heart of a praying man when wrestling with God with all earnestness; therefore he helpeth us in these agonies of spirit. Again, his praying is an encouragement against our imperfections. Christians, when we are alone with God, and our hearts are heavy as a log and stone, what a comfort is it to think Christ himself prayed, and that earnestly, and was once alone wrestling with God in human nature! Mat. xiv. 23. And when the enemy came to attack him, he was alone, striving with God in prayer. He takes all occasions for intercourse with God; and if you have the Spirit, you will do likewise.

3. I might argue from God's end in pouring out the Holy Ghost ; wherefore hath God poured out his Spirit? Zech. xii. 11–14, ' I will pour out the Spirit of grace and of supplication,' &c. He poureth out the Spirit, that it may break out by this vent: the Spirit of grace will presently run into supplication ; the whole house of Israel shall mourn. There is the church, they have the benefit of the pouring out of the Spirit; and every household hath benefit, that he and his family may mourn apart, and every person apart; that we may go and mourn over our case and distempers before God, and pour out our

hearts in a holy and affectionate manner. This argument I would have you to note, that this was God's end in pouring out his Spirit, for a double reason, both to take off excuses, and to quicken diligence.

Partly, to take off excuses, because many say they have no gifts, no readiness and savouriness of speech, and how can they go alone and pray to God? Certainly men which have necessities, and a sense of them, can speak of them in one fashion or other to God; but the Spirit is given to help. Such is God's condescension to the saints, that he hath not only provided an advocate to present our petitions in court, but a notary to draw them up; not only appointed Christ for help against our guilt and unworthiness, but likewise the Spirit to help us in prayer. When we are apt to excuse ourselves by our weakness and insufficiency, he hath poured out the Holy Ghost, that we may pray apart. Partly to this end, the more to awaken our diligence, that God's precious gift be not bestowed upon us in vain, to lie idle and unemployed, he hath poured out the Spirit; and therefore we should make use of it, not only that we may attend to the prayers of others, and join with them, but that we may make use of our own share of gifts and graces, and open and unfold our own case to God.

4. That it is a necessary duty, I plead it from the practice of saints, who are a praying people. Oh how often do we read in scripture that they are alone with God, pouring out their souls in complaints to him! Nothing so natural to them as prayer; they are called a 'generation of them that seek God:' Ps. xxiv. 6. As light bodies are moving upward, so the saints are looking upward to God, and praying alone to him. Daniel was three times a day with God, and would not omit his hours of prayer, though his life was in danger, Dan. vi. 10; and David, 'Seven times a day do I praise thee,' Ps. cxix. 164; and Cornelius, it is said that he prayed to God always, Acts x. 2, not only with his family, but alone in holy soliloquies. He was so frequent and diligent, that he had gotten a habit of prayer —he prayed always. Well, then, if this be the temper of God's people, then to be altogether unlike them—when we have no delight in these private converses with God, or neglect them, it gives just cause of suspicion.

5. Our private necessities show that it is a necessary duty, which cannot be so feelingly spoken to and expressed by others as by ourselves; and, it may be, are not so fit to be divulged and communicated to others. We cannot so well lay forth our hearts with such largeness and comfort in our own concernments before others. There is the plague of our own hearts, which every one must mourn over: 1 Kings viii. 38. As we say, no nurse like the mother; so none so fit humbly with a broken heart to set forth our own wants before the Lord as ourselves. There is some thorn in the flesh that we have cause to pray against again and again: 'For this I sought the Lord thrice,' saith St Paul, 2 Cor. xii. 7, 8. We should put promises in suit, and lay open our own case before the compassions of God. It is a help sometimes to join with others; but at other times it would be a hindrance. We have peculiar necessities of our own to commend to God, therefore must be alone.

Secondly, This closet and solitary prayer, as it is a necessary duty, so it is a profitable one.

1. It conduceth much to enlargement of heart. The more earnest men are, the more they desire to be alone, free from trouble and distraction. When a man weeps, and is in a mournful posture, he seeks secrecy, that he may indulge his grief. They were to mourn apart: Zech. xii., and Jer. xiii. 17, 'My soul shall weep sore for your pride in secret places.' So here, when a man would deal most earnestly with God, he should seek retirement, and be alone. Christ in his agonies went apart from his disciples. When he would pray more earnestly, it is said, 'He was withdrawn from them about a stone's cast:' Luke xxii. 41. It is said, 'He went apart.' Strong affections are loth to be disturbed and diverted, therefore seek retirement. And, it is notable, Jacob, when he would wrestle with God, it is said, Gen. xxxii. 24, 'And Jacob was left alone, and there wrestled a man with him until the breaking of the day.' When he had a mind to deal with God in good earnest, he sent away all his company.

A hypocrite, he finds a greater flash of gifts in his public duties, when he prays with others, and is the mouth of others; but is slight and superficial when alone with God; if he feels anything, a little overly matter serves the turn. But usually God's children most affectionately pour out their hearts before him in private; where they do more particularly express their own necessities, there they find their affections free to wrestle with God. In public we take in the necessities of others, but in private our own.

2. As it makes way for enlargement of heart on our part, so for secret manifestations of love on God's part. Bernard hath a saying, 'The church's Spouse is bashful, and will not be familiar and communicate his loves before company, but alone.' The sweetest experiences which God's saints receive many times are when they are alone with him. When Daniel was praying alone with great earnestness, the angel Gabriel was sent, and caused to fly swiftly to him to tell him his prayers were answered: Dan. ix. 21. And Cornelius, while he was praying alone, an angel of God came unto him, to report the hearing of his prayers: Acts x. 3; and, ver. 9, Peter, when he was praying alone, then God instructs him in the mystery of the calling of the Gentiles: then had he that vision when he was got upon the top of the house to pray. Before we are regenerated, God appeareth to us many times when we do not think of it; but after we are regenerated, usually he appeareth upon more eminent acts of grace—when we are exercising ourselves, and more particularly dealing with God, and putting forth the strength of our souls to take hold of him in private.

3. There is this profit in it: It is a mighty solace and support in affliction, especially when we are censured, scorned, and despised of men, and know not where to go to find a friend with whom we may unbosom our sorrow. Then to go aside, and open the matter to God, it is a mighty ease to the soul: Job xvi. 20, 'My friends scorn me; but mine eye poureth out tears unto God.' When we have a great burden upon us, to go aside and open the matter to God, it gives ease to the heart, and vent to our grief; as Hannah in great trouble falls

a-praying to God, and then was no more sad : 1 Sam. i. 13. As the opening of a vein cooleth and refresheth in a fever, so when we make known our case to God, it is a mighty solace in affliction.

4. It is a great trial of our sincerity, of our faith, love, and obedience, when we are alone, and nobody knows what we do, then to see him that is invisible : Heb. xi. 27 ;—when we are much with God in private, where we have no reasons but those of duty and conscience to move us. Carnal hypocrites will be much in outward worship. They have their qualms, and pray themselves weary, and do something for fashion sake when foreign reasons move them ; but will they so pray as to delight themselves in the Almighty ? Will they always call upon God ? Job xxvii. 10. That delight in God, which puts us upon converses with God, affects privacy.

5. It is a profitable duty, because of the great promises which God hath made to it. This secret and private prayer in the text shall have a public reward ; it will not be lost, for God will reward it openly. So Job xxii. 21 : ' Acquaint now thyself with him, and be at peace ; thereby good shall come unto thee.' Frequent correspondence with, and constant visits of God in prayer, what peace, comfort, quickening brings it into the soul ! So Ps. xlix. 32 : ' His soul shall live that seeks the Lord.' Without often seeking to God, the vitality of the soul is lost. We may as well expect a crop and harvest without sowing, as any liveliness of grace where there is not seeking of God. Could a man take notice of another in a crowd, whose face he never saw before ? So, will God own and bless you in the crowds of the assemblies of his people, if you mind not this duty when you are alone ?

APPLICATION.

Use 1. To reprove those which neglect closet-addresses to God ; they wrong God and themselves.

They wrong God ; because this is a necessary part of the creature's homage, of that duty he expects from them, to be owned not only in public assemblies, but in private. And they wrong themselves ; because it brings in a great deal of comfort and peace to the soul ; and many sweet and gracious experiences there are which they deprive themselves of, and a blessing upon all other things.

But more particularly to show the evil of this sin :—

1. It is a sin of omission ; and these sins are very dangerous, as well as sins of commission. Natural conscience usually smites more for sins of commission, than for sins of omission. To wrong and beat a father seems a more heinous and unnatural act, than not to give him due reverence and attendance. We are sensible of sins of commission ; but yet God will charge sins of omission as well as commission upon you ; and so will conscience too when it is serious, when, against the plain knowledge of God's will, you can omit such a necessary part of God's worship : James iv. 17, 'To him that knoweth to do good, and doeth it not, to him it is sin,'—that is, it will be sin with a witness. Conscience will own it so, when it is awakened by the word, or by providence, or great affliction, or cast upon your death-bed.

How will your own hearts reproach you then, that have neglected God, and lost such precious hours as you should have redeemed for communion with him! Sins of omission argue as great a contempt of God's authority as sins of commission; for the same law which forbids a sin, doth also require a duty from us.

And sins of omission argue as much hatred of God as sins of commission. If two should live in the same house, and never speak to one another, it would be taken for an argument of as great hatred as to fight one with another. So, when God is in us and round about us, and we never take time to confer with him, it argues much hatred and neglect of him.

And sins of omission are an argument of our unregeneracy, as much as sins of commission. A man which lives in a course of drunkenness, filthiness, and adultery, you would judge him to be an unregenerate man, and that he hath such a spot upon him as is not the spot of God's children. So, to live in a constant neglect of God, is an argument of unregeneracy, as much as to live in a course of debauchery. The apostle, when he would describe the Ephesians by their unconverted state, describes it thus: Eph. ii. 12, 'That they lived without God in the world.' When God is not owned and called upon, and unless the restraints of men, the law of common education, and customs of nations call for it, they live without God. So Ps. xiv. 1: 'They are corrupt, they have done abominable works; there is none that doeth good, they are altogether become filthy.' Every unregenerate man is that atheist. There is some difference among unregenerate men. Some are less in the excesses and gross outbreakings of their sins and folly. Some sin more, some less; but they all are abominable on this account, because they do not seek after God. And the apostle makes use of that argument to convince all men to be in a state of sin: Rom. iii. 11, 'There is none that seeketh after God.' The heart may be as much hardened by omissions (yea, sometimes more), than by commissions. As an act of sin brings a brawniness and deadness upon the heart, so doth the omission of a necessary duty. Not only the breaking of a string puts the instrument out of tune, but its being neglected and not looked after. Certainly by experience we find none so tender, so holy, so humble, and heavenly, as they which are often with God. This makes the heart tender, which otherwise would grow hard, dead, and stupid.

2. It is not only an omission in general, but an omission of prayer, which is, first, a duty very natural to the saints. Prayer is a duty very natural and kindly to the new creature. As soon as Paul was converted, the first news we hear of him, Acts ix. 11, 'Behold, he prayeth.' As soon as we are new-born, there will be a crying out for relief in prayer. It is the character of the saints: Ps. xxiv. 6, 'This is the generation of them that seek thee,' a people much in calling upon God. And the prophet describes them by the work of prayer: Zeph. iii. 10, 'My supplicants'; and, Zech. xii. 10, 'I will pour upon them the Spirit of grace and supplication.' Wherever there is a spirit of grace, it presently runneth out into prayer. Look, as a preacher is so called from the frequency of his work, so a Christian is one that calleth upon God. 'Every one that calleth on the name

of the Lord, shall be saved:' Rom. x. 13. In vain he is called a
preacher that never preacheth, so he is in vain called a Christian that
never prayeth. As things of an airy nature move upward, so the
saints are carried up to God by a kind of naturality, when they are
gracious. God hath no tongue-tied or dumb children ; they are all
crying, ' Abba, Father.' Then it is an omission of a duty which is of
great importance as to our communion with God, which lieth in two
things—fruition and familiarity; in the enjoyment of God, and in being
familiar and often with him. Fruition we have by faith, and familiarity is carried on by prayer. There are two duties which are never
out of season, hearing and prayer, both which are a holy dialogue
betwixt God and the soul, until we come to vision, the sight of him
in heaven. Our communion with God here is carried on by these two
duties: we speak to God in prayer, God answereth us in the word ;
God speaks to us in the word, and we return and echo back again to
him in prayer. Therefore the new creature delighteth much in these
two duties. Look, as we should be ' swift to hear,' James ix. 19,
until we come to seeing, we should take all occasions, and be
often in hearing. So in prayer we speak to God, and therefore should
be redeeming time for this work. In the word God comes down to
us, and in prayer we get up to God; therefore, if you would be
familiar and often with God, you must be much in prayer. This is
of great importance. You know the very notion of prayer. It is a
' visiting' of God: Isa. xxvi. 16, ' O Lord, in trouble have they visited
thee; they poured out a prayer when thy chastening was upon them.'
Praying to God, and visiting of God, are equivalent expressions. Now
it argueth very little friendship to God, when we will not so much as
come at him. Can there be any familiarity, where there is so much
distance and strangeness as never to give God a visit?

3. It is the omission of personal and secret prayer, which in some
respects should be more prized than other prayer.

Partly, because here our converse with God is more express as to
our own case. When we join with others, God may do it for their
sakes, but here, Ps. cxvi. 1, ' I love the Lord, because he hath
heard my voice and my supplication.' When we deal with him
alone, we put the promises in suit, and may know more it is we that
have been heard. We put God more to the trial ; we see what he
will do for us, and upon our asking and striving.

Partly, here we are more put to the trial what love we will express
to our Father in secret, when we have no outward reasons, no induce-
ments from respects of men to move us. In public duties (which
are liable and open to the observance of others), hypocrites may put
forth themselves with great vigour, quickness, and warmth, whereas
in private addresses to God, they are slight and careless. A Christian
is best tried and exercised in private, in those secret intercourses between God and his own soul ; there he finds most communion with
God, and most enlargement of heart. A man cannot so well judge of
his spirit, and discern the workings of it in public, because other
men's concernments and necessities, mingled with ours, are taken in,
and because he is more liable to the notice of others. But when he
is with God alone, he hath only reasons of conscience and duty to

move him.   When none but God is conscious and our own hearts, then we shall see what we do for the approbation of God, and acceptance with him.

And partly, in some respects, this is to be more prized, because privacy and retiredness is necessary, and is a great advantage, that men's spirits may be settled and composed for the duty.   Sinful distractions will crowd in upon us when in company, and we are thinking of this and that.   How often do we mingle sulphur with our incense— carnal thoughts in our worship!   How apt are we to do so in public duties!   But in private we are wholly at leisure to deal with God in a child-like liberty.   Now, will you omit this duty where you may be most free, without distraction, to let out the heart to God?

And partly, because a man will not be fit to pray in public and in company, which doth not often pray in secret: he will lose his savour and delight in this exercise, and soon grow dry, barren, sapless, and careless of God.   Look, as in the prophet Ezekiel, you read there that the glory of the Lord removed from the temple by degrees: it first removed from the holy place, then to the altar of burnt-offerings, then to the threshold of the house, then to the city, then to the mount which was on the east side of the city; there the glory of the Lord stood hovering a while, as loth to be gone, to see if the people would get it back again; this seems to be some emblem and representation of God's dealing with particular men.   First, God is cast out of the closet, private intercourses between God and them are neglected; and then he is cast out of the family, and within a little while out of the congregation; public ordinances begin to be slighted, and to be looked upon as useless things; and then men are given up to all profaneness and looseness, and lose all: so that religion, as it were, dieth by degrees, and a carnal Christian loseth more and more of the presence of God.   And, therefore, if we would be able to pray in company, we must often pray in secret.

4. Consider the mischief which followeth neglect of private converse with God.   Omissions make way for commissions.   If a gardener withholds his hand, the ground is soon grown over with weeds. Restrain prayer and neglect God, and noisome lusts will abound.   Our hearts are filled with distempers when once we cease to be frequent with God in private.   It is said of Job, chap. xv. 4, 'Thou restrainest prayer before God.'   That passage is notable, Ps. xiv. 4: 'They eat up my people as they eat bread, and call not upon the Lord.'   Omit secret prayer, and some great sin will follow; within a little while you will be given up to some evil course or other: either brutish lusts, oppression, or violence; to hate the people of God, to join in a confederacy with them which cry up a confederacy against God.   The less we converse with God in private, the more is the awe of God lessened.   But now, a man which is often with God dareth not offend him so freely as others do.   As they which are often with princes and great persons are better clothed and more neat in their apparel and carriage, so they which are often conversing with God grow more heavenly, holy, watchful, than others are; and when we are not with God, not only all this is lost, but a great many evils to be found.   It is plainly seen by men's conversations how little they converse with God.

But now, to avoid the stroke of this reproof, what will men do? Either deny the guilt, or excuse themselves.

First, Some will deny the guilt. They do call upon God, and use private prayer, therefore think themselves to be free from this reproof. Yea, but are you as often with God as you should be?

There are three sorts of persons :—

1. Some there are that omit it totally, cannot speak of redeeming any time for this work. These are practical atheists, 'without God in the world:' Eph. ii. 12. They are heathens and pagans under a Christian name and profession. We should 'pray without ceasing:' 1 Thes. v. 17; that is, take all praying occasions; therefore they which pray not at all, all the week long God hears not from them, surely come under the force of this reproof.

2. There are some which perform it seldom. Oh, how many days and weeks pass over their heads and God never hears from them! The Lord complains of it, Jer. ii. 32 : ' They have forgotten me days without number.' It was time out of mind since they were last with God.

3. The most do not perform it so often as they should. And therefore (that I may speak with evidence and conviction) I shall answer the case; what rules may be given; how often we should be with God; and when we are said to neglect God.

[1.] Every day something should be done in this kind. Acts x. 2 : Cornelius prayed to God always, every day he had his times of familiarity with God. Daniel, though with the hazard of his life, would not omit 'praying three times a day:' Dan. vi. 10. And David speaks of ' morning, evening, and noon :' Ps. lv. 17. Though we cannot bind all men absolutely to these hours, because of the difference of conditions, employments, and occasions, yet thus much we may gather from hence, that surely they which are most holy will be most frequent in this work.

[2.] Love will direct you. They which love one another, will not be strange one to another : a man cannot be long out of the company of him whom he loveth. Christ loved Lazarus, and Mary, and Martha, John xi. 5, and therefore his great resort was to Bethany, to Lazarus' house. Surely they which love God will have frequent recourse to him. In the times of the gospel, God trusts love : we are not bound to such particular rules as under the law. Why? For love is a liberal grace, and will put us upon frequent visits, and tell us when we should pray to God.

[3.] The Spirit of God will direct you. There are certain times when God hath business with you alone ; when he doth (as it were) speak to you as to the prophet in another case, Ezek. iii. 22, ' Go forth into the plain in the desert, and there I will talk with thee.' So, get you to your closets, I have some business to speak with you. ' Thou saidst, Seek ye my face : my heart answered, Thy face, Lord, will I seek :' Ps. xxvii. 8. God invites you to privacy and retirement ; you are sent into your closet to deal with God about the things you heard from the pulpit. This is the actual profit we get by a sermon, when we deal seriously with God about what we have heard. When God sends for us (as it were) by his Spirit, and invites us into his presence by these motions, it is spiritual clownishness to refuse to come to him.

[4.] Your own inward and outward necessities will put you in mind of it. God hath not stated what hours we shall eat and drink; the seasons and quantity of it are left to our choice. God hath left many wants upon us, to bring us into his presence. Sometimes we want wisdom and counsel in darkness: James i. 5, 'If any lack wisdom, let him ask of God, which giveth to all men liberally.' It is an occasion to bring us to God: God is the best casuist to resolve our doubts and guide us in our way. Sometimes we lack strength to withstand temptations; the throne of grace was set up for a time of need, Heb. iv. 16, when any case is to be resolved, and comfort to be obtained. We want comfort, quickening, counsel, and all to bring us to God. So for outward necessities too. Certainly if a man doth but observe the temper of his own heart, he cannot neglect God, but will find some occasion or other to bring him into his presence, some errand to bring him to the throne of grace. We are daily to beg pardon of sin, and daily to beg supplies. Now, certainly, when you do not observe these things, you neglect God.

Secondly, Others, to avoid it, will excuse themselves. Why, they would pray to God in private, but either they want time, or they want a convenient place, or want parts and abilities. But the truth is, they want a heart, and that is the cause of all; and, indeed, when a man hath no heart to the work, then something is out of the way.

1. Some plead they want time. Why, if you have time for other things, you should have a time for God. Shall we have a season for all things, and not for the most necessary work? Hast thou time to eat, drink, sleep, follow thy trading (how dost thou live else?), and no time to be saved—no time to be familiar with God, which is the greatest business of all? Get it from your sleep and food, rather than be without this necessary duty. Jesus Christ had no such necessity as we have, yet it is said, Mark i. 35, ' He arose a great while before day, and went out, and departed into a solitary place, and there prayed.' Therefore, must God only be encroached upon—the lean kine devour the fat —Sarah thrust out instead of Hagar—and religion be crowded out of doors? *Felix illa domus, ubi Martha queritur de Maria,—That is a happy house where Martha complains of Mary.* Martha, which was cumbered with much service, complained of Mary that she was at the feet of Jesus Christ, hearkening to his gracious counsel; but in most houses Mary may complain of Martha; religion is neglected and goes to the walls.

2. Some want a place. He that doth not want a heart will find a place. Christ went into a mountain to pray, and Peter to the top of the house.

3. Many say they want parts, they cannot tell how to pray. Wherefore hath God given his Spirit? In one fashion or other a man can open his case to God; he can go and breathe out his complaints, the Lord will hear breathings. Go, chatter out thy requests to thy Father: though you can but 'chatter like a crane,' yet do it with fervency and with a spirit of adoption. We have not only Christ given us for an advocate, but the Holy Ghost to help our infirmities. He hath given us ' the Spirit of his Son, whereby we may cry, Abba, Father:' Gal. iv. 6. A child can acquaint a father with his wants.

Use 2. To exhort God's children to frequency in this duty, and to much watchfulness and seriousness in the performance of it.

First, To frequency. For arguments again to press you :—

1. It argueth more familiarity to pray to God alone than in company. He that goeth to a prince alone, and upon all occasions hath access to him in private, when company is gone, hath nearer friendship and a greater intimacy with him than those which are only admitted to a speech with him in the company of others ; so, the oftener you are with God alone the more familiar. He loves to treat with you apart, as friends are most free and open to one another when they are alone.

2. Then you will have a more sensible answer of your own prayers ; you will see what God hath done upon your requests. Dan. ix. 21, 22. Daniel was praying for the church, and an angel comes and tells him, ' It is for thy prayers and supplications that I am come.' Therefore surely a man would take some time to go and plead the promises with God. But further, by way of means :—

[1.] Consider the omnipresence of God, which is the argument in the text : ' He is in secret, and seeth in secret.' If men were convinced of that, they would make conscience of secret prayer. Look, as Jesus Christ says of himself, John xvi. 32, ' You leave me alone, and yet I am not alone, for the Father is with me.' So when you are alone you are not alone ; there is a Father in secret ; though nobody to see and hear, yet God is there. We are apt to think all is lost which men are not conscious to, and done in their sight. Acts x. 4 : ' Thy prayers and thine alms are come up for a memorial before God.' God keeps a memorial of your private prayers ; there is a register kept in heaven, and never a prayer lost.

[2.] Consider the excellency of communion with God. Jer. ii. 32 : ' Can a maid forget her ornaments, and a bride her attire ?' Women are very curious and careful of their ornaments, and will not forget their dressing-attire, especially a bride upon the wedding-day, she that is to be set forth in most costly array—she makes it her business to put on jewels, to be seen in all her glory. God is as necessary to us as ornaments to a bride. We should be as mindful of communion with God as a bride of her dressing-ornaments. ' Yet they have forgotten me days without number.' Whatever is forgotten, God must not be forgotten.

[3.] Make God a good allowance ; resolve to be much in the practice of it. It is best to have set times for our religious worship. For persons which are *sui juris*, at their own dispose, it is lawful and very convenient to dedicate a certain part and portion of our time to the Lord of time. Lazy idle servants must be tasked and required to bring in their tale of brick ; so it is good to task the heart, to make God a fair, and reasonable, and convenient allotment of some part of our time. David had his fixed hours : ' Three times a day will I call upon thee.' And Daniel had his set times ; he prayed three times a day. Though we cannot charge you to observe these hours, yet you should make a prudent choice yourselves, and consecrate such a part of time as will suit with your occasions, your course of life, according to your abilities and opportunities. It is an expression of love to God to give him somewhat that is your own; and it will be of exceeding profit to you, and make your communion with him more seasonable and orderly. This will make you careful and watchful how you spend your other hours, that you may not be unfit when times of prayer come. 1 Pet. iii. 7: 'Husbands, dwell with your wives according to knowledge, that your prayers be not hindered.' But do not propose a task too great for your strength, and perplex yourselves with such an unreasonable allowance as will not suit with your occasions. Men create a trouble to themselves, and bind themselves with chains of their own making, when they propose more duty than they can well discharge.

The Second Part of the Use.

Do it seriously, with caution, and warily. Here Christ gives direction: 'When thou prayest, enter into thy closet, and shut thy door, and then think of thy Father which is in secret.' We need a great deal of caution; for:—

1. When you shut the door upon all others, you cannot shut the devil out of your closets; he will crowd in. When you have bolted the door upon you, and shut other company out, you do not lock out Satan; he is always at hand, ready to disturb us in holy duties; wherever the children of God are, he seeks to come at them. When the sons of God met together, Satan was in the midst of them: Job i. He meets in congregations, he gets into the closet. When Joshua the high priest was ministering before the Lord, Satan stood at his right hand, ready to resist him: Zech. iii. 1.

2. There needs caution; because in private duties there may be many failings and evils, which we are apt to be tainted with in our private addresses to God.

[1.] There may be danger of ostentation; therefore Christ gives direction here, that it should be managed with the greatest secrecy, both as for place, time, and voice. Let none but God be conscious to our drawing aside that we may be alone. Withdraw yourselves out of the sight and hearing of others, lest pride and ostentation creep upon you. The devil will seek to blast this serious acknowledgment to God, one way or other.

[2.] There may be customariness, for fashion sake. It is said of Christ, that 'he went into the synagogue on the Sabbath-day, as his custom was.' We may use accustomed duties; but we must not do them customarily, and for fashion sake, no more than Christ himself did; for though this was his custom, yet he was not customary in these his synagogue attendances. We are very apt to do so, because we have used it for these many years. Men go on in a tract of duty, and regard not the ends of worship—Zech. vii. 3—they come with a fond scruple and case of conscience to the prophet: they had an old custom among them to fast for the destruction of the temple; now when the temple was built again, 'Should I weep in the fifth month, separating myself, as I have done these so many years?'

[3.] Much slightness and perfunctoriness of heart you may be guilty of. Such is the wickedness of men, that they think God will be put off with anything; and though they would set off themselves with applause in the hearing of others, yet how slight are they apt

to be when they deal with God alone! Consider, you must sanctify
the name of God in private, as well as in public; you must speak to
God with reverence and fear, and not in an overly fashion. Take
heed of this slightness; it is a great wrong to the majesty of God.
When they offered a sickly offering, saith God, 'I am a great King,
and my name is dreadful among the heathen:' you do not consider
my majesty.

[4.] There may be this evil: resting in the work, in the tale and
number of your prayers: Luke xviii. 12, 'I fast twice in the week.'
Man is very apt to rest and dote upon his own worth, and to build all
his acceptance with God upon it; to come to God, and challenge him
for a debt, as the Pharisee did. It is very natural to rest in those
duties, and make them an excuse for other things.

[5.] There may be pride, even in the exercise of our gifts. There
is a delight in duties, which seems spiritual many times when it is
not;—as when a man delighteth in the exercise of his own gifts,
rather than in communion with God; when there is a secret tickling
of heart with a conceit of our own worth; as when, in the carriage of
a duty, we come off roundly, and parts have their free course and
career. This complacency and pride, it may be not only in public,
where we have advantage to discover ourselves with applause, but in
private, between God and our souls. When a man is conceited of his
gifts, they may end in the private exercise of them, to the wrong of
God. When invention is quick and free, he may have such a delight
as may make him rest in the work, as it is a fruit of parts, rather than
as a means of communion with God. Therefore there needs a great
deal of caution when we are alone with our heavenly Father.

----

*But when ye pray, use not vain repetitions, as the heathen do; for
they think they shall be heard for their much speaking. Be not
ye, therefore, like unto them; for your Father knoweth what
things ye have need of, before ye ask him.*—MAT. VI. 7, 8.

OUR Lord having spoken of the ostentation of the Pharisees, and
their vainglory, he cometh here to dissuade from another abuse, and
that is babbling and lip-labour. They prayed to be seen of men;
but the heathens were guilty of another abuse. Here take notice:—

1. Of the sin taxed.
2. The reasons which our Lord produceth against it.

First, the sin taxed is set forth by a double notion. Here is βαττολογια and πολυλογια: the first we translate, 'vain repetitions;' and
the last, 'much speaking.' Both may well go together; for when
men affect to say much, they will use vain repetitions, go over the
same things again and again, which is as displeasing to God as it is
irksome to prudent and wise men.

But let us see a little what these words signify. The first word is
βαττολογια, which we translate 'vain repetitions.' Battus was a
foolish poet, that made long hymns, consisting of many lines, but

such as were often repeated, both for matter and words; and Ovid brings in a foolish fellow, that would be often repeating the same words, and doubling them over:—

'Montibus, inquit, erant, et erant sub montibus illis.'

And again:—

'Et me mihi perfide prodis ?
Me mihi prodis ? ait.'

And from thence this word is taken, which is here used by the evangelist: βαττολογια, or idle babbling over the same thing. And the scripture representeth this vain going over of the same things: Eccles. x. 14, 'A fool also is full of words; a man cannot tell what shall be ; and what shall be after him, who can tell?' The most judicious interpreters do conceive there is a μιμησις, an imitation of the fool's speaking. Groundless, fruitless repetitions are here reproved, or the tumbling out of many insignificant words, and the same over and over again ; this is vain repetition. But the other word which Christ useth to tax the same abuse is πολυλογια, 'much speaking.' It signifieth affectation of length in prayer, or using many words, not out of fervency of mind, but merely to prolong the duty, as if the length of it made it more powerful or acceptable with God, or a more comely piece of worship. This is what our Lord here reproves ; vain repetitions and much speaking.

Secondly, here are the reasons produced against it ; they are two :—

1. That it is a heathenish custom, and that grounded upon a false supposition. The heathens were detestable to the Jews, and therefore their customs should not be taken up, especially when grounded upon an error, or a misapprehension of the nature of God. Now the heathens think they shall be heard for their much speaking, for their mere praying and composing hymns to their gods, with thundering names repeated over and over again.

2. It is inconsistent with the true nature of God: ver. 8, 'Be not therefore like unto them ; for your Father knoweth what things you have need of, before you ask him.' Here we learn three things:— (1.) Christianity and true religion takes up God under the notion of a father, that hath a care of his children. This will decide many questions about prayer, and what words we should use to God in the duty : go to God as children to their father. (2.) He is represented as an omniscient God—one that knows all things, our wants and necessities. (3.) As an indulgent father, who hath a propense and ready mind to help us, even before we ask.

From the words thus opened, that which we may observe is this, viz. :—

Doct. That certainly it is a sin needlessly to affect length of speech, or vain repetitions in prayer.

Our Lord dissuadeth us from it here, and his authority should sway with us. He knew the nature of prayer better than we do ; for he appointed it, and he was often in the practice and observance of it. So we are directed to the contrary : Eccles. v. 2, 'Be not rash with thy mouth, and let not thine heart be hasty to utter anything before God : for God is in heaven, and thou upon earth ; therefore let thy words be few.' Remember, you have to do with a great God, and do

not babble things over impertinently in his ears. It is a truth evident
by the light of nature: *Paucis verbis rem divinam facito* (Platinus).
If you be to worship God, a needless prolixity doth not become addresses to him.

But because this text may be abused, I shall endeavour to clear it a
little further. There are two extremes: the slight and careless spirit,
and babbling.

1. There is the slight and careless spirit, who doth the work of an
age in a breath, and is all for starts and sudden pangs, which pass
away like a flash of lightning in a dark room; whose good thoughts
are gone as soon as they rush into the heart. A poor, barren, and
slight spirit, which is not under the influence and power of that
celestial love which keeps the soul in converse with God, cannot
endure to be any while with God. Alas! we need stroke upon stroke
to fasten anything upon the heart. We are like green wood, that
will not presently take fire, until it lie long there, and be thoroughly
and well warmed; so until we have gone far in the duty, we can
hardly get any warmth of heart. They which are short in prayer had
need of much habitual preparation of heart.

2. The babbler is another extreme, who thinks the commendation
of a duty is to be long in it, and affects to say much rather than well;
whereas serious and short speech makes the best prayer: Prov. x. 19,
'In the multitude of words there wanteth not sin;' either to God or
men, it is true; but especially when affected. So they do but beat
the air, rather than pray to God.

These, then, are the two extremes: shortness, out of barrenness or
slightness; or length, out of affectation; and we must carefully avoid
these. Christ would not justify that shortness which comes from
slightness and barrenness of heart, nor, on the other side, indulge the
affectation of length in prayer.

Therefore let us a little see:—

I. What is the sin.

II. Give you the force of our Lord's reasons here urged, or how conclusive our Saviour's arguments are against this practice.

I. What is the sin? That is necessary to be known; for all repetitions are not vain, nor is all length in prayer to be accounted babbling.

First, for repetitions:—

1. When they express fervency and zeal, they may be used. And
so we read, Christ prayed over the same prayer thrice: Mat. xxvi. 44,
'O my Father, if it be possible, let this cup pass from me.' And
another evangelist showeth that he did this out of special fervency of
spirit: Luke xxii. 44, 'Being in an agony, he prayed more earnestly.'
And so we read of the prophet Daniel, chap. ix. 17–19, 'O our
God, hear the prayer of thy servant; O my God, incline thine ear,
and hear; O Lord, hear; O Lord, forgive; O Lord, hearken and do;
defer not for thine own sake, O my God.' All this was out of
vehemency; he goes over and over again the same request. When
we use many words of the same kind and signification, and it be out
of vehemency and fervency of spirit, it is not forbidden.

2. This repetition is not to be disproved[1] when there is a special

---

[1] That is, 'disapproved.'—ED.

emphasis and spiritual elegancy in it, as Ps. cxxxvi., you have it twenty-six times repeated, 'for his mercy endureth for ever;' because there was a special reason in it, his purpose there being to show the unweariedness and the unexhausted riches of God's free grace, that, notwithstanding all the former experiences they had had, God is where he was at first. We waste by giving, our drop is soon spent; but God is not wasted by bestowing, but hath the same mercy to do good to his creatures as before. Though he had done all those wonders for them, yet his mercy was as ready to do good to them still. All along God saved and blessed his people, 'for his mercy endureth for ever.' But as there are repetitions which have their use, so there are useless tautologies and vain repetitions. And such they are when they neither come from the heart nor go to the heart; when they come not from the abundance of the heart, but rather the emptiness of the heart; because we know not how to enlarge ourselves to God, therefore fall upon idle and useless repetitions of the same words and requests. As a man that hath small skill in music doth only play over the same note, so when men have not a full spiritual abundance, they waste themselves in prayer in these idle repetitions. And then they go not to the heart, they do not conduce to warm the affections. A vain, clamorous ingeminating the same thing, without faith and without wisdom, merely to fill up the tale of words, or to wear out a little time in a religious exercise, that is it which is here condemned under the notion of vain repetitions.

Secondly, For the other word, πολυλογία, or 'much speaking.' Every long prayer is not forbidden; for our Lord Jesus himself 'continued all night in prayer:' Luke vi. 12. And in extraordinary duties of fasting, length seems to be very necessary: Esther iv. 16, 'They fasted and prayed together for three days and nights, without eating any bread.' And Solomon prayed long at the dedication of the temple.

But that which is forbidden is, when men speak words without need and without affection; a needless lengthening out of prayer, and that upon a conceit that it is more acceptable to God.

1. In the general, prayer should be short, as all examples of scripture teach us. And the Lord's Prayer, you see how concise and short it is, for presently upon this our Lord teacheth his disciples to pray; for prayer is a spending rather than a feeding duty. Those which affect long speaking many times run into this: they make it a feeding duty, for they mingle exhortations with prayer, which is a great abuse. A man can bear up under the hearing of the word for an hour or two better than half an hour in prayer, with that necessary vigour of spirit which God hath required. Therefore the general rule is, let your words be concise, but full of affection. Look, as in vast and great bodies, the spirits are more diffused and scattered, and therefore they are more inactive than those which are of a smaller compass; so, in a long prayer, there may be more of words, but less of life.

2. The affectation of prolixity is naught. Usually it comes from some evil ground, either from pride and ostentation of gifts;—thus we read the Pharisees were taxed for making long prayers, Mat. xxiii.

14, that, under the colour of them, they might devour widows' houses; that is, be credited and trusted with the management of their estates; —or else it may come from superstition, such as is in the heathens, who had unworthy thoughts of God, as if he were harsh and severe, and delighted in much speaking, and needed to be quickened;—or it may come from folly, for folly abounds in words, though it be scanty in true affection and hearty respect to God. A wise man is content with words enough to express his mind: choice and measure of speech discovereth wisdom.

3. So much time should be spent in prayer, and so many words are necessary as may be convenient and profitable both for ourselves and others. For ourselves, when we are alone, so much as may express faith, and may argue a great plea in the promises, and so much as may reach fervent desire. While the fervency continues, the speech should continue; and so much as may express our filial dependence, that we have a sense that God is our Father, which are the ends for which prayer was appointed. And so as it may suit with the conveniency of others, that they may be warmed, but not tired, and may not be exposed to the temptations of weariness, and wanderings, and distractions in their mind, when things are spun out unto an unreasonable length; for then it is neither pleasing to God nor profitable to men. Thus I have stated the offence our Lord forbids, what are those vain repetitions and idle babblings, such as arise from weariness of soul and misconceit of God, or some other base grounds; not that plentiful expression which comes from a large and free heart, pouring out itself before the Lord. And if we be swayed by his authority, these things should be regarded by us, and we should remedy these sins in prayer.

II. Let us come to examine our Lord's reasons which are produced against it, and see how conclusive they are in the case, and you will discern the drift of Christ's speech.

Our Lord reasons:—

First, From the practice of the heathens: ' But when ye pray, use not vain repetitions, as the heathens do.' In this reason several propositions are couched and contained, which deserve to be weighed by us.

1. This is implied: that the heathens had a sense of the necessity of worship, as well as the being of a God. Though natural light be *inferioris hemisphœrii*, of the lower hemisphere, and chiefly reacheth to duties of the second table, of commerce between man and man; for that light which was left in the heart of man since the fall, more directly respects our carriage towards men, and there it is more clear and open; yet it so far reaches to the duties of the higher hemisphere, as that there is some discerning too of the duties of the first table, of piety as well as honesty; as that there is a God; and if there be a God, he is to be worshipped; for these two notions live and die together. The rude mariners were sensible of a divine power which was to be called upon and consulted with in case of extremity, and that the way of commerce was by worship: Jonah i. 5, when the storm arose, ' they called every man upon his god.'

2. Though heathens were sensible of the being of a God and the

necessity of worship, yet they were blind and dark in worship; for Christ saith, 'Be not as the heathen; for they think they shall be heard for their much speaking.' Usually a half light misleads men. The heathens, though they had some notions of an eternal Power, yet when they came to perform their worship, Rom. i. 21, 'They glorified him not as God; but became vain,' ἐν τοις διαλογισμοῖς, 'in their imaginations;' that is, in their practical inferences. They saw an infinite, eternal Power, which was to be loved, trusted, worshipped; but when they came to suit these notions to practice, to love, trust, and worship him, there they were vain, frivolous, and had misconceits of God.

3. Their errors in worship were many. Here our Lord takes notice but of one, that they thought to be heard for their much speaking. And there the original mistake of the heathens, and that which compriseth all the rest, was this, a transformation or changing of God into the likeness of man, which is very natural and incident to us. Upon all occasions we are apt to misconceive of God, and to judge him according to our own model and scantling: Ps. l. 21, 'Thou thoughtest I was altogether such an one as thyself.' So did these. Because man is wrought upon by much speaking, and carried away with a flood of words, therefore they thought so it would be with God. This transformation of the divine nature into an idol of our own shaping and picturing, the turning of God into the form of a corruptible man, this hath been the ground of all the miscarriage in the world.

But more particularly: their error in this matter was charging weakness and harshness upon God, or not worshipping him according to his spiritual nature.

[1.] Charging weakness upon God, as if many words did help him to understand their meaning, or to remember their petitions the better. Hence that practice of Baal's priests, 1 Kings xviii. 26, 'They called on the name of Baal from morning till night, O Baal, hear us.' They were repeating and crying again and again, 'O Baal,' as if their clamour would awaken their god. Whence Elijah's sarcasm, 'He sleepeth, and must be awaked.' As those that for two hours together cried out, 'Great is Diana of the Ephesians! Great is Diana of the Ephesians!' Acts xix. 34.

[2.] Their ascribing harshness to God, as if he were hard to be entreated, and delighted in the pain of his creatures, and would be more affected with them, because they wearied themselves with the irksomeness of a long prayer. Penal satisfactions are very natural. Superstition is a tyranny; it vexeth the soul with unreasonable duty, affects outward length to the weariness of the flesh. The general conceit is, that man thinks God must be served with some self-denial, and the flesh must be displeased; but it shall be displeased but in a little, and in an outward way, as Baal's priests gashed themselves; as if God were pleased with our burdensome and long exercises.

[3.] There was error in it. They did not conceive aright of the spiritual nature of God; as if he were pleased with the mere task, a long hymn, and an idle repetition of words, without sense and affection. Whereas the Lord doth not measure prayers by prolixity, but by the vehemency ; not by the labour of the external work, but by the inward affection manifested therein. And words are only accepted with him as they serve to quicken, continue, or increase our affection.

Secondly, Our Saviour's next reason is drawn from verse 8: ' Be not ye like unto them ; for your Father knoweth what things ye have need of before you ask him.' It is inconsistent with the true notion of God. Here are three propositions, all which are of force to draw us off from babbling, or affectation of many words in prayer. As:—

1. That God is a Father, and that both by creation and covenant. By creation, to all mankind ; so he will be ready to sustain that which he hath made. He that hath given life will give food; he that hath given a body will give raiment. Things expect supply thence from whence they received their being. But much more by covenant; so he is our Father in Christ: ' Doubtless thou art our Father, though Abraham be ignorant of us,' Isa. lxiii. 16. Well, but what is this to the present purpose, that God is a Father ? This is a check to babbling ; therefore we should go to him in an unaffected manner, with a child-like spirit and dependence, with words reverent, serious, and plain. Children do not use to make starched speeches to their fathers when they want bread, but only express their natural cry, and go to them for such things as they stand in need of. There they speak, and are accepted ; and a word from a child moves the father more than an orator can move all his hearers. Even such a naked address should we make to God in a plain manner ; for when we come to pray, Christ would have us take up God in the notion of a father, and to behave ourselves in a natural way to him ; for affected eloquence or loquacity in prayer is one of the main things Christ here disproves.[1] Prayer ought to be simple and plain; therefore the great business of ' the Spirit of adoption' is to make us cry, ' Abba, Father:' Rom. viii. 15.

2. He is such a Father as is not ignorant of our wants. The care of his providence is over all the creatures he hath made. God hath an inspection over them, to provide necessaries for them ; much more over his people. His eyes run to and fro, to find them out in all the places of their dispersion ; and he doth exercise his power for their relief : 2 Chron. xvi. 9. Now this thought should be rooted in our hearts when we come to pray to God : I go to a Father, which hath found me out in the throng of his creatures, and knows what is good for me. This is a great ground why we should not use battology, because God knows what my needs are. Words are not required for God's sake, but for ours ; not to inform God, but that we may perform our duty the better. Well, then, so far as they are useful, so far they should be used; to bound our thoughts, to warm our affections, to strengthen our faith. (1.) To bound our thoughts; for an interruption in speech is sooner discerned that an interruption in meditation. (2.) And to warm our affections. Words at first are vent to affection, but afterwards they continue to increase the affection ; as a hearth is first warmed by the fire, and then it serves to keep in the fire. (3.) And they conduce to strengthen our faith, while we plead promises in

---

[1] ' Disapproves.'—ED.

God's hearing. We wrestle with God, that we may catch a heat ourselves. And therefore words should be only used as they conduce to the strengthening our faith, or continuing our affection to God ; longer than they serve that end in prayer, they are babbling and vain repetitions, and much speaking, which Christ here forbids. Consider, there is not a change in God, but a change in us, wrought by prayer. It is neither to give information to God, that he may know our meaning, nor to move him and persuade him to be willing by our much speaking, but only to raise up our own faith and hope towards God.

3. He is such a Father as is not unwilling to relieve us. Your heavenly Father is very ready to give you such things as you stand in need of, as Christ expresseth it, Mat. vii. 11, 'If ye, being evil, know how to give good things unto your children, how much more shall your heavenly Father give good things to them that ask him ?' And, Luke xi. 13, it is, 'How much more shall your heavenly Father give his Holy Spirit ?' When you come to beg for grace, consider what earthly parents would do for a child. Their affections are limited, they are in part corrupt ; and poor straitened creatures have not such bowels of compassion as God; and yet, when a child comes to them with a genuine cry, with a sense of his want and confidence of his father, he cannot harden his bowels against his child. This also checks much speaking ; for we do not pray to stir up mercy in him, as if he needed much entreaty, and were severe, and delighted to put the creature to penance. No, he is ready before we ask ; he knows our wants and needs, and is ready to supply us with those things we stand in need of, only will have this comely order observed. Sometimes he prevents our prayers before we ask : 'Before they call, I will answer ; and I am found of them that sought me not.' Before we can have a heart to come, the Lord prevents us with his blessing. And sometimes he gives us what we ask. This is the condescension of God, that when you call he will answer ; and when you cry, he doth in his providence say, 'What will you have, poor creatures?' And he gives more than we ask ; as Solomon asked wisdom, and God gave him more than he asked—wisdom, riches, and honour.

Object. But here is an objection. These notions seem not only to exclude long prayer and much speaking, but all prayer. If God know our wants, and is so ready to give, whether we ask or no, what need we open them to him in prayer at all ?

I answer, it is God's prescribed course, and that should be enough to gracious hearts that will be obedient to their Father. Whatever he intends, though he knows our wants and resolves to answer them, yet it is a piece of religious manners to ask what he is about to give: Jer. xxix. 11, 'I know my thoughts towards you, thoughts of peace, yet will I be inquired of you for these things.' God knows his own thoughts, hath stated his decrees, and will not alter the beautiful course of his providence for our sakes, yet he will be sought unto. So Ezek. xxxvi. : God purposed to bless them, and therefore promiseth, 'I will do thus and thus for you'; yet, verse 37, 'I will yet for this be inquired of by the house of Israel, to do it for them.' I will do it, but you shall milk out the blessing by prayer. This course is also necessary, and that both for his honour, and our profit and comfort.

1. It is necessary for his honour, that God may still be acknowledged, that the creature may be kept up in a constant dependence upon God, and may go about nothing, but may ask his leave, counsel, and blessing: Prov. iii. 6, 'In all thy ways acknowledge him, and he shall direct thy paths.' We ask God's leave that we may do such a thing, for he hath the dominion over all events. And if we are doubtful, we ask his counsel, whether we may stay here or there, or dispose of ourselves and families, and we ask his blessing upon our resolution. Now that we may know God doth all, that he governeth all human affairs, that we may live upon his allowance and take our daily bread from his hands, and that we may see we hold all these things from our great landlord, therefore we pray unto him. We are robbers and thieves if we use the creature without his leave. God is the great owner of the world, who gives us our daily bread, and all our supplies; therefore he will have it asked, that we may acknowledge our dependence.

2. It is most for our profit. Partly, that our faith should be exercised in pleading God's promise, for there we put the promise in suit. Faith is begotten in the word, but it is exercised in prayer; therefore it is called the 'prayer of faith.' In the word, we take Christ *from* God; in prayer we present Christ *to* God. That prayer which is effectual, it is an exercise of faith: Rom. x. 14, 'How shall they call on him, in whom they have not believed?' And as it concerns our faith, so also our love, which is both acted and increased in prayer. It is acted, for it is delight in God which makes us so often converse with him. Thus the hypocrite: Job xxvii. 10, 'Will he always call upon the Lord? Will he delight himself in the Almighty?' They that love God cannot be long from him, they that delight in God will be often unbosoming themselves to him. It doth also increase our love, for by answers of prayer we have new fuel to keep in this holy fire in our bosoms. We pray, and then he gives direct answers: Ps. cxvi. 1, 'I love the Lord, because he hath heard my voice and my supplication.' So our hope is exercised in waiting for the blessing prayed for: Ps. v. 3, 'O Lord, in the morning will I direct my prayer unto thee, and will look up.' That looking up is the work of hope, when we are looking and waiting to see what comes in from pleading promises. It is much too for our peace of conscience, for it easeth us of our burthens. It is the vent of the soul, like the opening of a vein in a fever. When our hearts swell with cares, and we have a burthen upon us, and know not what to do, we may ease ourselves to God: Phil. iv. 6, 'Be careful for nothing; but in everything, by prayer and supplication, with thanksgiving, let your requests be made known to God; and the peace of God shall keep your hearts.' Oh, blessed frame, that can be troubled at nothing here in this world, where there are so many businesses, encounters, temptations! What is the way to get this calmness of heart? Be much in opening your hearts to God. Let your requests be made known to God. Look, as in an earthquake, when the wind is imprisoned in the bowels of the earth, the earth heaves, and shakes, and quakes, until there be a vent, and the wind be got out, then all is quiet; so we have many tossings and turmoilings in our minds, till

we open and unbosom ourselves to God, and then all is quiet. Also it prepareth us for the improvement of mercies, when we have them out of the hands of God by prayer : 1 Sam. i. 27, 28, ' For this child I prayed,' said Hannah, ' and I will lend him unto the Lord.' Those mercies we expressly prayed for we are more thoroughly obliged to improve for God.   What is won with prayer is worn with thankfulness.

APPLICATION.

Use 1. To caution us against many abuses in prayer, which may be disproved and taxed, either formally, or by just consequence. I shall instance in five.

1. An idle and foolish loquacity, when men take a liberty to prattle anything in God's hearing, and do not consider the weight and importance of prayer, and what a sin it is to be ' hasty to utter anything before God:' Eccles. v. 2. It is great irreverence and contempt of the majesty of God, when men go hand over head about this work, and speak anything that comes into their mind. As men take themselves to be despised when others speak unseemly in their presence, surely it is a lessening and a despising of God, when we pour out raw, tumultuous, undigested thoughts, and never think of what we are to speak when we come to God: Ps. xlv. 1, ' My heart is inditing a good matter.' The word signifieth, it ' boils or fries a good matter.' It is an allusion to the *Mincah,* or meat-offering, which was to be boiled or fried in a pan, before it was to be presented to the Lord, that they might not bring a dough-baked sacrifice and offering to the Lord. Such ignorant, dull, senseless praying, it is a blaspheming of God, and a lessening of the majesty of God.

2. A frothy eloquence, and an affected language in prayer, this directly comes under reproof. As if the prayer were more grateful to God, and he were moved by words and strains of rhetoric, and did accept men for their parts rather than graces. Fine phrases, and quaint speeches, alas ! they do not carry it with the Lord. They are but an empty babble in his ears, rather than a humble exercise of faith, hope, love, and child-like affections, and holy desires after God. If we would speak with God, we must speak with our hearts to him, rather than with our words. This is a sin of curiosity, as the other was of neglect. It is not words, but the spirit and life which God looks after. Prayer, it is not a work of oratory, the product of memory, invention, and parts, but a filial affection, that we may come to him, as to a father, with a child-like confidence. Therefore, too much care of verbal eloquence in prayer, and tunable expressions, is a sin of the same nature with babbling. Though men should have the wit to avoid impertinent expressions and repetitions, yet when prayer smells so much of the man rather than of the Spirit of God, alas ! it is but like the unsavoury belches of a rotten breath in the nostrils of God. We should attend to matter, to the things we have to communicate to God, to our necessities, rather than to words.

3. Heartless speaking, filling up the time with words, when the tongue outruns the heart, when men pour their breath into the air, but their hearts are dead and sleepy, or their hearts keep not time and

pace with their expressions. We oftener pray with our tongues than with our minds, and from our memories than our consciences, and from our consciences than our affections, and from our affections, as presently stirred, than from our hearts renewed, bended, and inclined towards God. Be the prayer long or short, the heart must keep pace with our tongues. As the poet said, *disticha longa facit*, 'his distichs were tedious,' so it is tedious and irksome to God, unless we make supplication in the spirit: Eph. vi. 18. Remember God will· not be mocked.

4. When men rest in outward vehemency and loud speech, saith Tertullian, *Quibus arteriis opus est, si pro sono audiamur !* 'What lungs and sides must we have, if we be heard to speak to heaven by the noise and sound!' In some there is a natural vehemency and fierceness of speech, which is rather stirred up by the heat and agitation of the bodily spirits than any vehemency of affection. There is a contention of speech, which is very natural to some, and differeth much from that holy fervour, the life and power of prayer, which is accompanied with reverence and child-like dependence upon God. It is not the loud noise of words which is best heard in heaven, but the fervent affectionate cries of the saints are those of the heart rather than of the tongue. Exod. xiv. 17, it is said, 'Moses cried to the Lord.' We do not read of the words he uttered ; his cry was with the heart. There is a crying with the soul and with the heart to God : Ps. x. 17, 'Lord, thou hast heard the desire of the humble.' It is the desires God hears : Ps. xxxix. 9, 'Lord, all my desire is before thee, and my groaning is not hid from thee.' The Lord needs not the tongue to be an interpreter between him and the hearts of his children. He that hears without ears can interpret prayers though not uttered by the tongue. Our desires are cries in the ears of the Lord of hosts. The vehemency of the affections may sometimes cause the extension of the voice, but alas ! without this it is but a tinkling cymbal.

5. Popish repetition, and loose shreds of prayer often repeated, as they have in their liturgy over and over again ; their *Gloria Patri*, so often repeated ; their *Lord have mercy ;* and in their prayer made to *Jesus, sweet Jesus, blessed Jesus ;* and going over the *Ave Maria*, and this to be tumbled over upon their beads, and continuing prayer by tale and by number : surely these are but vain repetitions, and this is that much speaking which our Lord aims at. Thus I have despatched the abuses of prayer.

Use 2. To give you direction in prayer, how to carry yourselves in this holy duty towards God in a comely manner.

I shall give you directions :—

1. About our words in prayer.
2. About our thoughts in prayer.
3. About our affections in prayer.

First, about our words. There is a use of them in prayer, to excite, and convey, and give vent to affection : Hosea xiv. 2, 'Take with you words, and turn to the Lord, and say, Take away all iniquity, and receive us graciously.' Surely the prophet doth not only prescribe that they should take affections, but take with them words. Words have an interest in prayer.

Now, these may be considered either when we are alone or in company.

1. When we are alone. Here take the advice of the Holy Ghost : Eccles. v. 2, ' God is in heaven, and thou art upon earth, therefore let thy words be few.' How few ? Few in weight, conscience, reverence. Few in weight, affecting rather to speak matter than words ; concisely and feelingly, rather than with curiousness, to express what you have to say to God. Few in conscience. Superstition is a bastard religion, and is tyrannous, and puts men upon tedious services, and sometimes beyond their strength. Therefore pray neither too short nor too long ; do it not merely to lengthen out the prayer, or as counting it the better for being long. The shortness and the length must be measured by the fervency of our hearts, our many necessities, and as it tendeth to the inflaming our zeal. As it can get up the heart, let it still be subservient to that. Few with reverence, and managed with that gravity, awfulness, and seriousness as would become an address to God. As Abraham, Gen. xviii. 31, had been reasoning with God before, therefore he saith, ' Let not God be angry if I speak to him this once,' when he renewed the suit. Thus alone.

2. In company. There our words must be apt and orderly, moving as much as may be, not to God, but to the hearers ; managed with such reverence and seriousness as may suit with the gravity of the duty, and not increase, but cure the dulness of those with whom we join. And what if we did in public duties choose out words to reason with God, as Job saith, chap. ix. 14, ' Choose out my words to reason with him ;'—if we did use preparation, and think a little beforehand, that we may go about the duty with serious advice, and not with indigested thoughts ? But this hath the smallest interest in prayer.

Secondly, Our thoughts ; that we may conceive aright of God in prayer, which is one of the greatest difficulties in the duty.

1. Of his nature and being.

2. Of his relation to us.

3. Of his attributes.

First, Of the nature and being of God. Every one that would come to God must fix this in his mind, that God is, and that God is a spirit ; and accordingly he must be worshipped as will suit with these two notions. Heb. xi. 6, ' He that cometh to God must believe that God is,' and then that God is a spirit ; for it is said, John iv. 24, ' God is a spirit, and they that worship him must worship him in spirit and in truth.' Oh, then, whenever you come to pray to God, fix these two thoughts, let them be strong in your heart : God is ; I do not speak to an idol, but to the living God. And God is a spirit ; and therefore not so much pleased with plausibleness of speech, or tunable cadency of words, as with a right temper of heart. Alas ! when we come to pray, we little think God is, or what God is. Much of our religion is performed to an unknown God, and, like the Samaritans, we worship we know not what. It is not speculations about the divine nature, or high-strained conceptions, which doth fit us for prayer : the discoursing of these things with some singularity, or terms removed from common understanding, this is not that which I press you to ; but such a sight of God as prompteth us to a reverent and serious worshipping of him.   Then we have right notions of God in prayer, when we are affected as Moses was, when God showed him his back-parts, and proclaimed his name : Exod. xxxiv., ' He made haste, bowed his head, and worshipped.'   When our worship suiteth with the nature of God, it is spiritual and holy, not pompous and theatrical.   Well, then, these two things must be deeply imprinted in our minds—that God is, and that he is a spirit; and then is our worship right.

For instance :—

[1.] For the first notion, God's being.   Then is our worship right, when it doth proclaim to all that shall observe us, or we that observe ourselves, there is a great, an infinite, eternal power, which sits at the upper end of causes, and governeth all according to his own pleasure.   Alas! the worship of many is flat atheism ; they say in their hearts either there is no God, or believe there is no God.   Therefore, do you worship him as becomes such a glorious being ?   Is his mercy seen in your faith and confidence, his majesty in your humility and reverence, his goodness in your soul's rejoicing, his greatness and justice in your trembling before his throne ?   The worship must be like the worshipped, it must have his stamp upon it.

[2.] For the other notion, God is a spirit, therefore the soul must be the chief agent in the business, not the body, or any member of the body.   Spirits they converse with spirits : the body is but employed by the soul, and must not guide and lead it, but be led by it.   Therefore see whether there be the spirit, otherwise that which is most essential to the worship is wanting.   To have nothing employed but the tongue, and the heart about other business, is not to carry yourselves as to a God, and a God that is a spirit.   Recollect yourselves ; where is my soul in this worship, and how is it affected towards God ?

Secondly, As there must be thoughts to direct us in his being and nature, so also in his relation as a father, as one that is inclinable to pardon, pity, and help you.   We have the spirit of adoption given us for this very end and purpose, that we may cry, ' Abba, Father ;' and, Gal. iv. 16, ' Because you are sons, therefore he hath sent forth the Spirit of his Son into your hearts, crying, Abba, Father ;' and, Rom. viii. 15, ' We have received the Spirit of adoption, crying, Abba, Father ;' that we may come to God in a child-like manner, dealing with him as with a father, acquainting him with our wants, necessities, burdens, with a hope of relief and supply.

Object. Ay, saith a distressed soul, if my heart be thus carried up to God, if I could discern such a Spirit of adoption prompting me to go to God as a father, then it would be better with me.

To this I answer :—

1. Many times there is a child-like inclination where there is not a child-like familiarity and boldness.   What is that child-like inclination ?   The soul cannot keep away from God, and that is an implicit owning him as a father: Jer. iii. 19, ' Thou shalt call me, My father ; and shalt not turn away from me.'   It is a child-like act to look to him for all our supplies, and to recommend our suit.   As when a child wants anything, he goes to his father.

2. There is a child-like reverence many times when there is not a child-like confidence. The soul hath an awe of God when it cannot explicitly own him as our God and Father, yet it owns him in the humbling way: Luke xv. 18, 'I have sinned against heaven and before thee, and am not worthy to be called thy son.' Though we cannot confidently approach to God as our reconciled Father, yet we come with humility and reverence. Lord, I would fain be, but I deserve not to be, called thy child.

3. There is a child-like dependence upon God's general offer, though we have not an evidence of the sincerity of our particular claim. God offereth to be a Father in Christ to all penitent believers. Now, when a broken-hearted creature comes to God, and looks for mercy upon the account of the covenant, though he cannot see his own interest; for then we come to God, though not as our Father, yet as 'the God and Father of our Lord Jesus Christ;' and that is a relief in prayer, as Eph. i. 3, 'Blessed be the God and Father of our Lord Jesus Christ;' and, ver. 17, 'The God of our Lord Jesus Christ, the Father of glory;' and, Eph. iii. 14, 'I bow my knees unto the Father of our Lord Jesus Christ.' Mark, when we come to him as the Father of Christ, we believe what God offereth in the covenant of grace—namely, that he will deal kindly with us as a father with his children; that he will be good to those that come to him by Christ. The term *Father* is not only to be considered with respect to the disposition or qualification of the persons, but the dispensation they are under. It is the new covenant. In the new covenant God undertakes to be fatherly—that is, to pity our miseries, to pardon our sins, to heal our natures, to save our persons. Now all that come for refuge to take hold of this hope set before them, may come to God as a father, if they believe the gospel in general, though they are not assured of God's love to themselves.

4. There may be a child-like love to God, when yet we have not a sense and assurance of his paternal love to us. God hath a title to our choicest and dearest love before we can make out a title to his highest benefits. We owe our hearts to him: Prov. xxiii. 26, 'My son, give me thy heart.' If you give him your hearts, you are sons, though you know it not. God may be owned as a father, either by our sense of his fatherly love, or by our choice and esteem of him, *optando, si non affirmando.* Come as fatherless without him: Hosea xiv. 3; or, to speak it in other words, the unutterable groans of the Spirit do discover the spirit of adoption, as well as the unspeakable joys of the Spirit: 1 Pet. i. 8. There is an option and choice, though we be not assured of our special relation.

5. God is glorified by an affiance, and a resolute adherence, where there is no assurance. When you are resolved, let him deal with you as an enemy, you will stick to him as a father: Job xiii. 15, 'Though he slay me, yet will I trust in him.' Faith can take God as a friend and father, and put a good construction upon his dealings, when he seems to come against us as an enemy. And we give glory to God when we can adhere to him as our only happiness, and trust his fatherly kindness and goodness, though he cover himself with frowns, and hide himself from our prayers; and you own him as the Father

of mercies, though it may be you have no sense and feeling of his
fatherly love to you.

6. There is a difference between the gift itself and the degree. We
cannot say we have not the spirit of adoption because we have not so
much of the spirit of adoption as others have—I mean as to the effects.
We may have the Spirit as a sanctifier, though not as a comforter;
though he doth not calm our hearts, and rebuke our fears, yet he doth
sanctify us, and incline us to God. The Spirit was only given to Christ
without measure, but to Christians in a different measure and proportion; and usually as you submit more to his gracious conduct, and
overcome the enemies of your peace, the devil, the world, and the
flesh. The impression is left upon some in a smaller, and upon
others in a larger character. All are not of one growth and size;
some are more explicitly Christians, others in a riddle. Much grace
doth more discover itself than a little grace under a heap of imperfection. Some are more mortified and heavenly-minded than others.

7. When all other helps fail, faith will make use of our common
relation to God as a Creator, as we may come to him as the workmanship of his hands. It is better to do so than keep off from him;
and we may come to him as the workmanship of his hands when we
cannot come to him as children of his family. The church saith,
Isa. lxiv. 8, ' Now, O Lord, thou art our father : we are the clay, and
thou our potter, and we all are the work of thy hand.' They plead
for favour and mercy by that common relation, as he was their potter,
and they his clay. And David, Ps. cxix. 73, ' Thy hands have made
me and fashioned me : give me understanding, that I may learn thy
commandments.' Surely it is some comfort to claim by the covenant
of Noah, which was made with all mankind, when we cannot claim
mercy by the covenant of Abraham, which was made with the family
of the faithful. The scriptures warrant us to do so : Isa. liv. 9, ' For
this is as the waters of Noah unto me.' All this is spoken to show
that, one way or other, we should bring our hearts to depend upon
him as a father, for succour and relief.

Thirdly, His attributes. This text offereth three. God's omni-
sciency, ' He *knows;*' His fatherly care, ' Your *Father* knows what
you stand in need of;' and his readiness to help, even *before we ask.*

[1.] He is omniscient : He knows our persons, for Christ calleth his
own sheep by name : John x. 3. He knoweth every one of us by head
and by poll, by person and name. Yea, and he knows our state and
condition : Ps. lvi. 8, ' Thou tellest my wanderings; put thou my
tears into thy bottle; are they not in thy book ?' All our wanderings
he tells them; all our tears he hath a bottle for them; to show God's
particular notice; they are metaphorical expressions. And he observes
us in the very posture when we come to pray, and where. Acts ix.
11 : Go to such a street, in such a place, and ' inquire for one Saul
of Tarsus; for, behold, he prayeth.' The Lord takes notice, in such
a city, in such a street, in such a house, in such a room, and what you
are doing when you are praying. And he seeth, not only that you
pray, but how you pray : Rom. viii. 27, ' And he that searcheth the
heart, knoweth what is the mind of the Spirit, because he maketh
intercession for the saints, according to the will of God.' He can dis-

cern between lusts and groans, words and affections, and such words as are the belches of the flesh, and such as are the breathings of the spirit.

[2.] There is his fatherly care , for it is said, ' Your *Father* knows what things you have need of.' He knows what pincheth and presseth you. It is said, 1 Pet. v. 7, ' Casting all your care upon him, for he careth for you.' It is not said, that he *may* take care of you, but he *doth* take care. God is aforehand with us, and our carking care doth but take the work out of God's hand which he is doing already. Our cares are needless, fruitless, burthensome ; but his are assiduous, powerful, blessed. A small matter may occasion much vexation to us, but to him all things are easy. Upon these considerations, ' We should be careful for nothing, but make known our requests unto God :' Phil. iv. 6. Praying for what we want, and giving thanks for what we have ; ' For your Father knoweth you have need of these things:' Mat. vi. 32. His fatherly love will not suffer him to neglect his children or any of their concernments. Therefore, if you have a temptation upon you to anxiety and carefulness of mind, and know not how to get out of such a strait and conquer such a difficulty, remember you have a father to provide for you : this will prevent tormenting thoughtfulness, which is good for nothing but to anticipate your sorrow.

[3.] The next is, his readiness to help. This should be deeply impressed upon your minds, and you should habituate these thoughts, how ready God is to help and to run to the cry : Ps. xxxii. 5, ' I said, I will confess my transgressions unto the Lord, and thou forgavest the iniquity of my sin.' Before his purpose could be brought to pass : Isa. lxv. 24, ' Before they call, I will answer, and whiles they are yet speaking, I will hear.' So Jer. xxxi. 20 : ' I heard Ephraim bemoaning himself,' &c. God's bowels were troubled presently. He is more ready to give than you to ask. This will help and direct you mightily in the business of prayer ; for God hath a care for his children, and is very ready to help the weak, and relieve them in all their straits.

Thirdly, For directions about our affections in prayer : three things are required, viz., fervency, reverence, confidence.

1. Fervency. That usually comes from two grounds, a broken-hearted sense of our wants, and a desire of the blessing we stand in need of. For the broken-hearted sense of our wants, especially spiritual. Weaknesses are incident to the best. All Christians have continual need to cry to God. We have continual necessities both within and without. Go cry to God your Father without affectation, but not without affection, and seek your supplies from him. Let me tell you, the more grace is increased, the more sense of wants is increased ; for sin is more hated, defects are less borne. And then, there must be a desire of the blessings, especially spiritual ; our needs must stir up fresh longings and holy desires after God : Mat. vii. 7, ' Ask, seek, knock ;' Luke xi. 8, ' For his importunity, he will rise and give.' We spend the earnestness of our spirits in other matters, in disputes, contests, earthly pursuits ; our importunate earnestness runs in a worldly channel. No, no ; it must be from simplicity and sincerity,

pouring out your hearts before him ; no sacrifice without fire : James v. 16, ' The effectual fervent prayer of a righteous man availeth much.'

2. Reverence. A reverent respectful carriage towards our heavenly Father : Ps. ii. 11, ' Serve the Lord with fear, and rejoice with trembling.' Mark, there is in God a mixture of majesty and mercy ; so in us there must be of joy and trembling. God's love doth not abase his majesty, nor his majesty diminish his love. We ought to know our distance from God, and to think of his superiority over us ; therefore we must be serious. Remember, ' God is greatly to be feared in the assembly of the saints, and to be had in reverence of all them that are about him,' Ps. lxxxix. 7.

3. With confidence : Eph. iii. 12, ' In whom we have boldness and access with confidence by the faith of him.' There is boldness in pouring out our requests to God, who will certainly hear us, and grant what is good. We must rely upon his goodness and power in all our necessities. He is so gracious in Christ that he will do that which is best for his glory and our good, and upon other terms we should not seek it. If you would not turn prayer into babbling, much speaking to affectation of words, take heed of these abuses, and labour to bring your hearts to God in this manner.

AN EXPOSITION

OF

THE LORD'S PRAYER.

Our Father which art in heaven.

I HAVE insisted upon the foregoing verses, which do concern the duty of prayer; let me now come to the Lord's Prayer itself. This prayer was formed and indited by Christ, and therefore to be highly esteemed by Christians: Jesus Christ, who was the wisdom of God, he knew both our necessities and the Father's good-will towards us; and therefore surely he would give us a perfect form and directory. We are not absolutely tied to this form. We do not read that it was ever used by the apostles, though we have many of their prayers upon record in the Acts and in the Epistles; yet they plainly differ as to the construction of the words; and this very prayer is diversely set down by the evangelists themselves: Mat. vi. 11, 'Give us this day our daily bread;' it is in other words, Luke xi. 3, 'Give us day by day our daily bread;' and ver. 12, 'And forgive us our debts, as we forgive our debtors;' in Luke xi. 4, it is, 'And forgive us our sins, for we also forgive every one that is indebted to us.' But, however, though we are not tied to this form, yet I think it may be humbly used; for Christ taught his disciples how to pray while as yet they were in their ignorance and tenderness, and had not received the Spirit. And God usually puts words into sinners' mouths: Hosea xi. 2, 'Take with you words, and say unto him, Receive us graciously.' Look, as Joseph is said to feed his father and his brethren as a little child is nourished (as it is in the margin), there is not only food provided, but it is put into their mouths, Gen. xlvii. 12; so did Christ teach his disciples to pray, not only as directing them what they should pray for, but putting a form of words into their mouths.

In this prayer there are three parts observable:—

1. The preface.
2. The petitions themselves.
3. The conclusion.

In the preface we have a description of God, as always we should begin prayer with awful thoughts of God. God is described partly from his goodness and mercy—*Our Father;* and partly from his greatness and majesty—*which art in heaven.*

I. His goodness and mercy: *Our Father ;* where is set forth:—

1. The relation wherein God standeth to his people, in the word *Father.*

2. Their propriety and interest in that relation, wherein, not the particular interest of a single believer is asserted, *My Father,* but the general interest of all the elect in Christ, *Our Father.*

I shall waive all which may be said concerning prayer in general; concerning the lawfulness or unlawfulness of a form in prayer; the disputes concerning the use of this form ; as also all the disputes concerning the object of prayer, which we learn from hence to be God alone. Surely prayer is a sacrifice, and belongeth only to God; it cannot be made to any other but to him, who knoweth all the prayers that are made in the world at the same time, and the hearts of all those that pray. I will also waive what might be spoken concerning preparation before petition; for here there is a preface before the prayer itself. Neither shall I speak concerning the necessity of conceiving right thoughts of God in prayer; how we may conceive of his goodness, to beget a confidence; of his majesty, to beget an awe and reverence.

That which I shall insist upon is, the notion and relation under which God is here expressed, which is that of Father—Our Father.

Observe, those that would pray aright must address themselves to God as a father in Jesus Christ.

Hypocrites, at the last day, will cry, 'Lord, Lord;' but Christ hath taught us to say, 'Our Father.'

Here I shall:—

I. Inquire in what sense God is a father.

II. What encouragements we have from thence in prayer, when we can take him up under this notion and appellation.

I. In what sense God is a father. This title may be given to God, either essentially, or with respect to personal relation.

1. Essentially; and so it is common to all the persons in the Godhead—Father, Son, and Holy Ghost; all three are God, and our Father. And thus, not only the first Person, but the second, is called 'the Everlasting Father:' Isa. ix. 6. And the Holy Ghost, being author of our being, is called our Maker. But,

2. It may be ascribed to God personally. And so the first Person is called God the Father ; and that either with relation to Christ or to us.

[1.] With relation to Christ, as the Son of God. So the first Person is called the Father, as he is the fountain of the Deity, communicating to and with him the divine essence : Ps. ii. 7, ' Thou art my Son, this day have I begotten thee.' The personal property of the Father is to beget; and of the Son, to be begotten. There is an eternal *now,* wherein God is said to beget him. Thus he may be called the Father of Christ, as he is the second Person, and not only as incarnate and Mediator. Though God be Christ's Father, as second Person, yet they are all equal in power, dignity, and glory;

but as Mediator, God is his Father in another respect. So it is said, John xiv. 28, ' My Father is greater than I '—not as God, for so he was equal; ' He thought it no robbery to be equal with God: ' Phil. ii. 6. But ' greater than I ; ' that is, consider him as man and mediator, in the state of his humiliation ; for it is notable to consider upon what occasion Christ speaks these words: ' If ye love me ye would rejoice because I said I go unto the Father; for my Father is greater than I ; ' that is, You admire me and prize my company exceedingly, because you see the power which I put forth in the miracles which I do ; ye would rejoice if you understood it aright; he is infinitely more glorious than I appear in this state of abasement and humiliation. Thus, with respect to Christ, God, the first Person, may be called the Father.

[2.] With respect to us ; for the first person is not only the Father of Christ, but our Father: John xx. 17, ' I go to my Father, and your Father.' We share with Christ in all his relations. As God was his God by covenant, so he is our God. And in this sense, personally, it may be taken here ; for our business lieth mainly with the first Person, with whom Christ intercedeth for us : 1 John ii. 1, ' We have an advocate with the Father, even Jesus Christ the righteous.' Before whom doth he appear ? Before the Father. And it is to him to whom we direct our prayers, though not excluding the other persons : Eph. iii. 14, ' I bow my knees unto the Father of our Lord Jesus Christ.' Though it be not unlawful to pray to Christ, or to the Holy Ghost, for that hath been done by the saints. Stephen saith, ' Lord Jesus, receive my spirit ;' and Jacob saith, ' The angel of the covenant bless the lads.' And all baptized persons are baptized in the name of the Son and Holy Ghost, as well as in the name of the Father. But usually Christian worship is terminated upon God the Father, as being chief in the mystery of redemption; and so it is said, Eph. ii. 18, ' Through him, by one Spirit, we have access to the Father.' We come to him through Christ, as the meritorious cause, who hath procured leave for us ; and by the Spirit, as the efficient cause, who gives us a heart to come ; and to the Father, as the ultimate object of Christian worship. Christ procureth us leave to come, and the Spirit gives us a heart to come : so that by the Spirit, through Christ, we have access to God. So that now you may see what is meant by the Father—' Our Father.'

But now let me distinguish again. God is a father to mankind, either :—

1. In a more general consideration and respect, by creation ; or,

2. In a more special regard, by adoption.

First, By creation God is a father. At first he gave a being to all things ; but to men and angels he gave reason : John i. 4, ' And this life was the light of man.' Other things had life, but man had such a life as was light ; and so by his original constitution he became to be the son of God. To establish the relation of a father, there must be a communication of life and likeness. A painter, that makes an image or picture like himself, he is not the father of it, for though there be likeness, yet no life. The sun in propriety of speech is not the father of frogs and putrid creatures, which are quickened by its heat ; though there be life, yet there is no likeness. We keep this relation for univocal generations and rational creatures. Thus, by creation, the angels are said to be the sons of God: Job xxxviii. 7, ' When he was laying the foundations of the earth, the sons of God shouted for joy ;' that is, the angels. And thus Adam also was called the son of God: Luke iii. 38. Thus, by our first creation, and with respect to that, all men are the sons of God, children of God. And (mark it) in respect of God's continual concurrence to our being, though we have deformed ourselves, and are not the same that we were when we were first created ; yet still, in regard of some sorry remains of God's image, and the light of reason, all are sons of God, and God in a general sense is a father to us ; yea, more a father than our natural parents are. For our parents, they concur to our being but instrumentally, God originally. We had our being, under God, from our parents : he hath the greatest hand and stroke in forming us in the belly, and making us to be what we are. Which appeareth by this : Parents, they know not what the child will be, male or female, beautiful or deformed ; they cannot tell the number of bones, muscles, veins, arteries, and cannot restore any of these in case they should be lost and spoiled ; so that he that framed us in the womb, and wonderfully fashioned us in the secret parts, he is our Father : Ps. cxxxix. 14. As the writing is rather the work of the penman than of the pen, so we are rather the workmanship of God than of our parents ; they are but instruments, God is the author and fountain of that life and being which we still have. And again, consider, the better part of man is of his immediate creation, and in this respect he is called ' the Father of spirits :' Heb. xii. 9. They do not run in the channel of carnal generation or fleshly descent, but they are immediately created by God. And it is said, Eccles. xii. 7, ' The spirit returneth to God which gave it.'

Well, then, you see how, in a general sense, and with what good reason, God may be called our Father. Those which we call fathers, they are but subordinate instruments ; the most we have from them is our corruption, our being depraved ; but our substance, and the frame and fashion of it, our being, and all that is good in it, that is from the Lord.

Now, this is some advantage in prayer, to look upon God as our father by virtue of creation, that we can come to him as the work of his hands, and beseech him that he will not destroy us and suffer us to perish : Isa. lxiv. 8, ' But now, O Lord, thou art our father ; we are the clay, and thou our potter; and we are all the work of thine hand.' There is a general mercy that God hath for all his creatures; and, therefore, as he gave us rational souls, and fashioned us in the womb, we may come to him and say, Lord, thou art our potter and we thy clay, do us good, forsake us not.

What advantage have we in prayer from this common interest or general respect of God's being a father by virtue of creation ?

[1.] This common relation binds us to pray to him. All things which God hath made, by a secret instinct they are carried to God for their supply : Ps. cxlv. 15, ' The eyes of all things look up to thee.' In their way they pray to him and moan to him for their supplies, even very beasts, young ravens, and fowls of the air. But much more is this man's duty, as we have reason, and can clearly own the first cause. And therefore upon these natural grounds the apostle reasons with them why they should seek after God: Acts xiv. 17.

[2.] As this common relation binds us to pray, so it draweth common benefits after it: Mat. vi. 25, 26, 'Is not the life more than meat, and the body than raiment? Behold the fowls of the air: for they sow not, neither do they reap, nor gather into barns; yet your heavenly Father feedeth them.' Where God hath given a life, he will give food; and where he gives a body, he will give raiment, according to his good pleasure. He doth not cast off the care of any living creature he hath made, as long as he will preserve it for his glory. Beasts have their food and provision, much more men, which are capable of knowing and enjoying God.

[3.] It giveth us confidence in the power of God. He which made us out of nothing is able to keep, preserve, and supply us when all things fail, and in the midst of all dangers. Saints are able to make use of this common relation. And therefore it is said, 1 Pet. iv. 19, that we should 'commit our souls unto him in well-doing, as unto a faithful Creator.' The apostle speaks of such times when they carried their lives in their hands from day to day. They did not know how soon they should be haled before tribunals and cast into prisons. Remember, you have a Creator, which made you out of nothing; and he can keep and preserve life when you have nothing. Thus this common relation is not to be forgotten, as he gives us our outward life and being: Ps. cxxiv. 8, 'Our help is in the name of the Lord, who made heaven and earth.' As if the psalmist had said, as long as I see these glorious monuments of his power, these things framed out of nothing, shall I distrust God, whatever exigence or strait I may be reduced to?

Secondly, More especially there is a particular sort of men to whom God is a father in Christ, and that is, to believers: John i. 12, 'To as many as received him, to them gave he power to be called the sons of God.' Those which in their natural state and condition were children of wrath, and slaves to sin and Satan, when they come, and are willing to welcome and receive Christ into their hearts, in a sense of their misery, are willing to make out after God and Christ; they have an allowance to call God Father, and may have child-like communion with him, and run to him in all straits, and lay open their necessities to him. 2 Kings iv. 19, When the child cried unto his father, he said, 'Carry him to his mother:' so when we are ill at ease and in any straits, this is the privilege of our adoption, that we have a God to go to; we may go to our Father and plead with him, as the church: Isa. lxiii. 16, 'Doubtless thou art our father, though Abraham be ignorant of us, and Israel acknowledge us not: thou, O Lord, art our father, our redeemer.' It is good to know God under this special relation of a father in Christ; and this is that which is the grace of adoption. Adoption is an act of free grace, by which we that were aliens and strangers, servants to sin and Satan, are, in and by Christ, made sons and daughters of God, and accordingly are so reckoned and treated with, to all intents and purposes. It is a great and special privilege, given to God's own children, by virtue of their interest in

Christ; and therefore it is said, 1 John iii. 1, 'Behold, what love the
Father hath bestowed upon us, that we should be called the sons of
God!' That is, behold it as a certain truth, and admire it as a great
privilege. This second relation is a very great privilege, and it will
appear to be so, if we consider :—

[1.] The persons that receive it. We that were aliens, and enemies,
and bond-slaves ; that were of another line and stock ; that might
'say to corruption, Thou art my father ; to the worm, Thou art my
mother, and my sister :' Job xvii. 14. We that were cousin-germans
to worms, a handful of enlivened dust, that we should be taken into
such a relation to God! We that might say indeed to the devil, Thou
art our father, and the lusts of our father we will do: John viii. 24.
Satan is the sinners' father, and God disclaims them. The Lord disclaims the people which were brought out of the land of Egypt, when
they rebelled against him : Exod. xxxii. 7, 'The Lord said unto
Moses, Go, get thee down, for thy people which thou broughtest out
of the land of Egypt have corrupted themselves.' *Thy* people, which
thou hast brought, in scorn and disdain, as if God did disavow them
from being his. And so it was with us all. When Adam had rebelled against God, God executed the law of the rebellious child
against him, which was this, that he should be turned out of doors.
So was Adam turned out of paradise, and lost his title and heritage ;
and we were reckoned to the devil. Now, 'behold, what manner of
love was this, that we should be called the sons of God!'

[2.] You will wonder at it, you will behold it as an excellent privilege, if you consider the nature of the privilege itself, to be sons and
daughters of God, to be able to call God Father. This was Christ's
own title and honour. When God had a mind to honour Christ, he
proclaims it from heaven: Mat. iii. 17. 'This is my beloved Son, in
whom I am well pleased.' Surely, if our hearts were as apprehensive
of heavenly privileges as they are of earthly, we would admire it more.
Earthly alliance, how is it prized! If a great man should match
into our blood and line, what an honour and glory do we reckon it to
us! 1 Sam. xviii. 23, 'Seemeth it to you a light thing to be a king's
son-in-law?' Do we account this a small matter, to be related to
kings, and princes, and potentates? No, no ; we have high thoughts
of it. And is not this an excellent thing, to be sons and daughters of
God? In all other cases, if men have children of their own, they do
not adopt. God had a Son of his own, in whom his soul found full
delight and complacency ; yet he would adopt and take us wretched
creatures, he would invest us with the title of sons ; and shall it be
said of this and that believer, here is the son of God? O behold what
manner of love! &c.

[3.] Then do but consider the consequents of it, both in this life and
the life to come. In this life, what immunities and privileges have
we! Free access to God ; we may come and treat with him when
we please, as children to a father, when we stand in need of anything.
'We have received the spirit of adoption, whereby we cry, Abba,
Father:' Rom. viii. 15. If we ail anything, we may go to our Father
and acquaint him with our case and grief. And we shall have a child's
allowance here in the world. The heirs of glory are well provided

for in their nonage ; they have a right to a large portion ; all the good
things of the world, meat, drink, marriage, such things they have by
a son's right.   They have a right to the creature, in and by him who
is heir of all things, so they are established in their right which Adam
lost : 1 Tim. iv. 3, 4.   And they are under the ministry of angels ;
the angels are sent forth to be their guardians, and to supply and provide for them.

And then, in the life to come (for we are not only sons, but heirs),
we have a right to the glorious inheritance !   Rom. viii. 17, ' If children, then heirs, heirs of God.'   Here all the children are heirs, male
and female, every son and daughter an heir and joint-heirs with Christ.
We do as it were divide heaven between us ; we have a great, blessed,
and glorious inheritance ; poor despicable creatures, ' chosen heirs of a
kingdom :' James ii. 5.

[4.] You will see it was a very great privilege, if you consider how
we come to be entitled to it : Eph. i. 5, ' Having predestinated us unto
the adoption of children, by Jesus Christ, to himself.'   We come to
it in and by Jesus Christ.   Christ was fain to come down, and to take
a mother upon earth, that we might have a Father in heaven.   He
comes down, and was made a man ; he became our brother, and so
layeth the foundation for the kindred : Heb. ii. 11.   Nay, not only
incarnate, but he died to purchase this title for us.   When the business was debated in the council of the Trinity, how lost man might
be restored in blood, and have a right and interest in God ; and when
justice put in exceptions against us, Jesus Christ was content to be
' made under the law, that we might receive the adoption of sons :'
Gal. iv. 4, 5.   There could be no reconciliation, no amity, no alliance,
until sin was expiated and justice satisfied ; therefore Christ was not
only ' made of a woman,' but ' made under the law ;' first our brother
by incarnation, and then our redeemer by his death and suffering.
As under the law, if a man had waxen poor, the next of kin was to be
his redeemer : Lev. xxv. 25 ; or if he had sold himself, ver. 47, one
of his brethren was to redeem him.   Christians, there was a kind of
sale and forfeiture on our part of the inheritance and right and title
of children ; therefore Jesus Christ, when he became a man, *jure propinquitatis*, by virtue of his kindred and nearness to us, came to redeem
his people, and purchase us to God.   And this is the relation which
is mainly intended in this place ; for mark, Christ taught his disciples
to pray, ' Our Father ;' others, they cannot speak of this relation ; and
in them all that believe, and all that walk in the Spirit, these alone
can come to God as a father.

II. What advantage have we in prayer by taking up God under
this notion and relation, when we can come to him and say, ' Our
Father ' ?

1. It conduceth to our confidence in prayer.

2. It furthereth our duty.

First, It conduceth to our confidence in prayer : for it is not an
empty title or a naked relation ; but this is the ground of all that
favour and grace which we stand in need of, and receive from God.
It is notable, 2 Cor. vi. 18, saith God, ' I will be a father unto you,
and ye shall be my sons and daughters.'   In other places it is said,

Ye shall be *called* my sons ; but here, You shall *be* my sons ; you shall
not only be called so, but be so.   He will really perform all the parts
of a father to us ; yea, no father like God.   The outward father is
but a shadow ; as in all comparisons, outward things are but the
shadow and similitude , the reality is in inward things.   A servant is
not always a servant, there may be a release ; a husband is not
always a husband, there may be a separation by divorce ; but a
father is always a father, and a child a child.   'I am the true vine.'
The outward vine is but a shadow, but Christ himself hath the true
properties of a vine.   So the outward father is but a shadow and
similitude, the reality is in God ; none so fatherly and kind as he :
Mat. vii. 11, ' If ye, being evil, know how to give good gifts unto
your children, how much more shall your Father which is in heaven
give good things to them that ask him ? '   There is a *how much more*
upon the fatherly care of God.   Natural parents, whose affections are
stinted and limited, nay, corrupt and sinful, when a son comes for a
fish, will not give him a scorpion, when he comes for bread, will not
give him a stone.   That were a monstrous thing, vile and unnatural.
So Isa. xlix. 15 : ' Can a woman forget her sucking-child, that she
should not have compassion on the son of her womb ? yea, they
may forget, yet will I not forget thee.'   Passions in females are more
vehement ; the mother hath stronger affections.   If the mother could
do so as totally to forget that ever she had such a child, yet she would
not forget her sucking-child—a poor, shiftless, helpless babe, that can
do nothing without the mother, a child which never provoked her,—
she would not forget such a child.   They may forget, yet will I not
forget thee.   Certainly, God which hath left such an impression upon
the hearts of parents, hath more of pity, bounty, and goodness in his
own heart ; for whatsoever of God is in the creature, is in God in a more
eminent manner.

But particularly, How will God perform the parts of a father ?

[1.] In allowing them full leave to come to him in all their necessities : Gal. iv. 6, ' Because ye are sons, God hath sent forth the Spirit
of his Son into your hearts, crying, Abba, Father.'   There is a spirit
that attendeth upon this state.   They which are sons shall have the
spirit of sons, and God will incline their hearts to come and call to
him for supplies.   This is a great advantage.   When he gives a spirit
of prayer, then he will be ready to hear and grant our requests ; not
only to give us a heart to ask them, but to incline his ear : Luke xi.
13, ' How much more shall your heavenly Father give the Holy Spirit
to them that ask him ? '   When we ask for the highest blessing ;
when we come and are importunate with him, and will take no nay.

[2.] In supplying all our wants : Mat. vi. 12, ' Your Father which
is in heaven knoweth you have need of these things.'   A father will
not let his child starve—certainly none so fatherly as God.   You have
not such a father as is ignorant, regardless of your condition, but
takes an exact notice of all your wants and pressures.   It is notable
to observe how God condescendeth to express the particular notice
he taketh of the saints : Isa. xlix. 16, ' Behold, I have graven thee
upon the palms of my hands.'   As we use to tie things about our hands,
that we may remember such a work and business ; so God doth, as it

were, put a print and mark upon his hands ; to speak after the manner of men. Nay, Mat. x. 30, ' The hairs of their heads are numbered.' God hath a particular notice of their necessities ; and Jesus Christ, he is his remembrancer, one that ever appeareth before him to represent their wants : Heb. ix. 24. As the high priest in the law was to go in with the names of the tribes upon his breast and shoulder when he did minister before God : Exod. xxviii.; which is a type how much we are in the heart of Christ, ever presenting himself before the Lord on the behalf of such and such a believer.

[3.] Pitying our miseries. As he taketh notice of them, so he will pity their miseries, as a father pitieth his children when he seeth them in an afflicted condition : Ps. ciii. 13, ' Like as a father pitieth his children, so the Lord pitieth them that fear him.' Nay, he will pardon their sins : Mal. iii. 17, ' And I will spare them as a man spareth his own son which serveth him.' An only son needs not fear much if his father were to be his judge, though he hath done unworthily. They may exhaust and draw up all their pity, their bowls may shrink when they meet with multitude of provocations. Now, God will spare us as a man spares his only son—nay, not only his only son, but his dutiful son which serves him. Many times we forget the duty of children, but God will not forget the mercy of a father. ' I will go to my father,' saith the prodigal. He had forgotten the duty of a child, he went into a far country and wasted his patrimony, and that basely and filthily upon harlots ; yet, upon his return, when he was a great way off, the father runs to meet him half-way, and kisseth him.

[4.] In disciplining and treating us with much indulgence, and wisdom, and care. A father takes a great deal of pains in forming his child, and fashioning its manners and behaviour ; so doth God with his children. If he afflicteth, it is as a father only, with purposes of good, and not so as an earthly father : Heb. xii. 10, ' For verily for a few days they chastened us after their own pleasure ; but he for our profit, that we might be partakers of his holiness.' They mingle a great deal of passion with their correction when they are inflamed ; but God never mingleth passion with his rod. When he gives a bitter cup he is a father still : John xviii. 11.

[5.] In providing able guardians for his children. None so attended as God's children are—those which are adopted and taken into grace and favour with Christ : Heb. i. 14, Angels are ' ministering spirits, sent abroad for the heirs of salvation.' They have a guard of angels to watch over them, that they dash not their foot against a stone.

[6.] In laying up an inheritance for them. The apostle saith, 2 Cor. xii. 14, ' Children ought not to lay up for their parents, but parents for their children.' Now, God hath laid up for us, as well as laid out much upon us : Luke xii. 32, ' Fear not, little flock, it is your Father's good pleasure to give you the kingdom.' He has a kingdom, a glorious inheritance to bestow upon us ; and we are kept for that happy state. Though he hath an heir already, Jesus Christ, the heir of all things, yet God hath made us ' co-heirs with Christ : ' Rom. viii. 17.

Thus, then, it is a mighty advantage. If we did take up God in this notion, to look upon him as a father, it would increase our confidence and dependence upon him. This is a sweet relation : the reality is more in God than can be in an earthly father; for he is a father according to his essence, knowing our necessities, pardoning our sins, supplying our wants, forming and fashioning our manners, providing able guardians for us, and laying up a blessed inheritance for us in heaven.

Secondly, As it encourageth us to pray, so it furthereth our duty in prayer, that we may behave ourselves with reverence, love, and gratitude.

[1.] With a child-like reverence and affection in prayer: Mal. i. 6, 'If, then, I be a father, where is mine honour? And if I be a master, where is my fear?' If we expect the supplies of children, we must perform the duty of children. God will be owned as a father, not with a fellow-like familiarity, but humbly, and with an awe of his majesty.

[2.] With love. Now, our love to God is mainly seen by subjection and obedience to his laws. Thus Christ would have us take up God in prayer under such a relation, that we might mind our duty to him: 1 Pet. i. 17, 'And if ye call on the Father, who without respect of persons judgeth according to every man's work, pass the time of your sojourning here in fear.' We never pray aright but when we pray resolving to cast off all sin. How can we call him Father, whom we care not continually to displease from day to day? So the Lord treats his people: Jer. iii. 5, 6, 'Thou hast said, Thou art my father. Behold, thou hast spoken and done evil things as thou couldest.' God takes it to be a contumely and reproach to himself when we do evil, yet come and call him Father. He takes it ill that men should come complimentally and flatter him with lying lips, and do not walk as children in holy obedience. Therefore, it is an engagement to serve God with holiness.

[3.] With gratitude. When we come to pray, we must remember not only what we want, but what we have received, acknowledging we have all from him; he is our father: Deut. xxxii. 6, 'Do ye thus requite the Lord, O foolish people, and unwise? Is not he thy father that hath bought thee? Hath he not made thee and established thee?' We must acknowledge the good we have, as well as that we expect to come from him. Therefore, if we would have a praying frame, and be eased of our solicitude, and that anxious care which is a disparagement to providence, it is good to take up God under the notion of a father, which makes us rest upon him for all things: Mat. vi. 25, 'Take no thought for your life, what ye shall eat, or what ye shall drink; nor yet for your body, what ye shall put on.' Why? 'For your heavenly Father knoweth that you have need of all these things.' You that are able fathers would think yourselves disparaged if that your children should filch and steal for their living, and beg and be solicitous, and go up and down from door to door for their maintenance and support, and not trust to your care and provision. A believer which knoweth he hath a heavenly Father will not be negligent in his calling, but be active and industrious in his way, and use those lawful means which, by the providence of God, he hath been brought up in; and then, 'be careful for nothing,' as the apostle's advice is, Phil. iv. 6, and 'in everything, by prayer and supplication, make your request known unto God.' Oh, could we turn carking into prayer, and run to our Father, it would be happy for us. Care, and diligence, and necessary provision, that is our work and labour: but, for the success and event of things, leave it to God. When we are carking in the world with such anxiousness, and troubled with restless thoughts, how we should be provided for in old age, and what will become of us and ours, we take God's work out of his hands. This is a disparagement to our heavenly Father, and a reproach to his providence and fatherly care. Well, then, certainly this is of great advantage in prayer.

APPLICATION.

Use. If it be a great advantage in prayer to take up God under the notion and relation of a father, then those that would pray aright, let this instruct and quicken them above all things. Clear up your adoption, that you may be able to call God Father, for otherwise, when you come to pray, it is a very lie to God. As Acts v. 4, when Ananias spake false to the apostle, saith Peter to him: 'Thou hast not lied unto men, but unto God.' Why? Because he knows all that is done in the world. But much more do they lie unto God here; this is a very disgrace and blasphemy, a contumely, rather than a prayer and supplication, when you will come and make God to father the devil's brats. When you that live in sin, and have no reverence and awe of God upon your hearts, shall come and pray to him, this is a lie which is told to the very face of God.

But if this be a truth, that all those which would pray aright must clear up their adoption and get a sense of it, then here will doubts arise. Therefore here I shall handle three cases :—

1. What shall natural men do? Must they desist from prayer? for they have no right to it.

2. What shall they do which have not as yet received the testimony of the Spirit? For a child of God may have the right of children, yet have not a sense of his adoption.

3. What are the evidences by which our adoption may be cleared up to us, how we may know we are taken into a child-like state?

First, What shall natural men do? Must they desist from prayer? for they have no right to it.

I answer, you may see here the miserable condition of wicked men, how much they are bound to pray, and yet what an impossibility lieth upon them of praying aright. Certainly none should desist from this duty of prayer because they cannot perform it aright, for though we have lost our power and fitness, yet there is no reason God should lose his right and his power to our obedience. There is an obligation and precept from God, as a father by creation, upon all mankind; all which are reasonable creatures, they are to own God as a father in this way. I say prayer is a homage we owe to God by natural right, therefore no doubt wicked men do sin when they cease to pray. It is one of the accusations brought against natural men, and is an aggravation of their sin: Ps. xiv. 1, 'They do not call upon God.' Rom. iii. 10, it is applied to natural men. This is the misery they have subjected themselves to, that their prayer is turned into sin. As a natural man must not omit hearing, because it is a means to bring him to be acquainted with God, though he cannot hear in faith, so he must not omit prayer, because it is one means to bring us to own God as a father by adoption. A man is not to turn the back upon him, but call him Father, as well as he can : Jer. iii. 19, ' But I said, How shall I put thee among the children, and give thee a pleasant land, a goodly heritage of the hosts of nations ? And I said, Thou shalt call me, My Father, and shalt not turn away from me.' Better to own God any way, than not to own him at all, than not to inquire after him ; to own him rationally, if not spiritually, to own him by choice, if not out of sense. If we cannot come and clear up our title to this great privilege by the spirit of adoption, yet any way ' Thou shalt not turn away from me.' We should not shut the door upon ourselves. It is required of a natural man, being weary of his sins, to fly to God in Christ Jesus, for his grace and favour, that he might become his God and Father.

Secondly, What shall they do which have not as yet received the testimony of the Spirit, that do not know their adoption ?

I answer, a child of God may have the effects and fruits of adoption, yet not always the feeling of it, to witness to him that God hath taken him into a child-like relation to himself. Certainly they are in a very uncomfortable condition, for they want a help in prayer. ' Doubtless thou art our Father.' Oh, what an advantage is that ! How much of eloquence and rhetoric is there in that, when we can speak to God as a father ! Yet they are not to neglect their addresses to God, for this is a means to obtain the Spirit of adoption : Luke xi. 13, ' He will give the Spirit to them that ask him.' Therefore, in whatever condition we be, we must pray ; otherwise we shut the door upon our hopes. You continue the want upon yourselves, and so wholly detain yourselves in a comfortless condition.

There is a fourfold spiritual art we must use in prayer, when we have not the sense of our adoption, that we may be able to speak to God as our Father.

[1.] Disclaim when you cannot apply. When you cannot clear up your own relation and interest, then disclaim all other confidences. If thou canst not say *Father ;* yet plead *fatherless ;* Hosea xiv. 3, ' In thee the fatherless find mercy.' Come as poor, helpless, shiftless creatures ; seek peace and reconciliation with God in Christ. It may be God may take you into his favour. He is a Father of the fatherless.

[2.] Own God in the humbling way. Learn the policy of the prodigal : Luke xv. 18, 19, ' Father, I have sinned against heaven, and before thee, and am no more worthy to be called thy son.' This is the policy and art of a humble faith, to call God Father. As Paul catcheth hold of the promise on the dark side : ' Jesus Christ came to save sinners ;' and presently he addeth, ' whereof I am chief : ' so a believer may come and say, ' Lord, I am not worthy to be called thy son, make me as one of thy hired servants.'

[3.] The third policy we should use in prayer is to call him Father in wish : *Optando, si non affirmando.* If we cannot do it by direct affirmation, let us do it by desire. Let us pray ourselves into this relation, and groan after it, that we may have a clearer sense that God is our Father in Christ.

[4.] Faith hath one art more,—it maketh use of Christ Jesus. God hath a Son whose name significth much in heaven, therefore if you cannot come to him as your Father, come to him as the God and Father of our Lord Jesus Christ: Eph. iii. 14, 'For this cause I bow my knees to the God and Father of our Lord Jesus Christ.' Let Christ bring you into God's presence. He is willing to change relations with us. Take him along with you in your arms. Go to God in Christ's name : 'Whatsoever you ask in my name, shall be given to you.'

Thirdly, But what are the evidences by which our adoption may be cleared up to us? How shall we know that we are taken into a child-like state?

[1.] Consider how it is brought about. How do we come to be related to God by Christ Jesus? By receiving Christ, as he is offered in the gospel : John i. 12, 'To as many as received him, to them gave he power to become the sons of God.' It is a prerogative, and special grant to those which receive Christ, even those that believe in his name, that is, those who, out of a sense of their own need, and sight of Christ offered in the promise, do really consent to take him for the ends for which God offereth him, to wit, as Prince and Saviour, that he might give you repentance and remission of sins, not in pretence, but in your hearts. These have full liberty to call God Father, to come to treat and deal with him, though they have not a sense of the blessedness of their state, for this followeth believing: 'After you believed, you were sealed by the Holy Spirit of promise,' Eph. i. 13, 14.

[2.] There is a witness which is given to the saints, that the thing may not always be dark and doubtful. The Holy Ghost is given as a witness. If you would know whether or no you are the children of God, see that of the apostle: Rom. viii. 16, 'The Spirit itself beareth witness with our spirit, that we are the children of God.' As under the law, in the mouth of two witnesses every doubtful thing was to be established, Deut. xvii. 6, so here the Spirit beareth witness, together with our spirits, that we are the children of God. Our spirits alone may be lying, deceitful ; we may flatter ourselves, and think we are the children of God, when we are children of the devil. All certainly comes from the Holy Ghost ; and, therefore, the great question which is traversed to and fro in the heart, is, whether we be God's children ? What is the Spirit's witness ?

(1.) He lays down marks in scripture, which are the ground and decision of this debate, for the scriptures are of the Holy Ghost's inditing, and so may be said to bear witness: Rom. viii. 14, 'For as many as are led by the Spirit of God, they are the sons of God:' 1 John iii. 10, 'In this the children of God are manifest, and the children of the devil: whosoever doth not righteousness, is not of God, neither he that loveth not his brother.' Thus the Spirit beareth witness to our spirits, by laying down such marks as we, by our own spiritual sense and renewed conscience, feel to be right within ourselves. And this is the main thing called the witness of the Spirit.

(2.) He worketh such graces as are peculiar to God's children, and are evidences of our interest in the favour of God ; and therefore it is called 'the sanctification of the Spirit,' 2 Thes. ii. 13 ; and 'the re-

newing of the Holy Ghost,' Titus iii. 5. Look, as John knew Christ
to be the Son of God by the Spirit's descending and abiding upon
him, John i. 32, so by the Spirit's work, and the Spirit's inhabitation,
we know whether we are the children of God or no; whether ' we
dwell in God, and God in us, because of his Spirit that he hath
given us;' that is, because of those graces wrought in us. And this
is called the seal of the Spirit; for the Holy Ghost, stamping the
impress of God upon the soul, working in us an answerable likeness to Christ, is said to be the seal; then we have God's impress
upon us.

(3.) The Spirit goes further : he helpeth us to feel and discover
those acts in ourselves. There is a stupid deadness in the conscience,
so that we are not always sensible of our spiritual acts. Hagar saw
not the fountain near her until God opened her eyes, so we may not
see the work of the Spirit without the light of the Spirit. We cannot
own grace in the midst of so much weakness and imperfection ; there
is a misgiving of conscience: therefore the Spirit of sanctification is
also a ' Spirit of revelation :' Eph. i. 17. The author of the grace is
the best revealer and interpreter of it: he works, and he gives us a
sight of it. As a workman that made a thing can best warrant it to
the buyer, he knows the goodness and strength of it, and how it is
framed and made ; so the Holy Ghost, which works grace, he reveals
and discovers this grace to us.

(4.) The Spirit helps us to compare them with the rule, and accordingly to judge of their sincerity. The Spirit opens our understandings, that we may be able to discern the intent and scope of
the scripture, that so we may not be mistaken. We must plough
with God's heifer if we would understand the riddle: ' In thy light
we shall see light.' We shall be apt to misapply the rule, so as to judge
of our own actions : Rom. ix. 1, ' I lie not, the Holy Ghost bearing me
witness ;' when he had spoken of some eminent thing wrought in him.
We are apt to lie, and feign and misapply rules, comforts, and privileges ; but now the Holy Ghost bearing witness with our spirits, by
this means we come to have a certainty. There are so many circuits,
wiles, turnings in the heart of man, that we are not competent judges
of what is wrought in us ; therefore it is usually ascribed to the Spirit
to be the searcher of the heart: Ps. cxxxix. 7, ' Whither shall I go
from thy Spirit ? or whither shall I flee from thy presence ?' Acts
v. 4, ' Thou hast not lied unto men, but unto God.' The Holy Ghost
is rather spoken of than any other person, because it is his personal
operation to abide in the hearts of men, and to search and try the
reins. It is more particularly ascribed to him, though it belongs to
all the persons.

(5.) As the Spirit helps us to compare that which is wrought with
the rule, the impression or thing sealed with the stamp or the thing
sealing, so he helps us to conclude rightly of our estate. For many
times when the premises are clear, the conclusion may be suspended,
either out of self-love, in case of condemnation ; or out of legal fear
and jealousy, in case of self-acquitment. Therefore the conclusion is
of the Holy Ghost: 1 John iv. 13, ' Hereby we know that we dwell
in him, and he in us, because he hath given us of his Spirit.' There

is a great deal ado to bring us to heaven with comfort. There needs a person of the Godhead to satisfy us as well as to satisfy God, and help us to determine concerning our condition.

(6.) He enlivens and heightens our apprehensions in all these particulars, and so fills us with comfort, and raiseth our joy upon the feeling of the sense of the favour of God; for all this is the fruit of his operation. Therefore it is said, Rom. v. 5, ' The love of God is shed abroad in our hearts by the Holy Ghost, which is given unto us.' Those unspeakable glimpses of God's favour, and sweet manifestations of God's love in the conscience which we have, these are given by the Holy Ghost. There is not one act of the soul, but the Holy Ghost hath a stroke in it for our comfort. In every degree, all comes from God. So that if you would know what the witness of the Spirit is, consider—What are the marks in scripture? what graces are wrought in your hearts? how doth the Spirit help you to discern those graces, to compare them to the rule, to make accordingly in these things a determination of our condition? and what joy and peace have you thereupon wrought in your hearts by the Holy Ghost? For an immediate testimony of the Spirit, the scripture knows of no such thing. All other is but delusion besides this.

[3.] There are certain fruits and effects which do more sensibly evidence it unto the soul. What are those fruits of the Spirit of adoption in our hearts, by which we may further evidence it, whether we are the children of God or not?

(1.) In prayer, by a kind of naturalness or delight in this duty of holy commerce with God: Rom. viii. 15, ' We have received the Spirit of adoption, whereby we cry, Abba, Father;' Gal. iv. 6, ' Because ye are sons, God hath sent forth the Spirit of his Son into your hearts, crying, Abba, Father;' and Zech. xii. 10, ' I will pour upon the house of David, and upon the inhabitants of Jerusalem, the Spirit of grace and of supplication.' Wherever the Spirit of God is dispensed, and dwelleth in the hearts of any, the heart of that man will be often with God. The Spirit of grace will put him upon supplication; he will be often acquainting God with his desires, wants, fears.

(2.) You will be mainly carried out to your inheritance in heaven. Those which are the children of God do look after a child's portion, and will look for an estate in heaven, and cannot be satisfied with present things. Worldly men, they have their reward: Mat. vi. 2. They discharge God for other things. If they may have plenty, honour, worldly ease, and delights here, they never look after heaven. As a servant hath his reward from quarter to quarter, but a child waits until the inheritance comes, so when we are begotten for this lively hope, when there is a heavenly-mindedness in you, this is a fruit of the Holy Ghost wrought in the heart, by which you might know you are the sons of God: Rom. viii. 23, ' Having the first-fruits of the Spirit, we groan within ourselves, waiting for the adoption, to wit, the redemption of our body.'

(3.) By a child-like reverence and dread of God, when we are afraid to offend God: Jer. xxxv. 5, 6. The sons of Rechab, their father had commanded them that they should drink no wine; now saith God by the prophet, ' Set pots full of wine, and cups, and say unto them,

Drink ye wine;' that is, present the temptation. No, they would not:
'Our fathers have forbidden us.' So when a child of God is put upon
temptation, his heart recoils, and reasons thus: 'How can I do this
wickedness, and sin against God ?' I dare not, my Father hath forbidden me. There is an awe of his heavenly Father upon him:
1 Pet. i. 17, 'If you call on the Father, who without respect of
persons judgeth according to every man's work, pass the time of your
sojourning here in fear.'

We now come to speak of the possessive particle—*Our* Father.
The word is used for a double reason:—

1. To comfort us in the sense of our interest in God.

2. To mind us of the common interest of all the saints in the same
God. It is not *my* or *thy* Father only, but *our* Father.

First, Observe the great condescension of Christ, that poor creatures
are allowed to claim an interest in God. If Christ had not put these
words in our mouths, we never had had boldness to have gone to
God, and said, 'Doubtless thou art our Father.' But he which was
in the bosom of God, and knew his secrets, hath told us it is very
pleasing to God we should use this compellation to him. This is a
privilege which cannot be sufficiently valued ; if we consider:—

[1.] The unworthiness of the persons which enjoy it: poor dust and
ashes, sinful creatures, that were children of the devil, that we should
lay claim and title to God for our Father. And,

[2.] If we consider the greatness of the privilege itself: 'Oh,
behold what manner of love the Father hath bestowed upon us, that
we should be called his children !' 1 John iii. 1. We think it much
when we can say, This field, this house is mine; but surely this is
more, to say, This God is mine.

Again, observe here that interest is a ground of audience. So
Christ would have us begin our prayers, 'Our Father.' God's interest
in us, and our interest in God. God's interest in us: when Christ
mediates for his disciples, he saith, John xvii. 6, 'Thine they were, and
thou gavest them me.' And David: Ps. cxix. 94, 'I am thine, save me.'
That is his argument: the reason is, because God, by taking them for
his own, binds himself to preserve and keep them. Everybody is
bound to look to his own : 'He that provides not for his own is worse
than an infidel.' Now what a sweet thing is it when we can go to
God and say, We are thine ! So it is the same, as to our interest in
God. It is an excellent encouragement: Ps. xlii. 11, 'Hope thou
in God,' saith David to his soul. Why? For he is my God. And
elsewhere, reasoning with himself: Ps. xxiii. 1, 'The Lord is my
shepherd, I shall not want.' First, his covenant-interest is built, and
then conclusions of hope. So 2 Sam. xxx. 6, 'David encouraged himself in the Lord his God.' It is sweet when we can go to God as *our*
God. Luther was wont to say, God was known better by the predic-
ament of relation than by his natural properties. Why is interest
such a sweet thing? Because by this relation to God we have a
claim to God, and to all that he can and will do. God hath made over
himself, *quantus quantus est*, as great as great he is, for his use and
comfort. Therefore the psalmist saith, Ps. xvi. 5, 'The Lord is the
portion of mine inheritance, and of my cup.' A believer hath as sure

a right and title to God, as a man hath to his patrimony to which he
is born, or as any Israelite had to that share which came to him by
lot; so he may lay claim to God, and live upon his power and goodness, as a man doth upon his estate.

Well, then, labour to see God is yours, if you would find acceptance
with him. It is not enough to know the goodness and power of God
in general, but we must discern our interest in him, that we may not
only say *Father*, but *Our* Father. It is the nature of faith thus to
appropriate and apply: John xx. 28, 'My Lord and my God.' How
is God made ours? How shall we know it, that we may come and
lay our claim to him? Behold, Christ teacheth us here to say, Our
Father, by taking hold of his covenant; and this is God's covenant
notion, 'I will be your God, and you shall be my people.' When we
give up ourselves to be God's, then he is ours. Resignation and appropriation go together. 'I am my beloved's;' there is the resignation
of obedience: 'And he is mine;' there is the appropriation of faith.
A believer cannot always say God is his, but, I am thine; however it
be with him, he would be no other's but the Lord's. If he cannot
say he is God's by an especial interest, yet he will be God's by the
resignation of his own vows. He knows God hath a better right and
title to him than he hath to himself.

Quest. But how shall we know that we do indeed resign up ourselves
to God?

I answer, When we make him our chief good and our utmost end—
that is, when we unfeignedly choose him for our portion, and set apart
ourselves to act for his glory.

1. When we choose and cleave to him as our all-sufficient portion:
'The Lord is my portion, saith my soul,' Lam. iii. 24. Sometimes the
Lord speaks to us: 'I am thy reward, I am thy salvation,' Ps. xxxv. 3.
So the soul speaks to God: 'Thou art my portion.' When we cleave
to God, 'He is my portion for ever,' Ps. lxxiii. 25; 'Whom have I in
heaven but thee?' &c. When our souls are satisfied in God, having
enough in him, this is to give up ourselves to him.

2. When we set apart ourselves to his use, to live and act for his
glory, this is also entering into covenant with God. As in that formal
matrimonial covenant that was used between the prophet and his
wife, Hosea iii. 3, 'Thou shalt not be for another man, so will I also
be for thee;' so in the covenant we resolve to renounce all others, and
to live and act for God: 'The Lord hath set apart him that is godly
for himself,' Ps. iv. 3. When we are thus set apart for God, to serve
him and glorify him by this special dedication of ourselves to his use,
this is the act of grace on our part. We were God's by election; but
he comes and takes possession for himself by the Spirit, and then the
soul sets himself apart for God.

Secondly, That all the saints have a common interest in the same
God; therefore Christ taught us to say, 'Our Father.' They have
one Father, as well as one Spirit—one Christ, one hope, and one
heaven: Eph. iv. 6. Questionless, it is lawful to say, *My* Father.
Some have disputed it, because they suppose this expression is used
to signify Christ's singular filiation: Christ could only say, *My
Father*. But it is lawful, provided we do not say it exclusively, and

appropriating it to ourselves. But here Christ, when he giveth us this perfect form, teacheth us to say, '*Our* Father.' As the sun in the firmament is every man's, and all the world's, so God is every single believer's God—the God of all the elect. But why would Christ put this in this perfect pattern and form of prayer?

[1.] To quicken our love to the saints in prayer. When we come to pray, there must be a brotherly love expressed ; now that is a distinct thing from common love: 'Add to brotherly kindness, charity,' 2 Pet i. 7. When we are dealing with God in prayer, we must express somewhat of this brotherly love. How must we express it? In praying for others, as well as for ourselves. Necessity will put men upon praying for themselves, but brotherly love will put them upon praying for others. Wherein must brotherly kindness be expressed in prayer? In two things :—

(1.) In a fellow-feeling of their miseries, in being touched with their necessities, as we would be with our own. To be senseless, it is a spiritual excommunication, a casting ourselves out of the body. Members must take care for one another. We must be grieved with their pains. 'Who is offended,' saith the apostle, 'and I burn not?' If there be any power in such a confession or title of a Father, we must be wrestling with God, how well soever it be with us, remembering we speak to him in whom others have a joint interest with ourselves.

(2.) It must be expressed in wishing the same good to others as to ourselves. Many that pray in their own case, with what earnestness and importunity are they carried out ! but how flat and cold in the case of others ! Now, a good Christian must be as earnest with God for others as for himself. Look, what earnestness and heedfulness of soul he showeth when he puts up prayers for himself; the same must he do 'for all saints:' Eph. vi. 18. Self-love and self-respect must not breathe only in our prayers ; they must be carried out with as much earnestness as if we would go to God in our own case.

[2.] Again, as it showeth us what brotherly love we should express in prayer, so it checketh many carnal dispositions which we are guilty of, and Christ would mind us of them. It checks strife and contention ; we are brethren—have one common Father. Everywhere meekness and love: it is a qualification for prayer. 'Let the husband live with his wife according to knowledge, that their prayers be not hindered:' 1 Pet. iii. 7. If there be such brawls in the family, how can the husband and wife call upon God with such a united heart as is requisite? So, 1 Tim. ii. 8, 'I will that men pray everywhere, lifting up holy hands, without wrath and doubting.' Not only lift up 'pure' hands to God, and that 'without doubting;' there must be confidence in our prayers. But that is not all : but 'without wrath ;' there must be nothing of revenge and passion mingled with your supplication. And then it checketh pride and disdain. Christ teacheth all, in all conditions, whether masters or servants, fathers or children, kings or beggars, all to say 'Our Father;' for we have all one Father. Thou hast not a better Christ, nor a better Father in heaven, than they have. The rich and the poor were to give one ransom under the law, Exod. xxx., to show they have all the same

Redeemer.   The weak should not despise nor disdain the strong, nor
the rich be ashamed to own the poor as brethren.   We should never
be ashamed to own him as a brother whom God will own as a son.

Which art in heaven.

WE have considered the title given to God with respect to his goodness and mercy: He is a Father—'our Father.' Now, let us consider
the titles given to him with respect to his greatness and majesty:
'Which art in heaven.' From thence note:—

  Doct. It is an advantage in prayer to look upon God as a Father
in heaven.

  By way of explication, to show:—

  First, What is meant by heaven. There are three heavens in the
computation of the scripture. There is, first, the lowest heaven, that
where the fowls of the air are, whence the rain descendeth; therefore
the fowls are called the 'fowls of heaven,' Job xxxv. 11; and, James
v. 18, 'Elijah prayed, and the heaven gave rain.' Secondly, the
luminary heaven, where the sun, moon, and stars are: therefore it is
said, Mark xiii. 25, 'The stars of heaven shall fall.' Thirdly, there is
the highest heaven, or the heaven of the blessed, spoken of Mat. vii.
21: 'Not every one that saith unto me, Lord, Lord, shall enter into
the kingdom of heaven;' that is, into the third heaven, the glorious
heaven, the blessed presence of God. Mat. xviii. 10: 'In heaven their
angels do always behold the face of my Father which is in heaven:'
in heaven, that is, 'the third heaven.' So it is called by Paul, 2 Cor.
xii. 2, which was the highest part, because he saw and heard things
which it is not lawful for a man to utter. In this heaven God is.

  Secondly, How is God there, since he is everywhere?

  Negatively; It is not to be understood so as if he were included
in heaven, or locally circumscribed within the compass of it; for 'the
heaven of heavens cannot contain him:' 1 Kings viii. 27. In regard
of his essence, he is in all places, being infinite and indivisible. He
is not included within the heavens, nor excluded from earth, but filleth
all places alike: Jer. xxiii. 24, 'Do not I fill heaven and earth?
saith the Lord.' But yet in an especial manner is God present in
heaven. That appears, because there is his throne: Ps. ciii. 19,
'He hath prepared his throne in the heavens.' Earthly kings, they
have their thrones exalted higher than other places, but God's throne
is above all, it is in heaven. He hath a more universal and unlimited
empire than all the kings of the earth; so he hath a more glorious
throne. Heaven is the most convenient place to set forth his majesty
and glory to the world, because of the sublimity, amplitude, and
purity of it. And so, Isa. lxvi. 1, 'Thus saith the Lord, The heaven
is my throne, and the earth is my footstool.' Heaven is his throne,
because there is his majestical presence, more of his glory and excellency is discovered: and the earth is his footstool, because there, in
the lowest part of the world, he manifesteth his powerful presence
among the lower creatures.

Briefly, to conceive how God is in heaven, we must consider :—

[1.] The several ways of his presence. He is in Christ, hypostatically, essentially, or (as the apostle speaks) bodily : Col. ii. 19, 'The fulness of God dwells in him bodily.' In the temple, under the law, there God was present symbolically, because there were the signs and tokens of his presence. The Jewish temple was a sacramental place and type of Christ, in whose name, and by whose merit, worship was acceptable to God. But now, in Christians, he is present energetically, and operatively, by his Spirit. And in heaven, he there dwells by some eminent effects of his wisdom, power, greatness, and goodness. God hath showed more of his workmanship in the structure of the heavens than in any other part of the creation, that being the most glorious part of the world : Ps. xix. 1–3, 'The heavens declare the glory of the Lord, and the firmament showeth his handiwork,' &c. Certainly it is meet God should dwell in the most glorious part of the world ; now heaven is the most glorious part of the creation. Heathens in their straits would not look to the capitol where their idols were ; but to heaven, where God hath impressed his majesty and greatness. Whenever we look upon these aspectable heavens, the vast expansion, the glorious luminaries, the purity of the matter, and sublimity of its posture, it cannot but raise our hearts to think of a glorious God that dwelleth there. When we come by a poor cottage, we guess the inhabitant is no great person ; but when we see a magnificent structure, we easily imagine some person of account dwells there. So, though the earth doth declare the glory of God, and show much of his wisdom and power, yet chiefly the heavens, whenever we look upon them, we cannot choose but have awful thoughts, and be struck with a religious horror, at the remembrance of the great God, which has stretched out these heavens by his wisdom and power.

[2.] Therefore God is said to dwell in heaven, because from thence he manifesteth his powerful providence, wisdom, justice, and goodness. God is not so shut up in heaven as not to mind human affairs, and to take notice of what is done here below : Ps. xi. 4, 'The Lord's throne is in heaven : his eyes behold, his eyelids try the children of men.' Though his throne be in heaven, yet his providence is everywhere ; his eyes behold, he seeth how we behave ourselves in his presence ; and his eyelids try the children of men. He may seem to wink now and then, and to suspend the strokes of his vengeance, but it is but for our trial. He owneth his children from heaven : Deut. xxvi. 15, 'Look down from thy holy habitation, from heaven, and bless thy people.' And from thence he punisheth the wicked : Rom. i. 18, 'The wrath of God is revealed from heaven.'

[3.] There is God most owned by the saints and glorified angels, therefore he is said to dwell there ; as a king is beloved by his subjects, but most immediately served and attended upon by those of his own court. So that in heaven, there we have the highest pattern of all that duty which doth immediately concern God. In this prayer, 'Hallowed be thy name, thy kingdom come, thy will be done,' these three petitions concern God more immediately. Now before we put them up, Christ would have us think of our Father in heaven, praised by angels and saints that fall down before his throne, crying, Honour, glory, and praise.   There he reigneth, his throne is there, and there he is perfectly obeyed and served without any opposition.

[4.] There God is most enjoyed, and therefore he dwells there, for there he doth more immediately exhibit the fulness of his glory to the saints and angels.   In heaven God is all in all.   Here we are supplied at second or third hand : Hosea ii. 18, 'I will hear the heavens, and the heavens shall hear the earth,' &c.   But there God is immediately and fully enjoyed.   Here there are many wants and vacuities to be filled up ; but 'in thy presence there is fulness of joy, and at thy right hand there are pleasures for evermore :' Ps. xvi. 11.   Look, as when the flood was poured out upon the world, you read that the windows of heaven were opened,' Gen. vii. 11 ; the drops of rain were upon earth, but the cataracts and floodgates were in heaven ; so when he raineth down drops of sweetness upon his people, the floodgates are above, they are reserved for that place where they are fully enjoyed.

Thirdly, Why hath God fixed and taken up his dwelling-place in the heavens ?   I answer,

[1.] Because mortal men they cannot endure his glorious presence : Deut. v. 23, 'When ye heard the voice out of the midst of the darkness, for the mountain did burn with fire, ye said, Behold, the Lord our God hath showed us his glory, and his greatness, and we have heard his voice out of the midst of the fire : now therefore why should we die ?   For this great fire will consume us ; if we hear the voice of the Lord our God any more, then we shall die.'   Any manifestations of God, how easily do they overset and overcome us !   A little spiritual enjoyment it is too strong for us.   If God pour out but a drop of sweetness into the heart, we are ready to cry out, Hold, Lord, it is enough ; our crazy vessels can endure no more.   Therefore, when Christ was transfigured, the disciples were astonished and fell back ; they could not endure the emissions and beamings out of his divine glory, because of the weakness and incapacity of the present state : therefore hath God a place above, where he discovereth his glory in the utmost latitude.   It is notable in scripture, sometimes God is said to 'dwell in light,' 1 Tim. vi. 16 ; and sometimes to 'make darkness his dwelling-place,' Ps. xviii. 11.   How doth he dwell in light, and how in darkness ?   Because of the glorious manifestations which are above, therefore it is said he dwells in light ; and because of the weakness and incapacity of our comprehension, therefore he is said to dwell in darkness.

[2.] To try our faith and our obedience, that he might see whether we would live by faith, yea or no ; whether a believer would love him and obey him, though he were invisible and withdrawn within the curtain of heaven.   You know when the Israelites saw the glory of God, then they cried, 'All that God hath commanded us we will do :' Deut. v. 27.   But as soon as that manifestation ceased, they were as bad as ever.   If all were liable to sense, there would be no trial of this world ; but God hath shut up himself, that by this means the faith of the elect might be manifested ; for 'faith is the evidence of things not seen :' Heb. xi. 1.   Where there is no sight there is exercise for faith.   And that our love might be tried : 1 Pet. i. 8, 'Whom

having not seen, ye love: in whom, though now ye see him not, yet
believing, ye rejoice with joy unspeakable, and full of glory.' And
this is that which discovereth the faithless and disobedient world:
Job xxii. 12-14, 'Is not God in the height of heaven? How doth
God know? can he judge through the dark cloud? Thick clouds are
a covering to him that he seeth not, and he walketh in the circuit of
heaven.'

[3.] It is fit there should be a better place into which the saints
should be translated when the course of their obedience is ended:
Eph. i. 3, 'He hath blessed us with spiritual blessings in heavenly
places.' The main of Christ's purchase we have in heavenly places.
It is fit the place of trial and place of recompense should differ; therefore the place of trial, that is God's footstool; and the place of recompense, that is God's throne. The world, that is a place of trial; it is
a common inn for sons and bastards, for the elect and reprobate; a
receptacle of man and beast: here God will show his bounty unto all
his creatures; but now, in the place of his residence, he will show his
love to his people. Therefore, when we have been tried and exercised,
there is a place of preferment for us.

Fourthly, What advantage have we in prayer by considering
God in heaven? Very much, whether we consider God absolutely, or with respect to a mediator; both ways we have an advantage.

First, If we consider the Father, Son, and Holy Ghost, who have
their residence in heaven; consider them without respect to a mediator. Why, the looking up to God in heaven:—

[1.] It showeth us that prayer is an act of the heart, and not of the
lips. That it is not the sound of the voice which can pierce the
heavens, and enter into the ears of the Lord of hosts, but sighs and
groans of the spirit. Christians! in prayer God is near to us, and yet
far from us, for we must look upon him as in heaven, and we upon earth.
How then should we converse with God in prayer? Not by the tongue
only, but by the heart. The commerce and communion of spirits is not
hindered by local distance; but God is with us, and we with him,
when our heart goeth up.

[2.] It teacheth the great work of prayer is to lift up the heart to
God. To withdraw the heart from all created things which we see
and feel here below, that we may converse with God in heaven:
Ps. cxxiii. 1, 'Unto thee lift I up mine eyes, O thou that dwellest in
the heavens;' and, Lam. iii. 41, 'Let us lift up our heart with our
hands unto God in the heavens.' Prayer doth not consist in a multitude and clatter of words, but in the getting up of the heart to God,
that we may behave ourselves as if we were alone with God, in the
midst of glorious saints and angels. There is a double advantage
which we have by this getting the soul into heaven in prayer. It is a
means to free us from distractions and doubts. To free us from
distractions and other intercurrent thoughts. Until we get our
hearts out of the world, as if we were dead and shut up to all present
things, how easily is the heart carried away with the thoughts of
earthly concernments! Until we can separate and purge our spirits,
how do we interline our prayers with many ridiculous thoughts! It

is too usual for us to deal with God as an unskilful person that will
gather a posy for his friend, and puts in as many or more stinking
weeds than he doth choice flowers. The flesh interposeth, and our
carnal hearts interline and interlace our prayers with vain thoughts
and earthly distractions. When with our censer we come to offer
incense to God, we mingle sulphur with our incense. Therefore we
should labour all that we can to get the heart above the world into
the presence of God and company of the blessed, that we may deal
with him as if we were by him in heaven, and were wholly swallowed
up of his glory. Though our bodies are on earth, yet our spirits
should be with our Father in heaven. For want of practising this in
prayer, these distractions increase upon us. So for doubts, when we
look to things below, even the very manifestations of God to us upon
earth, we have many discouragements, dangers without and difficulties within: till we get above the mists of the lower world, we can see
nothing of clearness and comfort; but when we can get God and our
hearts together, then we can see there is much in the fountain, though
nothing in the stream; and though little on earth, yet we have a God
in heaven.

[3.] This impresseth an awe and reverence, if we look upon the glory
of God manifested in heaven, that bright and luminous place. This
is urged by the Holy Ghost: Eccles. v. 2, 'Thou art upon earth, and
God is in heaven; therefore let thy words be few;' Gen. xviii. 27,
'Who am I that I should take upon me to speak unto the Lord, who
am but dust and ashes?' We are poor crawling worms, and therefore,
when we think of the majesty of God, it should impress a holy awe
upon us. Mean persons will behave themselves with all honour and
reverence when they supplicate to men of quality; so should we to
God, who is so high and so much above us; he is in heaven. It is a
diminution of his greatness (Mal. i. 14) when we put off God with
anything, and come slightly and carelessly into his presence.

[4.] It teacheth us that all our prayers should carry a correspondence
with our great aim. What is our great aim? To be with God in
heaven, as remembering that is the centre and place of our rest, to
which we are all tending: Col. iii. 1, 'If ye then be risen with Christ,
seek those things which are above, where Christ sitteth on the right
hand of God.' We come to our Father which is in heaven. He will
have his residence there, that our hearts might be there. Therefore
the main things we should seek of God from heaven are saving graces,
for these 'come down from above, from the Father of lights:' James
i. 17. We have liberty to ask supplies for the outward life, but
chiefly we should ask spiritual and heavenly things: Mat. vi. 22, 23,
'Your heavenly Father knoweth that ye have need of all these things.'
What then? 'First seek the kingom of God,' &c. If we have to do
with a heavenly Father, our first and main care should be to ask
things suitable to his being, and his excellency. If children should
ask of their parents such a thing as is pleasing to their palate,
possibly they might give it them; but when they ask instruction, and
desire to be taught, that is far more acceptable to them. When we
ask supplies of the outward life, food, raiment, God may give it us;
but it is more pleasing to him when we ask for grace. In every

prayer we should seek to be made more heavenly by conversing with our heavenly Father.

[5.] It giveth us ground of confidence in God's power and absolute dominion over all things, for God is in heaven above all created beings: Ps. cxv. 3, ' Our God is in the heavens, and doth whatsoever he pleaseth.' So 2 Chron. xx. 6, ' Art not thou God in heaven? and rulest not thou over all the kingdoms of the heathen? and in thine hand is there not power and might, so that none is able to withstand thee?' Oh, what an advantage is this in prayer, when we think of our all-sufficient God, who made heaven and earth, and hath fixed his throne there! What can be too hard for him?

[6.] Here is encouragement against carnal fear. Whatever the world doth against us, we have a Father in heaven, and this should bear us up against all their threatenings and oppositions. When there were tumults and confusions in the world, it is said, Ps. ii. 4, ' But God, which sits in heaven, shall laugh them to scorn.' An earthly parent may have a large heart, but a short hand; though they may wish us well, yet they cannot defend us, and bear us out in all extremities. But our Father in heaven will laugh at the attempts against his empire and greatness. Thus considering God absolutely, it is an advantage to reflect upon him as a Father in heaven.

But I suppose this expression hath respect to a mediator. Therefore,

Secondly, Let us look upon God with respect to a mediator, for so I think we are chiefly bound to consider our Father in heaven, because of Christ which sits there at his right hand: Heb. viii. 1. It is said there, ' He sat down on the right hand of the throne of the Majesty in the heavens, a minister of the sanctuary.' Oh, this is comfortable to think of. In heaven we have a Saviour, Jesus Christ, representing our persons and presenting our prayers to God, by which means God is reconciled and well pleased with us. So that our duty in prayer is to look up to heaven, and to see Christ at God's right hand as our high priest, mediating for us that we may be accepted with God.

A notable resemblance we have between God's presence in the tabernacle or temple, and God's presence in heaven.

"In the temple you know there were three partitions. There was the outward court, and the sanctuary, as the apostle calls it, where the table of shew-bread was set, and there was the holy place, the holy of holies. Just so in heaven there are three partitions; there is the airy heaven, and the starry heaven, and the heaven of heavens: the lower heaven, which answers to the outward court; the starry heaven which answers to the sanctuary; and the heaven of heavens, which answers to the holy of holies by a fit analogy and proportion. Well, in the holy of holies, saith the apostle, there was the golden censer and the mercy-seat: Heb. ix. 4. There you find God conspicuously manifesteth his presence, and gives answers to his people: ' At the mercy-seat, there will I answer thee, saith the Lord.' So here, in this heaven of heavens, there is a mercy-seat, there is a throne of grace, and there God will answer. We may ' come boldly to the throne of grace, that we may obtain mercy and find grace to help in time of need:' Heb. iv. 16.

Into this holy of holies none but the high priest did enter, and that once a year, after the sacrifice of atonement for the whole congregation : then the high priest was to come into the holy of holies, he was to pass through the veil with blood and with sweet incense in his hand. Just thus is Jesus entered into the heaven of heavens for us. He is gone there to present his blood and sufferings, to appear before God for us, to present himself as a sweet-smelling sacrifice: Heb ix. 24; Eph. v. 2. Now the high priest, when he went with this blood in to the mercy-seat, he went in with the names of the twelve tribes upon his breast and shoulder, as Jesus also doth appear before God for us, representing our persons continually before his Father. Now about the mercy-seat, there were cherubims, and figures of angels ; just about the ark, there they stooped down, to show the angels do attend about the throne, to despatch messages abroad into the world, and convey blessings to the saints. There is a throne of grace, a mercy-seat, a mediator there, angels at God's beck, ready to send up and down, to and fro, for the good of the saints. And mark, not only hath Jesus this liberty to enter into this heaven of heavens, but all the saints have a liberty to enter, and that not only at death, but in their life-time ; for saith the apostle, Heb. x. 19, 'Having therefore boldness to enter into the holiest, by the blood of Jesus.' All of us, not only when we die, and personally go to God, do we enter into the holy of holies, but now we have boldness. It relateth to prayer, for the word signifieth liberty of speech. This holy of holies, which was closed and shut up against us before, is opened by the blood of Jesus ; the veil is rent, and now all saints have a privilege to come freely to converse with God. It is good to observe the difference between the holy of holies, and the heaven of heavens. The Jews their *sanctum sanctorum* was earthly ; but our holy of holies is heavenly. Into theirs, which was as it were God's bed-chamber, the common people were not admitted; none but the high priest could enter into the holy of holies. But now into ours all believers may enter and converse with God. There the high priest could enter but once a year ; now we may come to the throne of grace as often as we have a cause to present to God. There the high priest he entered with the blood of beasts; but we enter by the blood of the Son of God. Oh, what a great privilege is this, that we have a Father in heaven ! In this respect the holy place is now open to us. Though we have not a personal access till death, yet by the blood of Jesus we may come with boldness, presenting ourselves before the Lord with all our wants and desires. The great distance between heaven and earth shall not hinder our communion with God, if we have a friend above."

Therefore it is very comfortable now to say, 'Our Father which art in heaven ; ' that is, our gracious and reconciled Father, in and by Christ.

APPLICATION.

If we have a Father in heaven, let us look up to heaven often.

1. If we have a Father in heaven, and a Saviour at his right hand, to do all things that are needful for us, let us look upon the aspectable heavens with an eye of sense, with our bodily eyes. It is good

to contemplate the glory of the heavenly bodies, or the outside of that court which God hath provided for the saints. It is not an idle speculation I press you to ; the saints of God have thought it to be worthy of their morning and evening thoughts. It is notable, David doth, in two psalms especially, contemplate heaven ; one seems to be a nightly, the other a morning, meditation. The night meditation you have Ps. viii. 3 : ' When I consider thy heavens, the work of thy fingers, the moon and the stars, which thou hast ordained.' David was got abroad in a moon-shining night, looks up, and had his heart affected. But now the 19th Psalm, that seems to be a morning meditation ; he speaks of the ' sun coming out like a bridegroom from his chamber in the east,' and displaying his beams, and heat, and influences to the world ; and then saith he, ver. 1, ' The heavens declare the glory of God.' Morning and evening, or whenever you go abroad to see the beauty of the outward heavens, say, I have a Father there, a Christ there ; this is the pavement of that palace which God hath provided for the saints. Christians, it is a sweet meditation when you can say, He that made all things is there. It will be a delightful, profitable thing sometimes, with an eye of sense, to take a view of our Father's palace, as much as we can see of it here below.

2. Let me especially press you to this : with an eye of faith to look within the veil; and whenever you come to pray, to see God in heaven, and Christ at his right hand. The great work of faith is to see him that is invisible ; and the great duty of prayer is to get a sight of God in heaven, and Christ at his right hand. What Stephen did miraculously, or in an ecstasy, we must do graciously in prayer. Now it is said of Stephen, Acts vii. 56, ' Behold, I see the heavens opened, and the Son of man standing on the right hand of God.' There is a great deal of difference about Stephen's sight: how the heavens could be opened, which are a solid body, and cannot be divided as fluid air, and so come together again ; how he could see the glory of God with his corporal senses, which is invisible ; how he could see Christ at such a distance, the eye not being able to reach so far. Some think it to be a mere intellectual vision, or a vision of faith ; that is, he did so firmly believe, and had the comfort of it in his heart, as if he had seen it with his eyes. So they think Stephen saw the glory of God, and Christ at his right hand, as Abraham saw Christ's day and rejoiced ; that is, he saw it by faith. Some think it to be a prophetical vision, by seeing those things objected to his fancy by imaginary species ; as Isaiah saw God in a vision—Isa. vi.—and as Paul's rapture. Some think it a symbolical vision ; that he saw these things represented by some corporal images, as John saw the Holy Ghost descending in the form of a dove. Some think his bodily eyes did pierce the clouds, and got a sight of the glory of Christ. Whatever it be, there must be such a sight in prayer, something answerable to this. In a spiritual way, this must ever be done : Ps. v. 3, ' I will pray,' saith the psalmist, ' and look up.' There is a looking up required in all prayer, a seeing the invisible God by faith. If you would have God look down upon you from his holy habitation, you must look up with an eye of faith, and converse with God in heaven: Ps. lxiii. 4, ' I will lift up my hands in thy name.' If you would have

God look upon you with an eye of compassion, you must look up, and see Christ at his right hand, by an eye of faith.

3. Let us love our Father; love God in Christ, and love the place for his sake, where his residence is.

[1.] Love God in Christ: Ps. lxxiii. 25, 'Whom have I in heaven but thee?' When God hath been so gracious to you! Christians, if I had no other argument to press you to love God but that he which is in heaven offereth to be your father in Christ Jesus, it might suffice; because it is a great condescension that the God of heaven will look upon poor broken-hearted creatures—that he whose throne is in heaven would look upon him that is of a trembling spirit: Isa. lxvi. 2. 'That the high and lofty One, that dwelleth in the high and holy place, will look to him that is of a contrite heart:' Isa. lvii. 15. That he that is the Lord of heaven and earth will be our Father, and own us and bless us! A great condescension on God's part, and a great dignity also is put upon us; and how should our hearts be affected with it! Therefore, though there be a great distance between heaven and earth, it should not lessen our affections to God. He is mindful of us, visits us at every turn; we are dear and tender to him; therefore let the Lord be dear to you. The butler, when he was exalted, forgot Joseph; but Christ is not grown stately with his advancement—he doth not forget us. Oh, let not us forget God. Let us manifest our love, by being often with him at the throne of grace, with our Father which is in heaven. A child is never well but when in the mother's lap or under the father's wing: so should it be with us, with a humble affection coming into the presence of God, and getting into the bosom of our heavenly Father. Never delight in anything so much as conversing with him, and serious addresses to him in prayer. Again:—

[2.] Love the place for his sake; God is there, and Christ is there. We have cause to love the place for our own sakes; and in a short time, if you continue patient in well-doing, you will be with God. It is not only God's throne, but it is your house: 2 Cor. v. 1, 'We look for an house in heaven, not made with hands.' It is a place appointed for our everlasting abode; therefore all our hopes, desires, and delights should run that way. But chiefly I would press you to love it for his sake, the place where your heavenly Father dwells. God hath not taken his denomination from earth, which is the place of corruption; but from heaven, which is the place of glory and happiness. Oh, let us not forget our heavenly Father's house. We are too apt to say, It is good to be here. Christians, let us draw home apace; let us grow more heavenly-minded every day; seek the things which are above; prize it rather upon this occasion, because if we were more heavenly in the frame of our hearts, we would be more heavenly in our solemn approaches to God. What is the reason a man is haunted with the world, and things which are of a worldly interest and concern, when he comes to prayer? It is because his heart is taken with these things.

Hallowed be thy name.

WE are now come to the first petition of the Lord's Prayer; there three things will fall under discussion:—

I. The order of this petition.

II. The necessity of putting up such a request to God.

III. The sense and meaning of the petition itself.

I. Of the order; it is the first of all the six. The petitions of the Lord's Prayer may thus be ranked:—The four first concern the obtaining of good; and the two last, the removal of evil—either the removal of evil past, and already committed, or the removal of evil future, and such as may be admitted by the temptation of the devil. Among the former, those things that do more immediately concern the glory of God, they have the first place. In this petition, the glory of God is both desired and promised on our part; for every prayer is both an expression of a desire, and also an implicit vow or a solemn obligation that we take upon ourselves to prosecute what we ask. Prayer, it is a preaching to ourselves in God's hearing. We speak to God to warm ourselves, not for his information, but for our edification.

From the order observe :—

Doct. That those things are to be desired in the first place, and with the greatest affection, which do concern the glory of God. The first petition is, ' Hallowed be thy name.'

Here to show :—

1. Why this petition is put first.

2. Present some reasons of the point.

First, This petition is put first, for a double reason:—

1. Partly to show that this must be the end of all our requests. All that we desire and pray for, in behalf of ourselves and others, must be subordinate to this end. All these things must be asked, that by the accomplishment of them God may be brought more in request in the world. See all the other petitions in this prayer, how they are suited to this end in scripture. When we say, ' Thy kingdom come,' what do we beg that for, but ultimately the glory of God? Phil. ii. 10, 11, ' God hath given him a name which is above every name, that every tongue should confess that Jesus Christ is Lord, to the glory of God the Father.' When we say, ' Thy will be done in earth, as it is in heaven,' it is still to the glory of God: Mat. v. 16, ' That our good works may still shine forth before men here upon earth, that they may glorify our Father which is in heaven.' When we ask our daily bread, and provisions for the present life, it is still that he may be glorified in our comfortable use of the creature : 1 Cor. x. 31, ' Whether therefore ye eat or drink, or whatsoever ye do, do all to the glory of God.' When we ask for the remission of sins, it is that God may be glorified in Christ : Rom. iii. 25, 26, ' Whom God hath set forth to be a propitiation through faith in his blood, to declare his righteousness for the remission of sins that are past, that he may be just,' &c. When we beg freedom from temptation, it is that we may not dishonour God : Prov. xxx. 9. ' Lest I be full, and deny thee, and say,

Who is the Lord ? or lest I be poor, and steal, and take the name of
my God in vain.' Still that God may be glorified in every condition.
When we ask deliverance from evil : Ps. l. 15, 'Call upon me in the
day of trouble ; I will deliver thee, and thou shalt glorify me.' So
that the glory of God, in all requests that we make to him, like oil,
still swims on the top, and must be the end of all the rest ; for other
things are but means in subordination to it.

2. It notes that our chiefest care and affection should be carried out
to the glory of God when we pray. We should rather forget ourselves
than forget God. God must be remembered in the first place. There
is nothing more precious than God himself, therefore nothing should
be more dear to us than his glory. This is the great difference
between the upright and the hypocrite : the hypocrite never seeks
God but when his necessities do require it, not in and for himself ;
but when the upright come to seek God, it is for God in the first
place—their main care is about God's concernments rather than their
own. Though they seek their own happiness in him, and they are
allowed so to do ; yet it is mainly God's glory which they seek, not
their own interests and concernments. See that : Ps. cxv. 1, ' Not
unto us, not unto us, O Lord, but unto thy name give glory, for thy
mercy, and for thy truth's sake.' It is not a doxology, or form of
thanksgiving, but a prayer ; not for our safety and welfare, so much
as thy glory ; not to reek and satisfy our revenge upon our adversaries ; not for the establishment of our interest ; but for the glory of
thy grace and truth, that God may be known to be a God keeping
covenant ; for mercy and truth are the two pillars of the covenant.
It is a great dishonouring of God when anything is sought from him
more than himself, or not for himself. Saith Austin, it is but a carnal
affection in prayer when men seek self more than God. Self and God
are the two things that come in competition. Now there are several
sorts of self ; there is carnal self, natural self, spiritual self, and glorified self. Above all these God must have the pre-eminence.

[1.] Carnal self. By a foolish mistake we take our lusts to be ourselves : Col. iii. 5, ' Mortify your members here upon earth.' And
these members he makes to be fornication, uncleanness, and the
like. Our sins are as dear to us as any essential or intregal part of
the body ; they are our members. Now, these should have no room
in our prayers at all, though usually they have the first place : James
iv. 3, ' Ye ask and receive not, because ye ask amiss, that ye may
consume it upon your lusts.' Our prayers should be the breathings
of the spirit, and usually they are but the belches and eructations of
the flesh. And for these it is we are so instant and earnest with God.
We would have God bless us in some revengeful and carnal enterprise. We deal with God as the thief that lighted his candle at the
lamps of the altar. So many would make God a party in their carnal
designs : Prov. xxi. 27, ' The sacrifice of the wicked is an abomination ; how much more when he bringeth it with a wicked mind ? '
It is an abomination when it is at the best ; but when he hath an ill
aim, then it is an abomination with a witness. Foolish creatures
vainly imagine to entice heaven to their lure. Balaam builded altars
and sacrificed, out of hope that God would curse his own people, and

engage in Moab's quarrel; like the man in the Gospel that would make no other use of Christ than to compose his civil difference: Luke xii. 13. He comes to him as a man of authority, ' Master, speak to my brother, that he divide the inheritance with me.' We all look upon God, *tanquam aliquem magnum*, as Austin said he did in his infancy, as some great power that would serve all our carnal turns. In this sense we make God to serve our sins, Isa. xliii. 24, when we would have God to contribute to our lusts, to our pride, wantonness, revenge. This is such a foolish request, as if a wife should beg of her husband to give her leave to go on with her adulteries. Survey all the petitions which are in this present platform of prayer, there is not one that is calculated for such an evil purpose as our revenge, pomp, pride, pleasure. Carnal self surely must give way to God.

[2.] There is a natural self, when we seek our own temporal felicity. Christ hath allowed these natural desires a room in our prayers ; but they must keep their order and their place: first, God's glory ; and then, our safety. The obtaining of natural good is put in the last place. And, therefore, when our thoughts only run upon temporal felicity and outward supplies, it is not prayer, but a brutish cry: Hosea vii. 14, ' They howl upon their beds for corn, wine, and oil.' Beasts are sensible of their pain, and are carried by natural instinct to seek their own welfare, as well as men. And, therefore, when this is our first and only request, it is a perversion of that order which Christ hath set down in this perfect form of prayer.

[3.] There is spiritual self, which is valuable either in point of justification or acceptance with God, or in point of sanctification and conformity to him. Now, as these blessings cannot be severed from God's glory where they are really enjoyed, so they must not be severed in our prayers, nor preferred before it. To ask pardon as a separate benefit as it concerns our ease and quiet, not as it concerns God's glory, is a perversion and a diversion of our prayers. The main thing which God intends should be the main thing in our requests, is, ' the praise of his glorious grace, wherein he hath made us accepted in the beloved,' Eph. i. 6. And, therefore, this is the main thing which the soul intends: Ps. lxxix. 9, ' Help us, O God of our salvation, for the glory of thy name ; and deliver us, and purge away our sins, for thy name's sake.' The argument is not taken from themselves merely, or from their own misery, but from God's glory. If God could not be more glorified in our pardon and acceptance with him than in our death and damnation, it were an evil thing to desire pardon. But now when God hath abundantly cleared up this to us, that he is no loser by acts of mercy ; that this conduceth more to the exalting of his great name, to accept poor sinners to mercy ; the soul goeth with the more confidence to beg it of God, that he would purge us from our filthiness for his name's sake. But now men's thoughts are wholly taken up with their own peace and safety, and take no care for God's honour. This is but a selfish request, or an offer of nature after ease. For the other part, to ask for grace and conformity to God's will, merely as it is a perfection of our nature abstractly from God's glory, it is not a right request. It is contrary to the very nature of grace, whose tendency is to God in the first place, that his name may be glorified, that we should be to the praise of his glorious grace. Grace wrought in us is but a creature, and not to be preferred before the Creator. See how the apostle prays: 2 Thes. i. 11, 12, 'We pray always for you, that our God would count you worthy of this calling, and fulfil all the good pleasure of his goodness, and the work of faith with power : that the name of our Lord Jesus Christ may be glorified in you, and ye in him, according to the grace of our God and the Lord Jesus Christ.' That is a regular prayer, when all our spiritual interests are swallowed up in God, and we beg that his name may be glorified in us and upon us.

[4.] There is glorified self, which standeth in the eternal fruition of God. Man was made for two ends—to glorify God, and to enjoy him. Now our crown of glory must be laid at God's feet; as the elders, Rev. iv. 10, ' Saying, Thou art worthy, O Lord, to receive glory, and honour, and power.' All our desires must give place to this, that he may be glorified in our eternal happiness ; and we are to beg it no further than as it may stand with his honour. Man's chief end, and so his chief request, in respect of himself, is, to enjoy God ; but with respect to God, so it is the highest only of subordinate ends ; for the highest, chiefly and absolutely, is the glorifying of God.

Well then, therefore, this is put first, to show that our chiefest care and affection should mainly run upon the glory of God, and that God might be advanced and lifted up on high.

Secondly, To give you some reasons why those things which concern the glory of God must be sought in the first place, and with the greatest affection :—

1. As we are reasonable creatures, it is fit it should be so. In all regular desires the end is first intended, and then the means. But now the glory of God, that is the end of all things : Prov. xvi. 4, ' The Lord hath made all things for himself ;' that is, for his own glory, for the manifesting of his excellency. And so our redemption : Luke ii. 14, ' Glory be to God on high.' When God came to show his good-will in Christ, it was to make way for his glory : as it begins in good-will, so it must end in glory. This is the end of all the privileges we have by nature and grace. Now God's glory is the end of our being and service, and therefore must be first taken care of in our prayers ; first his glory, and then our profit, for the end is the first thing intended by any rational agent.

2. As we are the children of God by adoption. The great duty of children is to honour their parents. God pleads for honour upon this account: Mal. i. 6, ' If I be father, where is my honour ?' So that if you consent to the preface, and say, ' Our Father ;' then the next request will be, ' Hallowed be thy name.' If we would own ourselves in such a relation, then we must make it our chief desire and care that God might be glorified by ourselves and others. Every kind of honour will not serve our heavenly Father. He must not be honoured as an ordinary father, in a common notion, but as an infinite and eternal Majesty ; and to prefer anything to his interest or glory, or to equal anything to him, it is to make an idol of it, and to renounce him to be our father. The case of earthly parents is not always so. But now you renounce God when an idol is set in the throne ; when

any interest or concernment of yours is preferred before God, and before his interest and concernment.

3. That which is of most value and consideration should be sought first. Now God's glory it hath an infinite excellency above all other things. The glory of God is of more worth than all creatures,—than their being and happiness. The end is more worthy than that which serveth and conduceth to the end. Meats and drinks they were made for the body, therefore are not so good as the body. Who would dig for iron with mattocks of gold ? The means or instrument is better worth than the purchase. Now no matter what becomes of us, so God may be glorified. As it is said of David, ' Thou art better than ten thousand of us ;' therefore, though they exposed their bodies to hazard, they thought it not safe for him. So is God better than the whole world of men or angels. Our first care must be that he may be glorified, then let other things succeed in their place.

4. The example of Christ shows how much the glory of God should be cared for, and preferred before the creature's good : John xii. 27, 28, ' Father, save me from this hour.' There was the innocent and sinless inclination of his human nature. ' But for this cause came I unto this hour ; Father, glorify thy name.' He doth not so earnestly insist upon that, but submits all his human concernments, though exceeding precious, that they might give way to the glory of God ; and he had no respect to his own ease, or to the innocent inclination of his human nature, or to the felt comforts of the Godhead. Now Christ's example it is the best instruction. He taught us how we should behave ourselves to our heavenly Father ; and, therefore, we should learn to prefer the honour of God before our own ease ; and if God but get up, though we be kept low and poor, yet we should be contented. Look, as all natural things will act against their particular inclination for a general good ; as to avoid a vacuity, the air will descend, and the water ascend, that there may not be a confusion or dissolution of the frame of nature : so hath Christ taught us still to prefer a general good. ' Father, glorify thyself ;' that is it we must insist upon, though it be with our loss, suffering, trouble, yea, sometimes with our trouble of conscience, we must be content.

5. From the nature of prayer. The whole spiritual life it is a living to God : Gal. ii. 19, ' I am dead to the law, that I might live unto God.' The whole tendency and ordination of all acts of the spiritual life they are to God. Even the natural life is overruled and directed to this end ; there is an eating and drinking to God ; the meat and drink we take, if God be not the last end of it, it is but a meat-offering and a drink-offering to our own appetite, and a sacrifice to Moloch. Now, much more in acts of immediate worship, there God will be principally regarded, for their respect and tendency is mainly to God. In our whole life we are God's, dedicated to him. Every godly man is set apart for God. A man that is a Christian must be ' holy in all manner of conversation,' 1 Pet. i. 15. A Christian must look upon himself as one that is dedicated to God, when he is at his meals, in his trade and calling ; and grace is to run out in every act. But much more is this tendency of grace to bewray itself in our solemn sequestration of ourselves when we make our nearer

approaches to him : Lev. x. 3, ' I will be sanctified in them that come nigh me, and before all the people will I be glorified.'   What is it to sanctify God ?   A thing is sanctified when it is set apart ; and God is sanctified when we set apart ourselves wholly for him—when he hath more than common affections and common respects.   And therefore in prayer, in the first place, we should go to God for God, and surely in such a request we are likely to speed.

6. Love to God, if it be unfeigned, and hath any strength in the soul, will necessarily put us upon this.   Love seeks the good of the party beloved, as much or more than its own.   Those which love have all things in common between them, and one counts it done to himself what is done to the other ; so it is in the love between us and God.   Look, as Christ loves the saints, and counteth whatever you do to them it is done to him, because done to those whom he loved— Mat. xxv. : so, reciprocally, the saint which loves God, what is done to God is done to us : when God is honoured, we are comforted as much or more than with our own benefit ; and when God is dishonoured, we have the grief and sorrow : Ps. lxix. 9, ' The reproaches of them that reproached thee are fallen upon me.'   Or if they hear God's name rent in pieces, and men dishonour him by their filthy lives, it goeth to their hearts ; for God and they have but one common interest—nay, they prefer God's interest before their own or any other's : John xxi. 15, ' Simon, son of Jonas, lovest thou me more than these ? '   By the world's maxim, love should begin at home ; but by Christ's direction, it beginneth with God   They are more tender of God's glory than their own lives and outward comfort : ' I count not my life dear to me,' saith Paul.   Thus you see what reason there is why our main care and thoughts should be taken up about the concernments of God, and about the glory of his holy name.

Use 1. To reprove us, that we are no more affected with God's glory.   Oh, how little do we aim at and regard it in our prayers !   We should seek it, not only above the profits and pleasures of this life, but even above life itself ; yea, above life present and to come.   But alas ! since the fall, we are corrupt, and wholly poisoned with self-love ; we prefer every base interest and trifle before God ; nay, we prefer carnal self before God.   Some are wholly brutish ; and so they may wallow in ease and pleasure, and eat the fat and drink the sweet, never think of God, care not how God is dishonoured, both by themselves and others.   And then some, oh, how tender are they in matters of their own concernment, and affected with it, more than for the glory of God !—John xii. 43.   They are more affected with their own honour, and their own loss and reproach, than with God's dishonour or God's glory.   If their own reputation be but hazarded a little, oh, how it stings them to the heart !   But if they be faulty towards God, they can pass it over without trouble.   A word of disgrace, a little contempt cast upon our persons, kindles the coals and fills us with rage ; but we can hear God's name dishonoured, and not be moved with it.   When they pray, if they beg outward blessings, if they ask anything, it is for their lusts, not for God ; it is but to feed their pomp and excess, and that they may shine in the pomp and splendour of external accommodations.   If they beg quickening and enlargement, it is

for their own honour, that their lusts may be fed by the con-
tributions of heaven; so, by a wicked design, they would even
make God to serve the devil.   The best of us, when we come to pray,
what a deep sense have we of our own wants, and no desire of the
glory of God!   If we beg daily bread, maintenance, and protection,
we do not beg it as a talent to be improved for our master's use, but
as fuel for our lusts.   If we beg deliverance, it is because we are in
pain, and ill at ease; not that we may honour and glorify God, that
mercy and truth may shine forth.   If we beg pardon, it is only to get
rid of the smart, and be enlarged out of the stocks of conscience.   If
they beg grace, it is but a lazy wish after sanctification, because they
are convinced there is no other way to be happy.   If they beg eternal
glory, they do not beg it for God, it appears plainly, because they can
be content to dishonour God long, provided they at length may be
saved.   Most of us pray without a heart set to glorify God, and to
bring honour unto his great name.   Though a man hath never so
much sense and feeling in his prayer, yet if his heart be not duly set
as to the glory of God, his prayer is turned into sin.   It is not the
manner or the vehemency only, for a carnal spring may send forth high
tides of affection, and motions that come from lust may be earnest and
very rapid; therefore it is not enough to have fervour and vehemency,
but when our aim is to honour and glorify God: Zech. vii. 5, 6,
'When ye fasted, did ye at all fast unto me, even to me?   And when
ye did eat, and when ye did drink, did you not eat for yourselves, and
drink for yourselves?'

Use 2.   For exhortation, to press us to seek the glory of God above
all things.   Take these arguments:—

1. How necessary it is the Lord should have his glory.   The
world serves for no other purpose; it is made and continued for this
end: Rev. iv. 11, 'Thou art worthy, O Lord, to receive glory, and
honour, and power; for thou hast created all things, and for thy
pleasure they are and were created.'   All that God hath made, it was
for his own glory; and, Rom. xi. 36, 'For of him, and through him,
and to him are all things; to whom be glory for ever.   Amen.'   *Of
him*, in a way of creation; *through him*, by way of providential influence and supportation; that they may be *to him* in their final tendency and result.   God did not make us for ourselves, but his own glory.

2. It is a singular benefit to be admitted to sanctify God's name.
Oh that poor worms should come and put the crown upon God's head!
and that he will count anything we can do to be a glory to himself:
1 Chron. xxix. 14, 'But who am I, and what is my people, that we
should be able to offer so willingly after this sort?   For all things
come of thee, and of thine own have we given thee.'

3. Consider how much it concerneth us, that we may make some
restitution for our former dishonouring of God; therefore we should
be more zealous in this work.   How forward have we been to dishonour God in thought, word, and deed, before the Lord wrought
upon us!   There is not a mercy but we have abused it, nor anything
we have meddled with, but one way or other we have turned it to the
Lord's reproach and dishonour.   Now when the Lord hath put grace
in our hearts, when we are 'a people formed for his praise'—Isa. xliii.

—when he hath made us anew, we should think of making some restitution, some amends to God, and should zealously affect his glory above all things.

Use 3. For trial. Do we prefer the glory of God in the first place? Take these marks:—

1. Then we would be content with our loss, provided the name of God may gain any respect in the world; and so he may be magnified, no matter what becomes of us, and our interest and concernment: Phil. i. 20. The apostle expresseth there a kind of indifferency: so 'Christ shall be magnified in my body, whether it be by life or by death.' Oh, then it is a sign you make it your purpose, drift, and care, when you are contented to do or be anything that God will have you to be or do. This holds good, not only in temporal concernments, when you are content to want necessary food, &c., but it holds also in spiritual concernments: as to sense of pardon, though God should suspend the consolations of his Spirit, yet, if it be for the glory of his grace, I am to be content; nay, in some cases God's glory is more to be cared for than our own salvation, if they two could come in competition; but that case never falls out with the creature—our salvation is conjoined with the glory of God. But yet, in supposition, if it should, as Paul and Moses puts the supposition—Exod. xxxii. 32, 'Blot me, I pray thee, out of the book which thou hast written'—so God might be honoured in saving that people. So Rom. ix. 3, 'For I could wish that myself were accursed from Christ for my brethren, my kinsmen according to the flesh.' It was not a rash speech, a thing spoken out of an unadvised passion: see but with what a serious preface it is ushered in, ver. 1, 'God is my witness, I lie not, my conscience also bearing me witness in the Holy Ghost.' He calls God to witness this was the real disposition of his heart, and he speaks advisedly, and with good deliberation.

Object. But is it lawful thus to wish to be accursed? Certainly Paul could not wish himself to love Christ less, or to be less beloved of him; for these things we cannot part with them without sin; but in our enjoyment of Christ there is a happy part, some personal happiness which resulteth to us. Now all this he could lay at God's feet. How so? What, for others? A regular love begins at home, and every man is bound to look to his own salvation first, and then the salvation of others. But that was not the case; it was not their salvation and Paul's salvation which was in competition, but the glory of God, and the common salvation of the Jews, and Paul's particular salvation. It was a mighty prejudice to the gospel that the people from whom Christ's messengers proceeded—for the law went out of Sion, the gospel came out from among the Jews—that so many of them were prejudiced, and a mighty eclipse to the glory of God. Now he could lay down all his personal happiness at God's feet, he speaks in supposition, if such a case falls out. But, however, this is a clear rule: the glory of God must be preferred before our own salvation. In some cases there will be need of this rule. For instance, there is many a man that possibly is convinced of a false religion; and the first question men make is, if they can be saved in such a religion, but many men are hardened in Popery. When, therefore, a man is contented to continue in a false religion, and dishonour God with his compliance there, provided he may be saved, he prefers his own salvation before the glory of God; and in case of the delay of repentance, when men dally with God, and put off the work of returning to the Lord until another time, or hereafter it is time enough to repent, these men prize their salvation before the glory of God. If it were true upon that supposition, that if ever they shall be saved, they are contented God shall be dishonoured a great deal longer, and that if they be saved at length this will satisfy them.

Quest. But how may we discern that we make the glory of God the first and chief thing we aim at in prayer?

1. Partly by the work of your own thoughts. The end is first in intention, though last in execution. When you are praying for a public mercy against an enemy, what runs in your thoughts? Revenge, safety, and your own personal happiness, or God's glory? 'What wilt thou do, O Lord, unto thy great name?' Josh. vii. 9. Are you pleasing yourselves with suppositions of your escape and deliverance, and reeking your wrath upon your adversaries? So in prayer for strength and quickening, what is it that runs in your mind? Are you entertaining your spirit with dreams of applause, and feeding your minds with the sweetness of popular acclamation?

2. By the manner of praying, absolutely for God's glory, but for all other things with a sweet submission to God's will: John xii. 27, 'Father, save me from this hour: but for this cause came I unto this hour. Father, glorify thy name. Then came there a voice from heaven, saying, I have both glorified it, and will glorify it again.' Christ is absolute in the request, and he receives an answer. Is this enough? Do you mainly press God with this, that he might provide for his own glorious name, that his name might not lie under reproach? But now carnal aims do make affection impetuous and impatient of check and denial. Rachel must have children, or die. When the heart is set upon earthly success, pleasure, or comfort, then they cannot brook a denial without murmuring. The children of God only accept of God's glory, and in all other things they leave themselves to God's disposal, and therefore this is the main thing.

3. Partly too by the disposition of your hearts when your prayers are accomplished, and God hath given any blessing you pray for. We do not ask it for God's glory, if we do not use it for God's glory. The time of having mercies is the time of trial, and therefore when we consume our mercies upon our lusts, when they do not conduce to check our sins, it is a sign God's glory is not the thing intended as it should be.

Thus for the order of this petition.

II. The necessity of putting up such a request to God. It is his charge to us in the third commandment, that we should sanctify his name: 'Thou shalt not take the name of the Lord thy God in vain.' The positive part of that commandment is, thou shalt sanctify it. Now here we make it matter of prayer to God: 'Hallowed be thy name.' From whence let me observe:—

Doct. Those that would have God's name hallowed and glorified, must seriously deal with God about it.

There are several reasons why we must put up such requests to God. I might argue from the utility and the necessity of it.

First, The utility. We put up these requests to God:—

1. That we may more solemnly warn ourselves of our own duty. In prayer there is an implicit vow, or solemn obligation, that we take upon ourselves to prosecute what they ask. It is a preaching to ourselves in God's hearing. So that every word we speak to God is a lesson to us, and our requests are so many exhortations to glorify his holy name. With what face can we ask that which we are wholly reckless and neglectful of? Then we shall certainly come under that character: Mat. xv. 7, 8, 'This people draweth nigh unto me with their mouth, and honoureth me with their lips; but their heart is far from me.' It is the greatest mockage of God to ask, unless we have a mind to pursue and diligently to attend to this work and business, that the name of God may be glorified in us and upon us.

2. That we may have a due sense and grief for God's honour. God's children they are troubled to see God dishonoured. Lot's righteous soul was vexed, not with Sodom's injuries, but with Sodom's sins, 2 Pet. ii. 8. And David saith: 'Rivers of tears run down mine eyes, because men keep not thy law,' Ps. cxix. 136. Many will scarce weep for their own sins, where they have advantage of remorse of conscience; but when they are zealously affected with God's glory, they will weep for others' sins. When his name is torn and rent in pieces, it is a grief of heart to them. Now God will have us ask this, that this holy sense of spiritual grief may be kept up; for when it is become the matter of our requests, then we are interested in the glory of God. We are loth to see things miscarry where we have petitioned and begged for others; so when we have begged the glory of his name, it will further this spiritual sense and grief of heart when his name is dishonoured.

3. That we may count it as great a blessing when God is glorified as when we are saved. 'Continue in prayer,' saith the apostle, 'and watch thereunto with thanksgiving.' When we have been instant with God in prayer, that he might be glorified, then we shall count it as great a blessing when he is glorified as when we are saved. Prayer makes way for the increase of our esteem, and engages us to observe the return. When we have asked it of God, we will be affected with it then. When we see all his works praise him, what a comfort will this be to the soul: 'Bless the Lord, O my soul,' Ps. ciii. 22.

But secondly, Let me show the necessity of dealing with God about it. The necessity will appear both in respect of persons and things; when we beg that God's name may be hallowed, we beg dispositions of heart and occasions.

First, The necessity will appear in respect of persons, both as to ourselves and others.

First, In respect of ourselves, there is a great necessity that we should deal with God about the hallowing of his name; because we need direction, sincerity, quickening, submission to God, humility, and holiness. To instance in these six things :—

1. We need direction. The habits of grace are God's gifts, and the exercise of grace is another thing; to actuate, quicken, guide, and direct it: 2 Thes. iii. 5, ' The Lord direct your hearts to the love of God.' And so in prayer, and in honouring of God. In prayer, ' we know not' how or ' what to pray for as we ought.' Though we have grace, yet we need direction. A ship that is well rigged, yet needs a skilful pilot: Rom. viii. 26, ' Likewise the Spirit also helpeth our infirmities; for we know not what we should pray for as we ought.' How much are we to seek to give God his due honour ! ' Of ourselves we cannot so much as think a good thought :' 2 Cor. iii. 5. There is an utter insufficiency in us to meditate of God, and conceive aright of his excellency, and give him the honour which is due to him. None of us but needs daily to go to God, that we may be taught how to hallow and sanctify his name.

2. We need quickening, being so backward to this duty. All the lepers could beg help, and but one returned to give God the glory. There is much dulness and deadness of heart as to the praising of God, and glorifying of God. Self-love will put us upon other things; but it is grace must quicken us to glorify him and praise him. When we go to God for ourselves, our necessities will sharpen our affections, and put a shrill accent upon our prayers. But now when we beg of God for God, then there is a greater restraint upon us. And therefore David saith, Ps. li. 15, ' Open thou my lips, and my mouth shall show forth thy praise.' We need God to open our mouths; that is, enlarge our hearts and quicken our affections. How apt are we to turn the back upon the mercy-seat ! Ezek. xlvi. 9. If a man came in at the north gate he was to go out at the south gate, but never at the same door. Why ? That he might not turn his back upon the mercy-seat. When we have prayed, we are apt to forget that God which hath blessed us; and therefore that our hearts might be enlarged and quickened, we need to go to God.

3. We need uprightness and sincerity, that we may mind the glory of God. This is not a work of nature, but grace : Phil. ii. 21, ' All men seek their own, not the things which are Jesus Christ's.' There is the fruit and effect of nature, it puts men upon seeking their own things, worldly ease, profit, and pleasure. Every creature naturally seeks its own welfare; but to make the glory of God our great aim and pursuit, it is grace puts upon that. Water ascends no higher than it descends, so nature cannot rise beyond itself. The stream cannot rise above the fountain, and above the principle. A man that hath nothing but nature, he cannot unfeignedly seek the things which are of God. The old man with the deceitful lusts, that is the natural man. The upright heart, that unfeignedly seeks God, needs grace from above. Without influence from God, our actions cannot have a tendency to God. We shall prefer our interest before God's glory, if we have no higher principle than what our hearts furnish us with.

4. We must go to God for submission. Now there is a double submission required, which if we have not, we shall find it marvellously difficult to glorify God. One, as to the choice of instruments; another, as to the way and means by which God will bring about his own glory.

[1.] As to the choice of instruments. There is in us an envy, and wicked emulation. Oh, how hard a matter is it to rejoice in the gifts, and graces, and services of others, and be content with the dispensation, when God will cast us by as unworthy, and use others for the glorifying of his name! Therefore that we may refer the choice of instruments to God, we need go to him and say, Lord, ' hallowed be thy name;' do it which way, and by whom thou pleasest. We are troubled, if others glorify God, and not we, or more than we ; if they be more holy, more useful, or more serious, self will not yield to this. Now by putting up this prayer to God, we refer it to him to choose the instrument whom he will employ. It was a commendable modesty and self-denial in John Baptist, which is described, John iii. 13, ' He must increase, I must decrease.' When we are contented to be abased and obscured, provided Christ may be honoured and exalted ; and be content with such a dispensation, though with our loss and decrease. Many are of a private station, and straitened in gifts, and can have no public instrumentality for God ; now these need to pray, ' Hallowed be thy name,' that they may rejoice when God useth others whom he hath furnished with greater abilities.

[2.] A submission for the way ; that we may submit to those unpleasing means and circumstances of his providence, that God will take up and make use of, for the glorifying of his holy name. Many times we must be content, not only to be active instruments, but passive objects of God's glory. And therefore if God will glorify himself by our poverty, or our disgrace, our pain and sickness, we must be content. Therefore we need to deal with God seriously about this matter, that we may submit to the Lord's will, as Jesus Christ did : John xii. 27, 28, ' Save me from this hour ; but for this cause came I unto this hour : Father, glorify thy name. And there was a voice from heaven that said, I have glorified it, and will glorify it again.' Put me to shame, suffering, to endure the cross, the curse, so thou mayest be glorified. This was the humble submission of Christ Jesus, and such a submission should be in us. The martyrs were contented to be bound to the stake, if that way God will use them to his glory. Phil. i. 20, saith Paul, ' So Christ shall be magnified in my body, whether it be by life, or by death :' if my body be taken to heaven in glory, or whether it be exercised or worn out with ministerial labour. We need to deal with God that we may have the end, and leave the means to his own choosing ; that God may be glorified in our condition, whatever it be. If he will have us rich and full, that he might be glorified in our bounty ; if he will have us poor and low, that he may be glorified in our patience ; if he will have us healthy, that he may be glorified in our labour ; if he will have us sick, that he may be glorified in our pain ; if he will have us live, that he may be glorified in our lives ; if he will have us die, that he may be glorified in our deaths : and therefore, ' Whether we live or die, we are the Lord's :' Rom. xiv. 9. A Christian is to be like a die in the hand of providence, content whether he be cast high or low, and not to grudge at it, whether he will continue us longer or take us out of the world. As a servant employed beyond the seas, if his master will have him tarry, there he tarries ; if he would have him come home,

home he comes : so that we had need to deal seriously with God about this submissive spirit.

[5.] Humility ; that we may not put the crown upon our own heads, but may cast it at the Lamb's feet ; that we may not take the glory of our graces to ourselves. God's great aim in the covenant is, ' that no flesh should glory in itself ; but whosoever glories, may glory in the Lord :' 1 Cor. i. 27–31. He would have us still come and own him, in all that we are, and in all that we do. As the good servant gave account of his diligence, Luke xix. 16, he doth not say, My industry, but, ' Thy pound hath gained ten pounds.' And Paul was a zealous instrument, that went up and down doing good; he ' laboured more abundantly than they all : yet not I, but the grace of God, which was with me :' 1 Cor. xv. 10. In this case if we would honour and glorify God, we must do as Joab did, when he was likely to take Rabbah : he sent for David to gather up more forces, and encamp against the city and take it, ' Lest I take the city, and it be called after my name :' 2 Sam. xii. 28. How careful was he that his sovereign might have the honour ! So careful should we be that the crown be set upon Christ's head, and that he may have the glory of our graces and services, that they may not be called after our own name, that God may be more owned in them than we. Now what more natural, than for creatures to intercept the revenues of the crown of heaven, and to convert them to their own use ? It is a vile sacrilege, to rob God of the glory of that grace he hath bestowed upon us ; and yet what more common ? The flesh is apt to interpose upon all occasions ; and therefore we need to put up this request, ' Hallowed be thy name.'

[6.] There is holiness required, that we may not be a disgrace to God and a dishonour to him. The Lord saith, Ezek. xx. 9, ' That his name should not be polluted before the heathen, among whom they (his people) were.' The sin of God's people doth stain the honour of God, and profane his name. When men profess much to be a people near God, and live carnally and loosely, they dishonour God exceedingly by their conversation. Men judge by what is visible and sensible, and so they think of God by his servants and worshippers ; as the heathens did of Christ in Salvian's time,—If he was a holy Christ, certainly Christians would live more temperately, justly, and soberly. They are apt to think of God by his worshippers, and by the people that profess themselves so near and dear to him ; therefore it concerns us to walk so, that our lives may honour him : Mat. v. 16, ' Let your light so shine before men, that they may see your good works, and glorify your Father which is in heaven.' As the loins of the poor (saith Job) blessed him, Job xxxi. 20, namely, as they were fed and clothed by his bounty ; so our lives may glorify God. David saith, Ps. cxix. 7, ' Then shall I praise thee with uprightness of heart, when I have learned thy righteous judgment.' There is no way to praise God entirely and sincerely until we have learned both to know and do his will. Real praise is the praise God looks after. Otherwise we do but serve Christ as the devil served him, who would carry him upon the top of the mountain, but it was with an intent to bid him throw himself down again. So we seem to exalt God much in our talk and profession; yea, but we throw him down, when we pollute him and deny him in our conversation. Our lives are the scandal of religion, and a pollution and blot to the name of God. So that with respect to ourselves, you see what need we have to go to God. that he will give us grace that we may please him and glorify his name.

Secondly, In regard of others. A Christian cannot be content to glorify God himself, but he would have all about him to glorify God. As fire turns all things round about it into fire; and leaven, it spreads still, until it hath subdued the whole lump: so is grace a diffusive, a spreading thing. As far as we can reach and diffuse our influence, we would have God brought into request with all round about us. ' Being converted,' saith Christ to Peter, ' strengthen thy brethren.' So it will be where there is true grace. Mules, and creatures which are of a mongrel and bastard race, they beget not after their kind : so bastard Christians are not for the calling in of others, and the gaining of those about them. But a true Christian will be earnest, and much in this matter. Now their hearts are not in our power, but in God's; therefore we need to be much in prayer, and make this our main request, Lord, ' hallowed be thy name.' For hereby,

1. We acknowledge God's dominion over the spirits of men, which is a great honour to God, and a quieting to us. It is a title often given to God in scripture, that he is the ' God of the spirits of all flesh.' If they had a magistrate to choose, they go to God : Num. xxvii. 16, ' Let the Lord, the God of the spirits of all flesh, set a man over the congregation.' If a judgment to be averted, Num. xvi. 22, ' O God, the God of the spirits of all flesh, shall one man sin, and wilt thou be wroth with all the congregation ? ' This is a great honour to God, when we acknowledge the power and dominion that he hath over the hearts and spirits of men. To roll a stone is not so much as to rule the creatures; and to keep the sun in its course is not so much as to rule the spirits of men, and to work them to the glorifying of his holy name. God can turn the hearts of men this way and that way, according as he pleaseth: Prov. xxi. 1, ' The king's heart is in the hand of the Lord, as the rivers of water; he turneth it whithersoever he will.' As a man can dispose of a watercourse, turn it hither and thither as the necessities of his field or garden require, so can God draw out the hearts and respects of men. Surely there would not be so many disorders in the world if we did often reflect upon this attribute, or did deal with God about his power over the spirits of men. We are wrathful, and think nothing but the confusion of men would serve the turn, and there is no riddance of our burden but by the destruction of those who stand in our way; whereas the conversion of men, a change of their spirits and hearts, would be a better cure, and bring more honour to God, and safety with it. The truth is, we look more to men than to God, and that is the reason why we pitch rather upon the destruction than the conversion of others. Destruction, that may be executed by the creature; but conversion, that is a power (to order and regulate the spirits of men) which God hath reserved in his own hands. One angel could destroy above a hundred and eighty thousand in Sennacherib's camp in one night ; but all the angels, with their united strength, cannot draw in one heart to God.

But now the God of the spirits of all flesh, who is too hard for him ?
Oh, did we often reflect upon this, we would be dealing with God about
this matter, that he would work upon the spirits of men. If there be
a wicked ruler, or an obstinate child or servant, &c., that he would
sanctify himself upon them, and change their hearts.

2. You discover much love to God, when, as you would not dishonour him yourselves, so you are careful others may not dishonour
him. 'Praise him, all ye ends of the earth,' Ps. xcviii. 4, and c. 1.
You would have all the world own him. Private spirits that would
impale and enclose religion, that they may shine alone, they do not
love God, but themselves, their own credit, and their own profit.
'Would to God all the Lord's people were prophets!' Num. xi. 29.
That was a free and noble speech. God is resembled to the sun, because it is he that must shine alone; but the church is compared
to the moon and stars, where all may shine, but every star in its own
glory. True Christians would have all to be as they are, unless it be
with respect to their bonds and incumbrances.

3. You discover love to others, you would have them glorify God.
The angels, they rejoice when a sinner is converted; they have a great
love to souls, Luke xv. 7. And so do Christians; the more spiritual
they are, the more they come near to the blessed spirits above, and
the more affected they are with the good done to others, and with
their conversion. Saith Paul, Rom. ix. 3: 'I could wish that myself were accursed from Christ for my brethren, my kinsmen according to the flesh.' Such a zeal and entire affection he had to the souls
of others, that he could lay all his personal happiness at Christ's feet.
And thus you see what need we have to deal seriously with God in
this business, if indeed we make this our aim. Especially those which
are in public relations, as Paul was, which had an office put upon
him to procure the salvation of others, how will their hearts run out
upon it!

Secondly, It is needful we should deal with God about the sanctifying of his name, as in regard of persons, so of things and events.
God hath the disposal of all events in his own hands. There are
many things which concern the glory of God that are out of our reach,
and are wholly in God's hands; and therefore it discovers our love
to his glory, and our submission to his wise and powerful government
of all affairs, when we deal with God about it, and refer the matter
to his disposal, and say, Lord, 'hallowed be thy name,' take the work
into thy own hands. We discover our love to his glory, because we
make it a part of our request that all these events may conduce to
the glory of his majesty. As Joshua, when Israel fell before their
enemies: Josh. vii. 9, 'Lord, what wilt thou do for thy great name?'
There was his trouble. And Moses: Num. xiv. 15, 16, What will the
nations say round about? 'Because the Lord was not able to bring
this people into the land which he sware unto them, therefore he hath
slain them in the wilderness.' It goeth near to the heart of God's
children when they see anything that will tend to God's reproach.

But that is not all; it is not enough we discover that, but also our
submission to his wise and powerful government, when we refer the
matter to his disposal, and can see that he can work out his own ends

out of all the confusions which happen there; out of sins, errors, wars, blood: Ps. lxxvi. 10, 'The wrath of man shall praise thee; the remainder of wrath shalt thou restrain.' In the Septuagint it is, the wrath of man shall keep holy day to thee, shall increase a festival for thee. God many times gets up in the world upon Satan's shoulders. When matters are ravelled and disordered, he can find out the right end of the thread, and how to disentangle us again; and when we have spoiled a business, he can dispose it for good, and make an advantage of those things which seem to obscure the glory of his name.

By the way, both these must go together, our love to his glory, and our submission to his providence. Our love to his glory; for we should not be altogether reckless and careless how things go; and yet not carking, because of the wisdom and power of his providence. The truth is, we should be more solicitous about duties than events. The glory of events belongeth to God himself, and we are not to take his work out of his hand, but mind him in it. Look, as some would learn their schoolfellows' lesson better than their own; so we would have things carried thus and thus. And so by murmuring we tax providence, rather than adore it, and we eclipse the glory of God. Yet we must be sensible of the reproaches cast upon God, and must pray to the Lord to vindicate and right his name, to take the way and means into his own hands.

Thus you have seen the necessity of putting up such a request to God, 'Hallowed be thy name.'

Use 1. Is for information. It informs us that whatever we bestow upon God, we have it from God at first: 1 Chron. xxix. 11, 'Of thine own have we given thee.' The King of all the earth, we cannot pay him any tribute but out of his own exchequer. When we are best affected to God's interest, and pray for God's concernments, we must beg the grace which maketh us to do so. It is his own gift. It is he must enable and incline us, quicken and direct us. So that in all things he is *Alpha* and *Omega*—we begin in him, whenever we end in him. And when we do most for God, we have all from him.

Use 2. For direction in the matter of glorifying God, in four propositions.

[1.] This life is not to be valued, but as it yieldeth us opportunities for this end and purpose, to glorify God. We were not sent into the world to live for ourselves, but for God. If we could make ourselves, then we could live to ourselves. If we could be our own cause, then we might be our own end. But God made us for himself, and sent us into the world for himself. Christ saith: John xvii. 4, 'Father, I have glorified thee on earth,' &c. It is not our duty only to glorify God in heaven, to join in concert with the angels in their hallelujahs above, where we may glorify him without distraction, weariness, and weakness; but here on earth, in the midst of difficulties and temptations. There are none sent into the world to be idle, or to 'bring forth fruit to themselves,' Hosea x. 1; to improve their pains [1] and strength, to promote merely their own interest; but God's glory must be our chief work and aim while we are here upon earth,—this must be the purpose and intent of our lives.

---

[1] Qu. 'gains'?—Ed.

[2.] Every man, besides his general calling, hath his own work and course of service whereby to glorify and honour God: John xvii. 4, 'I have finished the work which thou gavest me to do.' As in a great house one hath one employment, one another : so God hath designed to every man his work he hath to do, and the calling he must be in ; some in one calling, and some in another ; but they all have their service and work given them to do for God's glory.

[3.] In discharge of this work, as they must do all for God, so they can do nothing without God. Every morning we should revive the sense of it upon ourselves, as the care of our work and aim, so the sense of our impotency. This day I am to live with God; but how unable am I, and how easily shall I dishonour him ! ' The way of man is not in himself,' Jer. x. 23. When a Christian goeth abroad in the morning, he must remember he is at Christ's dispose ; he is not to do as he pleaseth, but to be guided by rule, and act for God's glory, and fetch in strength from Christ: Col. iii. 17, ' Whatsoever ye do in word or deed, do all in the name of the Lord Jesus.' Not only in our duties or immediate converses with God, but in our sports, business, recreation. What is it to do things in the name of Christ,— that is, to do it according to Christ's will and command ? He hath allowed us time for recreation, for conversing with God, and calling in Christ's help, and aiming at his glory. If we have anything to do for God, we must do it in his own strength, in every word and deed.

[4.] You are directed again, when the glory of God and sanctifying of his name either sticks with us, or sticks abroad, God must be specially consulted with in the case. When our hearts are backward, then, ' Lord, open thou my lips ; ' Lord, affect me with a sense of thy kindness and mercy. When it sticks abroad, when such events fall out, as for a while God's name is obscured, and seems to be clouded, ' Lord, what wilt thou do for thy great name ? '

III. Having opened the order of the words, and the reasons of putting up such a request to God, I now come to the sense of the petition, ' Hallowed be thy name.' Four things will come under consideration :—

1. What is meant by the *name* of God.

2. What it is to *hallow* and sanctify it.

3. I shall take notice of the form of the proposal, ἁγιασθήτω, *Hallowed*.

4. The note of distinction, *thy* name.

First, What is meant by God's name ?

1. God himself.

2. Anything whereby he is made known.

[1.] God himself. *Name*, by an Hebraism, is put for the person itself. Thus : Rev. iii. 4, ' Thou hast a few names even in Sardis, which have not defiled their garments ;' that is, many persons ; so : Acts i. 15, it is said there, ' The number of the names together were about one hundred and twenty,' that is of persons. So it is used in the present case. God's name is put for God himself : Ps. xx. 1, ' The name of the God of Jacob defend thee !' That is, God himself. So : Ps. xliv. 5, ' Through thy name will we tread them under that rise up against us ;' that is, by thee. And to believe in the name of Christ is to believe in Christ himself. *Name* is put for person, for the immediate object of faith is the person of Christ: John i. 12, 'To as many as received him, to them gave he power to become the sons of God, even to them that believe on his name.'

[2.] Anything whereby he is made known to us, *Nomen quasi notamen.* As a man is known by his name, so God's titles and attributes, his ordinances, his works, his word, are his name, chiefly the two latter. For his works, they are a part of the name of God: Ps. viii. 1, the burden of that psalm is twice repeated, 'O Lord, our Lord, how great is thy name in all the earth!' By the name there, is meant God made known in his works of creation and providence, for he speaks there of sun, moon, and stars, which proclaim an eternal power to all the world; and he speaks of such a name as is in all the earth. And, Ps. cxlvii. 19, 20, 'He hath not dealt so with any nation,' and given them his word, statutes, and ordinances; every one hath not that privilege. But, 'How great is thy name in all the earth!' That is, how manifestly art thou made known by thy works! But above all, by *name* is meant his word: Ps. cxxxviii. 2, 'Thou hast magnified thy word above all thy name.' There is more of God to be seen in his word, than in all the creatures of the world, and in all his other works besides. We understand more of God than can be taken up by the creation. It helps us to interpret the book of nature and providence; there we have his titles, attributes, ordinances; there we have his greatest work, in which he hath discovered so much of his name, the mystery of redemption, which is not elsewhere to be known. Thus by the name of God is meant God himself, as he hath made known himself in the word. We desire that he may be sanctified, that he may with honour and reverence be received everywhere.

Secondly, The second thing to be explained, what is meant by *hallowed?* In scripture God is said sometimes to be magnified, sometimes to be justified, sometimes to be glorified, and sometimes to be sanctified. Now it is not here said, *Magnificetur nomen tuum,* or *glorificetur,* but *sanctificetur*—let thy name be sanctified. All these terms do express how God is to be honoured by the creature, and they have all distinct notions. God is said to be magnified: Luke i. 46, 'My soul doth magnify the Lord.' To magnify God argueth a high esteem or a due sense of his greatness. Again, God is said to be justified: Luke vii. 29, 'The people and the publicans justified God.' What is it to justify God? To justify is to acquit from accusation, and when that word is applied to God, it signifieth our owning of him notwithstanding the prejudices of the world against him. To glorify God is to make him known to others, and to bring him into request with others, for glory it is *clara cum laude notitia,* a public fame or knowledge of excellency. Thus Christ saith, John xvii. 10, 'I am glorified in them;' speaking of his apostles, because by their means he was made known to the world. All these are included in the word of the text. Yet there is somewhat more intended by to be sanctified. When is God then said to be sanctified?

To hallow and to sanctify is to set apart from common use, and so to sanctify the name of God, is to use it in a separate manner, with that reverence and respect which is not used to anything else. So that when we pray that God's name may be hallowed or sanctified, we desire that, according as he hath made known himself in the word, so he may be known, reverenced, and esteemed in the world. Known to be the only true God : 1 Kings xviii. 36, 'Let it be known this day that thou art God in Israel,' and accordingly worshipped and glorified in the hearts and lives of men.

The third thing to open is the form of proposal, ἁγιασθητω. It is not *sanctificemus*, let us hallow, but *sanctificetur*, let it be hallowed, for in this form of speech, all the persons concerned in this work are included—God, ourselves, and others.

[1.] God is to be included in the prayer, that we may express our sense of his providence working all things for the glory of his holy name, yea, discovering his excellency, showing himself to be the holy God : Ezek. xxxviii. 23, ' I will magnify myself, and sanctify myself, and I will be known in the eyes of many nations, and they shall know that I am the Lord.' The Lord magnifieth himself by the more eminent effects of his care and providence, but he sanctifieth himself chiefly by blessing and defending the godly, and by punishing and afflicting the wicked, for thereby he declareth his holiness, the purity of his nature, and his love to saints ; so that when we say, ' Hallowed be thy name,' we mean, Lord, declare thyself to be a holy God, by putting a distinction between men and men in the course of thy providence, and owning thy people from heaven.

[2.] We include ourselves when we say, ' Hallowed be thy name,' for it is especially the duty of God's people : Isa. xxix. 23, ' They shall sanctify my name, and sanctify the Holy One of Jacob, and shall fear the God of Israel.' It is our duty, by our religious carriage, to evidence that we have a holy God. This must be our first care, that we ourselves be sanctified, and to sanctify our sanctifier, the Holy One of Israel. Some, they would have God glorified by others, but do not look to themselves how they sanctify God. Now God hath made this to be a great part of our care, that his own people should not only magnify and glorify him, but sanctify him; therefore he rather makes them good than great. When he would make men great, then he shows his magnificence, to be the almighty disposer of the riches of the world; but when he makes them good, then he expects to be sanctified, that his people should discover that he is a holy One ; that he is holy in himself, for we add nothing to him when we sanctify him, but only discover him to be such a one. In short, God sanctifieth us effectively by working grace and holiness in us, and we sanctify him relatively, objectively, declaratively, declaring him to be a holy God, and that we are a people belonging to this God.

[3.] The speech is so formed that others may be included, and that we may express our sense of their dishonouring God, as a thing that is grievous to us, that we may show how near it goeth to our heart to see the ignorance, atheism, and blasphemy that is in the world. They would have the holy God to be sanctified abroad, either by the conversion of men, or by their punishment. And so it is meant : Isa. v. 16, ' God that is holy shall be sanctified in righteousness.' That is, his holiness and hatred of sin shall appear, either in the conversion of obstinate sinners, that God may be sanctified by them, or else for punishment, that God may be sanctified upon them.

Fourthly, The next thing is the note of distinction, 'Hallowed be *thy* name,' not ours. There seems to be a secret opposition between our name and the name of God. When we come to pray, we should distinctly remember whose name is to be glorified, that God may be at the end of every request. We beg of God many times, but we think of ourselves; our hearts run upon our own name, and upon our own esteem. How often do we come to him with a selfish aim, as if we would draw God into our own designs and purposes! None are so unfit to glorify God, and so unwelcome to him, as those that are so wedded and vehemently addicted to their own honour and esteem in the world. Therefore Christ, by way of distinction, by way of opposition to this innate disposition that is in us, he would have us to say, 'Hallowed be *thy* name.' That which gives most honour to God is believing: Rom. iv. 19, 20, Abraham was 'strong in faith, giving glory to God.' Now, none so unfit for the work as they that seek glory for themselves: John v. 44, 'How can ye believe, which receive honour one of another, and seek not the honour that cometh from God only?' Affectation of vainglory, or splendour of our own name, is a temper inconsistent with faith, which is the grace that gives honour to God. I say, when we hunt after respect from men, and make that the chiefest scope of our actions, God's glory will certainly lie in the dust; when we are to suffer ignominy and abasement for his sake, the care of God's glory will be laid aside. The great sin of the old world was this: Gen. xi. 4, 'Let us make us a name.' There are many conceits about that enterprise, what that people should aim at there in building so great and so vast a tower, before God confounded their tongues. Some, interpreting that place, 'Let us build us a tower even to heaven,' think this was their intention, to make a way into heaven. But it is not likely they would be so foolish that had so late experience of the flood, and, when the ark rested upon the top of the highest mountains, found themselves to be at so great and vast a distance from heaven. Some think it was (as Josephus) to secure themselves from another flood; but that was sufficiently done by God's promise, who had engaged to them he would no more destroy the earth by water; and if that were their intention, why should they build in the plain, between the two rivers of Tigris and Euphrates? Moses gives the main reason there, that they might have an immortal name among posterity. But now see how ill they reckon that do reckon without God. Those that are so busy about their own name, how soon will God blast them! When in any action we do not seek glory to God, but ourselves, it is the ready way to be destroyed. This was the means to bury them in perpetual oblivion. Nebuchadnezzar, when he re-edified the city, Dan. iv. 30: 'Is not this great Babylon that I have built for the house of the kingdom, by the might of my power, and for the honour of my majesty?' How doth God disappoint him, and turn him out among the beasts! Thus are we sure to be disappointed and blasted, when our hearts run altogether upon our own name. But now Christ saith *thy name;* when we are careful of that, this is the way to prosper.

From the words thus illustrated, I shall only observe:—

Doct. That God will be so glorified in the world as that his name may be hallowed or sanctified.

Here I shall show:—

1. How many ways God's name is sanctified.

2. Why God will be so glorified as that he may be sanctified.

First, How many ways is God's name sanctified? I answer, either upon us, or by us.

[1.] Upon us, by the righteous executions and judgments of his providence: and so God is sanctified when he doth by a high hand of power recover and extort the glory of his holiness from the dead and stupid world; as by that notable stroke of the Bethshemites, when fifty thousand were slain for peeping into the ark: 1 Sam. vi. 20. This was the result of all: 'Who is able to stand before this holy Lord God?' There he discovered himself to be a holy God, to be one that hath a high displeasure against the creature's disobedience. Now when he doth by a high hand extort this from the wicked, or from his children, then he sanctifieth himself upon us.

[2.] By us. And so he is sanctified in our thoughts, words, and actions; in our heart, tongue, or life.

1. In our hearts: 1 Pet. 3, 15, 'Sanctify the Lord God in your heart.' How is God sanctified in our hearts?

[1.] When we have awful thoughts of his majesty: Ps. cxi. 9, 'Holy and reverend is his name.' Not only when we speak of the name of God, but when we think of it, we should be seriously affected. But,

[2.] More especially God is sanctified when, in straits, difficulties, and dangers, we can bear ourselves upon the power and sufficiency of God, and go on resolutely and cheerfully with our duty, notwithstanding discouragements. This is to sanctify the Lord God in our hearts. I shall prove it by two places where the phrase is used; one is, 1 Pet. iii. 15, 'Be ready always to give an answer to every man that asketh you a reason of the hope that is in you, with meekness and fear.' Mark, the Christians that did profess the name of God, which spake of God as their hope or object of their religion, were in great danger. Now what direction doth he give them, that they might not be afraid, but bear up? For he speaks before: 'Be not afraid of their terror, or be troubled; but sanctify the Lord God in your hearts.' See the same phrase used for the same purpose: Isa. viii. 13, 'Sanctify the Lord of hosts himself, and let him be your fear, and let him be your dread.' He opposeth it plainly there to carnal fear: ver. 12, 'Say ye not a confederacy to all them to whom this people shall say a confederacy; neither fear ye their fear, nor be afraid; but sanctify the Lord of hosts himself, and let him be your fear.' How comes this direction to be used in the present case? Thus; to sanctify is to set apart; and to sanctify God is to set apart, as the alone object of fear and trust, that he alone is to be feared and trusted, so that we can see no match for God among the creatures; therefore we are to embolden ourselves in the Lord, and go on cheerfully, when we can counterbalance all fears and dangers with his surpassing excellency. To glorify God is to do that which simply and absolutely tendeth to the manifestation of his excellency, without any relation to the creature; but to sanctify God is to set God above the creature, to do that which tends to exalt his greatness and excellency from and above all terrors, and all the discouragements that we can have from the creature; it is to ascribe that greatness, that power and glory, to God alone, which cannot be ascribed to anything else, and so to go on cheerfully with our duty, whatever difficulties we meet with.   Thus Moses was chidden, that was amazed with present difficulty : Num. xx. 12, ' And the Lord spake unto Moses and Aaron, Because ye believed me not, to sanctify me in the eyes of the children of Israel ; therefore ye shall not bring this congregation into the land which I have given them.' Because they were discouraged, and thought they should never carry on their business, therefore God saith, ' Ye believe not to sanctify me :' you sanctify not God, or set him aloft, as the alone and supreme object of fear and trust.   It is a practical acknowledgment of God's matchless excellency.   Thus we sanctify God in our hearts.

2. God is sanctified with our tongues, when we use God's name, titles, ordinances, and word, as holy things ; when we speak of the Lord with reverence, and with great seriousness of heart, not taking his name in vain ; especially when we are deeply affected with his praise.   It is no slight thing to praise God.   God's people, when they have gone about it, see a need of the greatest help : Ps. li. 15, 'O Lord, open thou my lips, and my mouth shall show forth thy praise.' And Ps. xlv. 1 : ' My heart is inditing a good matter ;' my heart fries or boils a good matter : when we will not give God dough-baked praise, nor speak of his name slightly, but so as becomes his greatness and surpassing excellency.

3. In our actions.   Our actions may be parted into two things,— worship, and ordinary conversation.

(1.) In our worship, there God especially will be sanctified.   Lev. x. 3, ' I will be sanctified in all that draw near unto me.'   God is very tender of his worship : *sancta sanctis*, holy things must be managed by holy men in a holy manner.   Therefore, what is it to sanctify God when we draw nigh to him ?   To have a more excellent frame of heart in worship than we have about other things.   As in prayer, the frame of our hearts must not be common ; we must not go about it with such a frame of heart as we go about our callings, worldly business, and converses with men : but there must be some special reverence, such as is peculiar to him.   When we draw near to God in the word, he will be sanctified.   The word must be received with meekness, and by faith applied to our souls, as an instrument designed to our endless good.   When we have a peculiar reverence for God, and a respect to God in all our approaches ; Eccles. v. 1, ' Look to thy feet when thou goest to the house of God :' we must not go about these holy services hand over head, but with great caution and heed.   Thus is God sanctified in worship, or in our immediate converse with him.

(2.) In our ordinary conversation.   Then God is sanctified ; when our life is ordered so that we may give men occasion to say, that surely he is a holy God whom we serve.   By two things you may know you sanctify God in your conversations : when you walk as remembering you have a holy God, and when you walk as discovering to others you have a holy God.

[1.] When you walk as remembering yourselves that you have a holy God, therefore you must be watchful and strict.   It is notable, when the Israelites were making a hasty promise, Joshua puts them in mind, chap. xxiv. 9, ' You cannot serve the Lord, for he is a holy God.' So we should remember when we give up ourselves to God, he is a holy and jealous God, that is narrowly observant, and he will not be put off with anything that is common.

[2.] As discovering you have a holy God. A carnal worshipper profaneth the memory of God in the world. But now a Christian that walks according to his holy calling, that is holy in all manner of conversation, he discovereth what a God he hath. 1 Pet. ii. 9, ' That ye should show forth the praises of him, who hath called you out of darkness into his marvellous light.' We are not only to conceive and make use of them to beget fear and reverence in our hearts of the all-seeing God, but are to show them forth, to evidence them to others. We should discover more than a human excellency, that so those which look upon us may say, These are the servants of the holy God.

Secondly, For the reasons why God will be so glorified, that he may be sanctified.

1. Because this is the glory that is due to his name. Ps. xcvi. 8, ' Give unto the Lord the glory due to his name.' Every glory will not serve the turn, but such glory as is proper and peculiar for that God we serve. It is a stated rule in scripture, that respects to God must be proportioned to the nature of God. God is a spirit, therefore will be worshipped in spirit and truth. God is a God of peace, therefore lift up your hands without wrath and doubting. God is a holy God, therefore will be sanctified. They which worship the sun, among the heathens, they used a flying horse, as a thing most suitable to the swift motions of 'the sun. Well, then, they that will glorify and honour God with a glory due to his name, must sanctify him as well as honour him. Why? For God is 'glorious in holiness,' Exod. xv. 11. This is that which God counteth to be his chief excellency, and the glory which he will manifest among the sons of men.

2. This is that glory which God affects, and therefore the saints will give it him, Isa. vi. 3. The holy angels, what do they cry out when they honour God? They do not acknowledge his power and dominion over all creatures as Lord of all; but they give him his peculiar glory, ' Holy, holy, holy is the Lord of hosts; the whole earth is full of his glory.' So David, Ps. ciii. 1, ' Bless the Lord, O my soul; yea, all that is within me, bless his holy name.' That is the notion upon which he pitcheth, he would praise God with such praise as is welcome and acceptable to him.

3. This is the attribute which is most eclipsed and most blotted out in the hearts of the sons of men, because of God's patience, because he doth not take vengeance of all the sins of men: ' Thou thoughtest I was altogether such a one as thyself,' Ps. l. 21. Certainly if men did not blot and stain God in their thoughts, if they did not fancy an unreasonable indulgence, such as is not comely and proper to his majesty, they could not go on in sin, and think God could be so pure; therefore he will be so glorified, that he may be sanctified.

Use. To press us so to glorify God, as we may also sanctify him. Let this be your care. To quicken you, remember—

1. God is much offended with his people that do not sanctify him.

Moses and Aaron, as choice and as dear to God as they were, yet you know what the Lord saith, Num. xx. 12, ' Because ye believed me not, to sanctify me in the eyes of the children of Israel ; therefore ye shall not bring this congregation into the land which I have given them.' When Moses and Aaron murmured, and spake unadvisedly, and did not sanctify him, nor carry God's excellency aloft, they shall not enter. And God remembereth this a great while after, in that, Deut. xxxii. 51, ' Because ye trespassed against me among the children of Israel, at the waters of Meribah-Kadesh, in the wilderness of Zin ; because ye sanctified me not in the midst of the children of Israel, thou shalt not go into the land which I give the children of Israel.' Well, then, though God's children should get to heaven, yet if they do not sanctify God they will want many a privilege. God will remember this against them ; for he takes it ill when his people will not sanctify him as becoming his peculiar excellency.

2. If you do not sanctify God, then you pollute God, and stain his memory in the world : Ezek. xxxvi. 20, ' Ye have profaned my holy name among the heathen.' How is God polluted ? Not intrinsically ; God cannot receive any pollution from us. It is here, as in that case, ' A man that lusteth after a woman, hath committed adultery already in his heart,' Mat. v. 28. The man pollutes the woman in his heart, while she remains spotless and undefiled. So in this case we blemish God in appearance, as much as in us lies we pollute and blot God, though he remains pure and undefiled. You make heathens think as if you had an unholy God. Well, then, glorify God.

For directions :—

1. Be holy. The praise of the wicked is a disgrace to him, it is an obscuring of his praise : 1 Pet. i. 15, ' As he which hath called you is holy, so be ye holy in all manner of conversation.'

2. Study his name, if ye would sanctify his name : Ps. ix. 10, ' They that know his name will put their trust in him.'

3. Submit to his providence without murmuring. When we can speak well of him, though he seem to deal most hardly ; as the Bethshemites, when there was such a slaughter made among them, fifty thousand slain ; they do not say, murmuringly, Who can stand before this severe, cruel God ? but before ' this holy God ?' They own his holiness in the dispensation, though it were so dreadful, 1 Sam. vi. 20. It is a great glory to God when you own him as just in all his ways, when he deals most hardly. Whatsoever be our lot and portion, yet he is a holy God. But to cavil and murmur, it is to tax and blemish God before the world.

4. Live to public ends, that is, to draw God into request with others. Let this be the aim of your conversation, not only to get holiness enough to bring you to heaven, but to allure others, and recommend God to them, that by the purity and strictness of your conversation you might gain upon others, and bring them to be in love with God, and acquainted with him.

And lastly, Be sensible when God's name is dishonoured by your-selves and others, not enduring the least profanation of it.

Thy kingdom come.

THE first petition concerneth the end, the rest the means. Now, among all the means, none hath such a near and immediate respect to the glory of God as Christ's kingdom ; for here there is more of God discovered, more of his infinite grace, justice, wisdom, and power than possibly can be elsewhere. All other things are for the church, and the church for Christ as head and king, and Christ for God, 1 Cor. iii. 22, 23. So that Christ's kingdom is the primary means of advancing God's glory ; and therefore among all the means it must be sought in the first place. Mat. vi. 33, ' Seek first the kingdom of God.' First, not above the glory of God, it doth not come in competition with that, but above all other things whatsoever, before pardon and grace.

In the words observe three things :—

I. We grant *a kingdom*.

II. By way of distinction and appropriation we say, *thy* kingdom.

III. By way of supplication, we beg of God that it may *come*.

The concession, the distinction, the supplication are the three things to be opened.

I. First, The concession of a kingdom, which our heavenly Father hath. A kingdom in the general signifieth the government of a people under one head or governor ; and therefore the term may be fitly applied to God, who alone is supreme, and we are all under his dominion.

Now, God's kingdom is twofold :—

1. Universal.

2. More particular and special.

First, There is a universal kingdom over all things ; over angels and devils ; over men elect and reprobate ; over beasts and living creatures ; and over inanimate things, sun, moon, and stars. This is spoken of : 1 Chron. xxix. 11, ' Thine is the kingdom, O Lord, and thou are exalted as head above all.' And again : Ps. ciii. 19, ' The Lord hath prepared his throne in the heavens ; and his kingdom ruleth over all.' There is no such monarch as God is, for largeness of empire, for absoluteness of power, and sublimity of his throne. This is not principally understood here, but is implied as a foundation and ground of faith, whereupon we may deal with God about that kingdom, which is specially intended in this request.

Secondly, More particularly and especially, God hath a kingdom over a certain order and estate of men. Of this especial kingdom there are two notable branches and considerations. One is that administration which belongeth to the present life, and is called ' the kingdom of grace ; ' and the other belongeth to the life to come, and is called ' the kingdom of glory.'

1. The kingdom of grace is spoken of in many places, specially that : Luke xvii. 20, 21, ' When he was demanded of the Pharisees when the kingdom of God should come, he answered them and said, The kingdom of God cometh not with observation. Neither shall they say, Lo here ! or, lo there ! for, behold, the kingdom of God is within you,' or ' among you.' He speaks of a kingdom of God that

was already come among them in the dispensation of his grace by Christ. And, then, the other belongeth to the life to come, called the kingdom of glory: Mat. xxv. 34, ' Come, ye blessed of my Father, inherit the kingdom prepared for you from the foundation of the world;' 1 Cor. xv. 50, ' Flesh and blood cannot inherit the kingdom of God.'

Now, the kingdom of grace may be considered two ways,—as externally administered, and as internally received.

[1.] As externally administered in the ordinances and means of grace, as the word and seals, and censures, and the like. In this sense it is said: Mat. xxi. 43, ' The kingdom of God shall be taken from you, and given to a nation bringing forth the fruits thereof.' The gospel or means of grace administered in the visible face of the church, they are called God's kingdom upon earth, and a very great privilege they are when they are bestowed upon any people. Surely, when Christ saith, ' The kingdom of God shall be taken from you,' he doth not mean it of the inward kingdom,—that they had not, that cannot be lost,—but of the outward and external means.

[2.] As internally received; and then by it is meant the grace of God, which rules in the hearts of the elect, and causeth their souls to submit and subject themselves unto the obedience of Christ, and unto his sceptre, and to his word and Spirit, that this is that kingdom properly which is within us. This is ' the kingdom of God which consisteth in righteousness, peace, and joy in the Holy Ghost,' Rom. xiv. 17. And this differeth from the kingdom of glory, not so much in nature as in degree.

Well, then, that by the kingdom of God is here meant, not his general empire over all the world, and all the things of the world, though that be not wholly excluded, but his special kingdom, which he doth administer by Christ: and that either as externally managed by ordinances and visible means of grace, or as internally received and administered in the hearts of the elect. This is that kingdom we beg that it may flourish and get ground more and more.

2. Then for the kingdom of glory, it is either begun and inchoate, or else consummate and perfect.

[1.] It is begun and inchoate upon our translation to heaven in the very moment of death, in which Christ reigns in the other world in the spirits of just men made perfect—that is, being perfectly freed from sin, and admitted into the clear and immediate vision and fruition of God, though our bodies abide in the grave, expecting full redemption and deliverance. That there is such a kingdom carried on many scriptures intimate: Phil. i. 23, ' I desire to depart, and to be with Christ.' As soon as the saints are loosed from the body, they are with Christ under his government: Luke xxiii. 43. ' This day shalt thou be with me in paradise.' As soon as Christ died he was in paradise, and there was the good thief with him. The scriptures do not establish any such drowsy conceit as the sleep of souls, or such an estate wherein they do not enjoy God. We read of ' the spirits of just men made perfect,' which make up the congregation which is above, of which Christ is head: Heb. xii. 23. As the spirits of the wicked are in prison, 1 Pet. iii. 19, that is, in hell. This is the kingdom of glory begun.

[2.] There is a kingdom of glory consummate, when sin and death is utterly abolished, and the elect perfectly separated from the reprobate, and conducted into heaven, and there remain with the Lord for ever. This is a kingdom : Mat. xxv. 34, ' Come, ye blessed of my Father, inherit the kingdom prepared for you.' The full and final estate we enjoy after the general judgment and resurrection, that is called a kingdom. Well, now, you see what is meant by the kingdom we pray for.

II. Secondly, Here is a note of distinction, *thy kingdom*, by which the kingdom here spoken of is limited by particular reference to God, not only to difference it from the kingdoms of men, which are subordinate to it, but those adverse kingdoms which are set up against God ; as the kingdom of sin, Satan, antichrist, the destruction of which we intend when we pray for the advancement of God's kingdom, as I shall show you.

III. Thirdly, Here is the supplication or the request which we make to God about this kingdom, ἐλθέτω, let it *come*. What do we mean by that ? This word must be applied to the several acceptations of Christ's kingdom.

1. If you apply it to the external kingdom of grace, then when we say, Thy kingdom come, the meaning is, let the gospel be published, let churches be set up everywhere, let them be continued and maintained against all the malignity of the world, and opposition of the devil : and in the publication of the gospel, where the sound of it hath not been heard, that God would come there in the power of his Spirit, and draw people into communion with himself : Mat. xii. 28, ' If I cast out devils by the Spirit of God, then the kingdom of God is come unto you,'—meaning in the public tenders thereof. Saith he, if this miracle doth clearly, as it doth in your consciences, evidence my mission, then you may know the kingdom of God is come—that is, that there is a publication of the gospel of grace. Then we pray for the continuance of this privilege, notwithstanding opposition, that Christ may stand his ground. This is that we seek of God, that he may maintain his interest among the nations of the world, that the gates of hell may not prevail against his kingdom.

2. If you refer to the internal part of this kingdom, then we beg the beginning, the progress, and the final consummation of it. First, The beginning or the erection of a throne for Christ in our hearts, and the hearts of others, that he may fully exercise regal power. Secondly, The increase of this kingdom by holiness and obedience, and sincere subjection to him ; for the kingdom of grace is so come already, that it will still be coming yet more and more. So long as we need to pray, so long shall we have cause to say, ' Thy kingdom come.' Thirdly, The consummation of it, when the fulness of glory in the second coming of Christ shall be revealed ; when our head shall be glorious, and his day shall come, ἡμέρα κυρίου. For the present it is man's day, so the scripture seems to call it ; but then it is the day of the Lord, when all the devils shall stoop, and enemies receive their final doom, and the saints shall have the crown of glory put upon their heads in the sight of all the world.

Well, the sum of all is this, that though this petition do mainly concern the special kingdom, which God administereth by Christ, yet God's universal kingdom, the kingdom of his power and providence, is a mighty support and prop to our faith in making this request to God. When we consider what an unlimited power God hath over all creatures, even devils themselves, to dispose of them for his own glory, and his church's good ; we need not be discouraged though Christ's kingdom be opposed in the world, but should with the more confidence deal with God about it.

That which I shall handle upon this petition will fall under these two points :—

1. That God hath a kingdom, which he will administer and manage for his own glory.

2. All those which are well affected to God's glory should desire the coming of this kingdom, and seriously deal with God about it.

For the first, namely—

Doct. 1. That God hath a kingdom, which he will administer and manage for his own glory.

I speak not of the kingdom of his power and providence, but of the dispensation of grace by Christ. The evangelical gospel state is compared to a kingdom ; as, Mat. iii. 2, ' The kingdom of heaven is at hand.' So to the disciples, Mat. x. 7, ' And as ye go, preach, saying, The kingdom of heaven is at hand.' And so Christ himself.

It may be called so with very good reason, for in this kingdom there is a monarch, Jesus Christ, to whom all power and authority is given. God the Father calls him 'my king:' Ps. ii. 6, ' I have set my king upon my holy hill.' And this king hath his throne in the consciences of men, where thoughts are brought into captivity to him : 2 Cor. x. 5. And he hath his royal sceptre, Ps. cx. 3, which is called ' the rod of his strength.' And he hath his subjects, and they are the saints: Rev. xv. 3, ' king of saints.' And he hath his laws and constitutions ; we read of ' the law of faith,' and ' the law of liberty.' And in this kingdom there are privileges, and royal immunities ; there is freedom from the curse of the law, and from the power of sin, and from the destructive influence of Satan and the world. And here are punishments and rewards both for body and soul; there is hell and heaven. Now, because all these things do so fitly suit, therefore is the gospel called a kingdom. It will not be amiss to insist upon some of these.

1. The state of the gospel, or evangelical state, it is God's kingdom, in regard of the monarch whom God hath set up, that is, Jesus Christ, the great Lord of all things. There is no king like him: God hath made him ' higher than the kings of the earth,' Ps. lxxxix. 27. How doth he exceed all other monarchs and potentates in the world ? Partly for largeness of command and territory. All kings and monarchs have certain bounds and limits by which their empire is terminated ; but Christ is the true catholic king, his government runs throughout the whole circuit of nature and providence; he hath power over all flesh, John xvii. 2, yea, devils themselves are to stoop to him : Phil. ii. 10, every thing under the earth is to bow the knee to Christ. Partly for the excellency of his throne. This king hath a double throne, one in heaven, the other in the heart of a humble

sinner, which is his second heaven: Isa. lvii. 15. And in both these
respects there is no monarch like Christ. ' He hath prepared his
throne in the heavens, and his kindom ruleth over all,' Ps. ciii. 19.
Earthly kings, that their majesty may appear to their subjects, have
their thrones usually exalted; there were six steps to Solomon's
throne ; a description of it you have in 1 Kings x. 18, 19. But what is
this to the throne of Christ, which God hath fixed above in the
heavens? The whole globe of sea and earth is but as one point, and
there are ten thousand times ten thousands of angels about his throne.
The supporters of this throne are justice and mercy. And in regard
of his other throne also in the hearts of men : the power of outward
potentates reacheth but to the bodies of men, they can take cogni-
sance of nothing but of external conformity to their laws : but
Christ gives laws to the thoughts : 2 Cor. x. 5. So for his royal
furniture : other princes, they have their chariots, and coaches, and
horses, &c. ; but ' he makes the clouds his chariot, and walketh
upon the wings of the wind,' Ps. civ. 3. Riding up and down in
the world, dispensing mercies and judgments. So for troops and
armies to support his dignity, all the hosts of heaven are obedient
to him ; one angel in one night destroyed in Sennacherib's army an
hundred fourscore and five thousand. Hostility against him must
needs be deadly. He is above in heaven, and can rain down fire and
brimstone upon us, and cannot be resisted. He is higher than the
kings of the earth too, because none hath so good a right and title
to rule as this king hath, whom God hath set upon his holy hill of
Sion. God's dominion over the creatures is founded in creation.
Other kings *find* their subjects; he *makes* them. He hath the first
and chief right, there is nothing we have but he made. We depend
upon him every moment for his providential assistance, therefore he
hath the highest right and title. No creature can be *sui juris*, at his
own dispose. And he hath a right by conquest and by purchase; he
hath bought us, and ' given his life a ransom for many,' Mat. xx. 28.
Christ is opposed there to worldly potentates; they must be served,
but he came to minister. Subjects, their blood and lives must go to
preserve the rights of the prince ; but he gave his life. And he hath a
right too by contract and covenant. All that are subjects of his
kingdom have sworn allegiance. He hath such an absolute right that
thou canst call nothing thy own. We think, indeed, our lips are our
own, Ps. xii. 4 : and our estates our own ; as Nabal, 1 Sam. xxv.
11, ' Shall I take my bread, and my water, and my flesh?' &c. All
you have it belongeth to this king by right of creation and providence. Therefore in all these respects he is higher than the kings of
the earth.

2. The gospel state is set forth as a kingdom, in regard of the
subjects and their privileges. The gospel doth not only reveal a king,
but maketh all kings : ' He hath made us to be kings and priests,' &c.,
Rev. i. 5. All those that submit to him. So that, indeed, Christ
may properly be styled *Rex regum*, King of kings. As the king of
Assyria made his boast, Isa. x. 8, ' Are not my princes altogether
kings ?' A vaunting speech of his, that his princes and favourites
were, for power and authority, as good as kings. But Christ may

say so. Are not my subjects altogether kings? Not only kings in
regard of their spiritual power and command they have over themselves, ruling their own spirits in the fear of God, while others are
slaves to their base affections; but in point of their privileges. They
have kingly privileges, they are made kings; they are royally
attended by angels, they are sent forth to be as guardians to the
heirs of promise: Heb. i. 14. They have royal immunities, from
the curse of the law, from the damnable influence of sin; they may
as well pluck Christ from the throne, as pluck the elect out of that
state wherein they are. As David said, 'Is it a small thing to be the
king's son-in-law?' so, is it a small thing to be the sons of God,
co-heirs with Christ? This honour and glory doth God put upon his
saints. And there is the greatest pleasure and contentment in this
state; for this kingdom, which all the saints are interested in, it
consisteth in 'righteousness, peace, and joy in the Holy Ghost:'
Rom. xiv. 17. And surely these consolations of God should not be
small to us. It is a state of most absolute freedom and sovereignty:
John viii. 36, 'If the Son shall make you free, then shall ye be free
indeed.' Many a monarch which ruleth over men may be a captive to
his own lusts; but these are free. There are the richest revenues
and increase which belong to Christ's subjects. 'All things are yours;
whether Paul, or Apollos,' &c.: 1 Cor. iii. 21. They are ours by covenant, and when they come into our possession, by the fair allowance
of God's providence, we have them with a blessing, and may use them
with a great deal of comfort.

3. In regard of the laws and manner of administration. I shall
not speak of the external political government of the church, which
questionless is monarchical, I mean in regard of Christ the Head;
though it be aristocratical in regard of officers, and, in some respect,
democratical, with reference to the consent of the people in all church
acts. But there are laws and sanctions by which this body of men
and this kingdom is governed: James ii. 8, 'If ye fulfil the royal
law.' It is called the royal law, not only as it requires noble work,
but in regard of the dignity of the author, and firmness of the obligation. All the precepts of faith, repentance, and gospel-walking, are
as so many royal edicts, which Christ hath set forth to signify his
pleasure to his people. How slightly soever we think of these gospel
injunctions, they are the laws and instructions of the great king.

4. In regard of punishments and rewards. Christ, who is a king
by nature, might rule us with a rod of iron; yet he is pleased to
govern us as a father and prince, that he might cast the bands of a
man upon us. Christ, as a king, punisheth, and, as a king, rewardeth:
Prov. xvi. 14, 'The wrath of a king is as messengers of death.'
When a king is angry it is as if a messenger should come and tell us
we must die. How great is the wrath of the king of kings! He
cannot endure to be slighted in his regal power: Luke xix. 27, 'But
those mine enemies, which would not that I should reign over them,
bring them hither, and slay them before me.' Christ himself will see
execution done, in his own sight and presence, upon those rebels that
will not submit to his rule and government. How should the hearts
of wicked men tremble, which have violated the laws of Christ, and

affronted his authority, when they consider how odious this is, how certainly Christ will see execution done upon them ! When Adonijah and his guests heard of Solomon sitting upon his throne, and the shouts and acclamations of joy and applause, they were stricken with fear, and fled every one several ways : 1 Kings i. 49. You that cherish your lusts, which stand out against the sovereignty of Christ, that will not let him rule over you, whose hearts say (though their tongues dare not), ' We will not have this man to reign over us ;' you that seem to put him by his kingdom, he is furnished with absolute and irresistible power to destroy you, and will one day come and say, Bring forth these drunkards, worldlings, voluptuous, that would not I should reign over them ; those that durst venture upon known sin against the checks of their own conscience : how will their hearts tremble in the last day at the shouts and acclamations of the saints, when they shall welcome this great king, when he shall come forth in all his royalty and sovereignty ! And as for punishment Christ will show himself as a king, so for rewards. Kings do not give trifles. Araunah ' gave like a king to a king :' 2 Sam. xxiv. 23. He was of the blood-royal of the Jebusites, and he gave worthy of his extraction. And so Christ will give like a king. God propounds nothing that was cheap and unworthy, but he ' gives you a kingdom :' Luke xii. 32. The poor of this world are ' heirs of a kingdom,' the fairest kingdom that ever was, or ever will be ; as poor and as despicable as now they are, yet they shall have a kingdom. What can you wish for and desire more than a kingdom ? All shall reign with Christ for evermore ; which shows the folly of carnal men that will hazard so great and so blessed hopes. Thus I have shown you why the gospel state is compared to a kingdom.

Now, let me tell you it is a spiritual kingdom, not such as comes with observation. Jesus Christ, when he was inaugurated into the throne, when he was to sit down at God's right hand, how doth he manifest it ? He gives gifts, as princes use to do at their coronation, but they are spiritual gifts : Eph. iv. 8. And he sent abroad ambassadors, poor fishermen, they and their successors, to go and treat with the world : 2 Cor. v. 19. Indeed, they had a mighty power with them, as becoming such a great king, as was under the vail of meanness and weakness ; it was carried on in a spiritual manner. And still he doth administer his kingdom, not by force ; he rules not by the power of the sword, but by his word and Spirit, so he governeth his people. The publication of the gospel is a ' sending forth the rod of his strength :' Ps. cx. 2. And the Holy Ghost, as Christ's viceroy, he governeth them, and administereth all things that are necessary to his kingdom ; he doth it by the Holy Ghost, as his deputy. The Father chooseth a sort of men, gives them to Christ ; the Son dieth for them, that they may be subjects of his kingdom, and he commits them to be governed and ruled by the Holy Ghost : he useth the ministry of men, and so unites them to Christ ; and Christ brings them to the Father by his intercession, committing them to his care and love ; and by a final tradition at last, which is the last act of Christ's mediatorial kingdom, 1 Cor. xv. 24, he shall deliver them up to the Father. The Spirit, blessing the ministry of men, works faith, by which we are united to Christ; and Christ intercedes for us, and will bring us to God again. And in this spiritual manner is this kingdom carried on. So that if we would enter into this kingdom, we must go to God the Father, and confess we are rebels and traitors, but desire he would not enter into judgment with us, but seek to be reconciled to God the Father. Now, as God bade the friends of Job to go to Job, chap. xlii. 8, so God sends us to Christ, in whom alone he is well pleased with the creature. If we go to the Son, he refers us to the Spirit, to be reclaimed from our impurity and rebellion. If we go to the Spirit, he refers us to Moses and the prophets, pastors and teachers; there we shall hear of him in Christ's way, and there we feel the rod of Christ's strength, the efficacy of his grace put into our hearts.

Thus are we brought into his kingdom, and made to be a mystical body and spiritual society, in whom Christ rules; and there we come to enjoy those freedoms I spake of; and our obedience to this kingdom is carried on in a spiritual manner. In worship, we give our homage to God; in the word, we come to learn his laws; in the sacraments, we renew our oath of allegiance to this king; in alms and charity, we pay him tribute; in prayer, we ask his leave, acknowledging his dominion; and praise, it is our rent to the great Lord, from whom we hold all things. And thus is Christ's kingdom carried on in a spiritual manner.

Use 1. The use is to press you to come under this kingdom. Consider what God hath proffered to draw you off from your carnal delights and sinful pleasures: no less than a kingdom to bear you out, to call you off from your sins. Oh, do not answer, as the olive-tree and the vine in Jotham's parable: Judges ix. 9, 'Shall I leave my fatness, and go to be promoted over the trees?' God comes to a worldling, and makes him a proffer of this blessed state, which is represented by a kingdom. Shall I leave all my sports and worldly hopes? (according as the man is affected). Shall I renounce my pleasures, live a strict and austere life? Must I leave off projects, saith a worldling, and depend upon the reversion of heaven? Oh, consider it is for a glorious kingdom. Men will do much for an earthly crown, though lined with cares,—for this golden ball, which all hunt after, and doth occasion so many stirs in the world. Turn your ambition this way. You may aspire to a crown, to the kingdom of heaven, without the crime of treason. This is a faithful ambition: it is indeed treason against the kingdom of heaven, not to look after this crown, and plot, contrive, and act, and offer violence for the obtaining of it. And, therefore, come under this kingdom; if you do not, you will be left under the power of a worse: 2 Chron. xii. 8, God saith, he would give them up to the king of Egypt; why? 'They shall be his servants, that they may know my service, and the service of the kingdoms of the countries:' that they might see what difference there is between serving God and serving others. If you refuse God's government, you are under a worse, under sin, and the power of darkness; you are under your own lusts; nay, and by a just judgment God may give you over to live in bondage to unmerciful men. How many kings and lords doth he serve that will not serve one Lord?

Oh, therefore, renounce those other lords that have dominion over you, and come under this kingdom which God hath set up.

Use 2. To press the children of God:—

1. To walk worthy of the gospel: it is a kingdom. The apostle hath an exhortation and charge to this purpose: 1 Thes. ii. 11, 12, 'That ye would walk worthy of God, who hath called you unto his kingdom and glory.' Walk in obedience to Christ, that is one thing. Christ is a king by a natural right; God hath chosen him, God hath set him upon his holy hill: 'The Lord hath made him to be head over all things,' Eph. i. 22. Nay, the church chooseth Christ: 'They shall appoint to themselves one head,' Hosea i. 11. And, therefore, for you that are called to his kingdom and glory, that have entered into covenant with Christ, that have subscribed to him as head and king; for you to be disobedient, give way to sin, it is worse in you. 'Will ye go away also?' saith Christ to his disciples. Christ hath a right to reign over wicked men; but you have actually chosen him. Treason is less culpable in those which have not submitted to a power and prince, and owned him for their king, than in those that have sworn faith and allegiance. You have passed under the bond of the holy oath; 'God hath called you to his kingdom and glory;' therefore you should be more obedient than to allow a disloyal thought or rebellious lust against Christ.

2. As you should be more holy, wary, watchful, that you do not break the laws of Christ, for you have consented to him; so live as kings, exercising all acts of regality within your own souls, ruling your own spirits, exercising judgment over your own hearts, and over every affection that will not be bridled. It is a disgrace to the regal estate of the gospel for you to be over-mastered by a lust, to lie under the power of any sin; yet thus it is, God's children are conflicting with one sin or other more than the rest. So far you have not experience of that truth: John viii. 32, 'And ye shall know the truth, and the truth shall make you free.' A man that liveth in bondage to his lusts, how can he choose but doubt of those glorious privileges? Have you found the state of the gospel to be a kingdom? do you walk worthy of the gospel?

3. It teacheth us contempt of the world and earthly things: Phil. iii. 14, 'I press toward the mark, for the prize of the high calling of God in Jesus Christ.' It is not for princes to embrace a dunghill, nor for eagles to catch flies. Remember, thou wilt one day be a king with God in glory, and therefore shouldst not be as low and base as the men of the world are, but walk worthy of God, who hath called you to a royal state.

4. A generous confidence in the midst of the troubles and abasements of the world. What though you be accounted as the scurf and offscouring of all things? Though your outward condition be low and mean, know the worth of your high calling in Christ. How poor and despicable soever you are in this world, yet you are heirs of a crown and kingdom. Therefore remember you are princes, that walk up and down in disguise in a foreign country. If you are kept in a mean condition, it is but a disguise God hath put upon you. We are the sons of God, though for the present it doth not appear what we shall

be. God's heirs make little show in the world. But there is a high
dignity, a mighty privilege put upon you ; you are called to be heirs
of this kingdom, and this blessed and royal estate, which God hath
provided for them that love him.

Use 3. Are we translated into this kingdom ? Col. i. 13, ' He hath
delivered us out of the power of darkness, and translated us into the
kingdom of his dear Son.' Every man naturally is under other lords,
the devil hath dominion over him, and he is under the government
of his own lusts; but now are we translated into the kingdom of
Christ.

The second point is :—

Doct. 2. All those that are affected with God's glory should desire
the coming of this kingdom, and seriously deal with God about it.

None else can rescue and pluck them out of the power of darkness,
and deliver them from the thraldom of those other lords that hold
them, and none else can defend and preserve them.

I shall handle the point :—

1. In a private respect.
2. In a public respect.

First, In a private respect. Every man should desire that the
kingdom of God should come down and be set up in his own heart.
Here I must repeat and apply the distinctions of Christ's kingdom.
He is to desire the kingdom of grace and the kingdom of glory may
come to himself and others.

1. The kingdom of grace, that it may be begun, continued, and
increased.

First, That this kingdom may be begun, and a throne erected for
Christ in our hearts. The great necessity of this request will be
evidenced in these considerations :—

[1.] That every man by nature is under another king, under the
kingdom of sin and Satan. Satan is the monarch, and sin is the
sceptre. Christ and the devil divide the world; either we belong to
the one or the other. Now the devil, by reason of the fall of Adam,
he hath the start of Christ, and the Lord Jesus coming to possess the
heart, doth not seize upon it as a waste which belongeth to the next
occupier, but he seizeth upon it as already possessed by Satan. The
devil quietly ruleth in the hearts of the unregenerate ; he keeps house,
and all the goods are in peace, Luke xi. 21; and therefore wicked
spirits are called, ' The rulers of the darkness of this world,' Eph. vi.
12. All the ignorant and carnal part of the world falls to his share,
and he doth not easily quit possession. Christ indeed employeth men
to wrestle with principalities and powers. The work of the ministry
is to shake and batter the empire of the devil. You must be turned,
you must be rescued. You must be turned: Acts xxvi. 18, ' To turn
them from the power of Satan unto God.' You must be rescued and
plucked out of this captivity by the strong hand: Col. i. 13, ' Who hath
delivered us from the power of Satan ;' who hath taken us out of
darkness by a powerful rescue. Even as the Israelites were brought
out of Egypt ' by a strong hand and stretched-out arm,' so are we
brought out of the power of darkness. By such an irresistible power
of grace must God recover you, otherwise men yield themselves up

to his sceptre. Look, as the Spirit of God works holy motions and
gracious desires in the hearts of God's children, so the devil is ' at work
in the children of disobedience,' Eph. ii. 2, framing wicked devices,
carnal desires, evil thoughts against God. Man is such a perfect slave
to the devil that he can do nothing but sin.

[2.] This kingdom which Satan exerciseth is an invisible kingdom.
The devil doth not sensibly appear to his vassals and slaves. When
Christ's kingdom and regiment was more external, so was the devil's
also. As when God was served by sacrifices, and delivered his mind
by oracles, so men did then more professedly own the devil by observing his prescribed rites of worship, and by being deluded by lying
oracles, and answers to their prayers and questions. But now, since
the kingdom of Christ is more spiritual, and managed by the Holy
Ghost in the hearts of his saints, so is Satan's kingdom invisible. So
that men may be Christ's subjects by external profession, and the
devil's by internal obedience and constitution of mind, though they
worship not by pagan rites, as he ruleth in their hearts, and takes
them off from obeying the gospel they profess. ' The god of this world
hath blinded their eyes:' 2 Cor. iv. 4. All carnal men, however they
defy Satan, and abominate the thought of serving him, yet while they
remain in their sin and ignorance, they still hold the crown upon
the devil's head. Look, as God's subjects may own him in verbal
pretence, yet their hearts may be far from him : Mat. xv. 8. So that
wicked men may defy the devil in pretence and words, and cannot
endure to hear of him ; but they are under the god of this world, he
hath blinded their hearts. So that this kingdom is to be fought for
in the heart. Christ made a great inroad upon the devil, beat him
out of his quarters ; yet, as the sea gets in one place what it loseth in
another, so though the devil hath lost ground in the Christian world
as to external profession, whilst people renounce the superstitions of
the Gentiles, yet still he gets ground in the hearts of wicked men by
their carnal dispositions ; his empire is upheld still, though professedly
they are subjects of Christ.

[3.] Until Satan be cast out of the throne, Christ can have no
entertainment in the heart. The ark and Dagon cannot sink and
stand together ; either the ark must be removed, or Dagon will down
upon his face : so 2 Cor. vi. 14, ' What communion hath Christ with
Belial, and light with darkness ?' It is impossible both kingdoms can
stand together, or both kings be set up in the same heart. The
marriage-bed will admit no partner nor rival. A man must be under
Christ or Satan. Until he be cast out, Christ hath no room to be
entertained : Mat. vi. 24, ' No man can serve two masters ; ye cannot
serve God and Mammon.' Look upon the devil under that notion,
as he is Mammon, as he doth entice to worldliness : it is impossible to
serve him and Christ. Both masters have work enough for their
servants, and their commands are contrary. If two masters consent
to employ one man in the self-same business, though they are two men,
yet they are but one master. But now to execute the wills of men
which differ in their design, and which have a several and full interest
in our labours and actions, it is as impossible as to move two contrary
ways at once. Well, then, Mammon and Christ, Belial and Christ,

divide the world. It is impossible to be under Belial and Christ; both have full work for us to do, and their designs are contrary. So that either it must appear we have changed masters, or we are under the power of the devil still. We must come out of the power of darkness, else we cannot be brought into the kingdom of the Lord Jesus, that we may obtain remission of sins.

[4.] Satan may be cast out in part, and yet still retain a supreme interest in the heart. I prove it out of that parable, Mat. xii. 43–45: 'When the unclean spirit is gone out of a man, he walketh through dry places, seeking rest, but findeth none. Then he saith, I will return into my house, from whence I came out,' &c. Out of that parable we may plainly conclude there may be a shaking of Satan's empire, Satan may be cast out of a man in some sort, yet the man not plainly renewed. Well, how may he be cast out, and yet his empire remain unbroken? He may be cast out partly by conviction and illumination; yet as long as any lust remaineth there unmortified and unsubdued, he still keeps his sovereignty in the heart. Many begin to be troubled, and to be thoughtful about eternity, that see better, yet they do that which is worse in the issue. When there is a conflict between corruption and conviction, corruption carrieth it away. As iron often heated and often quenched is so much the harder; so, when they had some wamblings of conscience, and the heart begins to boggle, and after this sin breaks out the more. This is the scope of that place: they were convinced of a better estate, and had some thoughts of the Messiah, but did not give him entertainment. Again, the devil may be cast out in regard of some external reformation. A man may a little wash his polluted life and abstain from gross sins, yet Satan have full possession of the inner man. A man may abjure his former ill life, and for a while carry it fair, but afterwards retain his former filthiness, and keep a secret league with his lusts, and so he is entangled again, and then 'his latter end is worse than his beginning;' and as it is in 2 Pet. ii. 22, 'The dog is turned to his own vomit again, and the sow that was washed to her wallowing in the mire.' A prisoner which hath made some escape, if ever the gaoler get him into his clutches, is sure to be laden with irons; so one that hath had some partial reformation, oh, when the devil gets such a man into his power again, he is ten times worse than he was before.

[5.] The difficulty of casting off the sovereignty of Satan, lieth partly in ourselves and partly in the devil.

Partly in ourselves. As in the Israelites going out of Egypt, the difficulty lay, not only in gaining the consent of Pharaoh, for he pursues after them when they were gone, but also in persuading the people to give their consent—it was long ere Israel desired to be gone—so in our natural condition, the mind of man is so depraved that he thinks his bondage to be his freedom, and that there is no such merry life as to wallow in carnal satisfactions; and our affections are so far engaged to this sinful estate, that we dote upon our shackles, and are unwilling to hear of a change. The first step of coming out of this kingdom of darkness is when we find it to be a heavy burthen, and grow weary of the devil's government, though it be but out of a principle of self-love, Isa. xxvi. 13: 'O Lord, other lords besides thee have had dominion over us; but by thee only will we make mention of thy name.' Yea, but as soon as we begin to have any serious thoughts of that miserable state in which we are, Satan interposeth, dealing with us as Pharaoh did with the Israelites. The Israelites complain their bondage was very sore; what doth Pharaoh? He doubles the burthen: Exod. v. 17, ' You are idle,' &c. ;—so that out of bondage of soul they would not hearken to Moses. Just so Satan deals with us. When souls begin to be serious, and to leave off fleshly and worldly lusts, and to give up themselves to God that they may be directed in the way of holiness and obtain eternal life, then he doubles our burthens. Corruptions are never more stirring than after some conviction: Rom. vii. 9, ' When the commandment came, sin revived, and I died ;' not only as to a deeper sense of the guilt of it, but as to its struggling for life. The bullock at the first yoking is most unruly; so we which are unaccustomed to the yoke, when we begin once to take it upon us, there is a mighty backwardness. Fire at first kindling makes abundance of smoke; so when conviction is stirring, corruption is more exasperated. The devil is very jealous of the first beam of light which breaks into the heart, and of every ordinance which conveys it; therefore sets corruptions at work, that it may appear to be a vain hope of ever escaping his clutches: so men are tired and give over, and think it is to no purpose. But if light increases to more trouble, the devil seeks to elude the importunity of it by delay; as Pharaoh put off Moses and Aaron still by delay: or else by compromising and compounding the business; as Pharaoh, when he saw the people would go, God would have them go, then they shall not go far : Exod. viii. 28. So if men will be thinking of Christ's service, and coming under his government, they shall go, but not far; they shall come and pray, and come and hear now and then, and make a general profession, but not too far in Christ's quarters; he is afraid of that. Just as Pharaoh stood hucking still; they must go a good way into the wilderness, otherwise it should be an abomination to the Egyptians, yet their little ones must stay. If people will not only hear and pray, but begin to reform and cleanse their lives, yet he must have a pledge, some lust, as a nest-egg, left in the heart, some darling sin that must keep up the devil's empire. Then they must leave their herds, then leave their flocks; no, not a hoof. Ah! how long is it, when we are under this power of darkness, ere we are free, and get rid of the government of Satan!

[6.] We can never be sure that Satan is wholly cast out until Christ be seriously received and entertained as Lord and King, until he dwell and rule in the heart by faith. Alas! there may be some brabble now and then between us and our sins, and some partial dislikes; but until you heartily consent to take another king, that you will be governed and ordered by, you are not his subjects, but remain in the same state: John i. 12, ' As many as received him, to them gave he power to become the sons of God, even to them that believe on his name.' We are children of the devil before, under his standard and government; but when we receive him, then we are under another king, another power: when we receive what God offered, receive Christ as Lord and King, when the whole soul opens the door to Christ, that the King of glory may come in, and dwell with us, and reign over us, then is his kingdom set up. The first offer of the gospel is Christ as Prince and Saviour: Acts v. 31. And the main thing the business sticks at is Christ's regal power: Luke xix. 14, ' We will not have this man to reign over us.' Now, when we receive him with all our hearts, and though before we had but mean thoughts of him, now he begins to be welcome to us, and with the dearest embraces of our souls we entertain him; and with a willing resignation we give up ourselves, not only by a consent of dependence, to rest upon him for reconciliation with God, but by a willing subjection to obey him, and give up the keys of the heart, and lay them at Christ's feet: as Paul, Acts ix. 16, 'Lord, what wilt thou have me to do?' When you desire nothing more but that his kingdom might come, the King of glory himself, than that he might bring righteousness, peace, and joy in the Holy Ghost; until then you are not entered into his kingdom.

[7.] Christ is not received and entertained as Lord and King, but where his laws are obeyed: Col. ii. 6, ' As ye have therefore received Christ Jesus the Lord, so walk ye in him.' If you receive him as Lord and King, so also obey him. And Heb. xii. 28, ' We receiving a kingdom which cannot be moved, let us have grace whereby we may serve God acceptably, with reverence and godly fear.' In this prayer, first, we say, ' Thy kingdom come,' and then presently we add, ' Thy will be done.' We do but prattle over the Lord's Prayer, and say it with our lips only, until we are resolved to do what God would have us to do—love and hate, fear and rejoice, as God directs. Until we are brought to this frame, we do not in good earnest say, ' Thy kingdom come.' An earthly king will ' do according to his will :' Dan. xi. 3. So Christ stands upon his will in his law. If you have taken God for your God, and Jesus Christ for your King, then say, with David, Ps. cxliii. 10, ' Teach me to do thy will, for thou art my God.' It is a universal maxim, ' His servants you are whom you do obey.' Where is your obedience? If subjects of grace, ' Every thought is brought in subjection :' 2 Cor. x. 5. You will watch not only against your irregular actions, but every thought which lifts up itself against the obedience of Christ. There will be a greater tenderness upon us not to break any of the holy laws which belong to Christ's government. Hereby you may know whether you come under another king, Do you fear a commandment? That is the description of a good man : Prov. xiii. 13. It is not he that feareth a punishment, but he that feareth a commandment, when the heart is brought under an awe of Christ's laws; so that when a man is tempted to sin, Oh, I dare not; the Lord hath commanded me the contrary. This is more than if a flaming sword stood in his way. When we have such workings of heart when we are tempted to this and that sin, so when we are doing any duty, though irksome to flesh and blood, yet it is the will of my Lord, to whom I have entirely given up myself in a way of subjection; this is a sign you are brought under his government.

[8.] None can obey his laws but by the virtue and power of his Spirit. The new covenant, it is not only a law, but ' the law of the Spirit of life which is in Christ.' So it is called by the apostle, Rom. viii. 2. It is not a bare literal command that shall urge us to duty;

but it giveth strength and efficacy to the heart. Other kings, they give laws, that men may keep them by their own strength; but now Christ, he would be owned as a king, not only in a way of subjection, but establish a constant dependence. He is a king, not only to *require*, but to *give* repentance, Acts v. 31; not only to make a law, but to write and work a sense of this new covenant-gift upon the heart, Heb. viii. 10. He doth not only set up his ordinances, laws, constitutions, but there is power goeth along with the dispensation of this kingdom, and thereby we are fitted and enabled to love, serve, and please God; and then are we under the kingdom of God, when we are under the spiritual power of it. It is not only necessary to obey his laws, but that we do it by virtue of his power and Spirit: ' The kingdom of God stands not in word, but in power,' 1 Cor. iv. 20. That we may both acknowledge his authority and wait for his strength. This is a true submission, when we look for all from him, and serve him in the strength of his own grace.

[9.] All those that act through the virtue and power of his Spirit, they do unfeignedly seek his glory, and make Christ to be not only their principle, but their end; for having a new principle, they have a new tendency; acting in the power of the Spirit, their hearts are carried out to seek Christ's interest and Christ's glory. When they can say with the apostle, Phil. i. 21, ' To me to live is Christ,' when their whole business is to set up Christ. We set up ourselves in the room of Christ, if he be not at the end of all: 2 Thes. i. 11, 12, ' That God might fulfil all the good pleasure of his goodness, and the work of faith with power, and that Christ may be glorified in you.' If you have the power of Christ's kingdom, this will be the immediate result and issue of it, that Christ may be honoured and set up, not only as a lawgiver and fountain of grace, but as the last end. If to us to live is Christ, then is the kingdom of God come into our heart. For this we pray, that the Lord would so break the yoke and government of Satan, that we may receive the Lord Jesus into our heart, that we may come under the awe of his laws, and in the power of his grace may seek his kingdom and glory.

To conclude : All this grace is offered to you; if you refuse the offer, your condition is worse than if it had never been tendered to you. The Lord hath sent his Son to help you out of the power of the devil, and bring you in heart and life again to himself; if you refuse this, then ' This is the condemnation, that light is come into the world, and men love darkness rather than light:' John iii. 19. The Lord Jesus, when he comes in flaming fire to render vengeance, it shall be upon them that do not obey his government, 2 Thes. i. 8, that did not acknowledge God to be their sovereign. There will be a sore vengeance on them which had the gospel tendered, and this wonderful provision brought home to them, and left to their choice, and yet have turned their backs upon it.

Secondly, We beg the continuance of it, that he would maintain this kingdom in our heart, and preserve us in this state; for those which can call God Father, are still to say, ' Thy kingdom come.' It is not enough to go to Christ to begin it, but to carry it on, and to keep and ' preserve us unto his heavenly kingdom,' 2 Tim. iv. 18; that we may not revolt to the devil's side after we have chosen God for our God, and so our latter end be worse than our beginning.

Thirdly, We pray for the increase of it, that it may get ground more and more. There are some relics of the kingdom of darkness yet left, and there is something wanting to the kingdom of grace ; we are troubled and molested still. Though sin doth not get the throne, though the regency of it is cast down, yet it is not cast out in regard of inherence. ' Sin shall not have dominion over you ;' that is all we can hope for: Rom. vi. 14. We cannot hope for an extinction of sin, but only that it shall not have dominion. As the beasts in Dan. vii. 12, though their dominion was taken away, yet their lives were prolonged for a season and time. The reign, power, and dominion of sin is taken down, yet it continues for our exercise and molestation. Now, we desire he might rule in us by his grace, and that of the increase of his government there may be no end.

II. For the kingdom of glory, which, in this private consideration (as it concerns each person), is to begin at death. And when we desire the coming of the kingdom of glory, we do two things: we express our readiness for it, or our desire after it.

1. Our readiness for it; at least, the kingdom of God is ready for us if we were ready for it ; as the apostle saith, 1 Pet. iv. 5. God is ready to judge, but we are not ready to be judged. And therefore we read of the kingdom of heaven prepared for us, and of men prepared for the kingdom of heaven. It is prepared for the saints : Mat. xxv. 34, ' A kingdom prepared for you from the foundation of the world.' And the saints prepared for it: Rom. ix. 23, ' Vessels of mercy, which he had afore prepared unto glory.' And this is that which the apostle gives thanks for unto the Father : ' Which hath made us meet to be partakers of the inheritance of the saints in light,' Col. i. 12. Before we come to heaven, there is a right to heaven ; we are made meet, more mortified and weaned from present things, often in communion with God here, and so for ever with the Lord hereafter. We are still to have our eyes to our rest and happy state, that we may be made ready for it. We express our readiness, or we beg it.

2. That we may express our desires after the enjoyment of it. A Christian is to desire the company of Christ: Phil. i. 23, ' I desire to be dissolved, and to be with Christ ;' and he is to hasten the coming of the day of God : 2 Pet. iii. 12.

Now because this cannot be but by our death, therefore here we may examine a case or two.

Case 1. First, about longing for death. Is it lawful to desire death ? The law doth not only forbid acts, but thoughts and desires ; therefore is it lawful to long for death ?

Ans. Yes ; but yet we are not anxiously to long after it till the time come ; not to grow weary of life out of desperation and tiresomeness of the cross, as Jonah did, chap. iv. 3 ; but in order to God s glory and accomplishment of our happiness. See more at large, Ps. cxix. verse 17.[1]

Case 2. Secondly, Do all that have an interest in Christ desire to

---

[1] In a subsequent volume.—ED.

die? Is not death terrible? Certainly death is terrible, both as a natural and a penal evil; as in itself it is the curse of the covenant; and as it depriveth us of life, the chiefest blessing. Yet we should train up ourselves in an expectation of death; we should look and long for it, that, when the time is come, we might be willing to give up ourselves into the hands of God. It is required of a Christian that he should not only be passive in his own death, to die in peace, but active. How? to hasten his death? No; but to resign up himself willingly into the hands of God, that his soul might not be taken away, but given up and commended to God. We should be willing to be in the arms of Christ, to be there where he is, to behold his glory. If Christ had such a good-will to men as that he longed to be with us, solacing his heart with the thought of it before all worlds, Prov. viii. 31—he was thinking of us, how he should come down, and converse with men—surely we should not be so backward to go to Christ. And, therefore, as Jacob's spirit revived when he saw the chariots Joseph sent to carry him into Egypt, so our hearts should be more cheerful and comfortable when death approacheth: especially since death is ours, it is changed; therefore we should be framing ourselves to such a temper of heart by degrees that we might be ready.

Use 1. For reproof to those that would be glad in their hearts if Christ's kingdom would never come. As to the kingdom of grace, in the external administration, they ' hate the light, and will not come to the light, lest their deeds should be reproved:' John iii. 20. A wicked man is loth to be troubled. God's witnesses are the world's torment: Rev. xi. 10, 'They tormented them that dwelt on the earth.' A man that is bodily blind would have a fit guide; but these wretchedly blind sinners, nothing so troublesome and hateful to them as one that would lead them to the kingdom of God. And then as to internal grace, when this kingdom of heaven breaks in upon their hearts, when any light and power darts in, they seek to put it out; they ' resist the Holy Ghost,' Acts vii. 51, and refuse his call. And for the kingdom of glory, they say, ' It is good to be here,' and would not change their portion here for their portion in paradise.

Use 2. To exhort us to desire the coming of Christ's kingdom to ourselves. If you have any love to the Lord's glory, or your own good, you should do it: Rev. iii. 20, ' Behold, I stand at the door and knock: if any man hear my voice, and open the door, I will come in to him, and will sup with him, and he with me.' Will you not open to God that hath the best right? Will you not set open the doors to the King of glory, when Christ comes to bring entertainment to you, to sup with you? Again, all men (will they, nill they) are subject to Christ: either they must come and touch his golden sceptre, or feel the bruises of his iron mace; they must own him as king: ' Every knee shall bow,' Phil. ii. 10. Therefore be more willing to have the kingdom of glory come. Again, if God be not your king, you will have a worse master, every sin, every lust: Titus iii. 3, ' Serving divers lusts and pleasures.' You will be at the beck of every lust and carnal motion, and the devil will be your master to purpose; for upon the refusal of Christ's government, there is a judicial tradition,

you are given up to your own heart's lusts : Ps. lxxxi. 12, ' Israel
would none of me ; so I gave them up to their own hearts' lusts, and
they walked in their own counsels.'   And to Satan, to be ensnared by
him : 2 Tim. ii. 26, ' Taken captive by him at his will and pleasure.'
Not to buffet them, as Paul was, but to ensnare and harden their
hearts.   Again, if you be not subject to God, you go about to make
God subject to you in effect.   You would have the kingdom of glory,
and yet continue in your lusts : Isa. xliii. 24, ' Thou hast made me
to serve with thy sins, thou hast wearied me with thine iniquities.'
When you would have God patient, hold his hand, and be merciful to
you, and yet would continue in your lusts, then you make God serve
with your sins.   Again, many temporal inconveniences will follow, if
we do not give way to the kingdom of Christ to seize upon us.   When
we make no difference between God's service and the service of other
lords, then he gives us up to the service of men, to a foreign enemy,
to an oppressive magistrate, or breaks the staff of government among
men, that we might know what it is to be under his service and
government.   Therefore give willing entertainment to the kingdom
of Christ.

So much for the private consideration of this request, ' Thy kingdom come ; ' that is, to us and our persons, both the kingdom of grace
and the kingdom of glory.

Secondly, Having spoken of the kingdom of Christ in a private,
now I come to speak of it in a public, consideration.   And that is
twofold :—

1. The public visible administration of the kingdom of grace.

2. The public and solemn administration of the kingdom of glory
at the day of judgment, when enemies shall have their final doom, and
saints have their crowns set upon their heads in the sight of all the
world.

I shall speak of both, but (because the discourse may be more fresh
and lively) upon other texts.

1. The public visible administration of the kingdom of grace, on
Ps. li. 18, ' Do good in thy good pleasure unto Zion : build thou the
walls of thy Jerusalem.'

2. The kingdom of glory, on Rev. xxii. 20, ' Surely I come quickly :
Amen.   Even so, come, Lord Jesus.'

For the first.   Though the church be never so afflicted, Ps. cii. 14,
when all is defaced, as to external appearance, lying in a ruinous
heap, yet it is beloved and pitied by God's servants : ' Thy servants
take pleasure in her stones, and favour the dust thereof.'   There is
nothing God's people desire so much as Zion's welfare : Ps. cvi. 5,
' That I may see the good of thy chosen, that I may rejoice in the
gladness of thy nation, that I may glory with thine inheritance.'   And
David in this psalm, Ps. li. 18, having prayed for himself, prayeth for
mercy to the church and state : ' Do good in thy good pleasure unto
Zion ; build thou the walls of thy Jerusalem.'   But how cometh David,
who was in the depth of private humiliation, so suddenly to fall upon
the case of the church ?   There was a special reason for annexing this
request to his own private complaints and confessions.   The reasons
will occasion so many observations.

[1.] Because of the offence, scandal, and mischief done to the church by his fall ; and to make amends, he prayeth the more earnestly, let not Zion fare the worse for my sake.   From thence observe, that the sins of particular persons oft bring a mischief upon the whole community.   David had made a breach in the walls of God's protection, and left them naked, and more in danger of judgment : ' Therefore do good,' &c.

[2.] David was not only a private member, but a prince, and their sins have a more universal influence.   The sins of magistrates draw down judgments on their people, all smart for their miscarriages. Hezekiah's pride cost Israel dear : 2 Chron. xxxii. 25, ' Wrath was upon him, and upon Judah and Jerusalem.'   It did not stay upon his person.   As a great oak cannot fall but all the shrubs about it suffer loss.   But,

[3.] David having some comfortable assurance of the pardon of his sins, doth now seek mercy for the church.   From thence observe, that we are never fit to pray for the public, till we have made our peace with God ; as the priests under the law offered sacrifice, ' first for their own sins, and then for the people's : ' Heb. vii. 27.

[4.] Because being brought by such a solemn but sad occasion into God's presence, he could not but have some thoughts of Zion.   And from thence observe, that we should never come to God upon any private occasion but we should remember the public.   We are to pray in love as well as faith.   Christ hath not taught us to say, ' *My* Father,' but, ' *Our* Father,' to show that we should take in the interests and concernments of the whole body, that there may be a spirit of communion breathing in our prayers.   David doth not only say, ' Have mercy upon me according to thy loving-kindness,' but, ' Do good unto Zion in thy good pleasure.'   Every living member will be careful for the body.   Members should be careful one for another, much more for the whole.   Is any member pained or grieved ?—all suffer.   If the toe be trod upon, the tongue complaineth, you have hurt me ; but now much more when all is concerned.   Therefore we should not altogether seek our own things, but wrestle with God for the public.

I. This reproveth divers sorts of people.   Some are enemies to the public welfare, as vipers eat out the dam's belly,—especially enemies to Zion : ' Down with it, down with it, even to the ground ! '   What monsters hath this age brought forth !   Others are indifferent and careless which goeth up, Christ or Antichrist ; they only mind the matters of their own interest and concernment : ' All seek their own things.'   As to the public interest of the church, let all go how it will.   Let me tell you, to be selfish is a sort of self-excommunication ; you cast yourselves out of the bundle of life.   And to be senseless, it is an implicit renouncing the body. Others there are that are gracious, but full of discontent at some passages of providence, and these seem to have lost their public affections.   It is a sad symptom when a praying people are discouraged from praying for public welfare.   God is very tender of the prayers of his people ; he is loth they should be lost, and sorry they cannot be granted.   We may sin in ceasing to pray.   It is a sad judgment when the hearts of God's people are taken off from praying.   Again, those that pray too coldly for the public, not as those that would do their work. There is a great decay of the spirit of prayer, which is also a sad presage. But now to show you :—

II. What we should pray for for Zion.

1. The dilatation or enlargement of it throughout the world. The more ample God's heritage is, the more is his glory known : Prov. xiv. 28, ' In the multitude of the people is the king's honour ; ' and the glory of a shepherd lieth in the number of his flock. So Christ's kingdom, the more it is enlarged, the more honour God hath : Ps. lxvii. 2, ' That thy way may be known among the heathen, and thy saving health among all nations.' Especially when the fulness of the Gentiles is brought in, Ps. liv. 2 ; and when the Jews are brought in, Hosea iii. 5. To be instrumental to enlarge Christ's kingdom, it is an honour to us to draw on Christ's triumphant chariot,—let us be sure to have a hand in it. These prayers, if sincere, are never in vain ; if they profit not others, they promote the kingdom of God in ourselves.

2. The preservation and defence of the churches already planted, frustrating the plots and power of the enemies : That God would be ' a wall of fire round about them,' Zech. ii. 5. *Qui comminus arceat et eminus terreat.* When at the weakest, God can protect them, bridling by his secret power the rage of adversaries, or defeating their attempts.

3. For comfort and deliverance in afflictions. We should pity the distressed church, as before ; that God would redeem them out of all their troubles. Every true member of the church hath life from Christ ; and that life giveth feeling, and that feeling affection and sympathy to rejoice and mourn. They that mourn for Zion rejoice with her : Isa. lxvi. 10, ' Rejoice ye with Jerusalem, and be glad with her, all ye that love her ; rejoice for joy with her, all ye that mourn for her.'

4. For the furniture of the church, a supply of all good, internal and external.

[1.] Internal. That God would bless them with ordinances, enrich them with graces, preserve truth and unity, and continue his presence with them : his ordinances, that they may enjoy them in purity, that the word, seals, and censures may be rightly administered till the Lord come. These are things pertaining to the kingdom of God, concerning which Christ spake to the disciples : Acts i. 3. These are to be kept till Christ's appearing : 1 Tim. vi. 14. It is an honour to God, and of great profit to the church, and a rejoicing to God's people, to see them pure and unmixed : ' Though absent in the flesh, yet I am with you in the spirit, joying and beholding your order,' Col. ii. 5. And then that God would enrich them with his presence : Mat. xxviii. 20, ' Lo, I am with you always, even unto the end of the world.' It is God that giveth the increase : ' Paul may plant, and Apollos water ; but God giveth the increase,' 1 Cor. iii. 6—for conviction, conversion, confirmation. It was not the ark, nor mercy-seat covered with cherubims, but the answer from between the cherubims, given immediately by God, that manifested his presence. It is not the sound of the gospel, or outward ministry, but the work of his Spirit : Ps. lxxxiv. 2, ' My soul longeth, yea, even fainteth for the courts of the Lord ; my heart and my flesh crieth out for the living God.' And

Acts x. 44, it is said, 'The Holy Ghost fell on all them which heard the word.' And then for unity : Christ hath called us into a body, not only into a family, but into a body. It was Christ's own prayer : John xvii., 'Let them be one.' Disputes will not heal, but prayers may.

[2.] For external helps. We should pray that God would give us pastors after his own heart : Mat. ix. 38, 'Pray ye the Lord of the harvest, that he would send forth labourers into his harvest.' Men that will discharge their duty with all faithfulness, men whose hearts are set to the building up of Christ's kingdom, labourers. And then for schools of learning. A man that hath many orchards will also have seminaries of young plants to maintain them. Schools are seminaries, without which the church falleth to decay. And then for good magistrates, to patronise and protect God's people, and promote his work with them : Isa. xlix. 23, there is a promise, 'Kings shall be thy nursing-fathers, and their queens thy nursing-mothers,' &c. Rest from persecution is a great blessing : Acts ix. 31, 'Then had the churches rest, and were edified ; and walking in the fear of God, and the comforts of the Holy Ghost, were multiplied.' It is a great mercy that the church hath any breathings. These are the things that we should pray for for Zion.

Thus much shall suffice to be spoken of the kingdom of Christ in a public consideration, with respect, first, to the public visible administration of the kingdom of grace.

I come now to speak of the second, viz., the public and solemn administration of the kingdom of glory ; and for that I shall insist on that portion of scripture : Rev. xxii. 20, 'Surely I come quickly. Amen. Even so, come, Lord Jesus.'

Here you have—

I. Christ's proclamation.

II. The church's acclamation in answer thereunto.

I. Christ's proclamation : 'Surely I come quickly.' Where take notice of two things :—

1. His asseveration : *Surely.*

2. His assertion : *I come quickly.*

1. His asseveration : *Surely.* It is a certain truth, though we do not so easily receive it. All notable truths, about which there is the greatest suspicion in the heart of the creature, you will find them thus averred in scripture ; as Isa. liii. 4, 'Surely he hath borne our griefs, and carried our sorrows.' The dying of the Son of God is so mysterious that the Holy Ghost propounds it with a note of averment, *Surely;* that is, how unlikely soever it seems, yet this is a certain truth. So here the coming of Christ is a thing so future, so little regarded by epicures and atheists, that it is propounded with a like note of averment, 'Surely I come quickly.' Herein secretly is our unbelief taxed, and also our confidence engaged.

2. You have his assertion : *I come quickly.* Let me explain what is meant by the coming of Christ. There is a twofold coming of Christ—a personal, and a virtual. Some think that the virtual coming is here meant,—his coming in the efficacy of his Spirit, or in the power of his providence, to accomplish those predictions. Here are many things prophesied of, and behold, 'I come quickly;' you shall find

these things presently produced upon the stage of the world. So some carry it. I think rather it is to be meant of his personal coming. There are two mystical scriptures which do express all the intercourse which passeth between God and the church in the world, and they are both closed up with a desire of Christ's coming. The Canticles is one, which declareth the communion and intercourse which is between Christ and his church; and you will find it thus closed up: Cant. viii. 14, 'Make haste, my beloved, and be thou like to a roe, or to a young hart upon the mountains of spices.' And so here, in this book of the Revelation, where are the like intercourses recorded, it is closed up with this: 'Even so, Lord Jesus, come quickly.' The personal coming, I suppose, is here meant. Now Christ's personal coming, it is but twofold—the first, and the second. The scripture knows of no other coming: Heb. ix. 28, 'He shall appear the second time without sin unto salvation.' It is but a fond dream to think of a personal reign before Christ's coming to judgment. They reckon without book that look for any other. There was his first coming, which was to suffer; his second coming is to reign. The first his gracious, and this his glorious coming. The former is past, and the latter is yet expected.

'I come quickly.' How shall we make good that?

[1.] In general, Christ's absence from the church is not long. Though you reflect upon the whole flux of time, from his ascension to his second coming, it is but a moment to eternity; some hundreds of years, that may be easily counted.

[2.] It is no longer than need requires. The high priest, when he was gotten within the veil, was to tarry there until his ministration was ended, until he had appeared before God, and represented himself for all the tribes, then he was to come out to bless the people. Jesus Christ tarrieth within the veil but until all the elect be gathered. 'He is not slack,' 2 Pet. iii. 9, but we are hasty. Our times are present with us, but we must leave him to his own time to go and come.

[3.] Christ speaks this of the latter end of the world, and then it will not be long when once he begins to set forth. The old prophecies are accomplishing apace; and how little preparation soever there seems to be for this work, it comes apace. It is said of the antichristian state, 'Her plagues shall come upon her in one day:' Rev. xviii. 8. And of the Jews it is said, 'A nation shall be born at once:' Isa. lxvi. 8. So much for the first part.

II. Here is the church's acclamation: 'Amen. So, Lord Jesus, come quickly.' This acclamation is double:—

1. Implicit, and enfolded in the word *Amen*.

2. Explicit, and unfolded: 'Even so, Lord Jesus, come quickly.'

1. For the implicit acclamation of the church, in the word *Amen*. The word sometimes is taken nominally: Rev. iii. 14, 'Thus saith the Amen, the faithful and true Witness.' He that is *Amen*, as it is explained there, true and faithful, that will certainly give a being to his promises. Sometimes it is used adverbially, and translated *verily*. It is either an affectionate desire—'Let it be,' or a great asseveration —'It shall be.' It hath in it an affectionate desire: Jer. xxviii. 6, the

prophet said, 'Amen, the Lord do so, the Lord perform thy words,' &c. When he had prophesied peace to the people : ' Amen, the Lord perform thy words;' not to confirm the truth of his prophecy, but to express his own wish and hearty desire, if it might stand with the will of God. Then it expresseth a firm belief that it shall be done. Thus Christ often saith, 'Amen, verily, verily I say unto you,' by way of strong asseveration. Well, then, the church expresseth her faith and desire implicitly : Amen, Lord, that it were so; and surely, Lord, it shall be so; we believe it, and we desire it with all our hearts.

2. Explicitly : ' Even so, Lord Jesus, come quickly.' From this latter clause I might observe many things.

[1.] The sweet and blessed harmony that is between Christ and the church. Christ's voice and the church's voice are unisons. Christ saith, ' I come.' And the church, like a quick echo, takes the word out of Christ's mouth, ' Even so, come.' There is the same Spirit in Christ and in the church; for it is his Spirit that resides with us. Christ, he speaks in a way proper to him, by way of promise, ' I come.' And the church in a way proper to her, by way of prayer, ' Even so, come.'

[2.] I might observe that, in the close of the world, we should most earnestly desire Christ's coming. We have the advantage of former times. To us Christ saith, ' I come quickly.' Now the set time almost is come, therefore our pulses should beat more strongly in putting up this request to Christ. Tertullian shows that the primitive Christians did pray *pro mora finis,* that the end might not come too soon, Christ having as yet but a small interest in the world, they expecting enlargement upon earth; but we have more cause to look for the accomplishment of his kingdom in heaven. They expected the revelation of Antichrist, and we expect the destruction of Antichrist. They, that God might be known in the world ; we, that he might be no longer dishonoured in the world. When great promises are near their accomplishment, there is a more lively spirit stirring in the hearts of the saints : Dan. ix. 2, 3, ' I understood by books the number of the years whereof the word of the Lord came to Jeremiah the prophet, that he would accomplish seventy years in the desolations of Jerusalem. And I set my face to the Lord God, to seek by prayer and supplication.'

But quitting these notes, I shall mainly insist upon this point, viz.:

Doct. That the church, and all the faithful members of it, do really and heartily desire Christ's second coming.

They look for it, they long for it, they wait for it. They look for it: Phil. iii. 20, 'Our conversation is in heaven; from whence also we look for the Saviour, the Lord Jesus Christ.' They reckon upon it, as Rebekah espied Isaac afar off. He is gone within the veil, he is appearing before God, but he will come out again. When they see the clouds, upon these one day will our Saviour come. / Then they long for it. It is their description : 2 Tim. iv. 8, ' They love his appearing.' Wicked men and guilty sinners hate and abhor it, he being to come to them as a terrible judge. Malefactors do not long for the assizes. But now the saints, who are absolved and washed in the blood of Christ, it doth them good to the heart to think of it, that one day Christ will appear in all his glory. And then they wait for it : 1 Thes. i. 10, ' They wait

for his Son from heaven, even Jesus, who hath delivered us from
wrath to come.' It is 'wrath to come,' something behind the coming
of Christ, which makes it so terrible. Hell makes the day of judgment terrible. The devil could not endure to hear of Christ's coming,
Mat. viii. 29, 'Art thou come to torment us?' &c. So wicked men
have the spirit of the devil; it is a torment and bondage to them to
think of the Judge's coming. But those which have their discharge,
they wait for it. It supports and bears up their hearts in the midst
of their present afflictions, and they go on cheerfully in their work,
notwithstanding lets and troubles.

To give some reasons why the faithful members of Christ so really
and heartily desire Christ's second coming. They are of three
sorts :—

1. Some in respect of the person who is to come.
2. Some in respect of the persons which desire his coming.
3. Some in respect of the coming itself.
I. In respect of him who is to come.
1. His person, that we may see him. The children of God have
delighted to look upon him through a veil, and have had a kind of
heaven upon earth from beholding his face in the glass of an ordinance.
Looking upon him in the veil of ordinances hath been a mighty comfort and refreshing to them; now they would desire to see his person
face to face. They know by hearsay this great Redeemer and Saviour
of theirs; he wooeth them by proxy. As Eliezer, Abraham's servant,
was to go abroad and seek for a match for his master's son, so the
great business of the ministers of God is to set forth our Master's Son.
Now the saints would fain see him. Nay, they have not only heard
of him, but believed in him, and received him into their hearts. Nay,
not only believed in him, but they have loved him greatly : 1 Pet. i.
8, 'Whom having not seen, ye love; in whom, though now ye see him
not, yet believing, ye rejoice with joy unspeakable, and full of glory.'
It hath been a ravishing thought to them to think of Christ. And
they have tasted : 1 Pet. ii. 3, 'If so be ye have tasted that the
Lord is gracious.' And they have felt him in the drawings of the
Spirit; they live by his life, they have found a virtue going out from
him. Now all that they desire is, that they may see this great person,
who hath been their Redeemer and Saviour.

2. Consider him as in his person, so in his relations to them. Here
are two titles: 'Even so, Lord Jesus.' He is *Lord*, and he is *Jesus*.
He is *Lord,* as a master and husband; as Sarah called Abraham,
Lord. As a *Master:* good servants will look for their master's coming:
Mat. xxiv. 46. And surely such a Master should be longed for and
looked for, for when he comes, he will not come empty-handed : ' Behold, I come quickly, and my reward is with me,' Rev. xxii. 12. Here
Christ's servants have their vales, but not their wages. Here they
have present maintenance, that is all they have now, but then they
shall have their reward and wages. Here they have their earnest, but
then they shall have the full sum. Under the law masters were charged
severely not to defraud their servants of their hire—why? He hath
lift up his soul to him ; that is, in the middle of his hard labours this
was his comfort: when the work of the day was over, he should have

his wages and his hire at night. So you have lift up your souls to him; the great pay-day will come, and this hath borne you up in all your labours and travail of your soul. Therefore, as he is our Lord, so we should look for him. And then as our *Husband;* this is a sweeter relation : 'The bride saith, Come,' Rev. xxii. 17. We are here contracted and betrothed to Christ : 'I will betroth thee to me,' Hosea ii. 19. But the day of solemn espousals is hereafter. Here we are betrothed to Christ in the covenant of grace ; Christ hath taken a token from us, and left a token with us. He hath taken human flesh, carried our nature to heaven, that he might be mindful of us, and hath left the Spirit with us. Now there will be a longing, looking, and waiting for this day of solemn espousals. And as he is Lord, so he is *Jesus,* a Saviour. With what melting wishes doth the captive long for a Saviour and Redeemer ! Now ' we look for a Saviour from heaven.' Christ is a Saviour now, but not a perfect Saviour to the uttermost; never till then. Therefore the day of judgment is called ' the day of redemption:' Eph. iv. 30. There is something left, that every coming of Christ might bring some benefit; something of misery left upon us to the last day. Here we have enemies within and without. Within, mighty lusts; and therefore his coming is ' like a refiner's fire,' Mal. iii. 2, 'and fullers' soap.' His first and second coming we find oft in the Old Testament put together. His coming is 'to present us holy, without spot and blemish:' Eph. v. 27. Our present state is but a convalescency, a recovery out of sickness by degrees. There is some fruit of sin left upon the body, until the day of the general resurrection, that we may have new matter of glorifying God just as we are entering into heaven. Therefore that every coming of Christ might bring us a new benefit, the body is to die. The old Adam is not quite abolished until God be all in all. And so for enemies without us. Here we dwell among wicked men, whose sins are a grievance to us, and whose injuries are a very great molestation and trouble. We live here, like Lot in Sodom : 'His righteous soul was vexed with their ungodly deeds,' their filthy conversation. But then there will be a perfect separation between the sheep and the goats. Here we are exposed to many persecutions; here Antichrist is but consuming; there he shall totally and utterly be abolished.

II. If we respect the persons desiring this coming, there is something in them to move them to it. There is :—

1. The Spirit of Christ.

2. Certain graces which do necessarily issue themselves into this work.

3. Certain experiences they have, which put them upon this longing.

1. There is the Spirit of Christ : 'The Spirit and the bride saith, Come,' Rev. xxii. 17. The Holy Ghost breedeth this desire in the church. Nature saith, it is good to be here ; but this is a disposition above nature, the Spirit in the bride. The flesh and corrupt nature saith, ' Depart ;' but the Spirit saith, ' Come.' The great work of the Spirit is to bring us and Christ together ; he comes from the Father and the Son, to bring us to the Father by the Son. All he doth is to bring Christ and the spouse together ; therefore he enkindleth

in the hearts of God's people a strong and earnest desire of his coming.

2. There are graces planted in us ; faith, hope, love, zeal. Faith, that is the ground of this desire. Christ saith he comes quickly; and this provokes and draws up the desire to believe Christ will be as good as his word: John xiv. 2, 3, ' I go to my Father, and will come again to receive you to myself.' Christ hath ever been plain-hearted with us : he saith, ' I come ;' and the church saith, ' Amen,' in a way of faith, ' Even so, come.' If Christ had gone away in discontent, and with a threatening in his mouth that we should never have seen his face more, then we could have had but cold hopes and faint desires; but he parted in love, and left a promise with us. The church and the believing soul saith, I have his word for it : he hath ever been punctual hitherto, and kept his word to a tittle, and hath said, ' I will come again.' This upholdeth the hearts of believers during his absence ; for they reason thus : What need had Christ to flatter or deceive us, or promise more than he will perform ? Would we flatter a worm that we can easily crush ? He can strike us dead if we do not please him; he hath been true in all things, and we have ever found him plain-hearted. Then there is hope planted in the saints. Hope is faith's handmaid, it looks for that which we believe: faith determines the certainty of the thing, then hope looks for it. This grace was made on purpose that we might reach out to heaven and see if our beloved be coming, that we might expect our full and future happiness. God not only provides a glorious estate for us, but grace to expect it; he works this hope in us that we might look after it: 1 Pet. i. 3, ' He hath begotten us again unto a lively hope.' Then there is love in the saints to Christ. This is an affection of union, it desires to be with the party beloved; he desireth to be with us, and we with him. Love awakeneth earnest longings : ' Oh, come, come ! why is his chariot so long a-coming ? ' As a loving wife stands upon the shore ready to welcome her expected husband, so doth love in the saints ; they desire to be with Christ, therefore they long for the kingdom of God coming to themselves out of love : Phil. i. 23, ' I desire to be dissolved, and to be with Christ.' And upon the same ground they desire the general resurrection of the church. Especially is this inflamed with the thoughts of Christ's love to us. He hath removed his bodily presence from us, yet he cannot be satisfied until he and we meet again: John xiv. 3, ' I will come again, and receive you to myself, that where I am, there ye may be also;' and John xvii. 24, ' And that you may be there with me, to behold my glory.' Christ is not satisfied in his glorious estate until we be with him, till he hath our company, and we be beatified with the sight of him. Before his coming in the flesh, he delighted to be with the saints before the world was : Prov. viii. 31. And when the world was made, before his incarnation, he took pleasure to come and appear in the fashion of a man, and converse with his people in human shape. In the days of his flesh, he delighted to spend his time and busy himself among them that are faithful. And when he was to go from us, he did assure us of returning, and cannot be quiet until we be with him. So, reciprocally, and according to our measure, doth love work

in us; we cannot be without Christ, therefore we long to be with him.

Then zeal is planted in the saints, and a tenderness for his glory. It is not their interest only which makes them desire his coming, but that the king may sit upon the throne, that Christ may reign in the most perfect manner, that the day of manifestation may come, that all mists and clouds which are upon his person may vanish. The saints that love the glory of God as well as their own salvation, nay, above their own salvation, are longing for that time when Christ shall be seen in all his glory, that he may be dishonoured no more, that sin and opposition may have an end. Here God hath not his perfect glory, neither from us nor from the wicked, neither from angels nor devils: not his perfect glory from us, and therefore the saints long for that time when Christ may be more admired in them; it is the comfort of their souls that God is glorified in their glory, that there will a time come when he shall be admired and glorified in their glory, and when they shall praise him for evermore, without weakness and distraction. And then the wicked, that they may oppose and dishonour him no more, that the whole course of justice may be seen in the history of the world, which shall be produced at the day of judgment; that his power may be seen, when devils and all ungodly men are trodden underfoot, and all offences taken away, and all opposite powers are abolished. First, Christ would zealously affect us to the glory of God: 'Hallowed be thy name;' then he would have us pray, 'Thy kingdom come,' that our zeal for God's glory might make us earnest and instant for his kingdom. Then,

3. There are certain experiences that we have here which set us a-longing and groaning for this time: Rom. viii. 23, 'We which have the first-fruits of the Spirit, groan within ourselves, waiting for the adoption, to wit, the redemption of our body.' When they have tasted of the clusters of Canaan, oh, they long to see the land; they long that Jesus, the captain of their salvation, the spiritual Joshua, may lead them into the good land. The church hath here enjoyed Christ in her house: 'I brought him into my mother's house,' Cant. iii. 4. Now they would enjoy him in his own house, have a more plentiful enjoyment of him. Wherefore have we a taste, but to long for a fuller banquet? Why doth God give out such a pittance, but to awaken our desires to look for more? Indeed these beginnings are sweet, and are a wonderful mercy; to hear Christ say in a promise, 'Come to me, that you may have life.' But when once they have embraced this, they will be longing for another call, for the great voice to say, 'Come, ye blessed of my Father,' &c. When Christ biddeth them welcome into the kingdom of heaven, to the crown of glory; when we can get any joy in the Holy Ghost, a little peace of conscience, any sweet experience of our being cleansed from sin, this is reviving and comfortable. But why is this given, but to set us a-longing for the whole harvest? for this is but the first-fruits. It is sweet now to find pardon of sin, and any comfortable feeling of God's love in the conscience; to have any doubt resolved, any fear silenced and suppressed; to have a glimpse of the light of God's countenance, a little elevation of the heart in duty. Now this draws on the soul to long

for more ; for we begin then to think, What a sweet reviving will it
be when we enjoy the full of all these things! If there be but one
promise now set home upon our hearts, though here we have only the
right, not enjoyment; if we have but our right cleared up to a promise, it is very reviving. God gives us this experience, that we may
long to enjoy the thing promised, the full possession of it. When you
have gone away feasted with loves at the Lord's table, thou hast said,
One hour's communion with God is better than all the world. If thy
heart was melted a little in duty, if it was affected with godly sorrow
for sin, it hath yielded thee more comfort than all the mirth and
music which fond worldlings cheer themselves withal, than all their
jollity. Now this is but given as a foretaste, as a prelibation, and to
awaken our desires after more. In the Lord's Supper many times we
come and drink of that cup which God hath tempered for us ; this is
but a dark presignification of the 'new wine we shall drink in our
Father's kingdom,' Mat. xxvi. 29, and of those eternal comforts we
shall have there, and those unmixed joys in the presence of Christ.
Therefore, because of the tastes they have had, and those beginnings
of glory, their hearts will be more enlarged and drawn out to look for
more, and long for that happy time when all this shall be accomplished.

III. There may be arguments taken and drawn from the coming
itself, that they long for his coming. Wherefore doth Christ come?
what are the ends of it? It is to manifest his love to the saints
mainly, as to punish his enemies and glorify his justice.

1. I will mention the first; to gather the saints together, to draw
all his scattered people into one holy body and communion: Ps. 1. 5,
' Gather my saints together unto me, those that have made a covenant
with me by sacrifice.' Now they are scattered up and down, as God
hath service for them to do ; one here, another there : they are spread
in several places, where they are like two or three berries in the upper-
most top of the bough. That psalm is generally acknowledged to be
spoken of the day of judgment; then they are gathered to meet in one
great assembly. The psalmist speaks of 'the great congregation of
the righteous,' where the 'sinners shall not stand:' Ps. i. 5. At that
great day when Christ comes, all the saints shall make but one
assembly and one congregation. As the wicked shall be bundled
together, and the tares cast into unquenchable fire, so all the saints
shall be gathered together into one great assembly, and this glads
their hearts. Therefore we are not feasted to the full, because we
have not all our company ; all the guests do not meet together until
the day the Son of God comes to bless the elect.

2. He comes to proclaim our pardon, and to pronounce the sentence of our acquittance juridically in court, as judge upon the throne.
Our pardon is passed and sealed as to conscience, then he will blot
out all our sins; therefore it is said, Acts iii. 19, ' That your iniquities
may be blotted out, when the times of refreshing shall come from the
presence of the Lord.' He comes then to comfort and refresh the
souls of the saints, by proclaiming their pardon in the ears of all the
world. To whomsoever the throne of Christ is terrible, it should not
be terrible to the saints : if he comes as a judge to them, he comes to
acquit them upon the throne ; he means no trouble to them.

3. He comes to crown us. Certainly there is a longing for this day and coming; for what is his work? He comes to crown the saints: 2 Tim. iv. 8, 'Henceforth there is laid up for me a crown of righteousness, which the Lord, the righteous judge, shall give me at that day.' Then he comes to put the crown of righteousness upon our heads, and invest us with all the fruits of his purchase; then the godly Christian comes to have his crown: 1 Pet. v. 4, 'When the chief Shepherd shall appear, ye shall receive a crown of glory, that fadeth not away.' He that hath been careful to honour God in his relation, then the great Shepherd comes to put the crown of glory, which fades not away, upon his head.

Are the children of God always in this frame, as to desire his coming? Many tremble at the thoughts of it, and can have no comfort, for want of assurance of God's love; and many times the saints do not feel such inclinations, and such ardent and strong desires.

I answer:—

1. The meanest saint hath some inclination this way; he cannot but desire Christ should come into his heart and bless him, in turning him from his sins; and that he should come to judgment, since comfort and reward is more naturally embraced than duty. Whoever is begotten to God, is 'begotten to a lively hope,' 1 Pet. i. 3; his heart is carried this way, though not with so much strength and lively motions as others are. Yet I grant,

2. Sometimes there may be a drowsiness and indisposition, when their lamps are not burning, when they are grown careless and fallen asleep; as the wise virgins slept, as well as the foolish, by a sluggish security. And the saints may find themselves indisposed, possibly by the remission of their watchfulness; they may contract an indisposition, yet there is a spirit stirring this way, which begins with the new birth, and still continues, though it doth not always alike put forth itself. A wife desires her husband's coming home, yet it may be all is not in such good order. Now, all Christians desire the coming of Christ; but they are not so watchful, therefore are not so lively. Security brings deadness, until God awakens them by some sharp affliction. The needle that is touched with the loadstone yet may a little be discomposed and turned aside, but it settles again. This is the right posture and frame of a gracious soul, to be thus earnestly bent and carried out after the coming of Christ.

3. I answer again: The church doth really and heartily desire this coming, though they may tremble at some circumstances of it. When we think of this great day, and of the book that shall be opened, and the impartial proceedings, there is some degree of bondage still left in the saints, that doth a little weaken their confidence and boldness. 1 John iv. 18 we are told: 'Perfect love casteth out fear, because fear hath torment.' Until our graces are perfect, there is something of fear.

APPLICATION.

Use 1. To reprove those that do not desire the coming of Christ, but put off the thoughts of it. Why? Because it casts a damp upon their fleshly rejoicing; which put far away the day of the Lord, the

evil day; it is so to them : Amos vi. 3.   They wish it would never
come, and would be glad in their hearts to hear such news.   Why ?
For Christ's coming is their torment and burden ; they look upon it
as a day of vengeance and an evil day, therefore are loth to entertain
the thought of it.   Saith Austin, ' Canst thou pray that the kingdom
of God may come, when thou art afraid the kingdom of God should
come ? '   A carnal man cannot say the Lord's Prayer without being
afraid ; they tremble at the remembrance of it; they are afraid it
should be true, and afraid to be heard.   If it might go by their voice,
Christ should never come.   The voice of corrupt nature is, ' Depart
from us; and what can the Almighty do for them ?' Job xxii. 17.
Or if they do desire it, it is but in a slight, formal manner; as those
in the prophet that would see the day of the Lord, yet they could not
bear it : Amos v. 18, ' Woe unto you that desire the day of the Lord ;
to what end is it for you ?   The day of the Lord is darkness, and not
light.'   They little consider what they are doing, and what is their
danger, when they are making such a prayer to God, ' Thy kingdom
come.'

Use 2. For trial.   How are you affected towards the coming of
Christ ?   Are you carried out with such an inclination and bent of
heart, as the day of your perfection, and the day of your solemn enjoyment of God, requireth ?   Is the bent of your heart carried out to
things to come ?   If there be looking, then there would :—

1. Be a preparing.   A man that expects and desires the coming of
a great person to his house will make all things ready, is careful to
furnish himself; when all is sluttish and nasty, and nothing of provision, do you look for your guest ?   What have you done as to the
day of Christ's coming ?   Have you judged yourselves ? 1 Cor. xi. 31,
' If we would judge ourselves, we should not be judged.'   Have you ever
seriously passed sentence upon yourselves, according to the law, that
you may be found in Christ ? Rom. viii. 1, ' There is no condemnation to them that are in Christ.'   That you may have Christ's righteousness to bear you out in that day against Christ's judgment ?   Are
you so as you would be found in him ?   Do you ' live soberly, righteously, and godly in this present world ' ?   Strict walking is a preparing and providing for this day ; you do but provide for terror
when you give way to sin : 2 Pet. iii. 10, 11, ' The day of the Lord will
come as a thief in the night ; therefore what manner of persons should
ye be in all holy conversation and godliness, looking for and hasting
unto the coming of the day of God?'   We should be trimming up our
lamps.

2. What kind of entertainment do you give to Christ now ?   Do
you entertain him for the present into your hearts, in his ordinances ?
A woman that never cares to hear from her husband, doth she long
for his coming ?   Oh, be careful now to get Christ into your hearts !

3. What doth this expectation produce ? what revivings in the fore-
thoughts of it ?   John viii. 56, ' Abraham rejoiced to see my day, and
he saw it and was glad.'   He means the day of his incarnation, the
day of his abode in the world.   Abraham foresaw, by the eagle eye of
his faith, through all mists, clouds, veils, and ceremonies ; he got a
sight of Christ's day, and it did him good at heart.   Do the appre-

hensions of it make your hearts spring and leap within you for joy? What groanings longings, what dealing with God about it doth it produce? Rom. viii. 19, ' For the earnest expectation of the creature waiteth for the manifestation of the sons of God.' What support and strength doth it give you against the burdens and sorrows of this present life, to remember Christ will come?

Use 3. To press us to this sweet affection and disposition of the saints. I might mention the profit of it; this longing, looking, and waiting for the coming of Christ, it will make us heavenly in our conversation. Christ is there: where should we converse most but where Christ is? And it makes us faithful in improving our talents: ' Our Lord will come, and reckon with his servants,' Luke xix. 15.

Thy will be done in earth, as it is in heaven.

WE are come to the third petition, which is fitly subjoined to the former. In the preface we own our relation to God, ' Our Father.' In the first petition we express our care of his glory; in the second, our desires of his kingdom; and now we beg obedience to his will. We may judge of our respect to his name and kingdom by our obedience to his will, without which we neither sanctify his name nor submit to his kingdom. The kingdom of God implieth two things,—his government over us, or the privileges which we enjoy thereby.

1. As it is taken for his government over us, so there is a fair connexion between these two requests. Before, we pray that God would rule us, and now, for a soft and pliable heart, that we may be ruled by him. Christ is not our king when we do our own will. These two are distinct; government is one thing, and obedience to it another: as, Mat. vi. 33, ' The kingdom of God,' and ' the righteousness thereof,' they are distinguished. The kingdom of God we plead for in the second petition, and here for the righteousness thereof; that Christ may not be a titular prince and sovereign, as certainly he is, when we do our own will. Every sovereign stands upon his own will, and the more absolute, still the more his will is to be looked upon as a law and rule. Now, God being so absolute a sovereign, it is but fit his will should be done in the perfectest manner: ' Thy will be done in earth, as it is in heaven.'

2. If you take the kingdom of God for the privileges of his government, especially if they be considered in their consummation and final accomplishment, for that which the scripture calls the kingdom of God, by doing God's will we enter into his kingdom: see Mat. vii. 21, ' Not every one that saith unto me, Lord, Lord, shall enter into the kingdom of heaven; but he that doeth the will of my Father which is in heaven.' It is not the blandishment of a spiritual compliment, but a true and hearty subjection to the will of God, that availeth in God's kingdom, and is intended by this petitionary clause, ' Thy will be done.'

Here consider—

I. The substance of the petition.

II. The circumstances thereof.

The substance of the petition, ' Thy will be done.' The circumstances are two : The place where, which indeed intimateth the persons by whom, by men here ' upon *earth.*' Then the manner is set down in a comparison, ' Upon earth, *as it is in heaven.*'

Let me first open these passages, then observe somewhat.

I. The substance of the petition, ' Thy will be done;' and there :—

1. The matter about which it is conversant, the *will* of God.

2. The request about it, *Thy will be done.*

First, The matter of the request, *Thy will.* God's name was under consideration in the first petition, his kingdom in the second, and now his will. And then here is a note of appropriation, *Thy* will, in contradistinction to all others.

God's will, it signifieth two things, either his decree concerning future events, or else that which God hath revealed concerning our duty—his intended or commanded will. The first is spoken of, Rom. ix. 19, ' Who hath resisted his will?' that is, his decree and his purpose; and the second, his revealed pleasure concerning our duty, is spoken of, 1 Thes. iv. 3, ' This is the will of God, even your sanctification.' The will not of his purpose, but it is his law, his revealed pleasure. Now it is not meant here of God's decree or secret will. Why? God's secret will, that is not known, therefore how can it be done upon earth ? To that all are subject,—reprobates, devils. But here this petition speaks of a will which is to be done in conformity to the good angels. Again, we may, without sin, will that which God wills not by his secret will, as the life of a sick parent, which God purposeth to take away. Nay, a man may fulfil this secret will and yet perish for ever, as Judas, and many which break his commandments and yet fulfil his decrees, that do that which God had determined before to be done in his secret purpose; as it is said, Acts iv. 28, ' To do that which his hand and counsel had determined before to be done.' Therefore his secret will is not here meant, but the will of God revealed. Therefore let me here distinguish again: The will of God is revealed two ways, in his word and in his works; the one to be done *by* us, the other to be done *upon* us: the one is *Voluntas de nobis,* God's will concerning us; the other, *Voluntas in nobis,* God's will in us, and to be done by us; the one maketh way for our active, the other for our passive obedience. Our active obedience hath respect to his laws and commands, but our passive to his providence. We show as much obedience in the one as in the other, in patience as in holiness: for as in holiness we own God as the supreme lawgiver, so in patience we own him as the supreme Lord, that hath a dominion over all events and all things which fall out in the world. In the one, we pray *Ut nihil Dei displiceat nobis,* that nothing which comes from God may provoke us to unseemly passion; in the other, we pray *Ut nihil nostrum displiceat Deo,* that nothing which comes from us may provoke God by unseemly and undutiful carriage. We principally pray for the latter here, that we may fulfil his will revealed in the word, and yet the other cannot be excluded. Take but this reason, because the saints in scripture express their subjection to God's providence in words very agreeable to this request, to the form of this petition; as those believers, when they saw God had determined Paul's

journey to Jerusalem, when he went bound in the Spirit, notwithstanding the dangers of it, and their loss by his departure, they said,
'The will of the Lord be done,' Acts xxi. 14. And Christ himself,
speaking of his passion, Mat. xxvi. 39, 'Not as I will, but as thou
wilt:' and 'not my will, but thine, be done,' Luke xxii. 42. So that
we pray both for the one and the other, though with a plain difference.
Why? For our active obedience must be even without a conditional
desire that the commands of God should be repealed; we cannot so
much as desire God should disannul his law, and repeal those statutes
he hath enacted. Yet we may desire conditionally, if God see fit, the
removal of our affliction, and that condition of life to which we are
determined by his providence: 'The commandment is not grievous'
in itself, 1 John v. 3, yet the affliction in its own nature is grievous,
Heb. xii. 11. We may desire more knowledge of God's law, yet we
may not desire more experience of affliction; the one is more absolutely necessary than the other. We are not only to obey actively,
but to love the commandments of God, and to have our hearts carried
out in a greater esteem, and to prefer them before liberty itself; but I
doubt whether we are so concerning our afflictions, to prefer them
before freedom and exemption, and the welfare of our nature.

Well, then, you see what is meant by the will of God, which is the
matter about which this is conversant.

Then here is the note of appropriation, *Thy* will, in opposition to our
own will, the will of Satan, the wills of men.

[1.] To our own will, which is the proudest enemy Christ hath on
this side hell, and the cause of all the mischief which doth befall us.
The great contest between us and God is, whose will shall stand, God's
will, or ours? In every sin we slight the will of God, and set up our
own. We 'despise the commandment,' 2 Sam. xii. 9: not grossly
and formally; David did not slight the commandment, and say, 'Tush!
it is a foolish law;' but by necessary interpretation we slight the law
of God, and set up our own will. Therefore, when we pray that God's
will may be done, we do in effect renounce our own will, those 'wills
of the flesh and mind,' Eph. ii. 3, which the apostle speaks of; so it is
in the Greek. The soul is never renewed until the will be renewed,
till the will be broken. And therefore self-denial is made one of the
first principles of Christianity, the denying of our own will. The will
is the leading part of the soul. Though the new creature begins with
the mind, yet it comes not to any perfection, it is not formed until
the will be subdued to God, until grace be seated in the heart. When
a man treadeth on a dry hide, one part or other will be apt to rebound
and leap up against him, till he stands in the middle and centre: so,
until grace be seated in the heart, corruption will recoil. When a
bird's wings are broken, it can fly no longer; so when the will is subdued, then the work of grace begins. The mind is the counsellor,
but the will is the monarch and prince, which sways and rules all in
the soul. Again, the will is more corrupted than the mind; the
understanding is much blinded, but the will is more depraved. The
mind hath a little light, and is apt to take God's part sometimes, by
suggesting good motions; but the will doth more abhor and refuse
good than the understanding is ignorant of it. We are convinced often

when not converted. Therefore this is the main thing, that our corrupt wills may be subdued to God : Let thy will be done, not our own.

[2.] Thy will, in opposition to Satan's will. Our lusts are called his lusts : John viii. 44, ' The lusts of your father the devil ye will do.' They are of his inspiring, of his cherishing ; the grand incubus of hell is the father of these brats and sinful productions. So, 2 Tim. ii. 26, the Holy Ghost speaks of carnal men, that they are ' taken captive by Satan at his will and pleasure.' Wicked men are at Satan's beck, and they do his will. The devil sets such a lust at work, the man obeys presently : the devil stirs such lusts by his arts and engines, and observes such a lust will be most prevalent at such a time ; the man is taken by Satan's will. Now, *Thy will*, &c., we desire the Lord's grace, that we may not comply with the devil's motions.

[3.] Thy will, in opposition to the wills of men : 1 Pet. iv. 2, ' That he no longer should live to the lusts of men, but to the will of God ;' not according to the wills of men, but according to the will of God. In our natural state we are apt to be swayed by the lusts and humours of others, according as the posture of our interest is determined ; and therefore it is a good piece of self-denial to cease from the lusts of men, from the humours and customs of those whom we fear and from whom we hope. And until we cease from men, in vain do we expect. to serve God.

Thus for the matter about which this request is conversant, ' Thy will.'

Secondly, Here is the request itself, *Be done;* what doth this imply, when we say, ' Let thy will be done '?

[1.] We beg a heart to do it : Deut. v. 29, ' Oh that there were such an heart in them, that they would fear me, and keep all my commandments always !' It is not enough to set ourselves to do what God hath commanded ; but we must get a renewed, sanctified heart.

[2.] We beg skill to do it : Ps. cxliii. 10, ' Teach me to do thy will, for thou art my God.' We beg that God would teach us, and lead us forth in the obedience of his will.

[3.] We beg strength to do it. It is said, Heb. xiii. 21, ' The God of peace, through the blood of the everlasting covenant, make you perfect in every good work, to do his will.' We beg strength, that we may do what is pleasing in his sight. In our will there is a double mischief ; it is opposite to and averse from God : Rom. viii. 7, ' The carnal mind is enmity against God ; for it is not subject to the law of God, nor indeed can be.' And it is strongly inclined to other things ; and this both by nature and by evil custom. There is an aversion from God, which is natural, and which is increased by custom ; therefore it is God must give us a heart to do his will, and skill and strength. Thus God he must draw us off from other things, which is called the ' circumcising of the heart,' Deut. xxx. 6. He must draw us off, and he must draw us on too. As he pares away the foreskin, the fleshiness which cleaves to our hearts, and inclineth us to seek our own will, in hunting after pleasures, honours, profits : so doth the Lord draw us to himself : Cant. i. 4, ' Draw me, and we will run after thee.'

II. Let us come to the circumstances of the petition, ' In earth, as it is in heaven.'

First, The place, wherein also the persons are noted, *in earth*, that is, by the men which live upon earth. Why is this mentioned, *on earth ?*

[1.] The earth is a place of our exercise and trial, and now is the time to show our self-denial and our obedience to God, to deny our own will and do the will of God : John xvii. 4, ' I have glorified thee upon earth.' This is a work that must not be suspended until we come to heaven; it will not be thankworthy then, when there is no interruption, no trouble, no molestation there : but here, ' I have glorified thee on earth,' where so few mind the work, and where there are so many distractions and temptations to divert us.

[2.] The earth is the only place where this work is begun, or else it shall never be done hereafter : instance in anything that is the will of God. Here we must believe, or there we shall never enjoy : Luke ii. 14, ' Peace upon earth.' Now God offereth grace, and now it is his will we should come out of our sins, and accept of Christ to the ends for which he hath appointed him. And here we must be sanctified, else we shall be filthy for evermore. Corn grows in the field, but it is laid up in the barn. Now is the time of minding this work, here upon earth.

[3.] That while we are upon earth, we might long for that happy estate we shall have in heaven, wherein we might serve God. Therefore Christ in his prayer would have us think how God is glorified and obeyed there, that we might send up hearty wishes after that perfect estate, when we shall serve God without weariness, and without distraction.

[4.] Upon earth, to show that we pray not for those in the other world, but for those upon earth. We do not pray for the saints departed, they are out of harm's way, past our prayers, being in their final estate. We pray not for the dead, but for the living. Thus for the first circumstance in this petition, the place where.

Secondly, There remains nothing but the last, and that is the manner how this is to be done : ' As it is in heaven.' Chrysostom observes that this clause may be referred to all the former petitions: ' Hallowed be thy name upon earth, as it is in heaven;' ' Thy kingdom come upon earth, as it is in heaven.' But certainly most proper it is to the matter in hand. But what is the sense ? How is God obeyed in heaven ?

There are in scripture three heavens, the airy heaven, the starry heaven, and the heaven of heavens. In all these heavens God's will is done. God is obeyed in the lower heaven, you shall see in Ps. cxlviii. 8, ' fire, hail, snow, and vapours, stormy winds, fulfilling his word.' Winds and storms, and all those things which seem to be most tempestuous and unruly, to be the disorders of nature, they are at God's beck. Then in the starry heaven, ver. 6, ' He hath made a decree which shall not pass :' they are under a law and statute, and are not exorbitant and eccentric, do not alter their path ; the sun riseth, sets, and knows the just point of his compass. But it is chiefly meant of the heaven of heavens, where angels and blessed spirits are, and they obey God perfectly : Ps. ciii. 20, 21, ' Bless the Lord, ye his angels, that excel in strength, that do his commandments, hearkening unto the voice of his word.   Bless ye the Lord, all ye his hosts, ye ministers of his that do his pleasure.'   The angels do his commandments, and are hearkening to the voice of his word, are at God's beck, to be sent up and down, to ascend and descend as God will have them ; so with respect to this doth Christ say, ' Thy will be done in earth, as it is in heaven.'

But here, again, why is this added, *As it is in heaven ?*

1. To sweeten our subjection to God's will.   We upon earth are not held to a harder law and task than they in heaven.   The angels, they are not *sui juris*, at their own dispose : they have many privileges above man, yet have no exemption from homage and duty to God.   They have an exemption and freedom from trouble, and sickness, and disease, and the necessities of meat and drink, and all the molestations and infirmities of the flesh which we lie under, but are not freed from the will of God, but they obey his commandments, hearkening to the voice of his word.   These courtiers of heaven are servants of God, and fellows with us in the same obedience ; none is too great to obey God.   The angels, which excel in strength, they obey his will, and so must we ; nay, they obey his will with a holy awe and fear, that they may not displease him in the least ; for it is said of Michael the archangel, Jude 9, that 'he durst not bring against the devil a railing accusation, but said, The Lord rebuke thee.'   He had not boldness to speak one uncomely word, or one unseemly word, to do anything that was displeasing to God.

2. As to sweeten our obedience, so to show us the reasonableness of this obedience.   We would have the happiness of the angels, and, therefore, certainly we should come into a fellowship in their duty ; it is but equal we should imitate their holiness.   If we would have communion with them in glory, we should have communion also with them in grace.   Mat. xxii. 30, it is said, we shall be ἰσάγγελοι, 'like the angels of God.'   We seek after the same glory and happiness which they have : to stand before the Lord and to behold his face ; that is their happiness.   Surely if we would have the reward of angels, which we upon earth are aspiring and looking after, it is but equal we should do the work of angels, and write after their copy.

3. Therefore doth Christ use this comparison, that we might not miscarry by a low example.   How apt are we to follow the track, and to take up with an easy and low rate of obedience : Luke xviii. 11, that put great confidence in that, ' God, I thank thee I am not as other men.'   Now because we have few good examples in the world, and those we have have their spots and defects, and are very susceptible of evils, and apt to miscarry by them, therefore Christ would carry us up to look after a heavenly and celestial pattern ; he propoundeth the angelical perfection as a pattern and example.   He that shoots at a star, will shoot higher than he that aims at a shrub : surely the higher the pattern that we aim at, the greater will our obedience be. Wicked men they think that everything is enough in religion, though it be never so little ; but the godly cannot so easily satisfy themselves, they are pressing and hastening on more and more.

4. To teach us that we are not only to look to the *quid*, but to the *quomodo* ; not only to *what* we do, but also in what *manner* we yield

obedience to God ; therefore Christ would not teach us to pray only, ' Thy will be done,' but ' as it is in heaven,' in such a manner. God respects not only the doing of what he hath required, but also the manner of it, that we may not only do good, but well ; it is the adverb which crowns the action. We are to consider with what heart we go about it : Prov. xvi. 2, ' The Lord weigheth the spirits.' That which he putteth into the balance of the sanctuary is, with what spirit, with what heart, we go about the work ; that is it he weigheth and regardeth. Now that we may look not only to the matter of obedience, but also to the manner how we do it, therefore doth Christ give us this pattern.

Object. But you will say, Our obedience is accompanied with many defects and infirmities ; therefore, how can we serve God as the angels do in heaven ? How shall we take comfort in our obedience if this be our pattern ?

I answer :—

1. Though we cannot do it in the same *measure*, yet we should do it in the same *manner ;* though there be not an exact equality, yet there should be some answerable resemblance. Our obedience should not be wholly different in the kind and manner of it from theirs which serve God in heaven, though for the degree and rate we cannot come up to their pattern.

2. Though we do not attain to this perfection in this life, yet we must aim after it, long for it, and pray for it. Aim after it, not sluggishly content ourselves with any low degrees of obedience, but aim at the highest. And to long for it : there is a time coming when we shall be perfect ; when we shall be not only as the angels are, but as Christ is : ' We shall be like him,' 1 John iii. 2. And we pray for that on earth which is expected in heaven ; we pray for what we do expect from the final and consummate estate, when we shall be as the angels of God, and perfectly do his will.

I come to the points ; they are three :—

1. It concerns them very much that would in prayer own God as a father, and pretend a respect to his glory and kingdom, to see that his will be done here upon earth.

2. It is the Lord that giveth to will and to do those things which are pleasing in his sight.

3. God doth not only look to this, that his will be done, but to the manner how it is done.

I. It concerneth them very much that would in prayer own God as a father, and pretend a respect to his glory and kingdom, to see that his will be done here upon earth.

I shall prove it :—

First, By the arguments intimated in the point.

1. As we pray to God, we should see his will be done, upon a double account—as real and successful.

[1.] As we would express a reality and sincerity in prayer. They mock God that pray they might do his will, yet have no care to do it, that declaim against their lusts, yet hug them and keep them warm in their bosoms. We oftener pray from our memories than our consciences, and oftener from our consciences than our affections.

From our memory, as we repeat words by rote, without sense, or feeling, or consideration of the importance of them. From our consciences, rather than affections. Austin observes of himself: while he was under the power of his lusts he would pray against concupiscence, but his heart would say, *At noli modo, timebam enim ne me exaudiret Deus;* 'But, Lord, not yet; for I am afraid lest God should hear me.' Conscience tells us that such things must be done and asked; thus we put a little of our conscience in prayer, but nothing of affection and serious desire. Many would be loth God should take them at their words, when they seem to resign up themselves to his will, and think of parting with their lusts; it is bitter and irksome to them: as Phaltiel, Michal's husband, 'went after her, going and weeping,' 2 Sam. iii. 16. Now if we would manifest our prayers to be real, we should labour to perform the same; otherwise we are but like those soldiers which spat upon Christ and buffeted him, yet cried, 'Hail, King of the Jews;' so it is but a mockage to say, 'Thy will be done,' yet have no care to do it: Mat. xv. 8, 'This people draweth nigh unto me with their mouth, and honoureth me with their lips, but their heart is far from me.' There is no reality in the prayer, whatever be in it, if the heart be not in it. Some men's prayers are but the fruit of wit and memory; others but the result of their judgments, what is fit to be done, rather than of their hearts, what they desire to be done; and they are only good so far as they do more solemnly express God's right, not their inward desires.

[2.] If we would have our prayers successful. Ps. lxvi. 18, 'If I regard iniquity in my heart, the Lord will not hear me.' Clearly, if we will not do God's will, there is no reason he should regard our will. If I regard iniquity in my heart, there may be sin in the heart; but if I regard it there, God will not hear me, if I entertain an affection to it. When the wind blows, some cold air will get into the chamber, though the door be shut never so close; but to leave the door open for it doth not argue such a care of health as is requisite. There will be sin in the children of God, but it is not allowed. Love to any known sin makes our prayers to God to be without success. So Prov. xxviii. 9, 'He that turneth away his ear from hearing the law, even his prayer shall be abomination.' God useth often the law of retaliation, will pay home sinners in their own coin: we will not hear him, therefore he will not hear us. The same argument we have to urge to God in prayer, that God hath to urge to us for duty and obedience. What argument will you use to awaken your confidence and affection? 'By the blood of Christ we have boldness to come to him,' Heb. x. 19, and Eph. iii. 12. This is not only an argument to be urged in expectation of mercy, but also in the enforcement of duty, when God beseecheth you by the bowels of Christ to do his will, and to mind his work. If the blood of Christ cannot prevail with us, to bring us up to the will of God, how can we expect it should prevail with God to bring us in returns of blessing? When God speaks we slight him, therefore when we speak God may cast off our prayers.

God speaks more wisely to us than we can to him; we stammer, and lisp, and speak foolishly in our prayers to God. There is far more reason why we should hear God than God hear us; for there is more equity in his precepts than there is reason in our prayers, and we are bound to obey God's will more than he is to grant our request; and therefore if we would not have God turn away his ear from our prayers, we should not turn away our ears from hearing his law and counsel: John ix. 31, 'Now we know that God heareth not sinners; but if any man be a worshipper of God, and doeth his will, him he heareth.' It is a general maxim, Those which were ready to deprave Christ's actions were possessed of the truth of this: 'If any man worship him, and do his will, him he heareth,' John ix. 31. It is not enough to keep up a form of worshipping, but we must be tender of his will; that is the way to get a gracious answer. Thus as we pray we are bound.

2. As God's children, so we must do his will: Mal. i. 6, 'If I be a father, where is mine honour? and if I be a master, where is my fear?' Relations to God are not bare titles and grounds, whereby we may expect favour from God; but they carry in their bosom obligations to duty on our part. Many will give God good words and fair titles, but there is no care had of complying with his will. Nay, your owning that relation will aggravate your sin, and be a witness against you. You owned me your father, and have not done my will. So Mat. xii. 50, ' Whosoever shall do the will of my Father which is in heaven, the same is my brother, and sister, and mother.' These may be sure of a comfortable relation to God, and that God will own them in that claim, when they make it their business to do his will; otherwise you reproach God rather than worship him. When you do your own will, and call God Father, you lay the devil's brats at his door; you pretend to God, and take his name upon you; therefore those that say, 'Our Father,' must also say, 'Thy will be done.'

3. Those that would have respect to God's glory must do his will. This is the honour of God, when you are at his command. God gloried in Abraham; rather Cyrus than Abraham is there meant, as the context shows: see Isa. xlvi. 11. Isa. xli. 2, ' The man from the east, whom I have called to my foot.' When you are at his beck, ready to go step by step with God, as God leads you, you are ready to follow. It was the honour of the centurion that had his soldiers at such a command, that ' when he said to one, Go, he went; and to another, Come, and he came,' Mat. viii. So it is God's honour, when he can bid you do nothing but you are ready to obey, though with the greatest hazard and loss of all.

4. Our subjection to his kingdom. God stands upon his authority. What is a king without obedience? Christ is never received as king but where his will is obeyed, otherwise we mock him with an empty title. The high priest's servants said, ' Hail, King of the Jews,' in mockage; thus it is to own him as king, when we will not yield obedience. Then do we desire that his kingdom may come indeed and in power, when we resolve to do his will, to love as God will have us, and hate, fear, and hope as God will: Ps. cxliii. 10, ' Thou art my God; teach me to do thy will.' If you own God as sovereign, you must be in subjection to his will. Thus this prayer will yield us arguments, as we own him as a father, as we profess respect to his glory and kingdom.

Secondly, I shall bring other arguments to persuade this, to make conscience of God's will.

1. The example of Christ Jesus, who wholly yielded up himself to the will of God; and wilt thou stand upon thy terms? John v. 30, 'I seek not mine own will, but the will of him that sent me.' Christ did not seek to please his human, his own natural will, but the will of his Father. This is true religion, to be like him whom we worship. Now, we are never like Christ until we make doing of God's will to be the great business of our lives. Wherefore doth he come into the world? He tells you; to do his Father's will: Luke ii. 49, 'Wist ye not that I must be about my Father's business?' This was his sole employment; so it should be ours, if we have the same mind which Christ had.

2. Consider God's right. We are not at our own dispose, but at the Lord's use. God hath a right in us, as he created us. The perfection of everything lieth in fulfilling the Creator's will, for that is the end wherefore they were made. The creatures 'are all thy servants, and continue this day according to thine ordinances,' Ps. cxix. 91. We owe our being, and all we have, from him. We see among men dependence begets observance; a man that lives upon another will be careful to please him. Thou holdest all by the indulgence and bounty of God, therefore it should be thy study to do his will. Jesus Christ hath bought thee: 1 Cor. vi. 20, 'Glorify the Lord in your souls and bodies, which are God's.' That is God's which he hath bought. A servant that was bought, when men were sold for slaves, he was his master's money; so his strength, time, service belonged to his master. We are God's, because he hath bought us, therefore we cannot live as we will; for this is the property of a servant, that he cannot live as he will. Again, as God hath begotten us anew, regenerated us, what is the aim of his grace? 'That we should no longer live in the flesh, to the lust of men, but to the will of God,' 1 Pet. iv. 2. It is the aim of grace to cure the disorders of the will, and to bring us to a stricter bond of duty and service to God. And indeed if grace hath had its fruit and power upon you, you will give up yourselves to God. Cant. vii. 10, 'I am my beloved's.' You are your beloved's, to be used by him as he pleaseth. So that unless you will retract your vows, you will make conscience of doing the will of God, for he hath a manifest right in you.

3. Consider our own incapacity. There is great reason why our wills should be given up to the will of God, because we are not able to manage them ourselves. By the law of nations, fools and madmen must have a guardian; they have lost the dominion and power over themselves, they are to be ruled by another, they are slaves by nature, that must be guided by another: Tit. iii. 3. We are all by nature fools, and it is the greatest mischief that can be to be left to our own wills; and therefore, when God requireth the resignation of our wills, it is but as the taking of a sword out of a madman's hand, which will be the cause of his own mischief and ruin. *Nemo læditur nisi a seipso,*—'No man is hurt by any but himself, though he may be troubled by others.' Now, since we cannot manage our own will, it is fit we should have a guardian; and who is more wise than God to govern

us? A merchant, though he owns the ship, and hath stored it with goods, yet because he hath no skill in the art of navigation, he suffereth the pilot to guide it. Certainly we shall but shipwreck ourselves unless we give up ourselves to be guided by the Spirit of God according to his will.

4. The benefit that accrueth to us by doing his will—we shall have his favour here and his glory hereafter. His favour here, which is that which endeareth us to God: Acts xiii. 22, ' I have found a man after mine own heart, which shall fulfil all my will.' These are men after God's own heart, that do his will. And though we have great infirmities, yet because we are bent to do his will, they will be passed over; as David had his infirmities, yet because it was in his heart to do the will of God, therefore this is a man after mine own heart. And you shall have the glory of God hereafter : 1 John ii. 17, ' The world passeth away and the lusts thereof : but he that doeth the will of God abideth for ever.' Those things that our wills carry us to they perish. The inclination of our heart carrieth us to the world, riches, honours, pleasures ; but the will of God carrieth us to an everlasting estate. ' The world passeth away, and the lusts thereof.' There will a time come when those things we will, and are so strongly addicted to and lust for, will be gone—we shall have no relish, no savour in them, no appetite to them. When men are leaving the world, then they cry out how the world hath deceived them; but now ' he that doeth the will of God abideth for ever.' Never any repented of doing the will of God; this will stick by us to all eternity, and bring us to everlasting happiness.

Use 1. To show how far they are from any sincere respect to God, that upon the least occasion transgress his will, and break through bonds and restraints God hath set to them. The heart is never right but when it lieth under the awe of a command. Many will fear a punishment; but it is said, Prov. xiii. 13, ' He that feareth the commandment:' if the commandment stands in his way he dares not break through, it is more than a hedge of thorns, or if lions stood in the way. But on the other side, when men make no bones of a commandment, when they will ' transgress for a pair of shoes ' (as the prophet saith), when every small temptation is enough to draw them off from God, it showeth how little sincere respect they have to God.

Use 2. It serves to press us to a more tender regard to the will of God. To this end consider these motives :—

1. His absolute authority to command: 1 Tim. vi. 15, ' Who is the blessed and only potentate, the King of kings, and Lord of lords ; ' his will is enough—I am the Lord, you shall do thus and thus.

2. Consider the equity of what he hath commanded : Rom. vii. 12, ' The commandment is holy, and just, and good.' Nothing God commandeth but what is agreeable to his own nature, and what is suited to our benefit. It is no burden to live justly, soberly, and holily in communion with God ; it is not a burden, but a great advantage. The yoke of Christ is a bountiful yoke. Our service and duty hath its own reward in the very mouth and bosom of it. It is no great wrong to us to govern our affections, to live soberly, chastely, and in the exercise of holy services; here is nothing but what raiseth

and sublimates the nature of man. If the commandment of God had been to offer our children in sacrifice, or any of those barbarities which were practised among the Gentiles, yet this had been enough, ' I am the Lord;' but when he hath given such holy and good commands, which makes you live more like men, like reasonable creatures, you should be tender of the Lord's will.

3. To be given up to our own will is a great judgment. When the Lord hath a mind to destroy a people, he gives them up to their own will : Ps. lxxxi. 12, ' Israel would none of me ; so I gave them up unto their own hearts' lust ; and they walked in their own counsels.' It is the greatest judgment which can be laid upon any creature, that he may have his own will. A man may be given up to Satan, yet recover : 1 Cor. v. 5, ' Deliver such an one to Satan for the destruction of the flesh, that the spirit may be saved in the day of the Lord Jesus.' He may be given up to Satan for his exercise and trial ; but when he is given up to himself, to the sway of his own heart, to be besotted with his own counsels, and to have his own lusts, what a heavy judgment is this ! When Balaam would not be satisfied, God said to him, 'Go,' Num. xxii. 35. He had his answer before, again and again, but he would be inquiring still ; ' Go,' and that was his punishment.

4. It is the truest liberty to be subject to the will of God. Then, ' when the Son of God shall make you free, you shall be free indeed,' John viii. 36. How doth the Son of God make us free ? Not *from* duty, but *for* duty. He that lieth under the dominion and power of any sin is a very slave. But then are we free indeed, when we are loosed, not from a due subjection to God, but from the power of the devil. It is not liberty to be free to do what we please, good or evil ; but the more determined we are to good, the more freedom—for that is a liberty which comes nearest to the liberty of God, who is a most free agent and yet cannot sin. Such a liberty is in God, Christ, and the angels in heaven : surely they do not live a slavish life that are ever praising and lauding of God. It will be the greatest pleasure in the issue to deny our own will and do the will of God. The more we are enlarged for this, the greater is our happiness. Then we have the happiness of the spirits of just men. None among men have greater happiness than glorified saints, yet none have less of their own will. Why should we account that a bondage which is part of our happiness ? In heaven glorified spirits there are not complaining of any burden, yet they have no will of their own, but they will and nill as God doth.

5. He that hath a heart bent to do the will of God, he hath the clearest knowledge of the mind of God : John vii. 17, ' He that will do the will of God, he shall know of the doctrine, whether it be of God.' It is not the sharpness of parts that pierceth into a truth, especially into a controverted truth, when the dust of contention is raised ; but he that is most close in walking with God, it is he that knoweth his mind. A blunt iron, when hot and in the fire, will pierce deeper into an inch board than a sharper tool that is cold ; so a man that hath pure affections for God, a heart to do the will of God, pierceth deeper many times into controverted truth, and sees more of

the mind of God in that truth than a man of parts doth. There are many mistakes about the will of God. Now make conscience of obedience, do not consult with the interest of your own private passions, and then you shall know the mind of God. It is just with God to withhold the light from them that consult with their lusts and interests and carnal humours, for these blind the mind, and only like and dislike things as they shall relish with their lusts.

6. God will surely punish the violation of his will. This implieth two things :—

[1.] That God takes notice of it; he observes whether his will be done, yea or no. The Rechabites were tender of the commandment of their dead father, who could not take cognizance of their actions; but it was the will of their father, and they would keep to the will of the dead : Jer. xxxv. 14. But now the Lord seeth whether his will be kept, yea or no : Prov. xv. 3, ' The eyes of the Lord are in every place, beholding the evil and the good.' Wherever you are, God is with you. As the prophet said to Gehazi, ' Went not mine heart with thee ? ' 2 Kings v. 26, meaning his prophetical spirit. The Lord's Spirit goeth along with us wherever we go, he observes what we do. When Jesus Christ was in the throng, he saith, ' Who is it that toucheth me ? ' He was sensible virtue passed out from him when one touched him by faith. So in the throng of creatures we depend upon God—he knows what virtue goeth out to preserve thee and me in being. These are fit instances to ingenerate in our minds a sense of God's omniscience.

[2.] He will severely punish : James iv. 12, ' There is one lawgiver, who is able to save and to destroy.' There are many lawgivers in the world, that have power of life and death, but that is only of life temporal; but there is one Lawgiver that can reward with eternal life, and punish with eternal death. So God truly and properly hath the power of life and death. Therefore, since he can punish so severely, we should not stand out against God's will. Many times the doing God's will is irksome to flesh and blood, but remember hell will be worse. When we press men to faith, repentance, and new obedience, and tell them this is the will of God concerning you, that you do believe in Christ, walk holily and humbly with God, what saith the man ? Shall I mope myself, and sit mourning in a corner, and spend my life in a dark melancholy manner, in going from one duty to another ? This is far better than to sit howling under the wrath of God for evermore.

For directions. If you would do the will of God, then—

1. There must be some solemn time of resigning and giving up thy will to him. Naturally we are averse. Now, whosoever is brought unto God, he comes and lays down the weapons of his defiance at God's feet. God hath a right to us, and he will have this right confirmed by our grant and consent : Rom. xii. 1, ' I beseech you by the mercies of God, that ye present your bodies a living sacrifice, holy, acceptable unto God.' There cannot be a more acceptable sacrifice to God than the resignation of our own will to him : See how Paul comes and layeth down the buckler, when God had him under : Acts ix. 6, ' And he, trembling and astonished, said, Lord, what wilt thou have me to do ? ' There will be a time when you will solemnly give up the keys

of your own hearts to God, and bid him come and enter. Paul, that now did nothing but threaten and breathe out terror ·to the children of God, when God had humbled him, then he lies at God's feet. When you are truly humbled, you will desire God to come and take possession of your hearts, and resolve to come under his yoke: Mat. xi. 28, 'Take my yoke upon you, and you shall find rest for your souls.' Christ will force it upon none. In the matrimonial contract, consent is not to be forced: ' *Take* my yoke.'

2. When you give up yourselves to God, it must be without bounds and reservations: 'That ye may stand perfect and complete in the will of God,' Col. iv. 42. That was his prayer for them: and, Acts xiii. 22, ' I have found David, the son of Jesse, a man after my own heart; he shall fulfil all my will.' We should so perfectly obey, as if we had no will of our own, not reserving a property in anything. Our thoughts are not our own to dispose, nor our desires nor delights, but as God will. The least sin reserved is a pledge of the devil's interest and right in us. And therefore give up all to God, resign up yourselves wholly to him, as remembering that every motion, every thought, every affection, is under a rule, and in every action we should say, Will God have this to be done, yea or no?

3. There are some special things concerning which God hath more expressly signified his will and given special charge, and these we should make greatest conscience of, how distasteful soever they be to flesh and blood, or prejudicial to our own interest. For instance, concerning repentance and turning from sin, Ezek. xxxiii. 11, you have God's oath that he delights in it: ' As I live, saith the Lord God, I have no pleasure in the death of the wicked, but that the wicked turn from his way, and live.' And God ' would not have any to perish, but that all should come to repentance,' 2 Pet. iii. 9. This is the will of God; he hath told you what a great deal of pleasure he takes in repentance, that you should come and mourn over your sins, and bewail your stragglings. When a profane Esau knew what his father desired, he takes his bow to go and kill venison; when we know anything more pleasing to God, we should do it. And then he takes pleasure also in the work of faith, believing in Christ: John vi. 29, ' This is the work of God, that ·ye believe on him whom he hath sent: and 1 John iii. 23, ' This is his commandment, that we should believe on the name of his Son Jesus Christ.' Therefore we should be much in the work of faith, and in receiving Christ, that we may accomplish the good pleasure of God in us. It is very pleasing to God we should thus repent, believe, and return to him. The very first motion, how welcome is it to the Lord! Ps. xxxii. 5, ' I said, I will confess my transgressions unto the Lord; and thou forgavest the iniquity of my sin.' So Luke xv. 20: the father ran to meet him when the prodigal thought of returning. So that you should live a sanctified life: 1 Thes. iv. 3, ' This is the will of God, even your sanctification.' That you should walk holily, God hath expressly declared his will. Then for duties of relations, God takes a great deal of pleasure in obedience to magistrates, parents, masters: 1 Pet. ii. 15, ' For so is the will of God, that with well-doing ye may put to silence the ignorance of foolish men.' Then, that we should observe providences, ever

be in a thankful frame: 1 Thes. v. 18, ' In everything give thanks;
for this is the will of God, in Christ Jesus, concerning you.' It is a
great rebellion and disobedience not to obey God's solemn charge.

4. We should be willing to obey God, whatever it cost us. The
least sin is not to be committed to avoid the greatest trouble. You
would think it were a small sin for Moses to tarry in Pharaoh's court,
where he might be helpful to the people of God, yet he ' chose rather
to suffer affliction with the people of God, than to enjoy the pleasures
of sin for a season,' Heb. xi. 25.

5. For the greatest good that possibly can come of it, we should not
cross God's revealed will. Many times this is a snare. Men think to
be justified by their good intentions. We must not do evil that good
may come thereof: Rom. iii. 8. If one lie could save the world, we
were not to do it, for the least evil is not to be done contrary to God's
will, though the greatest good come of it.

Use 3. Examine how you stand affected to God's will. This is very
needful, because—

1. There be many mistakes about it.

2. Hereby we may discern whether we are thus entirely affected
with the Lord's will.

Men flatter themselves with a pretence of obedience, and cry, ' Lord,
Lord,' but do not do his will. They give God good words, but do not
break out into an actual contest; as those wretches, Jer. xviii. 12,
' We will every one do the imagination of his evil heart:' and Jer.
xliv. 17, ' We will certainly do whatsoever thing goeth forth out of
our own mouth.' There are many things wherein we are apt to mistake. As,

[1.] We pretend to do God's will in general, but when it comes to
particulars we stick at it. Usually, when we take up duty by the
lump, it doth not exasperate opposite propensions and inclinations.
This is our great fault, we please and flatter ourselves with notions
and abstract conceits. What say you to this will of God concerning
you in particular? How forward were the Israelites! Oh, they
would do the whole will of God; they run away with the general
notion. Yea, but saith Joshua, chap. xxiv. 19, ' Ye cannot serve the Lord,
for he is an holy God, he is a jealous God; he will not forgive your
transgressions nor your sins.' We will do the will of God in general,
but when it comes to cross our lusts and private inclinations, these
make us grudge at it, and shrink back again.

[2.] Some commend and approve the will of God, and talk of it, but
do not practise it. It is here, ' Thy will be done;' it is not, Let it be
talked of, spoken and conferred of by me, but done. And it is not
giving good words. You know the parable of the two sons: One said,
' I will not, and did;' the other, ' I go, sir, and went not,' Mat. xxi.
29, 30. Where Christ prefers the open sinner before the hypocrite,
that is talking of God's will, and seems at a distance to be like the
carbuncle, all of a fire, but touch him, he is key-cold. When we are
approving much of the will of God in our judgments, and commending of it, and do it not, this is in effect to say, I know what my Father
commands me, but I will do as I list.

[3.] Another deceit about the will of God is this: For the present, while we are in a good humour, when our lusts lie low, when the heart is warm under the impulsions of a present conviction or persuasion, men have high thoughts of doing the will of God : Deut. v. 27, ' Speak thou unto us all that the Lord our God shall speak unto thee ; we will hear it, and do it.' There are several acts of our wills ; there is consent, choice, intention, and prosecution. It is not enough to consent : these things may be extorted from us by moral persuasion ; but there must be a serious choice, an invincible resolution, such an intention as is prosecuted with all manner of industry and serious endeavours, whatever disappointments we meet with from God and men. Then this intention or invincible resolution is such as will not be broken by difficulties, weakened by loss of interest, not discouraged by the many disappointments we meet with, even in our waiting upon God.

[4.] We have many times a seeming awe upon the conscience, and so are urged to do God's will, yet the heart is averse from God all the while ; therefore they strive to bring God's will and theirs together, to compromise the difference. A notable instance of this you have in Balaam. He had a message sent to him, and a great bribe. Now he had a carnal heart, which ran out upon the wages of unrighteousness, and, therefore, though he knew the people of Israel were blessed of the Lord, yet first he will go to God : Num. xxii. 8, ' Lodge here this night, and I will bring you word again, as the Lord shall speak unto me.' He is very tender, he durst not go with them, unless the Lord say, Go. But God denies him : ver. 12, ' Thou shalt not go with them.' What then ? The Lord refuseth to give him leave. Then Balak sends more honourable messengers, and propounds rewards again. Then his carnal will is for God : ver. 18, Balaam answered, ' If Balak would give me his house full of silver and gold, I cannot go beyond the word of the Lord my God, to do less or more.' Was not this spoken with an honest mind, think you ? This was the dictate of his conscience ; not for a houseful of gold durst he go against God the Lord. Yet you shall find it was a sore temptation to him, for he goes again to God : ver. 19, ' Tarry here this night, that I may know what the Lord will say unto me more.' Then saith God, Go, when he saw his heart was set for the wages of unrighteousness. There was a reluctancy in his conscience, he durst not go, therefore he would fain bring the will of God to his will. In many cases we are thus divided between our own affections and God's will, between our interests and the will of God.

It is a case often falls out, when there is a quarrel between conviction and corruption. When light is active and strong in conscience, men dare not go against the apparent will of God, yet their hearts hang another way. We have one carnal affection or other, and then all our business is to bring God's will and ours together ; and how to disguise and palliate the matter, that with greatest leave to conscience we may seem to contradict the will of God.

[5.] A fifth deceit about the will of God, and that is, a wish that we were brought under the power of it, as he that stretched himself upon his bed, and said, Oh, that this were to labour ! Many men have a velleity, a languid and incomplete will ; they have a wish, but not a volition, not a serious desire ; and sometimes they may draw it out to a cold prayer that God would make them better. It is just like a man that should lie down and complain, Oh, that I were at such a place ! and never travel. Would I had performed such a task ! yet puts not his hand to the work. Men *would*, but they *will* not, set themselves in good earnest to get the grace they wish for, there is not striving to accomplish their will. A chapman no doubt would have the wares, it is like he hath a cold wish, but will not come to the price ; I will buy it whatever it cost me. They have not those active and industrious resolutions, such a strong and serious bent of heart towards God, but only a few wishes.

[6.] Halving the will of God ; as in many cases many will do part of the will of God, but not all, they come not fully up to the mind of God. For instance, they will take notice of some great commandment, but not of the least. We cannot dispense with ourselves in the least : Mat. v. 19, ' Whosoever shall break one of the least commandments, and shall teach men so, he shall be called the least in the kingdom of heaven.' We are apt to say ' It is but a little one, and my soul shall live.' No sin is little which is committed against a great God. It argueth more wickedness to break with God for a trifle and a very small matter, it argueth more corruption ; as a little force will make a heavy body move downward. Again, in another case, the ceremonialist stands upon some lesser things ; as the Jews, John xviii. 28, 'would not go into the judgment-hall lest they should be defiled,' yet they could seek the life of the Lord of glory. They are not brought under the dominion of the Lord's grace, faith, repentance, holiness, and the weightier things of the law ; these are things they regard not. This is hypocrisy. Like one that comes into a shop to buy a pennyworth and steals a pound's worth ; so they are punctual in lesser things, that they may make bold with God in greater. Again, some will do the will of God in public, where they may be observed ; but not in private, and when alone. They make a fair show in the world, but in their families their converse is more loose and careless : Ps. ci. 2, ' I will walk within my house with a perfect heart.' A man that is truly holy will show it at home and abroad, in his closet and secret retirements, everywhere he makes conscience of the will of God. Many times we strain ourselves and put forth our gifts in public ; God will be served with our utmost in secret also ; and the will of God is expressed concerning the inward as well as the outward man, and we must make conscience of both : Isa. lv. 7, ' Let the wicked man forsake his way, and the unrighteous man his thoughts,' &c. Not only make conscience of our way, our outward course, but of our thoughts as well as our actions, for the thoughts fall under a law. So some will make conscience of the first-table duties, and neglect the second ; and some of the second, and neglect the first. Some are very punctual in dealing with men, but neglectful of God : Rom. i. 18, ' The wrath of God is revealed from heaven, against all ungodliness and unrighteousness of men.' Both tables are owned from heaven. Some will not wrong their neighbour of a farthing, but stick not to rob God of all that faith, fear, love, trust, worship, that is due to him. Many that will not defile their bodies with promiscuous copulation, yet are adulterers and adulteresses to God, their hearts straggling from God, doting upon the creature to the wrong of God. Many condemn the rebellion of Absalom, and rise up against their heavenly Father, and are murderers, that strike at the being of God. They are tender of wronging the reputation of men, yet dishonour God, and are never troubled. So, on the other side, others fear and worship, but in their dealings are very unconscionable ; they will not swear an oath, but are very uncharitable, censuring their brethren without pity and remorse. This is the fashion of the world, to be in with one duty and out with another.

[7.] A loathness to know the will of God, to search and inquire into it, argueth deceit, and that we are loath to come under the power of it. Some men shrewdly suspect it is true, but are loath to inquire into it : John iii 20, ' Every one that doeth evil hateth the light, neither cometh to the light, lest his deeds should be reproved.' They have a shrewd guess about the ways of God, but will not search to be satisfied : 2 Pet. iii. 5, ' They are willingly ignorant.' As Tertullian saith of the heathens, they would not search into the Christian religion, because they had a mind to hate it ; so these are loath to inquire further into the will of God. There is a great deal of deceit in it ; it shows we are afraid to come too near a suspected truth. Again, now and then when lusts are under some restraint, men seem to lie much under the will of God. A horse that is kept low is easily ruled by the rider, but when fed high he grows headstrong. Many times in a mean condition a man seems to make conscience of doing the will of God ; but when prosperous, he waxeth wanton and disobedient : Jer. v. 5, ' I will get me to the great men, but these have altogether broken the yoke and burst the bonds.'

So that there are a great many mistakes about doing the will of God, therefore you had need search.

Secondly, How shall we know we are rightly affected with the will of God ?

[1.] When God's will is reason enough for what he hath required of us ; when a man is so sensible of God's will that this is instead of all reasons. Obedience is never right but when it is done upon the mere sight of God's will. This is enough to a gracious heart, that this is the will of God, 1 Pet. ii. 15, 1 Thes. v. 18, though the duty be never so cross to our own desires and interests. This is to obey the commandment for the commandment's sake, without any other reason or inducement. There is, indeed, *ratio formalis* and *ratio motiva*, the formal reasons of obedience and the motives of obedience. The formal reason of obedience is the sight of God's will, the motives to obedience are rewards and a dread of punishment. The formal reason is God's will ; and this is pure obedience, to do what God wills because God wills it.

[2.] When a man is very inquisitive to know what is the will of his heavenly Father. When he doth not only practise what he knows, but searcheth that he may know more : Rom. xii. 2, ' That ye may prove what is that good and acceptable and perfect will of God ;' and, Eph. v. 17, ' Be ye not unwise, but understanding what the will of the Lord is.' When a man is desirous to know the whole will of God, not for curiosity but for practice, that he might do it. When the understanding hath a confused notion of a thing they will not know it distinctly, but when men search, and are willing to find out the counsel of God in all things that they may come up to it, this is a sign the heart is rightly affected to the will of God.

[3.] Hereby may you know your affection to God's will, by keeping yourselves from your sins : Ps. xviii. 23, ' I was upright before him, and kept myself from mine iniquity.' There is an iniquity that we may call ours, upon which the will is most passionately addicted; be it worldliness, sensuality, inordinate desire of reputation and respect with men. Now, when we are plucking out our right eye, and cutting off our right hand, Mat. v. 29—when we are mortifying and subduing our lusts—when we can deny ourselves in those things to which the heart is most wedded, that is a sign of compliance with the will of God.

The second point.

Doct. 2. That it is the Lord which giveth to will and to do those things which are pleasing in his sight.

Therefore we ask it of him, ' Thy will be done,'—that is, as I explained it, we ask of him a heart, skill, and strength to do his holy will.

Here I shall tell you :—

1. What I mean by the point.
2. Give you the proof of it.

I. What I mean by the point :—

1. I mean thus, that in the work of conversion God doth all : Ezek. xi. 19, ' I will give them one heart, and I will put a new spirit within you ; and I will take the stony heart out of their flesh, and I will give them an heart of flesh.' The benefit of a tender sanctified heart is God's gift : Ezek. xxxvi. 26, 27, ' A new heart also will I give you, and a new spirit will I put within you : and I will take away the stony heart out of your flesh, and I will give you an heart of flesh, and I will cause you to walk in my statutes.' Mark, a *new* heart— that is, *another* heart, a heart to understand, a heart to love, a heart to do the will of God, he *gives* it. He doth not only offer it, or prepare it, make way for it, but ' I will give you a heart of flesh.'

2. This is that I mean, that after conversion God still concurreth. He doth not only give the habit of grace, but actual help in the work of obedience. ' He worketh all our works in us,' Isa. xxvi. 12. His actual help is necessary to direct, quicken, strengthen, protect, and defend us. To direct us : Ps. lxxiii. 24, ' Thou shalt guide me by thy counsel, and bring me to thy glory.' In our way to heaven, we need not only a rule and path, but a guide. The rule is the law of God, but the guide is the Spirit of God. To quicken and excite us by effectual motions : a drowsiness and a deadness is apt to creep upon our hearts, and we see in the same duty it is a hard matter to keep up the same frame of spirit, the same vigour of affection, life, and warmth ; and therefore we had need go to God often, as David : Ps. cxix. 37, ' Quicken thou me in thy way.' It is God which doth renew the vigour of the life of grace upon all occasions, when it begins to languish and droop. To corroborate and strengthen what we have received : Eph. iii. 16, the apostle prays there that he would ' strengthen with might by his Spirit in the inner man ;' and, 1 Pet. v. 10, 'Make

you perfect, stablish, strengthen, settle you.' There are many words heaped up there to show how God is interested in maintaining and keeping afoot that which he hath planted in the soul. In protecting and defending them against the incursions and assaults of the devil, who always lieth in wait to surprise the soul, to withdraw us from God. The regenerate are not only escaped out of his clutches, but are advanced and appointed to be Satan's judges, which an envious and proud spirit cannot endure; therefore he maligns, assaults, and besiegeth them with temptations daily. Now, it is God that defends: John xvii. 11, ' Keep through thine own name those whom thou hast given me;' by thy *name*—that is, by thy *power*.

3. God must not only help us in the general, and upon weighty occasions, but in every act, from the beginning of the spiritual life to the end. It is not enough to say that the first principles and motions are of God, but the flowing forth of all motions and actions, according to those principles: Phil. ii. 13, ' It is God that worketh in you both to will and to do of his good pleasure.' God not only gives the desire and purpose, but he gives grace to the good which we will and purpose to do. These two are distinct; and we may have assistance in one kind and not in another; willing and doing, I mean, are different. Paul saith, Rom. vii. 18: ' To will is present with me; but how to perform that which is good I find not.' To *will* is more than to *think;* and to *exert,* and put forth our will into action, it is more than both; and in all we need God's help. We cannot think a good thought, nor conceive a holy purpose, much less perform a good action, without God, so that every moment we need renewed strength. As long as the work of grace is powerful and renewed in us, so long we are kept in a warm and healthful frame; but we grow vain, loose, earthly, carnal again, and off from God, when this heat and warmth of grace is withdrawn; and therefore God still concurreth in the whole business of our obedience to him.

II. Having showed what I mean, and how far God is interested in this work, what need we have to desire we may do his will; let us prove it. And because it is a weighty point, I shall prove it by parts.

1. As to the first grace, that it is God alone which frames our hearts to the obedience of his will.

2. That when we are thus framed by grace, after conversion, it is God still concurs, and must help us to do his will.

First, As to the first grace, I shall prove that it is God alone, by the power of his own Spirit, which frames our hearts to the obedience of his will. This will appear by considering:—

(1.) What man is by nature.

(2.) The words by which our cure is expressed, and the way God takes to put us into a course of obedience.

(3.) What the scripture speaks as to the utter impotency of man, to the framing of his heart to the obedience of God's will.

(1.) First, This will appear by those notions or emphatical terms by which the scripture doth set forth man's condition before God works upon him. He is one that is ' born in sin:' Ps. li. 5, ' Behold, I was shapen in iniquity, and in sin did my mother conceive me;' and things natural are not easily altered. And as he is born in sin, so he is greedy of sin: Job xv. 16, 'He drinketh in iniquity like water;' it noteth a vehement propension, as greedy to sin as a thirsty man to drink.   Thirst is the most implacable appetite, hunger is far better borne.   It is the constant frame of his heart: Gen. vi. 5, 'Every imagination of the thoughts of his heart is only evil continually.' Oh, how many aggravating and increasing circumstances are there named. There is a mint that is always at work; the mind is coining evil thoughts, and the heart evil desires and carnal motions; and the memory is the closet and storehouse where they are lodged and kept. This is the case of man, born in sin, greedy and thirsty of sin, and one whose thoughts are evil continually.

But may not a man be reclaimed?   Oh no, for he hath a heart of stone: Ezek. xxxvi. 26, 'I will take away the heart of stone.' Every man that comes to be converted hath a heart of stone; and what is that? insensible, inflexible.   Insensible, he hath no feeling of his condition; inflexible, he will not be moved and wrought upon by the word, and the Spirit, and providence.   How many means are wasted upon him, and to no purpose ! And Jer. xvii. 9, 'The heart is deceitful above all things, and desperately wicked : who can know it ?' It invents all kinds of shifts and excuses to elude God, or rather to cheat itself.   When God comes to work upon man, it slides away from under his hand, as if salvation itself should not save them.   Yea, but is not the New Testament more favourable to man than the Old ? Or, is not man grown better now there is so much of God's grace discovered ?   I answer, there is a perfect harmony between the Testaments: there he is styled 'a child of wrath by nature,' Eph. ii. 3; the elect as well as others were so.   There you will find him to be a 'servant of sin,' Rom. vi. 17.   Never such an imperious master as sin is, never such a willing servant as man is.   Sin never leaves commanding, and we love to work, and therefore are at its beck.   There you will find him to be represented as a man that hath a 'blind understanding,' and a 'hard heart,' and one that is 'averse from the life of God,' Eph. iv. 18.   There you will find him to be one that is an 'enemy to the law of God,' 'enmity' itself, Rom. viii. 7; one that neither will nor 'can please God.'   One that is blind, and knows not what to do : 2 Pet. i. 9, 'He that lacketh these things is blind,' and with such a blindness as is far worse than bodily.   A man that is blind in his bodily eyes, would think it to be a great happiness to have a fit guide : as in Acts xiii. 11, when Elymas was smitten blind, 'he sought about for somebody to lead him by the hand.'   But he that is spiritually blind, cannot endure to have a guide; or if one would lead him, and direct him in the right way, he is angry.   And as the scripture represents him as blind, so without strength : Rom. v. 9, 'Dead in trespasses and sins;' Eph. ii. 5, yea, worse than dead; a dead man doth no more hurt, his evil dieth with him; but there is a life of resistance and rebellion against God that goeth along. I have spoken but little, yet put all together, and then it shows what a miserable wretched creature man is.

The scripture doth not speak this by chance, it is not an *hyperbole* used once or twice, but everywhere, where it speaks of this matter, it sets out man to be blind, hard, dead, obstinate, and averse from God.

Certainly man contributes little to his own conversion, if the word of God sets him out everywhere to be such a one; he cannot hunger and thirst after Christ, that drinks in iniquity like water. Nothing in his nature to carry him to grace, who is altogether sinful.

If the scripture had only said that man had accustomed himself to sin, and was not born in sin : if it had said that man is very prone, and not greedy and thirsty in iniquity : if it had only said that man did often think evil, but not continually : if the scripture had said that man was somewhat obstinate, but not a stone, an adamant, and like the nether mill-stone : that he had been indifferent to God and the world, God and the flesh, and not a professed enemy : that he had been a captive of sin, and not a servant of sin : that man had been weak and not dead : only a neuter and not a rebel : then there might have been something in man ; and the work of conversion and reducing to God had not been so great. But the scripture saith the quite contrary, that man is all this and much more, therefore this clears it up, that his conversion is not in himself, but it is God must work this good work upon him, or else he can never be renewed.

(2.) Secondly, Let us consider the terms how the cure is wrought. Certainly to remedy so great an evil, requireth an omnipotent, an almighty power. Therefore see how conversion is described in scripture, sometimes by enlightening the mind : Eph. i. 18, ' The eyes of your understanding being enlightened, that ye may know what is the hope of his calling,' &c. Man, the best creature on this side heaven, is stark blind in the things of God. If he should go to see with the light of nature, how would he grope at noon-day ! If he should put on the spectacles of art he will but be little better. Nay, let him take further the glass of the word, yet how blind in a spiritual sense. Something there must be done upon the faculty ; the object must not only be revealed, but the eye must be enlightened. There are thick scales upon his eye, as Paul had in his blindness, that must be taken off, before he can see into the things of God.

But is this all, enlightening the eye ? No; the scripture describeth this work of God by opening of the heart : Acts xvi. 14, ' God opened the heart of Lydia, that she attended unto the things which were spoken of Paul.' God doth not only *knock* at the heart—that he doth by his word, and by the external means—but he *openeth* the heart ; he must open the door before he can come in, enter, and take possession.

As to the means, God trieth key after key, one providence after another. As when a man would open a door, he knows not what key will fit the lock, he trieth key after key ; so God trieth one cross, one affliction after another, one sermon, one message after another ; but until he puts his fingers upon the hole of the lock, we shall not open.

But these words are not emphatical enough, therefore it is expressed by a regeneration : John iii. 3, ' Except a man be born again, he cannot see the kingdom of God.' Mark, they must not only be re-formed, but must be regenerated and born again.

Now, because this is an ordinary work which falleth out in the course of causes, therefore there is a more solemn notion used, it is expressed by a resurrection : Eph. ii. 5, ' He hath raised you up to-gether with Christ.' Yea, but that which hath been may be again, therefore it is expressed not only by a resurrection, but by a creation : Eph. ii. 10, 'We are his workmanship, created in Christ Jesus unto good works :' 2 Cor. iv. 6, 'He that commandeth the light to shine out of darkness, hath shined in our hearts.' And we are called new creatures. And higher than this, it is expressed not only by a creation, but by a victory and overcoming. It is resembled by beating and binding of the strong man, and rescuing and taking away his prey from him : Luke xi. 21, 22; 1 John iv. 4. 'By bringing into captivity every proud thought to the obedience of Christ,' 2 Cor. x. 5.

These expressions the scripture useth to set out the mystery of grace, the power of God that worketh in us. What is wanting in one is supplied in another.

(3.) The third thing I shall produce ; That the scripture doth expressly deny any power in man to convert himself to God : 1 Cor. ii. 14, 'The natural man cannot know the things of the Spirit of God, because they are spiritually discerned ;' and as he cannot know, so he cannot obey: Rom. viii. 7, 'The carnal mind is enmity against God ; for it is not subject to the law of God, neither indeed can be ; and they cannot please God :' ver. 8. And they cannot come to Christ: John vi. 44, 'No man can come to me except the Father draw him.' And they cannot do anything without Christ, John xv. 15 ; and they cannot think a good thought, 2 Cor. iii. 5 ; and they cannot bring forth good fruit, Mat. vii. 18 ; and they cannot speak a good word, Mat. xii. 34 ; and they cannot believe, John xii. 39 ; and they cannot do that which is good, Jer. xiii. 23, 'Ye that are accustomed to do evil, cannot do good.' From whence doth all this deficiency in them arise ? Partly from nature, partly from custom. Besides the natural there is a customary and habitual depravation. By nature we are averse from God, and by custom we are more confirmed in this evil aversation from God. Man, by lying long in his unregeneracy, hath his averseness from God increased and strengthened upon him. Naturally we are in love with the world, and have declined God and the things of God. Consider him in his naturals, he 'cannot know the things of the Spirit:' 1 Cor. ii. 14. And the carnal mind cannot be subject to the law of God, being at enmity against him, Rom. viii. 7. There are other places express this *cannot*, which derive it from custom; they are become slaves to their lusts, and their sins have gotten such a hand over them that they know not how to break them off : Jer. xiii. 23, 'Can the Ethiopian change his skin, or the leopard his spots ? Then may ye also do good, that are accustomed to do evil.' And so where it is said: John xii. 39, 'They could not believe.' Naturally man is unable ; but that place speaks of another degree of impossibility through contracted obstinacy and judicial obduration. Thus you see man is wholly impotent as to this work, and it is the Lord alone must do it.

Object. But here is an objection. If it be so that man hath such an utter impotency to convert himself to God, how can it stand with the mercy of God, as the creator of mankind, to require the debt of obedience from him that is not able to pay? How can it stand with the justice of God to punish him with eternal death, for the neglect of that which he is not able to do ? and how can it stand with the wisdom of the supreme lawgiver, to exhort him by promises and threatenings, who hath no power to do what he is exhorted to do?

I answer:—

1. As to the first; how can it stand with the mercy of God to require the debt of obedience from him that is not able to pay? God hath not lost his *right*, though man hath lost his *power;* their impotency doth not dissolve their obligation. A drunken servant is a servant still. It is against all reason a master should lose his right by the servant's default. A prodigal debtor hath nothing to pay, yet he is liable to be sued for the debt without any injustice. God contracted with us in Adam, and gave us a power which we lost by his fall; and therefore though our power be gone, yet God may demand his due to obey and please him; especially since this obedience God required of Adam, was not only due by covenant and positive law, but by immutable right and natural justice of man. Men think it harsh to suffer for Adam's fault, to which they were not conscious and actually consenting.

Yea, but consider, every man will find an Adam in his own heart. The old man is there, we are still sinning away those relics of natural light in conscience, and those few moral inclinations which are left. There is a little ability and strength he hath as a man, and shall not God challenge the debt of obedience from a proud prodigal debtor, that is weakening and wasting himself more and more? We are proud, therefore God may exact it of us. We think we are able to obey and do his will, when we are weak; we are poor, yet think ourselves rich; therefore God may admonish us of our duty, demand his right to show our impotency and beggary, and that we may not pretend we were not called upon for what we owe. But man is not only a proud debtor, but we are prodigal debtors; those relics of conscience and moral and human inclinations, which escaped out of the ruins of the fall, we lose those things every day, and embezzle them away by the service of sin. Therefore it standeth fully with the clemency of God, as creator of mankind, to require the debt of him that wastes that little stock he hath.

2. As to the other part, how it can stand with the justice of God to punish him with eternal death, for the neglect of that he cannot do. I answer: Besides natural impotency, there is voluntary. We must not consider man merely as impotent to good, but as delighting in evil, as loving it with all his heart. This *cannot* indeed is a *will not*, it is a voluntary impotence. 'You will not come to me, that ye might have life:' John v. 40. Our impotency lies in our obstinacy. So man is left without excuse, because we freely refuse the grace offered, and by continuing in sin we increase our bondage, and draw an inveterate custom upon ourselves, and so grow every day more obstinate against God.

3. As to the last, how can it stand with the wisdom of God to exhort him with promises and threatenings, that hath no power to do that which he is exhorted to?

I answer: These exhortations, they carry their own blessing with them to those to whom God means them for good. As God's creating word carried with it its power: 'Be there light, and there was light;'

and as Christ's word carried forth his power, it was not in vain to say, 'Lazarus, come forth,' though he was dead, and could not hear it; there was a mighty power went with the word; so there is power goes along with the exhortations of the gospel, to work grace in the hearts of those to whom God intends it as a blessing.

Yea, but if this be for the elect's sake only, and to convey that power to them, to what use doth it stand to others? If the elect did dwell alone, and were a distinct community among themselves, the objection were plausible; but they are hidden among others: therefore reprobates are called *obiter*, by the by, as others are called according to purpose; and therefore they have the benefit of the common call and the common offer. The world stands for the elect's sake, yet others have the benefit of the world and worldly things. So the word is preached for the elect's sake, yet others have the benefit of an external call. The sun shines, though blind men see it not. The rain falls upon rocks and mountains, as well as fruitful valleys; so God may suffer these exhortations to light upon wicked men. And again, as to them, it is for their conviction; it is to bridle their corruptions; it is at least a means to civilise them, and keep them from growing worse: therefore such kind of doctrines and persuasions restrain their wickedness. Therefore it stands well enough with the wisdom of the lawgiver to call upon men, and invite them with promises and threatenings, to repentance.

Therefore now let me show how doth God reduce and frame our hearts to the obedience of his will. The ways God useth are of two sorts, moral and real.

[1.] God works morally, so as to preserve man's nature, and the principles thereof; therefore he works by sweet inclination, not with violence. So he comes with blandishments and comfortable words: Hosea ii. 14, 'I will allure her, and bring her into the wilderness, and speak comfortably unto her.' So, Gen. ix. 27, 'The Lord shall persuade Japhet, and he shall dwell in the tents of Shem.' By fair and kindly words, he draweth on men to the liking of the gospel. He offereth no violence to our natural principles, but to our corruptions. God doth not make the will to be *no* will, but to be a *good* will; he restoreth the faculties to their right use and exercise; he layeth forth the beauty and excellency of his grace, and a glorious estate he sets before our eyes, and so outbids temptation, and draweth our hearts to himself. And God not only doth work suitably to our general nature, as we are reasonable creatures, but suitably to the particular frame of the heart. Some are of a stout and stubborn temper, and will not be subdued by milder means and motives; therefore God breaks them with fears and terrors, and with a spirit of conviction; and others, he draws them on by love, and by a gentle application.

That God hath respect to men's particular tempers was figured in those extraordinary ways of appearance and manifestation; they are fitted according to the state of men. To Moses, that was a shepherd, and was acquainted with bushes, God appears in a bush of fire; and to the wise men, that were skilled in the motions of the heavenly bodies, he appears in a star; and to Peter, that was a fisherman, he appears to him, and shows his power first in the draught of fishes,

So still these are pledges of this kind of dispensation : that God will work suitably, not only to our general nature as men, but to our particular state and temper. Yea, yet further, to set on this moral way of working, there is a fit subordination of the circumstances of providence. God 'takes the wild asses in their month;' and he hath his season wherein to surprise the hearts of sinners : Prov. xxv. 11, 'A word fitly spoken is like apples of gold in pictures of silver.' God comes in in a fit season; as when a soul is humbled by some sudden accident; as one was converted by seeing a man fall down dead suddenly by him. God ordereth some providences to work, and awaken the hearts of men; or else by some great affliction : Hos. ii. 14, 'I will bring her into the wilderness, and speak comfortably unto her.' God finds many a sinner in the briars, as Abraham found the lamb. Stubborn humours are then most broken. Metal in the furnace is capable of any form. God may suit and dispose us so that he may come in in a fit season to the soul, or in terrors of conscience, when the heart is scourged with remorse for great sins. All this is God's moral work.

[2.] There is a real work, which goes along with this persuasion : there is an almighty power; for bare persuasion cannot make the blind to see, the dead to live, or open the heart of man, that is so desperately and obstinately wicked, until he puts his fingers upon the holes of the lock, until he begins to open the heart.

Concerning this real work, observe it is secret, yet thorough and prevailing, so as the effect doth follow, when God will convert. The exact manner of God's drawing is unknown. Austin calls it an inward, hidden, and unspeakable power, which God putteth forth together with the word. It is marvellous in our eyes; but he that knew how to create souls knows how to work upon them. This power, it is like the influences of the heavens, which so insinuate themselves with the operation of second causes, that they cannot be seen; so there is such a mighty power working in us, though we cannot tell how to express it. We cannot say there is no such power, because we do not know what it is.

And as this power is secret, so when this power is put forth it is prevailing : he works prevailingly, so as the effect must necessarily follow. The grace God gives to men, to convert them, it is not a power to be converted, repent, and believe, if they will; no, but he gives repentance, he gives faith, and works so as the effect shall succeed : he works efficaciously and determinately, so as to oppose all the resistance of the will, and accomplish his work.

That is the first branch.

Secondly, When we are thus framed by grace, after conversion God still concurreth, and must help us to do his will. He doth not only give us the habit of grace, but actual help in the work of obedience : Isa. xxvi. 12, 'Thou hast wrought all our works in us.'

But why is it that still the Lord worketh in us, both to will and to do, unto the last; and not only begins with us, but still keeps grace in his own hands, so as we shall have our supplies from heaven from day to day ?

There are several reasons :—

[1.] Because it endeareth God to a gracious soul. The more visits we have from God, and the more he is mindful of us at every turn, the more is God endeared to us. In such a duty, there we met with comfort and enlargement, because God was there; that is noted and regarded, so that the Lord is rendered the more precious. The experiment we have of God in every duty doth the more make us prize his grace. As David, Ps. cxix. 93, ' I will never forget thy precepts, for with them thou hast quickened me.' I shall never forget such a sermon, and such a prayer, because there I met with God. So in affliction, Rom. v. 3, ' Patience worketh experience;' or in such a conflict, we had such a support: this endeareth God to the soul. As mutual acts of kindness do maintain a friendship between man and man, so do these renewed acts of love, and of God's care and kindness over us, maintain a friendship between God and us.

[2.] It engageth us to a constant dependence upon God, and communion with him. It is dependence which maintains the commerce between heaven and earth. Now, if we did keep the stock ourselves, God and we should soon grow strangers. When the prodigal had his portion in his own hands, he goes out of his father's house: Luke xv. The throne of grace would lie neglected and unfrequented. If we did not stand in need of daily receivings, when would the Lord hear from us? And therefore, to oblige us to a constant dependence, God will keep the grace in his own hands, that ever we may have something to drive us to himself, some necessities upon us; for the throne of grace is for a time of need: Heb. iv. 16.

[3.] This is that which keeps us humble, and that upon several considerations. All we have, it is by gift; and then what can we be proud of ? Not only the habits of grace themselves, but also those actual incitements which are necessary to draw them forth into act. So that of all our excellencies we may say, Alas ! it is but borrowed; and if we be proud of them, we are but proud we are more in debt than others: when most enlarged and most assisted, it is from God. We would laugh if a groom should be proud of his master's horse and his master's cloak; shall we usurp that honour that is due to God? 'What hast thou that thou didst not receive?' 1 Cor. iv. 7. And then we have it from hand to mouth. That which we have received will not bear us out, unless God come in with new influences of grace. We should soon grow proud if God did not direct us, and give out the renewed evidences of his love day after day; and we should not acknowledge our benefactor if God should do all at once: therefore he lesseneth and weakeneth our corruptions by degrees, and by the renewed influences of his grace; and by this means we are made sensible of the mutability of our own nature. God left Hezekiah, ' to try him, that he might know all that was in his heart,' 2 Chron. xxxii. 31. God hath so dispensed grace that he will be going and coming as to actual influence; therefore sometimes he will leave us, that he may discover a man to himself. Though we have grace planted in our hearts, and are renewed, yet if God leave us, how weak and foolish are we ! We are renewed, but not fully recovered of that maim and bruise we got by the fall of Adam, and we cannot do as we will. If God withdraw his quickening, his strength, secret corruption will break forth, and our indisposition to holy things will soon appear.

[4.] Then it is for the honour of the Lord's grace. It doth abundantly provide for the glory of grace, that from first to last we are
indebted to God; not only for those permanent and fixed habits which
constitute the new creature, but for those daily supplies without which
the motions of the spirit are at a stand. And this is that which
makes the saints still to put the crown upon grace's head. When the
servants gave an account of improving of their talents, saith one of
them, Luke xix. 16, 'Lord, thy pound hath gained ten pounds:' he
doth not say, 'My industry,' but, 'thy pound.' So Paul, Gal. ii. 20,
'I live;' yea, but he interposeth presently, 'Yet not I, but Christ
liveth in me.' They are ever ascribing all to God, because they see
they can do nothing without him. When we come to heaven, it is a
question which we shall admire most, grace or glory, the glory of that
estate into which we are brought, or else grace, which was the foundation of it. Oh, when we see all that was done and suffered for God,
it was from God: 'Of thine own have we given thee.' How will the
soul admire the riches of his glorious grace! We have not only
traded with his money, but by his direction ; and when our stock was
embezzled he supplied us at every turn. For these ends the Lord
still keeps grace in his own hands, that we can do nothing to any purpose unless he be pleased to concur, by the influences and quickenings
of his own Spirit.

Use. The use shall only be in these two branches :—

1. In doing any good work, let us do all things in him as well as
to him. Let us not only make this our scope, that we may do it to
God, but let us make his grace our principle : otherwise, when we go
to work for God without God, it will befall us as it did Sampson, that
thought to go out and shake himself as in former times, but his locks
were cut and his strength gone. Men that have had former experiences, think to find a like vigour of affection, a like raisedness of
spirit, a like savouriness of expression ; but if they take not God along
with them, they find their strength is gone, their affections dead, that
all their spirits are dry and sapless, and that they do not go forth with
such life and power as formerly. Therefore, whenever you go about
a good work, say, as David, 'I will go forth in the strength of
God.'

2. It directs us in ascribing the honour of what we have done. It
is dangerous to assume divine honour to ourselves or accept it from
others ; but we must give the Lord the glory, whose concurrence doth
all the work. Remember, we have received all from God, and God must
have all the glory and honour ; if others should ascribe it to us, we
are not to take it. To conceal and receive stolen goods, brings us
within the compass of theft, as well as to steal them ourselves. So,
when others would ascribe anything to us, still let the Lord have the
glory of every work and business.

The third point.

Doct. 3. We are not only to look to this, that his will be done, but
to the manner how it is done.

It is not for the honour of his majesty to be put off with anything;
we must serve him with all our mind and strength: Mal. i. 14, 'When
ye brought that which was torn, and lame, and sick, should I accept

this of your hands? saith the Lord. I am a great king, saith the Lord of hosts, and my name is dreadful among the heathen.' We are to aim at the highest manner of serving God. There is an ardent desire in the saints to be perfect: ' If by any means they would attain to the resurrection of the dead,' Phil. iii. 11 ; that is, that happy and sinless state they shall enjoy hereafter. The manner is more considerable than the work itself. A man may sin in doing *good,* but he cannot sin in doing *well;* therefore the manner is that which is mainly stood upon in scripture. God doth not only look that we pray, but it must be fervent effectual prayer, not a drowsy devotion; not only *that* we hear, but take heed *how* we hear ; not only that we *serve* him, but serve him *instantly;* not only *run,* but *so* run. The great thing that is put into the balance of the sanctuary, when God comes to weigh the actions of men, what doth he consider ? He weighs the spirits : Prov. xvi. 2, ' All the ways of man are right in his own eyes; but the Lord weigheth the spirits ;' that is, he considers with what frame of heart, and in what manner, we go about anything we do for him. And therefore this is the main thing we should look after, in what manner we serve him, even as the angels do in heaven; not in an ordinary but perfect manner.

But wherein doth the resemblance hold ; how should we be as the angels ?

1. In conformity to the angels, we must serve God readily. The angels are represented as ' with wings,' Isa. vi. 2: and the angel Gabriel is said to ' fly swiftly' upon God's message ; they are hearkening for God's word, and go on God's errand. So we should be ready and speedy in our obedience : Ps. cxix. 60, ' I made haste, and delayed not to keep thy commandments.' It is not enough to keep God's commandments, but we must make haste ; that is, before the strength of the present impulsion be lost, and those fervours which are upon us be cooled.

2. Willingly and cheerfully, and without murmuring. Angels are ready at God's beck ; they are ministering spirits, even to the meanest saints ; God hath sent them abroad for the heirs of salvation ; they are as guardians to them, to look after them in all their ways. The devils, what Christ bids them do, do it murmuringly ; the unclean spirit would not come out without rending and tearing, Mark ix. ; Christ's presence was a burthen to them, Mat. viii. When we do things with reluctancy, murmuringly, we are more like the devils than the angels. When the devils obey his word, they are forced to it by the absolute power of Christ ; yet they do it not with willingness and freeness, as the good angels do. But we are to do it freely : ' I delight to do thy will, O my God,' Ps. xl. 8. And, John iv. 34, ' It is my meat and drink to do the will of him that sent me.' That was the dish Christ loved.

3. Constantly and unweariedly. Thus do the angels in heaven. The devils they abode not in the truth ; but angels, they do it without weariness ; they rest not day nor night, but are still lauding, praising, and serving God, and are never weary. God in communion is ever new and fresh to them ; the face of their heavenly Father is as lovely as at the first moment ; no weariness or satiety creeps upon those

good spirits. Thus should we do it without weariness, and then we shall reap if we faint not.

4. Faithfully, not picking and choosing: ' They hearken to the voice of his word,' whatever it be, be it to ascend or descend. So we, if it be to go backward for God, though it be against the bent of our hearts. David is said to be ' a man after God's heart,' because he did ' all God's will,' Acts xiii. 22 : all which should be a pattern for us, and we should strive to come up to it.

Give us this day our daily bread.

WE are now come to the second sort of petitions, that concern ourselves, as the former did more immediately concern God. Now you may observe the style in the prayer is altered. It was before, *Thy* name, *Thy* kingdom, *Thy* will ; now it is, Give *us*, and Forgive *us*, &c. Before, our Lord had taught us to speak in a third person, ' Thy will be done ;' and now in a second person, ' Give us this day :' which is not so to be understood as if we were not at all concerned in the former part of the Lord's Prayer. In those petitions, the benefit is not God's, but ours. When his name is sanctified, his kingdom cometh, and his will is done ; these things do not only concern the glory of God, but also our benefit. It is our advantage when God is honoured by the coming of Christ's kingdom and the subjection of our hearts unto himself. But these latter petitions do more immediately concern us. Now, among these, in the first place, we pray for the necessary provisions of the present life. Some make a scruple why such a prayer should be put in the first place. Surely not to show the value of these things above pardon and grace ; but this is the last of the supplications. The Lord's Prayer may be divided into supplications and deprecations. Among the supplications, there we prayed, first, for the glory of God ; next, for the kingdom of God ; next, for our subjection to that kingdom ; and, in the last place, we pray for daily bread, or sustentation of the present life. But the other two are deprecations ; and that either of evil already committed, and so we pray for pardon of sin, ' Forgive us our trespasses;' or deprecation of evil that is likely to be admitted, and so we pray against temptation, ' Lead us not into temptation :' so that this request is put into a fit order. First, we seek God's glory as the end ; his kingdom as the primary means ; our subjection to that kingdom as the next means ; and last of all, our comfortable subsistence in the world as a remote subservient help, that we may be in a capacity to serve and glorify God.

In this petition there is :—

I. The thing asked, and that is *bread*, by which is meant all things necessary for the maintenance of this life.

Now this is set forth :—

1. By a note of propriety, *our* bread.

2. By an adjunct of time, *daily* bread.

II. The manner of asking, *give ;* we ask it as a gift of God.

III. The persons for whom we ask, Give *us ;* as many as are

supposed to be in a family together. Those that can call God
Father by the Spirit, they may come with most confidence to God
about daily supplies.

IV. The renewing of our request, σήμερον, ' this day :' there is very
much in that ; we ask but from morning till night: ' Give us this
day our daily bread.'

Before I come to explain these circumstances, let me observe in
general :—

Doct. 1. That it is the Lord which doth bestow upon us freely and
graciously the good things of this life.

It is bread we ask, and we ask it of God, and to God we say,
' Give.' All which circumstances do fully make out the point.

This point again must be made good by parts :—

1. That God giveth it.

2. That he freely and graciously giveth it.

First, I shall show you how God is interested in the common
mercies we do enjoy ; and how every one, high or low, rich or poor,
full or in a mean condition, of what rank soever they be, even those
that have the greatest store and plenty of worldly accommodations,
they must come from morning to morning and deal with God for
daily bread.

Those common mercies which we do enjoy :—

[1.] God gives us the possession of them, for he is the absolute
Lord of all things both in heaven and in earth, and whatsoever is
possessed by any creature, it is by his indulgence ; for the primitive
and original right was in him : Ps. xxiv. 1, ' The earth is the Lord's,
and the fulness thereof ; the world, and they that dwell therein.' It
is all God's ; we hold it in fee from him, for he is the great landlord
who hath leased out all these blessings to the sons of men. The
earth is first the Lord's, and then by a grant he hath given it to men
to enjoy : Ps. cxv. 16, ' The heaven, even the heavens, are the Lord's ;
but the earth hath he given to the children of men.' He hath given
it to men partly by a general grant, and leave given to enjoy and
occupy it as the place of our service. But that is not all ; he doth
not only give the earth in general to men, but he makes a particular
allotment ; the particular designation of every man's portion of what
he shall enjoy in the world, it is of God. And so it is said, Acts
xvii. 26, ' He hath determined the bounds of their habitation.' God
hath not only appointed in general the earth to be the place of our
service for a while, but he hath determined how much every one shall
possess, what shall fall to his share. These things come not by
chance, or by the gift of others, or by our own industry, but by the
peculiar designation of God's providence. However they come to us,
God must be owned in the possession ; whether they come to us by
donation, purchase, labour, or by inheritance, yet they are originally
by God, who by these means bestoweth them upon us. If they
come by donation, or the gift of others, the hearts of men are in
God's hands, and he it was that disposed them to be bountiful to us,
that appointed them to be instruments of his providence, to nourish
us. He that sends a present, he is the giver, not the servant which
brings it. So, though others be employed as instruments, it is the

Lord which made them able and willing to do us good. If they come to us by inheritance, it is the providence of God that a man is born of rich friends and not of beggars: Prov. xxii. 2, ' The rich and poor meet together ; the Lord is the maker of them all.' He that hath cast the world first into hills and valleys, it was he that disposed of men, some into a high, and some into a low condition. If they come to us by our own labour and purchase, still God gave it to us: Deut. viii. 14–18, ' Take heed that thine heart be not lifted up, and thou forget the Lord thy God ; for it is he that giveth thee power to get wealth.' He doth not leave second causes to their own power and force, as if he were only an idle spectator in the world. No, he gives the skill and industry to manage affairs, and success upon lawful undertakings ; the faculty and the use, it is all from God. Though a man hath never so many outward advantages, yet, unless the Lord concur with his blessing, all would be to no purpose.

[2.] As God gives us the possession, so he gives us a right and title to them. There is a twofold right to these common blessings ; a providential and a covenant right. *Dominium politicum fundatur in providentia ;* ' Our civil right to things is founded upon God's providence:' but *Dominium evangelicum fundatur in gratia;* 'Our gospel right to things is founded upon God's grace.' (1.) He gives the providential right, and thus all wicked men possess outward things, and the plenty they enjoy is as the fruits and gifts of God's common bounty ; it is their portion, he hath given it to them: Ps. xvii. 14, ' Which have their portion in this life,' whatever falleth to their share in a fair way, and in the course of God's providence ; they are not usurpers merely for possessing, but for abusing, what they have. They have not only a civil right by the laws of men, to prevent the incroachment of others, but a providential right before God ; and are not simply responsible for possession, but for their ill use and administration. (2.) There is a covenant right to these blessings: so only believers have a right to creature comforts by God's special love ; and so, ' That little that a righteous man hath is better than the treasures of many wicked,' Ps. xxxvii. 16; as the mean fare of a poor subject is better than the large allowance of a condemned traitor. Every wicked man is a traitor to God, and hath only an allowance until he be destroyed. But that little which a man hath, seasoned with God's love, is better than all the mighty increase of wicked men. Now, this covenant right we have by Christ, who is ' heir of all things,' Heb. i. 2 ; Christ hath the original right to them, and we by him come to have a covenant right. So it is said, 1 Cor. iii. 23, ' Things present, and things to come, all are yours.' As things to come, the day of judgment is theirs ; so things present are theirs by a new title from him. So it is said, 1 Tim. iv. 5, marriage, meats, and drinks, and all creatures, are made for them that believe. They that believe have only a gospel right to them. To draw it to the present thing, we do not only beg a possession of these things, but a right; not only a providential, but a covenant right, that we may enjoy them as the gifts of God's fatherly love and compassion to us, that we may take our bread out of Christ's hands, that we may look upon it as swimming to us in his blood, and all our mercies as wrapt up in his bowels ; and then they will be sweet, and relish much better with a gracious soul, because he can not only taste the creature, but the love of God in the creature.

[3.] He gives the continuance of our blessings, that we may keep what we have ; for unless the Lord do daily support us, we cannot keep our comforts for one day. How soon can God blast them ! It is at his pleasure to do what he will with you. He gave Satan power over Job's estate: chap. i. 12, ' Behold, all that he hath is in thy power.' Our life, it is continued to us by the indulgence of God, and by his providential influence and supportation. For as the beams of the sun are no longer continued in the air than the sun shineth, or, as the water retains the impress and stamp no longer than the seal is kept on it, so when God takes off his providential influence, all vanisheth into nothing. Thus he is said, Heb. i. 3, to ' uphold all things by the word of his power.' As a weighty thing is upheld in the hand of a man, when he looseneth his hand all falls to the ground ; so it is said, Job xii. 10, ' In whose hand is the soul of every living thing, and the breath of all mankind.' God by his almighty grasp holdeth all things in his own hands, and if he should but let loose his hand, all would fall to nothing and disappear : Job vi. 9. For it is from the intimate support and influence of his providence that we have our lives. So our comforts, they are continued to us by God. Alas! in themselves they are poor fugacious things ! Haman was to-day high in honour, and to-morrow high upon the gallows. ' Riches make themselves wings, and fly away as an eagle towards heaven:' Prov. xxiii. 5. The Holy Ghost seems there to compare riches to a flock of birds, which pitcheth in a man's field to-night, but to-morrow they are gone. Who is the richer for a flock of wild fowls because they pitch in his field now ? So all these outward things are so flying that they are soon gone by many accidents, unless he preserves them and continues our possession of them. For God he can give a charge and commission to the fire, to the fury of men, one way or other, to deprive us of these things : ' Behold, all he hath is in thy hands,' Job i. 12. When a man hath gotten abundance of worldly comforts about him, and seemeth to be intrenched and provided against all hazards, the man is taken away, and cannot enjoy what he had heaped together with a great deal of care and solicitude.

[4.] We beg leave to use them. It is good manners in religion to ask God's leave in all things. It is robbery to make use of a man's goods, and to waste and consume them without his leave. We must ask God's leave upon this account, because, though God gives these good things to men, yet he still reserves the property in himself ; for by distributing blessings to the creature, he never intended to divest himself of the right. As a husbandman, by scattering his corn in the field, did not dispossess himself, but still keeps a right and means to have the increase ; so when the Lord scattereth his blessings, we only receive them as stewards, not as owners and proprietors : God still is the supreme Lord, and only hath the property and dominion. In life it is clear man is not *dominus vitæ*, but *custos ;* not lord of his life, but only the steward and guardian of it ; he cannot live or die at his own pleasure: if a man kills himself he runs the danger of God's law.

What is said of life is true also of his estate : he is not an owner so much as a steward ; that is the notion of our possession : we are stewards, and must render an account to God : Hos. ii. 9, ' I will return and take away my corn in the time thereof, and my wine in the season thereof, and will recover my wool and my flax.' Though God hath communicated these things to the children of men, yet he hath reserved the dominion in his own hands : so Hag. ii. 8, ' The silver is mine, and the gold is mine, saith the Lord of hosts.' He never disposed anything so into the creature's hands, but still he hath reserved a right and interest in it ; and therefore it is, Gen. xiv. 19, that the Lord is not only called the creator of heaven and earth, but ' possessor of heaven and earth.' He is not only the possessor of heaven where he dwells, which he hath reserved to his own use, but he is possessor of earth, which he hath committed to the use of men. And God will have his right acknowledged from day to day.

[5.] It is he that giveth us ability to use them : we beg that we may not only have the comforts, but life and strength to use them ; for God can blast us in the very midst of our enjoyments. It is the case of many, when they have hunted after a worldly portion, and begin to think, now I will sit down and enjoy it ; when the gain is come into his hands, and he thinks to waste[1] that which he hath got in hunting, death takes him away, and he hath not power to use them. Thus it was with the rich fool ; when he began to sing lullabies to his soul, and enjoy what he had got, he is taken away by death : Luke xii. 20, ' Thou fool, this night thy soul shall be required of thee ; then whose shall those things be which thou hast provided ? ' And it is said, Num. xi. 33, when those people had gotten quails, that ' while the flesh was yet between their teeth, ere it was chewed, the wrath of the Lord was kindled against the people ; and the Lord smote them with a very great plague.' And that nobleman which saw plenty in Samaria, but could not taste of it : 2 Kings vii. 19. So Job xxi. 23, ' One dieth in his full strength, being wholly at ease and quiet : ' when he has gotten abundance of worldly comforts about him, death seizes on him of a sudden.

[6.] God yet is further interested in these mercies, so as to give us a sanctified use of them, that we may take our bread out of God's hands with prayer and thanksgiving, and due acknowledgments of God. In 1 Tim. iv. 4, 5, ' Every creature of God is good, and nothing to be refused, if it be received with thanksgiving ; for it is sanctified by the word of God and prayer.' Then are the creatures sanctified to us, when we enjoy God in them ; when our hearts are raised to think of the donor, and can love him the more for every gift. Carnal men, like swine, raven upon the acorns, but look not up to the oak from whence they drop. In the Canticles, the spouse's eyes are compared to dove's eyes. They which make the allusion say this is the meaning : look, as a dove pecks, and looks upward ; so upon every grain of mercy, we should look up to the God of mercies : it is not enough to taste the sweet of the creatures, but also to own God, his love and bounty in them, so to have them sanctified to us. This is the privilege we have as men, that we can know the first cause, and who is the benefactor. All creatures subsist upon the first cause, but are not

[1] Qu. " taste ? "—ED.

capable of knowing it. And this is our privilege as Christians, to have this capacity reduced into act. It is of the Lord's grace to give us a sanctified use of these things.

[7.] We beg of God the natural blessing upon the holy use of outward comforts, so as they may continue us in health and vigour for the service of God; for nothing will prosper with us but by his blessing: Ps. cvi. 15, 'He gave them their request, but sent leanness into their souls;' that is, they had no natural comfort by that which they had obtained. God may give a man meat, yet not an appetite; he may not give him the comfortable use of it, a blessing with it. And therefore the apostle makes it to be an argument of God's bounty to the heathen, that as he gave them food, so he gave them gladness of heart: Acts xiv. 17, 'He gave them rain from heaven, and fruitful seasons, filling their hearts with food and gladness;' that is, gave them a comfortable use, a blessing upon the use of outward things. And Lev. xxvi., you will find a distinction between 'bread,' and the 'staff of bread.' We may have bread, yet not the staff of bread. Many have worldly comforts, but not with a natural blessing: Eccles. iii. 13, 'That every man should eat and drink, and enjoy the good of all his labour; it is the gift of God:' not only that he should have increase by his labour, but enjoy good; to have the comfortable use of that increase.

[8.] Contentation is one of God's blessings that we ask in this prayer, 'Give us this day our daily bread;' that is, such provisions as are necessary for us, contentment and quiet of mind in the enjoyment: Joel ii. 19, 'Behold, I will send you corn, and wine, and oil, and ye shall be satisfied therewith.' It is not only a blessing we should look after, but contentment, that our minds may be suited to our condition, for then the creature is more sweet and comfortable to us. The happiness of man doth not lie in his abundance, but in the suitableness of his mind to his estate: Luke xii. 15, 'A man's life consisteth not in the abundance of things which he possesseth.' There is a twofold war within a man, both which must be taken up before a man can have comfort; there is a war between a man and his conscience, and this breeds trouble of mind; and there is a war between his affections and his condition, and this breeds murmuring and envious repining. Say, Yea, Lord, and let us be contented with thy gift. This for the first thing, how God is concerned in these outward comforts.

Secondly, That the Lord doth freely and graciously give these good things to us, that is, merely out of his bounty and goodness. It is not from his strict remunerative justice, but out of his grace. The very air we breathe in, the bread we eat, our common blessings, be they never so mean, we have them all from grace, and all from the tender mercy of the Lord. Ps. cxxxvi. 25, you have there the story of the notable effects of God's mercy, and he concludes it thus: 'Who giveth food to all flesh; for his mercy endureth for ever.' Mark, the psalmist doth not only ascribe those mighty victories, those glorious instances of his love and power, to his unchangeable mercy, but our daily bread. In eminent deliverances of the church we will acknowledge mercy; yea, but we should do it in every bit of meat we eat, for the same reason is rendered all along. What is the reason his people smote Sihon king of the Amorites, and Og the king of Bashan, and rescued his people so often out of danger ? 'For his mercy endureth for ever.' And what is the reason he giveth food to all flesh ? 'For his mercy endureth for ever.' It is not only mercy which gives us Christ, and salvation by Christ, and all those glorious deliverances and triumphs over the enemies of the church ; but it is mercy which furnisheth our tables, it is mercy that we taste with our mouths and wear at our backs. It is notable, our Lord Jesus, when there were but five barley loaves and two fishes, John vi. 11, 'He lift up his eyes and gave thanks.' Though our provision be never so homely and slender, yet God's grace and mercy must be acknowledged.

But to evidence this by some considerations that certainly it is of the mercy of the Lord that he giveth bread to the creature : God giveth these mercies—

1. To those that cannot return any service to him.
2. To those that will not return any service to him.
3. When we are at our best we cannot deserve them.
4. We deserve the quite contrary.

[1.] He giveth these mercies to those that cannot return any service to him ; the beasts, and fowls of the air, the young ravens : Ps. cxlv. 16, 'Thou openest thy hand, and satisfiest the desire of every living thing.' What can the beasts, or fishes, or fowls of the air deserve at God's hand ? What honour and service can they bring to him? Only they have a bountiful Creator, from whom they receive their allowance.

So as to infants. Alas ! what can they deserve at his hand ? When God rocks their cradles, and nourisheth them from the dug, what service can they do to God ? Isa. xlvi. 3, 4, ' By me,' saith the Lord, 'you are borne from the belly, and carried from the womb ; and even to your old age, I am he ; and even to hoar hairs will I carry you.' Mark, not only in old age, when we have done God service, doth he maintain us ; but from the womb, the belly, before we could do anything for him, we were tenderly handled by him. He alludeth to parents and nurses, which carry their younglings in their arms. In infancy we are not in a capacity to know the God of our mercies, and look after him ; yet he looked after us then, when we could not perform one act of love and kindness to him. The psalmist takes notice of this : Ps. xxii. 9, 10, 'Thou art he that took me out of the womb ; thou didst make me hope when I was upon my mother's breasts. I was cast upon thee from the womb ; thou art my God from my mother's belly.' Christians, before ever you could do anything for him or yourselves, before you could improve his mercy, when you could not know who was your benefactor, who it was that nourished and cherished you, yet then God rocked your cradles, kept you from many dangers, nursed you, and brought you up, and carried you in the tender arms of his providence.

[2.] God gives these mercies to those that will not serve him when they can : Isa. i. 2, ' I have nourished and brought up children, and they have rebelled against me.' There are many in the world whom God protects, supplies, and provides them of all necessaries, yet they return nothing but disobedience, contempt, rebellion, and unthankful-

ness. The sun doth not shine by chance, but at God's disposal : Mat.
v. 45, ' He makes his sun to rise on the evil and on the good, and
sendeth rain on the just and on the unjust.' Most of those which are
fed at God's table, and maintained at his expense and care, they are
his enemies ; and many times the more men receive from him the
worse they are. Look, as beasts towards man, when they are in good
plight they grow fierce, and are ready to destroy those which nourish
them, so, when we are plentifully supplied, we kick with the heel,
wax wanton, and forgetful of God. Or as a froward child scratcheth
the breast which suckles it, so we rebel against God that nourished
us, and brought us up, and dishonour our heavenly Father that provides these blessings for us. Parisiensis hath a saying, ' They which
hold the greatest farms many times pay the least rent.' So the great
ones of the world, they which have most of God's bounty, give him
the least acknowledgment.

[3.] When we do our best we cannot deserve these mercies, or merit
aught at God's hands ; for all we do is already due to God, as we are
his creatures, and the paying new debts will not quit old scores. The
question is propounded : Job xxii. 2, ' Can a man be profitable unto
God, as he that is wise may be profitable unto himself ? ' See the
answer : chap. xxxv. 7, ' If thou be righteous, what givest thou him ?
or what receiveth he of thine hand ? ' And wherein is God profited if
a man's ways be perfect ? And, therefore, whatever God doth for
creatures, he doth it freely, because he cannot be obliged by any act
of ours and pre-engaged. Thus Adam in innocency could not obtain
the blessing but by virtue of the covenant, nor merit aught at God's
hands, that is, put any obligation upon God ; and, therefore, certainly
now we cannot. And partly, too, because whatever we do, it will not
carry a proportion with these common mercies. We are proud creatures, and think of a condignity of works, and to merit from heaven
these mercies. But, alas ! there is no comparison ; and if God would
deal with us upon merit and strict commutative justice, we cannot
give him a valuable compensation for temporal mercies : Gen. xxxii.
10, ' I am not worthy of the least of all the mercies which thou hast
showed unto thy servant.' Though none of God's mercies can simply
be said to be little, for whatsoever comes from a great God should be
great in our value and esteem, as a small remembrance from a great
person is much prized ; therefore no mercy is simply little, but comparatively. Now the least mercies some have, and others the greatest
temporal things. When we are put into the balance, we and all our
worth and deservings cannot counterpoise the least mercy, or merit
the daily bread we have from God. And then the little good we do,
it is merely by the grace that we have received. If one man differs
from another, who made him differ ? It is but a new gift, he is the
more indebted to God.

[4.] We deserve the contrary. We have forfeited our lives, and all
our comforts ; we have put ourselves out of God's protection by sin.
Death waylaid us when we were in our mother's womb ; and as soon
as we were born there was a sentence in force against us : Rom.
v. 12, ' Death came upon all, for that all have sinned.' And still we
continue the forfeiture. We provoke God to cut us off. It is a kind

of pardoning mercy by which we subsist every moment. This is sensible in case of sickness, when our lives and comforts slide from us, when there is but a step between us and death, when the old covenant comes to be put in suit, and God seems to be executing the sentence of the law. And that is the reason why the temporal deliverance of the wicked and impenitent is called a remission : as Ps. lxxviii. 38, ' But he, being full of compassion, forgave their iniquity, and destroyed them not.' And Mat. xviii. 26, 27, 28, ' Have patience with me, and I will pay thee all. And the lord of that servant was moved with compassion, and forgave him the debt.' Why is it called a remission ? Improperly, because it was a reprieve from the temporal judgment for a time ; it was not an executing the sentence which was in force against us ; and it was not from anything in the sinner, but from God's pity over his creatures. And a godly man, every time his life and comforts are in danger, hath a pardon renewed at that time : Isa. xxxviii. 17, ' Thou hast in love to my soul delivered it from the pit of corruption ; for thou hast cast all my sins behind thy back.' They are loved out of danger, and loved out of sickness ; the pardoning mercy of God is indeed renewed to them.

APPLICATION.

Use 1. For information, in two branches :—

First, That God will give his people temporal things. Not only pardon, and grace, and glory ; but ' no good thing will he withhold :' Ps. lxxxi. 11. Many say they can trust God for eternal life, but cannot trust him for daily bread. This is an utter mistake. Certainly it is far more easy to trust God for daily bread than for eternal life ; because there are more difficulties, more natural prejudices, against these greater mercies of pardon and eternal life, than there can be against the daily effects of God's bounty. It is a harder matter to work through our natural prejudices, which lie against eternal life, than to work through that distrust which lies against God's care over us and provision for us. Why ? For God's common bounty it reacheth to all his creatures, even to the smallest worm ; his mercy is over all his works. And surely it is more easy to believe his common bounty than his special love, which runs in a distinct channel to such a sort of men.

But because many have too weak a faith about temporal things, let us consider how willing God is to distribute and give out these supplies. Several things I might mention.

1. God's respect to the bodies of his people is a mighty ground and encouragement. God is in covenant with the body as well as the soul. Jesus Christ proves the resurrection from thence, that God is ' the God of Abraham, Isaac, and Jacob :' Mat. xxii. 32. This argument can never be made good, but upon the supposition that God is in covenant with Abraham's body, with the whole believer ; and therefore the mark of circumcision was in their flesh, as the water of baptism is sprinkled upon our bodies. Well, then, if the bodies of the saints be in covenant with God, certainly some of the promises of the covenant do concern the body and sustentation of the present life. But that is not all, but Jesus Christ hath purchased both body and

soul : 1 Cor. vi. 20, ' Ye are bought with a price ; therefore glorify
God in your body, and in your spirit, which are God's.' Not only the
soul is Christ's, but the body.

You will say, That is ground of service ; but what ! can it be in-
ferred that therefore God will provide for us ? It is not only a ground
of our service, but of Christ's care of us. If Christ had only purchased
our service, yet it were a ground of hope. If you expect work and
service from a body, you will give maintenance to that body. But
Christ's purchase implieth his care over that he hath purchased ; for
the interest God hath in us in redemption is a gracious interest. God
had an interest in us before we were redeemed ; we could not make
void his right by any rebellion of ours. But then God hath such an
interest in us as engaged and solicited him to destroy us. Look, as a
prince hath an interest in his subjects, if they rebel and revolt from
their obedience, they cannot disannul his right, but it is such a right
as binds him to pursue and chastise them until they return to their
duty, so God hath a right to the fallen creature, but it was such a
right as solicited vengeance. But the right Christ purchased was a
gracious right, that God might protect and preserve us. Well, then,
if Christ purchased body and soul, he hath obtained, not only that
God should be gracious to our souls, but gracious to our bodies ; then
the argument runs clearly for confirming the faith of the saints in
expectation of temporal benefits.

2. God hath given us greater things, therefore he will not stand
upon the less ; when a man hath been at great cost, he will not lose
it. The Lord hath given us his Christ: Rom. viii. 32, ' He that
spared not his own Son, but delivered him up for us all, how shall he
not with him also freely give us all things ? ' Can any man be so
illogical, so ill-skilled in consequences, as not to conclude from thence,
if God give us Christ, with him he will give us all things ? So
Mat. vi. 33, ' Seek first the kingdom of God, and his righteousness,
and all other things shall be added to you.'

3. These things are dispensed to inferior, yea, to the worst of his
creatures : Ps. cxlvii. 9, ' He giveth to the beast his food, and to the
young ravens which cry.' Will God maintain the beasts of the field,
and will he not maintain his children ? It is monstrous and unnatural to think thus, that God will not support you, and bear you out
in your work. This is Christ's own argument : Mat. vi. 34, ' Take
therefore no thought for the morrow ; for the morrow shall take
thought for the things of itself. Sufficient unto the day is the evil
thereof.' Daily bread is in your Father's power, and he gives it graciously to all his creatures, and therefore certainly he will give it to
you. Thus you may see with what confidence you may expect daily
supplies.

Secondly, It informs us that we may ask temporal things, if we ask
them lawfully. It is true, prayers to God for spiritual things are
more acceptable. As your child pleaseth you better when it comes
to you to be taught its book, rather than when it comes for an apple,
so it is more pleasing to God when you come for the Mediator's blessing and spiritual things : Acts iii. 26, ' God hath sent him to bless you,
in turning away every one of you from his iniquities.' But yet we may

ask other things. Why? For they are good and useful to us in the course of our service, and without them we are exposed to many temptations. And prayer easeth you of a deal of carking about them : Phil. iv. 6, ' Be careful for nothing ; but in everything by prayer and supplication, with thanksgiving, let your requests be made known unto God.' We may ask them, but it must be lawfully ; and that, for order, not in the first place. That is howling, when we come to God merely for corn, wine, and oil ; when we prefer these things before his favour and the graces of his Spirit. Then it must be lawful, too, as to the manner : a moderate proportion, not to set God a task to maintain you at such a rate, but to ask a moderate allowance. Christ teacheth us here to pray for bread, which is a necessary allowance : Prov. xxx. 8, ' Feed me with food convenient for me.' And, 1 Tim. vi. 8, ' If we have food and raiment, let us therewith be content.' And then ask them with humility and submission to the will of God. We ought to say, as in James iv. 15, ' If the Lord will, we will go to such a place, and get gain.' And then lawfully, too, as to the end ; not for an unlawful end, for ostentation and riot, that we may live at large and at ease : James iv. 3, ' Ye ask, and receive not, because ye ask amiss, that ye may consume it upon your lusts.' But we must ask it for a good end : Ps. cxv. 1, ' Not unto us, O Lord, not unto us, but unto thy name give glory, for thy mercy, and for thy truth's sake.' Lord, not for our ease, or our plenty, but that thy name may be glorified, that we may be supported in service. And then again, lawfully as to the plea. We must not come and challenge it, as if it were our due ; we must not use the plea of merit, but of mercy. Our Saviour doth not say, Let this bread come to us anyhow, as he saith, ' Let thy will be done ; ' our subjection to God is due ; but, ' Give us this day our daily bread,' acknowledging the Lord's mercy.

Use 2. Let us not place our confidence in second causes, but in God, by whose goodness and providence over us all temporal things do come unto us ; for without him all our carking and labour is nothing ; and if we have our wishes without labour, yet we shall not have our comfort and blessing without God : Mat. vi. 27. Which of you, by taking thought, can add one cubit to his stature ? ' By taking thought, he meaneth anxious care about success. We cannot change the colour of a hair by all our anxious thoughts. We cannot make ourselves stronger or taller. Many a man is pierced through with worldly cares, and still the world frowns upon him, so all his care comes to nothing. Prov. x. 4, it is said, ' The hand of the diligent maketh rich.' Compare it with ver. 22, and it is said, ' The blessing of the Lord, it maketh rich, and he addeth no sorrow with it.' Most commonly they that are diligent they thrive with their diligence ; yea, but if that be all, if they have not the Lord's blessing, they have not that sweetness and peace when they have gotten abundance. Oh, therefore, let us place our confidence, not in second causes, but in God.

Use 3. Let us be thankful to God for these worldly things that we enjoy. I urge this :—

First, Because of the danger of ingratitude. Usually we never forget God more than when he remembereth us most. When men have what they would have, then God is neglected ; they grow careless in prayer, or flat and cold in the performance of it. There is a great deal of difference between men poor and rich. When poor, they will seem to put a natural fervency into their prayers; but when rich, they grow cold and careless. Mark what the Lord saith, Hos. xiii. 6, 'They were filled, and their heart was exalted; therefore have they forgotten me.' Oh, how frequent is this, that many having been kept under a great sense of God in a low condition, but when they have been well at ease, then they bear it up as if they could live without God. The bucket comes to the river with an empty mouth, gaping to receive its fulness, as it were; but when it is full, the bottom is turned towards it. So it is very usual with men to turn their backs upon the mercy-seat, and when the Lord hath given them great increase in worldly things, and leased out a great estate to them, he hath very little rent from them. / Now, because this is usual, therefore those whom God hath blessed with the supplies of the present life, how should they study thankfulness!

Secondly, Because of the equity of it. Consider what an equity there is, that we should be thankful for outward blessings.

1. They are good in themselves.

2. They come from God.

3. They come from the Lord's grace and mercy.

[1.] They are good in themselves. Food and raiment is good, and 'every creature of God is good,' 1 Tim. iv. 4. They are good things, though not the best things. They are good for ourselves, that we may serve God more cheerfully. The Lord would have the Levites and priests have their portion, that they might be encouraged in the law of the Lord: 2 Chron. xxxi. 4. Now these things are good to encourage us, and support us in our work. Man consists of two parts, of a body and of a soul. Now whether we look to the one or the other, you will have many arguments to love and praise God, not only for what he hath done for our souls, but likewise for our bodies. And they are good, because they prevent many snares and temptations: Prov. xxx. 9, 'Lest I be poor and steal, and take the name of my God in vain.' Diseases which arise from fulness are more common; but diseases which arise from indigence and emptiness, they are more dangerous. So diseases of prosperity they are more common, it is a rank soil and yields more weeds; but diseases which arise from poverty breed atheism, irreligion, and rebellion against God. They are good, as they make us more useful for God and man. / For God, as having more advantages for the honouring of God: Prov. iii. 9, 'Honour the Lord with thy substance, and with the first-fruits of all thine increase.' And of doing good to others: 'That we may have to distribute to them that need,' Eph. iv. 28. Oh, we should all covet and affect mightily, to have wherewith to relieve the necessities of others.

[2.] As they are blessings, so they are blessings which do not come by chance, or by man's providence: 1 Tim. vi. 17, 'The living God, who giveth us richly all things to enjoy.' The people of God are plentifully provided for. Your tables are well furnished, backs well clothed; it is God which gives you richly to enjoy them, and he must be acknowledged. As David doth: 1 Chron. xxix. 14, 'For all things come of thee, and of thine own have we given thee.' Then, ver. 16, 'O Lord our God, all this store that we have prepared to build thee an house for thine holy name, cometh of thine hand, and is all thine own.' Though you yourselves have been purchasers of your own estate, and carvers of your own fortune (as man is most apt to forget God there), yea, but though you have prepared and brought together a great deal of store, yet, Lord, all comes from thee. It sweeteneth the mercy. When you are at the table, to be carved to by a great person, their remembrance is counted a greater favour than the meal itself. So it is not barely the comfort we have by the creature which sweeteneth it, but when we think of the donor, that the great God should think of us, that it is God who spreads our table for us, that doth put this meat and drink before us. It was he that 'gave seed to the sower, and bread for food,' 2 Cor. ix. 10. When we take it immediately out of God's hands, it is much sweeter. And not only so, but also it is the more sanctified. When we look to second causes, we shall surely abuse the mercy : Hosea ii. 8, ' For she did not know that I gave her corn, and wine, and oil, and multiplied her silver and gold.' What then ? ' Therefore she prepared it for Baal.' When God's kindness is not taken notice of, when we do not see God in our mercies, we shall not use them for God. That man will surely improve his comforts ill that doth not see God in them. Now that which comes from God leads the heart to God again, then the creature is sanctified. Therefore acknowledge God in these outward things. We should say of every morsel of bread, This is God's gift to me ; of every night's sleep, This is the Lord's goodness. When God is acknowledged in these outward things, he takes it the more kindly, and we are the better for it ; the mercy is the sweeter and the more sanctified.

[3.] They not only come from God, but from the Lord's free grace and mercy. These are two distinct notions, by which God's goodness is set out, and they are both significant and expressive in the present case : Grace, that doth all freely ; mercy, that pitieth the miserable.

(1.) Then we have them from grace. Grace is at liberty to give them to whom it will. Well, there is grace in these outward things ; for God gives them to whom he will ; to some, not to others. Oh, when we consider the distinction between us and others—every one hath not such liberal supplies, nay, many of those of whom the world is not worthy—surely this is merely the Lord's goodness. Prov. xxii. 2, ' The rich and the poor meet together, the Lord is the maker of them all.' They had the same maker that you had (others which are destitute), therefore why is it you have more than they ? It is merely from grace. Why is one vessel framed for an honourable use, and another for a baser use ? So it pleased the potter. God, as the great master of the scenes, appointeth to every man what part he shall act, merely out of his own grace ; he is bound to none. It was a good speech of Tamerlane, the great conqueror of the East, to Bajazet : What did God see in thee, that are blind in one eye, and me, that am lame of one leg, that he should make us, passing by many others, the lords of so many opulent and mighty kingdoms ? A savoury speech from an infidel ! What did God see in any of us, to exalt, cherish, and supply us, and let pass many others, who, for moral excellencies and virtuous endowments, do far exceed us? When we consider this distinction, then, 'Even so, Father, because it pleased thee.' There is a kind of election and reprobation in these common mercies; that is, God will dispense them to one and not to another; he will be glorified in their poverty and glorified in thy wealth; and therefore there is grace in it.

(2.) There is a mercy in it, that pitieth the miserable. How doth it appear these good things come from mercy? Because of our want, and because of our forfeiture.

(1st.) Our want and our indigence. Oh, when we think what shiftless creatures we should have been if he had not provided for us: Ps. xl. 17, 'I am poor and needy, yet the Lord thinketh upon me.' If we were but sensible of our own weakness, and emptiness, and manifold necessities, we would admire that God should think of us, such forlorn and wretched creatures; or that our baseness and poverty doth not make us contemptible to God: Ps. xxxiv. 6, 'This poor man cried, and the Lord heard him, and saved him out of all his troubles.' He doth not say, This *wise* man, this *eminent* saint, but this *poor* man. This was the doctrine of the Gentiles—That the divine power did only care for the great and weighty concernments of the world, but other things he left to their own event and to their own chance; as if God, in the great throng of business, were not at leisure to attend every private man's request. These were the fond surmises the Gentiles had of God; but we are taught better. 'This poor man cried unto the Lord, and he heard him.' Poor men in the world, when they have anything to do with great persons, they must look long, wait, pray, and pay to seek their face and favour, and at length meet with a rough answer and sour look. But God will not shut the door; the throne of grace lies open for every comer. You will say, this would sweeten mercies to the poor. Nay, it concerns not only those that are actually poor, but the great ones of the world (for they are poor and shiftless in themselves if God did not provide for them); others are but glasses where they might see their own misery. If they did well weigh the wants and necessities of others, they might see what would have been their own case if the Lord had not been merciful unto them. As Austin, when he saw a beggar frisking and leaping after his belly was filled, the spectacle wrought much upon him that he had not such rejoicing in God, who tasted so much of his abundance. Saith Chrysostom, If you are not thankful for health, go to the spittals and lazar-houses, and see what might have been your own case. Thus if you are not thankful for abundance, go to the families where there are children that want bread. It is the Lord's mercy to the richest, for they were miserable and indigent. It is a great mercy to relieve those from hand to mouth; but you that have abundance, it is a double mercy to you, for he prevents the necessity before it was felt. As Ps. xxi. 3, 'Thou preventest him with the blessings of goodness.' David takes notice of the goodness of God to him. Before the need is felt and observed, you are stored; and this should be a great endearment of the Lord's mercy to you.

(2d.) It is mercy, if we consider not only our want, but our forfeiture. It is not only mercy, but pardoning mercy; at least a reprieving from trouble, for we deserved the contrary. There is a kind of temporary pardon, which continueth all these blessings. It is as great a curse as possibly David could thunder out against obstinate sinners and God's implacable enemies : Ps. xxviii. 4, ' Give them according to their deeds, and according to the wickedness of their endeavours.' Do we think this would be matter of mischief only to David's enemies ? No ; every one of us, if we had our deserts, we should soon be shiftless, harbourless, begging from door to door, yea, howling for one drop of mercy to cool our tongues. Oh, then, surely the Lord is to be praised and acknowledged in bestowing the good things of this present life. Well, then—

As these blessings come from God, let them carry up your heart to God again. As all rivers they run from the sea, and they discharge themselves into the sea again, so let all be returned to God with thankfulness, with acknowledgments that you have received them from God. I shall urge it with one example : Jesus Christ, though he were heir, Lord of all things, ' Who thought it no robbery to be equal with God,' yet you find him ever giving thanks when he used the creatures : Mat. xv. 36. And it is the main thing John taketh notice of, and passeth by the miracle : John vi. 23, ' Where they did eat bread, after that the Lord had given thanks.' Nigh to Tiberias, there was the place where our Lord fed many with five loaves and two fishes ; but he only saith this, ' Where they did eat bread, after that the Lord had given thanks.' He saw this was a notable circumstance, so he doth but cursorily mention the miracle, only calls it eating bread, but expressly mentioneth Christ's blessing the creature. He would teach us that the blessing of all enjoyments is in God's hand.

Use 4. If the Lord be the donor and giver of all these outward things, let us beware we do not abuse these gifts of God, as occasions of sinning against the giver, that we fight not against him with his own weapons. Jesus Christ, speaking to his own disciples, though they were trained up with him, a company chosen out, and select family, who were to be his heralds and ambassadors to the world, yet he gives them this caution : Luke xxi. 34, ' Take heed to yourselves, lest at any time your hearts be overcharged with surfeiting and drunkenness, and cares of this life, and so that day come upon you unawares.' He saw it needful to warn his own disciples. We had two common parents, Adam and Noah, and one miscarried by eating, and the other by drinking ; these sins are natural to us. The throat is a slippery place, and had need well be looked unto. Mark, Christ there doth not mean surfeiting and drunkenness merely in a gross notion. When we hear of surfeiting and drunkenness, we think of spuing, staggering, reeling, vomiting, and the like ; but we are to consider it in a stricter notion : ' Take heed lest the heart be overcharged.' The heart may be overcharged when the stomach is not; that is, when we are less apt to praise God, grow more lumpish and heavy, or rather when we settle into a sensual frame of spirit, and by an inordinate delight in our present portion, are taken off from minding better things. Look, as the heart is overcharged with the cares of the world, so likewise with creature delights and comforts of this world, when it is set for ease and vanity. Many that would be loathers of the other drunkenness, yet are guilty of this kind of surfeiting and drunkenness; the heart is overcharged with an inordinate affection to present things. There cannot be a more heavy judgment than when our table is made our snare : Ps. lxix. 22.   A snare, it is God's spiritual judgment ; when the comforts of this life serve not so much to lengthen and strengthen life, but when their hearts are hardened in sin, and they grow neglectful of God and heavenly things.   Raining snares is an argument of God's hatred.   First, ' The Lord shall rain snares ;' and then, ' Brimstone and an horrible tempest shall be their portion,' Ps. xi. 6.   So it makes way for his eternal anger.

Use 5. Let us be contented with that portion which God hath given us of worldly things, if the Lord be the donor.   Why ?

1. Because God stands upon his sovereignty ; you must stand to God's allowance, though he gives to others more and to you less ; for God is supreme, and will not be controlled in the disposal of what is his own.   The goodman of the house pleaded, Mat. xx. 13–15, ' Friend, I do thee no wrong ; is it not lawful for me to do what I will with mine own ?'   The fulness of the earth and all is his ; and, therefore, though others have better trading, and finer apparel, and be more amply provided for than we are, God is sovereign, and will give according to his pleasure, and you must be content.

2. Nothing is deserved, and therefore certainly everything should be kindly taken.   If a man be kept at free cost, and maintained at your expense, you take it very ill if he murmur and dislike his diet. Certainly we are all maintained at free cost, and, therefore, we should with all humble contentation receive whatever God will put into our hands.

3. God knows what proportion is best for us ; he is a God of judgment, and knows what is most convenient for us, for he is a wise God. It is the shepherd must choose the pasture, not the sheep.   Leave it to God to give you that which is convenient and suitable to your condition of life.   A shoe may be too big for the foot, and a garment too great for the body, as Saul's armour was too large for little David : 1 Sam. xvii.   God will give you that which is convenient, that which is agreeable to you.   A garment, when too long, proves a dirty rag ; we may have too much ; and therefore God he carves out our allowance with a wise hand.

4. God doth not only give suitable to your condition, but suitable to your strength, such a portion as you are able to bear.   God layeth affliction upon his people, and he gives them mercies as they are able to bear ; if they had more, they would have more snares, more temptations.   You find it hard for a rich man to enter into the kingdom of heaven : Mat. xix. 24.   A man may take a larger draught than he is able to bear ; so God proportioneth every man's condition according to his spiritual strength ; every man is not able to bear a very high prosperous estate : Heb. xiii. 5, ' Let your conversation be without covetousness ; and be content with such things as ye have : for he hath said, I will never leave thee, nor forsake thee ;' then you will live upon the promise.   But when men set God a task, and he must maintain them at such a rate, that ends in mischief and distrust : Ps. lxxviii. 19, ' Can God furnish a table in the wilderness ?' &c.

5. Contentation is one of God's gifts that we ask in this prayer, ' Give us this day our daily bread;' that is, we ask to be contented with our portion. Contentment and quietness of mind with what we do enjoy, it is a great blessing: Joel ii. 19. See what the Lord saith there by his prophet : ' I will send you corn, and wine, and oil, and ye shall be satisfied therewith.' The bare and simple blessing doth not speak so much of God's love as when we are satisfied, when we have contentment in it; that is the greater blessing. When our minds are suited to our condition, then the creature is more sweet, more comfort-able. Your happiness lies not in abundance, but in contentment: Luke xii. 15. This doth not make a man happy, that he hath much ; but this, that he is contented; he hath what God will give him. All spiritual miseries may be referred to these two things : a war between a man and his conscience, and a war between his affections and his condition.

6. There may be as much love in a lesser portion as in a greater. There is the same affection to a small younger child, though he hath not so large an allowance as the elder brother; yet, saith he, My father loves me as well as him; not that I have a double portion, but I have as much of my father's love. So a child of God may say, God loves me, though he hath given another more and me less. Be content with what falls to your share, and with your allowance by the wise designa-tion and allotment of God's providence. Thus much for the first point.

A word of a second, viz. :—

Doct. 2. In asking temporal things, Christ hath stinted us to a day, ' Give us, σήμερον, *this day*, our daily bread.'

God in an extraordinary manner fed his people in the wilderness; the manna stank if they had kept it another day; they had it from day to day. What is the reason Christ saith, ' Give us *this day*' ?

1. That every day we may pray to God. Therefore it is not, Give us this month, or year, but day; because every day God will hear from us : 1 Thes. v. 17, ' Pray without ceasing.' God would not have us too long out of his company, but by a frequent commerce he would have us acquainted and familiar with him. This is required, that you should not let a day pass over your head but God must hear from you, for your patent lasts but for a day; you have a lease from God of your comforts and mercies, but it is expired unless you renew it again by prayer. How much do they differ from the heart of God's children, that could be contented, like the high priest of old, to come to the mercy-seat but once a year ! Now the Lord would have us come every day to the throne of grace.

2. Every day, because there should be family prayer; for all that take their meat together are to come, and say to God, ' Give us this day our daily bread.' It is not said, ' Give me,' but ' Give us.' There-fore you see how little of love and fear of God is there, where, week after week, they call not upon God's name.

3. To make way for our gratitude and thankfulness. Our mercies, they flow not from God all at once, but some to-day, and some to-morrow, for we take them day by day ; all together, they are too heavy for us to wield and manage: Ps. lxviii. 19, ' Who daily loadeth us

with benefits.' Our mercies, they come in greater number and a greater measure than we are able to acknowledge, make use of, or be thankful for. Therefore, this is the burden of gracious hearts, that mercies come so thick and fast they cannot be thankful enough for them ; but to help us, God distributes them by parcels. Who loadeth us daily, some to-day, some to-morrow, and every day, that we may not forget God, but may have a new argument to praise him.

4. To show us every day we should renew our dependence upon God for temporal things. There is no day but we stand in need of the Lord's blessing, of sanctification, of comfort, that they may not be a snare, that there is still need of new strength, new grace, and new supplies.

5. Again, 'Give us *this day*,' that we may not burden ourselves with overmuch thoughtfulness, that we might not solicitously cark for to-morrow: Mat. vi. 34, 'Sufficient unto the day is the evil thereof.' Every day affords business, trouble, care, and burden enough; we need not anticipate and pre-occupy the cares of the next day ; God would not have us overborne with solicitude, but look no further than this day.

6. Christ would teach us that worldly things should be sought in a moderate proportion ; if we have sufficient for a day, for the present want, we should not grasp at too much. Ships lightly laden will pass through the sea, but when we take too great a burden, the ship will easily sink with every storm. We have sore troubles to pass through in the world ; now when we are overburdened with present things we have more snares and temptations.

7. Christ would train us up with thoughts of our lives' uncertainty : James iv. 13, 'Say not, This and this I will do to-day or to-morrow : What is your life? it is but a vapour.' One being invited to dinner the next day, said, For these many years I have not had a to-morrow ; meaning he was providing every day for his last day. We do not know whether we have another day, but are apt to sing lullabies to our souls, and say, 'Soul, take thine ease, thou hast goods laid up for many years,' Luke xii. 19. We are sottishly secure, and dream of many years, whereas God tells us only of to-day.

8. To awaken us after heavenly things. When we seek bread for the present life, then give us 'this day ;' but now come to me, saith Christ, and I will give you bread that shall nourish you 'to eternal life,' bread that endureth for ever : John vi. 27, 'Labour not for the meat which perisheth, but for that meat which endureth unto ever-lasting life.' There is meat that will endure for ever, but for the present we beg only for this day: 1 Pet. i. 4, 'To an inheritance incorruptible, and undefiled, and that fadeth not away, reserved in heaven for you.' That is an eternal state, this but of a short and of a small continuance. You see what need you have to go to God, that he will most plentifully provide for you.

And forgive us our debts, as we forgive our debtors.

WE have now done with the supplications of this prayer, and are come
to the deprecations. The supplications are those petitions which we
make to God for obtaining of that which is good. The deprecations
are those petitions we make to God for removing of that which is evil.
Now of this latter sort there are two :—(1.) We pray for the remission
of evil that is already committed ; (2.) We pray for the prevention of
the evil which may be inflicted. The first of these is the petition we
have now in hand. Here,

1. The petition is proposed, ' Forgive us our debts.'

2. It is confirmed by an argument, ' As we forgive our debtors.'

In the first, take notice :—

    I. Of the object, or matter of this petition, and that is, *debts*.

    II. The subject or persons praying, *us*.

    III. The person to whom we pray, *our heavenly Father*, who alone
can forgive our sins.

    IV. The act of God about this object, *forgive*.

Then the petition is confirmed by an argument, which is taken
from our forgiving of others.

In which there is an argument.

1. *A simili*, from a like disposition in us. Thus, what is good in
us was first in God, for he is the pattern of all perfection. If we have
such a disposition planted in our hearts, and if it be a virtue in us,
surely the same disposition is in God, for the first being wanteth no
perfection.

2. The argument may be taken *à dispari*, or *à minori ad majus*,
from the less to the greater. If we, that have but a drop of mercy,
can forgive the offences done to us, surely the infinite God, that is
mercy itself, he hath more bowels and more pity : ' For his ways are
above our ways, as high as the heaven is above the earth,' Isa. lv. 9.
So it seems the argument is propounded : Luke xi. 4, ' Forgive us
our sins, for we also forgive every one that is indebted to us.'

3. The argument may be taken from the condition or the qualification of those that are to expect pardon. They are such that, out of a
sense of God's mercy to them, and the love of God shed abroad in
their hearts, are inclined and disposed to show mercy to others. So
Christ explains it, ver. 14, making it a condition or qualification on
our part: ' If ye forgive men their trespasses, your heavenly Father
will also forgive you.' But this will be more abundantly clear when
I come to examine that clause.

Before we come to the petition itself, the connexion is to be considered, for the particle *and* links it to the former petition. After
' Hallowed be thy name,' he doth not say, '*And* thy kingdom come ;'
they are propounded as distinct sentences : but, ' Give us this day our
daily bread, *and* forgive us our debts,' for three reasons :—

[1.] Without pardon all the good things of this life will do us no
good. They are but as a full diet, or as a rich suit, to a condemned
person ; they will not comfort him and allay his present fears. Until
we are pardoned, we are under a sentence, ready for execution and

therefore we cannot have that comfort in outward things until we have some interest in God's fatherly mercy. A man that is condemned hath the king's allowance until execution. So it is the indulgence of God to a wicked man to give him many outward things, though he is condemned already. We should not satisfy ourselves with daily bread without a sense of some interest in pardoning mercy.

[2.] To show us our unworthiness. Our sins are so many and grievous that we are not worthy of one morsel of bread to put in our mouths. When we say, 'Give us this day,' &c., we need presently to say, 'Forgive us our sins.' There is a forfeiture even of these common blessings: Gen. xxxii. 10, 'I am not worthy of the least of all the mercies, and of all the truth, which thou hast showed unto thy servant.' All that we have we have from mercy, and it is mercy undeserved. As we are creatures, there can be no common right between God and us to engage him to give temporal blessings, for we owe ourselves wholly to him, as being created out of nothing. Children cannot oblige their parents. But much more, as we are guilty creatures, it is merely of the mercy of the Lord.

[3.] These are joined together because sin is the great obstacle and hindrance of all the blessings which we expect from God: Jer. v. 25, 'Your sins have withheld good things from you.' When mercy comes to us, sin stands in the way and turns it back again, so that it cannot have so clear a passage to us. Therefore God must forgive before he can give, that is, bestow these outward things as a blessing on us.

Having spoken of this connexion, let me observe something from the petition itself.

The first thing I shall observe is the notion by which sin is set out, 'Forgive us *our debts*.' The point is:—

Doct. 1. That sins come under the notion of debts.

In Luke xi. 4, it is, 'Forgive us our sins.' There is a twofold debt which man oweth to God.

1. A debt of duty.
2. A debt of punishment.

[1.] A debt of duty, worship, and obedience; this is a debt we owe to God. In this sense it is said, Rom. viii. 12, 'We are debtors, not to the flesh, to live after the flesh.' In which negative the affirmative is clearly implied, that we are debtors to God, to live to God; debtors to the Spirit, to live after the Spirit. By the law of creation, we were not appointed to serve and please the flesh, but to serve God: Luke xvii. 10, 'When you have done all those things which are commanded you, say, We are unprofitable servants, we have done that which was our debt or duty to do.' Obedience, worship, and service, is a debt we owe to God, by virtue of that interest which he hath in us, and command he hath over us. And so you have that speech, Gal. v. 3, that we are debtors to the whole law, as we come under the obedience of it.

[2.] A debt of punishment, which we are fallen into through the neglect of our duty. Punishment is due to us as wages: Rom vi. 23, 'The wages of sin is death.' God hath, as it were, made a contract with us, that if we will sin we must take our wages; we must take what it comes to.

Now in this petition, when we say, 'Forgive us our debts,' we do not desire to be discharged of the duty we owe to God, but to be acquitted of the guilt and punishment. The faults or sins that we are guilty of oblige us and bind us to the punishment; and therefore sins are called debts. The original debt we owe is obedience; and in case of default, the next debt we owe is punishment. Look, as in a contract and bond, if the party observe not the condition, then he is liable to the forfeiture: so God dealt with man by way of covenant, and the tenor of it was exact obedience; and this covenant had a sanction or an obligation annexed: in case obedience was not exactly performed, we should be accursed, and suffer all manner of misery in this life and the next. Now, by the fall, we incurred this penalty; and therefore, as lost and undone creatures, we run to God's mercy, and beg him to forgive the debt, or the forfeiture of that bond of obedience wherein man standeth bound to God by the law.

A little to make it good, before I come to the body of the petition, let me show how sin is a debt, wherein it agrees. That will appear if you can consider:—

1. Our danger by sin.
2. Our remedy from sin.

In both the parts you will find sin is considered as a debt.

First, If you consider our danger by sin.

[1.] There is a creditor to whom the debt is due, and that is God: Luke vii. 41, when he would set out God's mercy he saith, 'There was a certain creditor which had two debtors,' &c. God is there set forth under the notion and similitude of a creditor. God is a creditor, partly as our creator, and partly as a lawgiver, and partly as a judge. As our creator and benefactor, from whom we have received all that we have: it was the Lord that gave to every man his talents to trade withal; to some more, to some less: Mat. xxv. Thus God hath trusted us with life, and all other blessings. But then, as a lawgiver: if God had given us life, strength, parts, wealth, that we should do with them what we would, though the gift would oblige us, in point of gratitude, to serve our benefactor, yet we had not been so responsible for our defaults. But we are under a law to serve him and honour him that made us and gave us what we have. God did not dispossess himself of an interest in them. He did not give them to us as owners and proprietors, to do with them what we would; but he gave them to us as stewards: our life and employment here is a stewardship. Nay, God is not only a lawgiver, but also a judge; he will call us to an account. He doth oblige us as a creator, but imposeth a necessity upon us of obeying and serving him as a lawgiver; and not only makes a law, but will take an account of men, how they observe the law of their creation. There will a time come when the lord of those servants will come and reckon with them, and require his own with usury: Luke xix. 23. He will require this debt and service at our hands, else we must endure the penalty. Well, this is the connexion: he that abuseth God's mercy as a creator offends him as a lawgiver, and is justly punished by him as a judge. There are many never think of this, therefore are not sensible of these great relations, nor that they shall answer for all their talents, strength, and time, and advantages they have in the world. Thus there is a creditor.

[2.] As a debtor is bound to make satisfaction to the creditor, or else is liable to the process of the law, which may be commenced against him, so are we all to God, bodies and souls; we are become ὑπόδικος τῷ Θεῷ, 'guilty before the Lord:' Rom. iii. 19. So we translate it. We are under the sentence of the law, liable to the process of his revenging justice, and one day God will pursue his righteous law against us. All the fallen creatures are quite become bankrupt; we can never pay the original debt of obedience, therefore must be left to lie under the debt of punishment.

[3.] Look, as debts stand upon record, and are charged upon some book of account, that they may not be forgot, so God hath his book of account—a book of remembrance, as it is called: Mal. iii. 16. All our words, speeches, actions, they are all upon record; what means we have enjoyed, what mercies, what opportunities, what calls, and what messages of his love and grace: Job xiv. 17, 'My iniquity is sealed up in a bag.' As men's writings or bonds, which they have to show for their debts owing to them, are sealed up in a bag, so Job useth that similitude. Thus is sin represented as a thing that is upon record, and cannot be forgotten. Many times we lose the memory of what we have done in childhood and infancy, but all is upon record; and your iniquities will one day find you out, though you have forgotten, and think never to hear of them more.

[4.] A day of reckoning will come, when God will put the bond in suit, and all shall be called to an account. Sometimes God reckoneth with sinners, in part, in this world, but surely in the next. Death is but the summons to come to an account with God: Luke xvi. 2, 'Give an account of thy stewardship, for thou mayest be no longer steward.' That passage of the parable is applicable to death: 'That when ye fail, they may receive you into everlasting habitations,' ver. 9. When the soul is turned out of doors, when it is cited to appear before the tribunal of God, then we give up our account. But especially at the great day: Rev. xx. 12, 'And I saw the dead, small and great, stand before God, and the books were opened;' that is, the book of conscience and the book of God's remembrance. There are two books, that are written within and without, upon which all our actions are stamped: they are now closed in a great measure; we know not what is in these great books. One of the books (that of conscience) is in our own keeping, yet we cannot deface and blot it out. These books at that day will be opened; conscience, by the power of God, shall be extended to the recognition of all our ways. Conscience writes when it speaks not: many times it doth not smite for sins we are guilty of; but there stands the debt charged, upon which we shall be responsible.

[5.] After this reckoning there is execution. A bankrupt that cannot satisfy his creditor is cast into prison; so God hath his prison for impenitent, disobedient, and obstinate sinners: 1 Pet. iii. 19, 'He went and preached unto the spirits in prison.' It is a dismal prison, where poor captive prisoners are held in chains of darkness; that is, under the horrors of their own despairing fears, looking for the judgment of the Lord, when they shall be cast into this prison, and no getting out again, until they have paid the utmost farthing: Luke xii. 50. And that will never be as to the sinner: he is, as it were, always satisfying, and can never be said to have satisfied, the justice of God.

Thus you see how sin is a debt, and what correspondence there is between them—the obligation of punishment that ariseth from sin. But now it differeth from all other debts.

(1.) No debt to man can be so great as our debt to God, both for number and weight. Mat. xviii. 24, compared with ver. 28: you shall see there the parable of the lord forgiving 'ten thousand talents;' and the servant goes and takes his brother by the throat, and requireth from him a debt of 'an hundred pence.' Mark, offences done to God are greater than offences done to us; for there is as much difference and disproportion as between an hundred and ten thousand. And then the debt of the fellow-servant was but pence, an hundred pence; but the debt due to the lord, that was talents; and a talent is reckoned to be one hundred and eighty-seven pounds ten shillings. Our sins against God are more and more heavy than any which our brethren can commit against us. Pence, talents; one hundred and ten thousand: there is the difference and disproportion. Oh that we had a due sense of what it is to sin against God, against an infinite majesty! To strike a private person is not so much as to strike an officer of justice; and that is not so much as to strike the supreme magistrate. What is it to sin against God? and how often do we? All our imaginations are only evil, and that continually; and therefore all our sins against God will arise to a vast and heavy debt, because of the infiniteness of the object against whom sin is committed.

(2.) In other debts there is a day of payment set them; in this debt there is none. God doth not tell us when he will put the bond in suit against us; he may surprise us ere we are aware. Luke xii. 20: when he dreamed of many years, 'Thou fool, this night.' The spirits now in prison did as little think of that doleful place as those sinners which are alive. It may be to-day, to-morrow, the next hour: Gen. iv. 7, 'Sin lieth at the door.' There is a sentence and curse that waylays him. Sin, for the punishment of sin; it is ready to seize upon him, and pluck him by the throat, and bring him into God's presence. Still the curse hovers over the head of obstinate and impenitent sinners.

(3.) In other debts, if the goods are taken by way of execution, and suffice, the person is free; but here God aims at the person, and the whole person. 'Body and soul are cast into hell fire,' Mat. x. 28.

(4.) Here there can be no shifting, no avoiding the danger. If you fly from God, you do but fly to God; from God, as willing to be a friend; to God, who is sure to be revenged. 'Whither shall I fly from thy Spirit? If I go into the depths, thou art there,' Ps. cxxxix. God is here, there, and everywhere.

(5.) All other debts cease at death; when a man dieth, we say his debts are paid: but here execution begins, then the law takes the sinner by the throat, and drags him to everlasting punishment, and doth in effect say, Pay me what thou owest. Death is God's arrest. As soon as the soul steps out of the world, presently it is attached and seized, and forfeited into the hands of God's justice. How many are there that lie under this danger and never think of it! Spiritual debts they are not so sensible of as literal. A man that is deeply in debt, and in danger of an arrest, cannot sleep, eat, walk abroad, but his fears are upon him. Augustus bought his quilt or bed, that could sleep soundly when he owed so many thousand sesterces. But poor senseless sinners never think of danger until they are plunged into it, and then there is no escape.

Secondly, The metaphor will also hold good as to our remedy and recovery, how we come out of this debt. A debtor that is insolvent is undone, unless there be some means found out to satisfy the creditor : so we must altogether lie under the wrath of God, unless satisfaction be made. Therefore, Jesus Christ, in the

[1.] Place, comes under the notion of a surety. Because he took the debt of man upon himself, therefore, Heb. vii. 22, he is called, ' the surety of a better testament.' When Christ undertook the business of our salvation, he did in effect say, as Paul to Philemon, ver. 18, ' If he hath wronged thee, or oweth thee aught, put that on mine account : ' so did Jesus Christ in effect say to God, Let me be made a sin, and made a curse for them. He that was a judge, was willing to become a party, and to pay what he owed. David, in the type of Christ, saith, Ps. lxix. 4, ' I restored that which I took not away.' He did not take away any honour from God : it was we that robbed God of the glory of his justice, authority, and truth ; that trampled them under our feet : but Christ made restitution and amends to God.

[2.] Having condescended to become our surety, he made full satisfaction, by suffering the punishment which was due to us : Isa. liii. 4, ' Surely he hath borne our griefs, and carried our sorrows.' That which we should have borne upon our own backs, and would have crushed us for ever, that he hath borne, and he hath carried. Christ was to be the sinner in law, and was to suffer in our stead. Solomon hath a passage concerning suretyship : Prov. xi. 15, ' He that is surety for a stranger, shall smart for it ; ' or, as the Hebrew will bear it, ' sore bruised ; ' or, as it is in the margin, 'shall be bruised and sore broken.' And the same word is used concerning Christ, that was our surety : Isa. liii. 10, ' It pleased the Father to bruise him.' Christ is our surety, therefore he was bruised and broken, he suffered what we should have suffered. It is true, there are some circumstances of our punishment which Christ suffered not, as a great part of our punishment in hell ; there is the worm of conscience and despair, and the eternity of torments ; but this was not essential to the punishment, but did only arise from the guilt and from the weakness of the party that is punished, because we cannot work through it otherwise. Christ paid the full price which divine justice demanded, and so made satisfaction for us.

[3.] Christ satisfying as our surety, all those which had an interest in his death, they are set free from the wrath of God, they have a release from this great debt owed. As when the ram was taken, Isaac was let go ; so when Christ was taken, the sinner is released and dis-

charged : Job xxxiii. 24, ' Deliver him from going down to the pit ;
I have found a ransom.'   Certainly God will not exact the debt twice,
of the surety and of the principal person ; our surety having paid the
debt for us, therefore we go free.   And, therefore, if our consciences
should pursue us at law, we may answer, Christ was taken for us, 'He
was bruised for our iniquities, and he bore the chastisement of our
peace.'

[4.] Christ hath not only satisfied for the punishment, but he hath
procured favour for us ; wherein he differeth from an ordinary and
common surety.   Christ does not only free us from bonds, but also
hath brought us into grace and favour with the creator, lawgiver, and
judge.   There is a double notion of Christ's death ; that of a ransom
for the delivery of a captive, and as a merit and price which was
given for eternal life.   The death of Christ did not only dissolve the
obligation which lay upon us to suffer the penalty for the breach of
the law, and so deliver us from the wrath to come ; but it was a price
that was given to purchase-grace, favour, and heaven for us, which is
called, Eph. i. 14, ' The purchased possession.'   Now, why must our
surety instate us thus into favour ?   Because Christ was such a surety
as did not only pay the forfeiture, but also the principal ; that is, he
did not only make satisfaction for the trespass and offence (which is
the payment of the forfeiture), but also he established a righteousness
answerable to the law (which is the payment of the principal), and of
that original debt which God first required of the creature ; for there
is a debt of duty and service which Christ performeth and establisheth
as a righteousness for us.

[5.] From hence in his name there is proclaimed redemption to the
captives, freedom to poor prisoners that were in debt, and weak, and
could not acquit themselves.   And therefore the publication of the
gospel is compared to the year of jubilee : Luke iv. 19, Christ came
' to preach the acceptable year of the Lord.'   It relates to the year of
jubilee, wherein all debts were cancelled ; it was a year of general
releasement, proclaimed by sound of trumpet, that every man should
return to his inheritance, and all debts dissolved and done away : Lev.
xxv. 9, 10.   So Jesus Christ saith, ' The Spirit of the Lord is upon me,
to preach the acceptable year of the Lord ;' that is, to proclaim to poor
captives a release of all debts, and all bonds which are upon them.

[6.] All those that come to God by Christ are interested in the
comfort of this offer and proclamation of grace, and may plead with
God about their discharge from this great and heavy debt.   I put it
mainly in that notion (those that come to God by Christ), because you
will find that is the description of those whom Christ means to save :
Heb. vii. 25, ' He is able to save them to the uttermost that come
unto God by him.'   Who are those that come unto God by him ?
Those that in Christ's name do seriously, and with brokenness of
heart, deal with him about a release and a discharge.   To come to
God by him, it is to come in his name, to plead his propitiation, or
his satisfaction, as the only meritorious cause ; and the promise of
God in Christ to blot out our offences, as the only ground of hope ;
and as to ourselves, acknowledging the debt ; that is, in confessing our
sins, and our desert of punishment, with a purpose to forsake them.

(1.) There is required an acknowledgment of the debt. God stands upon it, that his justice may be owned with a due sense, according to the tenor of the first covenant: for though the satisfaction be made by another, and that by a surety of God's providing; yet God will have the creature know they are under so heavy a debt, that he will have them feel it in brokenness of heart; not know it only in a general conviction, but confess their sins: 1 John i. 9, 'If we confess our sins, he is faithful and just to forgive us our sins.' When we come with true remorse, and confess we have offended so just, so holy, so merciful a Father, it must be grievous to us in the remembrance of it. You must not only confess sin as a wrong, but as a debt: sin hath wronged God, and it is also a debt binding you over to a punishment we could never endure, nor make God any satisfaction for. Therefore David, when he would have God's bond crossed and cancelled, see how he pleads: Ps. li. 2, 3, 'O Lord, blot out mine offences, for I acknowledge my transgressions; and my sin is ever before me.' Blot it out, for I acknowledge it; that is, I submit to thy instituted course; I submit to the justice of the first covenant.

(2.) The satisfaction of Christ must be pleaded also by a sinner in the court of heaven, in a believing manner, that there may be an owning of the surety. All parties that are interested in this business must consent. Now God and Christ they are agreed about the business of salvation: God hath agreed to take satisfaction from Christ, and Christ hath agreed to make this satisfaction to God: all the business now is about the sinner's consent, or about his ready acceptation of Jesus Christ; and we never heartily indeed consent to this, that Christ shall be our surety, and he the person that must release and discharge this debt, until we look upon him by an eye of faith, as one that tore the bond and handwriting that was against us. The law is called 'the handwriting that was against us;' there is the bond which was to be put in suit: now, Col. ii. 14, He hath torn, or 'blotted out the handwriting of ordinances, that was against us, which was contrary to us, and took it out of the way, nailing it to his cross.' He hath disannulled the law, which binds to suffer the wrath of God. The law was the bond by which our death was ratified.

(3.) There is required an unfeigned purpose to forsake sin. He that hath been released of his debt, must not still run into new arrears.

Christ never blotted out our debts that we might renew them, and go on upon a new score of offending God again; this is to dally with God, to run into the snare when he hath broken it for us and given us an escape, to plunge ourselves into new debts again.

In this prayer, 'Forgive us our debts,' then presently, 'Lead us not into temptation.' Therefore we must purpose to forsake sin, otherwise we do not draw nigh to God with a true heart: Heb. x. 22. We do but deal falsely with God in all the confessions we make, and in all the pleas of faith, unless there be an unfeigned purpose to renounce all sin, and cast it off as a thing that will undo our souls. Thus, Christians, must you sue out your release and discharge in your surety's name.

Use 1. The use is, first, to show us the misery of an impenitent, unpardoned sinner; he hath a vast debt upon him, that will surely undo him unless he doth in time get a discharge. He is bound over to suffer the wrath of God for evermore, and no hand can loose him but God's. Many times they think of no such matter, and cry, ' Peace, peace,' to themselves; but it is not the debtor which must cancel the book, but the creditor. Have you a discharge from God? where is your legal qualification? poor creatures, what will you do? Many take care that they may owe nothing to any man; oh! but what do you owe to God? To live in doubt and in fear of an arrest, oh, what misery is that! But when sin lieth at the door, ready to attack you every moment and hale you to the prison of hell, that is most dreadful. Therefore think of it seriously; how do accounts stand between God and you? Sinners are loth to think of it. When the lord came to reckon with his servants, Mat. xviii. 24, it is said, ' One was brought to him which owed him ten thousand talents:' he was loth to come to an account, he would fain keep out of the way, but he was brought to him. So we are unwilling to be called to account, we shift and delay, and will not think of our misery: but the *putting off* sin will not *put it away;* our not thinking of our misery will not help us out, and will not be a release and discharge.

2. If sins be debts, and an increasing debt, so that man is ever treasuring up wrath against the day of wrath; it presseth us to be more careful to get out of this condition. Saith Solomon, Prov. vi. 3–5 : If thou beest in debt, ' flee as a swift roe from the hand of the hunter, and as a bird from the hand of the fowler.' Oh, it is a sad thing to lie in our sins! If you be under this debt, ' give not sleep to thine eyes, nor slumber to thine eyelids; get away like the swift roe from the hand of the hunter,' &c. And what I say concerning a state of sin, I say concerning daily failings; make your peace with God betimes; if you have contracted a new debt, make all even between God and your souls, that you may not sleep in your sins.

3. This should make us more cautious that we do not commit sin : why? it is a debt that will render you obnoxious to the wrath of God; in itself it merits eternal death : oh, therefore, sin no more, do not run again into the snare! When you give way to sin, you hazard the comfort of your acquittance by Christ : Ps. lxxxv. 8, ' The Lord will speak peace unto his people, and to his saints; but let them not turn again to folly.' If the Lord hath given you your peace, and some hope of your being discharged of this heavy debt, take heed of meddling with forbidden fruit, and running into debt again.

II. From the subject or persons which make this prayer, ' Forgive *us*,' observe,

Doct. Even those that call God Father, ought to beg, daily and humbly, pardon of their sins.

Forgive us ; who is that *us* that can say in faith, *Our Father*, daily? For this is a pattern for daily prayer, as the word σήμερον in the former petition noteth. We need beg, for Christ hath taught us here to sue out our discharge: in which begging there is an exercise of faith eyeing Christ : Rom. iii. 25, ' God hath set forth him to be a propitiation through faith in his blood.' And there is an exercise also of repentance, as to mourning for sin : 1 John i. 9, and Prov. xxviii. 13, ' He that confesseth and forsaketh his sin, shall have mercy :' and as to loathing of sin, Acts iii. 19, ' Repent ye therefore, and be converted, that your sins may be blotted out.' And certainly it must be humbly begged ; for if we seek pardon we must seek it in God's way. We do not beg God to rescind and make void his laws, and those wise constitutions he hath appointed whereby the creature shall receive this grace ; and the manner wherein he will deal and transact this business with the offending creature : but we seek it as exercising our renewed repentance ; that is, mourning for sin, and loathing of sin. But of this more hereafter.

Now, that the best of God's children should be dealing with God about a pardon of their sins, I shall argue it :—

1. From the necessity.

2. The utility and profit of such a course.

First, The necessity of this will appear two ways :—

[1.] From the condition of God's children here in the world.

[2.] From the way wherein God will give out a pardon.

[1.] From the condition of God's children here in this world. The best are not so fully sanctified in this life but there is some sin found in them ; not only they who walk with no care, but even they that set the most narrow watch over their ways, they are not so sanctified but they need daily to go to God.

(1.) They have original sin which remaineth with them to the last, they have the sinning sin which the apostle speaks of. Paul complains of the body of death : Rom. vii. 23, 24, ' Who shall deliver me from it ?' The Hebrews were wont to propound their wishes by way of question ; as, ' Oh that salvation were come out of Zion !' It is in the Hebrew, ' Who shall bring salvation out of Zion ?' So, ' Who will lead me into Edom ?' that is, ' Oh that I were led into Edom,' that I might display the banner there, because of God's truth. So, ' Who shall deliver me from the body of this death ?' that is, ' Oh that I were delivered !' Where the reign of sin is broken, yet there it remains ; though it be cast *down* in regard of regency, yet it is not cast *out* in regard of inherency. As the ivy that is gotten into the wall, cut away the boughs, branches, stubs, yet still there will be some sproutings out again until the wall be pulled down ; so until these earthly tabernacles of ours be tumbled in the dust, though we are mortifying and subduing of sin, yet there will be a budding and sprouting out again.

(2.) There are many actual sins : James iii. 2, ' In many things we offend all ;' and Eccles. vii. 20, ' There is not a just man upon earth, that doeth good, and sinneth not :' that is, that sins not either in omitting of good or committing of evil : our offences are either total or partial. Partial offences ; though a child of God loves God, fears God, trusts in God, yet not in that purity and perfection that he hath required of him ; though he serves God and obeys him, yet not with that liberty, delight, reverence, which he hath required. There is an omission in part in every act : there is not that perfection which God deserveth, who is to be served with all our might, with all our strength. Our principles are divided ; there is flesh and spirit ; there is a mixture in all our actions. Sometimes there is a total omission, the spiritual life is at a stand, many times all acts of respect are intermitted.   Then for commissions, sometimes, out of ignorance, they do not see what is to be done.   Though they have a general resolution to do the whole will of God, yet many times they mistake.   Our light is but in part :   And ' who can understand his errors ?   Cleanse me from secret sins :' Ps. xix. 12.   We sin out of ignorance, as a man in the dark may jostle against his friend.   Sometimes by imprudence and inconsideration, as a man that is not heedful, though he knows it, he may mistake his way.   Many are overtaken in a fault : Gal. vi. 1 ; that is, unawares, and besides their intention.   Sometimes, out of incogitancy and sudden incursion, they may not only be overtaken but overborne, ' drawn away by their own lusts,' James i. 14 : overcome by the prevalency of passion and corrupt affection ; so sin gets the upper hand.   Thus it is with the children of God.   Look, as it was said of the Romans, that in battle they were overcome, but never in war ; though a child of God hath the best of it at last, yet in many particular conflicts he is overborne by the violence of temptation and his own corrupt lusts.   Thus there is a necessity of begging daily pardon, if we consider the condition of the saints while they are here in the world, who carry a sinning nature about them, a corrupt issue that will never be dried up while they are in the world ; and also they are guilty of many actual sins, both of omission and commission.

Secondly, The necessity of it will appear from the way wherein God gives a pardon, which is upon the creature's humble submission, and seeking of terms of grace ; so that whatsoever right we have to remission in Christ, though we have a general right to remission and pardon of sin, yet we must seek to apply that right, and beg the use of it for our daily pardon and acceptance with God.   This will appear by considering—(1.) The nature of this request ; (2.) The right that a justified person hath to the pardon of his daily sins.

1. What we beg for when we say, Forgive us our sins.   Five things we ask of God :—

[1.] The grant of a pardon.

[2.] The continuance of this privilege.

[3.] The sense and comfort of it.

[4.] The increase of that sense.

[5.] The effects of pardon, or a freedom from those penal evils that are fruits of sin.

(1.) The grant of a pardon, that God would accept the satisfaction of Christ for our sins, and look upon us as righteous in him.   Jesus Christ himself was to sue out the fruits of his purchase : Ps. ii. 8, ' Ask of me, and I will give thee the heathen for thine inheritance, and the uttermost parts of the earth for thy possession.'   Though he had a right to be received into heaven, to sit down at the right hand of God, and administer the kingdom for the comfort of his elect ones, yet ' ask of me.'   And so we are to sue out our right : Ps. xxxii. 5, ' I said, I will confess my transgressions unto the Lord ; and thou forgavest the iniquity of my sin.'   What then ?   ' For this cause shall every one that is godly pray unto thee.'   Though God be so ready to forgive—as soon as we conceive a purpose he gives out a pardon—yet we are to call upon God.   God will have us to sue out the grant of a pardon.   Why ?   Because he would deal with us as a sovereign, therefore

doth he require the submission of our faith.   It was of grace that he
would appoint a satisfaction for us, which he did not for the fallen
angels ; and it was much more grace that he would give that satisfaction, give that price, out of his own treasury.   Christ was not
a mediator of our choosing, but God's ; and therefore, though
justice be fully satisfied, yet the debt is humbly to be acknowledged
by the creature, and we are to sue out terms of grace.   And again,
the application to us is merely grace, when so many thousands perish
in their sins ; therefore we are to beg, to sue out this grace, that we
may have the benefit of Christ's death.   God doth it, that in begging
we may acknowledge our own misery, and how unable we are to make
satisfaction : Ps. cxliii. 2, ' In thy sight no flesh can be justified ;' and
Ps. cxxx. 3, 4, ' If thou shouldest mark iniquities, O Lord, who shall
stand ?   But there is forgiveness with thee, that thou mayest be
feared.'   Before God will give us an interest in this forgiveness, we
are to come and confess ourselves utterly to be insolvent, and also to
own Jesus Christ as the means, that we may solemnly and explicitly
own our Redeemer, who was appointed by God, and procured this
benefit for us : 1 John ii. 1, ' And if any man sin, we have an advocate
with the Father, Jesus Christ the righteous.'   God hath required
we should sue it out, and own our advocate, as well as confess ourselves unable to satisfy, that we might know who is our advocate.
In the type of the brazen serpent, Num. xxi. 8, ' And the Lord said
unto Moses, Make thee a fiery serpent, and set it upon a pole : and it
shall come to pass, that every one that is bitten, when he looketh upon
it, shall live.'   Mark, though God set up a sign of salvation (as it is
called elsewhere), yet when you shall look upon him you shall live.   So
God would have us sue out the grant by looking to Christ, that so our
interest may be established : John iii. 14, 15, ' And as Moses lifted up
the serpent in the wilderness, even so must the Son of man be lifted
up ; that whosoever believeth in him should not perish, but have
eternal life.'   That whosoever ' believeth in him,' that was the intent
of looking upon it, that we might fix our faith on Christ, and come
under the shelter of his wing.   We beg, upon a sense of our own
unworthiness, the acceptance of Christ's satisfaction for us.

(2.) We pray for the continuance of pardon ; though we are already
justified, yet ' Forgive us our sins.'   As in daily bread, though we have
it by us, and God hath stored us with blessings in our houses, yet we
beg the continuance and use of it ; so whatever right we have to
pardoning mercy, yet we beg the continuance of it, for two reasons :
—Partly because justification is not complete until the day of judgment, but mercy is still *in fieri*, that is, God is still a-doing : Acts
iii. 19, ' That your sins may be blotted out, when the times of refreshing shall come from the presence of the Lord.'   Then are our sins
blotted out, then is this privilege complete.   We read of forgiveness
in this world, and forgiveness in the world to come, Mat. xii. 32.
Forgiven in this world, when accepted to grace and favour with
God ; and forgiven in the world to come, when this privilege is complete, and fully made up to the elect.   Some effects of sin remain till
then ; as death, which came into the world by sin, remains upon the
body till then—then our sin is blotted out, when all the fruits of it

are vanished and done away. So that whilst any penal evils that are introduced by sin remain, we ought to pray for pardon, that God would not repent of his mercy. Look, as when we are in a state of sanctification, we pray for the continuance of sanctification, as well as the increase of it, because of the relics of sin, though our perseverance in grace and sanctification be as much secured by God's promise as our perseverance in God's favour, and the gift of justification ; so we pray for the continuance of pardon, because the evils of sin yet remain in part. And partly, because God, for our exercise, will make us feel the smart of old sins, which are already pardoned ; as an old bruise, though it be healed, yet ever and anon we may feel it upon change of weather. Accusations of conscience may return for sins already pardoned ; as Job xiii. 26, ' Thou makest me possess the iniquities of my youth.' Though a man be reconciled to God, and in favour with him, yet the sins of his youth will trouble him after he hath obtained the pardon of them. God may make these return with a horrible and frightful appearance upon the conscience ; their visage may be terrible to look upon. Though these sins are blotted out, Satan may make the remembrance of them very frightful ; and God, in his holy, wise dispensation, may permit it for our humiliation. Though this be no intrenching of the pardon already past, yet it may exceedingly terrify the soul, and overcloud our comfort, and therefore we must beg the continuance of this benefit. Go to God as David did : Ps. xxv. 6, 7, ' Remember, O Lord, thy tender mercies and thy loving-kindness, for they have been ever of old. Remember not the sins of my youth, nor my transgressions.' He begs God's ancient mercies would continue with him. He acknowledged he had received mercy of old ; he could run up to eternity, that had been for ever of old ; yet, Lord, remember not against me the sins of my youth. When the sense of old sins are renewed, we must renew petitions for the pardon of them. It is usual with God, when we are negligent, to permit the devil to make use of affliction to revive old sins, that they may stare afresh in the view of the eye of conscience ; therefore we had need to beg the continuance of this privilege, for it is not complete. Though the pardon itself be not abrogated, yet the comfort of it may be much intrenched upon, and old sins may come and terrify the soul with a very hideous aspect.

(3.) We beg here the sense and manifestation of pardon, though it be not the only thing we pray for. ' Forgive us our sins,' that is, let us know it. God may blot sins out of his book, when he doth not blot them out of our consciences. There is the book of conscience, and the book of God's remembrance. The book of God's remembrance may be cancelled (to speak after the manner of men) ; as soon as we believe and repent, then the handwriting which was against us is torn ; but he blots it out of our consciences when the worm of conscience is killed by the application of the blood of Christ through the Spirit, when we are ' sprinkled from an evil conscience,' as the expression is, Heb. x. 22. And David is earnest with God for this benefit, the sense of his pardon : Ps. li. 8, 12, ' Make me to hear joy and gladness ; that the bones which thou hast broken may rejoice ; and restore unto me the joy of thy salvation.' Nathan had told him his sins were pardoned, yet he wanted the joy of God's salvation, that ancient free spirit, that comforting, enlarging spirit he was wont to have. God may forgive in heaven, when he does not forgive in our sense and feeling; therefore we beg the manifestation of it by the comforts of the gospel.

(4.) We beg the increase of that sense, for this sense is given out in a different latitude. Spiritual sense is not in all alike quick and lively; many have only a probable certainty, but have many doubts —some have comfort, but never arrive to peace. Comfort, you know, is that thing which holds up itself against encounters when we are confronted; so there may be many doubts when the preponderating part of the soul inclineth to comfort. Some have peace for the present, rest from trouble of conscience; others have joy, which is a degree above peace and comfort.

(5.) We beg the effects of pardon, or freedom from those penal evils which are continued upon God's children, and are the fruits of sin. Clearly this is intended, for we beg of God to pardon us as we pardon others; that is, fully, entirely to forgive, forget. We beg of God to forgive us our sins; that is, to mitigate those troubles, evils, and afflictions, which are the fruits of sin. It is true, when a man is justified, the state of his person is altered; yet sin is the same in itself, it deserves all manner of evils; therefore we beg not only a release from wrath to come, but from those other temporal evils that dog us at the heels. Sin is the same still, though the person is not the same. It is still the violation of a holy law, an affront done to a holy God, an inconvenience upon the precious soul; it brings a blot upon us, an inclination to sin again; nay, it brings eternal death. Though it do not bring eternal death upon pardoned persons, yet it may occasion temporal trouble. God hath still reserved this liberty in the covenant: that he will 'visit their transgression with the rod, and their iniquity with stripes; nevertheless my loving-kindness will I not utterly take from him, nor suffer my faithfulness to fail,' Ps. lxxxix. 32, 33. And Prov. xi. 31, ' The righteous shall be recompensed in the earth; ' that is, he shall smart for his evil-doings. A child of God, when he sinneth against him, though he be not executed, yet he may be branded, he may have a mark of shame put upon him, his pilgrimage may be made uncomfortable, and these may be fully consistent with God's grace and love. Therefore we beg a release from these penal evils, that as the guilt, so the punishment also may be abolished.

2. The right that a justified person hath to the pardon of his daily sins.

Pardon of sin is to be considered: (1.) in the impetration of it; (2.) the offer; (3.) the judicial application, or legal absolution of the sinner.

[1.] In the impetration and purchase of it. So when, Heb. x. 14, ' By one offering he hath perfected for ever them that are sanctified,' there needed no more to expiate them to satisfy justice.

[2.] In the offer of it. So God hath proclaimed pardon upon the condition of repentance: Ezek. xxxiii. 11, ' Say unto them, As I live, saith the Lord God, I have no pleasure in the death of the wicked; but that the wicked turn from his way and live: turn ye, turn ye from your evil ways; for why will ye die, O house of Israel?'

[3.] In the judicial application, or legal absolution of a sinner. God in his word hath pronounced the legal absolution of every one that believeth in Christ. As soon as we repent and believe, a threefold benefit we have :—

(1.) The state of the person is altered; he is a child of God: John i. 12, 'To as many as received him, to them gave he power to become the sons of God, even to them that believe on his name.' He hath full leave to call God Father, a kind of fatherly dealing from him. Translated from a state of wrath to the state of grace, from a child of the devil he is made a child of God, never to be cast out of his family.

(2.) The actual remission of all past sins: Rom. iii. 25, 'To declare his righteousness for the remission of sins that are past, through the forbearance of God.' It would be a license to sin if his sins were remitted before committed.

(3.) A right to the remission of daily sins, or free leave to make use of the fountain of mercy, that is always running, and is opened in the house of God for the comfort of believers: Zech. xiii. 1, 'In that day there shall be a fountain opened to the house of David, and to the inhabitants of Jerusalem, for sin and for uncleanness.'

Secondly, The utility and profit of such a course. See Sermon on Psalm XXXII. 1. Sermon xx.[1]

Use. The use is to press us to be often dealing with God about the pardon of our sins, by a general and daily humiliation; none are exempted from bewailing the evil of sin. The death of Christ doth not put less evil into sin; it is still damning in its own nature; it is still the violation of a holy law, an affront to a holy God, an inconvenience to thy precious soul. When Christ paid the price for our sins, it was upon this condition: that we should renew our faith and repentance; that we should sue out our discharge in his name; that when we sin we may come and humble ourselves before the Lord. Under the law, if a man were unclean, he was to wash his clothes before evening; he was not to sleep in his uncleanness. So if you have defiled yourselves, you should go wash in the laver that God hath appointed. The Lord taught his people under the law the repeating a daily sacrifice, morning and evening. If one be fallen out with another, God hath advised us, before the sun be set, to go and be reconciled to our brother; and wilt thou lie under the wrath of God for one night? If we would oftener use this course, the work of repentance would not be so hard. Wounds are best cured at first, before they are suffered to fester and rankle into a sore; so are sins before they grow longer upon us. And if we did oftener thus reckon with ourselves, we should have less to do when we come to die. Therefore do as wise merchants; at the foot of every page draw up the account, so help it forward; so it will not be hard to sum up a long account, and reckon up our whole lives, and beg a release of all our debts; therefore daily come and humble yourselves before the Lord. The oftener you do this, the sooner you will have the comfort of pardon; but when you keep off from God, and delay, you suffer the loss of peace, and the loss of God's favour; and hardness of heart, and atheism, and carnal security increase upon you.

[1] In a subsequent volume.—ED.

As we forgive our debtors.

I come to the last branch. Hence observe:—

Doct. 3. Those that would rightly pray to be forgiven of God, they must forgive others.

First, I shall give you the explication; Secondly, The reasons.

For explication, I shall speak to three things:—

1. Who are debtors.

2. What respect our forgiving of others hath to God's forgiving of us.

3. In what manner we must forgive others.

First, Who are our debtors. It is not meant in a vulgar sense, of those only which stand engaged for a sum of money due to us; but of all such as have offended us in word or deed. There is a duty we owe to one another, which, when we omit, or act contrary unto it, we are not only debtors to God, but to one another; and the doers of the injury are bound to repair the wrong, and to make restitution. In this large sense is the word *debtors* here taken, with respect to the person that hath done the injury. He becomes a debtor, is to make satisfaction, and suffer the punishment which the wrong deserves.

Secondly, What respect hath our forgiving of others to God's forgiving us?

I shall speak to it negatively and positively.

1. Negatively.

[1.] It is not a meritorious cause, or a merit and price given to God, why he should pardon us, for that is only the blood of Christ. Every act of ours is due, it is imperfect, and no way proportionate to the mercies we expect; and therefore it cannot be meritorious before God. It is due, it is a duty we are bound to do, and paying off new debts doth not quit old scores. God hath laid such a law upon us, that we are to forgive others. That cannot expiate former offences. And it is imperfect too. The remembrance of injuries sticks too close to us. When we do most heartily and entirely forgive others, even then we have too great a sense of the injury and wrong that is offered to us. Now that which needs pardon cannot deserve pardon. And it is disproportionate to the mercy which we expect. What a vast disparity and difference is there between God's pardoning of us and our pardoning of others, whether we respect the persons that are interested in this action, or the subject-matter, or manner and way of doing, or the fruit and issue of the action.

First, In the persons pardoning. What proportion can there be between God and man, the Creator and the creature? God he is most free, and bound to none, of infinite dignity and perfection, which can neither be increased nor lessened by any act of ours, for him or against him; but we live in perfect dependence upon God's pleasure, are subject to his command, and bound to do his will; and therefore what is our forgiving our fellow-creatures, made out of the same dust, animated by the same soul, and every way equal with us by nature, when they wrong us in our petty interests? What proportion is there between this forgiving and God's forgiving? he that is of so infinite a majesty, his forgiving the violations of his holy law?

And secondly, To the subject-matter, that which is forgiven, there is no proportion. When we compare the multitude or magnitude, the greatness, and the number of offences forgiven of the one side and the other, we see there is a mighty disproportion. We forgive pence, and God talents; we an hundred pence, he ten thousand talents: Mat. xviii.

So, thirdly, The manner of forgiving: on God's part, by discharging us freely, and exacting a full satisfaction from Christ; therefore our forgiving can hold no comparison with it, which is an act of duty, and conformity to God's law.

And fourthly, As to the fruit and issue of the action. Our good and evil doth not reach to God. Though our forgiving of others be an action of profit to ourselves, yet no fruit redounds to God. And therefore there being no proportion between finite and infinite, there can be no such proportion between our forgiving and God's forgiving, as that this act may be meritorious before God. Thus it is not brought here as merit, as that which doth oblige and bind God meritoriously to forgive us.

[2.] It is not a pattern or rule. We do not mean our forgiving should be a pattern of forgiving to God. So *as* is taken, indeed, ver. 10, 'Thy will be done on earth, as it is in heaven;' there it implies a conformity to the pattern. But when we say, 'Forgive us, *as* we forgive,' it doth not mean here a pattern or rule. We imitate God, but God doth not imitate us, in forgiving offences; and it would be ill with us if God should forgive us no better than we forgive one another. God is matchless in all his perfections; there is no work like his: Ps. lxxxvi. 8. As God is matchless in other things, so in pardoning mercy. 'As the heavens are above the earth, so are his ways above our ways, and his thoughts above our thoughts:' Isa. lv. 9. And upon this very occasion the Lord will multiply to pardon: 'As far as the heavens,' &c. This is the greatest distance we can conceive. The heavens, they are at such a vast distance from the earth, that the stars, though they be great and glorious luminaries, yet they seem to be but like so many spangles and sparks. This is the distance and disproportion which is made between God's mercy and ours: Hosea xi. 9, 'I will not return to destroy Ephraim; for I am God, and not man.' If God should forgive but only as man doth, it would be ill for Ephraim if he had to do with revengeful man. God acteth according to the infiniteness of his own nature, far above the law and manner of all created beings. Therefore it is not put here as a pattern and rule.

[3.] It doth not import priority of order, as if our acts had the precedency of God's; or as if we did or could heartily forgive others before God hath shown any mercy to us. No; in all acts of love, God is first; his mercy to us is the cause of our mercy to others. As the wall reflects and casts back the heat upon the stander-by when first warmed with the beams of the sun, so, when our hearts are melted with a sense of God's mercy, his love to us is the cause of our love and kindness to others: 1 John iv. 19, 'We love him, because he first loved us;' that is, we love him, and others for his sake; for love to God implies that. Why? Because he hath been first with us. And then it is the motive and pattern of it. In that parable, Mat.

xviii. 32, 33, God's forgiving is the motive to our forgiving: 'I forgave thee all thy debt; and shouldest not thou have compassion on thy fellow-servant?' In those that have true pardon it causeth them to forgive others out of a sense of God's mercy; that is, they are disposed and inclined to show mercy to others. But in others that think themselves pardoned, and have only a temporary pardon and reprieve (such as is there spoken of), it is a motive which should prevail with them, though it doth not. Nay, it is the pattern of our love to others: Eph. iv. 32, 'Forgiving one another, even as God for Christ's sake hath forgiven you;' in that manner, and according to that example.

[4.] It doth not import an exact equality, but some kind of resemblance. *As*, it is a note of similitude, not equality, either of measure or manner; it only implieth that there is some correspondent action, something like done on our part. So, Luke vi. 36, 'Be merciful, *as* your heavenly Father is merciful.' *As*, notes the certainty of the truth, though not the exact proportion; there will be something answerable to God.

2. But positively to show what respect it hath.

[1.] It is a condition or moral qualification which is found in persons pardoned: Mat. vi. 14, 'For if ye forgive men their trespasses, your heavenly Father will also forgive you:' but, ver. 15, 'If ye forgive not men their trespasses, neither will your Father forgive your trespasses.' These two are inseparably conjoined, God's pardoning of us, and our pardoning of others. The grant of a pardon, that is given out at the same time when this disposition is wrought in us; but the sense of a pardon, that is a thing subsequent to this disposition. And when we find this disposition in us, we come to understand how we are pardoned of God.

[2.] It is an evidence, a sign or note of a pardoned sinner. When a man's heart is entendered by the Lord's grace, and inclined to show mercy, here is his evidence: Mat. v. 7, 'Blessed are the merciful, for they shall obtain mercy.' The stamp or impression shows that the seal hath been there; so this is an evidence to us whereby we may make out our title to the Lord's mercy, that we have received mercy from the Lord.

[3.] It is a necessary effect of God's pardoning mercy shed abroad in our hearts; for mercy begets mercy, as heat doth heat: Titus iii. 2, 3, 'Show meekness to all men; for we ourselves also were sometimes foolish, disobedient,' &c. There is none so tender to others as they which have received mercy themselves; that know how gently God hath dealt with them, and did not take the advantage of their iniquity.

[4.] It is put here to show that it is a duty incumbent upon them that are pardoned. God hath laid this necessity upon men. And that may be one reason why this clause is inserted, that every time we come to pray and beg pardon, we may bind ourselves to this practice, and warn ourselves more solemnly of our duty, and undertake it in the sight of God. So that when we say, 'Forgive us our debts, as we forgive our debtors,' it is a certain undertaking or solemn promise we make to God, if he will show mercy to us, this will incline us to

show mercy to others. In earnest requests, we are wont to bind ourselves to necessary duties.

[5.] It is an argument breeding confidence in God's pardoning
mercy. When we, that have so much of the old leaven, that sour,
revengeful nature, in us, yet when we have received but a spark of
grace, it makes us ready to forgive others; then what may we
imagine in God! What is our drop, to that infinite sea of fulness
that is in him! Clearly thus it is urged in that clause, Luke xi. 4,
'And forgive us our sins; for we also forgive every one that is
indebted to us.' There is a special emphasis upon that, *for we also ;*
that is, we that have so little grace, we that are so revengeful and
passionate by nature, we also forgive those that are indebted to us.
Therefore the gracious God, in all goodness, and in all moral
perfections, doth far exceed the creature; and if this be in us, what
is there in God? This kind of reasoning is often used in scripture ;
as Mat. vii. 11, 'If ye then, being evil, know how to give good
gifts unto your children, how much more shall your Father which is
in heaven give good things to them that ask him?' If evil men
hath such bowels and affections towards their children, certainly there
is more of this goodness and kindness in God.

Thirdly, Wherein this forgiving of others doth consist?

1. In forbearing others.

2. In acquitting others.

3. In doing good to them.

[1.] In forbearing one another and withholding ourselves from
revenge. This is a thing that is distant from forgiving, and accordingly we shall find it so propounded by the apostle: Col. iii. 13,
'Forbearing one another, and forgiving one another, if any man have
a quarrel against any ; even as Christ forgave you, so also do ye.'
Mark, there is first forbearing and then forgiving. What is forbearing? A ceasing from acts of revenge, which, though they be sweet to
nature, yet they are contrary to grace. Some men will say, We will
do to him as he hath done to us: Prov. xxiv. 29, 'Say not, I will do
so to him as he hath done to me ; I will render to the man according
to his work.' Corrupt nature thirsteth for revenge, and hath a strong
inclination this way ; but grace should give check to it : 'Say not,' &c.
Men think it is a base thing, and argueth a low, pusillanimous spirit,
to put up with wrongs and injuries: oh, it argueth a stupid baseness.
But this is that which giveth a man a victory over himself ; nay,
it gives a man the truest victory over his enemy, when he forbears to
revenge. It gives a man a victory over himself, which is better than the
most noble actions amongst the sons of men : Prov. xvi. 32, 'He that
overcometh his own spirit is more than he that taketh a city.'
There is a spirit in us that is boisterous, turbulent, and revengeful,
apt to retaliate and return injury for injury. Now, when we can bridle
this, this is an overcoming of our own spirits. But that is the true
weakness of spirit, when a man is easily overcome by his own passion.
And then hath our enemy a true victory over us, when his injuries
overcome us so far as we can break God's laws to be quit with him.
Therefore the apostle saith : Rom. xii. 21, 'Be not overcome of evil,
but overcome evil with good.' Then is grace victorious, and then

hath a man a noble and brave spirit, not when he is overcome by evil (for that argueth weakness), but when he can overcome evil. And it is God's way to shame the party that did the wrong and to overcome him too : it is the best way to get the victory over him. When David had Saul at an advantage in the cave, and cut off the lap of his garment, and did forbear any act of revenge against him, Saul was melted, and said to David, ' Thou art more righteous than I,' 1 Sam. xxiv. 17.   Though he had such a hostile mind against him, and chased and pursued him up and down, yet when David forebore revenge when it was in his power, it overcame him, and he falls a-weeping.   So the captains of the Syrians, when the prophet had blinded them, and led them from Dothan to Samaria, what saith the king of Israel ? is he ready to kill them presently ? No : 2 Kings vi. 22, ' Set bread and water before them, that they may eat and drink, and go to their master.'   He was kind to them ; and what followeth ? ' They did no more annoy Israel.'   This wrought upon the hearts of the Syrians, so that they would not come and trouble them any more.

[2.] In forgiving, it is not only required of Christians to forbear the avenging of themselves, but also actually to forgive and pardon those that have done them wrongs.   They must not only forbear acts of revenge, but all desires of revenge must be rooted out of their hearts.   Men may tolerate or forbear others for want of a handsome opportunity of executing their purposes; but the scripture saith, ' Forbearing one another, forgiving one another.'   This forgiving implieth the laying down of all anger, and hatred, and all desire of revenge.   Now this should be done, not only in word, but sincerely and universally.

(1.) Sincerely, and with the heart.   In the conclusion of that parable, Christ doth not say, If ye do not forgive, thus it shall be done to you ; but, ' If ye from your hearts forgive not every one his brother their trespasses, so also shall my heavenly Father do to you.'   We must not only do this, but do it from the heart.   Joseph, when his brethren came to him and submitted themselves, did not only remit the offence, but his bowels yearned towards them, and his heart was towards them : Gen. l. 17.   Then,

(2.) It must be done universally, whatever the wrong be, be it to our persons, names, or estates.   To our persons : Acts vii. 60, Stephen, when they stoned him, he said, ' Lord, lay not this sin to their charge.' Though they had done him so great an injury as to deprive him of his life and service, yet, ' Lord, lay not this sin to their charge.'   So to our names : When Shimei came barking against David—the poor man was driven out of Jerusalem by a rebellious son, and this wicked wretch takes advantage against David and rails at him—yet David forgives him when restored to his crown : ' He shall not die,' 2 Sam. xix. 23.   Nay, he sware to him.   So his estate : When a debtor is not able to pay, and yet submits.   So Paul bids Philemon to forgive the wrongs of Onesimus : ' Put it on my score,' Philem. 18, that is, for my sake forgive this wrong.

[3.] We must be ready to perform all offices of love to them : Luke vi. 27, ' Love your enemies, do good to them which hate you.'   Mark, do not only forbear to execute your wrath and revenge upon them, but do good to them; yea, though they be enemies upon a religious ground; though religion be made a party in the quarrel, and so engage us to the greater fury, when that which should bridle our passions is the fuel to them: 'Pray for them which despitefully use you and persecute you,' Mat. v. 44. Miriam, when she had wronged Moses, yet he falls a-praying for her, Num. xii. 13, that the Lord would forgive the sin and heal her.

For the reasons why those that would rightly pray to be forgiven of God must forgive others—it should be so, it will be so—there is a congruency and a necessity.

1. The congruency, it should be so. It is fit that he that beggeth mercy should show mercy; it is exceedingly congruous. For this is a general rule: that we should do as we would be done unto; and, therefore, if we need mercy from God, we should show mercy to others, and without it we can never pray in faith. He that doth not exercise love can never pray in faith. Why? His own revengeful disposition will still prejudice his mind, and make him conclude against the audience of his prayers; for certainly we muse on others as we use ourselves. And that is one reason of our unbelief, why we are so hardly brought to believe all that tender mercy which is in God; because it is so irksome to us to forgive seven times a day, we are apt to frame our conclusions according to the disposition of our own heart. Can we think God will forgive when we ourselves will not forgive? A man's own prayers will be confuted. What is more equal than to do as we would be done unto? And therefore it is but equal, if he entreat mercy for himself, he should show it unto others. Look, as the centurion reasoned of God's power, from the command that he had over his soldiers: Mat. viii. 9, 'I am a man under authority, and I say to one, Go, and he goeth; and to another, Come, and he cometh.' Those things we are accustomed to, they are apt to run in our minds when we come to think of God. Now he that kept his soldiers under discipline that if he said, Go, they go, he reasons thus of God: Surely God hath power to chase away diseases. So accordingly should we reason of God's mercy according to the mercy that we find in ourselves. Therefore it is very notable that when Christ had spoken of forgiving our brethren, 'not only seven times, but seventy times seven,' the disciples said unto the Lord, 'Increase our faith,' Luke xvii. 5. How doth this come in? In the 4th verse Christ had spoken that they should forgive not only seven times, but seventy times seven; and they do not say, Lord, increase our charity, but our faith; implying that we cannot have such large thoughts of God when our own hearts are so straitened by revenge and our private passions.

2. In point of necessity; as it should be so, so it will be so; for God's mercy will have an influence upon us to make us merciful. All God's actions to us imprint their stamp in us. His election of us makes us to choose him and his ways; his love to us makes us love him again, who hath loved us first; so his forgiving of us makes us to forgive our brethren. There is an answerable impression left upon the soul to every act of God. Why? For a true believer is God's image: 'The new man is created after God,' Eph. iv. 24; and therefore he acts as

God. Certainly, if there be such a disposition in our heavenly Father, it will be in us if we have an interest in him. Look, as a child hath part for part, and limb for limb, answerable to his father, though not so big in stature and bulk ; so hath a child of God, which is created after God, he hath all the divine perfections in some measure in his soul. And this consideration is of more force, because the new creature cannot be maimed and defective in every [1] part, but is entire, lacking nothing. And therefore, if God forgive others, certainly the godly will be inclinable to forgive too.

Use 1. Here is a ground of trial whether we are pardoned or no: Is our revengeful disposition, that is so natural and so pleasing to us, mortified ? That is one trial or evidence whether we are forgiven of God ; can we freely from the heart forgive others ?

Object. But it may be objected against this : Do you place so much in this property of forgiving others ? It doth not agree only to pardoned sinners, because we see some carnal men are of a weak and stupid spirit, not sensible of injuries. And, on the other side, many of God's children find it hard to obtain [2] to the perfect oblivion of injuries that is required of them.

Ans. As to the first part, I answer: We do not speak of this disposition as proceeding from an easy temper, but as it proceedeth from grace ; when, in conscience towards God, and out of a sense of his love to us in Christ, our hearts, being tendered and melted towards others, to show them such mercy as we ourselves have received from the Lord ; that is the evidence. And again, we do not press to judge by this evidence single and alone, but in conjunction with others; when they are humbly penitent, and confessing their sins, and turn to the Lord, which is the great evangelical condition: Job xxxiii. 27, ' If any say, I have sinned, and perverted that which was right, and it profited me not,' then will he restore light to him. When a man is soundly touched with remorse, and seeth the folly of his former courses, and asketh pardon of God, then is God gracious to him. But this is that we say, that this disposition of pardon, in conjunction with the great evangelical condition of faith and repentance, it helpeth to make the evidence more clear.

2. As to the other part of the objection, which was this : it will be a great weakening of the confidence of God's children who cannot get such a perfect oblivion of injuries they have received, but find their minds working too much this way :—

I answer : As long as we live in the world there will be flesh and spirit, corruption as well as grace ; there will be an intermixture of the operations of each. Carnal nature is prone to revenge, but grace prevaileth and inclineth to a pardon. Well, then, if this be the prevalent inclination of the soul, and that which we strive by all good means to cherish in us, this meek disposition, passing by of wrongs we receive by others, then we may take comfort by this evidence, though there be some reluctances and regrudgings of the old nature.

Use 2. To press us to this ready inclination to forgive wrongs and injuries. We are not so perfect but we all need it from one another. There will be mutual offences while we are in the world, especially in

---

[1] That is, 'any.'—ED.   [2] Qu. 'attain'?—ED.

a time when religious differences are on foot; therefore it concerns us to look after this disposition of forgiving others, as we would be forgiven of God. Human society cannot well be upheld without this mutual forbearance and forgiving. Now imitate your heavenly Father. No man can wrong us so much as we daily trespass against him, and yet God pardoneth us. He doth not only pardon the lesser failings, some venial errors, and sins of incogitancy and sudden surreption, which creep upon us we know not how; but he pardons the greatest sins, though they be as scarlet: Isa. i. 18. Those that are of a crimson hue, God can wash them out in the blood of Christ. And mark, what is it then that you will stand upon? Is it the greatness of the offence? God pardons great sins. Or is it the baseness of those that injure you—(this is the circumstance)—when we have received wrong from those which are our inferiors, that owe us more reverence and respect? What are we to God? Notwithstanding the baseness of those which affront him daily, all men to him are but ' as the drop of the bucket, and the small dust of the balance,' Isa. xl. 15; yet God pardons them. And then again, cast in the consideration of God's omnipotency. He is able to right himself of the wrongs done to him, and no man can call him to an account. Many times it is not in our power: 'He can cast body and soul into hell,' Mat. x. 28. God is thus offended, and by saucy dust that is ready to fly in his face, inconsiderable man; and yet the Lord pardons, and this he doth freely: Luke vii. 42, 'He frankly forgave them both.' And he pardons fully, as if it were never committed: Micah vii. 19, 'He casts all our sins into the depths of the sea.' Then he pardons frequently: His 'free gift is of many offences unto justification,' Rom. v. 16. And he ' multiplies to pardon,' Isa. lv. 7. And mark, he pardons too (in some sense) before they repent; there is a purpose; he provided Christ before we were born. And he gives us grace to repent, or else we could never humble ourselves at his feet, the offended God; he gives them the grace whereby they shall acknowledge the offence. Christ prayed for his persecutors when they had no sense of the injury they had done him; they were converted by that prayer afterwards: Luke xxiii. 34, 'Father, forgive them, for they know not what they do;' therefore certainly much more when they repent and submit. Oh, therefore, let us not be drawn hardly to this duty; or, at least, we should not upon every petty offence cherish hatred and rancour against our brethren.

But here are certain cases that would come into debate.

First Case. Whether it be consistent with this temper, forgiving of others, to seek reparation of wrongs in a way of justice, and pursue men at law for offences they have committed against us?

Ans. Yes. For,

1. Certainly one law doth not cross another. By the law of charity the law of justice is not made void. A magistrate, though he be a Christian, and bound to forgive others, is not bound up from executing his office against public offenders. Nor yet are private men tied from having recourse to the magistrate for restoration to their right, or reparation of their wrong. For to demand one's right is not contrary to love, nor to seek to amend and humble the party nocent by the magistrate's authority, who is ' the minister of God for good,' Rom.

xiii. 4; and that others may 'hear and fear,' Deut. xix. 20; and the party damnified may for the future live in peace. Forgiving is an act of private jurisdiction. The offence, as far as it is private to us, it may be forgiven; but there are many such offences as are not only an offence to us, but to the public order, and that must be left to the process of the law.

2. Whosoever useth this remedy must look to his own heart, that he be not acted with private revenge, nor with a spirit of rigour or rancour against the party offending; but that he be carried out with zeal to justice, with pity to the person, that he and others may not be hardened in sin. For this is the general law of Christ, that 'all things should be done in love,' 1 Cor. xvi. 14. Therefore when we are acted by our private passion and secret desires of revenge, we abuse God's ordinance of magistracy, and make it to lacquey upon our lusts. And therefore there must be a taking heed to the frame of our own hearts, that they be upright in these things. Though it seem hard to flesh and blood, yet remember flesh and blood shall not inherit the kingdom of God. Grace must frame your hearts to the obedience of God's will.

3. These remedies from authority must be in weighty cases, and in matters of moment and importance. Their contending in law one with another about the smallest matters is that which the apostle taxeth: 1 Cor. vi. 7. Not upon every trifling occasion. It must be after other means are tried and used; as the help of friends to compound the matter, for charity trieth all things: 1 Cor. xiii. 4. And the apostle saith, 1 Cor. vi. 5, 'Is there none to judge between you?' that is, none to decide and arbitrate the difference, for the refuge to authority should be our last remedy. And it must be too when the party wronging is able to make satisfaction, otherwise it is rigour and inhumanity: 2 Kings iv. 1. As when the creditors came to take the sons of the widow for bondmen. When you are rigorous with those that come to poverty, not by their own default, but by the discharge of their duty brought poverty upon themselves, it is contrary to Christianity. Look, as physicians deal with quicksilver, after many distillations they make it useful in medicines; so, after many preparations is this course to be taken.

Second Case. Whether, in forgiving injuries, we are bound to tarry for the repentance of the party? The ground of doubting is, because Christ saith, Luke xvii. 3, 'If thy brother trespass against thee, rebuke him; and, if he repent, forgive him;' and because of God's example, who doth not forgive an obstinate sinner, but him that repents. Certainly, even before repentance, we are bound to lay aside revenge, and in many cases to go and reconcile ourselves with others. Saith our Saviour, 'If thou hast aught against any one, go reconcile thyself to him, and then come and offer thy gift.' It is not said, If any have aught against thee, but, If thou hast aught against any one.[1] I confess, in some cases, it is enough to lay it aside before the Lord. But at other times, we are to seek reconciliation with the party which hath wronged us. But this case is mightily to be guided by spiritual prudence. As for God's example, God is superior, bound to none, he acts

---

[1] This seems to be inaccurate.—ED.

freely; it is his mercy that pardons any; and yet God gives us a heart to repent of his good pleasure,—he begins with a sinner. But this is nothing to our case who are under law, who are bound to forgive others.

III. The person to whom we pray, Our heavenly Father.

The note is, that God doth alone forgive sin.

There is a double forgiveness of sin—in heaven and in a man's own conscience; and therefore sometimes compared to the blotting out of something out of a book, sometimes to the blotting out of a cloud. To the blotting out of a book: Isa. xliii. 25, 'I, even I, am he that blotteth out thy transgressions, for mine own sake, and will not remember thy sins;' that it may be no more remembered or charged upon us. To the blotting out of a cloud: Isa. xliv. 22, 'I have blotted out as a thick cloud thy transgressions, and as a cloud thy sins;' as the sun when it breaketh forth in its strength dispelleth the mists and clouds. Sin interposeth as a cloud, hindering the light of God's countenance from shining forth upon us. Both these are God's work; to blot the book and to blot out the cloud.

1. Pardoning of sin in the court of heaven, it belongeth to God peculiarly: Dan. ix. 9, 'To the Lord our God belong mercies and forgivenesses,' &c. It is God alone can do it, for two reasons:—

[1.] He is the wronged party.

[2.] He is the supreme judge.

(1.) He is the wronged party, against whom the offence is committed: Ps. li. 4, 'Against thee, against thee only, have I sinned.' He had sinned against Bathsheba, against Uriah, whose death he projected. How is it said 'against thee only'? There may be wrong and hurt done to a creature, but the sin is against God, as it is a breach of his law, and a despising of his sovereign authority; the injury done to the creature is nothing in comparison of the offence done to God, against so many obligations wherein we stand bound to him. Amongst men, we distinguish between the crime and the wrong. And a criminal action is one thing, and an action of wrong and trespass is another. If a man steal from another, it is not enough to make him restitution, but he must satisfy the law.

(2.) He is the supreme judge. Father, Son, and Holy Ghost, as one God, are the judge of all the earth, to whom they must be accountable for the offence: Gen. xviii. 25, 'Shall not the judge of all the earth do right?' But in the mystery of redemption, the Father, as first in order of the persons, is represented as the judge, to whom the satisfaction is tendered, and who doth authoritatively pass a sentence of absolution. And therefore it is said, 1 John ii. 1, 'We have an advocate with the Father, Jesus Christ the righteous.' He is to deal with him as the supreme judge; and 'it is God that justifieth,' Rom. viii. 33. The whole business of our acquitment is carried on by the Father, who is to receive the satisfaction, and our humble addresses for pardon.

But to answer some objections that may arise.

Object. 1. It is said, Mat. ix. 6, 'The Son of man hath power on earth to forgive sins.'

I answer: That is brought there as an argument of his Godhead. He that was the Son of man was also very God; and therefore upon earth, in the time of his humiliation, he had power to forgive sins, for

he ceased not to be God when incarnate. And it became him to discover himself, as by his divine power in the work of miracles, so his
divine authority in the forgiveness of sins.

Object. 2. Is taken from the text, ' Forgive us our debts, as we forgive those that trespass against us.'

I answer : In sin, there is the obliquity or fault in it, and the hurt
or detriment that redounds to man by it. As it is a breach of the law
of God, or an offence to his infinite majesty, God can only pardon it,
or dispense with it. As it is a hurt to us, so restitution is to be made
to man, and man can pardon or forgive it.

Object. 3. It is said, John xx. 23, ' Whosesoever sins ye remit, they
are remitted unto them ; and whosoever sins ye retain, they are
retained.' So that it seemeth man hath a power to remit sins.

I answer: They do it declaratively, and by commission from God.
The officers of the church have the keys of the kingdom of heaven
committed to them ; the key of knowledge or doctrine, and the key of
order and discipline. Accordingly this power is called, ' The keys of
the kingdom of heaven,' Mat. xvi. 19. And the use of them is to
open or shut the doors of God's house, and to ' bind or loose,' as the
expression is, Mat. xviii. 18. That is, to pronounce guilty and liable
to judgment, or to absolve and set free declaratively and in God's
name ; or, as it is literally expressed in the place alleged, to remit or
retain. The key of doctrine is exercised about all sin as sin, were it
never so secret and inward ; and the key of order and discipline about
sin only as it is scandalous and infectious. Now what they act minis-
terially, according to their commission, it is ratified in heaven, for it is
a declaration or intimation of the sentence already passed there. So
that a declarative and ministerial power is given to the church ; but
the authoritative power of forgiving sins, that God hath reserved to
himself. Man can remit doctrinally, and by way of judicial procedure,
but that is only by way of commission and ministerial deputation.
Such as are penitent, and feel the bonds of their sins, they do declaratively absolve and loose them, or take off the censure judicially inflicted
for their scandalous carriage. This ministerial forgiving, however
carnal hearts may slight it, both in doctrine and discipline, yet being
according to the rules of the word, is owned by God, and the penitent
shall feel it to their encouragement, and the obstinate to their terror.

2. As he pardoneth sin in the conscience ; and there God alone
can forgive sin, or speak peace to the soul upon a double account :—

[1.] Because of his authority.

[2.] Because of his power.

(1.) Because of his authority. Conscience is God's deputy, and till
God be pacified, conscience is not pacified upon sound and solid terms.
Therefore it is said, where conscience doth its office, 1 John iii. 20, 21,
' If our hearts condemn us, God is greater than our hearts, and
knoweth all things ; if our hearts condemn us not, then have we confidence towards God.' God is greater than our consciences. His
authority is greater, for God is supreme, whose sentence is decisive.
Now, though conscience should not do its office, 1 Cor. iv. 4, ' For I
know nothing by myself, yet am I not hereby justified : but he that
judgeth me is the Lord.' All depends upon God's testimony.

(2.) Because of his power, who only can still the conscience: Isa. lvii. 19, 'I create the fruit of the lips to be, peace, peace;' that is, the lips of his ministers or messengers, who bring the glad tidings of peace, or the reconcilement of God to his people: and therefore it is called 'the peace of God,' Phil. iv. 7, as wrought by him. The gospel is a sovereign plaster, but it is God's hand that must make it stick upon the soul, otherwise we hear words and return words: it is by the lively operation of his Spirit that our hearts are settled. God cometh in with a sovereign powerful act upon the soul, otherwise one grief or sad thought doth but awaken another. Till he 'command loving-kindness,' Ps. xlii. 8, we are still followed with temptation; as the rain swells the rivers, and rivers the sea, and in the sea one wave impelleth another, so doth one temptation raise another.

Use 1. It reproveth those that do not deal with God about the pardon of their sins. If God alone pardon sins, then God must be sought to about it. For though there be none in earth to call us to an account, yet God may call us to an account; and then what shall we do? Many, if they escape the judgment of man, think they are safe; but alas! your iniquities will find you out. You think they are past, and never more to be remembered; but they will find you out in this world or the next; our business lieth not with man so much as with God. Therefore this should be the question of your souls: Job xxxi. 14, 'What then shall I do when God riseth up? and when he visiteth, what shall I answer him?' Which way shall I turn myself when God calleth me to an account? He will come and inquire into our ways; are you provided of an answer? David's sin was secret; his plot for the destruction of Uriah closely carried. Nathan tells him, 2 Sam. xii. 12, 'Thou didst it secretly.' But, 'against thee have I sinned.' Many escape blame with men, but God's wrath maketh inquisition for sinners. You cannot escape his search and vengeance if you do not treat with him about a pardon.

Use 2. It shows the folly of those that have nothing to show for the pardon of their sins, but their own secure presumptions; it is God's act to pardon sin. Man may forget his sin, but if God remember it he is miserable. Man may hide his sin, but if God bring it to light; man may put off the thoughts, but if God doth not put away; man may excuse his sin, but if God aggravate it; the debtor may deny the debt, but if the book be not crossed, he is responsible: Ps. xxxii. 1, 2, 'Blessed is he whose transgression is forgiven, whose sin is covered; blessed is the man to whom the Lord imputeth not iniquity,' &c. We must have God's act to show for our discharge, then we may triumph: 'It is God that justifieth, who is he that condemneth?' &c., Rom. viii. 33, 34. God is the offended party, and the supreme judge. Then conscience hath nothing to do with us, nor Satan, neither as accuser or executioner. Not as an accuser, for then he is but a slanderer; not as an executioner, for he is turned out of office: Heb. ii. 14, 'That he might destroy him that had the power of death, even the devil.' Have you your pardon from God? Is your discharge from him? When have it we from God?

1. Have it you from his mouth, in the word, or prayer, upon suing

to him in Christ's name, and earnest waiting upon him? If men would consider how they come by their peace, they would sooner be undeceived. You were praying and wrestling with God, and so your comfort came. God speaketh peace. But when it groweth upon you, you know not how; it was a thing you never laboured for; like Jonah's gourd, it grew up in a night; it is but a fond dream.

2. Have it you under his hand? Is it a peace upon scripture terms?—of faith: Rom. v. 1, 'Therefore being justified by faith, we have peace with God through our Lord Jesus Christ:'—repentance: Luke xxiv. 47, 'That repentance and remission of sins should be preached in his name among all nations,' &c.;—and the exercise of holiness,—then have you God's word to show for it. But if it be not a peace consistent with scripture rules, nay, you are afraid of the word, John iii. 20, you are loth to be tried,—it is a naughty heart.

3. Have it you under his seal? 2 Cor. i. 22, 'Who hath also sealed us, and given us the earnest of the Spirit in our hearts.' Have you the impress of God upon you, God's seal, his image? Doth the Spirit of promise assure your hearts before God, that you can live in the strength of this comfort and go about duties cheerfully? Then it is God's pardon; otherwise it is but your own absolution, which is worth nothing.

Use 3. It showeth that we need not fear the censures of men, nor the hatred of the ungodly; for it is God pardoneth, and who can condemn? God will not ask their vote and suffrage who shall be accepted to life and who not: 1 Cor. iv. 3, 'But with me it is a very small thing that I should be judged of you, or of man's judgment,' &c. A man must expect censure that will be faithful to God; but if he acquit us, it is no matter what our guilty fellow-creatures say.

Use 4. Is comfort to broken-hearted sinners; to those that need and desire pardon. It is well for them that God doth not put them off to others, but reserveth this power of pardoning sins to himself.

1. It is his glory to forgive sins: Exod. xxxiii. 18, 'And he said, I beseech thee show me thy glory;' compared with Exod. xxxiv. 6, 7, 'And the Lord passed by before him, and proclaimed, The Lord, the Lord God, merciful and gracious, long-suffering, and abundant in goodness and truth, keeping mercy for thousands, forgiving iniquity, transgression, and sin,' &c. It is not only the glory of a man, who is so offensive himself and so passionate, that this passion will draw him to what is unseemly, but of God.

2. It is his glory, not only above the creatures, but above all that is called god in the world: Micah vii. 18, 'Who is a God like unto thee, that pardoneth iniquity, and passeth by the transgression of the remnant of his heritage? He retaineth not his anger for ever, because he delighteth in mercy.' The heathen gods were known by their terrors rather than their benefits, and feared rather for their revenges than their mercies. We may boast of him above all idol gods upon this account. He is known among his people, not so much by acts of power, as acts of grace, and the greatness of his mercy, in pardoning sins for Christ's sake.

3. He is willing to dispense a pardon: Micah vii. 18, 'He delighteth in mercy.' God delighteth in himself, and all his attributes, and

the manifestation of them in the world; but above all in his mercy. Justice is 'his strange act,' Isa. xxviii. 21. There is not anything more pleasing to him. It is the mercy of God that he hath drawn up a petition for us; he would never have taught us to have asked mercy by prayer, if he had not been willing to show us mercy.

4. God will do it for his own sake, and not for any foreign reasons: Isa. xliii. 25, 'I, even I, am he that blotteth out thy transgressions for mine own sake,' and out of a respect to his own honour. See how God casts up his accounts. It is mercy: Jer. iii. 12, 'I am merciful, saith the Lord, and I will not keep anger for ever.' So his truth: Ps. cvi. 45, 'He remembered for them his covenant, and repented according to the multitude of his mercies.' Not from any desert of theirs, who do so neglect him and wrong him; God will do it upon his own reasons.

5. He will do it in such a way as man doth not, in a way of infinite mercy: Hosea xi. 9, 'I will not execute the fierceness of mine anger; for I am God, and not man.' It is the great advantage of us sinners that we have to do with God and not man in our miscarriages; for man's pity and mercy may be exhausted, be it never so great. What! seven times a day? But God is infinite. Man may think it dishonourable to agree with an inferior when he stoops not to him; but God is so far above the creature that we are below his indignation. Man is soon wearied, but not God: Isa. lv. 8, 9, 'For my thoughts are not your thoughts, neither are your ways my ways, saith the Lord. For as the heavens are higher than the earth, so are my ways higher than your ways, and my thoughts than your thoughts.'

I now come to the fourth and last consideration.

IV. That forgiveness of sins is one great benefit that we must ask of God in prayer. Here it will be needful to show:—

First, The necessity of treating with God about forgiveness.

Secondly, The nature of this benefit.

Thirdly, The terms how God dispenseth it.

First, The necessity will appear in these propositions:—

1. Man hath a conscience: Rom. ii. 15, 'Thoughts accusing or excusing,' &c. A beast cannot reflect.

2. A conscience inferreth a law.

3. A law inferreth a sanction.

4. A sanction inferreth a judgment.

5. A judgment inferreth a condemnation to the fallen creature.

6. There is no avoiding this condemnation, unless God set up a chancery, or another court of grace.

7. If God set up another court, our plea must be grace. Of this see more at large, 'Twenty Sermons,' Sermon 1 on Ps. xxxii. 1, 2.

Secondly, The nature of this benefit, or manner how God forgiveth.

1. Freely.

2. Fully.

[1.] Freely, and merely upon the impulsions of his own grace: Isa. xliii. 25, 'I, even I, am he that forgiveth your iniquities for my name's sake.' Nothing else could move him to it but his own mercy; and he could have chosen whether he would have done so, yea or no—for he

spared not the angels, but offereth pardon to man, and all men are
not actually pardoned. And, therefore, the only reason why he showeth
us mercy and not others, is merely his own grace. The intervention
of Christ's merit doth not hinder the freedom of it, though dearly
purchased by Christ, yet freely bestowed on us. For it is said, Rom.
iii. 24, 'Justified freely by his grace, through the redemption that is
in Christ.' Why? Partly because it was mercy that he would not
prosecute his right against us. Partly because he found out the way
how to recompense the wrong done by sin unto his majesty, and out
of his love sent his Son to make this recompense for us: John iii. 16.
It was love set all a-work. And lastly, not excited hereunto by any
worth on our parts, but the external moving cause was only our
misery, and the internal moving cause his own grace. Nor is the
freedom of this act infringed by requiring faith and repentance on our
part, because that only showeth the way and order wherein this grace is
dispensed, not the cause why. It is not for the worth of our repentance,
or as if there were any merit in it. A malefactor, that beggeth his
pardon on his knees, doth not deserve a pardon; only the majesty of
the prince requireth that it should be submissively asked. These are
not conditions of merit, but order; not the cause, but the way of
grace's working. And these conditions are wrought in us by grace:
Acts v. 31; not required only, but given. In all other covenants, the
party contracting is bound to perform what he promiseth by his own
strength. But in the covenant of grace, God doth not only require
that we should believe and repent, but causeth it in us. Conditions
of the covenant are conditions *in* the covenant. God requireth faith
and repentance, and giveth faith and repentance. Compare Isa. lix.
20, with Rom. xi. 26. It is Christ's gift as well as his precept; so
that when we come about pardon of sin, we have only to do with
grace. We beg pardon, and a heart to receive it. It is a free
pardon.

[2.] It is a full pardon. It is full in several respects. (1.) Because
where the party is forgiven, he is accepted with God as if he had
never sinned: Ps. ciii. 12, 'As far as the east is from the west, so far
hath he removed our transgressions from us.' And Micah vii. 19,
'Thou wilt cast all their sins into the depth of the sea;' Isa. xxxviii.
17, 'Thou hast cast all my sins behind thy back.' It shall not be
remembered nor laid to their charge any more. It is true, for a while
after they may trouble the conscience, as when the storm ceaseth, the
waves roll for a while afterwards; so may sin in the consciences of
God's children work trouble, after the fiducial application of the blood
of Christ. But the storm ceaseth by degrees; and it is possible that
the commitment of new sins may revive old guilt, as a new strain
may make us sensible of an old bruise. Yet we must distinguish
between the full grant of a pardon, from the full sense of it. When
we are not thankful, humble, fruitful, former sins may come into
remembrance, and God may permit it, as matter of humiliation to
us, and to quicken us to seek after new confirmation of our right and
interest. Yet God's pardon is never reversed, nor will the sin be
charged again, or put in suit against him, to the final condemnation
of the person so pardoned. Once more: though the sins of the justified

should be remembered at the day of judgment, it will not be to the confusion of their faces, but the exaltation and praise of the Lord's grace. Then is this acquittance in all respects full. (2.) It is full, because where God forgiveth one sin, he will forgive all : Ps. ciii. 3, ' Who pardoneth all thy sins;' and Micah vii. 19, ' Thou wilt cast all their sins into the depth of the sea.' Sins original, actual; of omission, commission; small, great; secret, open; lust that boileth in the heart, and breaketh out in the life; sins of worship, of ordinary conversation. Look in the bill—what owest thou? A Christian is amazed when he cometh to a serious account with God; but the self-judging sinner needeth not be discouraged when he cometh to God. For where God pardoneth all that is past, the fountain stands daily open for him to flee unto, with all his faults as they are committed; and upon the renewing of his faith and repentance, he shall obtain his pardon. All sins are mortal, all of them damnable. Therefore if all sins be not pardoned, he remaineth in danger of the curse, and one sin let alone is sufficient to exclude us out of heaven. Therefore all is pardoned, first or last. Justice hath no more to seek of Christ. And we have all leave to sue out our pardon in Christ's name. He is under that covenant that will pardon all.

[3.] It is full; because where God forgiveth the sin, he also forgiveth the punishment. It will not stand with God's mercy to forgive the debt, and yet to require the payment. It is a mocking to say, I forgive you the debt, and yet cast the man into prison; and to pardon the malefactor, and yet leave him liable to execution. Here in the text, God forgiveth us, as we are bound to forgive our brother, not in part, but in whole. Guilt is nothing but an obligation to punishment (1.) As to eternal punishment, it is clear: Rom. v. 9. The eternal promises and threatenings, being of things absolutely good and evil, are therefore absolute and peremptory, that is certain. (2.) But now as to temporal afflictions, there is some difficulty, for where the whole punishment is done away, such grace and payment of any part of the debt cannot stand together. That pardon which is given upon valuable and sufficient price is full and perfect. Jesus Christ satisfied the justice of God for all our sins. How is it, then, that the saints are subject to so many afflictions? (1.) So far as sin remains, so far some penal evil remains: when the dominion of it is broken, there remains no condemnation, but yet some affliction, and when it is wholly gone, there is no evil at all. We are not yet purged from all sin; and, therefore, (2.) these afflictions are not satisfactory punishments, and need not, as to the completing of our justification, but are helps to us, as the furtherance of our sanctification; and so are of great use—[1.] To make us hate sin more. If we only knew the sweetness of it, and not the bitterness, we would not be so shy of it. Now the bitterness of it is seen by the effects: Jer. ii. 19, ' Thine own wickedness shall correct thee, and thy backslidings shall reprove thee; know therefore, and see, that it is an evil thing and bitter, that thou hast forsaken the Lord thy God, and that my fear is not in thee, saith the Lord God of hosts.' [2.] It will cause us to prize our deliverance by Christ. If affliction be so grievous, what would hell be? 1 Cor. xi. 32, ' But when we are judged, we are chastened of the Lord, that we should not be condemned with the world.' It is a gentle remembrance of hell-pains, or a fair warning to avoid them, when scorched or singed a little. [3.] To make us walk more humbly. We forget ourselves, and are apt to be puffed up. Paul saith, 2 Cor. xii. 7, ' Lest I should be exalted above measure through the abundance of the revelations, there was given to me a thorn in the flesh, the messenger of Satan to buffet me, lest I should be exalted above measure.'

[4.] It is full, because where God forgiveth sin, there are many consequent benefits.

(1.) God is reconciled: Rom. v. 1, ' Therefore being justified by faith, we have peace with God through our Lord Jesus Christ.' This is the great blessing, and our great work is to make and keep peace with God; to have no cloud between us and his face. Light is pleasant: what then is the light of his countenance, that filleth us with a peace that passes understanding? We would have a powerful friend, especially if we need him: Acts xii. 20; they sought peace with Herod, ' because their country was nourished by the king's country;' so should we do: we cannot live without God. If sin be pardoned, then we are at peace with God, and may have free access to him, with a free use of all that is his.

(2.) A heart sanctified is a connexed benefit: 1 Cor. vi. 11, ' And such were some of you; but ye are washed, but ye are sanctified, but ye are justified in the name of the Lord Jesus;' and 1 John i. 9. Sin is considerable in the guilt and filth of it, as it rendereth us obnoxious to God's justice, or as it tainteth our faculties and actions. According to this double respect, Christ destroyeth sin, and no man hath benefit by him that is not freed from the guilt and filth thereof. Christ was sent into the world to restore God's image in us. But the image of God consisteth in the participation of holiness, as well as the participation of blessedness; for God, that is happy and blessed, is also holy and good. The filthiness of sin is opposite to holiness, and the guilt of it to blessedness; so that either Christ must restore but half the image of God, or he must give us this double benefit. If he should give us one without the other, many inconveniences would follow; therefore both are given: he justifieth that he may sanctify, and he sanctifieth that he may glorify.

(3.) Providence is blessed: the curse is taken out of our blessings, and the sting out of our afflictions. As long as sin remains unpardoned our blessings are cursed: Mal. ii. 2, ' If ye will not hear, and if ye will not lay it to heart, to give glory to my name, saith the Lord of hosts, I will even send a curse upon you, and I will curse your blessings; yea, I have cursed them already, because ye do not lay it to heart.' There will be a worm in our manna, our ' table will become a snare,' Ps. lxix. 22. But when once sin is pardoned, the sting of misery is taken away: 1 Cor. xv. 56, ' The sting of death is sin, and the strength of sin is the law: but thanks be to God, which giveth us the victory through our Lord Jesus Christ.' Crosses are not curses.

(4.) We have a right to heaven, which is the great ground of hope: Rom. v. 10, ' For if, when we were enemies, we were reconciled to God by the death of his Son, much more, being reconciled, we shall be saved by his life.'

Thirdly, The terms upon which it is dispensed are faith and repentance.

1. Faith: Acts x. 43, ' To him give all the prophets witness, that, through his name, whosoever believeth in him shall receive remission of sins.' Faith is necessary to honour the mercy of God, to own the surety, to consent to his undertaking, to encourage the creature to look after this benefit.

2. Repentance, which implieth a sorrow for sin, with a serious purpose of forsaking it. Sorrow for sin: no man can seriously desire a pardon but he that is touched with a sense of his sin, moved and troubled at it. And then, for purpose of forsaking: Ezek. xxxiii. 12, ' As for the wickedness of the wicked, he shall not fall thereby in the day that he turneth from his wickedness.' Sin pardoned must be left; otherwise, a pardon given to a wicked man would be a confirmation of his sin, or a concession of leave to sin. Well, then, let us seek pardon of God in this way.

And lead us not into temptation.

WE are now come to the sixth petition, which is doubly expressed :—

1. Negatively, *Lead us not into temptation.*

2. Affirmatively, *But deliver us from evil.*

The first part doth more concern preventing grace, that we may not fall into evil; and the second, recovering grace, that if we fall into evil we may not be overcome of it, nor overwhelmed by it, but may find deliverance from the Lord. Here we pray : (1.) that we may not be tempted ; or, (2.) if the Lord see it fit we should be tempted, that we may not yield ; or, (3.) if we yield, that we may not totally be overcome. As the former petition concerned the guilt of sin, so this concerns the reign and power of it.

In this first part, take notice :—

First, Of the evil deprecated, or that which we pray against, and that is, *temptation.*

Secondly, The manner of deprecation, *Lead us not.*

In which there is something implied, and something formally asked.

1. Something implied ; and that is :—

[1.] God's providence. When we say to God, ' Lead us not,' we do acknowledge he hath the disposal of temptation.

[2.] God's justice, and our desert ; that for former sins, God may suffer this evil to befall us. We have so often provoked the Lord, that in a judicial manner he may suffer us to be tempted.

[3.] Our weakness ; that we are unable to stand under such a condition by our own strength, therefore we go to God.

2. Something formally asked ; that is, either that God would prevent the temptation, or, if he should use such a dispensation towards us, give us grace to overcome it.

Of these things I shall speak in their order.

First, Of the evil deprecated ; and from thence observe :—

Doct. 1. That temptations are a usual evil, wherewith we encounter in the present world.

Here I shall:—

    I. Open the nature of temptations.

    II. I shall give you some observations concerning them.

    III. The reasons of it.

    I. For the nature of temptations.

Temptation is a proving or making trial of a thing or person; what he is, and what he will do. And thus sometimes we are said to tempt God, and at other times God is said to tempt us.

1. We are said to tempt God when we put it to the proof whether he will be as good as his word, either in the comminatory or promissory part thereof: Ps. xcv. 9, 'When your fathers tempted me, proved me, and saw my works;' they tempted God, as they put him often upon the trial. To note that, by the way, there is a twofold tempting or proving of God, either in a way of duty or sin. (1.) In a way of duty, when we wait to see his promise fulfilled; and so, Mal. iii. 10, 'Prove me now herewith, saith the Lord of hosts, if I will not open you the windows of heaven, and pour you out a blessing.' Come pay your tithes and offerings: he would have the portion which belonged to himself: 'and prove me now herewith,' &c. God submits to a trial from experience, when we wait for the good promised. Thus we try God, and try his word: Ps. xviii. 30, 'The word of the Lord is a tried word; he is a buckler to all those that trust in him.' All those which build upon it, that wait to see what God will do, they will find it, upon experience, to be accomplished to a tittle; never did any build upon it, or wait for the accomplishment of it, in vain. (2.) In a way of sin. Many ways we are said to tempt God. When we set God a task, in satisfying our conceits and carnal affections: Ps. lxxviii. 18, 'They tempted God in their hearts, by asking meat for their lusts;' and when we will not believe in him, but upon conditions of our own making; or when we confine him to our means, or time, or manner of working; or would have some extraordinary proof of his being, and power, and goodness; or see whether God will punish us though we sin against him. All these ways we are said to tempt God in a way of sin. But that is not my business now. Therefore,

2. As man tempts God, so is man himself tempted. Now man is either tempted:—

First, By God.

Secondly, By Satan.

Thirdly, By his own heart.

First, Man is tempted by God: Gen. xxii. 1, 'And it came to pass, after these things, that God did tempt Abraham.' How is God said to tempt man? When he trieth what is in us: Deut. viii. 2, 'To humble thee, and to prove thee, to know what was in thine heart;' either what of grace, or what of sin, is in our heart.

[1.] What of grace. Thus the Lord tries us by afflictions, by delays of promises, and other means becoming his holy nature. By afflictions, for they are called a trial: 1 Pet. i. 6, 'Now for a season, if need be, ye are in heaviness through manifold temptations.' The afflictions of the gospel are called temptations. And so by delay of promises: God trieth us sometimes by delaying the accomplishment of his promise; as in Ps. cv. 19, 'Until the time that his word came, the word of the Lord tried him;' that is, until the promise was fulfilled and accomplished. A man is put to trial of all the grace that is in his heart.

[2]. God tries what corruption there is in us. He trieth this either by offering occasions, or withdrawing his grace, or by permitting Satan to tempt us.

(1.) By offering occasions in the course of his providence: God puts us upon trial there; sometimes by want, sometimes by fulness. By want: John vi. 5, 6, 'Whence shall we buy bread, that these may eat?' saith Christ to Philip. 'And this he said to prove him; for he himself knew what he would do.' Christ will have the weakness of his followers tried, as well as their strength. And he trieth his people often by this kind of trial, when there are many mouths and no meat, and a man cannot see which way his visible supplies shall come in: this he doth to prove them, to see whether they will look only to outward likelihood and probabilities, or rest themselves upon God's promise and all-sufficiency; or else, by fulness and outward prosperity, to see if they will forget him. I confess I do not remember where this is called a trial in scripture, unless there be somewhat in that place, Deut. viii. 16, 'He fed thee with manna in the wilderness, that he might humble thee, and that he might prove thee, to do thee good at thy latter end.' Possibly the trial there might lie in this: because they had but from hand to mouth, or because it was not that meat which their lusts craved, but that which God saw fit for them. But, however, though prosperity be not called so, yet certainly it is in itself a trial: Prov. xxx. 9, 'Give me not riches, lest I be full, and deny thee, and say, Who is the Lord?' Lust in us makes it to be a temptation, and the godly have been often foiled by it; and they need learn 'how to abound, as well as how to be abased,' Phil. iv. 12. They need learn how to avoid the snares of a prosperous condition. David, it was a trial to him; while he was wandering in the wilderness, he had such tenderness, that his heart smote him when he cut off the lap of Saul's garment, while he was chased like a partridge upon the mountains, wandering up and down, from forest to forest. But when he was walking at ease upon the terrace of his palace in Jerusalem, then he falls into blood and uncleanness; and therefore his estate was a trial, and he lieth in it, notwithstanding all his former tenderness of heart, until he was roused up by Nathan the prophet. And certainly, as to the wicked, it is a very great temptation, judicially inflicted, disposed of to them by God's judgment: they are plagued by worldly felicity; and it is part of their curse that they 'shall be written in the earth,' Jer. xvii. 13; and suitable to this purpose, God saith, Jer. vi. 21, 'Behold, I will lay stumbling-blocks before this people, and the fathers and the sons together shall fall upon them.' How doth God lay stumbling-blocks? If men will find the sin, God may with justice enough find the occasion; he will give them some outward condition that is a snare to them. As we may try a servant whom we have just cause to suspect, by laying something in the way, that his filching humour may be discovered, without any breach of justice;

so the wicked, that harden their hearts against God, God may give them their hearts' desire, and worldly happiness, and so it may cause them to stumble.

(2.) God trieth us also by withdrawing his grace, as in 2 Chron. xxxii. 31, 'God left him to try him, that he might know all that was in his heart.' It is needful sometimes that we should see our weakness as well as our strength, and how unable we are to stand without grace, that we may be sensible whence we stand, and which without temptation could not so well be.

(3.) God tries us, by permitting the temptations of Satan and his instruments; for surely these things do not befall us without a providence. Job xii. 16, 'The deceived and the deceiver are his,' his creatures; and nothing can be done or suffered in this kind without God's providence. See it in Christ's instance, Mat. iv. 1, it is said, 'He was led up of the Spirit into the wilderness, to be tempted of the devil;' that is, led by the good and Holy Spirit to be tempted by the evil spirit. So, 2 Sam. xxiv. 1, compared with 1 Chron. xxi. 1: God moved David, and Satan provoked David, to number the people; that is, God did let loose Satan upon David, to accomplish the righteous ends of his providence. And many of those arrows which are shot at us, though they come immediately from Satan's bow, yet they are taken out of God's quiver. God, as a just judge, may give us up to Satan as his minister and executioner. Well, then, this is one way of God's tempting, permitting of Satan to tempt. And as Satan, so his instruments, God tries us by them. Deut. xiii. 1–3, 'If there arise among you a prophet, or a dreamer of dreams, thou shalt not hearken unto him.' Why? 'For the Lord your God proveth you, to know whether ye love the Lord your God with all your heart, and with all your soul.' God proveth. When there are delusions abroad and errors broached, it is 'that the approved may be made manifest,' 1 Cor. xi. 19. God letteth loose these winds of error and delusion that the solid grain may be distinguished from the light chaff, and that he may discover his own people, and whether we have received truths upon evidence, or taken them up only upon hearsay. All these ways may God be said to tempt.

Now concerning this, take these rules :—

(1.) God's tempting is not to inform himself, but to discover his creatures to themselves and others. Not to inform himself, for 'he knows our thoughts afar off,' Ps. cxxxix. 2; that is, he knows not only the conclusion and event, and management of things near, but he knows the very remote preparation aforehand; he knows what kind of thoughts we will have, and workings of spirit. As a man that is up in the air may see a river in its rise, and fountain, and course, and fall of it—seeth it all at once; whereas another which stands by the banks can only see the water as it passeth by. God seeth all things in their fountain and cause, as well as in their issue and event— he seeth all things together; therefore it is not for his own information. But the meaning is, therefore doth God try us, that what is known to him, and yet unknown to ourselves, that that which lodgeth and lieth hid in our heart may be discovered to us. That we may not be conceited of more than we have, and that the evil which before lay hid and was unseen may be cured when it is discovered. And, on the other hand, that grace may not lie sleeping in a dead and inactive habit, but be drawn out into act and view, for his glory and praise.

(2.) God's tempting is always good, and for good; his tempting is either in mercy or in judgment. In mercy : and so when he trieth the graces of his people ; or when he means more especially to discover the failings of his people, it is all good. When he tries the graces of his people, there is no doubt of that. When God hath furnished a man with grace, that he may, without any impeachment of his goodness, put him upon trial, and use creatures for that end for which he hath fitted them ; as a man which hath made and bought a thing may prove it and try the strength of it. Or when the intent of the dispensation is to try their weakness, that is good also, and for good ; as when a man tries a leaky vessel, with an intent to make it stanch. So when God tempts us by sharp afflictions, or any other course, it is for good: Heb. xii. 10, ' He, verily, for our profit, that we might be partakers of his holiness.' A man that hath a disease upon him, it may be by walking or stirring the humours the disease may appear, it is for good ; it is better it should be discovered, that he may in time look after a remedy, than lurk and lie hid in the body to his utter undoing ; so it is for good our corruptions and weaknesses should be discovered, that they may be made sound. Ay, but when God brings it in judgment, yet that is for good ; that is, for his own glory and his church's good, though not for the good of the party. For the church's good, that naughtiness where it is might in time be discovered : Prov. xxvi. 26, ' Whose hatred is covered by deceit, his wickedness shall be showed before the whole congregation,' lest men get a name that they might do religion a mischief. And it is for the glory of God that men may appear what they are. Here is no stain upon God's justice for all this. He that pierceth a vessel, if it run dreggy with musty or poisonous liquor, the fault is not in him that pierceth it, but in the liquor itself: he that pierceth or broacheth it doth only discover what is within, that if it be unsavoury he may cast it into the kennel. So, it is not the fault of God which pierceth, discovereth, and letteth out our corruption ; the fault is in ourselves : we have those things within which are discovered as soon as God puts us upon a trial.

(3.) God tempts no man, as temptation is taken properly for a solicitation to sin : James i. 13, ' Let no man say, when he is tempted, I am tempted of God: for God cannot be tempted with evil, neither tempteth he any man.' Mark, the apostle proves it, that in this sense God cannot tempt, because of the unchangeable holiness of his nature. In temptation we must distinguish between the mere trial, and the solicitation to sin ; the mere trial, that is from God ; but the solicitation to sin, that is from Satan and ourselves. God solicits no man to sin. It is true, God may try us, trouble us, toss us, exercise our faith, hope, and patience. God is the author of our trouble ; but the devil is the author of our sin, who sinneth himself, and soliciteth others to sin.

(4.) When we say, ' Lead us not into temptation,' we do not beg a total exemption from God's trials, but only a removal of the judgment of them. Not a total exemption, for then we must go out of the world, for while we are here every condition is a trial to us, and every enjoyment. Afflictions and trouble more or less put to trial, and therefore temptation in this sense is a necessary part of that warfare we must encounter and grapple withal while we are in the world. Prosperity tries us, to see if we be then mindful of God when all things succeed well ; and adversity tries us, to see if we can patiently depend upon God. But it is the judgment of trials that we deprecate, that they may not come upon us as a judgment, or that our trial may be so moderate that we may stand our ground. When doth a trial come as a judgment ? When it is immoderate and beyond our strength, either in a way of prosperity or adversity, but chiefly in a way of adversity ; for that is most commonly set out in a way of trial in scripture. When it is immoderate and beyond our strength, 1 Cor. x. 13, God hath promised to his people that ' they shall not be tempted above that they are able to bear ; but will with the temptation also make a way to escape, that they may be able to bear it.' God's conduct is very gentle. As Jacob drove on as the little ones were able to bear, so doth God proportion his dispensations to his people's strength, not to their deservings, but he considers what they are able to bear. Either God keeps off greater trials, or gives in greater strength ; a sweeter sense of his love, or a greater measure of gracious support. A child would sink under that load that a strong back bears without any grudging. Now, this is that we ask of God, according to his promise, that our temptation may be not immoderate and too hard for us. Or else it is a judgment when it proves a provocation to sin ; and so God's temptation, which was meant for our good, we may abuse it, and take occasion thence to sin ; as when we murmur under the cross, or turn our worldly comforts into an occasion to the flesh. Now, to prevent the judgment which may be in these temptations ; in all the trials which befall us, we should fear more the offence against God than our own smart, or the power of the devil, or any inconvenience that may accrue to us in natural evils which we feel. When we are under afflictions, we should be more solicitous that we do not offend God, that he would keep us from murmuring and dishonouring his name, then we should be about our ease and safety ; for this is to prevent the judgment of the temptation. This was Paul's comfort when he was drawing to the conclusion of his life : 2 Tim. iv. 18, ' The Lord hath delivered me out of the mouth of the lion, and he shall deliver me from every evil work, and will preserve me unto his heavenly kingdom.' And so, in good things that we enjoy, we should fear more offending God with them than the losing of them ; for the loss of his favour is more than the loss of our comforts. A man that loseth his worldly portion, this loss may be recompensed ; but he that loseth the favour of God, that breach cannot be made up by any worldly comforts whatsoever.

(5.) In passive evils, which are the usual trials of God's people, we are not to seek them, but to submit to them when they come upon us. We are not to seek them : Mat. xvi. 24, ' If any man will be my disciple, let him take up his cross.' When clearly it is our cross, that is, when it lies in our way, and we cannot decline it, then take it up and fit his back to it. So James i. 2, ' My brethren, count it all joy when ye fall into divers temptations.' He doth not say when ye *run* into them, but *fall* into them. We are not to draw them upon ourselves. Afflictions are not to be sought and desired, but improved. Christians, we never know when it is well with us : sometimes we question God's love, because we have no afflictions and trials ; anon we are questioning his love, because we have nothing but afflictions. In all these things we should refer ourselves to God ; not desire troubles, but bear them patiently and quietly when he lays them upon our backs.

(6.) Again, for those trials which come from God. When God tempts us, or trieth his people in mercy, he hath a great deal of care of them under their trials. As a goldsmith, when he casts his metal into the furnace, he doth not lose it there, and look after it no more ; but sits, and pries, and looks to see if it be not too hot, that nothing be spilt, nothing lost. So it is said, Mal. iii. 3, ' And he shall sit as a refiner and purifier of silver : and he shall purify the sons of Levi, and purge them as gold and silver, that they may offer unto the Lord an offering in righteousness.' The Lord will observe his people when they are under trial, how to moderate affliction, how to refresh them with seasonable comfort, that all this might better them, and bring them to good.

(7.) Though in our trials we manifest weakness as well as grace, yet that weakness is to be done away. You must remember weakness is manifested that it may be removed, and grace manifested that it may be strengthened. When gold and silver is tried in the furnace, there is not only pure metal discovered, but also the drossy part mingled with it ; but it is so discovered that it may be severed from the gold. Such is our trial ; it may discover a great deal of dross and sin in us. But this is our comfort, that as it doth discover sin, so it conduceth to mortify sin. Therefore saith Job, chap. xxiii. 10, ' When he hath tried me, I shall come forth as gold ;' that is, purified and refined, and having the drossy part eaten out.

(8.) God permits us to be tempted of Satan and his instruments for his glory and our good. For his glory ; that his power may be discovered in our preservation, in upholding that grace he hath put into us : 2 Cor. xii. 10, ' Therefore I take pleasure in infirmities, in reproaches, in necessities, in persecutions, in distresses, for Christ's sake : for when I am weak, then am I strong.' We should be glad that God be glorified, though with our great inconvenience. And it is for our good ; to correct our pride and vainglory. When Peter presumed of his strength, then God left him to be tempted of the damsel, Mat. xxvi. 33, 70.

(9.) When God permitteth Satan to exercise us, though he suspends the victory, yet if he give us grace to fight and to maintain the combat, it is a great mercy. For so he dealt with Paul when he had to do with the messenger of Satan—(Satan was in that trouble, be it what it will)—he had only this answer, 2 Cor. xii. 9, ' My grace is sufficient for thee : for my strength is made perfect in weakness.' Three times he had been with God, and then he gets his answer, and it was only this, ' My grace,' &c. Jesus Christ in his conflict and combat was answered as to support, and so was heard in the things he feared. So if God give strength to the soul, it is an answer, though he do not take off the trial.

Secondly, There are temptations from Satan, as well as from God,
who is called the tempter: Mat. iv. 3. Now the devil's temptations
they are evil, and for evil. How doth the devil tempt?

[1.] By propounding objects; as Luke iv. 5, ' He showed unto him
all the kingdoms of the world in a moment of time.' He had nothing
to work upon within, therefore he propounds outward objects. So
still the devil tempts us with a curious eye to take in the object, that
it may be a bait and snare to the soul. Achan takes notice of it himself: Josh. vii. 21, ' When I saw among the spoils a goodly Babylonish
garment, and a wedge of gold, then I coveted them, and took them.'
I *saw*, I *coveted*, and I *took*: the eye awakens desire, and desire that
inclines to practise. So Prov. xxiii. 31, ' Look not thou upon the wine
when it is red, when it giveth his colour in the cup, when it moveth
itself aright.' Unless we shut the windows of the soul, this pestilent
plague gets in by the senses. The heart is corrupted by objects that
we take in by the senses, as it corrupted Eve, dealt with her first by
the sense; the forbidden fruit was full in her way, then the devil sets
upon her.

[2.] He tempts by the persuasion of instruments, who are the devil's
spokesmen: thus was Joseph tempted by the enticements and blandishments of his mistress, Gen. xxxix. 7. And many times the devil sets
nearest friends and relations to weaken their zeal, and withdraw their
hearts from God: Mat. xvi. 23. Saith Christ to Peter, ' Get thee behind me, Satan.' It was Peter said it, yet Christ rebuked Satan, for
the devil had a hand in it; he makes one of Christ's disciples his instrument.

[3.] He doth it by internal suggestion: 1 Chron. xxi. 1, ' And Satan
stood up against Israel, and provoked David to number Israel;' that
is, by internal suggestion. John xiii. 2, ' The devil put it into the
heart of Judas to betray him.' He haunts and pesters the hearts of
men by vain thoughts and carnal imaginations. So ' the god of this
world' is said to ' blind their minds,' 2 Cor. iv. 4.

[4.] By stirring up the humours of our body. When he seeth men
inclined to wrath, and angry motions, or lust, the devil joins, and
makes the tempest the more violent. He knows what use to make of
an angry look, a wanton glance; he knows how to tempt, by awakening the humours of our own body against us.

Take some observations here.

(1.) In all sins Satan joineth; he is not idle, but makes use of every
inclination of ours; as he sees the tree leaning, he joins issue. But
some sins are purely of his suggestion; horrid sins, and such as are so
very evil, that they could come from no other but from the devil: such
sins as could not be acted by man in an ordinary course of sinning.
As Judas his treason: though he were devil enough to plot such a
thing, yet it is said, Satan put it into his heart. And such singular
diabolical suggestions may be darted into the bosom of believers sometimes; thoughts of atheism, blasphemy, unnatural sins, self-murder,
suspicion of the gospel; these things the devil throws in. Therefore,
Eph. vi. 16, believers are warned to quench these fiery darts, that the
devil hurls into the souls of men.

(2.) Every man is haunted with special temptations, from temper, sex, age, custom, calling, company, course of affairs ; these things are often spoken of in scripture. From temper : God makes use of temper ; for though he plants all grace in the hearts of the regenerate, yet there are certain graces wherein they are eminent; as Timothy for temperance, Moses for meekness, &c. Thus Paul speaks of the law in his members : Rom. vii. 23. The devil may find forces from the temper of the body to destroy the soul. So also from sex; as he ' beguiled Eve,' 2 Cor. xi. 3. And from age: we read of ' youthful lusts,' 2 Tim. ii. 22. And how strong the devil is about young ones : 1 John ii. 13, ' I have written unto you, young men, because ye have overcome the wicked one.' They are most assaulted with pride, with youthful lusts suitable to their age. So from custom and education : Ps. xviii. 23, ' I kept myself from mine iniquity.' Every man hath *his* iniquity ; that is, such as his education and custom hath wrought upon him, which makes the sin prevail over other sins. A child of God hath a predominant sin, not over grace, for that is inconsistent with sincerity ; but some master-sin which prevails over the rest ; according as the channel is cut, so corrupt nature runs, but some in this channel, and some in that : every man hath his special sin, and accordingly the devil plies him. Then our calling is a special temptation : 1 Tim. iii. 6, the apostle speaks that a bishop should ' not be a novice, lest, being lifted up with pride, he fall into the condemnation of the devil ; '—pride, and ostentation of gifts, and vainglory in such public service. Many other sins follow every calling: therefore if you would be skilled in Satan's enterprises, you must mind temper, age, calling. So company : as a man's company is, his soul is insensibly tainted. As a man that walks in the sun is tanned before he is aware, so are the souls of men sullied and defiled by carnal company before they be aware. A man would think, of all sins, passion is so uncomely that it should not tempt another man : yet it is said, Prov. xxii. 24, 25, ' Make no friendship with an angry man, and with a furious man thou shalt not go ; lest thou learn his ways, and get a snare to thy soul :' for the more accustomed to them, the less odious they seem ; so by little and little, our spirits are shaped and fitted for such a sin. There are certain sins that are more special temptations. Look, as every disease hath a diet which suits with it, so all sins in the soul. Satan knows what baits we will catch at. It may be, a man that is addicted to the pleasures of the flesh may despise profit, and therefore the devil will not ply him that way. So a man that is addicted to gain despiseth pleasure. The devil suits him with a bait that suits the disease of his soul. It is an opinion the devils have their several wards and quarters ; some for such a sort of sinners, others for another sort. Look, as the heathens had several gods (which were indeed devils), as Bacchus, the god of riot, or patron of good-fellowship; and Venus, of wantonness and love ; and Mars, the devil of revengeful and angry spirits : and we read of Mammon for wealth : Mat. vi. 24. I know it is a *fictio personæ*, to make the matter more sensible ; there is a person feigned. But there may be something of this truth in it, that the devils have several quarters, some to humour the covetous, others enticing the wanton, others lie leigers in taverns and drinking-houses, to draw men to beastly excess; and others

about the revengeful, to awaken their rage. But all this, however it
be (it is the opinion of some), should make us watchful over our
own desires and inclinations, for that is it the devil makes use of to
set upon us.

(3.) The sin of the devil tempting must be distinguished from our
sin in consenting. If the devil tempt, and we consent not, it is his
sin. The envious man may throw weeds over the garden wall ; but if
we do not suffer them to root there, it is not the gardener's fault, but
the fault of the envious man : so the devil may fling in temptations,
fiery darts, atheistical or blasphemous thoughts; yet if we throw them
out with indignation, and give no harbour and entertainment to them
there, it is our misery, but the devil's sin ; and therefore, if our hearts
abhor them at the very first rising, though they be man's cross, they
will be put upon Satan's account.

(4.) Satan, if he cannot prevail by the first temptation to draw us to
sin, he will seek to prevail by a second or subsequent temptation, to
draw us to trouble and discomfort. If he cannot weaken grace, he
may molest and disturb our comfort by flinging in a blasphemous
thought, which is abhorred by a Christian. If he cannot draw you to
deny God, then he will seek to cloud things, that you may suspect
your own estate ; and thus our way is made wearisome to us. Look,
as a candle which sticks to a stone wall, though it cannot burn the
wall, yet it smutcheth and defileth it ; so the children of God, when
the devil seeks to make their temptations stick, though he doth not
burn their hearts with these fiery darts of blasphemy and atheism—
they catch not there—yet they weaken our comfort ; and then his
second temptation is to bring us to doubt of God's love, to doubt of
our own faith, and to draw us to impatiency and murmuring at God's
hand. Therefore it should be our care, not only to withstand the
devil's first temptation, but his second also.

(5.) Certainly they cannot stand long that seem to give up themselves
to Satan's snares. How may this be done ? Any carnal affection
unmortified layeth us open to the devil : 1 Tim. vi. 9, ' They that
will be rich, fall into temptation and a snare, and into many foolish
and hurtful lusts, which drown men in destruction and perdition.' If
a man cherish his worldliness, and do not mortify it, he lieth ready
to be seized upon as a ready prey for Satan. Judas, he had the bag,
and he lay open to the devil ; his worldliness increased upon him, so
the devil entereth into him. Again, when we ride into the devil's
quarters and will parley with temptation, when we freely open the windows of the senses unto alluring objects, and can dally with the snare
and play about the temptation, then we do but tempt God to leave us,
and tempt the devil to surprise us. And therefore ' be sober, be watchful, for your adversary, the devil, walketh about like a roaring lion,
seeking whom he may devour,' 1 Pet. v. 8. ' Be sober;' what is
sobriety ? A holy moderation in the use of worldly things. Be sure
not to leave any carnal affection unmortified. And then be watchful ;
take heed not to play about the temptation, nor put yourselves upon
occasions of sin, for then we lie open to the devil, and give him an
advantage against us. Thus much for the second sort of temptations,
such as come from Satan.

The *third* sort of temptations are those which arise from our own hearts ; so we call these urgings and solicitations to sin which we feel in our bosoms. Concerning this also I shall give some observations.

[1.] If there were no devil to tempt us, yet the heart of man is fruitful enough of all that is evil : Mat. xv. 19, ' Out of the heart proceed evil thoughts, murders, adulteries, fornications, thefts, false witnesses, blasphemies.' There is a black catalogue, and all comes out of the heart of man. And among the rest, observe, there is murder, which strikes at the life of man ; and blasphemy, which strikes at the honour and being of God. Though the devil should stand by and say nothing to us, we have enough within us to put us upon all kind of evil : Jer. xvii. 9, ' The heart is deceitful above all things, and desperately wicked ; who can know it ?' As to actual sins, there is a difference ; but as to original sin, it is the same in all. All the sins that ever have been or shall be committed in the world, they are virtually in our natures, they are but original sin acted and drawn out this way and that way, as all numbers are but one multiplied : Cain's murder, Judas's treason, Julian's apostasy and enmity to Christ, the seed and root of all is in our nature ; and if we were but left to ourselves, and had the same temptations and occasions, we should be as bad as others ; such as we would not imagine that ever we should commit is in our heart : 2 Kings viii. 13, ' Is thy servant a dog, that he should do this great thing ?' when he had been told of those horrid cruelties he should act upon the women and children of Israel. No man knows the depth of his own wickedness, if loosened of his chain and the restraints are taken off. At first nature abhors them in the conceit of them ; but when God permits us to lie under the temptation, and fair occasion, man is not to be trusted. We see, in this respect, what need there is to pray that God would not leave us under the power of temptation, because the heart of man is prone, naturally inclinable, to all evil. There are new actual sins, but there is no new original sin, that is but one and the same in all persons and at all times ; the root of all the mischief which hath been in the world is within us.

[2.] That without the flesh, the world and the devil can have no power over us. A man cannot be compelled to sin against his own consent ; he may be compelled to suffer temptation, but he is a sinner by his own choice. The world would not hurt us were it not for lust in the heart : 2 Pet. i. 4, ' Escaping the corruption of the world through lust.' I say, it is not the beauty or sweetness of the creature, but lust, which is our ruin and undoing, and that makes the world so dangerous unto us. A spider sucketh poison from the same flower from which a bee would suck honey ; the fault is not in the flower, but in the spider : the devil can do nothing unless we give him leave. The fire is kindled in our own bosoms, Satan only doth blow it up into a flame. Saith Nazianzen, we have the coals in our own hearts, the devil doth but come and blow them up : suggestion doth nothing without consent. In vain doth one knock at the door, and none within to look out and make answer ; so, all other temptations would be in vain, if there were not somewhat within that would close with what is suggested from Satan : James i. 14, ' Every man is tempted, when he

is drawn away of his own lust, and enticed,' by his own concupiscence.
If your hearts did not yield, if you did resist, the devil and the world
could not force you.   When Satan came to Christ, he might molest
him, but he 'found nothing in him,' John xiv. 30; as a glass of pure
water may be shaken, but there is no filth, no mud there discovered.
But now, the best of men, they have somewhat within them, naughtiness and corruption enough in their own hearts, upon which Satan
may work and inflame them with his fiery darts.   In short, we may
commit sin without Satan, but Satan cannot betray us to sin without
ourselves ; cannot have his desire upon us without us.

[3.] The flesh doth not only make us flexible and yielding to temptations, but is active and stirring in our hearts, to force and impel us
thereunto.   There is ' a law in our members,' Rom. vii. 23, a powerful active principle within us, that is always urging us to sin.   We
think and speak too gently of our own corrupt hearts when we think
the corruption is sleepy, and works not until it be irritated by outward
objects and Satan's suggestions.   No, there is an active, stirring
principle within us, that poureth out sin as a fountain doth waters,
though nobody comes to drink of them ; as Gen. vi. 5, ' Every imagination of the thoughts of his heart is only evil continually.'   There
is a mint in man's heart that is always at work coining evil thoughts,
evil desires, evil motions ; and 'the flesh lusteth against the spirit,'
Gal. v. 17 : And ' Sin wrought in me all manner of concupiscence,'
Rom. vii. 8.   Though there were no other occasion to irritate, but
God's law and the motions of his Spirit, yet there is a continual fer-
mentation wrought by these corrupt humours in our hearts.   Natural
concupiscence doth not lie idle in them, but is active and warring ; and
the objects that are in the world, and the solicitations of the devil make
it more violent.

[4.] The temptations of the flesh and the world go in conjunction,
and do mutually help one another.   And therefore it is said, 1 John
ii. 16, ' For all that is in the world, the lust of the flesh, the lust of
the eyes,' &c.   Mark, whatever is in the world, he doth not
mention the object, but the lusts, because these are complicated and
folded up together in the temptation.   The bait is the world; but
the appetite and desire we have from the flesh.   And this is intimated
in that passage, James i. 14, ' Every man is tempted when he is
drawn away of his own lust, and enticed.'   There are two words there,
drawn away, and *enticed :* the drawing away notes the vehemency
of desire or inclination of our own hearts ; and the enticement, that is
from the object.   Both ways doth corruption work, by force and
flattery.   The great bait is pleasure, the contentment that we take
in outward enjoyments.   And we are carried out to it by the
vehement propension of corrupt nature.

[5.] This vehement propension of corrupt nature to outward things
is set at work by a hope of gaining them, or a fear to lose them ;
and so we are assaulted on every hand, by right-hand and left-hand
temptations.   By right-hand temptations, from the flatteries and
comforts of the world, which are the more dangerous because of their
easy insinuation into, and strong operation upon our hearts, and so
our comforts prove a snare to us, and ' an occasion to the flesh,' as

the apostle saith, Gal. v. 13.   And then there are left-hand temptations, which arise from shame or fear of worldly evils, as the other did arise from a desire or hope of good.   So the apostle : Gal. vi. 12, 'As many as desire to make a fair show in the flesh, they constrain you to be circumcised; only lest they should suffer persecution for the cross of Christ.'   That was their temporising then to comply with the Jews, who had some national privileges under the Roman government, and had better security to their worldly interests than possibly thorough Christians could have.   Now, to avoid both these, the apostle, when he presseth Christians to all those graces which are necessary, he presseth them to temperance and patience : 2 Pet. i. 5, 6, 'Add to knowledge temperance, and to temperance patience.' Both these are armour of proof against worldly temptations; temperance against the delights, and patience against the evils and troubles of the world.   It was never yet so well with the world but that Christians (those that are so in good earnest, that mean to go to heaven and keep a good conscience) will be assaulted on both sides.

[6.] That there is no avoiding either of these snares and temptations as long as any carnal affection remaineth unmortified.   For until a man be dead to worldly comforts, and hardened against worldly sorrows, he doth but lie naked and open to Satan: 1 Tim. vi. 9, ' He that will be rich, falls into temptation and a snare.'   And what is said of riches, the same is true of pleasure : he that is vehemently addicted that way will soon come to put God out of the throne, and make his belly and his pleasure his God: 2 Tim. iii. 4, ' Lovers of pleasures more than lovers of God.'   Any lust that is cherished and indulged will betray us.   As for honour: John v. 44, ' How can ye believe, which receive honour one of another, and seek not the honour that cometh from God only ?'   True faith cannot be planted in that heart that is not purified, until there be a prevailing interest established for Christ over all carnal affections.   Grace bears no sway in us, and hath no power over us.   The ambition and love of respect from men will necessarily make us unsound in the profession of godliness.   Well, then, it stands us upon to allow and cherish no secret sin, but to observe what are the tender parts of our hearts, or which way our corruptions lie, where subjection to God is most apt to stick with us : Ps. cxix. 133, ' Order my steps in thy word ; and let not any iniquity have dominion over me.'   Though we seem to have a zeal in other things, yet if one lust be indulged, we shall soon swerve from our duty.   True obedience to God is inconsistent with the dominion of any one lust or corrupt affection.   I say, though a man, out of some slender and insufficient touch of religion upon his heart, may go right for a while, and do many things gladly, yet that corruption which is indulged, and under the power of which a man lieth, will at length draw him off from God ; and therefore no one sin should have dominion over us.   When doth sin reign or have dominion over us ?   When we do not endeavour to mortify it, and to cut off the provisions that may feed that lust.   Chrysostom's observation is: The apostle doth not say, Let it not *tyrannise* over you, but, Let it not *reign* over you ; that is, when you suffer it to have a quiet reign in your hearts.

[7.] The more we sin upon the mere impulsion of the flesh, and without an external temptation, the more heinous is our offence, for then the heart is carried of its own accord to sin: Ezek. xvi. 33, 34, 'They give gifts to all whores; but thou givest thy gifts to all thy lovers, and hirest them, that they may come unto thee for thy whoredoms. And the contrary is in thee from other women in thy whoredoms, whereas none followeth thee to commit whoredoms: and in that thou givest a reward, and no reward is given unto thee, therefore thou art contrary.' These are expressions to set forth their idolatry. But that which is intended there is this: that they were not desired or solicited, but merely carried to sin by their own proper motion, which exceedingly aggravateth sin. Why? For then it is a sign the heart is carried of its own accord by its own weight, as a heavy body is moved downward, not by the impression of outward force, but by its own natural propension.

Now, when do men thus merely sin upon the impulsions of the flesh? I will instance in three cases :—

(1.) When the temptation is so small and inconsiderable that it should not sway with any reasonable man. It is said in Amos ii. 6, 'They sold the poor for a pair of shoes.' And 'for a piece of bread will that man trangress,' Prov. xxviii. 21. When pleasure and profit is so inconsiderable as that it could not rationally make up a temptation, then men sin merely upon the corruptions of their own flesh. When the devil hath to do with great souls, such as Christ was, he propounds the glory of all the world: Mat. iv. Oh! but a lesser price will serve the turn with those that are deeply engaged already, that are biased with their own propension. For instance, a little ease and carnal satisfaction, a slothful humour, is enough to take them off from the sweetness of communion with God, and the pleasure and contentment that they might enjoy with him in holy exercises. Look, as in general, it is a great aggravation of all sin that for such paltry trifles we turn the back upon God and his grace. All sinners do so; they part with all their hopes by Christ for a mess of pottage, for a little present pleasure; that is profaneness indeed: Heb. xii. 16. So in particular things, when the smallest temptation seems to be strong enough to draw off our hearts from our duty, to bring us to a sin of omission, when it is needful to go and converse with God in secret; a little ease and sloth hangs upon us, and we cannot shake it off: or when we are drawn to a sin of commission by an inconsiderable matter, by the smallest worldly interest as can be mentioned, for a piece of bread, and a pair of shoes.

(2.) When men tempt themselves, or provoke Satan to tempt them. As those which 'make provision for the flesh, to fulfil the lusts thereof,' Rom. xiii. 14; that cater for their lusts, and contrive how to feed them, and how to cherish those inordinate affections in their hearts; that run into the devil's quarters, that bespeak a temptation; or, as it is, James v. 5, that 'nourish their hearts, as in a day of slaughter.' To nourish our hearts, is to feed our lusts, to put strength into the enemy's hand. When a commander sent to his prince to know how he should keep such a rebellious town in order, he sent him this answer: That he should starve the dog, and strengthen the clog;

that he should weaken the city, and strengthen the garrison, that
was his meaning. Truly, what was his advice in that outward case,
that is the duty of a Christian; to weaken his lusts, and still to be
strengthening grace. He should be increasing the better part, and
putting the spirit in heart by godly exercises; by treasuring up
promises, getting arguments and fresh encouragements against sin;
and by weakening the flesh, starving and cutting off provisions for
the flesh. But, on the contrary, when men cater for the flesh, provide
for it, indulge carnal distempers, and feed them with that diet which
they affect, these tempt themselves, and seem willing to lie under
their bondage, and to be glad of it.

(3.) When a man is a sinner to his loss, and hath reasons of nature
to dissuade him, as well as reasons of grace, not only religion, but his
civil interests, would counsel him to do otherwise; as he that brings
a blot upon his name or ruin upon his estate by evil courses; when
men ' draw on iniquity with a cart rope,' as the expression is, Isa.
v. 18; that is, when it is not pleasure, but a very toil and burden and
temporal inconvenience to them to be sinful; that industriously make
it their business ; those that are ' holden with the cords of their own
sins,' Prov. v. 22. He speaks of such as did bring temporal inconveniences upon themselves, as did consume their flesh and their own
bodies; these certainly are those that have cause to complain of their
own hearts, not to put it on Satan, but themselves.

II. Having opened the nature of temptations, I come now to give
the reasons why this is so usual an evil we encounter with in the
world—temptation.

1. God permits it for his own glory, to discover the power, the
freeness and riches of his grace, that men may be driven the more
earnestly to sue out their peace in the name of Jesus Christ. Luther
propounds this reason : Though man be prone to sin of himself of
his own accord, yet God suffers the tempter to be in the world,
because man is backward to seek mercy and grace by Christ; and
therefore God urgeth him with sore temptations. Certainly this
reason was given by him not amiss. You know, when Paul felt those
paroxysms and sad counter-buffs in his own spirit, this makes him
bless God for Jesus Christ: Rom. vii. 25. ' But thanks be to God,
through Jesus Christ our Lord.' It makes him reflect upon the
grace of God in Christ. We keep off from the throne of grace till
temptations drive us thither. As when the sheep wander, the
shepherd lets loose his dog upon them; not to worry them, but to
bring them back to the fold again : so God lets loose Satan to drive
us to himself.

2. For the trial of that grace which he hath wrought in us. Grace
doth better appear in temptation than out of it. The greatness of
the woman of Canaan's faith would never have been discovered, had
it not been for Christ's answer and denial: Mat. xv. 25-28 ; then,
' O woman, great is thy faith.' The glory of that grace which God
hath wrought in his people would not be discovered so much, were it
not for the great trials he puts them upon: Heb. xi. 17, ' By faith
Abraham, when he was tried, offered up Isaac.' Before we go to heaven
we shall have our trials, and shall be tried in our dearest comforts,

and choicest worldly contentments; and all to see what faith we have, and what loyalty to God in the midst of these trials. A great tempest discovereth the goodness of a ship and skill of the pilot; and so these great trials they discover the soundness of our hearts, and the fruit of that grace which God hath wrought in us. Gold is most tried in the fire, and discovered to be pure and perfect. Stars that lie hid in the day shine in the night. We have but dry notions of the comforts of Christianity, and make them matter of talk, until we are put upon great trials, then is our belief and sense of them proved. A gilded potsherd may shine until it comes to scouring, but then the varnish and paint is worn off. The valour and worth of a soldier is not known in times of peace and when he is out of action. When we are put to some difficulty and straits, then is faith seen. Now this is a very pleasing spectacle to God, to see them approve their faith and loyalty to his majesty.

3. Temptations, as they serve to prove, so also to humble us, that we may never be proud of what we have, or conceited of what we have not. As Paul, that he might not be exalted above measure, he was buffeted with a messenger of Satan: 2 Cor. xii. 7. Poor bladders we are, soon blown up and swollen into vanity and vain conceits of ourselves, therefore had need be pricked, that we may let out those swelling winds. A ship that is laden with precious ware, needs to be ballasted with wood, stones, or contemptible stuff. But why will God humble us by temptations, and such kind of temptations as are solicitations to evil? *Answer.* Spiritual evils need a spiritual cure. Outward afflictions they humble, but not so much as temptations do; they are not so conducible to humble a gracious heart as temptations to sin. Why? For then the breach is made upon our souls, and the assault is given to that which a gracious man counts to be dear, and therefore these are suffered to come upon us. If anything will humble a child of God, this will do it. It may be he may bear up under losses tolerably, but when his peace comes to be assaulted, and his grace, this will humble him to purpose. Worldly men, they value their estate by their outward interest, but a child of God by his peace of conscience, and his thriving in grace. Oh, this wounds him to the heart, when in either of these he suffers loss; this sets him a-praying and groaning to God, as Paul groans bitterly when he felt those gripes of sin, and those reluctances in his heart: 'O wretched man!' &c. Afflictions, they conduce to 'humble and prove' us, Deut. viii. 16. And besides, too, the Lord loves to make the cause of our mischief to be the means of our cure. This giveth us the sight of some corruption we saw not before.

4. God permits this exercise to his people to conform us to Christ. We must pledge him in his own cup, it must go round; he himself was tempted: Heb. ii. 7. Christ hath felt the weight, burden, and trouble of temptations, and knows the danger of them. Now the disciple is not above his lord, nor the scholar above his master. The devil, that did set upon Christ, will not be afraid of us.

5. By temptations to sin God mortifieth sin; not only that sin to which we are tempted, but others, that we may not be so heedless. When we have smarted under temptation, we are not so indulgent to

corruption as before; we do not let our senses nor affections run loose. As David speaks, that he got this by his fall: Ps. li. 6, ' In the hidden part thou shalt make me to know wisdom.' Oh, I shall be wiser and more circumspect for this all my life. When men have smarted they grow more cautious; and so, by the overruling and good hand of God, our sins do us service in our passage to heaven, as well as our graces; and God's children may say, they had sinned more if they had sinned less: they are more acquainted with the wiles and depths of Satan and naughtiness of their own hearts, and so are more solicitous.

6. To make us more meek to others: Gal. vi. 1, ' If any man be fallen, ye which are spiritual, restore such a one in the spirit of meekness, considering thyself, lest thou also be tempted.' We are very apt to be severe and fierce upon the failings of others; but now, when we are tempted ourselves, we learn more pity and compassion towards them. Severe censurers are left to some great temptation, that they may be acquainted with their own frailties; they are tempted to some sins, to which their hearts were not so inclinable before. Well, then, that we may pity others, mourn over them, and have a fellow-feeling of their condition, God will make us know the heart of a tempted man, that we may have more compassion over poor tempted souls. Possibly that may be a part of the apostle's sense: 2 Cor. i. 6, ' Whether we be afflicted, it is for your consolation and salvation; or whether we be comforted, it is for your consolation and salvation.' Persons in office in the church, they are afflicted and tempted; and, it may be, have a greater measure of afflictions and temptations, that they may show more pity to other souls. Therefore Luther was wont to say, three things made a minister, viz., prayer, meditation, and temptation. When he is much in communion with God, much in the study of the word, and hath been exercised in temptation, then he will be of a tender and compassionate heart over others; and that he may help them out of the snares of the devil, he is more fitted to his work by temptation.

7. It occasions much experience of the care and providence of God, and the comforts of his promises. A man doth not know what the comforts of faith mean till he be exercised by temptation. And spiritual experiences will countervail all other troubles. This is an hour of temptation: Rev. iii. 10. What should we do in this hour of temptation? Be not over-confident, nor over-diffident, in an hour when God casts us upon trying times. Not over-confident, in casting yourselves upon needless troubles without cause: Mat. xiv. 28. Peter said, ' Lord, if it be thou, bid me come unto thee on the water.' Peter thought he could do anything in the strength of Christ's word; Peter seeks a call before it be given him. Nor yet be over-backward and diffident to own God, and the truths of God. As Paul taxed Peter for dissembling: Gal. ii. 12. When those false brethren were likely to bring great trouble, Peter dissembled, and runs with them, and separates himself from the purer sort of Christians, he is taxed there for it. We should not run into them without cause, nor yet be ashamed to own the ways of God, those which are most agreeable to his holy word. Not be solicitous so much about events as duties; for God is

far more concerned than we, and hath a greater interest than we can have. What is our interest, and the interest of our families and our children, to the great interest of God, the safety of his children, the safety of his glory, and cause of his church? Be not troubled about events, for all our business is to understand our duty, that we may not sin, but keep blameless in the hour of temptation.

Use. If temptations be a usual evil, wherewith we encounter in the present world, then—

First, We should not be dismayed at them.

Secondly, We should be prepared for them.

First, We should not be dismayed at them, as if some strange thing did befall us. When we enter into the lists with Satan, resist the devil. Why? 1 Pet. v. 9, ' For all those things are accomplished in your brethren that are in the flesh.' They are all troubled with a busy devil, a naughty world, and a corrupt heart! And why should we look for a total exemption, and to go to heaven in an unusual way?

That we may not be dismayed by temptation, I shall give you several considerations.

[1.] We took an oath to fight under Christ's banner. Baptism it is *sacramentum militare,* our military oath, which we took to fight in Christ's cause, against all the oppositions and difficulties we meet with in the world: 1 Pet. iii. 21. The apostle calls baptism ' The answer cf a good conscience towards God.' An answer supposeth a question. It is an allusion to the questions propounded by the catechist to the catechumen. When they came to desire baptism, they asked them, *Abrenuncias?* Dost thou renounce the world, the flesh, and the devil? And they answered, *Abrenuncio,* I do renounce them. So *Credis?* Dost thou believe in Jesus Christ with all thy heart? as Philip pro-pounds the question to the eunuch; and they answered, *Credo,* I do believe. Wilt thou undertake to walk in all holy obedience? and the answer is, I do undertake before God. Conscience, which is God's deputy, puts the question, in God's name, to those which take the seals of his covenant, Are you willing to renounce the flesh and worldly vanities? Will you cleave to God, and his ways, whatever they cost you? Whosoever makes this answer,, is supposed that he makes it knowingly, that he doth understand the difficulties of salvation, and what he must meet with in his way to heaven. So the apostle saith, ' You are not debtors to the flesh,' Rom. viii. 12. A man is a debtor to another, either by the obligation of some received benefit, or by his solemn promise and engagement; both are of use in that place. They that would seek the well-being of their souls, need not gratify the flesh. They that are engaged to walk after the Spirit, and come under the bond of a holy oath, and that are thus solemnly engaged, cannot expect to carry on the profession of godliness without conflicts and multiplied difficulties.

[2.] That is not the happiest condition which is most quiet and free from the temptations of Satan; for Luke xi. 21, ' When the strong man armed keepeth his palace, his goods are in peace.' When the devil hath quiet possession, he doth not trouble men. The sea must needs be smooth and calm when wind and tide go one way. There are some which suspect their condition, because of continual temptation; and others, because they have no temptation. Neither is a safe rule, for the time of our conflict may not yet be come. But if any have cause to suspect themselves, it is the last sort; for they that are least troubled may be most hurt; they are quiet and secure, because Satan hath got them into his snare, and hath a quiet dominion in their souls.

[3.] Jesus Christ himself was tempted, and therefore we should not be dismayed with temptations. Upon several accounts is this a comfort to us; partly, as it shows that we cannot look for an exemption, for the captain of our salvation was thus exercised, Heb. ii. 10. Be not disconsolate, it becomes good soldiers to follow their captain. We are to pledge him in this cup. *He* was tempted, therefore *we* shall be tempted. Partly and chiefly, because now he is more likely to pity us. It is said, Heb. ii. 18, 'Wherefore he is able to succour those that are tempted.' Jesus Christ hath felt the weight and trouble of temptations, therefore sure he will pity us if we lie under griefs and dangers; as a man that hath been shipwrecked himself is the more likely to pity others in their distress when they have lost all. One that knows evils by guess and imagination, knows them only at a distance, and doth not know how evil they are; but he that knows them by experience, he knows them at hand, and by such a smart sense as must needs leave a deep stroke and impression upon the soul. So Jesus Christ, that hath had an experimental knowledge, that knows the heart of a tempted man, can more feelingly succour those that are tempted; his heart becomes tender by experience; he knows the danger and troubles we are subject unto; therefore be not dismayed. And partly too, because by suffering this evil in his own person, he hath pulled out the sting of temptation. Christ sanctified every condition that he passed through; his being poor hath pulled out the sting of poverty. It is the more comfortable now to a godly {poor man, one that hath an interest in Christ. His dying hath pulled out the sting of death; so that what is to him a prison (Isa. liii. 8, 'He shall be taken from prison and from judgment') is to us a bed of ease: Isa. lvii. 2, 'They shall rest in their beds;' so his being tempted hath unstung temptations, and hath made them not so grievous. And partly too, as he hath directed us how to stand out, and with what kind of weapons to foil Satan. Christ, that is a pattern of doing and suffering, is also a pattern of resisting. He that left us an example of doing the will of God, and of suffering with meekness, and when he was reviled, reviled not again; so in resisting temptations hath he left us an example, hath taught us how to grapple with the devil, and in what manner to repress his temptation; therefore we should not be altogether dismayed.

[4.] Consider the comforts of the tempted. Abundantly hath God provided for his servants in their conflicts.

(1.) Jesus Christ, our general, the captain of our salvation, in whose quarrel we are engaged, hath overcome all our enemies, we are interested in his victory: John xvi. 33, 'In the world ye shall have tribulation; but be of good cheer, I have overcome the world.' We may have many pressing and searching troubles, but the sting of

them is gone. *Non pugna sublata est, sed victoria :* Christ hath not
taken away the combat, we must fight; but the victory is sure, he
hath overcome the world. This is our comfort when we are full of
faintings and fears, that all things are vanquished and overcome by
Christ; that though they terrify us, yet they shall not hurt us.
Though Christ will not exempt us from battle, yet we have to do with
the devil, the world, and death, which are all vanquished enemies.

(2.) He hath a tender sense and knowledge of our estate. Christ
saith to Peter, ' Satan hath a desire to have you, that he may sift you
as wheat; but I have prayed for thee, that thy faith fail not,' Luke
xxii. 32. Christ's love and mercy is never more at work for his people
than when they are most assaulted by Satan; then is he interceding for
them: John xiii. 1, 'Jesus having loved his own which were in the world,
he loved them unto the end.' When Christ was about to go to heaven,
he thought, My own are to be left in the world, they are exposed to
great temptation; and that set his heart a-work, as if he had said,
Poor creatures! they are undone if I help them not. So, Zech. iii. 1, 2,
' And he showed me Joshua, the high priest, standing before the
angel of the Lord, and Satan standing at his right hand to resist him.
And the Lord said unto Satan, The Lord rebuke thee, O Satan; even
the Lord that hath chosen Jesusalem rebuke thee: is not this a
brand plucked out of the fire?' 'And he showed me!' Our whole case
and danger it is clearly known to Christ. He knows how Satan
molests and troubles you in your approaches to God; how he seeks
to divert your thoughts, to weaken your confidence. We have a
friend and advocate that puts forth the strength of his mediation and
intercession, and is zealous and affectionate for the welfare of his
people. ' The Lord, that hath chosen Jerusalem, rebuke thee.'

(3.) He is engaged in the battle, and fights with us, by renewing
the strength of his own grace: Phil. iv. 13, ' I can do all things
through Christ which strengtheneth me.' He gives relief and help,
according to the nature of the conflict. If there be duty to be done,
burden to be borne, or battle to be fought, Christ is giving in supply.
As the olive-trees (Zech. iv. 11, 12) were always dropping into the
lamps, so is he dropping in strength and grace into the heart: Ps. xvi.
8, ' I have set the Lord always before me; because he is at my right
hand, I shall not be moved.' When a man hath an able second, he
doth with the more courage go to the conflict. God is on our right
hand, he is our second; his grace comes into the combat, and then the
field cannot be lost. If we would exercise faith in God we might be
the more confident.

(4.) He will reward us when we have done. Hold fast to the end,
and I will give thee a crown of life, a garland of immortality, that
shall never wither. If you will but hold out, continue to fight the
good fight of faith, there will a time of triumph come. He that is
now a soldier shall be a conqueror, when the crown of righteousness
shall be put upon his head, 2 Tim. iv. 8. And mark that: Rom. xvi.
20, ' And the God of peace shall bruise Satan under your feet shortly.'

It is troublesome to be in the world, but shortly God shall bruise
Satan. Mark, he doth not only say, God shall tread Satan, but tread
him under your feet, triumph over him. As Joshua called upon his

companions, Come set your feet upon the necks of these kings, when they were hid in the cave ; so the God of peace shall tread Satan under your feet shortly. Then your comfort will be greater, the more dangers you have gone through. As travellers, when they are come to their inn, and to their home, they sweetly remember the trouble and danger of the road ; so, when we are come to heaven, these temptations will increase our rejoicing, and our triumph in God.

(5.) Even before the battle a believer may be sure of victory. In other fights the event is uncertain. *Non æque glorietur accinctus, ac discinctus,* ' Let not him that girdeth on his harness boast himself as he that putteth it off,' 1 Kings xx. 11. When a field is won then they will rejoice. But a believer, when he goes to fight, is sure to have the best of it beforehand, *in bello,* the war, though not *in prælio,* the particular conflict. Why ? Because the Father and Jesus Christ are stronger than all his enemies ; they cannot pluck the believer out of his hands : John x. 28, 29, ' I give to them eternal life, and they shall never perish, neither shall any pluck them out of my hand. My Father, which gave them me, is greater than all ; and none is able to pluck them out of my Father's hand.' This is the privilege which Christ conferreth upon his sheep, upon those which have an interest in him ; though they have many shakings and tossings in their condition, yet their final perseverance is certain. Christ is so unchangeable in the purposes of his love, ' I will give to them eternal life ;' and so invincible in the power of his grace, ' None shall pluck them out of my Father's hand ;' nothing shall be able to hinder their perseverance. Now, though the fight be long and troublesome, yet this is one of God's encouragements, you are sure of victory at last. Therefore how much doth it concern us to get an interest in Christ, that we may keep on in this way and in this hope.

Secondly, Let us be provided and prepared against temptations. And to this end I shall—

First, Give some directions how to resist temptations in general.

Secondly, What to do in a special hour of temptation which comes upon the world :—

When there are terrors without, and we know not what evil may be a-coming, and our hearts are full of doubt, how we may support and bear up ourselves.

First, To direct you as to temptations in general.

[1.] You must be completely armed : Eph. vi. 11, ' Put on the whole armour of God, that ye may be able to stand against the wiles of the devil.' Not a piece only, but the whole armour of God, otherwise you will never come off with honour and safety from the spiritual conflict. The poets feign of their Achilles that he was vulnerable only in the heel, and there he got his death-wound. A Christian, though he be never so well furnished in other parts, yet if any part be left naked, you are in danger. Our first parents were wounded in their heel. Who would have thought, that they which had such vast knowledge of God and his creatures, that they should be enticed by appetite ? And Solomon, who had the upper part of his soul so well guarded, that he should be enticed by women ? To see men of great knowledge to be unmortified and miscarry by their sensual appetite, is sad.

A Christian must have no saving grace wanting: 2 Pet. i. 5, 'Add to your faith, virtue; and to virtue, knowledge,' &c. There is all the graces, and they must come out in their turn. We need faith and virtue, zeal and holiness; and knowledge to guide it, and patience to arm it against the troubles of the present life; and we need temperance to moderate our affections to our worldly enjoyments; and godliness, that we may be frequent in communion with God; and brotherly-kindness, that we may preserve peace among our brethren, and may not make fractions and ruptures in the church; and we need charity, that we may be useful to all that are about us. There is use and work for all graces, one time or other: sometimes we shall be tempted to a neglect of God, at other times we shall be tempted to make a breach upon brotherly-kindness, at other times there will be a breach of charity. Sometimes the devil seeks to tempt us to fleshly wickedness, therefore we need temperance; sometimes to spiritual wickedness, to error, therefore we need knowledge; sometimes to raging with despair, then we need faith. We need the whole armour of God, for Satan hath his various ways of battery and assault: sometimes through ignorance we miscarry and run into error; sometimes for want of faith we run into despair and discomfort; sometimes for want of temperance violent corrupt lusts overset the soul.

[2.] We must often pray to God for renewed influences; we must not only get habits of grace, but pray for a renewed influence. It is notable, next to the spiritual armour, the apostle mentioneth prayer: Eph. vi. 18, 'Praying always with all prayer and supplication in the Spirit, and watching thereunto with all perseverance.' We never receive so much from God upon earth as to stand in need of no more. And therefore though you put on the whole armour of God, yet 'praying always with all supplication in the Spirit.' Why? Because without the Lord's special assistance, whereby he actuates those graces, we can never defend ourselves nor offend the adversaries, or do anything to purpose in the spiritual life. Strength of grace inherent will not bear us out against new assaults. Habitual grace it needs actual influence; partly, that these graces may be applied and excited to work: Phil. ii. 13, 'He giveth to will and to do.' God giveth to do; that is, excites that strength you have, and carrieth it out to work; and then that it may be directed in work: 2 Thes. iii. 5, 'And the Lord direct your hearts into the love of God, and into the patient waiting for Christ.' Every time we would make use of the helmet of salvation, when we would lift up the head and wait for the mercy of God. The Lord direct you; we must be directed: and not only so, but that it may be supplied with new strength, for it is said, Isa. xl. 29, 'He giveth power to the faint, and to them that have no power he increaseth strength.' And he doth continue it: Luke xxii. 32, 'I have prayed for thee, that thy faith fail not.' Thus will God keep us in dependence for those liberal aids and constant supplies of his grace, without which we cannot use the grace that we have.

[3.] You must resist: 1 Pet. v. 9, 'Whom resist, steadfast in the faith;' James iv. 7, 'Resist the devil, and he will flee from you.' Stand your ground, and then Satan falls.

In all those assaults, Satan hath only weapons offensive, as fiery darts; none defensive. We have not only the sword of the Spirit, which is an offensive weapon, but the shield of faith, that is a de-fensive piece of armour; therefore your safety lieth in resisting.

Now, this resistance must be :—

(1.) Not faint and cold, but strong and vehement.

(2.) Thorough and total.

(3.) Constant and perpetual.

(1.) Not faint and cold. Some kind of resistance may be made by general and common grace. The light of nature will rise up in defiance of many sins, especially at first; but this must be earnest and vehement; it is against the enemies of your soul. Paul's resist-ance was with serious dislikes and deep groans: Rom. vii. 15, 24, ' The evil that I hate;' and ' O wretched man! how shall I be de-livered?' In most cases, a detestation or peremptory denial is enough. When the devil tempts Christ to worship him: Mat. iv. 10, ' Get thee behind me, Satan.' In other cases, there must be serious dis-putes and repulses. When Eve speaks faintly and coldly, the devil renews his assaults with more violence: Gen. iii. 1–3, ' Hath God said, Ye shall not eat of every tree of the garden? And the woman said unto the serpent, We may eat of the fruit of the trees of the garden; but of the fruit of the tree which is in the midst of the garden, God hath said, Ye shall not eat of it, neither shall ye touch it, lest ye die.' She speaks there warmly, and with too impatient a re-sentment of the restraint, and too cold in the commination and threatening. Therefore the devil works upon her, when he saw she amplifieth the restraint; for she saith more indeed : ' We must neither eat nor touch it.' A faint denial is a kind of grant, and therefore your repulse to Satan must be vehement and strong. In many cases, slight Satan—answer with indignation; as though a dog barks, yet the traveller goes by: Satan cannot endure contempt. At other times, argue for God strongly. Now, the great argument that quickens you to this lively and vehement resistance is, to consider thy soul is in danger, and all thy eternal concernments. So some ex-pound that, Eph. vi. 12, ' We fight not against flesh and blood, but against spiritual wickedness in high places;' in ' heavenly places ' it is in the original. No worldly concernments must go so near as that which concerns the eternal good and salvation of your souls. What would the devil have from thee but thy soul and thy precious enjoy-ments, thy peace of conscience, communion with God, thy hopes of eternal life? And when Satan comes, and bids nothing but worldly vanities, we should repel them with indignation. A merchant that hath a precious commodity, and a chapman bids him a base price, he puts up his wares with indignation, and will not so much as regard him or hear him; so when the devil comes, and would cheat you of your precious enjoyments, you should repel him with indignation, when there is such base and unworthy trifles to come in competition with your great hopes: as Christ, Mat. xvi. 26, ' What is a man profited if he shall gain the whole world and lose his soul? or what shall a man give in exchange for his soul?' What! shall I lose my soul, my hopes, and happiness and all for such paltry things, for a little temporal advantage?

(2.) It must be a thorough and total resistance: when you yield, the devil encroacheth upon you. We are bid, in the Canticles, to 'take the little foxes,' to dash Babylon's brats in pieces: we should not yield to Satan a little. The devil at first cannot hope to prevail for greater things, therefore he seems more modest in his temptations; ay, but lesser sticks set the greater on fire: when ye entertain lesser temptations, this kindles in your souls, and it is easily blown up into a great flame in your conscience. At first, when the devil came to our first parents, 'Hath God said?' and then, 'You shall not surely die.' 'Hath God said you shall not eat of the fruit of the garden?' The first temptation was more modest. The approaches of Satan to the soul are gradual—he asks but a little; ay, but it is a great matter if we grant it. Consider, the evil of temptation is better *kept* out than *got* out. The stone on the top of the hill, when it begins to roll downward, it is a hard thing to stay it; we cannot say how far it will go. Saith the deceived heart, I will yield but little, and never yield again. The devil will carry thee further and further, until he hath left no tenderness in thy conscience. As many that thought to venture but a shilling or two, yet, by the secret witchery of gaming, they play away their estate, clothes and all; so many that think they will sin but little at first, at last sin away all principles of conscience and profession of godliness.

(3.) It must not be temporary, for a while, but perpetual. It concerns us not only to stand out against the first assault of Satan, but a long siege. Satan, what he cannot gain by argument, seeks to procure by importunity. But 'resist him,' saith the apostle, 'steadfastly in the faith,' 1 Pet. v. 9. As his instrument spake to Joseph, 'from day to day,' she ceased not, Gen. xxxix. 10. Deformed objects, when accustomed to them, seem not so odious; so the devil hopes to prevail at last, at least temptation will not seem so odious. But you must keep your zeal to the last, as we rate away an importunate beggar that will not be answered: to yield at last is to lose the glory of the conflict. Grace must not only have its work, but 'its perfect work,' James i. 4; so let all our graces, temperance, godliness, and brotherly kindness, have their perfect work.

[4.] There is required watchfulness: 1 Pet. v. 8, 'Be sober, be vigilant.' You that are not ignorant of Satan's devices should watch that you give not him an advantage, 2 Cor. ii. 11; nor an occasion, 2 Cor. xi. 12, lest Satan tempt you; nor a pretence, Gal. v. 13, to the flesh. Certainly, he that would not be foiled needs a great deal of holy moderation, and constant jealousy over his heart; he had need to guard his senses: Ps. cxix. 37, 'Turn away mine eyes from beholding vanity;' and to look to his company: Ps. cxix. 115, 'Depart from me, ye evil-doers, for I will keep the commandments of my God;' and to avoid all occasions of sin, not rush into them, but keep out of the way: Prov. iv. 14, 'Enter not into the path of the wicked, and go not in the way of evil men;' for this is to ride into the devil's quarters, to run into the mouth of danger. Heretofore these were wholesome instructions, and why should they not be so now? The devil is not less subtle, or sin less odious and dangerous; only we are more foolhardy, therefore stand not at such a distance as we should

from occasions. It is easier to avoid the occasion than the sin when
occasion is offered; as it is easier for a bird to fly from the snare than,
when entangled, to avoid danger.   Therefore, when you run into
harm's way, you tempt Satan to tempt; and when you look not to
yourselves, it is just with God to let you fall into the snare.

Secondly, There are special times of temptation, when Christians
should look to themselves.   There is an *evil day :* Eph. vi. 13, ' That
ye may be able to stand in the evil day.'   And there is an *hour* of
temptation upon the world: Rev. iii. 10, 'I will keep thee from the
hour of temptation which shall come upon all the world.'   There are
certain times when God is proving what men will do, and when the
devil is likely to make a great advantage of our discontents and afflictions, when things fall cross to our desires, and we know not what evil
waits for us ; how should we do to behave ourselves ?

[1.] Be not over-confident or over-diffident. Not over-confident, in
running beyond the bounds of our calling, to cast ourselves into dangers
and hazards of temptation.   Nor over-diffident, by base flying from, or
giving way when God calls for valiant resistance.   Both ways is the
devil likely to assault us; either by making us foolhardy. So Satan
seeks to drive us beyond the bounds of our calling, to put us out of
our place, that we may be a prey to him.   As men use to trouble the
water, that they may rouse the fish, and draw them into the snare,
and drive them out of places of safety where they rest; so the devil
seeks to put us out of our safety.   Peter would needs come to Christ :
Mat. xiv. 28, ' Lord, if it be thou, bid me come unto thee on the
water ; ' and we see he sinks before he could accomplish his purpose.
So when we are over-confident, and run out of our calling upon hazards,
then we are ever and anon ready to sink.   But we should not turn
back when God calls us to a valiant resistance : ' Should such a man
as I flee ? ' Neh. vi. 11.   Observe Peter's dastardliness when he ven-
tures without a call into the priest's hall ; a question of the damsel's
overturns him.   He that was so cowardly when he was out of his way,
look upon his boldness when he was in his work : Acts iv. 7 unto ver.
13, ' When they saw the boldness of Peter and John, they marvelled.'
John was the disciple of love, and Peter was the fearful disciple; yet
how full of boldness, courage, and zeal when they were called and
singled out to give proof of the reality of God's grace !   And therefore
we should never be over-forward, nor over-backward, but own God in
his truth when we are in our calling.   Let not Satan bring you out of
your place to cast yourselves as a prey to him.

[2.] In an hour of temptation, we should be more solicitous about
duties than events, and about sins than dangers.   As to events, God
is concerned as well as you, and he will order them for his own glory.
It should be your great care that you may be kept blameless to his
heavenly kingdom : 2 Tim. iv. 17, 18, ' The Lord, that hath delivered
me out of the mouth of the lion, shall deliver me from every evil
work, and will preserve me unto his heavenly kingdom.'   However
God deal with you as to events, and whatever dangers attend you, this
should be your care mainly, that you may not sin, but be kept blameless.   David often begged direction, that he might be guided in his
trouble, and not falter, and do anything unseemly.

[3.] Be more jealous of Satan's wiles than of his open assaults.
Natural courage, and the bravery of a common and ordinary resolution, together with deep engagement of credit and interest, may do
much to make us stand out against assaults, against open force and
violence of evil men ; but there needs a great deal of judgment to
stand out against the wiles and crafts of the devil. Flesh and blood
will not so easily bear us out against the secret ensnarings of the
heart. The young prophet doth thunder out his message against the
king, 1 Kings xiii. 3, yet was enticed by the wiles of the old prophet.
So we may stand out against an open assault and apparent violence,
but take heed of the secret wiles of Satan.

[4.] The wiles of Satan are to enforce and draw us into those corruptions which are incident to the season. Here is the great point of
spiritual wisdom, to be seasoned in our mortification, and to withstand
the spiritual evil that is apt to grow upon us in the time of our fears :
Ps. lvi. 3, ' What time I am afraid, I will trust in thee.' Then our
great business is, to cherish our dependence upon God, to prevent
distrust and unbelieving thoughts of God's providence. As, on the
other side, in a time when we are likely to be corrupted with ease and
prosperity, then our business is to watch against security and deadness
of heart, which is apt to grow upon us. As Nazianzen said, When
things go prosperous with me, I read the Lamentations of Jeremiah,
I remember the mournful passages which befall the people of God,
and that is my cure. So to prevent despondency in a time of fears,
to encourage our souls to dependence.

Now, when our wills are crossed, dangers attend us on every side,
and we know not how far evil will break out to the overturning of all.
What are the sins incident to such a time of trouble ? and how do the
wiles of Satan come upon us ?

(1.) Impatience : Gen. xxx. 1, when the will of Rachel was crossed,
she said unto Jacob, ' Give me children, or else I die.' When we im-
patiently fret against the Lord : Ps. xxxvii. 1, ' Fret not thyself
because of evil-doers; neither be thou envious against the workers of
iniquity.'

(2.) Murmuring and repining against the Lord, that is another
snare : Jonah iv. 9, ' I do well to be angry, even unto death;' when
he was crossed. Discontent at God's providence gratifieth Satan
exceedingly ; when we will justify ourselves, and think it a kind of
zeal to be angry, and pet against providence.

(3.) A spirit of revenge against instruments, when we do not sweetly
calm the heart with the remembrance of God's hand : 2 Sam. xvi. 9,
' Why should this dead dog curse my lord the king ? Let me go over,
I pray thee, and take off his head.' Thus when wicked men disturb
order, the heart is apt to rise in revenge, therefore we are to calm our
hearts.

(4.) There is fainting in duty ; when we begin to give over prayer,
and are discouraged, and are loth to wrestle with God in an ordinance :
Heb. xii. 12, ' Lift up the hands which hang down, and the feeble
knees.' When a man's hands begin to wax feeble, and he is discouraged in the ways of the Lord : ' My foot had well-nigh slipped,'
saith David, Ps. lxxiii. 2.

(5.) There is closing with sinful means, and running to them for an escape; as Saul, when he was crossed : 1 Sam. xxviii. 7, ' Seek me a woman that hath a familiar spirit, that I may go to her, and inquire of her.' When we go to carnal shifts, and unworthy means, these are very natural to us.

(6.) Despair and distrustful thoughts of God, though we have had much experience of his goodness. David, 1 Sam. xxvii. 1, ' I shall now perish one day by the hand of Saul,' after all his experience.

(7.) Questioning our interest in God, by reason of crosses, or the doubtful posture of our affairs: Judges vi. 13, ' If the Lord be with us, why then is all this befallen us ? '

These are the wiles of Satan. Ride out the storm upon gospel encouragements. This will bear us up, it is but a moment to eternity. It is but ' a light affliction, and will work for us a far more exceeding and eternal weight of glory,' 2 Cor. iv. 17.

The second point is this:—

Doct. 2. That if we would not be overcome by the evil of temptations, we should earnestly deal with God about them.

For so doth our Lord direct us here (' Lead us not into temptation ') to come to God himself.

There are two reasons I shall consider of in this discourse :—

First, We cannot be tempted without the will of God.

Secondly, Nor resist without the power of God.

Therefore we should deal with God earnestly in all our temptations.

First, We cannot be tempted without the will of God. That God hath a providence in and about temptations, is clear from the scripture : Mat. iv. 1, ' Then was Jesus led up of the Spirit into the wilderness, to be tempted of the devil.' The Holy Spirit had a hand in it, as well as the evil spirit. So, 2 Sam. xxiv. 1, ' God moved David to number Israel and Judah;' but in 1 Chron. xxi. 1, it is said, ' And Satan stood up against Israel, and provoked David to number Israel.' Satan, he cannot tempt without leave from God. As a lion cannot stir out of his cage, until the keeper brings him out, so the devil, this roaring lion, is held by the irresistible chains of God's providence, and cannot stir until God brings him out.

Consider two things :—

[1.] To be led into temptation is more than simply to be tempted. God's permitting us to be tempted is not so much as God's leading us into temptation, for these are two distinct phrases. God may permit or suffer us to be tempted, as a lord or sovereign, which hath power over his own creature, for the trial and exercise of grace, and can absolutely dispose of it according to his own will; but he leads us into temptation as a judge. And therefore this is one of the comforts which Job propounds to himself, when Satan had a liberty to molest him : Job ix. 12, ' He taketh away, who can hinder him ? who shall say unto him, What doest thou ? ' The general of an army may, according to his discretion, lead which band he pleaseth, and set them in the forlorn hope, in a place of the greatest danger, and appoint for reserves which part of the army he pleaseth. So God may single out his champions to combat for his glory, and may leave others in a more quiet posture, according as he pleaseth. Thus, as a sovereign agent, God may suffer to be tempted. But now, to lead into temptation, that is another thing, and implieth something of punishment, or as it is expressed, Mat. xxvi. 41, 'Pray that ye enter not into temptation.' We enter into it by our own voluntary motion, as having forfeited his protection. But then God leads us in as a judge, puts the malefactor into the executioner's or officer's hands : so doth God lead us into temptation ; it is a judicial act, especially when left to perish under the weight of a temptation.

[2.] Consider God as a judge ; he may lead us into temptation two ways : either he may act in way of correction, to manifest his fatherly indignation ; or by way of strict punishment. And so, in respect of his fatherly correction, God may give us up to a vexing, or to an ensnaring temptation. He may lead the godly into temptation, that they may be molested and troubled ; and may lead the wicked into temptation, that they may be seduced and led away for their eternal ruin. There is a vexing temptation God useth for the correction of his own children ; and thus Paul was buffeted by Satan, lest he should be exalted above measure : 2 Cor. xii. 7. The shepherd sets his dog upon the strayed sheep, not to worry him, but to lodge him, and bring him back again into the fold : so doth God suffer his children to be buffeted and exercised by Satan, to their great trouble, but for their good in the issue ; for he knoweth how to turn all these things for good. Then there is an ensnaring temptation, by which the wicked are entangled in a way of sin ; and so Satan, as God's executioner, is said sometimes to blind the eyes of wicked men, lest the light of the glorious gospel of Christ should shine unto them, 2 Cor. iv. 4 ; and sometimes to harden their hearts, John xii. 40, 'lest they should be converted and healed.' For the punishment of former sins, God may give up the wicked to be blinded and hardened by Satan to their own destruction, which is one of the most dreadful acts of God, as a judge, on this side hell.

Certainly then, when we are tempted, we have great cause to deal with God about the temptation, for he hath a hand : either he may suffer us to be tempted, as lord and sovereign ; or may lead us into temptation, either in a way of fatherly correction, or as a mere punishment, that we may more ruin and destroy ourselves.

I come now to the second reason.

Secondly, God alone can give strength to resist and overcome the temptation ; and therefore we should deal with him very earnestly about it : Rom. xvi. 20, 'The God of peace shall bruise Satan under your feet shortly.' It is *God* that treads down Satan, but under *your* feet. We fight it out, but the author of the victory is the God of peace. We are interested in it (for we trample upon Satan with our own feet), but God's is the grace. Our faculties are not only exercised, but our graces.

Briefly, two ways doth God concur with the saints in resisting temptations.

First, God plants all those graces in their hearts that are necessary to the conflict. To speak of those three essential graces, faith, fear, and love ; these are all necessary for the resistance of a temptation.

That faith is necessary, 1 Pet. v. 9, 'Whom resist, steadfast in the faith.' And fear and love, that they also are necessary, I shall prove thus : Satan's weapons against us, and his way of assaulting, are either subtile wiles or fiery darts : 'That ye may be able to stand against the wiles of the devil, and quench all the fiery darts of the wicked,' Eph. vi. 11, 16. As he assaults us by fiery darts, by raging and boisterous temptations, take the shield of faith, cover all with the righteousness of Christ, and with a sense of your privileges by Christ, and that is it which maintains the heart, and keeps it against the fiery darts of the devil. But as he assaults us by his wiles, there fear and the love of God comes in, and is necessary for us. For there are two sorts of wiles that Satan useth for the destroying of our souls : one is, to convey the temptation by such means as are most taking with the person tempted ; and the other is, disguising and turning himself into an angel of light, colouring the temptation.

For the first, namely, as he suiteth every distemper of our souls with a proper diet or food, or tempts us by such means as are likely to prevail, as if a man were tempted by sensual delight ; there the love of God is necessary. Why ? For nothing but the love of God will make us deny that which is so near and pleasing to us, or that affection which grows upon the apprehension of his grace in Christ ; therefore the grace of God is said to teach us to 'deny all ungodliness and worldly lusts :' Titus ii. 12.

[2.] For the other wile. As Satan doth transform himself into an angel of light, and cover his base designs with plausible pretences ; for instance, revenge shall be accounted zeal ; he will disguise it so as that the very apostles shall count it zeal for the glory of God when they called for 'fire from heaven to consume them, even as Elias did :' Luke ix. 54. And carnal counsel shall be counted pity and natural affection : Mat. xvi. 22, 'Peter took him and began to rebuke him, saying, Be it far from thee, Lord : this shall not be unto thee.' He shall be the devil's agent to tempt Christ, and his carnal counsel shall be looked upon as pity to his Master. And licentiousness shall be Christian liberty, and our liberty by Christ shall be used as an occasion to the flesh : Gal. v. 13. And an immoderate use of carnal pleasure shall be Christian rejoicing or Christian cheerfulness. Therefore, as there needs love to withstand the potency of temptation, by the suitableness of the bait to our own affections, so there needs the fear of God : Prov. xiv. 27, 'The fear of the Lord is a fountain of life, to depart from the snares of death.' When the devil, by his wiles, is laying snares for us, snares of death, the fear of the Lord is a fountain of life. A man that is afraid to offend God, and to abuse his liberty, or run into any excess, under colour of grace, is very cautious and watchful, and thereby is not so soon surprised. Thus, when the soul is inflamed by the vehement heat of boiling lusts, or raging despair, faith is necessary : Luke xxii. 31, 32, 'Satan hath desired to have you, that he may sift you as wheat ; but I have prayed for thee, that thy faith fail not.' Faith laying hold upon Christ's righteousness, and waiting for his grace, teaches us to overcome in such conflicts.

But why should I instance in these three graces only, when we are bidden to 'put on the whole armour of God'? Eph. vi. 11, 13. If we would come off with honour in this conflict, we must be completely armed; no power of the soul or sense of the body must be left naked and without a guard, therefore not one saving grace can be wanting.

A Christian is set forth as armed from head to foot. There is for the head a helmet of salvation, which is hope; a breastplate of righteousness; the girdle of truth; for shoes, the gospel of peace; the shield of faith; the sword of the Spirit. These are the graces necessary to resist temptation, and these we have from God. A Christian hath not only weapons offensive, but defensive; not only a sword, but also a shield. Satan hath only weapons offensive, as darts; he hath darts to wound the soul. Again, observe, there is no piece of armour for the back. Why? Because there is no flight in this spiritual warfare; we must stand to it: James iv. 7, 'Resist the devil, and he will flee from you.'

But let us see what are the pieces of the spiritual armour. The apostle begins with 'the girdle of truth,' by which is meant, not truth of doctrine (for that is the sword of the Spirit), but sincerity, or an honest intention; when a man endeavoureth to be both to God and man what he seems to be. Now, it is the Lord that must renew the right spirit within us. Satan he assaults us with wiles, but our armour of proof against him is the girdle of truth. We stand against the wiles of Satan, but we must not fight against him with his own weapons, and put off wiles with wiles; sincerity and honest intention, that is our strength; this is the girdle to the loins, it gives strength and courage to the soul. And then there is 'the breastplate of righteousness,' or that grace which puts us upon a holy conversation, suitable to God's will revealed in his word, whereby we endeavour to give God and man their due; it secures the breast and vital parts, the seed of inherent grace in the heart; an honest fixed purpose to obey God in all things. The next thing, the feet must be shod; we shall meet with rough ways in our passage to heaven, and what is that which is armour of proof for our feet? 'The preparation of the gospel of peace,' a sense of our peace and friendship made up between God and us through Christ. Without this we shall never follow God in the way of duty when we meet with difficulties and hardships, But 'above all, take the shield of faith.' A shield covers the body, but that which gives defence to all is faith: without this a man is naked. Destitute of Christ's imputed righteousness, he wants his covenant-strength; it applieth Christ's righteousness, and engageth the power of God on our behalf. Then there is 'the helmet of salvation,' which is hope: 1 Thes. v. 8. A well-grounded hope of salvation, it makes us hold up the head in the midst of all waves and sore assaults; that is, it is our great motive and encouragement in the work of sanctification. Then there is 'the sword of the Spirit,' which is both offensive and defensive; it wardeth off Satan's blows, and makes him fly back from us as one wounded and ashamed. These are the graces. Now God gives them to us, and therefore he is called 'The God of all grace,' 1 Pet. v. 10. Why? because he requires it only? No, but because he giveth it also. And it is called 'The armour of God,' ver. 11. God is the author, God is the maker, God is the inventor of this armour, and he doth freely bestow it upon us. The apostle bids us 'take the whole armour of God,' ver. 13, that is, take it out of God's hand. This armour is not of our making and procuring, but made to our hands by God himself.

Secondly, He actuates these graces by putting good motions into our hearts, or sweet and gracious thoughts, whereby all the fore-mentioned graces are drawn out. When we are conflicting with sin in an hour of temptation, faith is set a-work: 'That God may fulfil all the good pleasure of his goodness, and the work of faith with power,' 2 Thes. i. 11; that is, by a divine power and influence quickening it into acts. Joseph, when he was assaulted by a grievous temptation, he had a gracious motion and thought put into his mind: 'How can I do this wickedness, and sin against God?' Gen. xxxix. 9. Still there is a seasonable remembrance of things by the Spirit, whose office it is to bring all things to remembrance: John xiv. 26. The Spirit doth 'not only teach us all things, but brings things to our remembrance, when we have need of any truth to be set home upon the heart; either such a truth as forbids the evil to which we are tempted, or that speaketh comfort and encouragement to us under such a cross; or pressing such a duty as we hang off from. The seasonable remembrance of truths is the great actual help which we have from God. Jesus Christ himself, by seasonable urging the scriptures, defeated the temptation wherewith he was assaulted: Mat. iv. 10, 11. The word quickeneth in affliction: Ps. cxix. 50. Some proper comfort is borne in upon the soul by the power of God. It is not the bare remembrance of truth, but the secret power of God which enliveneth it, and makes it effectual in its season to defeat the temptation.

Use. It directs you what to do in temptations, to go to God for help and strength against them. Briefly, when you treat with God, it should be under a threefold notion :—

1. As the author and giver of grace.

2. As the sovereign giver and disposer of it, according to his own will.

3. As a judge, by temptation correcting some foregoing sin by the present temptation.

1. Treat with God as the author and giver of grace: James i. 17, 'He is the father of lights, from whom every good and perfect gift cometh down.' And so—

[1.] We ought to come to him as renouncing our strength, and waiting for his grace as able to help us. That address Jehoshaphat made in a temporal case is good also in a spiritual: 2 Chron. xx. 12, 'Lord, we have no might; our eyes are unto thee.' There is a renouncing of their own strength, and a dependence upon God. There must be a renouncing of all self-dependence, for God 'gives grace to the humble,' James iv. 6. The word *humble* is to be understood not morally, to those that are of a lowly carriage towards men, of a meek spirit; but it is understood spiritually, of those that, in the brokenness of their hearts, acknowledge their own nothingness and weakness: to these he gives grace. God withholdeth and withdraweth his influences when we do not acknowledge the daily and hourly necessity of grace—when we do not desire it with such vehemency as we were wont, nor receive it with such thankfulness and rejoicing. In these three last petitions of the Lord's Prayer: 'Give us this day our daily bread;' then, 'Forgive us our trespasses;' then, 'Lead us not into temptation:' we beg daily bread, daily pardon, daily strength. We can neither live without the one nor the other: we cannot *live* without daily bread, nor live *comfortably* without daily pardon, nor live *holily* without daily grace. And therefore you are to 'wait upon God all the day,' Ps. xxv. 5; and Ps. xvi. 8, 'I have set the Lord always before me.' Now, we may be said to set the Lord before us, either in point of reverence, when we are sensible of his eye and presence, or in point of dependence, when we are still waiting for his strength; and that is the meaning there, 'He is at my right hand, I shall not be moved.' Look, as a glass without a foot falls to the ground, and is broken as soon as it is set out of hand, such a sensible Christian apprehends himself to be if he be out of the hands of God; he is broken, and falls to pieces. Therefore, in this sense, he goes to God, and desires him to keep him from temptation. Dependence begets observance. If the creature could once but live of himself, though it were but for a while, God would seldom hear from him. This is that which is the bridle upon the new creature, to keep up his constant commerce with God.

[2.] We must go to him with confidence, in an actual dependence upon the all-sufficiency of his grace. It is not enough to apprehend our weakness, but we must also go forth in the strength of God; that is, hold up our hearts with a sense of this, that God is able to bear us up, and defeat all our spiritual enemies. God would not take off the temptation from Paul, 2 Cor. xii. 9, but saith, 'My grace is sufficient for thee.' He can either weaken temptation, or give in further supply of strength; therefore encourage yourselves in the power of the Lord. The devil cannot tempt us one jot further than the Lord will permit him; his malice is limited and restrained: if you be in Satan's hands, Satan is in God's hands, and can do nothing without his leave and permission; he begs leave to enter into the herd of swine, much less can he enter into the sheep of his pasture.

2. Look upon God, not only as the giver of grace, but as the sovereign giver and disposer of it according to his own will: Phil. ii. 13, 'It is God that worketh in you both to will and to do of his good pleasure.' His giving of grace is altogether free, as what measure of assistance we shall have, and by what means it shall be supplied. God may enlarge or abate the degree of his influence, according to his own will. Now, thus we must come to him, with submission to his good pleasure, either for taking off the temptation, or continuing it for your exercise, or the measure of your supply. When you murmur and fret, it is a sign you have too good thoughts of yourselves; when we prescribe to God, it argues some ascribing to ourselves. You are to endeavour, indeed, to pray, and use all good means to come out of temptation; but submit, if the Lord be pleased to continue his exercise upon you. Nay, though God should continue the temptation, and for the present not give out those measures of grace necessary for you, yet you must not murmur, but lie at his feet; for God is Lord of his own grace.

3. You are to look upon God as a judge, correcting some foregoing sin by your present temptation. And therefore—

[1.] You must humble yourselves under his mighty hand, when you are exercised with great and sore temptations, and accept the punishment of your iniquity without murmuring; that is the only way to get it off, when you own it as the fruit of sin: Lev. xxvi. 41, 'If then their uncircumcised hearts be humbled, and they then accept of the punishment of their iniquity;' and Micah vii. 9, 'I will bear the indignation of the Lord, because I have sinned against him.' Acknowledge the justice of his providence in this trouble that is brought upon you. A Christian must not only look to the malice of Satan in his temptations, but to the justice of God. Look, as in outward afflictions, we are not to reflect upon instruments:—Job did not say, 'The Chaldean and Sabean hath taken,' but 'The Lord hath taken,' chap. i. 23—so in these spiritual afflictions, take the temptation out of God's hand, as a judge. Though Satan pursue you with fiery darts, with temptations horrible and terrible, yet look upon it as the fruit of some foregoing sin. If he should tempt you by injection of despairing fears or blasphemous thoughts, these are not your sins, but they may be a punishment for your sins; so you ought to humble yourselves under the mighty hand of God. When you are vexed with such temptations as pierce and prick you in your veins, as David speaks; when the devil bears in blasphemous thoughts upon the heart, they are his sins, but your corrections, justly ordered by God. It may be it is for the correction of your sin that you have provoked God to afflict you thus; and this rod, if it smart, it was dipped in your own guilt, and it is a fruit of God's fatherly indignation for your folly and vanity; for God may thus manifest it, by giving thee up to this severe discipline, to be tempted and vexed by Satan. Now, it is your duty to be sensible of your sin, and say, as Sion in her troubles, Lam. i. 18, 'The Lord is righteous, for I have rebelled against his commandment.'

[2.] Find out and remove the cause of sin, when God lets loose Satan upon us. Paul discerned it presently—as usually God's rod brings light along with it—when he was buffeted with a messenger of Satan; it was that he might not be 'exalted above measure,' 2 Cor. xii. 7. Now that which hath provoked God to exercise us with this discipline, that may be known sometimes by the time when this temptation surpriseth us: if it tread upon the heels of some immediate and foregoing provocation—that is the sin you should humble yourselves for; or by that ill frame and posture of spirit wherein the temptation found you, as Paul's heart was likely puffed up and exalted with his spiritual enjoyments; therefore God lets loose Satan. Sometimes by the nature of the temptation itself, for God suits punishments to sins, and apt and proper remedies to every disease; or else the sin will be cast up by workings of conscience in a way of remorse, as in a tempest that which is at bottom comes on top; or God will discover it by his Spirit, when you go and seek to him. When temptation is grievous and sore, go to God and say, Lord, why is it thus with me? Job xxxiv. 31, 32, 'Surely it is meet to be said unto God, I have borne chastisement, I will not offend any more. That which I see not, teach thou me; if I have done iniquity, I will do no more.' Pray for a discovery of your secret sin, and what is the mind of God in the dispensation. Now, when you have found out the cause of the sin, this is the direction, to remove the cause; for until we let the sin go, God will continue the punishment; though we strive, pray, and ask counsel, our burden will still be continued upon us, until sin be mortified in us, though in some measure it be removed out of our hearts.

But deliver us from evil.

WE come to the close. The words ἀπὸ τοῦ πονηροῦ may be rendered, either 'from the *evil one*,' or 'from the *evil thing*.'

First, From the evil one: Mat. xiii. 19, 'Then cometh, ὁ πονηρὸς, *the evil one*, and catcheth away that which was sown in his heart;' and 1 John ii. 13, 'I will write unto you, young men, because ye have overcome, τον πονηρὸν, *the wicked one* ;' and 1 John v. 18, 'He that is begotten of God keepeth himself, and, ὁ πονηρὸς, *that wicked one*, toucheth him not;' Eph. vi. 16, 'Take the shield of faith, wherewith ye shall be able to quench all the fiery darts of *the wicked*,' τοῦ πονηροῦ, of that wicked one. In all these places the devil is so called, because his great business is to draw, and drive others to sin; and therefore, as God is 'the holy one,' so Satan is called 'the wicked one.'

Secondly, It may be rendered that *evil thing* : Mat. v. 37, 'Whatsoever is more than these cometh, ἐκ τοῦ πονηροῦ, *of evil;*' Mat. v. 39, 'But I say unto you, μὴ ἀντιστῆναι τῷ πονηρῷ, resist not evil.' We are commanded to resist the devil, and therefore in that place clearly it is put for the evil thing; and so in many other places. Now which of these senses shall we prefer?

First, If it be meant of the evil one, or Satan, the words will bear a good sense, thus: If God, for our trial and further humiliation, shall suffer us to be tempted by the devil, yet we desire that he may not have his will upon us, that we be not kept under his power.

To make good this interpretation, know the devil may fitly be called 'the evil one,' for he is the oldest sinner; he sins from the beginning: 1 John iii. 8. And he is the greatest sinner, therefore he is called, Eph. vi. 12, 'spiritual wickedness;' his sins are in the highest degree sinful, every sin of his is a sin against the Holy Ghost, against full light, and with malice and spite against God and the saints. And he is the father of sin, John viii. 44. As Jubal was 'the father of all such as handle the harp and organ,' Gen. iv. 21; that is, he was the first that taught the use of that instrument: so all the sins in the world are by his furtherance, both actual and original; therefore he may be fitly called the evil one.

Again, he hath a great stroke in temptation, that he is the artificer, the designer, the improver of them; therefore he is called, ὁ πειράζων, 'the tempter,' Mat. iv. 3. Well, then, 'Lead us not into temptation, but deliver us from the *evil one*.'

Secondly, we may render it indefinitely, as we do, 'Deliver us from *evil,*' that is, from *sin.* And fitly is this so called, because it is the greatest evil, above poverty, sickness, and worldly loss. Everything which doth harm us, that may be called evil. Now sin doth most hurt; nothing so much as sin. Why? Because it doth endamage our inward man, and endanger our everlasting hopes.

[1.] It doth endamage our inward man, and hindereth and diminisheth our comfortable communion with God. Other things may harm the man, but they do not touch the Christian; and therefore saith the apostle, 2 Cor. iv. 16, ' For which cause we faint not; but though our outward man perish, yet the inward man is renewed day by day.' Breaches made upon the outward man come not so near as a breach made upon the inward man; therefore we faint not, so long as the inward man is safe.

[2.] It doth endanger our everlasting hopes and concernments, and therefore it is the greatest evil. All afflictions do but reach our temporal, but sin reacheth our eternal concernments; and therefore the apostle promiseth himself this kind of deliverance, as that which was most worthy: 2 Tim. iv. 17, 18, ' I was delivered out of the mouth of the lion. And the Lord shall deliver me from every evil work, and will preserve me unto his heavenly kingdom.' Well, then, you see it may be rendered *the evil one,* or *the evil thing.* The word carrieth it for sin; κακὸν denoteth the evil of afflictions, and *malum pœnæ,* as well as *malum culpæ;* but πονηρὸν never but evil of fault. And we need not anxiously dispute whether the one or the other, for one cannot be understood without respect to the other. Therefore I shall take it in a general sense—that evil which results from temptations, whether they arise from Satan, the world, or our own hearts.

From the words thus opened, the points will be two :—

First, That while we are in this valley of tears and snares, we should with earnestness and confidence pray to be delivered from evil.

Secondly, To be kept from the evil of sin is a greater mercy than to be kept from the trouble of temptation.

I observe the first point, because Christ thus directed us to pray to God. The second, because the evil of sin is intended. For the first, we should pray with earnestness, because of our danger, and with confidence, because of God's undertaking. The Lord Jesus knows what requests are most acceptable to his Father. Now when he would give a perfect pattern and platform of prayer, he bids you pray thus: ' Deliver us from evil.' Nay, we have not only Christ's direction, but Christ's example: John xvii. 15, ' I pray not that thou shouldest take them out of the world, but that thou shouldest keep them from the evil.' He did not absolutely pray for an exemption from temptation, though he knew the world would be a tempestuous place, that his people must expect strong assaults—Lord, take them not out of the world, but keep them from the evil; so here, ' Deliver us from evil.'

First, We should pray with earnestness, because of our danger from the enemies of our salvation, which are the devil, the world, and the flesh; in respect of all which, we pray to be delivered from evil.

[1.] From the evil which the devil designs against us. Both bad and good men have need to make this prayer: bad men have need; good men will have a heart certainly to pray thus to God, if they consider their danger.

(1.) Natural and unconverted men, they are under the power of the devil, if they were sensible of it; for the devils are said to be 'rulers of the darkness of this world,' Eph. vi. 12. By which is meant the wicked, ignorant, and carnal part of the world, whether they live in Gentilism, or within the pale and line of Christ's communion; over all those that live in their unrenewed state of sin and ignorance, over all these, Satan hath an empire and dominion. And mark, when God carried on his kingdom in a way of sensible manifestation, by visions, oracles, and miracles, so did Satan visibly govern the pagan world by apparitions, oracles, lying wonders, and sensible manifestations of himself. But now, when God's kingdom is spiritual,—'the kingdom of God is within you,' Luke xvii. 21,—so by proportion, Satan's kingdom is spiritual too; he rules in the hearts of men, though they little think of it. All natural men, whether they be pagans or Christians, though outwardly and apparently they may renounce the devil's kingdom, and do not seem to have such open communion with him, as the Gentiles that consulted with his oracles, and were instructed by his apparitions, acted by his power, and offered sacrifice to him: but spiritually, all natural men are under the devil; for, 1 John iii. 8, 'He that committeth sin is of the devil;' that is, he belongeth to him. How is he of the devil? They are his children: Acts xiii. 10, 'O thou child of the devil.' And they are his subjects, he ruleth in them, he hath a kingdom among men, which by all means he goeth about to maintain: Mat. xii. 26, 'If Satan be divided against himself, how then can his kingdom stand?' And they are his workhouses, he worketh in them: Eph. ii. 2, 'The spirit that worketh in the children of disobedience.' The devil is hard at work in a wicked man's heart, framing evil thoughts, carnal motions; urging them to break God's laws; drawing them on to more sin and villainy; fills their hearts with lying, and all manner of sins: Acts v. 3, 'Why hath Satan filled thine heart to lie to the Holy Ghost?' He binds them with prejudices, and will not suffer them to hearken to the glorious gospel: 2 Cor. iv. 4, 'In whom the god of this world hath blinded the minds of them which believe not, lest the light of the glorious gospel of Christ should shine unto them.' He blinds and holds them captive at his will and pleasure, their souls are fettered: 2 Tim. ii. 26. And sometimes he oppresses their bodies (for Satan carrieth on his kingdom by force, tyranny, fears, and bondage); and therefore it is said, Acts x. 38, that Christ 'went about doing good, and healing all that were oppressed of the devil.' Yet further, as God's executioner, he hath the power over death for their torment: Heb. ii. 14, 'That through death he might destroy him that had the power of death, that is, the devil.' And unless the Lord be merciful, he never ceaseth carrying on wicked men, until both they and he are for ever in hell: Mat. xxv. 41, 'Depart from me, ye cursed, into everlasting fire, prepared for the devil and his angels.' All this is spoken, to show carnal men their condition. Oh that they would seriously think of it! When they do evil, when they slight the motions of God's grace, they are under Satan; and not only by force, as a child of God may be sometimes, but they are willingly ignorant: 2 Pet. iii. 5. The more willingly we commit sin, still the more we are under the power of the devil. Well, then, if any have need to say, ' Deliver us from evil,' certainly unrenewed carnal men have need to go to God, and say, ' Lord, pluck us out of evil;' as the same expression is used, Col. i. 13, ' Who hath delivered us from the power of darkness,' "Ὅς ἐρρύσατο, who hath delivered us with a strong hand. Oh, go to God, in the name of Christ; there is no way of escape until God pluck you out by main force. And mark, this power by which we are delivered, God conveyeth by the preaching of the word, which was appointed to turn us from darkness unto light, and from the power of Satan unto God, Acts xxvi. 18; and therefore hearken to God's counsel before your condition grow incurable, and wait upon the ordinances; for the more you neglect and contemn the means of your recovery, your misery increaseth upon you; for every day you are still more given up to Satan by the just judgment of God, and to be captivated and taken by him at his will and pleasure by the snares he sets for you.

(2.) Good men, or God's own children, though they are delivered from the power of Satan, and brought into the kingdom of Christ, yet they are not wholly free in this world, but are sometimes caught by Satan's wiles, Eph. vi. 11, sometimes wounded by his fiery darts, ver. 16. Their lusts and their consciences are sometimes set a-raging; though he hath no allowed authority over their hearts, yet he exerciseth a tyrannical power; though he cannot rule them, yet he ceaseth not to assault them, if it were but to vex and trouble them. Briefly, the children of God have cause to pray, Deliver us from evil, in regard of Satan, because Satan hath a hand in their persecutions, and likewise a hand in their temptations to sin. It is he that instigateth their enemies to persecute them, and it is he that inflameth their lusts.

(1st.) In stirring up their enemies to persecute them. All the troubles of the children of God, they come originally from the devil: Luke xxii. 53, ' This is your hour, and the power of darkness.' We do not read that Satan did immediately vex Christ; and how was that hour then said to be the power of darkness? Why, by setting his instruments a-work to crucify him. And as he dealt with the head, so with the members: Rev. xii. 12, ' The devil hath great wrath, for he knoweth he hath but a short time.' When his kingdom begins to totter and shake, then he stirs up all his wrath, and inflames his instruments, as dying beasts bite hardest. So, Rev. xvi. 14, we read of the spirits of devils that go forth unto the kings of the earth, to stir them up against the saints. If you could behold, with your bodily eyes, this evil spirit hanging upon the ears of great men, and buzzing into them, and stirring them up, and the common people, and animating them against the children of God, you would more admire at the wonders of God's providence that you do subsist. Oh, how they are acted by this wrathful spirit!

(2d.) By inflaming our lusts and corruptions. So, 1 Cor. vii. 5, lest Satan tempt you by your incontinency, sets lusts a-boiling, either to vex the saints or to ensnare them. It is possible he may sometimes prevail with God's own children to draw them to some particular act of gross sin, as 2 Sam. xi. 4, as when David defiled himself with lust,

that thereby he may dishonour God; for by this means the name of
God was blasphemed, 2 Sam. xii. 14. Or that thereby he may disturb their peace, for this made David lie roaring, Ps. xxxii. 3, 4; his
radical moisture was even wasted and exhausted. Or else to spiritual
sins, as murmuring, repining against God, distrust of providence when
under crosses. Or when they are in their comforts, to drive them to
carnal complacency and neglect of holy things, disuse of communion
with God. Or to inordinate passions or spiritual wickedness, such as is
not conversant about carnal passions or fleshly lusts, but spiritual pride,
error, and unbelief. Certainly those that have anything of experience
of the spiritual life cannot be ignorant of Satan's enterprises.

Well, then, we had need go to God to deliver us from evil: for
outward evils; for the protection of his providence; for these God hath
undertaken: Ps. l. 15, 'Call upon me in the day of trouble; I will
deliver thee.' Satan is in God's chains; he could not enter into the
herd of swine without leave; therefore certainly he cannot get among
the sheep of Christ's fold. It is the saying of Tertullian, If the bristles
of swine be numbered, the hairs of our head are numbered; therefore
you had need go to God ('Deliver us from evil'), that persecution
may not rage over you, that he may hedge you in by his providence, Job i. 10, and that he would be as a wall of fire round about
you.

As to inward evils, so we go to God for wisdom and strength; for
Satan assaults us both ways, by wiles and darts: when he comes in a
way of violence, he comes with fiery darts; but when he doth lie in
ambush, there he hath his wiles to entice us with a seeming good.
We—

(1.) Beg wisdom, that you may espy the wiles of Satan, and may
not be caught unawares, for he is 'transformed into an angel of light,'
2 Cor. xi. 14. Mark, the devil doth not care so much to ride his own
horses, to act and draw wicked men to evil; he hath them sure enough;
but he laboureth to employ the saints in his work, if he can, to get
one which belongs to God to do his business; therefore he changeth
himself into an angel of light. The temptation is disguised with very
plausible pretences; then a child of God may be a factor for Satan,
and an instrument of the devil. For instance, would Peter have ever
made a motion for Satan if he had seen his hand? Oh, no; the temptation was disguised to him when he persuaded his Master from suffering. He covereth his foul designs with plausible pretences. Carnal
counsel shall be pity and natural affection: Mat. xvi. 22, 23, 'Let not
these things be; be it far from thee, Lord: this shall not be unto
thee. He said unto Peter, Get thee behind me, Satan; thou art an
offence unto me.' At another time, the disciples, when their Master
was slighted and contemned, they thought certainly they should do as
Elias did, call for fire from heaven to consume them, Luke ix. 54.
Revenge will often go for zeal for God. Revenge, or storming at personal affronts or injuries done to ourselves, is looked upon as zeal;
then the disciples may not know what spirit they are of. Many times
we are acted by the devil when we think we are acted by the Spirit of
God, and that which seems to be zeal is nothing but revenge. Therefore we had need go to God: Lord, deliver us from evil; we are

poor unwary creatures; that we may not be ensnared by fair pretences and surprised by his enterprises. And thus we beg wisdom.

(2.) We pray for strength to withstand his darts, that we may take the armour of God and withstand the evil one, Eph. vi. 13. Alas! of ourselves we cannot deliver ourselves from the least evil, or stand out against the least assault; therefore it is God alone that must keep the feet of his saints, 1 Sam. ii. 9. Therefore we go to him, that we may get his covenant strength, that we may be 'strong in the power of his might,' to conflict with Satan. Well, then, in regard of the first enemy of our salvation, the devil, we had need pray earnestly, that we may not be prevailed over by his arts; it is God alone that can keep us.

[2.] The world, that is another evil which is, as it were, the devil's chessboard; we can hardly move backward or forward but he is ready to attack us and surprise us by one creature or another, and draw us into the snare. Therefore it is said, Gal. i. 4, that Christ 'gave himself for us, that he might deliver us from this present evil world.' That is one way of being delivered from evil, when we are delivered from an evil world. It concerns us, and it is a great point of religion, to be 'kept unspotted from the world,' James i. 27. The whole world is full of evils and temptations, and we cannot walk anywhere but we are likely to be defiled. The things of the world, the men of the world.

(1.) The things of the world. All conditions of life become a snare to us, prosperity, adversity: Prov. xxx. 8, 9, 'Give me neither poverty nor riches; feed me with food convenient for me,' &c., 'lest I be full, and deny thee,' &c. Either condition hath its snares. A garment too short will not cover our nakedness, and too long proves *lacinia prœpendens*, ready to trip up our heels; and therefore both the one and the other condition are very dangerous. Many carry themselves well in one condition, but quite miscarry in another. As Ephraim was as a cake not turned, baked on the one side, Hosea vii. 8, quite dough on the other. Or as it is said of Joab, 1 Kings ii. 28, 'He turned after Adonijah, though he turned not after Absalom.' Some miscarry in adversity, others in prosperity. Indeed more under prosperity. Diseases which grow out of fulness are more rife than those which grow out of want; and fat and fertile soils are more rank of weeds. God's children most miscarry when all things are prosperous and flow in upon them, when they have lived in plenty. David was not soiled while he wandered up and down in the wilderness; but when he walked upon the terrace of his palace in Jerusalem, then he fell to lust and blood. The unsoundness of a vessel is not seen when it is empty; but when filled with water, then we see whether it be stanch, or leaky or no.

But the other condition is not without its snares neither. In adversity we are apt to be impatient, as well as in prosperity to be forgetful of God; and therefore we had need learn how to go up hill and down hill, to 'know how to abound, and how to be abased,' Phil. iv. 12. Look, as the wind doth rise from all corners, so do temptations. When we are kept low and bare, or in danger, then we are full of worldly fears, distrusts, cares, grow base, pusillanimous, and have not the spirit and generosity of a Christian. In a high condition we are proud, secure, forgetful of changes, vain, wanton; and press towards heaven less, and grow dead to good things.

(2.) As from the things of the world, so from the men of the world. We are apt to be poisoned by their bad example, and easily catch a sickness one from another. Good men may receive a taint: Isa. vi. 5, 'I am a man of unclean lips, and I dwell in the midst of a people of unclean lips.' Open excesses do soon manifest their own odiousness. I confess, a man that runs into open excess, we are not so much in danger of being enticed by him to the like practice; but we learn of one another secretly to be cold, careless, and less mortified. I say, though we are not carried into inordinate practices and gross wickednesses by the example of others, yet we learn to be cold in the profession of godliness, formal, less stirring in the way of holiness, and sometimes ensnared by their counsels. The flood and torrent of evil examples and counsels is so great, that it carrieth away men: Gal. ii. 13, 'Barnabas also was carried away with their dissimulati·n.' And the wills of men is one of our snares, 1 Pet. iv. 2. And besides, we are in danger to be terrified by their frowns, and act unseemly: Isa. viii. 13, 'Fear not their fear, nor be afraid.' Out of the fear of men we are apt to miscarry in our duty to God. Well, then, we need to go to God to be delivered from the evil of the world, that we may not be infected nor terrified by the men of the world; or, which is the more usual temptation, corrupted by the things of the world. The world doth secretly and slightly insinuate with us; and therefore keep us from evil.

Now how comes the world to be evil?

In two things, when both our care and our delight is lessened towards heavenly things.

(1.) When our care is lessened, when we are not so serious, so frequent in communion with God as we were wont to be; as Martha, that was 'cumbered about many things,' but Mary 'had chosen the better part,' Luke x. 42. When you begin to lessen your cares of duty, and Hagar thrusts Sarah out of doors, when the son of the bond-woman begins to mock at the son of the free-woman, when religion begins to be looked upon but as mopishness; to be so nice, precise, and so careful to maintain constant commerce with God; and begin to have lessening thoughts of God, and religion goes to the walls. So,

(2.) When our delight is less in heavenly things, when we have lost our savour of the word, and ordinances, and Sabbaths, and they are not so sweet as before: 1 John ii. 16, 'If any man love the world, the love of the Father is not in him.' When the love of the world hath made you weary of the love of God, when your heart goes a-whoring from God, the chief good. As when the affections are scattered, a man is tempted to look upon other objects, the wife of the bosom is defrauded of her right; so God is defrauded by an over-delight in the creature, the world intercepts your delight: Ps. lxxiii. 27, 28, 'Thou hast destroyed all them that go a-whoring from thee; but it is good for me to draw nigh to God.' When our delight in communion with God is lessened by delight in the creature, it is spiritual adultery. Now when worldly objects are so continually with us, soliciting our affections, and drawing us away from God, oh what need have the best of us to pray, ' Lord, keep us from evil!' The soul doth easily receive a taint from the objects to which we are accustomed; therefore they which live in the world had need to take heed of a worldly spirit. The continual presence of the object doth secretly entice the heart; as long suits prevail at length, and green wood kindles by long lying in the fire. Insensibly is the heart drawn away from God, and you shall find less savour in holy things.

[3.] We had need to pray earnestly, Lord, keep us from evil, because we are in danger of that other enemy, the flesh. There is not only an evil without us, as the devil and the world, but an evil within us: ' An evil heart of unbelief, in departing from the living God,' Heb. iii. 12. An evil heart, that is full of urgings and solicitations to sin. There are not only snares and temptations in the world, but there is a flexibleness in the party tempted: James i. 14, ' Every man is tempted, when he is drawn away of his own lust, and enticed,' ὑπὸ τῆς ἰδίας ἐπιθυμίας, of his own lust. The fire burns in our own hearts, Satan doth but blow up the flame. There is bad liquor in the vessel, Satan doth but only give it vent, and set it abroach with violence. We carry sinning natures about with us, therefore, Lord, ' Deliver us from evil.' The evil of the world would do no more hurt than the fire doth to a stone, if we were not combustible matter: ' The corruption that is in the world through lust,' 2 Pet. i. 4. The danger of living in the world doth not stand in this, because here are so many enticements and baits for every sense; but it is the corruption through lust; as the venom is not in the flower, but in the spider. The Philistines could not prevail against Samson if Delilah, on whom he doted, had not lulled him asleep; or as Balaam first corrupted Israel before he could curse them or bring them any harm: so corruption in the heart makes us liable to Satan's malice. There is a treacherous party within to open the door to Satan, without which all outward force could not annoy us.

Well, then, we had need go to God: Lord, ' Deliver us from evil.' Where we beg:—

(1.) That God would weaken the strength of inbred corruption, that we may not be foiled by it. Paul groans sadly, Rom. vii. 24, ' O wretched man that I am! who shall deliver me from the body of this death?' It is a question, but it implieth a wish, for the Hebrews propose their wishes by way of question; that is, Oh that I were delivered! It is a great mercy to be kept from falling into sin: ' kept from every evil work,' 2 Tim. iv. 18.

(2.) If we be foiled by our corruption, we beg that we may not lie in it, nor grow weary of our resistance, nor cast away our weapons, and suffer sin to have a quiet reign: Ps. cxix. 133, ' Let not any iniquity have dominion over me.' We cannot hope for a total exemption from sin, but, O Lord, let it not reign over us. How shall we know when sin reigns? When there is no course of mortification set up against it, to break the power, force, and tyranny of it. Take this distinction: There are *remaining* and *reserved* corruptions; sin remains where it doth not reign; but reserved corruption, that is reigning. I will explain it thus: sin remains when, notwithstanding all our endeavours, yet it still haunts and pesters us, though praying, watching, striving, waiting, and depending upon God for strength ; but it is reserved when you let it alone and are loth to touch it, but rather cherish, dandle, and foster it in the heart, and make provision for it. Therefore then are we delivered from evil when we recover by repentance ; and though we suffer by the tyranny of sin, we will not let it alone to have a quiet reign in our hearts, do not live under the power of corruptions. Sin let alone will do us further mischief.

Secondly, As we have reason to pray to God with earnestness, because of our danger; so with confidence, because of God's undertaking : 2 Thes. iii. 3, ' The Lord is faithful, who shall stablish you, and keep you from evil.' God hath undertaken to keep those who, with humble and broken hearts, do come to him to be kept from evil ; that are watchful, serious, and careful to get evils redressed as soon as discerned ; therefore we may come with an assured confidence to be delivered from all evil.

How far hath God undertaken to keep his people from evils and dangers in this life ? I answer :—

[1.] So far as may be hurtful to their souls : 1 Cor. x. 13, ' God is faithful, who will not suffer you to be tempted above that ye are able ; but will with the temptation also make a way to escape, that ye may be able to bear it.' It is part of God's faithfulness to keep you from evil, to proportion and temper temptation to your strength. God suits the burden to every back, he drives on as the little ones are able to bear ; therefore certainly he will mitigate temptation, or give in supply of strength.

[2.] God will keep you from the evil of sin so far as it is deadly ; that is, that it be not a sin unto death, 1 John v. 16 ; and that it may not reign in our mortal bodies, for you are dead to it : Rom. vi. 14, ' For sin shall not have dominion over you ; for ye are not under the law, but under grace.'

[3.] God undertakes for our final deliverance from all evil upon our translation to heaven. This is included in this prayer, that we may at length come to that state where is no sorrow, no sin, no assault and temptation from Satan, that we may be kept from all wickedness : Ps. xxxiv. 19, ' Many are the afflictions of the righteous; but the Lord delivereth him out of them all.' There is a time when God delivereth us from all at once, and that is by death and our translation into heaven.

Well, then, let us fly to God for deliverance, waiting for his help.

Doct. That to be kept from the evil of temptation is a greater mercy than to be kept from the trouble of temptation.

' Lead us not into temptation, but deliver us from evil ;' that is, if we be led into temptation, let us be kept from the evil of it.

First, It is a more wonderful providence to be kept from evil than from temptation ; *esse bonum facile est, ubi quod vetat esse remotum est.* It is no great matter to be chaste or honest, when there is no temptation to the contrary. Ay, but to keep our integrity in the midst of assaults and temptations, there is the wonder. If a garrison be never assaulted, it is no wonder that it standeth exempt from the calamity of war. This is like the bush that was burned, yet not consumed ; exercised with temptation from day to day, and yet kept from evil.

And in this sense God's power is more glorified than in keeping the angels ; for the angels are out of gun-shot and harm's way, and not liable to temptations. But to preserve a poor weak creature in the midst of temptation, oh, how is the power of God 'made perfect in weakness !' 2 Cor. xii. 9 : perfected, that is, gloriously discovered.

Secondly, The evil of sin is greater than the evil of affliction or trouble.

[1.] The evil of sin is the greater evil, because it separateth from God : Isa. lix. 2. It is an aversion from the chiefest good. Affliction doth not separate from God, it is a means to make us draw nigh to him. Poverty, sickness, blindness, loss of goods, let a man be never so low and loathsome, yet if in a state of grace, the Lord taketh pleasure in him, and he is near and dear to God ; God kisseth him with the kisses of his mouth ; nothing is loathsome to God but sin.

[2.] Sin is evil in itself, whether we feel it or no ; affliction is not evil in itself, but in our sense and feeling : Heb. xii. 11. Sin is evil, whether we feel it or no ; it is worse when we do not feel it : 'Past feeling,' Eph. iv. 19, when our conscience is benumbed.

[3.] Affliction, or *malum pœnœ*, is an act of divine justice; but *malum culpœ* is an act of man's corruptness. For the first, affliction, Amos vi. 3, ' Is there any evil, and the Lord hath not done it ?' But sin is the devil's work in us : 1 John iii. 8, 'He that committeth sin, is of the devil ; for the devil sinneth from the beginning. For this purpose the Son of God was manifested, that he might destroy the works of the devil.' And John viii. 34, ' Whosoever committeth sin, is the servant of sin.' The one cometh from a just God, the other from our corrupt hearts. The one is the act of a holy God, the other the act of a sinful creature.

[4.] The death of Christ falls more directly upon this benefit—exemption from sin : Mat. i. 21, ' He shall save his people from their sins ;' Acts iii. 26, ' God having raised up his Son Jesus, sent him to bless you, in turning away every one of you from his iniquities ;' not troubles or sorrows, but sins.

[5.] Affliction is a more particular temporal evil, but sin is an infinite universal evil. Sickness depriveth us of health, poverty of wealth, &c., and every adverse providence doth but oppose some particular temporal good ; but sin depriveth us of God, who is the fountain of our comfort ; the other but of some limited comfort.

[6.] Afflictions are sent to remove sin : Heb. xii. 11, ' Now no chastening for the present seemeth to be joyous, but grievous ; nevertheless afterward it yieldeth the peaceable fruit of righteousness unto them which are exercised thereby ;' Isa. xxvi. 9, ' When thy judgments are in the earth, the inhabitants of the world will learn righteousness:' but sin is not sent to remove affliction. Now the end must be greater than the means, both as to prosecution and aversation. As to prosecution ; to dig for iron with mattocks of gold and silver. So in aversation ; if death were not worse than the pain of physic, no man would take physic to avoid death.

[7.] Affliction is the effect of God's love : Heb. xii. 6, ' Whom the Lord loveth he chasteneth.' But to be left to sin is an effect of God's anger. God doth not always exempt from troubles ; yet if he keep from spiritual hurt thereby, if he sanctify the trouble, support us with sufficient grace, 2 Cor. xii. 9; if preserved from evil, howsoever tempted and exercised, it is enough.

Use 1. To reprove our folly. We complain of other things, but we do not complain of sin, which is the greatest evil. This is contrary to the spirit of God's children, who rejoice in troubles, but not in sins: 2 Cor. xii. 9, ' Most gladly therefore will I rejoice in infirmities, that the power of Christ may rest upon me.' They groan bitterly under sins : Rom. vii. 23, ' O wretched man !' &c. If any man had cause to complain of afflictions, Paul had : in perils often, whipped, persecuted, stoned. But the body of sin and death was the greatest burden : lusts troubled him more than scourges ; his captivity to the law of sin more than prisons. When affliction sitteth too close, sin sits loose. In affliction there is some offence done us, but in sin the wrong is done to God. And what are we to God ? Afflictions may be good, but sin is never good. The body suffereth by affliction, but the soul suffereth by sin loss of grace and comfort, which are not to be valued by all the world's enjoyments. The evil of affliction is but for a moment—like rain, it drieth up of its own accord; but the evil of sin is for ever, unless it be pardoned and taken away. Sin is the cause of all the evils of affliction ; therefore when we complain, we should complain, not so much of the smart, as of the cause of it.

2. It directeth us :—

[1.] How to pray to God against sin rather than trouble. This is indeed to be delivered from evil : 2 Tim. iv. 18, Paul reckoned upon that, ' He will deliver me from every evil work.' When afflicted, you should rather desire to have the affliction sanctified than removed ; you will be most careful for that ; saints do not pray for the interests of the old man rather than the new man. To be freed from trouble is a common mercy, but to have it sanctified is a special mercy. Carnal men may be without affliction, but carnal men cannot have experience of grace. Bare deliverance is no sign of special love.

[2.] In our choice. It was a heavy charge they put upon Job: Job xxxvi. 21, ' Thou hast chosen iniquity rather than affliction.' Sometimes we are put upon the trial, to lose the favour of God or the favour of men, duty and danger: here content myself, gratify my lusts and interests ; there offend God. Out of the temptation, we could easily judge that all the misery in the world is to be endured rather than commit the least sin. But how is it upon a trial, when a worldly convenience and a spiritual inconvenience is proposed ? By choosing sin, a man cannot altogether escape affliction here or hereafter. Wickedness, though it prosper a while, yet at length it proveth a snare.

3. It directeth us to submit to God's providence, and to own mercy in it. Though God doth not exempt us from troubles, yet if he keep us from hurt thereby, if he sanctify the trouble, and support us with grace sufficient, it is his mercy to us. For Daniel to be put into the lions' den was not so great a judgment as for Nebuchadnezzar to have the heart of a beast. To be given up to our own hearts' lusts, to commit any sin, it is a greater cross than any misery that can light upon us ; therefore let us be patient under affliction. Our great care

should be, not to dishonour God in any condition. God hath promised to be with his people in their afflictions to comfort them; but hath never promised to be with his people in their sins: ' I will be with you in the fire, and in the water,' as the Son of God was with the three children in the fiery furnace. But God is departed when they sin; I will go to my own place. Sin hindereth prayer, but afflictions quicken it: Isa. xxvi. 16, ' Lord, in trouble have they visited thee; they poured out a prayer when thy chastening was upon them.' In affliction it is a time to put the promises in suit; it doth not hinder our access to God and the throne of grace, but driveth us to it. But sin increaseth our bondage, maketh us stand at a distance, and grow shy of God. The fruit of sin is shame, Rom. vi. 21.

4. It teaches us how to wait and hope for the issue of our prayers. Pray that ye enter not into temptation; yet be not absolute in that, but to be kept from evil, that what way soever we are tried we may be kept from the evil of sin.

For thine is the kingdom, and the power, and the glory, for ever.
Amen.

IN these words we have the conclusion of all, and that which giveth us confidence in the requests we make to God.

First, The confirmation is taken from the excellency of God, to whom we pray; where there is a declaration of what belongeth to God:—

Secondly, The duration and perpetuity, *for ever.*

Three things are mentioned as belonging to God—*kingdom, power, and glory.*

1. By *kingdom* is meant God's right and authority over all things, by which he can dispose of them according to his own pleasure.

2. By *power* is meant his sufficiency to execute this right, and to do what he pleaseth, both in heaven and earth.

3. The final cause of all is his *glory.* ' Thine is the glory,' or the honour of all things in the world belongs to thee. Glory is excellency discovered with praise. We desire that he may be more honoured and brought into request and esteem.

Secondly, We have the obsignation and sealing of our requests in the word *Amen;* which is, *signaculum fidei,* an expression of our faith and hope. And *actus desiderii,* the strength of our desire. There is the *Amen* of faith, and the *Amen* of hearty desire; as by and by.

Now let us look upon this conclusion, first, as a doxology or expression of praise to God: and the note is:—

Doct. That in every address to God, lauding or praising of God is necessary.

For in this perfect form of prayer Christ teacheth us, not only to ask things needful for ourselves, but to ascribe to God things proper to him.

There are two words used in this case in scripture, *praise* and *blessing.* Praise relateth to God's excellency, and blessing to his benefits: Ps. cxlv. 10, 'All thy works shall praise thee, O Lord; and thy saints shall bless thee.' All the works of God declare his excellency; but the saints will ever be ascribing to God the benefits they have received from him. So they are spoken of as things, though somewhat alike, yet as distinct: Neh. ix. 5, 'Blessed be thy glorious name, which is exalted above all blessing and praise.' Our praise cannot reach the excellency of his nature; nor our blessing express the worth of his benefits. Both may be here intended. For *thine is kingdom and power,* relateth to his excellency, and *thine is the glory,* to his benefits; for God's glory is the reflex of all his works, and so expresseth the benefits showed to the sons of men, especially to his people. Well, then, whenever you would pray to God to bless you, you must bless God again, and praise his name: Eph. i. 3, 'Blessed be the God and Father of our Lord Jesus Christ, who hath blessed us with all spiritual blessings in heavenly places in Christ.' It is the echo and reflex of his grace and mercy to the creatures. God blesseth us, and we bless God; as the echo returneth the word, or the wall beateth back the beams of the sun. Only consider, we bless God far otherwise than he blesseth us: God's blessing is operative, ours declarative; his words are accompanied with power: *benedicere* is *benefacere.* He doth good; we speak good when we remember the blessed effects of his grace, and tell what he hath done for our souls.

The reasons why we are to mingle praises and thanksgivings with our requests are these:—

[1.] Because this complieth more with the great end of worship; which is not so much the relief of man as the honour of God; therefore we should not only intend the supply of our necessities, for that is but a brutish cry, howling for corn, wine, and oil, Hosea vii. 14; but we should intend also the honour of God: Ps. l. 23, 'Whoso offereth praise glorifieth me.' A man may offer requests to God, yet not honour him, but seek himself; but he that offereth praise glorifieth me. He that doth affectionately, and from his heart, give God the honour of his attributes and titles in scripture, he glorifieth him; and therefore worship being for the glory of God, that should not be left out.

[2.] This is the most effectual spiritual oratory, or way of praying: Ps. lxvii. 5, 'Let the people praise thee, O God, let all the people praise thee.' What then? 'Then shall the earth yield her increase; and God, even our own God, shall bless us.' We have comforts increased the more we praise God for what we have already received. The more vapours go up, the more showers come down; as the rivers receive so they pour out, and all run into the sea again. There is a constant circular course and recourse from the sea unto the sea. So there is between God and us; the more we praise him the more our blessings come down; and the more his blessings come down the more we praise him again; so that we do not so much bless God as bless ourselves. When the springs lie low we pour a little water into the pump, not to enrich the fountain, but to bring up more for ourselves.

[3.] It is the noblest part of worship, and most excellent and acceptable service. It is a great honour to creatures to bestow blessing upon God. In other duties God is bestowing something on us; but in praise (according to our manner, and as creatures can) we bestow something upon God. In prayer, we come as beggars, expecting an alms; in hearing, we come as scholars and disciples, expecting instruction from God. Here (according to our measure and ability) we give something to him; not because he needs it, being infinitely perfect, but because he deserves it, being infinitely gracious. This is the work of angels and glorified saints. Other duties more agree with our imperfect state, as hearing and prayer, that our wants may be supplied; but this duty agrees with our state when we are most perfect. Love is the grace of heaven, and praise the duty of heaven; we are for vials, they harps; prayer is our main work, and praise theirs.

Use. To reprove us, that we are altogether for the supply of our necessities, but little think of giving God the honour due to his name. Either we meddle not with it at all, or do it in a very flighty fashion. In this perfect form the glory of God is the *Alpha* and *Omega*, the beginning and the ending of this short prayer. The first petition it is for God's glory, and the final conclusion also. And therefore it is verily a fault that God is no more praised. In our addresses to him (Ps. xxii. 3) it is said, 'O thou that inhabitest the praises of Israel;' the meaning is, dwellest in Israel, where he is praised of them, because it is the great work they are about.

Surely our assemblies should more resound with the praises of God. In church worship there should be a mixture of harps, which are instruments of praise, as well as 'vials full of odours, which are the prayers of the saints,' Rev. v. 8. But usually we thrust gratulation, thanksgiving, and praise, into a narrow room, and are scanty therein, but can be large and copious in expressing our wants and begging a supply. This duty is made too great a stranger in your dealings with God. What are the reasons of this defect?

[1.] Self-love. We are eager to have blessings, but we forget to return to give God the glory. Prayer is a work of necessity, but praise a work of duty and homage. Self-love puts us upon prayer, but the love of God upon praise. Now, because we are so full of self-love, therefore are we so backward to this duty.

[2.] A second cause is our stupid negligence; we do not gather up matter of thanksgiving, and observe God's gracious dealing with us, that we may have wherewith to enlarge ourselves in giving glory to his name: Col. iv. 2, 'Continue in prayer, and watch in the same with thanksgiving.' We should continually observe God's answers and visits of love, and what attributes he makes good to us in the course of his providence. But out of spiritual laziness we do not take notice of these things, therefore no wonder if we are backward to speak good of his name, but are always whining, murmuring, and complaining.

Secondly, It is not only a doxology, but a full one, and very expressive of the excellency of God. From whence note :—

Doct. The saints are not niggardly and sparing in praising of God;

kingdom, power, and glory, and all that is excellent, they ascribe to him.

A gracious heart hath such a sense of God's worth and excellency that he thinks he can never speak honourably enough of it. See how David enlargeth himself very suitably to what is spoken here: 1 Chron. xxix. 10-13, ' And David said, Blessed be thou, Lord God, for ever and ever : thine, O Lord, is the greatness, and the power, and the glory, and the victory, and the majesty : thine is the kingdom, O Lord, and thou art exalted as head above all. Now therefore, our God, we thank thee, and praise thy glorious name.' Oh, when once a child of God falls upon speaking of God, he cannot tell how to come out of the meditation : he seeth so much is due to God that he heaps words upon words. So 1 Tim. i. 17, ' Now unto the king eternal, immortal, invisible, the only wise God, be honour and glory, for ever and ever. Amen.' And in many other places of scripture. Now, this copiousness in praising of God is, partly, because of the excellency of the object : Neh. ix. 5, ' Blessed be thy glorious name, which is exalted above all blessing and praise.' When they have done what they can to bless God, remember his benefits, or praise God, and recount his excellencies, still they come too far short ; therefore when we cannot do all, we should do much. And partly, it is from the greatness and largeness of their affection ; they think never to have done enough for God, whom they love so much. David saith, ' I will praise him yet more and more.' They cannot satisfy themselves by taking up the excellency of God in one notion only ; therefore majesty, greatness, glory, wisdom, and power, they mention all things which are honourable and glorious.

Use. The use is again to reprove us for being so cold and sparing this way. It argueth a want of a due sense of God's excellency and straitness of spiritual affection ; therefore we should study God more, and observe his manifold excellencies. Get a greater esteem of him in your hearts, for ' out of the abundance of the heart, the mouth will speak.' We should be calling upon ourselves, as David, Ps. ciii. 1 : ' Bless the Lord, O my soul ; and all that is within me, bless his holy name.'

Thirdly, I observe again, it is brought in with a *for,* as relating to the foregoing petitions : ' Lead us not into temptation, but deliver us from evil : *for* thine is the kingdom,' &c.

What respect hath this doxology to the foregoing requests ?

First, It serves to increase our confidence in prayer.

Secondly, Our reverence and affection.

Thirdly, To regulate and direct our prayers :—

[1.] As to the person to whom we pray.

[2.] As to the manner of asking.

[3.] As to the persons praying.

Let us see all these requests.[1]

First, The great end is to increase our confidence. Observe,

Doct. It is a great relief to a soul, in praying to God, to consider that his is the kingdom, power, and glory ; and all these for ever.

His is the kingdom.

---

[1] Qu. ' respects ? '—ED.

God hath the sovereign government of all things. And then his right to govern is backed with all-sufficient power and strength; and so he can dispose of his sovereignty for the bringing to pass what we expect from him.

Authority is one thing, and power another, but they both meet in God; he hath all power and authority.

And then, his is the glory: he is concerned as well as we; yea more, his interest is greater than ours, for the glory of all belongs to him: and all this, not for a time, but for ever. These are the encouragements to raise our confidence that our prayers shall be heard and granted when we ask anything according to his will.

There are two things that give us confidence in any that we sue to— if he be able and willing. Now God is able to grant our requests, and very prone and willing also. We are taught it sufficiently in this prayer; for we begin with him as *Father*, and we end with him as a glorious and powerful *king;* his fatherly affection, on the one hand, shows that he is willing; and his royal power, on the other, that he is able: so that if we ask anything according to his will, we need not doubt. We may gather his power and will out of this very clause: His power; for his is the kingdom, and power, or a right and authority, backed with absolute all-sufficiency. Then his will, 'Thine is the glory;' it is his glory to grant our petitions, not only matter of happiness to us, but of glory to God, therefore we need not doubt.

But more particularly :—

[1.] There is confidence established by that, that his is the kingdom. God's kingdom is either universal, over all men or things; or particular and special, which notes his relation to the saints, to those which have given up themselves to his government, to be guided by him to everlasting glory: and both these are grounds of confidence.

(1.) His universal kingdom over all persons and things in the world. This kingdom is an absolute monarchy, with a plenary dominion and propriety grounded upon his creation of them. There is a twofold dominion—*dominium jurisdictionis,* and *dominium proprietatis.* The one is such as a king hath over his subjects; the other, such as a king hath in his goods and lands: the latter is greater than the former. A king hath a dominion of jurisdiction over his subjects to command and govern them; but he hath not such an absolute propriety in their persons as he hath in his own goods and lands; he may dispose of *them* absolutely at his own pleasure, but his jurisdiction is limited. In short, we must distinguish of his dominion as a ruler, and as an owner. But both these, they concur in God, and that in the highest degree, for God is owner as well as ruler; he made all things out of nothing, therefore hath a more absolute dominion over us than any potentate or king can have, not only over his subjects, but his goods; and can govern all things, men, angels, and devils, according to his pleasure. It is more absolute than any superiority in the world, and more universal, as comprising all persons and things. God hath right to be king, because he gave being to all things, which no earthly potentate can: therefore the author must be owner. All other kings are liable to be called to account and reckoning by this great king, for their administration; but God is absolute and supreme.

Now this is a great encouragement to us, that we go to a God that hath an absolute right, for which he is responsible to none. We go not to a servant or a subordinate agent, who may be controlled by a higher power, and whose act may be disannulled; but to an absolute lord, to whom none can say, 'What doest thou?' Job ix. 12. Here is the comfort of a believer, that he goes immediately to the fountain and owner of all things; the absolute lord of all the world is his father; the sovereign and free disposing of all things is in his hand. If we expect anything from subordinate instruments, God's leave must first be asked, or they can do nothing for us; but he can do what he pleaseth, it is his own: Mat. xx. 15, 'Is it not lawful for me to do what I will with mine own?' None can call him to an account.

(2.) His relation to the saints. It is the duty of a king to defend his subjects, and provide for their welfare; so God, being king, will see that it be well with those that are under his government. It concerns you much to get an interest to be under this king, then to mention it in prayer: Ps. xliv. 4, 'Thou art my king, O God; command deliverances for Jacob.' If you want anything for yourselves or the church, put God in mind of his relation to you: 'Thou art my king.' Let not this interest lie neglected or unpleaded. All the benefit which subjects can expect from a potent king you may expect from God.

Again, the word *command* is notable, and expresseth the case to the full: 'command deliverances.' All things are at God's command and beck; if he do but speak the word, or give out order to second causes, it is all done in a trice. So Ps. v. 2, 'Hearken unto the voice of my cry, my king and my God: for unto thee will I pray.' To thee, and to none other. Why should we go to servants, when we may go to the king himself? So Ps. lxxiv. 12, 'For God is my king of old, working salvation in the midst of the earth.' God will defend his kingdom, and right his injured subjects. Therefore, if we would have any blessing to be accomplished for ourselves, or for the public, let us go to God: 'Thine is the kingdom.' And more especially, if we would have any good thing to be done by those in authority and subordinate power over us, do not so much treat with them as with God. Let us beseech God to persuade and incline their hearts, for his is the kingdom; he can move them to do what shall be for the glory of his name, and the comfort and benefit of his afflicted people. Let us go to God, who is the sovereign king; he can give you to 'live a quiet and peaceable life, in all godliness and honesty,' 1 Tim. ii. 2. Or, he can give you favour; dispose of their hearts to do good to his people: Neh. i. 11, 'Prosper, I pray thee, thy servant this day, and grant him mercy in the sight of this man; for I was the king's cup-bearer.' The sovereign disposal of all things is in the hand of God.

[2.] Thine is the power. This also is an argument of confidence, that God hath not only a kingdom, but power to back it. Titles without power make authority ridiculous, and beget scorn, not reverence and respect. But now God's kingdom is accompanied with power and all-sufficiency. He hath right to command all, and no creature can be too hard for him. Earthly kings, when they have authority and power, yet it is limited: 2 Kings vi. 27, When the woman came to the king of Israel, 'Help, my lord, O king. And he said, If the Lord do not help thee, whence shall I help thee?' But God's is an unlimited power: an absolute right and an unlimited power, they meet fitly in God; therefore this is an encouragement to go to him. Christians, that power of God which educed all things out of nothing, which established the heavens, which fixed the earth; that power of God, it is the ground of our confidence: Ps. cxxi. 2, 'My help cometh from the Lord, which made heaven and earth.' This power should we depend upon.

We can ask nothing but what God is able to give, yea, above our asking: Eph. iii. 20, 'Now unto him that is able to do exceeding abundantly above all that we ask or think.' Our thoughts are vast, and our desires very craving, and yet beyond all that we can ask or think, 'According to the mighty power that worketh in us.' We cannot empty the ocean with a nut-shell, nor comprehend the infinite God, and raise our thoughts to the vast extent of his power, only we must go to some instances of God's power; that power which made the world out of nothing, and that power which wrought in you, where there is such infinite resistance. We may go to God and say, Mat. viii. 2, 'Lord, if thou wilt, thou canst make me clean.' You need not trouble yourselves about his will; he is so good and gracious, prone and ready to do good; so inclinable: he is your heavenly Father. But that which is most questioned is the sufficiency of God; can you believe his power? Now determine but that, *Lord, thou canst,* and that is a great relief to the soul. Our wants are not so many but God is able to supply them; our enemies and corruptions not so strong but God is able to subdue them: surely your heavenly Father will do what is in the power of his hand. A beggar, when he seeth an ordinary man coming, lets him pass without much importunity; but when he seeth a man well habited, well attended, and with rich accoutrements, he runs close to him, and will not let him alone, but follows him with his clamour, knows it is in his power to help him. So this should encourage us to go to the mighty God, which made heaven and earth, and all things out of nothing.

The third argument which Christ propounds, 'Thine is the glory.' The honour and glory of all will redound to God, as the comfort accrueth to us; it is for God's honour to show forth his power in our relief, and to be as good as his word. Now this is a ground of confidence, that he hath joined his glory and our good together; and that God's praise waiteth, while our deliverance waiteth: Ps. lxv. 1, 'Praise waiteth for thee, O God, in Zion.' You think your comfort stays, and all this while God's honour waits. So Ps. cxii. 1, 'Praise ye the Lord; blessed is the man that feareth the Lord.' It is the Lord's praise that his servants are the only and blessed people in the world; and this is a wonderful ground of confidence. Think, surely God's glory he will be chary and tender of; he will provide for the glory of his great name. There is nothing God stands upon more than upon the glory of his name; nothing prevaileth with God more than that. If God were a loser by your comforts, if he could not save or bless thee without wrong done to himself, we might be discouraged. But when you come and plead with him, as Abigail, It will be no grief of heart unto my lord to forgive thy servant;' so it will be no loss to God if he show mercy and pity to such poor creatures as we are; you then may pray more freely and boldly. If thy comforts were inconsistent with his glory, or were not so greatly exalted by it, then it were another matter; but all makes for the glory of his name. If our good and happiness were only concerned in it, there might be some suspicion; but the glory of God is concerned, which is more worth than all the world. We are unworthy to be heard and accepted, but God is worthy to be honoured. It is for the honour of God to choose base, mean, and contemptible things, and to show forth the riches, goodness, power, and treasure of his glory. Much of our trouble and distrust comes only from reflecting upon our own good in the mercies that we ask, as if God were not concerned in them, whereas the Lord is concerned as well as you. As the ivy wrapped about the tree cannot be hurt, except you do hurt to the tree, so the Lord hath twisted our concernment about his own honour and glory. Thus the saints plead God's glory as an argument: Jer. xiv. 7, ' O Lord, though our iniquities testify against us, do thou it for thy name's sake.' They do not tell him what he shall do, but do thou that which shall be for thy glory. So Ezek. xxxvi. 22, 'Thus saith the Lord God, I do not this for your sakes, O house of Israel, but for mine holy name's sake;' so Isa. xlviii. 9, 'For my name's sake will I defer mine anger, and for my praise will I refrain for thee, that I cut thee not off.'

[4.] The duration, *for ever*. All excellencies which are in God, they are eternally in God. God is an infinite, simple, independent being, the cause of all things, but caused by none; therefore he was from everlasting, and will be to everlasting: Ps. xc. 2, ' Before the mountains were brought forth, or ever thou hadst formed the earth and the world, even from everlasting to everlasting, thou art God.' If there were a time when God was not, then there was a time when nothing was; and then there would never have been anything, unless nothing could make all things. Therefore God is eternally glorious; for whatever is in God is originally in himself, and absolutely without dependence on any other, to everlasting. How loosely do honours sit upon men! Every disease shakes them out of their kingdom, power, and glory; and within a little while the state, show, and all the command of earthly kings will fade away, and come to nothing. Governors and government may die, principalities grow old and infirm, and sicken and die, as well as princes; kingdoms expire, like kings, and they like us: Ps. lxxxii. 6, 7, 'I have said, Ye are gods; and all of you are children of the Most High: but ye shall die like men.' 'But thy throne, O God, is for ever and ever,' Ps. xlv. 6. His kingdom, and power, and glory, they are without beginning and without end. Now this is also a ground of confidence and dependence upon God. Earthly kings, when they perish, their favourites are counted offenders: 1 Kings i. 21, 'When my lord the king shall sleep with his fathers, that I and my son Solomon shall be counted offenders.' When other governors are set up, they and their children will be found offenders. But our king lives for ever; therefore this should encourage us to be

oftener in attendance upon God, performing it with all diligence and
seriousness, rather than court the humours and lusts of earthly potentates, who die like one of the people, and leave us exposed to the rage
and wrath of others that do succeed them.   But God is the same that
ever he was, to all those that ever called upon his name.   God is where
he was at first: I AM is his name; there is no wrinkle upon the brow
of eternity. 'His arm is not short, that it cannot save; or his ear
heavy, that it cannot hear,' Isa. lix. 1.   Whatever he hath been to his
people that have called upon him in former ages, he is the same still.
So Isa. li. 9, 'Awake, awake, put on strength, O arm of the Lord;
awake, as in the ancient days, in the generations of old.   Art thou not
it that hath cut Rahab, and wounded the dragon?'   God hath done
great things for his people: he smote Rahab, and killed the dragon
(meaning Pharaoh); and God is the same God still—his kingdom,
power, and glory are for ever; and God will be your God too for evermore.   Look, as this doth increase the terror of the damned in hell,
that they 'fall into the hands of the living God,' Heb. x. 31—God
lives for ever to see vengeance executed upon his enemies—so it is a
comfort to have an interest in the living God, that can and will keep
you, and bring you to heaven, where you shall be with him for evermore, that will ever live to see his friends rewarded.

Secondly, It directeth and regulateth our prayers.

[1.] It directs us to the object of prayer; to whom should we pray,
but to him that is absolute and above control?   To God, and God
alone; not to angels and saints.   To whom should we go in our necessities, but to him that hath dominion over all things, and power to
dispose of them for his own glory?   Will you think it a boldness to
go immediately to God?   It were so indeed if we had not a Mediator,
for a fallen creature can never have the impudence; and wicked men
that have not got an interest in Christ cannot expect relief from God;
but it is no impudence to come with a Mediator: Heb. iv. 16, 'Let
us therefore come boldly to the throne of grace, that we may obtain
mercy, and find grace to help in time of need.'

[2.] It directs us how to conceive of God in prayer.   Right thoughts
of God in prayer are very necessary and very difficult.   No one thing
troubleth the saints so much as this, how to fix their thoughts in the
apprehensions of God when they pray to him.   Now here is a direction how we should look upon God: look upon him as the eternal
being, and first cause, to whom belongs kingdom, power, and glory.
We cannot see God's essence, and therefore we must conceive of him
according to his praises in the word.   Now take but the preface and
the conclusion, and then you have a full description of God.   Look
upon him as an eternal being, whose is the kingdom, absolute right
to dispose of all things in the world, backed with all-sufficiency and
strength.   And look upon him as your Father that is in heaven; for
Our Father which art in heaven relates to Christ, that is, in the
heavenly sanctuary, appearing before God for us.   This will help you
in your conceptions of God, that you may not be puzzled nor entangled
in prayer.

[3.] It directs us as to the manner of praying: with reverence, with
self-abhorrency, and with submission.

(1.) With reverence, for he is a great, powerful, and glorious king : ' Thine is the kingdom, power, and glory.' Oh, shall we serve God then in a slight and careless fashion ? Mal. i. 8, ' If ye offer the blind, the lame, and sick for sacrifice, is it not evil ? Offer it now unto thy governor, will he be pleased with thee, or accept thy person ? saith the Lord of hosts.' Go to an earthly king, would you come to him with rude addresses, not thinking what to say, tumbling out words without sense and understanding ? And compare this with ver. 14 : saith God, when they brought him a sickly offering, ' I am a great king,' implying it is a lessening of his majesty. You do as it were dethrone God, you put him besides his kingdom, you do not treat him as he doth deserve, if you do not come into his presence with a holy trembling.

(2.) With self-abhorrency, and a sense of your own nothingness. I observe this, because all the arguments in prayer are not taken from us, but from what is in God, from his attributes : ' Thine is the kingdom, power, and glory.' It is a blessed thing to have God's attributes on our side ; to take an argument from God when we can take none from ourselves. Christ teacheth us to come with self-denial. The two first words, *kingdom* and *power*, show that all things come from God, as the first cause. And the last word, ' Thine is the *glory*,' shows all must be referred to God, as the last end ; so that self must be cast out. So that all the reasons of audience and acceptance are without us, not from within us : Dan. ix. 8, 9, ' To us belongeth confusion of face ; to the Lord our God belong mercies and forgivenesses.' Therefore thus it directs us to place all our confidence in God's fatherly affection, in his power, goodness, and glory, and in his absolute authority ; nothing to move God from ourselves.

(3.) To come with submission. Thine is the kingdom ; that is, he hath an absolute power to dispose of all blessings, therefore it is lawful for him to do with his own as he pleaseth. We must come, not murmuring or prescribing to God, but expecting the fulfilling of our desires, as it shall seem good to the Lord, according to his wisdom and power, by which he exercises his kingdom over all things, as may be for the glory of his name : Ps. cxv. 1, ' Not unto us, O Lord, not unto us, but unto thy name give glory, for thy mercy, and for thy truth's sake.' Not to satisfy our revenge, not to gratify our private interest and passions ; but, Lord, for thy name's sake, as may be for manifesting thy mercy and truth, so do it : not too passionate for our own ends, but confident that God, who hath the kingdom and government of the world in his own hands, will administer and carry on all things for his own glory.

[4.] It directs us, again, what are the duties of the persons praying.

(1.) Freely to resign up ourselves to God's service. Otherwise we mock God, when we acknowledge his dominion over all the world, and we ourselves will not be made subject to God. Therefore certainly a man that useth this prayer, ' Thine is the kingdom, power, and glory,' will also say, ' I am thine, save me,' Ps. cxix. 94. Let us freely resign up ourselves for him to reign over us. Can you say, with any face, to God, ' Thine is the kingdom,' yet cherish rebellious lusts in your own hearts ? It is the most unsuitable thing that can be.

' Thine is the power : ' He is able to bear you out in his work, however the world rage. And therefore we should not think scorn of his service, for his is the glory : the service of such a king will put honour upon you.

(2.) Another duty of him that is to pray is to depend upon God's all-sufficiency. Shall we speak thus of God, and say, ' Lord, thine is the power,' and yet not rely upon him ? He that cannot rely upon him for this life and the other, doth but reproach God when he saith, ' Thine is the power '—thine is the power, yet I will not trust thee, but fly to base shifts, as if the creature had power, and man had power—as if they could better provide for us than God. Therefore we are to live upon him, and cast ourselves into the arms of his all-sufficiency.

(3.) Another duty of them that would pray this prayer is, sincerely to aim at and seek the Lord's glory in all things. Why ? For the glory is thine. Wilt thou say, ' Thine is the glory,' and yet give and take the glory which is due to God to thyself? All is due to him, from whom we have received all things. But he that prides himself in gifts and graces, cannot be in good earnest. Wilt thou rob God of the honour, and wear it thyself? Did men believe all glory belongs to God, they would not take vainglory to themselves. Herod was eloquent, and the people cried out, ' The voice of a god, and not of a man.' He did but receive this applause, and usurped the glory due to God, and God blasted him. Therefore, when we pride ourselves in our sufficiencies, and abuse our comforts to our own lusts, we cannot with a good conscience say, ' Thine is the glory.'

For ever.   Amen.

ALL this is sealed up to us in the last word, *Amen ;* which may signify, either so be it, so let it be, or so it shall be.

The word *Amen* sometimes is taken nominally: Rev. iii. 14, ' Thus saith the *Amen*, the faithful and true Witness, the beginning of the creation of God.' Sometimes it is taken adverbially, and so it signifieth verily, and truly ; and so either it may express a great asseveration, or an affectionate desire. Sometimes it expresseth a great and vehement asseveration: John vi. 47, ' Amen, amen, verily, verily, I say unto you.' In other places it is put for an affectionate desire : Jer. xxviii. 6. When the false prophets prophesied peace, and Jeremiah pronounced war, ' Amen ! the Lord do so; the Lord perform thy words which thou hast prophesied.' Amen, it is not an asseveration, as confirming the truth of their prophecy, but expressing his own hearty wish and desire, if God saw it good.

Two things are required in prayer—a fervent desire and faith. A fervent desire ; therefore it is said, James v. 16, ' The effectual fervent prayer of a righteous man availeth much.' And then faith : James i. 6, ' But let him ask in faith, nothing wavering.' What is that faith required in prayer ? A persuasion that those things we ask regularly according to God's will, that God will grant them for Christ's sake.

Now both these *Amen* signifies : our hearty desire that it may be so; and our faith, that is, our acquiescency in the mercy and power and wisdom of God concerning the event.

Christ would have us bind up this prayer, and conclude it thus: Amen, so let it be, so it shall be. Observe hence,

That it is good to conclude holy exercises with some vigour and warmth.

Natural motion is swifter in the end and close: so should our spiritual affections, as we draw to a conclusion, put forth the efficacy of faith and holy desires, and recollect, as it were, all the foregoing affections; that we may go out of the presence of God with a sweet savour and relish, and a renewed confidence in his mercy and power.

Again, this *Amen* relateth to all the foregoing petitions, not to one only. Many, when they hear, ' Lord, give us this day our daily bread,' will say, ' Amen ; ' but when they come to the petition, ' Thy will be done on earth, as it is in heaven,' they are cold there, and have not hearty desires and earnest affections. Many beg pardon of sin ; but to be kept from evil, to bridle and restrain their souls from sin, they do not say Amen to that. Many would have defence, maintenance, and victory over their enemies; but not with respect to God's glory. They forget that petition, ' Hallowed be thy name ;' but this should be subordinated to his glory. Nay, we must say Amen to all the clauses of this prayer. Many say, ' Lord, forgive us our debts,' but do not like that, ' as we forgive our debtors:' they are loth to forgive their enemies, but carry a rancorous mind to them which have done them wrong. But now we must say Amen to all that is specified in this prayer. Then,

Mark, this Amen it is put in the close of the doxology. Observe hence,

There must be a hearty Amen to our praises as well as our prayers, that we may show zeal for God's glory, as well as affection to our profit.

Your Allelujahs should sound as loud as your supplications; and not only say Amen when you come with prayers and requests, things you stand in need of, but Amen when you are praising of God.

CHRIST'S

TEMPTATION AND TRANSFIGURATION

PRACTICALLY EXPLAINED AND IMPROVED

IN SEVERAL SERMONS.

TO THE READER.

THE following discourses on those important subjects of the temptation and transfiguration of our blessed Saviour, together with the sermons on the first chapter of the Epistle to the Colossians, from the fourteenth to the twenty-first verse, having been carefully perused, and transcribed from the reverend author's own manuscripts, are now, at the earnest request of divers persons that were the happy auditors thereof, offered to public view. Had the author lived to publish these himself, they had come forth into the world more exact; but yet as they are now left, I doubt not but they will be very acceptable to all that have discerning minds, for the peculiar excellency contained in them.

Thus much was thought necessary to be said by way of preface, the work sufficiently commending itself, especially coming from such an author as Dr Manton.

THE TEMPTATION OF CHRIST.

Then was Jesus led up of the Spirit into the wilderness, to be tempted of the devil.—MAT. IV. 1.

THIS scripture giveth us the history of Christ's temptation, which I shall go over by degrees.

In the words observe :—

1. The parties tempted and tempting. The person tempted was the Lord *Jesus* Christ. The person tempting was *the devil.*

2. The occasion inducing this combat, *Jesus was led up of the Spirit.*

3. The time, *then.*

4. The place, *the wilderness.*

From the whole observe :—

Doct. The Lord Jesus Christ was pleased to submit himself to an extraordinary combat with the tempter, for our good.

1. I shall explain the nature and circumstances of this extraordinary combat.

2. The reasons why Christ submitted to it.

3. The good of this to us.

I. The circumstances of this extraordinary combat. And here—

1. The persons combating—Jesus and the devil, the seed of the woman and the seed of the serpent. It was designed long before : Gen. iii. 15, ' I will put enmity between thee and the woman, and between thy seed and her seed : it shall bruise thy head, and thou shalt bruise his heel;' and now it is accomplished. Here is the Prince of Peace against the prince of darkness, Michael and the dragon, the Captain of our salvation and our grand enemy. The devil is the great architect of wickedness, as Christ is the Prince of life and righteousness. These are the combatants : the one ruined the creation of God, and the other restored and repaired it.

2. The manner of the combat. It was not merely a phantasm, that Christ was thus assaulted and used: no, he was tempted in reality, not in conceit and imagination only. It seemeth to be in the spirit,

though it was real; as Paul was taken up into the third heaven, whether in the body or out of the body we cannot easily judge, but real it was. I shall more accurately discuss this question afterwards in its more proper place.

3. What moved him, or how was he brought to enter into the lists with Satan? He was 'led by the Spirit,' meaning thereby the impulsion and excitation of the Holy Spirit, the Spirit of God. For it is said, Luke iv. 1, 'Jesus, being full of the Holy Ghost, returned from Jordan, and was led by the Spirit into the wilderness.' He did not voluntarily put himself upon temptation, but, by God's appointment, went up from Jordan farther into the desert.

We learn hence :—

[1.] That temptations come not by chance, not out of the earth, nor merely from the devil; but God ordereth them for his own glory and our good. Satan was fain to beg leave to tempt Job: Job i. 12, 'And the Lord said unto Satan, Behold, all that he hath is in thy power, only upon himself put not forth thine hand;' there is a concession with a limitation. Till God exposeth us to trials, the devil cannot trouble us, nor touch us. So Luke xxii. 31, 'Simon, Simon, Satan hath desired to have you, that he may sift you as wheat.' Nay, he could not enter into the herd of swine without a patent and new pass from Christ: Mat. viii. 31, 'So the devils besought him, saying, If thou cast us out, suffer us to go away into the herd of swine.' This cruel spirit is held in the chains of an irresistible providence, that he cannot molest any creature of God without his permission; which is a great satisfaction to the faithful: all things which concern our trial are determined and ordered by God. If we be free, let us bless God for it, and pray that he would not 'lead us into temptation:' if tempted, when we are in Satan's hands, remember Satan is in God's hand.

[2.] Having given up ourselves to God, we are no longer to be at our own dispose and direction, but must submit ourselves to be led, guided, and ordered by God in all things. So it was with Christ, he was led by the Spirit continually: if he retire into the desert, he is 'led by the Spirit,' Luke iv. 1; if he come back again into Galilee, ver. 4, 'Jesus returned in the power of the Spirit into Galilee.' The Holy Ghost leadeth him into the conflict, and when it was ended leadeth him back again. Now there is a perfect likeness between a Christian and Christ: he is led by the Spirit off and on, so we must be guided by the same Spirit in all our actions: Rom. viii. 14, 'For as many as are led by the Spirit of God, they are the sons of God.'

[3.] That we must observe our warrant and calling in all we resolve upon. To put ourselves upon hazards we are not called unto, is to go out of our bounds to meet a temptation, or to ride into the devil's quarters. Christ did not go of his own accord into the desert, but by divine impulsion, and so he came from thence. We may, in our place and calling, venture ourselves, on the protection of God's providence, upon obvious temptations; God will maintain and support us in them; that is to trust God; but to go out of our calling is to tempt God.

[4.] Compare the words used in Matthew and Mark, chap. i. 12,

'And immediately the Spirit driveth him into the wilderness.' That shows that it was a forcible motion, or a strong impulse, such as he could not easily resist or refuse, so here is freedom—he was *led* ; there is force and efficacious impression—he was *driven*, with a voluntary condescension thereunto. There may be liberty of man's will, yet the victorious efficacy of grace united together : a man may be taught and drawn, as Christ here was led, and driven by the Spirit into the wilderness.

3. The time.

[1.] Presently after his baptism. Now the baptism of Christ agreeth with ours as to the general nature of it. Baptism is our initiation into the service of God, or our solemn consecration of ourselves to him ; and it doth not only imply work, but fight : Rom. vi. 13, ' Neither yield ye your members as instruments, ὅπλα, of unrighteousness unto sin : but yield yourselves unto God, as those that are alive from the dead, and your members as instruments of righteousness unto God ;' and, Rom. xiii. 12, 'Let us cast off the works of darkness, and let us put on the armour of light.' Christ's baptism had the same general nature with ours, not the same special nature : the general nature is an engagement to God, the special use of baptism is to be a seal of the new covenant, or to be to us ' the baptism of repentance for the remission of sins.' Now this Christ was not capable of, he had no sin to be repented of or remitted ; but his baptism was an engagement to the same military work to which we are engaged. He came into the world for that end and purpose, to war against sin and Satan ; he engageth as the general, we as the common soldiers. He as the general : 1 John iii. 8, 'For this purpose the Son of God was manifested, ἵνα λύσῃ, that he might destroy the works of the devil.' His baptism was the taking of the field as general ; we undertake to fight under him in our rank and place.

[2.] At this baptismal engagement the Father had given him a testimony by a voice from heaven : ' This is my beloved Son, in whom I am well pleased ;' and the Holy Ghost had descended upon him in the form of a dove, Mark iii. 16, 17. Now presently after this he is set upon by the tempter. Thus many times the children of God, after solemn assurances of his love, are exposed to great temptations. Of this you may see an instance in Abraham : Gen. xxii. 1, ' And it came to pass after these things, that God did tempt Abraham ;' that is, after he had assured Abraham that he was ' his shield, and his exceeding great reward,' and given him so many renewed testimonies of his favour. So Paul, after his rapture, ' lest he should be exalted above measure through the abundance of revelations, there was given to him a thorn in the flesh, the messenger of Satan to buffet him,' 2 Cor. xii. 7. So Heb. x. 32, ' But call to remembrance the former days, in which, after ye were illuminated, ye endured a great fight of afflictions ;' *i.e.*, after ye were fully convinced of the Christian faith, and furnished with those virtues and graces that belong to it. God's conduct is gentle, and proportioned to our strength, as Jacob drove as the little ones were able to bear it. He never suffers his castles to be besieged till they are victualled.

[3.] Immediately before he entered upon his prophetical office.

Experience of temptations fits for the ministry, as Christ's temptations prepared him to set a-foot the kingdom of God, for the recovery of poor souls out of their bondage into the liberty of the children of God : ver. 17, 'From that time Jesus began to preach, and to say, Repent, for the kingdom of heaven is at hand.' Our state of innocency was our health, the grace of the Redeemer our medicine, Christ our physician; for the devil had poisoned our human nature. Therefore, when he sets a-foot his healing cure, it was fit and congruous that he should experimentally feel the power of the tempter, and in what manner he doth assault and endanger souls: Christ also would show us that ministers should not only be men of science, but of experience.

[4.] The place or field where this combat was fought, the wilderness, where were none but wild beasts: Mark i. 13, 'And he was there in the wilderness forty days tempted of Satan, and was with the wild beasts; and the angels ministered unto him.' Great question there is in what wilderness Christ was; their opinion is most probable who think it was the great wilderness, called the desert of Arabia, in which the Israelites wandered forty years, and in which Elijah fasted forty days and forty nights. In this solitary place Satan tried his utmost power against our Saviour.

This teacheth us :—

(1.) That Christ alone grappled with Satan, having no fellow-worker with him, that we may know the strength of our Redeemer, who is able himself to overcome the tempter without any assistance, and to 'save to the uttermost all that come unto God by him,' Heb. vii. 25.

(2.) That the devil often abuseth our solitude. It is good sometimes to be alone; but then we need to be stocked with holy thoughts or employed in holy exercises, that we may be able to say, as Christ, John xvi. 32, 'I am not alone, because the Father is with me.' Howsoever a state of retirement from human converse, if it be not necessary, exposeth us to temptations; but if we are cast upon it, we must expect God's presence and help.

(3.) That no place is privileged from temptations, unless we leave our hearts behind us. David, walking on the terrace or house-top, was ensnared by Bathsheba's beauty: 2 Sam. xi. 2–4. Lot, that was chaste in Sodom, yet committed incest in the mountain, where there were none but his own family: Gen. xix. 30, 31, &c. When we are locked in our closets, we cannot shut out Satan.

II. The reasons why Christ submitted to it.

1. With respect to Adam, that the parallel between the first and second Adam might be more exact. They are often compared in scripture, as Rom. v., latter end, and 1 Cor. xv.; and we read, Rom. v. 14, that the first Adam was τύπος τοῦ μέλλοντος, 'the figure of him that was to come.' And as in other respects, so in this; in the same way we were destroyed by the first Adam, in the same way we were restored by the second. Christ recovereth and winneth that which Adam lost. Our happiness was lost by the first Adam being overcome by the tempter; so it must be recovered by the second Adam, the tempter being overcome by him. He that did conquer must first be conquered, that sinners might be rescued from the captivity wherein

he held them captive. The first Adam, being assaulted quickly after his entrance into paradise, was overcome; and therefore must the second Adam overcome him as soon as he entered upon his office, and that in a conflict hand-to-hand, in that nature that was foiled. The devil must lose his prisoners in the same way that he caught them. Christ must do what Adam could not do. The victory is gotten by a public person in our nature, before it can be gotten by each individual in his own person, for so it was lost. Adam lost the day before he had any offspring, so Christ winneth it in his own person before he doth solemnly begin to preach the gospel and call disciples; and therefore here was the great overthrow of the adversary.

2. In regard of Satan, who by his conquest got a twofold power over man by tempting, he got an interest in his heart to lead him 'captive at his will' and pleasure, 2 Tim. ii. 26; and he was made God's executioner, he got a power to punish him: Heb. ii. 14, 'That through death he might destroy him that had the power of death, that is, the devil.' Therefore the Son of God, who interposed on our behalf, and undertook the rescue of sinners, did assume the nature of man, that he might conquer Satan in the nature that was conquered, and also offer himself as a sacrifice in the same nature for the demonstration of the justice of God. First, Christ must overcome by obedience, tried to the uttermost by temptations; and then he must also overcome by suffering. By overcoming temptations, he doth overcome Satan as a tempter; and by death he overcame him as a tormentor, or as the prince of death, who had the power of executing God's sentence. So that you see before he overcame him by merit, he overcame him by example, and was an instance of a tempted man before he was an instance of a persecuted man, or one that came to make satisfaction to God's justice.

3. With respect to the saints, who are in their passage to heaven to be exposed to great difficulties and trials. Now that they might have comfort and hope in their Redeemer, and come to him boldly as one touched with a feeling of their infirmities, he himself submitted to be tempted. This reason is recorded by the apostle in two places: Heb. ii. 18, 'For in that he himself hath suffered, being tempted, he is able to succour them that are tempted.' Able to succour; that is, fit, powerful, inclined, effectually moved to succour them. None so merciful as those who have been once miserable; and they who have not only known misery, but felt it, do more readily relieve and succour others. God biddeth Israel to pity strangers: Exod. xxii. 21, 'Thou shalt neither vex a stranger, nor oppress him; for ye were strangers in the land of Egypt.' They knew what it was to be exposed to the envy and hatred of the neighbours in the land where they sojourned: Exod. xxiii. 9, 'For ye know the heart of a stranger, seeing ye were strangers in the land of Egypt.' We read that when King Richard the First had been, on the sea near Sicily, like to be drowned, he recalled that ancient and barbarous custom, whereby the goods of shipwrecked men were escheated to the crown, making provision that those goods should be preserved for the right owners. Christ being tossed in the tempest of temptations, knows what belongs to the trouble thereof. The other place is, Heb. iv. 15, 'We have not an

high priest which cannot be touched with the feeling of our infirmities, but was in all points tempted like as we are, yet without sin.' Christ hath experienced how strong the assailant is, how feeble our nature is, how hard a matter it is to withstand when we are so sorely assaulted. His own experience of sufferings and temptations in himself doth entender his heart, and make him fit for sympathy with us, and begets a tender compassion towards the miseries and frailties of his members.

4. With respect to Christ himself, that he might be an exact pattern of obedience to God. The obedience is little worth, which is carried on in an even tenor, when we have no temptation to the contrary, but is cast off as soon as we are tempted to disobey: James i. 12, ' Blessed is the man that endureth temptation, for when he is tried, he shall receive the crown of life, which the Lord hath promised to them that love him.' And Heb. xi. 17, ' By faith Abraham, when he was tried, offered up Isaac : and he that had received the promises offered up his only-begotten son.' Now Christ was to be more eminent than all the holy ones of God, and therefore, that he might give an evidence of his piety, constancy, and trust in God, it was thought fit some trial should be made of him, that he might by example teach us what reason we have to hold to God against the strongest temptations.

III. The good of this to us. It teacheth us divers things, four I shall instance in.

1. To show us who is our grand enemy, the devil, who sought the misery and destruction of mankind, as Christ did our salvation. And therefore he is called ὁ ἐχθρὸς, *the enemy ;* Mat. xiii. 39, ' The enemy that sowed them is the devil.' And he is called also ὁ πονηρὸς, *the wicked one*, Mat. xiii. 19, as the first and deepest in evil. And because this malicious cruel spirit ruined mankind at first, he is called ' a liar and murderer from the beginning,' John viii. 44. A liar, because of his deceit ; a murderer, to show us what he hath done and would do. It was he that set upon Christ, and doth upon us, as at first to destroy our health, so still to keep us from our medicine and recovery out of the lapsed estate by the gospel of Christ.

2. That all men, none excepted, are subject to temptations. If any might plead for exemption, our Lord Jesus, the eternal Son of God, might ; but he was assaulted and tempted ; and if the devil tempted our Saviour, he will be much morebold with us. The godly are yet in the way, not at the end of the journey ; in the field, not with the crown on their heads ; and it is God's will that the enemy should have leave to assault them. None go to heaven without a trial : ' All these things are accomplished in your brethren that are in the flesh,' 1 Pet. v. 9. To look for an exempt privilege, or immunity from temptation, is to list ourselves as Christ's soldiers, and never expect battle or conflict.

3. It showeth us the manner of conflict, both of Satan's fight and our Saviour's defence.

[1.] Of Satan's fight. It is some advantage not to be ignorant of his enterprises : 2 Cor. ii. 11, ' Lest Satan should get an advantage of us, for we are not ignorant of his devices.' Then we may the better stand upon our guard. He assaulted Christ by the same kind of temptations by which usually he assaults us. The kinds of temptations are reckoned up: 1 John ii. 16, 'The lusts of the flesh, the lusts of the eye, and the pride of life.' And James iii. 15, 'This wisdom descendeth not from above, but is earthly, sensual, devilish.' With these temptations he assaulted our first parents: Gen. iii. 8, 'When the woman saw that the tree was good for fruit, and that it was pleasant to the eyes, and a tree to be desired to make one wise, she took of the fruit thereof, and did eat.' And with the same temptations he assaulted Christ, tempting him to turn stones into bread, to satisfy the longings of the flesh ; to fall down and worship him, as to the sight of a bewitching object to his eyes ; to fly in the air in pride, and to get glory among men. Here are our snares, which we must carefully avoid.

[2.] The manner of Christ's defence, and so it instructeth us how to overcome and carry ourselves in temptations. And here are two things whereby we evercome :—

(1.) By scripture. The word of God is 'the sword of the Spirit,' Eph. vi. 17, and 1 John ii. 14, 'The word of God abideth in you, and ye have overcome the wicked one.' It is good to have the word of God abide in our memories, but chiefly in our hearts, by a sound belief and fervent love to the truth.

(2.) Partly by resolution : 1 Pet. iv. 1, 'Arm yourselves with the same mind,' viz., that was in Christ. When Satan grew bold and troublesome, Christ rejects him with indignation. Now the conscience of our duty should thus prevail with us to be resolute therein ; the double-minded are as it were torn in pieces between God and the devil : James i. 8, 'A double-minded man is unstable in all his ways.' Therefore, being in God's way, we should resolve to be deaf to all temptations.

4. The hopes of success. God would set Christ before us as a pattern of trust and confidence, that when we address ourselves to serve God, we might not fear the temptations of Satan. We have an example of overcoming the devil in our glorious head and chief. If he pleaded, John xvi. 33, 'In the world ye shall have tribulation, but be of good cheer, I have overcome the world ; ' the same holdeth good here, for the enemies of our salvation are combined. He overcame the devil in our natures, that we might not be discouraged : we fight against the same adversaries in the same cause, and he will give power to us, his weak members, being full of compassion, which certainly is a great comfort to us.

Use. Of instruction to us :—

1. To reckon upon temptations. As soon as we mind our baptismal covenant, we must expect that Satan will be our professed foe, seeking to terrify or allure us from the banner of our captain, Jesus Christ. Many, after baptism, fly to Satan's camp. There are a sort of men in the visible church, who, though they do not deny their baptism, as those did, 2 Pet. ii. 9, 'Who have forgotten that they were purged from their old sins,' yet they carry themselves as if they were in league with the devil, the world, and the flesh, rather than with the Father, Son, and Holy Ghost; with might and main they oppose Christ's kingdom, both abroad and at home, in their own hearts, and are wholly governed by worldly things, the lusts of the flesh, and the lusts

of the eye, and the pride of life. Now these are the devil's agents, and the more dangerous because they use Christ's name against his offices, and the form of his religion to destroy the power thereof; as the dragon in the Revelation, pushed with the horns of the Lamb. Others are not venomously and malignantly set against Christ, and his interest in the world, or in their own hearts, but tamely yield to the lusts of the flesh, and go 'like an ox to the slaughter, and a fool to the correction of the stocks,' Prov. vii. 22. We cannot say that Satan's work lieth about these. Satan needeth not besiege the soul by temptations; that is his already by peaceable possession; 'when a strong man armed keepeth his palace, his goods are in peace,' Luke xi. 21. There is no storm when wind and tide goeth together. But then there is a third sort of men, that begin to be serious, and to mind their recovery by Christ: they have many good motions and convictions of the danger of sin, excellency of Christ, necessity of holiness; they have many purposes to leave sin and enter upon a holy course of life, but 'the wicked one cometh, and catcheth away that which was sown in his heart,' Mat. xiii. 19. He beginneth betimes to oppose the work, before we are confirmed and settled in a course of godliness, as he did set upon Christ presently upon his baptism. Baptism in us implieth avowed dying unto sin and living unto God; now God permitteth temptation to try our resolution. There is a fourth sort, of such as have made some progress in religion, even to a degree of eminency: these are not altogether free; for if the devil had confidence to assault the declared Son of God, will he be afraid of a mere mortal man? No; these he assaulteth many times very sorely: pirates venture on the greatest booty. These he seeketh to draw off from Christ, as Pharaoh sought to bring back the Israelites after their escape; or to foil them by some scandalous fall, to do religion a mischief: 2 Sam. xii. 14, 'By this deed thou hast given great occasion to the enemies of the Lord to blaspheme;' or at least to vex them and torment them, to make the service of God tedious and uncomfortable to them: Luke xxii. 31, 'Simon, Simon, behold, Satan hath desired to have you, that he might sift you as wheat'—to toss and vex you, as wheat in a sieve. So that no sort of Christians can promise themselves exemption; and God permitteth it, because to whom much is given, of them the more is required.

2. The manner and way of his fight is by the world, *per blanda et aspera*, by the good or evil things of the world. There is 'armour of righteousness on the right hand and on the left,' 2 Cor. vi. 7, as there are right-hand and left-hand temptations. Both ways he lieth in ambush in the creature. Sometimes he tempts us by the good things of the world: 1 Chron. xxi. 1, 'And Satan stood up against Israel, and provoked David to number Israel,' so glorying in his might, and puissance, and victory over neighbour kings. So meaner people he tempteth to abuse their wealth to pride and luxury; therefore we are pressed to be sober: 1 Pet. v. 8, 'Be sober, be vigilant; because your adversary the devil, as a roaring lion, walketh about, seeking whom he may devour.' The devil maketh an advantage of our prosperity, to divert us from God and heaven, and to render us unapt for the strictness of our holy calling. Sometimes he tempts us

by the evil things of this world : Job i. 11, ' Put forth thine hand now, and touch all that he hath, and he will curse thee to thy face.' Satan's aim in bringing the saints into trouble is to draw them to fretting, murmuring, despondency, and distrust of providence, yea, to open defection from God, or blasphemy against him ; and therefore it is said, 1 Pet. v. 9, ' Knowing that the same afflictions,' &c., because temptations are conveyed to us by our afflictions or troubles in the flesh.

3. His end is to dissuade us from good, and persuade us to evil. To dissuade us from good by representing the impossibility, trouble, and small necessity of it. If men begin to apply themselves to a strict course, such as they have sworn to in baptism, either it is so hard as not to be borne, as John vi. 60, ' This is a hard saying, who can bear it ? ' Whereas, Mat. xix. 29, ' Every one that hath forsaken houses, or brethren, &c., for my name's sake, shall receive an hundredfold, and shall inherit everlasting life.' Or the troubles which accompany a strict profession are many. The world will note us : John xii. 42, ' Nevertheless, among the chief rulers also many believed on him ; but because of the Pharisees, they did not confess him, lest they should be put out of the synagogue.' Whereas we must not be ashamed of Christ : 2 Tim. ii. 12, ' If we suffer, we shall also reign with him ; if we deny him, he also will deny us.' Or that we need not be so strict and nice, whereas all we can do is little enough : Mark xxv. 9, ' Not so, lest there be not enough for us and you.' In general, the greatest mischiefs done us by sin are not regarded, but the least inconvenience that attendeth our duty is urged and aggravated. He persuadeth us to evil by profit, pleasure, necessity ; we cannot live without it in the world. He hideth the hook, and showeth the bait only ; he concealeth the hell, the horror, the eternal pains that follow sin, and only telleth you how beneficial, profitable, and delightful the sin will be to you : Prov. ix. 17, 18, ' Stolen waters are sweet, and bread eaten in secret is pleasant. But he knoweth not that the dead are there, and that her guests are in the depths of hell.'

4. While we are striving against temptations, let us remember our general. We do but follow the Captain of our salvation, who hath vanquished the enemy, and will give us the victory if we keep striving : ' The God of peace shall bruise Satan under your feet shortly,' Rom. xvi. 2. Not *his* feet, but *ours :* we shall be conquerors. Our enemy is vigilant and strong : it is enough for us that our Redeemer is merciful and faithful in succouring the tempted, and able to master the tempter, and defeat all his methods. Christ hath conquered him, both as a lamb and as a lion : Rev. v. 5, 8. The notion of a lamb intimateth his sacrifice, the notion of a lion his victory : in the lamb is merit, in the lion strength ; by the one he maketh satisfaction to God, by the other he rescueth sinners out of the paw of the roaring lion, and maintaineth his interest in their hearts. Therefore let us not be discouraged, but closely adhere to him

SERMON II.

*And when he had fasted forty days and forty nights, he was after-
wards an hungered. And when the tempter came to him, he said,
If thou be the Son of God, command that these stones be made
bread. And he answered and said, It is written, Man liveth not by
bread alone, but by every word that proceedeth out of the mouth of
God.—MAT. IV. 2–4.*

In these words there are three branches:—

First, The occasion.

Secondly, The temptation itself.

Thirdly, Christ's answer.

First, The occasion of the first temptation, in the second verse,
'When he had fasted forty days and forty nights, he was afterwards
an hungered.' Where take notice:—

I. Of his fasting.

II. Of his hunger.

And something I shall speak of them conjunctly, something distinctly and apart.

1. Conjunctly. In every part of our Lord's humiliation, there is an
emission of some beams of his Godhead, that whenever he is seen to
be true man, he might be known to be true God also. Is Christ
hungry? There was a fast of forty days' continuance preceding, to
show how, as God, he could sustain his human nature. The verity of
his human nature is seen, because he submitted to all our sinless infirmities. The power of his divine nature was manifested, because it
enabled him to continue forty days and nights without eating or drinking anything, the utmost that an ordinary man can fast being but
nine days usually. Thus his divinity and humanity are expressed in
most or all of his actions: John i. 14, ' The word was made flesh, and
dwelt among us, and we beheld his glory, as the glory of the only-begotten Son of God.' There was a veil of flesh, yet the glory of his
divine nature was seen, and might be seen, by all that had an eye and
heart to see it. He lay in the manger at Bethlehem, but a star
appeared to conduct the wise men to him ; and angels proclaimed his
birth to the shepherds: Luke ii. 13, 14. He grew up from a child, at
the ordinary rate of other children ; but when he was but twelve years
old, he disputed with the doctors: Luke ii. 42. He submitted to
baptism, but then owned by a voice from heaven to be God's beloved
Son. He was deceived in the fig-tree when an hungered, which shows
the infirmity of human ignorance; but suddenly blasted, this manifested the glory of a divine power: Mat. xxi. 19. Here tempted by
Satan, but ministered unto and attended upon by a multitude of
glorious angels: Mat. iv. 11 ; finally crucified through weakness, but
living by the power of God: 2 Cor. xiii. 4. He hung dying on the
cross ; but then the rocks were rent, the graves opened, and the sun
darkened. All along you may have these intermixtures. He needed
to humble himself to purchase our mercies ; but withal to give a discovery of a divine glory to assure our faith. Therefore, when there

were any evidences of human frailty, lest the world should be offended, and stumble thereat, he was pleased at the same time to give some notable demonstration of the divine power; as, on the other side, when holy men are honoured by God, something falleth out to humble them : 2 Cor. xii. 7.

2. Distinctly and apart. Where observe :—

[1.] That he fasted forty days and forty nights ; so did Moses when he received the law : Exod. xxxiv. 28 ; and at the restoring of the law Elias did the like : 1 Kings xix. 8. Now what these two great prophets had done, Christ, the great prophet and doctor of the Christian church, did also. For the number of forty days, curiosity may make itself work enough ; but it is dangerous to make conclusions where no certainty appeareth. However this is not amiss, that forty days were the usual time allotted for repentance : as to the Ninevites, Jonah iii. 4 ; so the prophet Ezekiel was to bear the sins of the people for forty days ; and the flood was forty days in coming on the old world : Gen. vii. 17. This was the time given for their repentance, and therefore for their humiliation; yet the forty days' fast in Lent is ill-grounded on this example, for this fast of Christ cannot be imitated by us, more than other his miracles.

[2.] At the end of the forty days he was an hungered, sorely assaulted with faintness and hunger, as any other man at any time is for want of meat. God's providence permitted it, that he might be more capable of Satan's temptations; for Satan fits his temptations to men's present case and condition. When Christ was hungry, he tempteth him to provide bread, in such a way as the tempter doth prescribe. He worketh upon what he findeth : when men are full, he tempteth them to be proud, and forget God ; when they are destitute, to distrust God : if he sees men covetous, he fits them with a wedge of gold, as he did Achan ; if discontented, and plotting the destruction of another, he findeth out occasions. When Judas had a mind to sell his Master, he presently sendeth him a chapman. Thus he doth work upon our dispositions, or our condition; most upon our dispositions, but here only upon Christ's condition. He observeth which way the tree leaneth, and then thrusteth it forward.

Secondly, The temptation itself, verse the third. Where two things are observable :—

I. The intimation of his address, ' And when the tempter came to him.'

II. The proposal of the temptation, ' If thou be the Son of God,' &c.

I. For the address to the temptation, ' And when the tempter came to him,' there two things must be explained :—

1. In what manner the tempter came to Christ.

2. How he is said to come then to him.

[1.] How he came to him. Whether the temptations of Christ are to be understood by way of vision, or historically, as things visibly acted and done? This latter I incline unto ; and I handle here, because it is said, προσελθὼν αὐτῷ ὁ πειράζων,—' The tempter came to him.' This importeth some local motion and accession of the tempter to Christ, under a visible and external form and shape. As afterwards, when the Lord biddeth him be gone, 'then the devil leaveth him,' ver. 11; a retiring of Satan out of his presence, not the ceasing of a vision only. Yea, all along, he 'taketh him,' and 'sets him on a pinnacle of the temple,' and 'taketh him to an high mountain.' All which show some external appearance of Satan, and not a word that intimateth a vision. Neither can it be conceived how any act of adoration could be demanded by Satan of Christ—'fall down and worship me'—unless the object to be worshipped were set before him in some visible shape. The coming of the angels to Christ when the devil left him, ver. 11, all understand historically, and of some external coming. Why is not the coming and going of the devil thus to be understood also? And if all had been done in vision, and not by converse, how could Christ be an hungered, or the devil take that occasion to tempt him? How could answers and replies be tossed to and fro, and scriptures alleged? So that from the whole view of the frame of the text, here was some external congress between Christ and the devil. If you think it below Christ, you forget the wonderful condescension of the Son of God; it is no more unworthy of him than crucifixion, passion, and burial was. It is true, in the writing of the prophets, many things historically related were only done in vision; but not in the Gospels, which are an history of the life and death of Christ; where things are plainly set down as they were done. To men the grievousness of Christ's temptations would be much lessened, if we should think it only a piece of fantasy, and imaginary rather than real. And if his temptations be lessened, so will his victory, so will our comfort. In short, such as was Christ's journey into the wilderness, such was his fast, such his temptation; all real. For all are delivered to us in the same style and thread of discourse. Yea, further, if these things had been only in vision and ecstacy, there would have been no danger to Christ in the second temptation, when he was tempted to throw himself down from the pinnacle of the temple. Surely then he was truly tempted, and not in vision only; yea, it seemeth not so credible and agreeable to the dignity and holiness of Christ, that Satan should tempt by internal false suggestions, and the immission of *species* into his fancy or understanding; that Christ should seem to be here and there, when all the while he was in the desert. For either Christ took notice of these false images in his fancy, or not. If not, there is no temptation; if so, there will be an error in the mind of Christ, that he should think himself to be on the pinnacle of the temple, or top of an high mountain, when he was in the desert. It is hard to think these suggestions could be made without some error or sin; but an external suggestion maketh the sin to be in the tempter only, not in the person tempted. Our first parents lost not their innocency by the external suggestion, but internal admission of it, dwelling upon it in their minds. To a man void of sin, the tempter hath no way of tempting but externally.

[2.] How is this access to Christ said to be after his fasting, when, in Luke iv. 2, it is said, 'Being forty days tempted of the devil, and in those days he did eat nothing; and when they were ended, he afterward hungered'?

I answer—(1.) Some conceive that the devil tempted Christ all the forty days, but then he tempted him invisibly, as he doth other men, striving to inject sinful suggestions; but he could find nothing in him to work upon: John xiv. 30. But at forty days' end he taketh another course, and appeareth visibly in the shape of an angel of light. He saith he came to him, most solemnly and industriously to tempt him. This opinion is probable.

(2.) It may be answered, Luke's speech must be understood: 'Being forty days in the wilderness, and in those days he did eat nothing, and was tempted;' that is, those days being ended. There is, by a prolepsis, some little inversion of the order. But because of Mark i. 13, where it is said, 'He was in the wilderness forty days, tempted of Satan, and was with the wild beasts,' take the former answer.

II. The proposal of the temptation, 'If thou be the Son of God, command that these stones be made bread.' Certainly every temptation of the devil tendeth to sin. Now where is the sin of this? If Christ had turned stones into bread, and declared himself by this miracle to be the Son of God, there seemeth to be no such evil in this. Like miracles he did upon other occasions; as turning water into wine at a marriage feast, multiplying the loaves in the distribution for feeding the multitude. Here was no curiosity; the fact seemed to be necessary to supply his hunger. Here is no superfluity urged—into bread, not dainties or occasions of wantonness, but bread for his necessary sustenance. I answer, Notwithstanding all this fair appearance, yet this first assault which is propounded by Satan was very sore and grievous.

1. Because manifold sins are implied in it, and there are many temptations combined in this one assault.

[1.] In that Christ, who was led by the Spirit into the wilderness to fast, and so to be tempted, must now break his fast and work a miracle at Satan's direction. The contest between God and the devil is, who shall be sovereign? therefore it was not meet that Christ should follow the devil's advice, and do anything at his command and suggestion.

[2.] That Christ should doubt of that voice that he heard from heaven at his baptism, 'Thou art my beloved Son;' and the devil cometh, 'If thou be the Son of God.' That it should anew be put to trial by some extraordinary work, whether it were true or no, or he should believe it, yea or no. No temptation so sore, no dart so poisonable, as that which tendeth to the questioning of the grounds of faith; as this did the love of God, so lately spoken of him. Therefore this is one of the sharpest arrows that could come out of Satan's bow.

[3.] It tendeth to weaken his confidence in the care and love of God's fatherly providence: being now afflicted with hunger in a desert place, where no supply of food could be had, Satan would draw him to suspect and doubt of his Father's providence, as if it were incompatible to be the Son of God and to be left destitute of means to supply his hunger, and therefore must take some extraordinary course of his own to furnish himself.

[4.] It tended to put him upon an action of vainglory, by working a miracle before the devil, to show his power; as all needless actions are but a vain ostentation.

2. Because it was in itself a puzzling and perplexing proposal, not without inconveniences on both sides, whichsoever of the extremes our Lord should choose; whether he did, or did not, what the tempter suggested. If he did, he might seem to doubt of the truth of the oracle, by which he was declared to be the Son of God, or to distrust God's providence, or to give way to a vain ostentation of his own power. If he did not, he seemed to be wanting, in not providing necessary food for his sustentation when it was in his power to do so; and it seemed to be unreasonable to hide that which it concerned all to know, to wit, that he was the Son of God. And it seemeth grievous to hear others suspicious concerning ourselves, when it is in our power easily to refute them; such provocations can hardly be borne by the most modest spirits. This temptation was again put upon Christ on the cross: Mat. xxvii. 40, ' If thou be the Son of God, come down from the cross.' But all is to be done at God's direction, and as it becometh our obedience to him, and respect to his glory. Satan and his instruments will be satisfied with no proofs of principles of faith, but such as he and they will prescribe, and which cannot be given without entrenching upon our obedience to God, and those counsels which he hath wisely laid for his own glory. And if God's children be surprised with such a disposition, it argueth so far the influence of Satan upon them, namely, when they will not believe but upon their own terms: as Thomas, John xx. 25, ' Except I see in his hands the print of the nails, and put my finger into the print of the nails, and thrust my hand into his side, I will not believe.' If we will not accept of the graces of faith as offered by God, but will interpose conditions of our own prescribing, we make a snare to ourselves. God may in condescension to a weak believer grant what was his fault to seek, as he doth afterwards to Thomas, ver. 27; but there is no reason he should grant it to the devil, he being a malicious and incorrigible spirit, coming temptingly to ask it.

3. This temptation was cunning and plausible; it seemed only to tend to Christ's good, his refection when hungry, and his honour and glory, that this might be a full demonstration of his being the Son of God. There is an open solicitation to evil, and a covert; explicit and implicit; direct and indirect. This last here. It was not an open, direct, explicit solicitation to sin, but covert, implicit, and indirect, which sort of temptations are more dangerous. There was no need of declaring Christ's power by turning stones into bread before the devil, and at his instance and suit. It was neither necessary nor profitable. Not necessary for Christ's honour and glory, it being sufficiently evidenced before by that voice from heaven, or might be evident to him without new proof. Nor was it necessary for Christ's refection, because he might be sustained by the same divine power by which hitherto he had been supported for forty days. Nor was it profitable, none being present but the devil, who asked not this proof for satisfaction, but cavil; and that he might boast and gain advantage, if Christ had done anything at his instance and direction. And in this peculiar dispensation all was to be done by the direction

of the Holy, and not the impure spirit. I come now to the third branch.

Thirdly, Christ's answer, ver. 4, ' And he answered and said, It is written, Man liveth not by bread alone, but by every word that proceedeth out of the mouth of God.' Christ's answer is not made to that part of the proposal, ' If thou be the Son of God,' but to the urgent necessity of his refection. The former was clear and evident, the force of the temptation lay not there; but the latter, which Satan sought to make most advantage of, is clearly refuted. Christ's answer is taken out of Deut. viii. 3 ; and this answer is not given for the tempter's sake, but ours, that we may know how to answer in like cases, and repel such kind of temptations. In the place quoted, Moses speaketh of manna, and showeth how God gave his people manna from heaven, to teach them that though bread be the ordinary means of sustaining man, yet God can feed him by other means, which he is pleased to make use of for that purpose. His bare word, or nothing ; all cometh from his divine power and virtue, whatever he is pleased to give for the sustentation of man, ordinary or extraordinary. The tempter had said that either he must die for hunger, or turn stones into bread. Christ showeth that there is a middle between both these extremes. There are other ways which the wisdom of God hath found out, or hath appointed by his word, or decreed to such an end, and maketh use of in the course of his providence. And the instance is fitly chosen ; for he that provided forty years for a huge multitude in the desert, he will not be wanting to his own Son, who had now fasted but forty days. In the words there is :—

I. A concession or grant, that ordinarily man liveth by bread ; and therefore must labour for it, and use it when it may be had.

II. There is a restriction of the grant, that it is not by bread only : ' But by every word that proceedeth out of the mouth of God.' The business is to explain how a man can live by the word of God, or what is meant by it.

1. Some take *word* for the word of precept, and expound it thus : if you be faithful to your duty, God will provide for you. For in every command of God, general or particular, there is a promise expressed or implied of all things necessary : Deut. xxviii. 5, ' Blessed shall be thy basket and thy store ;' and Mat. vi. 33, ' Seek ye first the kingdom of God, and his righteousness, and all these things shall be added unto you.' Now we may lean upon this word of God, keep ourselves from indirect means, and in a fair way of providence refer the issue to God.

2. Some take the *word* for the word of promise, which indeed is the livelihood of the saints: Ps. cxix. 111, ' Thy testimonies have I taken as an heritage for ever ; they are the rejoicing of my heart.' God's people in a time of want can make a feast to themselves out of the promises ; and when seemingly starved in the creature, fetch not only peace and grace and righteousness, but food and raiment out of the covenant.

3. Rather, I think, it is taken for his providential word or commanded blessing ; for as God made all things by his word, so ' he upholdeth all things by the word of his power ': Heb. i. 3. His powerful word doth all in the world : Ps. cxlvii. 15, ' He sendeth forth his com-

mandment on the earth; his word runneth very swiftly; he giveth snow like wool.' And then, in the 18th verse, 'He sendeth out his word, and melteth them.' As the word of creation made all things, so the word of providence sustaineth all things. This word is spoken of Ps. cvii. 20, 'He sent his word, and his word healed them; and delivered them from all their destructions.' It is *dictum factum* with God; if he speak but the word, it is all done: Mat. viii. 8, 'Speak but the word, and thy servant shall be whole.' So Luke iv. 36, 'What a word is this! for with authority and power he commandeth the unclean spirits, and they come out.' So of Joseph it is said, Ps. cv. 19, 'Until the time that his word came; the word of the Lord tried him;' that is, his power and influence on the hearts of the parties concerned for his deliverance. Well, then, the power of sustaining life is not in bread, but in the word of God; not in the means, but in God's commanded blessing, which may be conveyed to us by means, or without means, as God pleaseth. There is a powerful commanding word which God useth for health, strength, sustentation, or any effect wherein the good of his people is concerned. He is the great commander of the world. If he say to anything Go, and it goeth; Come, and it cometh.

Thus you have the history of the first temptation. Now for the observations.

Observe, first, That God may leave his children and servants to great straits; for Christ himself was sorely an hungered: so God suffereth his people to hunger in the wilderness before he gave them manna. Therefore it is said, Ps. cii. 23, 'He weakeneth the strength of the people in the way.' He hath sundry trials wherewith to exercise our faith, and sometimes by sharp necessities. Paul and his companions had continued fourteen days, and had taken nothing: Acts xxvii. 33. Many times God's children are thus tried: trading is dead, and there are many mouths to be fed, and little supply cometh in; yet this is to be borne: none of us more poor than Christ, or more destitute than was Christ.

Secondly, That the devil maketh an advantage of our necessities. When Christ was an hungered, then the tempter came to him; so unto us. Three sorts of temptations he then useth to us, the same he did to Christ:—

[1.] Either he tempteth us to unlawful means to satisfy our hunger; so he did to Christ, who was to be governed by the Spirit, to work a miracle to provide for his bodily wants at Satan's direction; so us. Poverty hath a train of sinful temptations: Prov. xxx. 9, 'Lest I be poor, and steal, and take the name of my God in vain.' Necessities are urging, but we must not go to the devil for a direction how to supply ourselves, lest he draw us to put our hand to our neighbour's goods, or to defraud our brother, or betray the peace of our conscience, or to do some unworthy thing, that we may live the more comfortably. You cannot plead necessity; it is to relieve your charge, to maintain life; God is able to maintain it in his own way. No necessity can make any sin warrantable. It is necessary thou shouldst not sin; it is not necessary thou shouldst borrow more than thou canst pay. or use any fraudulent means to get thy sustenance. If others be unmerciful, thou must not be unrighteous.

[2.] To question our adoption, as he did the filiation of Christ : ' If thou be the Son of God.' It is no wonder to find Satan calling in question the adoption and regeneration of God's children, for he calleth in question the filiation and sonship of the Son of God, though so plainly attested but a little before : Heb. xii. 5, 'Ye have forgotten the exhortation which speaketh unto you as children, My son,' &c. Certainly whatever moveth us to question our interest in God's fatherly love, bare afflictions should not ; for to be without afflictions is a sign of bastards. God hath no illegitimate children, but God hath degenerate children, who are left to a larger discipline.

[3.] To draw us to a diffidence and distrust of God's providence : this he sought to breed in Christ, or at least to do something that might seem to countenance it, if he should upon his motion work a miracle. Certainly it is Satan's usual temptation to work in us a disesteem of God's goodness and care, and to make us pore altogether upon our wants. A sense of our wants may be a means to humble us, to quicken us to prayer ; but it should not be a temptation to beget in us unthankfulness, or murmuring against God's providence, or any disquietness or unsettledness in our minds. And though they may be very pinching, yet we should still remember that God is good to them that are of a clean heart : Ps. lxxiii. 1. God hath in himself allsufficiency, who knoweth both what we want, and what is fittest for us, and is engaged by his general providence as a faithful Creator : 1 Pet. iv. 19, ' Let them that suffer according to the will of God, commit the keeping of their souls to him in well-doing, as unto a faithful Creator ; ' but more especially as related to us as a Father : Mat. vi. 32, ' Your heavenly Father knoweth that you have need of all these things.' And by his faithful promise, Heb. xiii. 5, ' He hath said, I will never leave thee, nor forsake thee.' And he will give us every good thing while we fear him : Ps. xxxiv. 9, 10, ' O fear the Lord, ye his saints : for there is no want to them that fear him. The young lions do lack and suffer hunger : but they that seek the Lord shall not want any good thing.' And walk uprightly : Ps. lxxxiv. 11, ' For the Lord God is a sun and a shield : the Lord will give grace and glory : no good thing will he withhold from them that walk uprightly.' And seek it of him by prayer : Mat. vii. 11, ' Ask, and it shall be given you ; seek, and ye shall find ; knock, and it shall be opened unto you.'

But you will say, You preach only to the poor and destitute. I answer, I speak as my subject leadeth me : it will put the point generally ; Satan maketh an advantage of our condition. Christ had power to do what was suggested ; every condition hath its snares, a full condition most of all : Ps. lxix. 22, ' Let their table be a snare, their welfare for a trap.' He hideth his snares and gins to catch our souls. In all the comforts men enjoy they are apt to grow proud, to forget God, to become merciless to others who want what they enjoy ; to live in vain pleasures, and to forget eternity ; to live in sinful security, in the neglect of Christian duties ; to be enslaved to sensual satisfactions, to be flat and cold in prayer. This glut and fulness of worldly comforts is much more dangerous than our hunger.

Thirdly, observe, In tempting, Satan pretendeth to help the tempted party to a better condition; as here he seemeth careful to have bread provided for Christ at his need, yea, pretendeth respect to his glory, and to have him manifest himself to be the Son of God, by such a miracle as he prescribeth.   This seeming tenderness, counselling Christ to support his life and health, was the snare laid for him. Thus he dealt with our first parents : he seeketh to weaken the reputation of God's love and kindness to man, and to breed in the woman's mind a good opinion of himself.   That his suggestions might make the greater impression upon her, he manageth all his discourse with her, that all the advice which he seemeth to give her proceeded of his love and good affection towards her and her husband, pretending a more than ordinary desire and care of man's good, Gen. iii. 5, as if he could direct him how to become a match for God himself.   So still he dealeth with us ; for alas ! otherwise ' in vain is the snare laid in the sight of any bird,' Prov. i. 17.   He covereth the snare laid for man's destruction with a fair pretence of love to advance man to a greater happiness, and so pretendeth the good of those whom he meaneth wholly to destroy.   He enticeth the covetous with dishonest gain, which at length proveth a real loss : the sensual with vain pleasures, which at length prove the greatest pain to body and soul : the ambitious with honours, which really tend to their disgrace.   Always trust God, but disbelieve the devil, who promoteth man's destruction under a pretence of his good and happiness.   How can Satan and his instruments put us upon anything that is really good for us ?

Fourthly, That Satan's first temptations are more plausible. He doth not at first dash come with ' fall down and worship me ; ' but only pretendeth a respect to Christ's refection, and a demonstration of his sonship.   Few or none are so desperate at first as to leap into hell at the first dash, therefore the devil beginneth with the least temptations. First men begin with less evils, play about the brink of hell : a man at first taketh a liking to company, afterwards he doth a little enlarge himself into some haunts and merry meetings with his companions, then entereth into a confederacy in evil, till he hath brought utter ruin upon himself, and what was honest friendship at first proveth wicked company and sure destruction at last.   At first a man playeth for recreation, then ventureth a shilling or two, afterwards, by the witchery of gaming, off goeth all sense of thrift, honesty, and credit. At first a man dispenseth with himself in some duty, then his dispensation groweth into a settled toleration, and God is cast out of his closet, and his heart groweth dead, dry, and sapless.   There is no stop in sin, it is of a multiplying nature, and we go on from one degree to another ; and a little lust sets open the door for a greater, as the lesser sticks set the greater on fire.

Fifthly, There is no way to defeat Satan's temptations but by a sound belief of God's all-sufficiency, and the nothingness of the creature.

[1.] A sound belief of, and a dependence on, God's all-sufficiency : Gen. xvii. 1, ' I am the Almighty God ; walk before me, and be thou perfect.'   We need not warp, nor run to our shifts, he is enough to help to defend or reward us ; he can help us without means, though there be no supply in the view of sense, or full heaps in our own keeping. God knoweth when we know not: 2 Pet. ii. 9, 'The Lord knoweth how to deliver the godly out of temptations,' &c., or by contrary means, curing the eyes with spittle and clay. He can make a little means go far. As he blessed the pulse to the captive children, Dan. i. 15, and made the widow's barrel of meal and cruse of oil to hold out, 1 Kings xvii. 14, and his filling and feeding five thousand with a few barley loaves and a few fishes, Mat. xiv. 21; on the other side he can make abundance unprofitable: Luke xii. 15, 'A man's life consisteth not in the abundance of the things which he possesseth.' No means can avail unless God giveth his blessing; therefore we should not distrust his providence, nor attempt anything without God's warrant, lest we offend him, and provoke him to withdraw his blessing.

[2.] The nothingness of the creature: 'Not by bread alone.' It is nothing by way of comparison with God, nothing by way of exclusion of God, nothing in opposition to God. It should be nothing in our esteem, so far as it would be something separate from God, or in co-ordination with God: Isa. xl. 17, 'All nations before him are as nothing, less than nothing and vanity;' Job vi. 21, 'Now ye are nothing.' All friends cannot help, our foes cannot hurt us, not the greatest of either kind: Isa. xxxiv. 12, 'All her princes shall be nothing.' In regard of the effects which the world promiseth to its deluded lovers, all is as nothing; not only that it can do nothing to our needy souls to relieve us from the burden of sin, nothing towards the quiet and true peace of our wounded consciences, nothing to our acceptance with God, nothing for strength against corruptions and temptations, nothing at the hour of death; but it can do nothing for us during life, nothing to relieve and satisfy us in the world without God. Therefore God is still to be owned and trusted

---

SERMON III.

Then the devil taketh him up into the holy city, and setteth him on a pinnacle of the temple, and saith unto him, If thou be the Son of God, cast thyself down: for it is written, He shall give his angels charge concerning thee; and in their hands they shall bear thee up, lest at any time thou dash thy foot against a stone.—MAT. IV. 5, 6.

IN this second temptation I shall give you—(1.) The history of it; (2.) Observations upon it.

I. The history of it. There,
1. What Satan did.
2. What he said.
3. The soreness of the temptation.

1. What he did: 'Then the devil taketh him up into the holy city, and setteth him on a pinnacle of the temple.' There—(1.) Take notice of the ground which the devil chose for the conflict: 'He taketh him up into the holy city, and setteth him on the pinnacle of the

temple.' By *the holy city* is meant Jerusalem, for this name is given to it in other scriptures: Isa. lviii. 2, 'They call themselves of the holy city.' And Isa. lii. 1, 'O Jerusalem, the holy city;' and in many other places. It was so called, because it was the seat of God's worship, and the place where God manifested his gracious presence with his people. If you ask why now it was called the holy city, since it was a city of blood, the seat of all wickedness, in which the law of God was depraved, their religion corrupted, their religion polluted? I answer, Yet there was the temple of the Lord. Some relics of good and holy men, some grace yet continued, and the only place that owned the true God, though with much corruption. The more especial place which the devil chose for the conflict was πτερύγιον τοῦ ἱεροῦ, 'the pinnacle of the temple,' or, 'the wing of the temple;' meaning the border round about the flat covering of the temple to hinder any one from falling off easily, which might be adorned with pinnacles and spires, from whence one might easily fall. (2.) How the devil got him there? Whether Christ was carried through the air, or went on his feet, following him of his own accord? The last seemeth to be countenanced by Luke; that he led him to the pinnacle of the temple, Luke iv. 9, ἤγαγεν αὐτὸν; yet the former is preferred by most ancient and modern interpreters, and not without reason. For Christ voluntarily to follow the devil, and to go up to the top of the temple, and stand on one of the pinnacles thereof, it seemeth improbable, and would take up more time than could be spent on this temptation. He that would not obey the devil persuading him to cast himself down, that he might not tempt God, would not voluntarily have gone up with him, for that would have been the beginning of a temptation, to yield so far. Most probably, then, Satan was permitted to carry him in the air, without doing him any hurt, to Jerusalem, and one of the pinnacles of the temple and battlements thereof. But how Christ was carried in the air, visibly or invisibly, the scripture showeth not: it affirmeth the thing, but sets not down the manner. We must believe what it asserteth, reverence what it concealeth. Here was a real translation, a transportation from place to place, not imaginary, for then Christ had been in no danger. And again, not violent, but voluntary—a carrying, not a haling—a leading, not a forcing, as the wrestler is drawn on to the combat. As he suffered himself to be drawn to death by Satan's instruments, so by the devil to be translated from place to place. The officers of the high priest had power to carry him from the garden to Annas, from Annas to Caiaphas, from Caiaphas to Pilate, from Pilate to Herod, from Herod to Pilate again, and then from Gabbatha to Golgotha, which could not have been unless this power had been given them from above, as Christ himself telleth Pilate, John xix. 11. So God, for his greater glory and our instruction, permitted this transportation; therefore this translation is not to be imputed to the weakness of Christ, but his patience, submitting thus far that he might experience all the machinations of Satan; and the transporting is not to be ascribed to the tempter's strength, but his boldness. Christ did not obey him, but submitted to the divine dispensation, and would fight with him not only in the desert, but in the holy city: and no wonder if Christ suffered Satan to carry him, who suffered his instruments to crucify him.

2. What he said to him, ver. 6, where take notice—(1.) Of the temptation itself, 'If thou be the Son of God, cast thyself down.' (2.) The reason alleged to back it, 'For it is written, He shall give his angels charge concerning thee,' &c.

[1.] The temptation itself: 'If thou be the Son of God, cast thyself down.' Mark what was the mote in the devil's eye, that Christ was declared to be the Son of God, the Messiah and Saviour of the world. He would have him to put it to this proof in the sight of all Jerusalem, wherein, if he failed, and had died of the fall, the Jews would think him an impostor; if he had escaped, he had submitted to the devil's methods, and so had run into the former sins mentioned before in the first temptation, his doing something at the devil's direction; his disbelief of the divine oracle, unless manifested by such proof as Satan required; and besides a tempting of divine providence—the ordinary way was down stairs. He would have him leap, and throw himself over the battlements. It would be too long to go down stairs; he will teach him a nearer way: to cast himself down and fear no hurt, for if he were the Son of God he might securely do so. But chiefly Christ was not to begin his ministry by miracles, but doctrine—not from a demonstration of his power, but wisdom. The gospel was to be first preached, then sealed and confirmed by miracles; and Christ's miracles were not to be ludicrous, but profitable—not fitted for pomp, but use— to instruct and help men, rather than strike them with wonder. Now this would discredit the gospel, if Christ should fly in the air; besides, we must not fly to extraordinary means, where ordinary are present.

Only, before I go off, observe that Satan did not offer to cast him down; that God did not suffer him to do, because he sought to bring Christ to sin. If Satan had cast him down, Christ had not sinned.

[2.] The reason by which he backeth the temptation. It is taken from scripture: 'For it is written, He shall give his angels charge concerning thee.' The scripture is in Ps. xci. 11, 12, where the words run thus: 'He shall give his angels charge over thee, to keep thee in all thy ways. They shall bear thee up in their hands, lest thou dash thy foot against a stone.' Where,

First, Observe the devil's cunning in citing scripture. The apostle telleth us that Satan is sometimes transformed into an angel of light, 2 Cor. xi. 14. And we read that once he took the habit and guise of a prophet, 1 Sam. xxviii. 18; and indeed he deceiveth more by the voice of Samuel than by the voice of the dragon. We read of τὰ βάθη τοῦ Σατανᾶ, 'The depths of Satan,' Rev. ii. 24. Here he cometh like a divine, with a Bible in his hand, and turneth to the place; here the enemy of God cometh with the word of God, and disguiseth the worst of actions with the best of words, opposeth God to God, and turneth his truth to countenance a lie. Being refuted by scripture, he will bring scripture too, and pretendeth to reverence that which he chiefly hateth. Christians, you have not to do with a foolish devil, who will appear in his own colours and ugly shape, but with a devout devil, who, for his own turn, can pretend to be godly.

Secondly, That he citeth such a scripture, which exceedingly conduceth to commend the happiness of the godly; for God will not only be the keeper and guardian of them that fear him, but hath also appointed the ministry of angels; and the argument of the tempter seemeth to be taken from the less to the greater; for if it be true of every one that trusts in God, and dwelleth in the shadow of the Almighty, that God will have such a care of him, much more will he have a care of his beloved Son, in whom he is well pleased. Therefore, you that are declared to be so from heaven, and having such an occasion to show yourself to be the Son of God with so much honour and profit, why should you scruple to cast yourself down?

But wherein was the devil faulty in citing the scripture? Some say in leaving out those words, *in all thy ways.* This was Bernard's gloss—*in viis, non in præcipitiis;* will keep you in your ways or duties, not in your headlong actions; these were none of his ways, to throw himself down from the battlements of the temple. This is not to be altogether rejected, because it reaches the sense; yet this omission was not the devil's fault in citing this scripture; for, *all thy ways* signifieth no more but in all thy actions and businesses, and that is sufficiently implied in the words cited by Satan. But the devil's error was in application. He applieth the word of God, not to instruct, but deceive; rather to breed a contempt, disdain, and hatred of scriptures, than a reverent esteem of them; to make the word of God seem uncertain; or if a reverence of them, to turn this reverence into an occasion of deceit; more particularly to tempt God to a needless proof of his power. We are not to cast ourselves into danger, that providence may fetch us off. God will protect us in the evils we suffer, not in the evils we commit—not in dangers we seek, but such as befall us besides our intention.

3. The soreness of this temptation, which appeareth in several things.

[1.] The change of place. For a new temptation, he maketh choice of a new place; he could do no good on him in the wilderness, therefore he taketh him and carrieth him into the holy city. Here was a public place where Christ might discover himself with profit, and the edification of many, if he would but submit to the devil's methods. In the temple the Messiah was as in his own house, where it was fit the Messiah should exhibit himself to his people. There was an old prophecy, Mal. iii. 1, 'The Lord, whom ye seek, shall suddenly come into his temple, even the messenger of the covenant, whom ye delight in.' And he was to send forth his rod out of Zion, even the law of his kingdom: Ps. cx. 2. If he would yield to this advice and vainglorious ostentation of his power before that numerous multitude which continually resorted to the holy things performed in the temple, how soon should he be manifested to be the Son of God, or the power of the great God. The devil doth not persuade him to cast himself from a rock or top of a tree in the desert—that had been temerity and rashness—but from a pinnacle of the temple, an holy place, and a place of much resort. But the Son of God was not to be discovered to the world by the devil's methods. That had been such a piece of ostentation and vainglory as did not become the Son of God, who came to teach the world humility. But, however, the temptation is grievous:

in so good a design, in such an holy place, there could no ill happen
to the Son of God, nor a better occasion be offered of showing himself
to many, so to confirm the Jews in the truth of the oracle they had of
late heard from heaven.

[2.] The change of temptations. Since he will trust, the devil will
put him upon trusting; he shall trust as much as he will. There he
tempted him to the use of unlawful means to preserve his life, here to
the neglect of things lawful. There, that God would fail him if he
were still obedient to the Spirit, and did not take another course than
divine providence had as yet offered to him; here, that God would not
forsake him, though he threw himself into danger. There, that he
would fail though he had promised; here, that he would help though
he had not promised. That faith which sustained him in his hunger
would preserve him in this precipice; if he expected his preservation
from God, why not now? He had hitherto tempted him to diffidence,
now to prefidence, or an over-confident presumption that God would
needlessly show his power. It is usual with the tempter to tempt man
on both sides; sometimes to weaken his faith, at other times to neglect
his duty. He was cast out of heaven himself, and he is all for casting
down.

[3.] The temptation was the more strong, being veiled under a pretence of scripture, and so Christ's weapons seem to be beaten back
upon himself. The devil tempted him to nothing but what he might
be confident to do upon the promise of God. Now it is grievous to
God's children, when the rule of their lives and the charter of their
hopes is abused to countenance a temptation.

II. The observations.

1. Observe, that the first temptation being rejected by Christ, Satan
maketh a new assault. Though he get the foil, he will set on us again;
like a troublesome fly that is often beaten off, yet will return to the
same place. Thus the devil, when he could do no good upon his first
patent against Job's goods and children, cometh and sueth for a new
commission, that he might touch his flesh and bones: Job ii. 4, 5,
'Skin for skin, yea, all that a man hath will he give for his life. But
put forth thine hand now, and touch his bone and his flesh, and he
will curse thee to thy face.' Satan is incessant in his attempts against
the saints, and is ready to assault afresh upon every occasion. Now
this cometh to pass by Satan's unwearied malice, who is a sworn
enemy to our peace and welfare—he still 'seeketh to devour' us,
1 Peter v. 8; also from God's providence, who permitteth this that we
may not be careless and secure after temptation, though we have gotten
the victory; for our life is a continual warfare: Job vii. 1, 'Is there
not an appointed time for man upon earth?' The same word signifieth also a warfare. Man's life is a perpetual toil, and a condition of
manifold temptations and hazards, such as a soldier is exposed to;
therefore we must perpetually watch. We get not an absolute victory
till death. Now this should the more prevail with us, because many
of God's people have failed after some eminent service performed for
God. Josiah, after he had prepared the temple, fell into that rash
attempt against Pharaoh Necho which cost him his life: 2 Chron. xxxv.
20, 'After all this, when Josiah had prepared the temple, Necho, king

of Egypt, came up to fight against Carchemish by Euphrates; and
Josiah went out against him.' And Peter, after he had made a
glorious confession, giveth his Master carnal counsel: Mat. xvi. 18,
'Thou art Peter, and upon this rock will I build my church,' &c.; and
yet, ver. 23, 'Get thee behind me, Satan.' Many, after they have
been much lifted up in consolation, do readily miscarry. First, he
made a glorious confession, a sign of great faith; then carnal wisdom
vents itself in some counsel concerning the ease of the flesh. Oh, what
need have we to stand upon our guard, till God tread Satan under our
feet! As one of the Roman generals, whether conquering or conquered, *semper instaurat pugnam*, so doth Satan.

2. Observe, God may give Satan some power over the body of one
whom he loveth dearly. For Satan is permitted to transport Christ's
body from the wilderness to the holy city, and to set it on a pinnacle
of the temple. As it is very consistent with God's love to his people
to suffer them to be tempted in their souls by the fiery darts of Satan,
so he may permit Satan to afflict their bodies, either by himself, or by
witches, who are his instruments. Thus he permitted Satan to afflict
Job, chap. ii. 6, 7, 'And the Lord said unto Satan, Behold, he is in
thy hand, but save his life. So went Satan forth from the presence of
the Lord, and smote Job with sore boils, from the sole of his foot
unto his crown.' The devil may have a threefold power over the
bodies of men :—

[1.] By transportations, or carrying them from one place to another,
which usually is not found but in those that give up themselves to
his diabolical enchantments. Or,

[2.] In possessions, which were frequent and rife in Christ's time :
'My daughter is sorely vexed with a devil,' Mat. xv. 22. Or,

[3.] In diseases, which is more common. Thus he afflicted Job's
body with ulcers; and what we read, Ps. xli. 8, 'An evil disease
cleaveth fast unto him.' It is דְּבַר־בְּלִיַּעַל 'a thing of Belial,' as if it
were a pestilential disease from the devil. So some understand that,
Ps. xci. 3, 'Surely he shall deliver thee from the snare of the fowler,
and from the noisome pestilence.' As if those sudden darts of venom
by which we are stricken in the plague came from Satan. Certainly evil angels may have a great hand in our diseases : Ps. lxxviii.
49, 'He cast upon them the fierceness of his anger, wrath, and indignation, and trouble, by sending evil angels among them.' But I press
it not much. Only,

(1.) A word of patience, that we would submit to God, though our
trials be never so sharp. We must yield to that measure of humiliation which it shall please God to prescribe. If he should give leave
to Satan to inflame our blood and trouble the humours of our body,
we must not repine; the Son of God permitted his sacred body to be
transported by the devil in the air.

(2.) A word of comfort. Whatever power God permitteth Satan
to have over our bodies, or bodily interests, yet it is limited; he cannot
hurt or molest any further than God pleaseth. He had power to set
Christ on a pinnacle of the temple, but not to cast him down. He
had a power to touch Job's skin, but a charge not to endanger his

life : Job ii. 6, ' Behold, he is in thine hand, but save his life.' God
sets bounds and limits to the malice of Satan, that he is not able to
compass all his designs. Job was to be exercised, but God would not
have him die in a cloud, his life was to be secured till better times.

(3) A word of caution. Let not the devil make an advantage of
those troubles which he bringeth upon our bodies, or the interests of
the bodily life, yet let him not thereby draw you to sin. Here the
devil may set Christ upon a precipice, but he can do him no further
hurt ; he may persuade us to cast down ourselves, but he cannot cast
us down unless we cast down ourselves, *Nemo læditur nisi a seipso.*
His main spite is at your souls, to involve you in sin. God may give
him and his instruments a power over your bodily lives, but he doth
not give him a power over the graces of the saints. The devil aimeth
at the destruction of souls ; he can let men enjoy the pleasures of sin
for a season, that he may deprive you of delight in God and celestial
pleasures ; he can be content that you shall have dignities and
honours if they prove a snare to you. If the devil seek to bring you
to poverty, trouble, and nakedness, it is to draw you from God. He
careth not for the body but as it may be an occasion to ruin the soul.

3. Observe, If Satan lead us up, it is to throw us down. He
taketh up Christ to the pinnacle of the temple, and saith unto him,
'Cast thyself down.' He bringeth up many by little and little to
some high place, that by their aspiring they may at length break
their necks. Thus he did Haman, and so he doth many others, whose
climbing maketh way for their greater fall. The devil himself was
an aspirer, and fell from heaven like lightning : Luke x. 18, ' I
beheld Satan as lightning fall from heaven.' And though in show he
may seem to befriend many that hearken to his temptations, yet in
the end he crieth, ' Down with them, down with them, even to the
ground.' God's manner is quite contrary ; when he meaneth to exalt
a man, he will first humble him, and make him low : Mat. xxiii. 12,
' Whosoever shall exalt himself shall be abased ; and he that shall
humble himself shall be exalted.' But the devil's way is to lift them
up to the clouds, that he may bring them down to the lowest pit of
destruction. Adam, in conceit, must be like God, that indeed he may
be like the beasts that perish : Ps. xlix. 20, ' Man that is in honour,
and understandeth not, is like the beasts that perish.'

4. Observe, ' If thou be the Son of God, cast thyself down.' The
temptation is quite contrary to what it was before. Then it was to
preserve life by unlawful means, now to endanger life by the neglect
of means lawful ; there to distrust God's care of our preservation
when he hath set us about any task or work, here to presume on his
care without warrant. The devil tempts us sometimes to pamper
the flesh, sometimes to neglect it in such a way as is destructive to
our service. Thus the devil hurrieth us from one extreme to another, as
the possessed man ' fell oft-times into the fire, and oft into the water,'
Mat. xvii. 15. Those that are guided by Satan reel from one extremity to another ; either men slight sin and make light of it, or
sinners are apt to sorrow above measure, as the incestuous Corinthian :
2 Cor. ii. 17, ' Lest perhaps such an one should be swallowed up with
overmuch sorrow.' And the apostle showeth there that these were the

enterprises of Satan.   Some men are careless of God's interest in the world, or else heated into the activity of a bitter zeal.   Some are of a scrupulous spirit, that they may make conscience of all things ; and the devil hurrieth them into a large atheistical spirit, that they make conscience of nothing.   How often have we known a fond scrupulosity to end in a profane licentiousness, when they have been wearied out of that kind of frame of spirit !   Some are dead and heartless, like Gallio,—' care for none of these things ;' fight Christ, fight Antichrist, it is all one to them ; and usually they are such as formerly have been heated with a blind and bold madness : as Peter at first refused to have his feet washed by Christ, and then would have head, hands, feet and all washed, John xiii. 8, 9, being out in both.   What sad work is there made in the church of God by Soli-fidians and Nullifidians : heretofore it was all faith and free grace misapplied and misunderstood ; and now it is all morality and virtue, while Christ is neglected, and the mystery of the gospel little set by or valued.   It is ever the devil's policy to work upon the humour of people.   If they will reform the church, it shall be to a degree of separation, and condemning all churches and Christians that are not of their mode ; if they be for uniting, Christ's unquestionable interests must be trodden underfoot, and all care of truth and reformation must be laid aside.   If he can destroy religion and godliness no other way, he will be religious and godly himself ; but it is either, as to private Christians, to set them upon overdoing, that he may make them weary of the service of Christ ; or, as to the public, by crying up some unnecessary things, which Christ never commanded.   If men be troubled with sin, and see a necessity of the gospel, and prize the comforts of it, the gospel must be over-gospelled, or else it will not serve their turns ; and that over-gospel must be carried to such a length as to destroy the very gospel, and free grace itself.   The devil first tempted the world to despise the poor fishermen that preached the gospel ; but the world, being convinced by the power of the Holy Ghost, and gained to the faith, then he fought by riches and grandeur to debase the gospel ; so that he hath got as much or more by the worldly glory he puts upon Christ's messengers as by persecution.   Then, when that is discovered, the devil will turn reformer ; and what reformation is that ? the very necessary support and main-tenance of ministers must be taken away.   All overdoing in God's work is undoing.   If Christ will trust, the devil will persuade him to trust, even to the degree of tempting God.

5. Observe, That the devil himself may pretend scripture to put a varnish upon his evil designs ; for here he seeketh to foil Christ with his own weapons : which serveth to prevent a double ex-treme.

[1.] One is, not to be frighted with the mere noise and sound of scriptures, which men bring to countenance their errors.   See whether they be not wrested and misapplied ; for the devil may quote scripture, but he perverts the meaning of it.   And usually it is so by his instru-ments ; as that pope, who would prove a double power to be in him-self, temporal and spiritual, by that scripture, *Ecce duo gladii !* ' Behold, here are two swords !' Luke xxii. 38.   It is easy to rehearse the words of scripture, and therefore not the bare words, but the meaning must be regarded.

[2.] The other extreme is this: Let none vilify the scriptures, because pleaded by Satan; for so he might as well vilify human reason, which is pleaded for all the errors in the world; or law, because it is urged sometimes to justify a bad cause. For it is not scripture, that is not a nose of wax, as Papists say. It is a great proof of the authority and honour of scriptures, that Satan and his greatest instruments do place their greatest hopes of prevailing by perverting and misapplying of it.

6. Observe, That God hath given his angels a special charge about his people, to keep them from harm. Here I shall show :—

[1.] That it is so.

[2.] Why it is so.

First, That it is so is evident by the scripture, which everywhere shows us that angels are the first instruments of his providence, which he maketh use of in guarding his faithful servants: Heb. i. 14. The apostle saith, 'Are they not all, λειτουργικὰ πνεύματα, ministering spirits, sent forth to minister to them that shall be the heirs of salvation?' Their work and employment is to attend us at God's direction, not to be worshipped and served by us by any devotion. They are 'ministering spirits,' not ours, but Christ's; he that serveth hath a master whom he serveth, and by whom he is sent forth: their work and employment is to attend us indeed, but at the command and direction of their own Master. They are not at our beck to go and come at our pleasure, neither do they go and come at their inclination, but at the commission of God: their work is appointed by him, they serve us as their Master's children, at his command and will; and whom do they serve? 'The heirs of salvation.' They are described, Titus iii. 7, 'That being justified by grace, we should be made heirs according to the hope of eternal life.' They are not ministers of conversion and sanctification: to this ministry Christ hath called men, not angels; but in preserving the converted the angels have a hand. Therefore it is notable they are sometimes called God's angels: Ps. ciii. 21, 'Bless the Lord, all ye his hosts, ye ministers of his that do his pleasure;' sometimes their angels: Mat. xviii. 10, 'Take heed that ye despise not one of these little ones, for I say unto you, that in heaven their angels do always behold the face of my Father which is in heaven.'

But whether every one hath an angel-guardian is a curious question. Sometimes one angel serveth many persons: Ps. xxxiv. 7, 'The angel of the Lord encampeth round about them that fear him, and delivereth them;' and sometimes many angels are about one person: 2 Kings vi. 17, 'And, behold, the mountain was full of horses and chariots round about Elisha.' And here in the text quoted by Satan, 'He shall give his angels charge concerning thee.' There is not mention made of one, but many angels, and the angels in general are said to be ministering spirits. When soldiers are said to watch for a city, it is not meant that every citizen hath a soldier to watch for him.

The only place which seemeth to countenance that opinion is Acts xii. 15, 'Then said they, It is his angel.' But if Peter had a peculiar angel to guard him, and look after him then, when he was in great trouble, and detained in prison, it doth not follow that every person and everywhere should have an angel-guardian.   Besides, an assertion in scripture must be distinguished from men introduced speaking in scripture.   It showeth, indeed, that it was the opinion of the Jews at that time, which these holy men had imbibed and drunk in.   Or it may be the word *angel* is only taken for a *messenger* sent from Peter. Why should an angel stand knocking at the door, who could easily make his entrance ?   And is it credible that the guardian angels do take their shape and habit whose angels they are ?   It is enough for us to believe that all the angels are our guardians, who are sent to keep us and preserve us, as it pleaseth God.

But what is their ministry and custody ?   It is not *cura animarum*, care and charge of souls ; that Christ taketh upon himself, and performeth it by his Spirit ; but *ministerium externi auxilii*, to afford us outward help and relief : it is *custodia corporis*, they guard the bodily life chiefly.   Thus we find them often employed.   An angel brought Elijah his food under the juniper-tree : 1 Kings xix. 5.   An angel stirred the waters at the Pool of Siloam : John v. 4.   An angel was the guide of the way to Abraham's servant : Gen. xxiv. 7, ' He will send his angel before thee, and thou shalt take a wife unto my son from thence.'   Angels defend us against enemies : Ps. xxxiv. 7, ' The angel of the Lord encampeth round about them that fear him, and delivereth them ; ' 2 Kings xix. 35, ' The angel of the Lord went out, and smote in the camp of the Assyrians an hundred fourscore and five thousand.'   An angel opened the prison doors to the apostles : Acts v. 19, and xii. 7.

But were not all these services extraordinary and miraculous, which we may not now expect ?

Ans. The visible ministry was extraordinary, proper to those times; but the invisible is perpetual and ordinary, as Abraham's servant did not see the angel in the journey.   The devil worketh in and about wicked men invisibly, so do the good angels.

Secondly, Reasons why it is so.

(1.) To manifest the great love and care which God hath over his people ; therefore he giveth those blessed spirits, which behold his face, charge concerning his people on earth ; as if a nobleman were charged to look to a beggar by the prince of both.

(2.) We understand the operation of finite agents better than infinite. God is so far out of the reach of our commerce, that we cannot understand the particularity of his providence.

(3.) To counterwork the devil : evil angels are ready to hurt us, and therefore good angels are ready to preserve us.   Well might the devil be so well versed in this place ; he hath often felt the effects of it ; he knew it by experience, being so often encountered by the good angels in his endeavours against the people of God.

(4.) To begin our acquaintance, which in heaven shall be perfected : Heb. xii. 22, ' Ye are come to an innumerable company of angels.'

Use 1. To show the happy state of God's people.   No heirs of a crown have such guards as they have.   Christ dwelleth in their hearts as in a throne : Eph. iii. 17, ' That Christ may dwell in your hearts

by faith.' The Holy Spirit guardeth them against all cares and fears:
Phil. iv. 7, 'And the peace of God, which passeth all understanding,
shall keep your hearts and minds through Jesus Christ.' And the
good angels are as a wall and camp about them: Ps. xxxiv. 7, 'The
angel of the Lord encampeth round about them that fear him, and
delivereth them;' Mat. xviii. 10, 'Despise not one of these little ones,
for verily I say unto you, that in heaven their angels do always behold
the face of my Father which is in heaven.' If the angels make an
account of them, surely men should not despise them; yea, rather,
God esteemeth so much of the meanest of these little ones, that the
good angels, who daily enjoy God's glorious presence, are ministering
spirits appointed to attend them. If the Lord and his holy angels set
such a price on the meanest Christians, we should be loth to despise
and offend them.

2. It should breed some confidence and comfort in Christians in
their sore straits and difficulties, when all visible help seemeth to be
cut off. This invisible ministry of the angels is matter of faith: 2
Kings vi. 16, 17, 'And he answered, Fear not: for they that be with
us are more than they that be with them. And Elisha prayed, and
said, Lord, I pray thee, open the young man's eyes, that he may see.
And the Lord opened the young man's eyes, and he saw: and, behold,
the mountain was full of horses and chariots of fire round about
Elisha.' These were no other but the angels of God, which were as an
host to defend them. Open the eye of faith, you may see God, and
his holy angels to secure you.

3. Take we heed how we carry ourselves, because of this honourable
presence. In congregations there should be no indecency, 'because of
the angels,' 1 Cor. xi. 10. In all our ways let us take heed that we
do not step out of God's way. Do nothing that is unseemly and dishonest; they are spies upon us. And it is profitable for us, that they
may give an account of us to God with joy, and not with grief.

SERMON IV.

*Jesus said unto him, It is written again, Thou shalt not tempt the
Lord thy God.*—MAT. IV. 7.

HERE is Christ's answer to the second temptation, where two things
are observable:—

First, That Christ answered.

Secondly, What he answered.

First, That Christ answered. Christ answered, the more to convince and confound this old deceiver, that he might not think that he
was ignorant of his sleights, or that he fainted in the conflict; as also
to instruct us what to do in the renewed assaults of the devil, to keep
up our resistance still, not letting go our sure hold, which are the
scriptures.

Secondly, What he answered, 'It is written,' &c.　But would it not have been more satisfactory to have said, It is sufficiently manifest to me that I am the Son of God, and cared for by him, and that it is not for the children of God to run upon precipices?

I answer: It is not for human wisdom to interpose and prescribe to Christ, who was the wisdom and power of God.　His answer is most satisfactory, for two reasons :—

1. It striketh at the throat of the cause.

2. It doth with advantage give us other instructions.

1. Christ cutteth the throat of the temptation by quoting a passage of scripture, out of Deut. vi. 16, ' Ye shall not tempt the Lord your God, as ye tempted him in Massah.'　If we must not tempt God, then it doth not become Christ to tempt his Father's providence for a new proof of his filiation and care over him.　Therefore the devil's temptation was neither good nor profitable, to put either his sonship or the care of God's providence to this trial ; as if he had said, I shall not require any more signs to prove my filiation, nor express any doubt of his power and goodness towards me, as the Israelites did : Exod. xvii. 7, 'And he called the name of the place Massah, and Meribah, because of the chiding of the children of Israel, and because they tempted the Lord, saying, Is the Lord among us, or not?'　To which story this prohibition of tempting God alludeth.

2. He doth with advantage give us other instructions ; as,

[1.] That we must not esteem the less of scripture, though Satan and his instruments abuse it ; and that nothing is more profitable to dissolve doubts and objections raised from scripture, than to compare one scripture with another.　For scripture is not opposite to scripture ; there is a fair agreement and harmony between the truths therein compared ; and one place doth not cross another, but clear and explain another.　One place saith he hath a great care of his people, and useth the ministry of angels for that end and purpose ; but another place saith, ' Thou shalt not tempt the Lord thy God ; ' they must not seek out dangers, and forfeit their protection by unreasonable presumption.

[2.] It teacheth us that what the scripture speaketh to all, is to be esteemed as spoken to every singular person, for they are included in their universality.　In Deuteronomy it is, ' Ye shall not tempt the Lord *your* God ; ' but Christ accommodateth it to his own purpose, ' Thou shalt not tempt the Lord *thy* God.'　He that is not to be tempted by a multitude, is not to be tempted by any one.　So Ps. xxvii. 8, ' When thou saidst, Seek ye my face, my heart said unto thee, Thy face, Lord, will I seek.'　God's words invite all, but David maketh application to himself.

[3.] Christ subjects himself to the moral law, and did apply the precepts thereof to himself, no less than to us ; and so is a pattern of obedience to us, that we ought to direct and order all our actions according to the law and word of God.

Doct. Tempting of God may be a usual, but yet it is a great and heinous sin.　In speaking to this point, I shall show :—

I. What this tempting of God is.

II. The heinousness of the sin.

I. What is this tempting of God?   And here let me speak:—

1. To the object.

2. To the act.

First, The object, *The Lord thy God.*   To us Christians there is but one only true God, Father, Son, and Holy Ghost.   Now sometimes we are said to tempt God, and sometimes Christ, and sometimes the Spirit of God.

[1.] In scripture we are said to tempt God, as Ps. xcv. 9, 'When your fathers tempted me, proved me, and saw my works.'   We tempt God either explicitly or implicitly.

(1.) Explicitly, by plain and direct words, which tend to God's dishonour ; or a doubting of his prescience, power, and providence, if they have not all things given them according to their fancies and humours.   As Ps. lxxviii. 18, 19, 'They tempted God in their hearts, by asking meat for their lusts.   Yea, they spake against God, and said, Can God provide a table in the wilderness?'   So Exod. xvii. 7, 'Is the Lord in the midst of us, or no?'   They doubted whether God's presence were among them, when they had continually such pregnant proofs of it.   The words may either bear this sense, Who knows that God is present? or, Now see whether God be present, or takes any care of us, yea or no.

(2.) Implicitly, or by interpretation, which is a more secret way of tempting God, when the act speaketh it, whatever be the intention of the doer.   As those who were about to lay the burden of the rites of Moses's law on the new converts of the Gentiles : Acts xv. 10, 'Now, therefore, why tempt ye God, to put a yoke upon the necks of the disciples, which neither our fathers nor we were able to bear?'   That is, why do you not acquiesce in the will of God, apparently manifested, as if ye did go about to try whether God did require anything of his servants besides faith in Christ?   His will was clearly evident in the case by what happened to Cornelius ; or as if ye would try whether God will take it well that ye should impose upon his disciples a yoke that he approveth not.

[2.] We are said to tempt Christ ; and he may be considered either as in the days of his flesh, or in his state of glory, and with respect to his invisible presence:—

(1.) In the days of his flesh he was frequently tempted by the scribes and Pharisees, who would not be satisfied in his mission, notwithstanding all the signs and wonders that he had wrought among them ; or else sought to accuse and disgrace him, and prejudice the people against him ; so Mat. xvi. 1, 'The Pharisees with the Sadducees came, and tempting him, desired him that he would show them a sign from heaven.'   So Mat. xxii. 18, 'Why tempt ye me, ye hypocrites?' when the Pharisees and the Herodians came to question him about paying tribute.   So Luke x. 25, 'A certain lawyer stood up, and tempted him,' &c.

(2.) In his state of glory, and with respect to his invisible presence. So the Israelites in the wilderness tempted him before his coming in the flesh, and Christians may now tempt him after his ascension into heaven.   Both are in one place : 1 Cor. x. 9, 'Neither let us tempt Christ, as some of them also tempted, and were destroyed of serpents.'

What was their tempting of Christ in the wilderness ?   If he be considered as God, he had a subsistence before he was incarnate of the
Virgin ; and in this sense, as they tempted God, so they may be said
also to tempt Christ; for all the affliction, shame, and disgrace done
to that people are called the reproach of Christ : Heb. xi. 25, 26,
'Choosing rather to suffer affliction with the people of God, than to
enjoy the pleasures of sin for a season; esteeming the reproach of
Christ greater riches than the treasures of Egypt.'   So their murmuring might be called a tempting of Christ.   Christ was the perpetual
head of the church, who in his own person did lead the people, and
was present in the midst of them under the notion of the angel of the
covenant.   The eternal Son of God guided them in the wilderness :
Exod. xxiii. 20–23, 'Behold, I will send an angel before thee, to keep
thee in the way, and to bring thee into the place which I have prepared.   Beware of him, and obey his voice, provoke him not; for he
will not pardon your transgressions ; for my name is in him.   But if
thou shalt indeed obey his voice, and do all that I speak, then I will
be an enemy to thy enemies, and an adversary unto thine adversaries ;
for mine angel shall go before thee, and bring thee in unto the land
of the Amorites,' &c.   This angel can be no other than Christ, whose
office it is to keep us in the way, and to bring us into the place which
Christ hath prepared for us ; he it is that must be obeyed by the
people of God, and pardon their transgressions; in him is God's
name, for he will not communicate it to any other that is not of the
same substance with himself : God is in him, and he in the Father,
and his name is 'Jehovah our Righteousness.'   So Exod. xxxiii. 14,
'My presence shall go with thee, and I will give thee rest.'   My
presence, that is, my angel, spoken of before, called 'the angel of his
presence :' Isa. lxiii. 9, 'In all their affliction he was afflcted, and the
angel of his presence saved them.'   This angel is called Jehovah :
Exod. xiii. 21, 'And the Lord went before them by day in a pillar of
a cloud,' &c.   This angel of God's presence was no other than Jesus
Christ, the conductor of them in the wilderness, who safe-guarded
them, and secured them all the way from Egypt to Canaan.   And we
Christians may also tempt Christ, for the apostle warneth us against
it : we tempt Christ, now he is ascended into heaven, when we disobey
his laws, question his authority, doubt of his promises, after sufficient
means of conviction, that he is the Messias, the Son of God ; grow
weary of his religion, loathing spiritual manna, and begin to be glutted
with the gospel, and are discouraged in the way to our heavenly
Canaan, whither we are travelling.

    [3.] The Holy Ghost is said also to be tempted : Acts v. 9, 'How is
it that ye have agreed together to tempt the Spirit of the Lord ?'
—namely, by their hypocrisy and dissimulation, putting it to the trial,
whether he could discover them in their sin, yea or no ; they had
endeavoured, as much as in them lay, to deceive the Spirit by keeping back part of the price; that is, by that practice they would put it
to the trial, whether the Holy Ghost, yea or no, could find out that
cheat and fallacy.   It is not barely to deceive the apostles, who were
full of the Holy Ghost, and had a discerning spirit, though to them
they brought their lie.   No, saith the apostle, 'Ye have not lied unto

men, but unto God,' ver. 4; and therefore they are said to 'tempt the Holy Ghost,' whether he could find them out or no, though they had so many experiences of his care and respect to the church, and all affairs belonging thereunto; and so the injury was done, not to the apostles, but to the Holy Ghost himself.

Secondly, The act. What is this temptation of God? Temptation is the proving and making trial of a thing or person, what he is, and what he will do. Thus we tempt God when we put it to the trial whether God will be as good as his word, and doubt of the comminatory and promissory part thereof, or whether he will be such an one as he is taken to be. Now, this is lawful or unlawful according as the trial is made humbly and dutifully, or else proudly and sinfully, whether God will do such a thing as we have prescribed him. And again, as the trial is made necessarily or unnecessarily. Sinfully we are said to tempt God when we make an unnecessary experiment of his truth, goodness, and power, and care of us, having had sufficient assurance of these things before.

[1.] There is a tempting or proving of God in a way of duty. So we are bidden, Mal. iii. 10, ' Bring ye all the tithes into the storehouse, that there may be meat in mine house, and prove me now therewith, saith the Lord of hosts, if I will not open you the windows of heaven, and pour you out a blessing, that there shall not be room enough to receive it.' God there submitteth to a trial upon experience; though we are to believe him upon his bare word, yet he will have us to wait for the good things promised; and in this sense it is said, ' The word of the Lord is a tried word, he is a buckler to all them that trust in him,' Ps. xviii. 30. All those that build any hope upon it, and wait to see what the Lord will do, will find that God will stand to his word. This is a constant duty to observe God's truth and faithfulness. To suspend our belief till the event is distrust; but to wait, observing what God will do as to the event, is an unquestionable duty.

[2.] There is an allowed trying of God in some cases. I cannot say it is a duty, because it is only warrantable by God's special indulgence and dispensation; and I cannot say it is a sin, because of God's gracious condescension to his people: Judges vi. 39, ' And Gideon said unto God, Let not thine anger be hot against me, and I will speak but this once: let me prove, I pray thee, but this once with the fleece; let it now be dry only upon the fleece, and upon all the ground let there be dew.' The request was not of distrust and malice, but of infirmity and from a weak faith; not out of infidelity to tempt God, but out of humility; being sensible of his own weakness, he desired this help, for the further confirmation of his faith concerning his calling to this work, as an instrument authorised, and the issue and success of it; and also to assure others who followed him. To this head I refer Thomas his proof and trial: John xx. 25, ' Except I see in his hand the print of the nails, and put my finger into the print of the nails, and thrust my hand into his side, I will not believe.' Here was weakness in Thomas, to suspend his faith upon such a condition; but an apostle was to be αὐτόπτης, an eye-witness of those things which were done, especially of his resurrection; and, therefore, Christ meekly condescended to his request, ver. 27, ' Reach hither thy finger, and behold my hands, and reach hither thy hand, and thrust it into my side, and be not faithless, but believing.' I put it among infirmities: he alloweth him his trial of sense, but with some rebuke. To this head may be referred that of Hezekiah, who, when he was sick of a mortal disease, and the Lord had extraordinarily promised him, on his mourning, that he should be recovered again, he asks a sign for the confirmation of his faith, and God grants it him: 2 Kings xx. 8, 9. And the instance of Ahaz, who, when the prophet bid him 'ask a sign,' he said, Isa. vii. 12, 'I will not ask, neither will I tempt the Lord.' He believed nothing of what the prophet had spoke, and was resolved to go on in his way, but he pretended a reverent and religious respect to God. This kind of tempting God is tolerable, being an act of condescension in God to the weakness of his people.

[3.] There is a sinful tempting of God, and this is done two ways:—

(1.) Generally every transgression, in a general sense, is a tempting of God: Num. xiv. 22, 'They have tempted me now these ten times, and have not hearkened to my voice.' Every eminent and notable provocation of theirs is called a tempting of God. Hereby they make trial of God's justice, whether he will execute vengeance upon them or no. Thus we tempt Christ when we fall into any voluntary and known sin, we put it to the trial what he will or can do; we enter into the lists with God, provoke him to the combat: 1 Cor. x. 22, 'Do we provoke the Lord to jealousy? are we stronger than he?' We try whether God will be so severe as his threatening speaks him to be, as if we would make some experiment of his anger, justice, and power. This kind of tempting of God is compounded of infidelity and presumption. There is infidelity in it when we dare sin against the clear light and checks of conscience, and venture upon his threatenings. You cannot drive a dull ass into the fire that is kindled before him: Prov. i. 17, 'Surely in vain the net is spread in the sight of any bird.' And there is presumption in it, therefore these voluntary acts of rebellion are called presumptuous sins: Ps. xix. 13, 'Keep back thy servant also from presumptuous sins.' Gross and scandalous sinners are described to be such as tempt God: Mal. iii. 15, 'And now we call the proud happy; yea, they that work wickedness are set up; yea, they that tempt God are even delivered.' And Ananias and Sapphira are said to 'tempt the Holy Ghost,' Acts v. 9. By open voluntary sins men dare God to his face; by secret sins we put it to the trial whether God be an all-seeing God, and will discover this hypocrisy. Both conclude they shall do well enough, though they break his laws, and run wilfully upon evil practices forbidden by his law.

(2.) More particularly we tempt God two ways—in a way of distrust or presumption. Both these arise from unbelief, though they seem to be contrary extremes; for though presumption may seem to arise from an over-much confidence, yet if it be narrowly searched into, we shall find that men presume upon unwarrantable courses, because they do not believe that God will do what is meet to be done in his own time or in his own way. As, for instance, had the Israelites believed that God, in his own time, and in his own way, would have destroyed the Canaanites, they would not have presumed, against an express charge, to have gone against them without the ark and with-

out Moses, as they did: Num. xiv. 40, to the end: they presumed to
go up unto the hill-top, and then they were discomfited. But presumption in some being most visible, in others distrust, therefore we
make two kinds of them.

[1st.] In a way of distrust. And that is done several ways, but all
agree in this : not content with what God hath done already to settle
our faith, we prescribe means of our own, and indent with him upon
terms of our own making. So the Israelites, Exod. xvii. 7, 'And he
called the name of the place Massah, and Meribah, because of the
chiding of the children of Israel, and because they tempted the Lord,
saying, Is the Lord among us, or not ?' They had sufficient signs
of God's presence—the pillar of a cloud and fire, that went before them
by day and by night; but they would have signs of their own. So the
Jews are said to tempt Christ, because they sought a sign from
heaven : Mat. xvi. 1, 'The Pharisees also, with the Sadducees, came,
and, tempting, desired him that he would show them a sign from
heaven.' He had given sufficient evidence of his mission and divine
power in casting out devils and healing the sick and diseased; but they
would have a sign from heaven, some sign of their own prescribing.
The devil is ready to put such thoughts into our minds. If God be
with us, let him show it by doing this or that ; and we are apt to require stronger proofs of God's power and presence with us than he
alloweth. This is a frequent sin now-a-days, and men are many ways
guilty of it.

First, Some will not believe the gospel except they see a miracle or
hear an oracle. Christ representeth their thoughts, Luke xvi. 30,
'Nay, father Abraham, if one went to them from the dead, then they
would repent.' They would have other ways of assurance than God
alloweth, and are not content with his word and works, by which he
revealeth himself to us, but will, at their own pleasure, make trial
of his will and power, and then believe. These tempt God, and
therefore no wonder if God will not do for them that which they
require.

Secondly, Some will not believe God's providence, but make question
of his power and goodness, and care over us and our welfare, when he
hath given us sufficient proof thereof. When he hath taken care to
convince our infidelity by supplying our wants, and hath done abundantly enough already for evidencing his power, justice, and truth, and
readiness to help us, we will not believe unless he give us new and
extraordinary proof of each, such as we prescribe to him : Ps. xcv.
9, 10, 'When your fathers tempted me, proved me, and saw my works.
Forty years long was I grieved with this generation, and said, It is a
people that do err in their hearts, and they have not known my ways.'
They saw his works, were fed with miracles, and clothed with miracles,
yet they must have new proof still. Two ways of tempting him as to
his providence the scripture mentions : —

One was their setting God a task of satisfying their conceits and
carnal affections : Ps. lxxviii. 18, 'And they tempted God in their
hearts, by asking meat for their lusts.' Of this sin they are guilty that
must be maintained at such a rate, must have such provision for them
and theirs, or else they cannot believe his truth and care of them. As

the Israelites, God must give them festival diet in the wilderness, or
else they will no longer believe his power and serve him.

The other way of tempting God, with respect to his providence,
was by confining him to their own time, manner, and means of
working: Ps. lxxviii. 41, 'Yea, they turned back, and tempted God,
and limited the Holy One of Israel.' To limit the Holy One is to confine him within a circle of their own making, and if he doth not help
them by their means, and at their time, as those in the text, they will
not tarry God's leisure, they think there is no depending on him for
any succour. Thus they set bounds to his wisdom and power, as if he
could do no more than they conceive to be probable. Thus also we
prescribe means and time to God, take upon us to set rules to him how
he should govern the world. And one usual way of tempting God now
is, when we will not go fair and softly in the path and pace of God's
appointing, but are offended at the tediousness thereof, and make haste,
and take more compendious ways of our own : Isa. xxviii. 16, ' He that
believeth will not make haste ;' but he that believeth not is precipi-
tant, must have God's mercy, power, and goodness manifested to them
in their own way and time.

Thirdly, Some will not be satisfied as to their spiritual estate without some sensible proof, or such kind of assurance as God usually
vouchsafeth not to his people. As suppose they must be fed with
spiritual dainties, and overflow with sensible consolation in every holy
duty, or else they are filled with disquieting thoughts about their
acceptance with God. We must have matters of faith put under the
view and feeling of sense, or else we will not take comfort in them.
But we must not limit God to give proofs of his love, nor prescribe
such signs as are not promised by him, but study our case in the
word. For God will not always treat us by sensible experience.
Thomas is allowed to touch Christ, but Mary is not allowed to touch
him : John xx. 17, compared with ver. 27.

[2dly.] In a way of presumption; so we tempt God when, without any
warrant, we presume of God's power and providence. As here the
devil tempted Christ to cast himself down from the pinnacle of the
temple, to try if he would take the charge of him in the fall ; whereupon Christ replieth, 'Thou shalt not tempt the Lord thy God.'
Now this is done several ways.

First, When we presume upon God's help, forsaking the ordinary
way and means. Christ would not throw himself down, when he could
go down by the stairs or steps of the temple. Down-stairs and over
the battlements is not all one. Christ, that could walk upon the sea
in the distress of his disciples, in ordinary cases taketh a ship. Whosoever will not use the ordinary means that God hath appointed, but
in ordinary cases expects extraordinary supplies, tempteth God. God
is able to bring water out of the rock, when there is nothing but rock
and stone ; but when we may hope to find spring-water, we must dig
for it. God can rain manna out of heaven ; but when the soil will
bear corn, we must till it. When Elisha was in a little village, not
able to defend him from the Syrians, he had chariots and horsemen of
fire to defend him, 2 Kings vi. 17 ; but when he was in Samaria, a
strong, walled town, and the king of Israel sent to fetch his head, he

said to those that were with him, 'Shut the door,' ver. 32.   Christ in
the wilderness miraculously fed many ; but near the city he ' sent his
disciples to buy bread,' John iv. 8.   When the Church of God had
need of able helps at first, gifts were miraculously conferred ; but
afterwards every man to his study, 1 Tim. iv. 15, 'Meditate upon
these things, give thyself wholly to them, that thy profiting may
appear to all.'   In short, God's omnipotency is for that time discharged, when we have ordinary means to help ourselves.   To disdain
ordinary means, and expect extraordinary, is as if a man should put
off his clothes, and then expect God should keep him from cold.

Secondly, When we expect the end without the means.   If Hezekiah had refused the bunch of figs, or Paul's companions to tarry in
the ship, they had tempted God.   When we desire any blessing, we
must not refuse or neglect any good means for attaining of it.   In
spiritual things this is very usual ; men hope to have the end without
the means.   In temporal things we will soon confess there must be
means used, for ' if any would not work, neither should he eat,' 2 Thes.
iii. 10.   In warfare no victory is to be hoped for without fighting ;
only in spiritual matters we think to do well enough, though we never
put to our endeavours to cry for knowledge, and to dig for it ; this is
a tempting of God : Prov. ii. 3-5, ' If thou criest after knowledge, and
liftest up thy voice for understanding ; if thou seekest her as silver,
and searchest for her as for hid treasures ; then shalt thou understand
the fear of the Lord, and find the knowledge of God.'   We dream of
heaven when there is no mortification, no exercising ourselves unto
godliness.   A great many say as Balaam did, ' Let me die the death
of the righteous, and let my last end be like his,' Num. xxiii. 10 ; but
they care not for living the life of the righteous.   If they can but charm
themselves into a secure presumption of salvation, they never give
diligence to make their calling and election sure.   This cometh from
hardness of heart, not strength of faith.   Many defer their conversion
to the last, and then think that in the twinkling of an eye they shall
in a trice be in heaven with Elias in whirlwind.   It was a prayer of
Sir Thomas More, *Domine, Deus, fac me in iis consequendis operam
collocare, pro quibus obtinendis te orare soleo*—' Lord ! make me to
bestow pains in getting those things, for the obtaining of which I use
to pray to thee.'   Otherwise we tempt God.

Thirdly, When without call we rush into any danger, or throw
ourselves into it, with an expectation God will fetch us off again.   As
if Christ, when nobody went about to thrust him down, should wilfully have cast himself down.   Whether the danger be certain, or
inevitable, or very probable, we must not throw ourselves on it ; but,
when God calls us, then we may expect his help according to his promise ; as to go into places or houses infected.   In spiritual cases it is
often done ; men that by often experience have found such and such
things to be occasions to them of sinning, yet presume to do the same
again ; these tempt God, ride into the devil's quarters, go into dangerous places and companies where they are like to be corrupted ; as
Peter went into the high-priest's hall, and those that go to live in
Popish families.   We pray that we be not led into temptations,
but when we lead ourselves, what shall become of us ? as we do,

when we cast ourselves upon temptations, and dangerous occasions of sin.

Fourthly, When we undertake things for which we are not fitted and prepared, either habitually or actually : as to speak largely without meditation. When an unlearned man undertakes the handling a weighty controversy, and a good cause wanteth shoulders, we tempt God. When we undertake things above bodily strength, all will condemn us ; so to undertake things that we have no ability to perform is unlawful. The sons of Sceva would take upon them to exorcise the devil, ' And the man in whom the evil spirit was leaped on them, and overcame them, and prevailed against them, so that they fled out of that house naked and wounded,' Acts xix. 16.

Fifthly, Another sort of tempting God is, when we come to him with an idol in our hearts ; that is, when people are resolved of a thing, they will go and ask counsel of God. In all matters we resolve on we are to take God's leave, and counsel, and blessing ; but they first resolve and then ask God's counsel. And, therefore, God saith, Ezek. xiv. 4, ' Every man of the house of Israel that setteth up his idols in his heart, and putteth the stumbling-block of his iniquity before his face, and cometh to the prophet, I the Lord will answer him that cometh according to the multitude of his idols.' Balaam had a mind to the wages of unrighteousness, but yet he durst not go without God, and, till God had permitted him, he would be asking again and again : Num. xxii. 12, compared with the 20th and 22d verses. God answered him in wrath, according to the idol of his heart. Thus you see men tempt God, when, either out of diffidence or presumption, they seek an experience of his wisdom, power, justice, truth, goodness, against his word and command, and the order he hath established ; as the Israelites, when means failed, murmured and prescribed time, means, and manner of deliverance, as if they would subject God to their lusts.

II. The heinousness of the sin.

1. Because it is a great arrogancy when we seek thus to subject the Lord to our direction, will, and carnal affections. Prescribing to God argueth too great an ascribing to ourselves. Certainly the Lord cannot endure that his people, who ought wholly to depend upon him, submit to him, and be ruled by him, should prescribe as they please how and when he should help them ; and that his power and goodness should lacquey upon, and be at the beck of, our idle and wanton humours. The direction of the affairs of the world is one of the flowers of God's crown. Now to dislike of his holy government is a presumptuous arrogancy in the creature ; we will take upon us to model our mercies and choose our means, and will not tarry the time that he hath appointed. for our relief, but will anticipate it, and shorten it according to our own fancies. God is sovereign, we are as clay in his hands ; he is our potter, and must prescribe the shape in which we must be formed, and the use we must be put to, Jer. xviii. 6 : ' O house of Israel, cannot I do with you as the potter, saith the Lord ? Behold as the clay is in the potter's hand, so are ye in mine hand, O house of Israel.' He hath full right to dispose of the creature as he pleaseth, and according to the counsel of his own will, to which

we are to be subject without murmuring or repining. We cannot say to him, ' What makest thou ? or why dost thou this ? ' Isa. xlv. 9 : ' Woe unto him that striveth with his maker ! let the potsherd strive with the potsherds of the earth: shall the clay say to him that fashioneth it, What makest thou ? or thy work, He hath no hands.' Tempting before the event is the same almost with murmuring after the event.

2. It is great unbelief, or a calling into question God's power mercy, and goodness to us. We should entirely depend upon God for salvation, and whatsoever is necessary to salvation, and that he will supply our wants, and bring us out of every strait, in a way most conducing to our own welfare and his honour. But now we are not satisfied with the assurance God hath given us in those laws of commerce, which are established between him and us; we must have extraordinary proofs, or else we question all. Tempting God seemeth rather to be opposed to the fear and reverence that we should have of him ; yet, primarily and in itself, it is rather opposite to our trust. And though we take it for a sin which argueth too much trust, or an unwarrantable boldness in expecting unusual ways of help from God, yet generally it belongeth to unbelief and diffidence, and ariseth from it. For, therefore, we put him to proof, tempt, or make trial of God, because we distrust his help, and are not satisfied with his goodness and power, till we have other testimonies thereof, than are ordinarily dispensed. Therefore this reason is given of their tempting God, because ' they believed not God, and trusted not in his salvation,' Ps. lxxviii. 22. They must have their own salvation, their own way of supply or deliverance, or else they cannot trust God if he doth not help them at their time and by their means.

3. It looseneth the bonds of all obedience, because we set up new laws of commerce between God and us; for when we suspect God's fidelity to us, unless he do such things as we fancy, we suspect our fidelity to him. Therefore disobedience is made the fruit of tempting God: Ps. lxxviii. 56, ' Yea, they tempted and provoked the most high God, and kept not his testimonies.' They that tempt God cast away God's rule, and God's terms of obedience, and make others to themselves. The question is, whether God shall direct us, or we him? We say, unless God will do thus and thus, we will no longer believe his power and serve him.

4. It is great ingratitude, or a lessening God's benefits and works already done for us : Ps. lxxviii. 20, ' Behold he smote the rock, that the waters gushed out, and the streams overflowed ; can he give bread also ? can he provide flesh for his people ? ' As if what he had done formerly were nothing. Now, God cannot endure to have his benefits lessened, or his former works forgotten and despised.

5. It is wantonness, rather than want, puts us upon tempting of God. There is a humour in men ; we are very desirous to try conclusions, condemning things common, and are fond about strange novelties. It was told the Israelites, as plain as could be, that they should not reserve manna till the morning ; and they need not to have reserved it, they had fresh every day ; yet they would needs keep it for experiment's sake, to try whether it would stink or no : Exod. xvi.

20. And though they were forbidden to gather it on the Sabbath-day, having on the evening before enough for two days, and it was told them they should find none on the Sabbath-day, yet they must try. Where need is, there a man may commit himself to the providence of God, and rely upon him ; and where means fail us, God can help us by prerogative, that we may say with Abraham, when we have no help present, ' In the mount of the Lord it shall be seen,' Gen. xxii. 14 ; and with Moses, when the Red Sea was before them, and the enemy was behind them, ' Fear ye not, stand still, and ye shall see the salvation of the Lord, which he will show to you to-day,' Exod. xiv. 13. When Elias was in distress, the angel brought him meat, 1 Kings xix. 5, 6 ; when Hagar and Ishmael were in the wilderness, and the bottle spent, then God comforted her from heaven, Gen. xxi. 17 ; when the three children were in the fiery furnace, then God sent an angel to be their deliverer, Dan. iii. 28. But now, in wantonness to desire extraordinary proofs of God's care over us, when he hath in ordinary ways provided for us, is to tempt the Lord : Ps. cvi. 14, ' They lusted exceedingly in the desert, and tempted God in the wilderness.' When they had so many convictions of God's power and providence over them, which should in reason have charmed them into a full and cheerful resignation and dependence upon him, they, remembering the flesh-pots in Egypt, must have their luxuriant appetites gratified ; and because they had not that festival plenty, which could not be expected in the wilderness, they reproached Moses for having brought them out of Egypt, to die in the wilderness ; and now God must show them a miracle, not for the supply of their wants, but to pamper and feed their lusts : Ps. lxxviii. 18, 19, ' And they tempted God in their heart, by asking meat for their lust : yea, they spake against God ; they said, Can God furnish a table in the wilderness ?' A table must be prepared ; he must give them festival diet in the wilderness.

6. It argues impatiency : Ps. cvi. 13, 14, ' They soon forgat his works ; they waited not for his counsel, but lusted exceedingly in the wilderness, and tempted God in the desert.' The word signifies they made haste, took it ill they were not presently brought into that plenty that was promised : Num. xx. 5, ' Wherefore have ye made us to come up out of Egypt, to bring us in unto this evil place ? it is no place of seed, or of figs, or of vines, or of pomegranates, neither is there any water to drink,' which was the plenty that was promised in the land of Canaan. Thus they made haste, were impatient of staying God's time of giving them this inheritance ; and because they had it not presently, they wished themselves back again in Egypt. Tempting is because we cannot attend the performance of God's promise in his own time. They went out passionately in the pursuit of their plenty, which they looked for ; and as soon as they discovered any difficulty, conclude they were betrayed, not waiting with patience God's time, when he should accomplish his promises made to them.

7. The greatness of the sin is seen by the punishments of it. One is mentioned : 1 Cor. x. 9, ' Neither let us tempt Christ, as some of them also tempted, and were destroyed of serpents.' They were bitten of serpents, because they tempted God, and murmured because of the length of the way, that they could not get presently into

Canaan ; and the apostle tells us that all the things which happened
to Israel of old happened to them ὡς τύποι, as patterns of providence.
A people might easily read their own doom and destiny, if they would
blow off the dust from the ancient providences of God, and observe
what proofs and characters of his justice, wisdom, and truth are
engraven there.   The desert of sin is still the same, and the exactness
of divine justice is still the same ; and therefore what hath been is a
pledge and document of what may be, if we fall into like crimes.
God is impartially and immutably just ; he is but one : Gal. iii. 20.
God is one, always consonant unto himself, and doth like unto himself : his power is the same, so is his justice.   Even the historical
part of the word is a kind of prophecy, not only a register and chro-
nicle of what is past, but a kind of calendar and prognostication of
what is to come.   As other histories in scripture are left upon record
for our learning, so especially the history of Israel's passage through
the wilderness into Canaan.

Use. Let us not tempt God in any of the kinds mentioned.

1. Not by requiring new grounds of faith, when God hath given
sufficient already ; not by cherishing scepticism and irresolution in
point of religion, till new nuncios come from heaven, with a power to
work miracles, and to be endowed with extraordinary gifts, as the
Seekers do.   Many waver in religion, would fain see an apparition,
and have some extraordinary satisfaction, which God would not give
them upon every trifling occasion.   The Pharisees must have a sign from
heaven ; the Papists would have the Protestant teachers show their
commission by miracles ; the Jews would believe if Christ came down
from the cross.   To suspend our faith till God gives us our own
terms is to tempt God ; and to dispossess you of this conceit, consider : —

[1.] Signs and wonders done in one age and time for the confirmation of the true religion, should suffice all ages and times afterwards ;
and it is a tempting God to ask more signs and wonders for the confirmation of that truth, which is sufficiently confirmed already, if
there be a good and safe tradition of these things to us.   The giving
of the law was attended with thunderings and lightnings, and the
sound of a terrible trumpet, Exod. xix., by which means the law was
authorised, and owned as proceeding from God.   Now, it was not
needful this should be repeated in every age, as long as a certain
report and records of it might convey it to their ears.   In the setting
up a new law, signs and wonders are necessary to declare it to be of
God ; but when the church is in the possession of it, these cease.   So
in the Christian church ; when the gospel was first set on foot, it was
then confirmed with signs and wonders, but now they are unnecessary.
See the law and gospel compared : Heb. ii. 2–4, ' For if the word
spoken by angels was stedfast, and every transgression and disobedience received a just recompense of reward ; how shall we escape, if we
neglect so great salvation ; which at the first began to be spoken by
the Lord, and was confirmed unto us by them that heard him ; God
also bearing them witness, both with signs and wonders, and with
divers miracles, and gifts of the Holy Ghost, according to his own will ? '

[2.] If you had lived in the age of signs and wonders, there were
hard hearts then, unbelievers then, and blasphemers then, and tempters

of God then: Ps. lxxviii. 22-24, ' Because they believed not in God, and trusted not in his salvation, though he had commanded the clouds from above, and opened the doors of heaven, and had rained manna upon them to eat, and had given them of the corn of heaven,' &c., to ver. 32, ' For all this they sinned still, and believed not for his wondrous works.' Extraordinary works will not work upon them upon whom ordinary works will not prevail.

Object. But for them that have to do with the conversion of Indians and remote parts of the world, is it a tempting of God to ask the gift of miracles?

Ans. I cannot say so. God may be humbly sought unto about direction in the gifts of tongues, and healing, being so necessary for the instruments employed, as well as the conviction of the nations. I dare not determine anything in the case, but I am satisfied with Acostus his reasons why miracles are not afforded by God now, as well as in the primitive times. Then simple and unlearned men were sent to preach Christianity among the nations, where many were armed and instructed against it with all kind of learning and philosophy; but now learned men are sent to the ignorant, and are superior to them in reason, and in civility and authority; and, besides, present them a religion far more credible than their own, that they cannot easily withstand the light of it.

2. Do not run into any wilful and known sin, as if you would try how far the patience of God will go, nor abuse his fatherly goodness by going on still in your trespasses. When a man will try the patience of God without any regard of his threatenings, or the instances of his wrath, which are before his eyes, he puts it to the proof whether God will punish him, yea or no. Remember you are no match for him: Isa. xlv. 9, ' Woe unto him that striveth with his maker! let the potsherds strive with the potsherds of the earth.' As Abner said to Asahel: 2 Sam. ii. 21, 22, ' Turn thee aside to thy right hand or to thy left, and lay thee hold on one of the young men, and take thee his armour. But Asahel would not turn aside from following of him. And Abner said again to Asahel, Turn thee aside from following me: wherefore should I smite thee to the ground?' So if you will needs be tempting and trying conclusions, and making experiments, let men meddle with their match, those who are equal to themselves, not challenging one infinitely above them; let frail man cope with man, but let him take heed of meddling with God: Ezek. xxii. 14, ' Can thine heart endure, or can thine hands be strong in the days that I shall deal with thee?' Many foolish people say, as those in the prophet, ' It is an evil, and I must bear it;' endure it as well as I can. What! endure the loss of heaven! endure the wrath of the Almighty God! If Rachel could not endure the loss of her children, nor Jacob the supposed loss of Joseph, but, says he, ' I will go down into the grave unto my son mourning,' Gen. xxxvii. 35. If Achitophel could not endure the rejectment of his counsel, and Haman could not endure to be slighted by Mordecai, and many cannot endure the loss of a beloved child; how wilt thou endure the loss of eternal happiness? The disciples wept bitterly when Paul said, ' Ye shall see my face no more,' Acts xx. 38. What will ye do, then, when God

shall say, Ye shall see my face no more? Ah wretch! how canst thou endure the wrath of God? Thou canst not endure to be scorched a few days with feverish flames; thou canst not endure the acute pains of stone and gout, when God armeth the humours of thine own body against thee; thou canst not endure the scorching of a little gunpowder casually blown up; thou canst not endure the pains of a broken arm or leg; and can you endure the wrath of God, when God himself shall fall upon you with all his might?

3. When we are destitute and sorely distressed, let us wait upon God with patience, according to the tenor of his promises, and tarry his leisure, without prescribing time and means. God knoweth the fittest season, and delighteth oftentimes to show our impatience and try our faith: Mat. xv. 28, ' O woman, great is thy faith!' And that his help may not be ascribed to chance or our industry, and that we may the more prize blessings, consider you cannot be more distressed than Christ was, who seemed abandoned to Satan's power, distressed with sore hunger through his long fasting. The devil was permitted to have power over his body, to carry him to one of the pinnacles of the temple, and yet he discovered an invincible confidence and trust in God, that he would not step the least step out of God's way for his preservation in so imminent a danger.—

Now that you may not tempt God:—

[1.] Let your heart be deeply possessed with apprehensions of the goodness, wisdom, and power of God. The scripture telleth us for his goodness: Ps. cxix. 68, ' Thou art good, and doest good;' and again, Ps. cxlv. 9, ' The Lord is good to all.' For his wisdom: Isa. xxviii. 29, ' He is wonderful in counsel, and excellent in working.' His purposes are often hidden from us, but he doeth all things well; God can do more for us than seemeth probable at the present; and therefore let us not tempt him by confining him to our time, means, and manner. He may love us, and yet delay our help: John xi. 5, 6, ' Jesus loved Lazarus,' and yet, ver. 6, ' When he heard that he was sick, he abode two days still in the same place where he was.' Then, for his power and sovereign dominion, there is not a better argument for confidence than the preface and conclusion of the Lord's Prayer. Whatsoever state you are reduced to, God is still to be trusted, who is ' Our Father, which is in heaven,' and ' whose is the kingdom, power, and glory:' 2 Tim. i. 12, ' I know whom I have believed, and I am persuaded that he is able to keep that which I have committed unto him against that day.' Whatsoever our straits be, he is a God still to be trusted.

[2.] Be firmly persuaded of God's care and providence over his people, and so careth for you in particular. This is assured to us by promises and by experiences. By promises: 1 Pet. v. 7, ' Casting all your care upon him, for he careth for you;' Phil. iv. 6, 7, ' Be careful for nothing: but in everything by prayer and supplication, with thanksgiving, let your requests be made known unto God; and the peace of God, which passeth all understanding, shall keep your hearts and minds through Jesus Christ.' By experiences: Mat. xvi. 8, 9, ' O ye of little faith! why reason ye among yourselves, because ye have brought no bread? Do ye not yet understand, neither remember the five loaves of the five thousand, and how many baskets ye took up?' Christ was angry with his disciples, that they should be troubled about bread, since they had lately such experience of his power to provide bread at pleasure.   Use the means God puts into your hands, and refer the success to him.   You need not be anxious about anything in this world.

[3.] Let all this produce in you an holy obstinacy of trust and obedience, or an invincible confidence in God, and close adherence to him, whatever your dangers, straits, and extremities be, and this will guard your heart against all tempting of God :—

(1.) A resolute trust and dependence : Job xiii. 15, 'Though he slay me, yet will I trust in him.'   This is the soul that is prepared to be true to God, and contentedly to bear whatever he sendeth.

(2.) A constant adherence to our duty: 'Wait on the Lord, and keep his way,' Ps. xxxvii. 34.   Do not go one step out of God's way for all the good in the world.   The greatest extremities are to be borne rather than the least sin yielded to: Dan. iii. 17, 18, 'Our God, whom we serve, is able to deliver us from the burning fiery furnace; and he will deliver us out of thine hand, O king.   But if not, be it known unto thee, O king, that we will not serve thy gods, nor worship the golden image which thou hast set up.'   Please God, and God will be always with you, when you seem to be left destitute : John viii. 29, 'And he that sent me is with me : the Father hath not left me alone; for I do always those things that please him.'

SERMON V.

*Again, the devil taketh him up into an exceeding high mountain, and showeth him all the kingdoms of the world, and the glory of them; and saith unto him, All these things will I give thee, if thou wilt fall down and worship me.—*Mat. IV. 8, 9.

This is the third temptation.   In handling it I shall use the former method, give you the history of the temptation, and observations thereupon.

In the history.

I. The introduction, ver. 8.

II. The temptation itself, with the grievousness of it, ver. 9.

III. Christ's reply, ver. 10.

First, In the introduction we have—

1. The place the devil taketh him unto: *an   exceeding   high mountain.*

2. The fact : he *showeth him all the kingdoms of the world, and the glory of them.*

1. The place chosen for the conflict, ' an exceeding high mountain.'   For the mountain, the scripture would not name it, and we need not anxiously inquire after it, whether any near Jericho, as some say, or as others, some mountain near Jerusalem ; and possibly the

highest above the rest was chosen by the tempter. The pinnacle of
the temple was not proper, because Jerusalem was surrounded with
higher mountains on all sides: Ps. cxxv. 2, 'As the mountains are
round about Jerusalem,' &c. He chose an high mountain, because of
the fairer prospect, where the horizon might be as spacious as was
possible, and the sight not hindered by any interposing object. God
took Moses into Mount Pisgah, and showed him the land of Canaan,
Deut. xxxiv. 1. The devil, who affecteth to do in evil as God doth
in what is good, taketh Christ into a mountain. He leadeth us high,
and promiseth us high things, that suiteth with his disposition; but
it endeth in a downfall that suiteth with his condition. The close is
still 'cast thyself down,' or else, as here, 'fall down and worship me.'
The devil's taking him up thither is to be explained the same way
with his taking him up to the pinnacle of the temple.

2. The fact, and 'showeth him all the kingdoms of the world,
and the glory of them.' But how could the devil from one mountain show him all the kingdoms of the world, when there is
none so high as that we can see the latitude of one kingdom, much
less through all, partly through the unequal swellings of the earth,
and partly through the weakness of the eye, which cannot reach so
far? The sight could go no further than the horizon, and the other
hemisphere is not to be seen at all; that part which we see is much
less than that part which we see not. Therefore how could he show
him all the kingdoms of the world, and the glory thereof ? *Ans.* These
words must not be taken rigorously; but that he showed them :—(1.)
In compendio. (2.) *In speculo.* (3.) *In colloquio.*

[1.] *In compendio.* It may be understood of so many kingdoms as
could fall under the sight of a man looking round about him from
some eminent place ; as God is said to show Moses all the land of
Canaan, when he did actually see only a part thereof. From that
high mountain the devil gave him a view of all that was to be seen
from thence ; many castles, towns, and fruitful fields might be seen
as a sample of the rest. It is a synechdochical hyperbole, he that
showeth a part of a thing, and the chiefest part, may be said to show
the thing itself.

[2.] *In speculo*, besides what he might reach by his sight. By way
of representation and external visible species, he represented to Christ
all the rest of the kingdoms of the world and the pomp and glory
thereof as in a map. For Satan can object to the eyes of men the
species and images of divers things ; and there is no absurdity to think
that this way he showed his utmost art and cunning to represent the
world to Christ in as splendid and inviting a manner as he could.
If you ask, therefore, why he carried him to a high mountain—he
might have done this in a valley or any other place as well? I answer,
it is true if the discovery had been only by representation, or if the
devil could have deluded Christ's fancy or imagination, so as to
impress these species upon it so far as that he should seem to see what
he did not see, a valley would have served turn as well as a mountain;
but this was done without it, and with it, showing the glory of the
world as in a map and picture, and therefore a convenient place is
chosen.

[3.] *In colloquio*, by discourse.   The temptation might be helped on by the devil's pointing at the several quarters of the world, with words relating the glory thereof, what splendour and glory the kings and nations had which adored him, all which Christ should have if he would fall down and worship him.   Now all this while Satan is but making way for his purpose, thinking Christ would be ravished with this glorious sight.   Possibly it was not a mere dumb show, but the tempting objects were amply set forth by Satan's speech.

Secondly, The temptation itself, where we may consider the nature and the grievousness of it.

1. The nature of the temptation, where observe two things:—

[1.] An offer or a promise: *all these things will I give thee.*

[2.] A postulation or demand: *if thou wilt fall down and worship me.*

[1.] An offer or promise : ' all these things will I give thee.'   This is a vain boast of the tempter, who ascribeth to himself that which was proper to God, and promiseth to Christ those things which were all his before.   God had said, Ps. ii. 8, ' Ask of me, and I will give thee the heathen for thine inheritance, and the uttermost parts of the earth for thy possession.'   This the devil, who affecteth to be like God, arrogateth unto himself, as if he would make him the universal king of the world.   In Luke it is, chap. iv. 6, ' All this power will I give thee, and the glory of them ; for that is delivered unto me, and to whomsoever I will I give it.'   But you must not always look for truth in the devil's speeches : he is not lord of the world to dispose of it at his own pleasure.   And yet it is not to be supposed he would come with a downright untruth to the Son of God, if there were no pretence or varnish for it.   Therefore we must distinguish between the devil's lie and the colour thereof.

(1.) Certain it is that God doth govern all the affairs of this world, and doth put bounds and limits to Satan's power, beyond which he cannot pass, and doth often hinder his endeavours, and turn them to the quite contrary end and purpose ; and if he doth not hinder them, yet he directeth them for good to his people.   Therefore that power that Satan hath is not given, but permitted ; not absolute, but limited. It is a lie that Satan can give these things at pleasure ; see these scriptures : Ps. xxiv. 1, ' The earth is the Lord's, and the fulness thereof ; the world, and they that dwell therein ;' Dan. ii. 21, ' He changeth the times and the seasons ; he removeth kings, and setteth up kings ;' and ver. 37, ' The God of heaven hath given thee a kingdom, power, and strength, and glory.'   All the alterations that are in the earth are of the Lord ; he pulleth down, and raiseth up, as seemeth good unto him.   Therefore this power of disposing kingdoms belongeth unto God.

(2.) That the Son of God is the right heir of the world : Heb. i. 2, ' Whom he hath appointed heir of all things.'   To whom the nations are given : Ps. ii. 8, ' Ask of me, and I will give thee the heathen for thine inheritance, and the uttermost parts of the earth for thy possession ;' Mat. xxviii. 18, ' All power is given unto me in heaven and in earth.'   And therefore it was impudence in him to arrogate this power, and to promise these things to the Lord which were his before.

(3.) Though this was a lie, yet here is the colour of the lie. God permitteth that men sometimes by indirect means become great in honour and dignity in this world; all which are done by the instinct of Satan and his help. And evil men often succeed in their attempts, and from hence Satan is called the prince of this world: John xii. 31, ' Now shall the prince of this world be cast out;' John xiv. 30, ' The prince of this world cometh, and hath nothing in me;' John xvi. 11, ' Of judgment, because the prince of this world is judged.' Yea, Paul goeth higher, and calleth him ' the god of this world:' 2 Cor. iv. 4, ' In whom the god of this world hath blinded the minds of them which believe not.' But this is by usurpation, not just right. And the devils are called, Eph. vi. 12, ' The rulers of the darkness of this world,' as the wicked consent to his empire and evil suggestions. But all this implieth but a limited and restrained kingdom; and the devil's impudence and falsehood lieth in this, that he interprets God's permission for a commission, his connivance for a conveyance. Indeed, there are two lies in the devil's offer: one assertory, as if the power and glory of the world were at his disposal; the other promissory, as if he would invest Christ in the full and peaceable possession thereof; whereas indeed he went about to divest and dispossess the Son of God of his right, or to tempt him to do a thing contrary to his kingdom; for he knew the abasement of Christ was the way to his glory, the cause of man's happiness, and the ruin of the kingdom of the devil; therefore he seeketh to prevent this by these magnificent promises.

[2.] The postulation or demand: ' if thou wilt fall down and worship me.' Here the devil appeareth in his own likeness. Before it was, ' if thou be the Son of God;' now it is, ' fall down and worship me.' Before he appeared as a friend to advise him in his hunger; then as a divine to instruct him how to discover himself as the Messiah; now as a plain usurper of God's worship. And he demands but one act of prostration, such as was given to the kings of the East; and the Jews in that manner did worship God. Therefore this was the vilest and most blasphemous suggestion which Satan could devise, that the Son of God should stoop to God's rebel. Here we see the devil not only importunate, but impudent.

2. The grievousness of the temptation, that will appear in these considerations :—

[1.] Because it was represented in a matter grateful and pleasing. It was unnecessary to turn stones into bread, dangerous to throw himself down from a pinnacle of the temple; but it might seem sweet and grateful to behold the kingdoms of the world and the glory thereof ; for surely the glory of the world is a bewitching object, and would much move a carnal heart. And therefore he produceth this tempting object, and sets it before Christ himself. Mark, he showed him the glory only, not the burdens, the labours, the cares, those storms of jealousy and envy which those encounter with who are at the top. This way did he now choose wherewith to assault Christ. Had he really represented the world, with all the vexations attending it, the temptation had not been so great; but he showeth the kingdoms of the world, and the glory thereof : the bait, not the hook; he talketh highly of small things, commendeth what is pleasing, but hideth the

bitter of these luscious sweets; he offereth Christ the glory of the
kingdoms of the world, but dissembleth the cares, the troubles, the
dangers.   Alas ! we see the best side of those that live in courts, their
gorgeous apparel, their costly entertainments, their power and greatness; but their fears of being depressed by superiors, jostled by equals,
undermined by inferiors, are hidden from us.

Therefore the temptation was dexterously managed by the devil, in
that he showed him the kingdoms of the world and the glory thereof.
Temptations of the right hand are more dangerous than those of the
left hand.

[2.] He showeth the bait before he offereth the temptation, that the
world might speak for him before he spake for himself, and prepared
the mind of Christ by this bewitching object before he cometh either
with his offer or demand.   And then afterwards, before he maketh his
demand, he premiseth his offer : ' All these things will I give thee.'
The offer is made before the spiteful condition is mentioned.   Observe
the different methods of Christ and Satan :—Satan maketh show of
glory first, but Christ of the cross.   Satan offereth the benefit before
he seemeth to require the service, as here he doth first offer and then
ask; but fallaciously, for indeed he requireth a present act, but only
promiseth a future compensation : ' I will give thee' all these things.
Christ telleth us the worst at first: Mat. xvi. 24, ' If any man will
come after me, let him deny himself, and take up his cross, and follow
me.'   The issue showeth the fraud of the tempter, and the misery of
those poor deluded souls who hearken to him.   On the contrary, the
sincerity of our Lord, and the happiness of those who obey him, will
soon appear.   The devil will have all paid before he part with anything ; no worship, no glory.   But I am carried too far : my purpose
was only to show his dexterity and cunning, how he sets a colour upon
sin before he mentions it, by glorious promises, and the manifold
pleasure and profit which comes by it.

[3.] He doth not seek to move him by naked words, but by the
sight of the thing itself.   Objects move the senses, senses draw away
the mind ; nor are they the porters of the soul so much as the cor-
rupters : Ps. cxix. 37, ' Turn away mine eyes from beholding vanity,
and quicken thou me in thy way.'   If we let loose our senses without
a guard, we soon contract a deadness of heart.   There is nothing so
soon led away as the eye, it is the broker between the heart and the
object; the eye gazeth and the heart lusteth ; this is the window by
which Satan hath crept in, and all manner of taint hath been conveyed into the soul.   In the first sin, Eve was corrupted this way :
Gen. iii. 6, ' And when the woman saw that the tree was good for
food, and that it was pleasant to the eyes, &c., she took of the fruit
thereof, and did eat.'   Gazing on the fruit with delight, her heart
was ensnared.   We read of Potiphar's wife, ' She cast her eyes on
Joseph,' Gen. xxxix 7 ; Achan, Josh. vii. 21, ' When I saw among
the spoils a goodly Babylonish garment, and two hundred shekels of
silver, and a wedge of gold of fifty shekels weight, then I coveted them,
and took them.'   First he *saw*, then he *coveted*, then he *took* them,
then he *hid* them, then Israel falls, and he is attached by lot.   So it
is said of Shechem and Dinah : Gen. xxxiv. 2, ' He saw her, and

took her, and lay with her, and defiled her.' So of Samson: Judges xvi. 1, ' He went to Gaza, and saw there an harlot, and went in unto her.' David was ensnared by his eyes: 2 Sam. xi. 2, ' From the roof he saw a woman washing herself, and the woman was very beautiful to look upon.' Naboth's vineyard was ever in Ahab's eye, as being near his palace, therefore he is troubled and falls sick for it, 1 King xxi. 1, 2. Now, because so many have been betrayed by their senses, the devil taketh this way to tempt Christ, as knowing this is the next way to the heart.

[4.] He taketh him into an high mountain, that he might look far and near, and see the more provinces, cities, and kingdoms, to move him the more. The devil was sensible that small things were not to be offered to Christ, and therefore dresseth out the temptation in as glorious a manner as he can. The chapman of souls is grown thirsty of late, he doth not offer all the kingdoms of the earth and the glory thereof, he knoweth that we will accept of less with thanks. The devil buyeth many at a very easy price; he needeth not carry them so high as the mountain; they are contented with a little gain that is got by a fraudulent bargain in the shop. If we stand in our window, or at our doors, we meet with temptations enough to carry us away. He needeth not come with kingdoms, or with the glory of all the world: thirty pence, the price of a slave, is enough to make Judas betray his master, Mat. xxvi. 15 ; and the prophet telleth us of some that will transgress for handfuls of barley and pieces of bread, Ezek. xiii. 19. And those pretended prophets, too, making God the author and maintainer of their lies and deceits. And, again, of those that respect persons, whether magistrates or ministers: Prov. xxviii. 21, ' To have respect of persons is not good, for for a piece of bread will that man transgress.' And another prophet telleth us of those that ' sell the poor for a pair of shoes,' Amos ii. 6, and viii. 6. Those will take any price. And the apostle saith of Esau, Heb. xii. 16, ' For one morsel of meat he sold his birthright.' So that the devil may abate a great deal of what he offered Christ. He need not say to such, You shall have ' all these things.' Nay, hold you ! You shall have this petty gain, that slight pleasure and carnal satisfaction. It is a wonder to consider what small things make up a temptation to many, yea, to most. The world is so corrupt that they will violate conscience with a small hire. We are not tempted with great things, less will serve the turn. But the devil knew that small matters were no temptation to Christ, therefore he carrieth him to the mountain, that he might see the glory of all the earth, to make the temptation the more strong.

[5.] He showeth him the kingdoms of the world, ἐν στιγμῇ χρόνου, Luke iv. 5, in a moment of time,—that circumstance is not to be passed over. When many objects and glorious come together of a sudden, they do the more surprise us. Therefore, the more to affect Christ with the splendour of these things, and on a sudden to prevail upon him, which otherwise he was not likely to do, he did not represent the glory of these kingdoms of the world to Christ that he might see them one after another, but all together, that there might be less time for consideration, that so his mind might be the more blinded by the appearing splendour of the tempting object, and his heart the

more captivated thereby. Diverse things seen in one view do more
surprise us than if viewed by a leisurely contemplation. Alas! we
are sometimes overborne by the violence of a temptation, sometimes
overtaken by the suddenness of it: Gal. vi. 1, 'Brethren, if one be
overtaken in a fault,' προληφθῇ, inconsiderately and suddenly surprised
by a sin. We do many things preposterously and in haste, which we
repent of by leisure. Thus the devil thought to surprise Christ, but
he was aware of him.

[6.] In other temptations the tempter doth only ask a thing to be
done, but here he doth ask and promise things glorious, profitable, and
pleasing to carnal sense, and such as seem every way desirable. The
offers of gain and glory are promised to the temptation.

[7.] He craveth but one thing, a very small thing, and this under
the hope of the greatest advantage: one act of external adoration,
easy to be performed; if Christ would but kneel to him, not as supreme
God; an inferior adoration would have contented him: yield but a
little, do but 'fall down and worship,' it shall be enough. As the
heathens of old said to the Christians, Do but touch the censer. The
commendation of God's servants was, that 'they had not bowed the
knee to Baal,' Rom. xi. 4. The devil knoweth if he can get us to a
little he shall get us to more; and the least reverence is too much to
such an impure spirit.

Secondly, The observations.

I. Observe from that *again the devil taketh him*, That we must
expect not only to be tempted, but to be often tempted. Satan
hath both his wiles and darts: Eph. vi. 11, 16. He sometimes
assaulteth us with the one, sometimes with the other. Therefore—

1. Be not secure, but watch, and stand upon your defence. It is
a careless soul that can sleep in so great a danger. There is yet a
malicious tempting devil alive, who would 'sift you as wheat,' Luke
xxii. 31; and somewhat within you which would betray you to him if
you be not wary; and you may meet with such snares as you have
not yet met withal.

2. Be not overmuch troubled and dejected if you be assaulted
afresh. You must make your way to heaven almost every step by
conflict and conquest. Remember your baptismal vow, the obligation
of which ceaseth not till your life be ended; and then you shall be out
of gunshot and harm's way. Therefore still follow the captain of
your salvation wherever he leadeth you. The more trials the more
glory.

3. Avoid rash judgment and censure, if the same happen to others.
Pirates do not use to set upon an empty vessel. The best are most
assaulted. God permitteth it for their trial, and Satan hath the
greatest spite at them.

II. Observe, That the more grievous temptations follow the lighter
ones, and the last assaults and trials are usually the greatest. This is
so, if you respect either the dexterity and cunning of the tempter,
represented before, or the foulness of the temptation, viz., to idolatry.
The best of God's children may be tempted to the most execrable sins.
Thus usually doth Satan reserve his worst assaults for the last, and his
last temptation is commonly the sorest. Dying beasts bite shrewdly;

so Satan rageth most when he hath but a short time. Therefore, since our warfare is not over, let us prepare for the worst brunt, and the last efforts of Satan. If God will crown us fighting, we have no cause to complain. Many of God's servants, whom he could not draw to worldliness, sensuality, or vainglory in their lifetime, he will seek to inject blasphemous thoughts into their minds at last. But, though it be grievous, be not dismayed, your conquest is sure and near.

III. Observe, The world and worldly things are the bait and snare which the tempter offereth to Christ and his followers. As here, when he would make his last onset upon Christ, he sets before him 'the kingdoms of the world, and the glory of them,' as the matter of the temptation.

1. There are three enemies of our salvation, the devil, the world, and the flesh:—they are reckoned up together, Eph. ii. 2, 3, 'Wherein in time past ye walked according to the course of this world, according to the prince of the power of the air, the spirit that now worketh in the children of disobedience. Among whom also we all had our conversation in times past in the lusts of our flesh, fulfilling the desires of the flesh and of the mind.' The devil is the deceiver and grand architect of all wickedness ; the flesh is the principle that he worketh upon, or that rebelling faculty within us that would be pleased before God ; the world is the bait by which the devil would deceive us and steal away our hearts from God, for it suiteth with our fleshly appetites and desires. More distinctly that Satan is an enemy appeareth from his name, that signifieth an adversary, and in many places of scripture he is so called; as Mat. xiii. 25 ; ' While men slept, the enemy came and sowed tares among the wheat,' compared with the 39th verse, ' the enemy that sowed them is the devil.' He is the great enemy to God and man : 1 Pet. v. 8, ' Your adversary the devil like a roaring lion walketh about,' &c. The flesh is an enemy, yea, our greatest enemy, for it warreth against the soul : 1 Pet. ii. 11, ' Abstain from fleshly lusts, which war against the soul.' If you indulge the flesh, you are willing to lose your souls. Yea, it warreth against the spirit or better part, as contrary to it : Gal. v. 17, ' For the flesh lusteth against the spirit, and the spirit against the flesh : ' other things could do us no harm without our own flesh. We are tempted to sin by Satan, encouraged to sin by the example and custom of the world, but inclined to sin by our own flesh. The world is an enemy of our salvation, as well as the devil and the flesh; all the other enemies get strength by it. By the bait of worldly things the devil pleaseth the flesh ; we are in continual danger of being everlastingly undone by it. Whosoever is a lover of the world is presumed to be a professed enemy of God : James iv. 4, 'Know ye not that the friendship of the world is enmity with God ? whosoever will be a friend of the world is the enemy of God ;' 1 John ii. 15, ' If any man love the world, the love of the Father is not in him.' It is an enemy, because it keepeth us from God, who is our chief good, and the enjoyment of him among his blessed ones, which is our last end. There is a neglect of God and heavenly things where the world prevaileth.

2. The devil maketh use of the world to a double end.

[1.] To divert us from God and heavenly things, that our time, and

care, and thoughts may be wholly taken up about things here below :
Luke xii. 19, ' Soul, thou hast much goods laid up for many years;
take thine ease, eat, drink, and be merry ;' Phil. iii. 19, 20, ' They
mind earthly things ; but our conversation is in heaven.' These are
perfectly opposite. Some are of the world, and speak of the world,
and wholly mind the world, and are governed by the spirit of this
world, seldom look higher, or very coldly and slightly. Thus that
which should be thought of in the first place is scarce thought of at
all. But, remember, he doth but offer you worldly things to deprive
you of heavenly.

[2.] To draw us to some open sin for the world's sake, as here he
tempted Christ to idolatry, and Demas to defection from the faith :
2 Tim. iv. 10, ' Demas hath forsaken us, having loved this present
world.' Others to some carnal, fraudulent, oppressive course, whereby
they are spotted by the world. The whore of Babylon propoundeth
her abominations ' in a golden cup,' Rev. xvii. 4; and the great motive
here is, ' All this will I give thee.' Though the devil cometh not in
person to us with his offers, he doth by his instruments; as Balak, when
he sent to Balaam to curse the Israelites, he promised him great
rewards : Num. xxii. 17, ' I will promote thee unto very great
honour, and I will do whatsoever thou sayest unto me : come therefore, I pray thee, curse me this people.' So when he doth entice you
by the motions of your own hearts to anything that is unlawful, to
falsehood, deceit, or unjust gain, or to get and keep wealth by any base
or unjust means, or doing something that is base and unworthy of
your religion.

[3.] I observe that temptations from the world may prevail with us.
Satan maketh use of a twofold artifice. The one is to greaten the
worldly object, the other is to make us large promises of success,
happiness, and contentment in our evil enterprises.

(1.) He useth this sleight here; he doth in the most enticing manner lay the world before Christ as a splendid object, to greaten it in
Christ's thoughts and apprehensions. Therefore, when we begin to
magnify the riches, pomp, and pleasures of the world, the devil is at
our elbow, and we are running into the snare. And therefore, if we
begin to say, ' Happy is the people that is in such a case,' it is time to
correct ourselves and say, ' Yea, happy is the people whose God is the
Lord,' Ps. cxliv. 15. Take heed the devil doth not gain this advantage
over you, to make you follow the world with the greatest earnestness,
and spiritual and heavenly things in a slight and overly manner.
Esteem, desires, resolutions of worldly greatness, though not upon base
conditions, begin the temptation. You think it is a fine thing to live
in pomp and at ease, to swim in pleasures, and begin to resolve to
make it your business. The devil hath you upon the hip, it is an hour
of temptation.

(2.) His next course is to make large offers and promises by his instruments or your own thoughts, that though you neglect God and
heaven, and do engage in some sinful course, you shall do well in the
world, and enjoy full satisfaction. There is a double evil in Satan's
offers and promises:—

First, They are false and fallacious : ' All these things will I give thee.' Satan maketh fair offers of what he cannot perform. He promiseth many things, but doth only promise them. He offereth the kingdoms of the world to Christ, but cannot make good his word; he showeth them to Christ, but cannot give them. And this is the devil's wont, to be liberal in promises, to fill the minds of those that hearken to him with vain hopes, as if he could transfer the riches and honours of the world to whom he pleaseth, whereas they are shamefully disappointed, and find their ruin in the very things in which they sought their exaltation, and their projects are crossed, for 'the earth is the Lord's, and the fulness thereof,' 1 Cor. xi. 26.

Secondly, All the devil's offers and promises have a spiteful condition annexed. He pretendeth to give, but yet selleth at the dearest rates. It is but a barter and exchange; a flat bargain, but no gift. He must have our souls, God is dishonoured, his laws broken, his Spirit grieved. The devil staineth his grant with unjust covenants, and exacteth more than the thing is worth.

Two ways then must we defeat the temptation :—

(1.) Not believing his promises, that I must be beholden to sin to make me happy. Those that by unlawful means get up to honour and wealth seem to have accepted the devil's offer ; they think he is lord of the world, and all the kingdoms and the glory thereof. Do not look upon wealth as the devil's gift, as a thing to be gotten by fraud, flattery, corruption, bribery: alas! it is put into 'bags with holes,' Hag. i. 6. It is called the 'deceitfulness of riches,' Mat. xiii. 22. They promise that contentment and happiness which they cannot give. There is sure dependence on the Lord's, but none on Satan's promises. Young men that are to begin the world, take up this resolution : take what God sendeth, but resolve never to take wealth out of Satan's hands ; what God sendeth in the fair way of his providence, by his blessing on your lawful endeavours : Prov. x. 4, 'The hand of the diligent maketh rich ;' and ver. 22, 'The blessing of the Lord it maketh rich, and he addeth no sorrow with it.' When you deal righteously, and do not barely heap up treasure to yourselves, but seek to grow rich toward God, to subordinate all to heaven and a better pursuit: otherwise God can find a moth and a thief for your estates.

(2.) The other way is, to consider what a sad bargain you make by gratifying the devil, and hearkening to his counsel: Mat. xvi. 26, 'What is a man profited, if he shall gain the whole world, and lose his own soul? or what shall a man give in exchange for his soul?' A man never gets anything with Satan, but he shall lose that which is more precious ; he never maketh a proffer to our advantage, but to our loss and hurt. Follow the world as hard as you can, lie, cozen, cheat, and you shall be rich ; put the case, It is so, but I must lose my soul, not in a natural, but legal sense: Job xxvii. 8, 'What is the hope of the hypocrite, though he hath gained, when God taketh away his soul?' He hath far better things from us than we have from him; a birthright for a mess of pottage, the hopes of heaven for an opulent condition here below. The bird buys the fowler's bait at a dear rate when his life must go for it. Thy soul must be lost, which all the gold and silver in the world cannot redeem and recover.

[4.] I observe again that Christ by his refusal hath taught us to tread the world under our feet, and all the glory of it should be an ineffectual and cold motive to a sanctified soul. If we have the same spirit that was in Christ, it will be so. All the kingdoms of the world, and the glory of them, was far too little to make up a temptation to him. A mortified heart will contemn all this in comparison of our duty to God, and the comfort of a good conscience, and the hopes of glory. Surely they have not the spirit of Christ who are taken with small things, with a Babylonish garment, or some petty temptation.

Uses. The use is to teach us how to counterwork Satan.

1. Since he worketh upon the fleshly mind, we are to be mortified and grow dead to the world. We profess faith in a crucified Lord; we must be like him, crucified as he was crucified; then shall we glory in the cross of Christ, when we feel the virtue of it, and are planted into the likeness of it: Gal. vi. 14, 'God forbid that I should glory, save in the cross of our Lord Jesus Christ, by whom the world is crucified unto me, and I unto the world.' Grow more dead to the riches, honour, pomp, pleasure, the favour, fear, love, wrath, praise and dispraise of men, that we may readily deny these things, so far as opposite to the kingdom of Christ, or our duty to God, or as they lessen our affections to him. We die as our esteem of those things doth decay ; till the man's temper be altered there is no hope to prevail by argument. Only they that are made partakers of a divine nature do escape the corruption that is in the world through lust.

2. Since he worketh by representation and promise, you must be prepared against both.

[1.] As he worketh by representation of the fair show and splendid appearance of worldly things, you must check it :—

(1.) By considering the little substance and reality that is in this fair appearance: 1 Cor. vii. 31, 'The fashion of this world passeth away,' σχῆμα. It is but a draft, an empty pageantry ; so it is called, Ps. xxxix. 6, 'A vain show;' an image, shadow, or dream, that vanisheth in a trice. So Prov. xxiii. 5, 'Wilt thou set thine eyes upon that which is not ?' It was not a while ago, and within a little while it will not be again, at least to us it will not be ; we must shortly bid good-night to all the world: 1 Pet. i. 24, 'All flesh is grass, and the glory thereof as the flower of the grass.' David saith, Ps. cxix. 86, 'I have seen an end of all perfection.' It is good often to intermingle these serious thoughts of the frailty of all sublunary enjoyments, to keep us modest in what we have, or desire to have, that we may not be blinded with the delusions of the flesh, and enchanted with an admiration of worldly felicity.

(2.) As the devil seeketh to open the eye of sense, so must we open the eye of faith : 2 Cor. iv. 18, 'We look not at the things which are seen, but at the things which are not seen ; for the things which are seen are temporal, but the things which are not seen are eternal.' Things unseen must be every day greatened in our eyes, that all our pursuit after things seen may be subordinated to our desires of, and labour after, things unseen. There we must see the greatest reality, or else we have not the true Christian faith : Heb. xi. 1, 'Faith is the substance of things hoped for, and the evidence of things not seen.'

It is such an evidence of the worth and reality of the unseen glory as draweth off the heart from things seen, which are so pleasing to the flesh. Faith sets it before the eye of the soul in the promises of the gospel: Heb. vi. 18, 'Who have fled for refuge to lay hold upon the hope set before us.' Heb. xii. 2, 'Who for the joy that was set before him endured the cross,' &c.

[2.] As he dealeth with us by promise. Everything we hope to get by sin is a kind of promise or offer of the devil to us; as suppose by unconscionable dealing in our calling. Here consider two things:—

(1.) The falsity of the devil's promises.

(2.) The truth and stability of God's promises.

(1st.) The falsity of Satan's promises. Either he giveth not what he promised, as he promised our first parents to be as gods: Gen. iii. 5, 'Ye shall be as gods;' and what ensued? Ps. xlix. 12, 'Man that is in honour and understandeth not, is like the beasts that perish;' degraded to the beasts, as the brutish and bestial nature prevailed in him when he fell from God. Or else, if we have them, we were better be without them; we have them with a curse, with the loss of better things: Jer. xvii. 13, 'O Lord, all that forsake thee shall be ashamed, and they that depart from me shall be written in the earth.' They are condemned to this felicity: we have them with stings of conscience:—Mat. xxvii. 4, 5, 'I have sinned, in that I have betrayed innocent blood; and he cast down the pieces of silver in the temple, and went and hanged himself;'—which are most quick and sensible when we come to die: Jer. xvii. 11, 'He that getteth riches, and not by right, shall leave them in the midst of his days, and at his end shall be a fool.' Now rise up in indignation against the temptation. Shall I sell my birthright? lose my fatness to rule over the trees? —as the olive-tree in Jotham's parable, Judges ix. 9.

(2dly.) The sufficiency and stability of God's promises.

First, Sufficiency: Gen. xvii. 1, 'I am the Almighty God; walk before me, and be thou perfect;' 1 Tim. iv. 8, 'Godliness is profitable for all things, having the promise of the life that now is, and of that which is to come;'—of heaven and of earth: Mat. vi. 33, 'Seek ye first the kingdom of God, and the righteousness thereof, and all these things shall be added to you.' It may be you have less than those that indulge themselves in all manner of shifts and wiles, but you shall have enough, not to be left wholly destitute: Heb. xiii. 5, 'He hath said, I will never leave thee, nor forsake thee.' And you shall have it with contentment: Prov. xv. 6, 'In the house of the righteous is much treasure, but in the revenues of the wicked is trouble;' and 'better is a little with righteousness, than great revenues with sin,' Prov. xvi. 8. And you have it so as not to lose other things.

Secondly, Stability: 2 Cor. i. 20, 'All the promises of God in him are Yea, and in him Amen;' and Heb. vi. 18, 'That by two immutable things, in which it was impossible for God to lie, we might have strong consolation,' &c.; Ps. cxix. 111, 'Thy testimonies have I taken as an heritage for ever: they are the rejoicing of my heart.'

IV. Observe—*Fall down*—The pride of the devil: he sinneth from the beginning, 1 John iii. 8. The sin of pride was fatal to him at first, and the cause of those chains of darkness in which now he is held; yet still he sinneth the same sin, he requireth adoration, and would be admitted into a partnership of divine worship. He obtained it from pagans and idolaters, not from Christ. The angel deprecates and detests it : Rev. xix. 10, ' And I fell at his feet to worship him. And he said unto me, See thou do it not ; for I am thy fellow-servant, and of thy brethren that have the testimony of Jesus : worship thou God.' So Rev. xxii. 9, 'I fell down to worship before the face of the angel that showed me these things. And he said to me, See thou do it not : for I am thy fellow-servant, and of thy brethren the prophets, and of them that keep the sayings of this book: worship God.' Paul, when the priests at Lycaonia were about to sacrifice to him : Acts xiv. 14, 15, ' When the apostles heard of it, they rent their clothes, and ran in among the people, crying out, and saying, Sirs, why do you these things ? We also are men of like passions with you, and preach unto you that ye should turn from these vanities unto the living God.' But the evil angels they are apt to invade the right of God.

SERMON VI.

Then saith Jesus unto him, Get thee hence, Satan : for it is written, Thou shalt worship the Lord thy God, and him only shalt thou serve.—Mat. IV. 10.

Thirdly, Christ's answer and reply, which is double :—

I. By way of rebuke, defiance, and bitter reprehension : *Get thee hence, Satan.*

II. By way of confutation : *For it is written, &c.*

1. The rebuke showeth Christ's indignation against idolatry: ' Get thee hence, Satan.' This was not to be endured. Twice Christ useth this form of speech, ὕπαγε Σατανᾶ,—to Satan tempting him to idolatry here, and when his servant dissuaded him from suffering : Mat. xvi. 23, ' Get thee behind me, Satan, for thou art an offence to me ; for thou savourest not the things that be of God, but those that be of men.' This suggestion intrenched or touched upon the glory of God, the other upon his love to mankind ; and Christ could endure neither; Satan is commanded out of his presence with indignation. The same zeal we see in his servants: in Moses in case of idolatry, Exod. xxxii. 19, He brake the tables ; so in case of contradiction to the faith of Christ, Paul taketh up Elymas, Acts xiii. 10, ' O full of subtilty and all mischief, thou child of the devil, thou enemy of all righteousness, wilt thou not cease to pervert the right ways of the Lord ? ' Open blasphemy must be abhorred, and needeth not only a confutation but a rebuke. Besides, it was an impudent demand of Satan to require adoration from him, to whom adoration is due from every creature; to ask him to bow down before him, to whom every knee must bow : and therefore a bold temptation must have a peremptory answer. There is no mincing in such cases. It is no way contrary to that lenity that was in Christ ; and it teacheth us, in such open cases

of blasphemy and downright sin, not to parley with the devil, but to
defy him.

2. By way of confutation : ' For it is written, Thou shalt worship the
Lord thy God, and him only shalt thou serve.' Where observe :—

[1.] Christ answereth to the main point, not to by-matters. He
doth not dispute the devil's title, nor debate the reality of his promises ;
to do this would tacitly imply a liking of the temptation. No ; but he
disproveth the evil of the suggestion from this unclean and proud
spirit : a better answer could not be given unto the tempter. So that
herein we see the wisdom of Christ, which teacheth us to pass by
impertinent matters, and to speak expressly to the cause in hand in all
our debates with Satan and his instruments.

[2.] He citeth scripture, and thereby teacheth that the word of
God, laid up in the heart and used pertinently, will ward off the blows
of every temptation. This weapon Christ used all along with success,
and therefore it is well called, ' The sword of the Spirit,' Eph. vi. 17.
It is a sword, and so a weapon both offensive and defensive : Heb. iv.
12, ' The word of God is quick and powerful, sharper than any two-
edged sword, piercing even to the dividing asunder of soul and spirit,
and of the joints and marrow, and is a discerner of the thoughts and
intents of the heart.' And ' a sword of the Spirit,' because the Spirit
is the author of it : 2 Pet. i. 21, ' Holy men of God spake as they
were moved by the Holy Ghost.' He formed and fashioned this weapon
for us ; and because its efficacy dependeth on the Spirit, who timeously
bringeth it to our remembrance, and doth enliven the word and
maketh it effectual. Therefore it teacheth us to be much acquainted
with the Lord's written word. The timely calling to mind of a word
in scripture is better than all other arguments,—a word forbidding or
threatening such an evil : Ps. cxix. 11, ' Thy word have I hid in my
heart, that I might not sin against thee ; ' pressing the practice of
such a duty when we are slow of heart : Ps. cxix. 50, ' Thy word hath
quickened me ; ' or a word speaking encouragement to the soul exercised with such a cross : Heb. xii. 5, ' Ye have forgotten the exhortation which speaketh unto you as unto children, My son, despise not
thou the chastening of the Lord, nor faint when thou art rebuked of
him ; ' Ps. cxix. 92, ' Unless thy law had been my delight, I should
then have perished in mine affliction ; ' still it breaketh the strength of
the temptation, whatsoever it be.

[3.] The words are cited out of the book of Deuteronomy. Indeed
out of that book all Christ's answers are taken, which showeth us the
excellency of that book. It was of great esteem among the Jews, and
it should be so among all Christians, and it will be so of all that read
it attentively. The church could not have wanted it.

[4.] The places out of which it is cited are two: Deut. vi. 13,
' Thou shalt fear the Lord thy God, and serve him, and swear by his
name ; ' and again, Deut. x. 20, ' Thou shalt fear the Lord thy God,
and serve him, and to him shalt thou cleave.' Christ, according to
the Septuagint, ' Thou shalt worship the Lord thy God, and him only
shalt thou serve.' Μόνῳ, only, which is emphatical, seemeth to
be added to the text, but it is necessarily implied in the words of
Moses ; for his scope was to bind the people to the fear and worship

of one God.   None was so wicked and profane as to deny that God was
to be feared and worshipped ; but many might think that either the
creatures or the gods of the Gentiles might be taken into fellowship of
this reverence and adoration.   *Him* is *only him ;* αὐτῷ is exclusive, if
μόνῳ were left out.   See the place, Deut. vi. 13, 14, ' Thou shalt fear
the Lord thy God, and serve him, and shalt swear by his name ; ye
shall not go after other gods, of the gods of the people which are round
about you.'   And in other places it is expressed ; as 1 Sam. vii. 3, ' If
you prepare your hearts unto the Lord, and serve him only.'   The
devil excepts not against this interpretation, as being fully convinced
and silenced by it.   And it is a known story that this was the cause
why the pagans would not admit the God of the Jews, as revealed in
the Old Testament, or Christ, as revealed in the New, to be an object
of adoration, because he would be worshipped alone, all other deities
excluded.   The gods of the heathens were good-fellow gods, would
admit partnership ; as common whores are less jealous than the married wife : though their lovers went to never so many besides themselves, yet to them it was all one, whensoever they returned to them
and brought their gifts and offerings.

[5.]   In this place quoted by our Saviour there is employed a distinction of inward and outward worship.   *Fear* is for inward worship,
serve is for outward worship, and the profession of the same.   *Fear* in
Moses is expounded *worship* by Christ ; so Mat. xv. 9, compared with
Isa. xxix. 13, ' In vain do they worship me, teaching for doctrines the
commandments of men ; ' but in the prophet it is ' Their fear towards
me is taught by the precepts of men.'   He that worshippeth feareth
and reverenceth what he worshippeth, or else all his worship is but a
compliment and empty formality.   So that the *fear* of God is that
reverence and estimation that we have of God, the *serving* of God is
the necessary effect and fruit of it ; for service is an open testimony of
our reverence and worship.   In this place you have worship and
service, both which are due to God only.   But that you may
perceive the force of our Saviour's argument, and also of this
precept, I shall a little dilate on the word *service*, what the scripture
intendeth thereby.   Satan saith, ' Bow down and worship me : '
Christ saith, ' Thou shalt worship the Lord thy God, and him only
shalt thou serve.'   Under *service*, prayer and thanksgiving is comprehended : Isa. xliv. 17, ' And the residue thereof he maketh a god,
even his graven image : he falleth down unto it, and worshippeth
it, and prayeth unto it, and saith, Deliver me, for thou art my god.'
This is one of the external acts whereby the idolater showeth the
esteem of his heart : so Jer. ii. 27, ' Saying to a stock, Thou art my
father ; and to a stone, Thou hast brought me forth.'   So, under *serving*, sacrifice is comprehended : 2 Kings xvii. 35, ' Ye shall not fear
other gods, nor bow yourselves to them, nor serve them, nor sacrifice
to them.'   Again, burning of incense : Jer. xviii. 15, ' My people
have forgotten me, they have burnt incense to vanity.'   Preaching
for them ; Jer. ii. 8, ' The pastors also have transgressed against
me, and the prophets prophesied by Baal.'   Asking counsel of them :
Hosea iv. 12, ' My people ask counsel at their stocks, and their staff
declareth unto them ; for the spirit of whoredoms hath caused them to

err, and they have gone a whoring from under their God.' So building temples, altars, or other monuments unto them : Hosea viii. 14,
' Israel hath forgotten his Maker, and buildeth temples ; ' and xii. 11,
' Their altars are as heaps in the furrows of the fields.' Erecting of
ministries, or doing any ministerial work for their honour : Amos v.
26, ' Ye have borne the tabernacle of your Moloch and Chium your
images, the star of your god, which ye made to yourselves ; ' as God
appointed the Levites to bear the tabernacle for communion in the
service of them : 1 Cor. x. 18, ' Are not they that eat of the sacrifices
partakers of the altar ? ' ver. 21,. ' Ye cannot drink the cup of the
Lord and the cup of devils ; ye cannot be partakers of the Lord's table
and of the table of devils.' So 2 Cor. vi. 16, 17, ' What agreement
hath the temple of God with idols ? ' In short, for it is endless to
reckon up all which the scripture comprehendeth under service and
gestures of reverence : Exod. xx. 5, ' Thou shalt not bow down thyself
to them, nor serve them.' Bowing the knee : 1 Kings xix. 18, ' I have
left me seven thousand in Israel, which have not bowed the knee to
Baal.' Kissing them : Hosea xiii. 18, ' They kiss the calves.' Lifting
up the eyes : Ezek. ii. 15, ' He hath not lift up his eyes to the idols of
the house of Israel.' Stretching out the hand : Ps. xliv. 20, ' If we
have stretched our hands to a strange God.' So that you see all
gestures of reverence are forbidden as terminated to idols. Thus
strict and jealous is God in his law, that we might not bow down and
worship the devil, or anything that is set up by him.

Doct. That religious service and religious worship is due to God
only, and not to be given to saint, or angel, or any creature.

Thus Christ defeateth the devil's temptation, and thus should we
be under the awe of God's authority, that we may not yield to the
like temptation when the greatest advantages imaginable are offered
to us. Here I shall show :—

  I. What is worship, and the kinds of it.
  II. I shall prove that worship is due to God.
  III. Not only worship, but service.
  IV. That both are due to God alone.

1. What is worship ? In the general it implieth these three
things : an act of the judgment, apprehending an excellency in the
object worshipped ; an act of the will, or a readiness to yield to it,
suitably to the degree of excellency which we apprehend in it ; and an
external act of the body whereby it is expressed. This is the general
nature of worship, common to all the sorts of it.

2. The kinds of it. Now worship is of two kinds—civil and
religious. Religious worship is a special duty due to God, and commanded in the first table. Civil honour and worship is commanded
in the second table. They are expressed by ' godliness and righteousness,' 1 Tim. vi. 11 ; and ' godliness and honesty,' 1 Tim. ii. 2.

[1.] For religious worship. There is a twofold religious worship.
One when we are right for the object, and do only worship the true
God ; this is required in the first commandment. The other when
we are right for the means, when we worship the true God by such
means as he hath appointed, not by an image, idol, or outward representation. Opposite to this there is an evil idolatrous sinful worship,

when that which is due to the Creator is given to any creature; which is primary or secondary. Primary, when the image or idol is accounted God, or worshipped as such, as the sottish heathens do. Or secondary, when the images themselves are not worshipped as having any godhead properly in themselves, but as they relate to, represent, or are made use of, in the worship of him who is accounted God. We shall find this done by the wiser heathens, worshipping their images, not as gods themselves, but as intending to worship their gods in these and by these. So also among some who would be called Christians. Thus the representing the true God by images is condemned, Deut. iv. 15–17, ' Take ye good heed unto yourselves, for ye saw no manner of similitude on the day that the Lord spake unto you in Horeb, out of the midst of the fire, lest ye corrupt yourselves, and make you a graven image, the similitude of any figure, the likeness of male or female.' Again, sinful worship is twofold: more gross of idols, representing false gods, called worshipping of devils; or more subtle, when worship is given to saints or holy men : Acts x. 25, 26, ' As Peter was coming in, Cornelius met him, and fell down at his feet, and worshipped him. But Peter took him up, saying, Stand up ; I myself also am a man.' Acts xiv. 14, 15, ' Paul and Barnabas, when they heard this, rent their clothes, and ran in among the people, crying out and saying, Sirs, why do you these things ? we also are men of like passions with you,' &c. Or to angels: Rev. xxii. 8, ' When John fell at the angel's feet to worship him, he said, See thou do it not ; for I am thy fellow-servant, and of thy brethren the prophets.'

[2.] Civil worship is when we give men and angels due reverence, and—

(1.) With respect to their stations and relations, whatever their qualifications be, as to magistrates, ministers, parents, great men ; we are to reverence and honour them according to their degree and quality : according to the fifth commandment, ' Honour thy father and thy mother ;' 1 Thes. v. 13, and to ' esteem them very highly in love for their work's sake.' Or,

(2.) A reverential worshipping or esteeming them for their qualifications of wisdom and holiness : Acts ii. 47, Good men had ' favour with all the people.' Such respect living saints get, such angels may have when they appear : Gen. xviii. 2, Abraham ' bowed himself towards the ground :' and Gen. xix. 1, Lot ' rose up to meet them, and bowed himself with his face towards the ground.'

Now, whether the worship be civil or religious may be gathered by the circumstances thereof ; as if the act, end, or other circumstances be religious, the action or worship itself must be so also. It is one thing to bow the knee in salutation, another thing to bow in prayer before an image.

II. That worship is due to God. These two notions live and die together—that God is, and that he ought to be worshipped. It appeareth by our Saviour's reasoning, John iv. 24, ' God is a spirit, and they that worship him must worship him in spirit and in truth.' He giveth directions about the manner of worship, but supposeth it that he will be worshipped. When God had proclaimed his name and manifested himself to Moses, Exod. xxxiv. 8, ' Moses made haste, and bowed himself and worshipped.' It is the crime charged upon the Gentiles,

that   when they knew God, they glorified him not as God,' Rom. i.
21.   They knew a divine power, but did not give him a worship, at
least competent to his nature.   God pleadeth his right : Mal. i. 6, ' If
I be a father, where is mine honour ?   If I be a master, where is my
fear?'   And God, who is the common parent and absolute master of
all, must have both a worship and honour, in which reverence and fear
is mixed with love and joy ; so that if God be, worship is certainly
due to him.   They that have no worship are as if they had no God.
The psalmist proveth atheism by that : Ps. xiv. 1, ' The fool hath
said in his heart, There is no God ;' and ver. 4, ' They call not upon
God.'   The acknowledgment of a king doth imply subjection to his
laws ; so doth the acknowledgment of his God imply a necessity of
worshipping him.

III.   That both worship and service is due to God : ' Him shalt thou
worship, and him shalt thou serve.'   The worship of God is both internal and external : the internal consisteth in that love and reverence
which we owe to him; the external, in those offices and duties by which
our honour and respect to God is signified and expressed : both are
necessary, both believing with the heart, and confession with the mouth:
Rom. x. 9, 10, ' If thou shalt confess with thy mouth the Lord Jesus,
and shalt believe in thy heart that God raised him from the dead, thou
shalt be saved.   For with the heart man believeth unto righteousness,
and with the mouth confession is made unto salvation.'   The soul and
life of our worship and godliness lieth in our faith, love, reverence, and
delight in God above all other things ; the visible expression of it is
in invocation, thanksgiving, prayers, and sacraments, and other acts of
outward worship.   Now, it is not enough that we own God with the
heart, but we must own him with the body also.   In the heart : ' Serve
the Lord with fear, and rejoice with trembling,' Ps. ii. 11.   Such as
will become the greatness and goodness of God ; with outward and
bodily worship you must now own him in all those prescribed duties in
which these affections are acted.   The spirit must be in it, and the body
also.   There are two extremes.   Some confine all their respect to God to
bodily worship and external forms : Mat. xvi. 8, ' This people draweth nigh unto me with their mouth, and honoureth me with their lips;
but their hearts are far from me.'   They use the external rites of
worship, but their affections are no way suited to the God whom they
worship : it is the heart must be the principal and chief agent in the
business, without which it is but the carcase of a duty, without the life
and the soul.   The other extreme is, that we are not called to an
external bodily worship under the gospel.   Why did he then appoint
the ordinances of preaching, prayer, singing of psalms, baptism, and
the Lord's supper ?   God, that made the whole man, body and soul,
must be worshipped of the whole man.   Therefore, besides the inward
affections, there must be external actions, whereby we express our
respect and reverence to God.

IV.   That both these, religious worship and service, are due to God
alone.   I prove it by these arguments :—

1. Those things which are due to God as God are due to him alone,
and no creature, without sacrilege, can claim any part and fellowship in
that worship and adoration, neither can it be given to any creature with-

out idolatry. But now religious worship and service is due to God as God: 'He is thy Lord, and worship thou him,' Ps. xlv. 11. Our worship and service is due to him, not only for his super-eminent excellency, but because of our creation, preservation, and redemption. Therefore we must worship and serve him, and him only: Isa. xlii. 8, 'I am the Lord; that is my name: and my glory will I not give to another, nor my praise to graven images.' God challengeth it as Jehovah, the great self-being, from whom we have received life and breath, and all things. This glory God will not suffer to be given to another. And therefore the apostle showeth the wretched estate of the Galatians, chap. iv. 8 : 'When ye knew not God, ye did service to them that by nature are no gods;' that is, they worshipped for gods those things which really were no gods. There is no kind of religious worship or service, under any name whatsoever, to be given to any creature, but to God only ; for what is due to the Creator as Creator cannot be given to the creature.

2. The nature of religious worship is such, that it cannot be terminated on any object but God ; for it is a profession of our dependence and subjection. Now, whatever invisible power this worship is tendered unto must be omniscient, omnipresent, omnipotent. Omniscient, who knows the thoughts, cogitations, secret purposes of our heart, which God alone doth: 1 Kings viii. 39, 'Give unto every one according to his ways, whose heart thou knowest ; for thou, even thou only, knowest the hearts of all the children of men.' It is God's prerogative to know the inward motions and thoughts of the heart, whether they be sincere or no in their professions of dependence and subjection. So omnipresent, that he may be ready at hand to help us and relieve us: Jer. xxiii. 23, 24, 'Am I a God at hand, and not a God afar off? Can any hide himself in secret places, that I shall not see him? saith the Lord. Do not I fill heaven and earth? saith the Lord.' The palace of heaven doth not so confine him and enclose him but that he is present everywhere by his essential presence, and powerful and efficacious providence. Besides omnipotent: Ps. lvii. 2, 'I will cry unto God most high, unto God who performeth all things for me.' Alas! what a cold formality were prayer if we should speak to those that know us not, and who are not near to help us, or have no sufficiency of power to help us! Therefore these professions of dependence and subjection must be made to God alone.

3. To give religious worship to the creatures, it is without command, without promise, and without examples, and therefore without any faith in the worshipper, or acceptance of God. Where is there any command or direction, or approved example, of this in scripture? God will accept only what he commanded, and without a promise it will be unprofitable to us: and it is a superstitious innovation of our own to devise any religious worship for which there is no example at all whereby it may be recommended to us. Certainly no action can be commended to us as godly which is not prescribed of God, by whose word and institution every action is sanctified which otherwise would be common ; and no action can be profitable to us which God hath not promised to accept, or hath accepted from his people. But giving religious worship to a creature is of this nature.

4. It is against the express command of God, the threatening of scripture, and the examples recorded in the word. Against the express command of God—both the first and second commandments, the one respecting the object, the other the means ; that we must not serve other gods, nor go after them, nor bow down unto them. It is against the threatenings of the word in all those places where God is said to be ' a jealous God.' God is said to ' put on jealousy as a cloak,' Isa. lix. 17 ; that is, the upper and outmost garment. He will be known, and plainly profess himself to be so. So Exod. xxxiv. 14, ' The Lord, whose name is Jealous, is a jealous God.' Things are distinguished from the same kind by their names, as from different kinds by their natures. Now, from the λεγόμενοι θεοὶ, God will be distinguished by his jealousy, that he will not endure any partners in his worship. It is against examples : Rev. xix. 10, and xxii. 8, ' When I had heard and seen, I fell down to worship before the feet of the angel which showed me these things. And he said unto me, See thou do it not,' &c. The argument is, ' I am thy fellow-servant, and of thy brethren the prophets, and of them which keep the sayings of this book : worship God.'

Use 1. To condemn those who do not make conscience of the worship of God. There are an irreligious sort of men that never call upon him, in public or in private, in the family or in the closet ; but wholly forget the God that made them, at whose expense they are maintained and kept. Wherefore had you reasonable souls, but to praise, honour, and glorify your Creator? Surely if God be your God, that is, your Creator and preserver, the duty will presently fall upon you : ' Thou shalt worship the Lord thy God.' If you believe there is a God, why do not you call upon him ? The neglect of his worship argueth doubting thoughts of his being ; for if there be such a supreme Lord, to whom one day you must give an account, how dare you live without him in the world ? All the creatures glorify him passively, but you have a heart and a tongue to glorify him actually. Man is the mouth of the creation, to return to God the praise of all that wisdom, goodness, and power which is seen in the things that are made. Now you should make one among the worshippers of God. A heathen could say, *Si essem luscinia*, &c. Are you a Christian, and have such advantages to know more of God, and will you be dumb and tongue-tied in his praises?

2. To condemn the idolatry of the Papists. Synesius said that the devil is εἰδωλοχαρὴς, that he rejoiceth in idols. Here we see what was the upshot of his temptations, even to bring men to worship and bow down before something that is not God. Herein he was gratified by the heathen nations, and no less by the Papists. Witness their worshipping of images, their invocation of the Virgin Mary and other saints, the adoring before the bread in the Eucharist, &c. I know they have many evasions ; but yet the stain of idolatry sticketh so close to them, that all the water in the sea will not wash them clean from it. This text clearly stareth them in the face, ' Thou shalt worship the Lord thy God, and him only shalt thou serve.' Not saints, not angels, not images, &c. They say, Moses only said, and Christ repeateth it from him, ' Thou shalt worship the Lord thy God ;' but not *only*, so that the last clause is restrictive, not the first, but some worship may be given to the creature. Civil, we grant, but not religious ; and

worship is the most important word. They distinguish of $\Lambda a\tau\rho\epsilon ia$ and $\Delta o\nu\lambda\epsilon ia$. The devil demanded of Christ only $\pi\rho o\sigma\kappa\nu\nu\acute{\eta}\sigma a\iota$, 'fall down and worship me;' not as the supreme author of all God's gifts, but as subordinate: 'all these things are delivered unto me.' But then Christ's words were not apposite to refute the tempter's impudency. Besides, for the distinction of $\Delta o\nu\lambda\epsilon ia$ and $\Lambda a\tau\rho\epsilon ia$, the words are promiscuously used; so their distinction of absolute and relative worship; besides that they are groundless, they are unknown to the vulgar, who promiscuously give worship to God, saints, images, relics. Some of the learned of them have confessed this abuse, and bewailed it :—Espencæus, a Sorbonnist: ' Are they well and godly brought up, who, being children of an hundred year old, that is, ancient Christians, do no less attribute to the saints, and trust in them, than to God himself, and that God himself is harder to be pleased and entreated than they ?' So George Cassander : ' This false, pernicious opinion is too well known to have prevailed among the vulgar, while wicked men, persevering in their naughtiness, are persuaded that only by the intercession of the saints whom they have chosen to be their patrons, and worship with cold and profane ceremonies, they have pardon and grace prepared them with God ; which pernicious opinion, as much as was possible, hath been confirmed by them by lying miracles. And other men, not so evil, have chosen certain saints to be their patrons and helpers, have put more confidence in their merits and intercession than in the merits of Christ, and have substituted into his place the saints and Virgin mother. Ludovicus Vives : ' There are many Christians which worship saints, both men and women, no otherwise than they worship God ; and I cannot see any difference between the opinion they had of their saints, and that the Gentiles had of their gods.' Thus far he, and yet Rome will not be purged.

3. Use is to exhort us to worship and serve the Lord our God, and him only.

[1.] Let us worship him. Worship hath its rise and foundation in the heart of the worshipper, and especially religious worship, which is given to the all-knowing God. Therefore there must we begin; we must have high thoughts, and an high esteem of God. Worship in the heart is most seen in two things—love and trust. Love : Deut. vi. 5, ' Thou shalt love the Lord thy God with all thy heart, and with all thy soul, and with all thy might.' We worship God when we give him such a love as is superlative and transcendental, far above the love that we give to any other thing, that so our respect to other things may give way to our respect to God. The other affection whereby we express our esteem of God is trust. This is another foundation of worship : Ps. lxii. 8, ' Trust in the Lord at all times, pour out your hearts before him.' Well, then, inward worship lieth in these two things—delightful adhesion to God, and an entire dependence upon him. Without this worship of God we cannot keep up our service to him. Not without delight, witness these scriptures : Job xxvii. 10, ' Will he delight himself in the Almighty ? will he always call upon God ?' Isa. xliii. 22, ' But thou hast not called upon me, O Jacob; but thou hast been weary of me, O Israel !' They that love God, and delight in him, cannot be long out of his company, they will seek all occasions to meet with God, as Jonathan and David, whose souls were knit to each other. So for dependence and trust, it keepeth up service, for they that will not trust God cannot be long true to him : Heb. iii. 12, ' Take heed lest there be in any of you an evil heart of unbelief in departing from the living God.' They that distrust God's promises will not long hold out in God's way, for dependence begets observance. When we look for all from him, we will often come to him, and take all out of his hands, and be careful how we offend him and displease him. What maketh the Christian to be so sedulous and diligent in duties of worship? so awful and observant of God? His all cometh from God, both in life natural and spiritual. In life natural : Ps. cxlv. 15-20, ' The eyes of all things wait on thee, and thou givest them their food in due season. Thou openest thy hand, and satisfiest the desire of every living thing,' &c. ; ' The Lord is nigh unto all them that call upon him, to all that call upon him in truth. He will fulfil the desire of them that fear him ; he will hear their cry and will save them. The Lord preserveth all them that love him,'—implying that because their eyes are to him, the author of all their blessings, therefore they call upon him and cry to him.

[2.] Serve him. That implieth external reverence and worship. Now we are said to serve him, either with respect unto the duties which are more directly to be performed unto God, or with respect to our whole conversation.

(1.) With respect unto the duties which are more directly to be performed unto God, such as the word, prayer, praise, thanksgiving, sacraments, surely these must be attended upon, because they are acts of love to God, and trust in God ; and these holy duties are the ways of God, wherein he hath promised to meet with his people, and hath appointed us to expect his grace, and therefore they must not be neglected by us. Therefore serve him in these things ; for, Mark iv. 24, ' With what measure ye mete, it shall be measured to you.' It is a rule of commerce between us and God.

(2.) In your whole conversation : Luke i. 74, 75, ' That we might serve him without fear, in holiness and righteousness before him, all the days of our life.' A Christian's conversation is a continual act of worship ; he ever behaveth himself as before God, doing all things, whether they be directed to God or men, out of love to God, and fear of God, and so turneth second table duties into first table duties. 'Pure religion and undefiled, before God and the Father, is this, to visit the fatherless and the widows in their affliction, and to keep himself unspotted from the world,' James i. 27, Eph. v. 21, 22, ' Submitting yourselves one to another in the fear of God ;' and next verse, ' Wives, submit yourselves unto your own husbands, as unto the Lord.' So alms are a sacrifice : Heb. xiii. 16, ' But to do good and to communicate, forget not ; for with such sacrifices God is well pleased.'

[3.] Worship and serve God so as it may look like worship and service performed to God, and due to God only, because of his nature and attributes. His nature : John iv. 24, ' God is a Spirit, and they that worship him must worship him in spirit and in truth.' When hearts wander, and affections do not answer expressions, is this like worship and service done to an all-seeing Spirit? His attributes: Greatness, goodness, holiness—

(1.) His greatness and glorious majesty: Heb. xii. 28, 'Let us serve him acceptably, with reverence and godly fear.' Then is there a stamp of God's majesty on the duty.

(2.) His goodness and fatherly love : Ps. c. 2, 'Serve the Lord with gladness, and come before his presence with singing.'

(3.) His holiness: 2 Tim. i. 3, 'I thank God, whom I serve from my forefathers, with pure conscience;' 2 Tim. ii. 22, 'With them that call on the Lord out of a pure heart.'

SERMON VII.

Then the devil leaveth him, and behold angels came and ministered unto him.—MAT. IV. 11.

IN these words you have the issue and close of Christ's temptations. The issue is double :—(1.) In respect of the adversary ; (2.) In respect of Christ himself.

I. In respect of the adversary : *then the devil leaveth him.*

II. In respect of Christ himself : *behold angels came and ministered unto him.*

I shall consider in both the history and the observations.

First, The history of it, as it properly belongeth to Christ: and there—

1. Of the first branch, the recess of Satan : 'Then the devil leaveth him.'

[1.] It was necessary to be known that Christ had power to chase away the devil at his pleasure ; that, as he was an instance of temptations, so he might be to us a pattern of victory and conquest. If Satan had continued tempting, this would have been obscured, which would have been an infringement of comfort to us. The devil being overcome by Christ, he may be also overcome by us Christians: 1 John v. 18, 'He that is begotten of God keepeth himself, and the wicked one toucheth him not.' That is, he useth all care and diligence to keep himself pure, that the devil draw him not into the sin unto death, and those deliberate, scandalous sins which lead to it. Christ having overcome Satan, in our name and nature, showeth us the way how to fight against him and overcome him.

[2.] Christ had a work to do in the valley, and therefore was not always to be detained by temptations in the wilderness. The Spirit, that led him thither to be tempted, led him back again into Galilee to preach the gospel: Luke iv. 14, 'Jesus returned in the power of the Spirit into Galilee.' All things are timed and ordered by God, and he limiteth Satan how far and how long he shall tempt.

[3.] In Luke it is said, chap. iv. 13, ' He departed from him, ἄχρι καιροῦ, for a season.' He never tempted him again in this solemn way hand to hand; but either abusing the simplicity of his own disciple: Mat. xvi. 22, 23, 'Then Peter took him, and began to rebuke him, saying, Be it far from thee, Lord ; this shall not be unto thee. But he turned and said unto Peter, Get thee behind me Satan ! thou art an offence unto me ;' or else by his instruments, laying plots to take away his life ; as often, but especially in his passion : Luke xxii. 53, ' This is your hour, and the power of darkness.' So John xiv. 30, ' The prince of this world cometh, and hath nothing in me.' Satan shall join with the Jews to destroy me, but they shall find nothing to lay to my charge ; nor, indeed, have they power to do me any hurt, but that, in obedience to my Father's will, I mean voluntarily to lay down my life for sinners. So he had a permitted power over him, and was the prime instrumental cause of his sufferings ; set aside his voluntary condescension to be a ransom for sinners, Satan had not any power over him, or challenge against him. Well, then, though he lost his victory, he retained his malice.

2. The second branch, the access of the good angels : ' And behold the angels came and ministered to him.' There observe three things :

[1.] The note of attention : *behold*. The Holy Ghost would ex- cite our minds, and have us mark this : the angels are always at hand to serve Christ, but now they come to him in some singular manner—some notable appearance there was of them, probably in a visible form and shape ; and so they presented themselves before the Lord to minister to him, as the devil set himself before him to molest and vex him. As Christ's humiliation and human nature was to be manifested by the devil's coming to him and tempting assaults, so the honour of his divine nature by the ministry of angels, lest his temp- tations should seem to derogate from his glory. When we read the story of his temptations, how he was tempted in all parts like us, we might seem to take scandal, as if he were a mere man ; therefore his humiliation is counterbalanced with the special honour done to him : he was tempted as man, but, as God, ministered unto by angels.

[2.] Why they came not before the devil was departed ? I answer :—

(1.) Partly to show that Christ had no help but his own when he grappled with Satan. When the temptations were ended, then the good angels came, lest the victory should seem to be gotten by their help and assistance. They were admitted to the triumph, but they were not admitted to the fight : they were not spectators only in the conflict (for the battle was certainly fought before God and angels), but partners in the triumph : they went away to give place to the combat, but they came visibly to congratulate the conqueror after the battle was fought and the victory gotten. Our Lord would alone foil the devil, and, when that was done, the angels came and ministered unto him.

(2.) Partly to show us that the going of the one is the coming of the other. When the devil is gone, the angels come. Certainly it is true on the contrary : 1 Sam. xvi. 14, ' The Spirit of the Lord departed from Saul, and an evil spirit from the Lord troubled him ;' and it is true in this sense, if we entertain the temptation, we banish the good angels from us : there is no place for the good angels till the tempter be repulsed.

[3.] Why now, and to what end, was this ministry ?

(1.) To put honour on the Redeemer, who is the head and lord of the angels : Eph. i. 20, 21, ' He hath set him at his own right hand in the heavenly places, far above all principalities and powers, &c., and gave him to be the head over all things to the church.' So 1 Pet. iii. 22, 'Who is gone into heaven, and is on the right hand of God; angels, and authorities, and powers, being made subject to him.' Christ, not only as God, but as mediator, hath all of them subject to him: Heb. i. 6, 'And unto the Son he saith, Let all the angels of God worship him.' They, as subjects and servants, are bound to obey him. Therefore, on all occasions they attend on Christ; at his birth: Luke ii. 13, 14, 'A multitude of the heavenly host praised God, saying, Glory be to God on high, on earth peace, good will towards men.' Now, in his temptations, 'The angels came and ministered unto him.' At his passion: Luke xxii. 43, 'There appeared to him an angel from heaven, strengthening him.' At his resurrection, 'An angel rolled away the stone from the grave,' and attested the truth of it, Mat. xxviii. 2. At his ascension, the angels declared the manner of his going to heaven, and return to judgment, Acts i. 10, 11. So now they come to attend Christ, as subjects on their prince, to tender their service and homage to him, and receive his commands.

(2.) For his consolation, inward and outward.

First, Inward, as messengers sent from God; and so their coming was a token of God's special love and favour to him, and care over him. The devil had mentioned in one of his temptations, 'He shall give his angels charge over thee.' This is a truth, and in due time to be verified; not at Satan's instance, but when God pleased. Therefore it was a comfort to Christ to have solemn messengers sent from heaven to applaud his triumph.

Secondly, Outward, they were sent to serve him, either to convey him back from the mountain, where Satan had set him, or to bring him food, as they did to Elijah: 1 Kings xix. 5, 6, 'And as he lay and slept under a juniper-tree, behold then an angel touched him, and said unto him, Arise and eat. And he looked, and behold there was a cake baken on the coals, and a cruse of water at his head: and he did eat and drink, and laid him down again.' Διακονεῖν, the word here used, is often taken in that sense in the New Testament: Mat. viii. 15, 'She arose and ministered unto them,' that is, served them at meat. So Mat. xxv. 44, 'When saw we thee an hungered, &c., and did not minister unto thee?' The name of *deacons* is derived hence, as they 'served tables,' or provided meat for the poor, Acts vi. 2. So Luke x. 40, 'My sister hath left me, διακονεῖν, to serve alone,' meaning, to prepare provisions for the family: so Luke xvii. 8, 'Gird thyself and serve me,' that is, at the table: again, Luke xxii. 27, 'Whether is greater, he that sits at meat, or he that serveth?' or ministereth. So John xii. 2: 'They made a supper, and Martha served, but Lazarus was one of those that sat at the table with him.' Thus the angels ministered unto Christ. This sort of ministry agreeth with what was said of his hunger, which was the occasion of Satan's temptations.

Secondly, The observations. As Christ is a pattern of all those providences which are dispensed to the people of God.

Doct. 1. That the days of God's people's conflicts and trials will not always last.

There are alternative changes and vicissitudes in their condition upon earth; sometimes they are vexed with the coming of the tempter, and then encouraged and cheered by the presence of angels; after storms come days of joy and gladness,—' the devil departeth, and the angels came and ministered to him:' So Ps. xxxiv. 19, 'Many are the afflictions of the righteous, but the Lord delivereth him out of them all.' Here is their present conflict and their final conquest. Look on a Christian on his dark side, and there are afflictions, and afflictions many for number and kind; look on his luminous part, and there is the Lord to take care of him, to deliver him; and the deliverance is complete,—' the Lord delivereth him out of them all.' God will put an end to their conflict sooner or later; sometimes visibly in this life, or if he doth not deliver them till death, or from death, he will deliver them by death; then he delivereth them from all sin and misery at once, for death is theirs. The reasons are these :—

1. God considereth what will become himself, his pity and fidelity.

[1]. His own pity and mercy: James v. 11, 'Ye have heard of the patience of Job, and have seen the end of the Lord, that the Lord is very pitiful, and of tender mercy.' God will give an happy end to our conflicts and trials, as he did to Job, that he may be known to be a God pitiful and merciful : Job is set up as a public visible instance and monument of God's tender mercy. We must not measure our afflictions by the smart, but the end of them; what the merciful God will do at length : the beginning is from Satan, but the end from the Lord. If we look to the beginning, we draw an ill picture of God in our minds, as if he were harsh, severe, and cruel to his creatures, yea, to his best servants; but in the end we find him very tender of his people, and that sense hath made lies of God. At the very time when we think God hath forgotten us, he is ready to hear and to remove the trouble: Ps. xxxi. 22, 'I said in my haste, I am cut off'; nevertheless thou heardest the voice of my supplications.' The Son of God was hungry, transported and carried to and fro by the devil, from the pinnacle of the temple to a high mountain, tempted by a blasphemous suggestion to fall down and worship the impure spirit; but at length ' the devil leaveth him, and the angels came and ministered to him.'

[2.] His fidelity, which will not permit him to suffer you to be tempted above measure. We do not stand to the devil's courtesy, to tempt us as long as he list, but are in the hands of the faithful God: 1 Cor. x. 13, 'There hath no temptation taken you but what is common to man: but God is faithful, who will not suffer you to be tempted above that ye are able; but will with the temptation also make a way to escape, that ye may be able to bear it.' What a heap of consolations are there in that one place—as (1.) That temptations are but ordinary and to be looked for: there is no πειρασμὸς, but it is ἀνθρώπινος, *incident to human nature;* it hath nothing extraordinary in it. If the Son of God in human nature was not exempted, why should we expect a privilege apart to ourselves, not common to others ? (2.) That God's conduct is gentle; he inflicteth nothing and permitteth nothing to be inflicted upon you beyond measure, and above strength; but, as Jacob drove as the little ones were able to bear, so God proportioneth trials to our strength. Before you have final deliverance, you shall have present support. (3.) That he will, together with the temptation, give ἔκβασιν, *a passage out*, a way to escape. And all this is assured to us by his faithfulness; the conflict shall be tolerable when it is at the highest, and the end comfortable. God doth bridle the malice and hatred of Satan and his instruments; he hath taken an obligation upon himself to do so, that he may omit no part of his care towards us. A good man will not overburden his beast.

2. The Lord considereth also our frailty, both with respect to natural and spiritual strength.

[1.] Natural strength. The Psalmist telleth us, that ' He will not always chide, and keep his anger for ever,' Ps. ciii. 9. Why? One reason is, that ' He knoweth our frame, and remembereth we are dust,' ver. 14. He may express his just displeasure, and correct us for our sins for a while; but he taketh off his punishing hand again, because he knoweth we are soon apt to faint and fail, being but a little enlivened dust, of a weak constitution, not able to endure long troubles and vexations. Job pleadeth, chap. vi. 12, ' Is my strength the strength of stones? or is my flesh of brass?' We have not strength to subsist under perpetual troubles, but are soon broken and subdued by them.

[2.] With respect to spiritual strength, the best are subject to great infirmities, which oft betray us to sin, if our vexations be great and long: Ps. cxxv. 3, ' The rod of the wicked shall not rest on the lot of the righteous, lest the righteous put forth their hands to iniquity.' The oppressions of wicked men shall not be so lasting and durable as that the temptations should be of too great force; this might shake the constancy of the best. He knoweth nothing in divinity that knoweth not that God worketh congruously, and attempereth his providence to our strength, and so will not only give an increase of internal grace, but lessen and abate the outward temptation; that his external government conduceth to the preservation of the saints, as well as his internal, by supporting their spirits with more liberal aids of grace. Therefore God will cause the temptation to cease when it is overpressing. But all must be left to his wisdom and holy methods.

3. With respect to the devil and his instruments, to whose malice he sets bounds, who otherwise would know no measure.

[1.] For the devil, see Rev. ii. 10: ' Fear none of those things which thou shalt suffer. Behold! the devil shall cast some of you into prison, that you may be tried; and ye shall have tribulation ten days.' Mark how they are comforted against the persecution coming upon them: Partly because the cause was clearly God's, for all this trouble was by the instigation of the devil, making use of his instruments;—Eph. ii. 2, he is called ' the prince of the power of the air, the spirit that worketh in the children of disobedience:' Partly because the persecution raised would not be universal—some of you, not all —and those not persecuted unto the death, but only cast into prison: Partly from the end, that they should be tried—it was not penal or castigatory, but probatory;—the devil would destroy you, but God would suffer you only to be tried, so that they should come forth like the three children out of the furnace, without singeing of their garments, or like Daniel out of the lions' den, without a scratch or maim, or as Christ here—the devil got not one jot of

ground upon him : Partly from the duration, ten days—that is, in prophetical account, ten years, reckoning each day for a year : Num.
xiv. 34.   It was not long ; the saddest afflictions will have an end.
All which showeth how God bridleth and moderateth the rage of
Satan, and his evil influence.

[2.] For his instruments, God saith, Zech. i. 15, 'I am very
sorely displeased with the heathen that were at ease ; for I was
but a little displeased, and they helped forward the affliction.'   The
instruments of God's chastisements lay on without mercy, and being
of cruel minds and destructive intentions, which are heightened in
them by Satan, are severe executioners of God's wrath ; and if God
did not restrain them by the invisible chains of his providence,
we should never see good day more.   Well, then, you see the reasons
why the children of God, though they have many troubles and conflicts, yet they are not everlasting troubles.

Use of instruction to the people of God.   It teacheth them three
lessons—comfort, patience, obedience.

1. Comfort and encouragement to them that are under a gloomy
day.   This will not always last.   He may try you for a while, and
you may be under great conflicts, and wants, and difficulties, as he
tried the woman of Canaan with discouraging answers ; but at last,
'Woman, great is thy faith ; be it unto thee even as thou wilt,' Mat. xv.
28.   He tried his disciples when he meant to feed the multitude : John
vi. 5, 6, 'Whence shall we buy bread that all these may eat? This he said
to prove them, for he himself knew what he would do.'   A poor believer
is tried, children increase, trading grows dead in hard times ; how shall
so many mouths be filled ?   He promiseth Abraham a numerous posterity, but for a great while he goeth childless.   He promiseth David
a kingdom, yet for a while he is fain to shift for his life, and skulk up
and down in the wilderness.   He intended to turn water into wine,
but first all the store must be spent.   He meaneth to revive the hearts
of his contrite ones, but for a while they lie under great doubts
and fears.   Moses' hand must be made leprous before it wrought
miracles.   Jesus loved Lazarus, and meant to recover him, but he
must be dead first.   But I must not run too far.   There will be
tedious conflicts and trials, but yet there is hope of deliverance :
God is willing and God is able.   He is willing, because he is sufficiently inclined to it by the grace and favour that he beareth his
people : Ps. cxlix. 4, 'The Lord taketh pleasure in his people ; he
will beautify the meek with salvation.'   The Lord loveth their persons, and he loveth their prosperity and happiness : Ps. xxxv. 27,
'He hath pleasure in the prosperity of his servants.'   He is able
either as to wisdom or power.   Wisdom : 2 Pet. ii. 7, 'The Lord
knoweth how to deliver the godly out of temptation.'   Many times
we know not which way, but God knoweth ; he is never at a loss.
Then for his power : power hath a twofold notion, of authority and
might.   He hath authority enough.   The sovereign dominion of
God is a great prop to our faith.   All things in the world are at
his disposal to use them for his own glory : Ps. xliv. 4, ' Command
deliverances for Jacob.'   Angels, devils, men, the hearts of the greatest
men, are all at his command.   He hath might and strength : Dan. iii.

17, ' Our God, whom we serve, is able to deliver us,' and what then can let?

2. Patience: we must be contented, with the Son of God, to tarry his leisure, and undergo our course of trial, as Christ patiently continued, till enough was done to instruct the Church : Isa. xxviii. 16, ' He that believeth will not make haste.' The people of God miscarry in their haste : Ps. xxxi. 22, ' I said in my haste, I am cut off, but thou heardest the voice of my supplication :' Ps. cxvi. 11, ' I said in my haste, All men are liars ;' even Samuel and all the prophets who had assured him of the kingdom. It will come in the best time when it cometh in God's time, neither too soon nor too late; it will come sooner than your enemies would have it, sooner than second causes seem to promise, sooner than you deserve, soon enough to discover the glory of God to you : Ps. xl. 1, ' I waited patiently for the Lord, and he inclined unto me, and heard my cry.' God will not fail a waiting soul; his delay is no denial, nor a sign of want of love to you : John xi. 5, ' Jesus loved Lazarus ;' and yet, ver. 6, ' When he had heard that he was sick, he abode two days still in the same place where he was.' It may come sooner than you expect : Ps. xciv. 18, ' When I said, My foot slippeth, thy mercy, O Lord, held me up.' David was apt to think all was gone, help would never come more to him, and in that very season God delivered him.

3. Obedience: the son of God submitted to the Holy Spirit while the impure spirit tempted him. If you would look for a ceasing of the conflict, do as he did, carry it humbly, fruitfully, faithfully to God.

[1.] Humble carriage will become you under your conflicts : 1 Pet. v. 6, ' Humble yourselves therefore under the mighty hand of God, that he may exalt you in due time.' The stubbornness of the child maketh his correction double to what it otherwise would be. The more submissive you are, the more the cross hath its effect ; whether you will or no, you must passively submit to God.

[2.] Carry it fruitfully, otherwise you obstruct the kindness of the Lord. He proveth us, that we may be fruitful : John xv. 2, ' Every branch in me that beareth not fruit he taketh away ; and every branch that beareth fruit he purgeth it, that it may bring forth more fruit.' The rod hath done its work when it maketh us more holy ; then the comfortable days come : Heb. xii. 11, ' Now no chastening for the present seemeth to be joyous, but grievous ; nevertheless afterward it yieldeth the peaceable fruit of righteousness unto them which are exercised thereby.' Righteousness brings peace along with it, inward and outward. This maketh amends for the trouble. Then God beginneth to take it off.

[3.] Carry it faithfully to God, still opposing sin and Satan ; for the more you give way to Satan, the more you are troubled with him, and your misery is increased, not lessened. But if you repel his temptations, he is discouraged : Eph. iv. 27, ' Neither give place to the devil.' The devil watcheth for a door to enter and take possession of your hearts, that he may exercise his former tyranny. If he gaineth any ground, he makes fearful havoc in the soul, and weakeneth not only our comfort but our grace. Therefore imitate Christ's resolution and resistance here. But this will deserve a point by itself. Therefore :

Doct. 2. When the devil is thoroughly and resolutely resisted, he departeth.

As here, when the adversary was put to the foil, he went his way. Therefore this is often pressed upon us in scripture: James iv. 7, 'Resist the devil and he will flee from you.' If you resist his suggestions to malice, envy, and strife, he is discouraged; so 1 Pet. v. 9, 'Whom resist, stedfast in the faith.' We must not fly nor yield to him in the least, but stoutly and peremptorily resist him in all his temptations. If you stand your ground, Satan falleth. In this spiritual conflict Satan hath only weapons offensive, cunning wiles, and fiery darts, none defensive; a believer hath weapons both offensive and defensive, sword and shield, &c.; therefore our safety lieth in resisting.

About which is to be considered :—

1. What kind of resistance this must be.
2. Arguments to persuade and enforce it.
3. What graces enable us in this resistance.

1. For the kind of resistance.

[1.] It must not be faint and cold. Some kind of resistance may be made by general and common graces; the light of nature will rise up in defiance of many sins, especially at first, before men have sinned away natural light; or else the resistance at least is in some cold way. But it must be earnest and vehement, as against the enemy of God and our souls. Paul's resistance in his conflicts was with serious dislikes and deep groans: Rom. vii. 9, 'The good that I would I do not, but the evil which I would not, that I do;' and ver. 24, 'Oh wretched man that I am! who shall deliver me from the body of this death?' In apparent cases a detestation and vehement indignation is enough,—'Get thee behind me, Satan!' in other cases there need strong arguments and considerations, that the temptation may not stick when the tempter is gone, as the smutch remaineth of a candle stuck against a stone wall. When Eve speaketh faintly and coldly, the devil reneweth the assault with the more violence: Gen. iii. 3, 'Ye shall not eat of it, neither shall ye touch it, lest ye die.' As to the restraint, she speaketh warmly, and with some impatience of resentment, 'not eat' 'nor touch,'—in the commination too coldly, 'lest ye die,' when God had said, 'ye shall *surely* die.' A faint denial is a kind of grant; therefore slight Satan's assaults with indignation. Though the dog barketh the traveller passeth on. Satan cannot endure contempt. At other times argue for God stoutly; thy soul and eternal concernments are in danger. No worldly concernment ought to go so near to us as that which concerneth our eternal good and the salvation of our souls. What would the devil have from thee but thy soul, and its precious enjoyments, peace of conscience, hope of everlasting life? What doth he bid?—worldly vanities. As the merchant putteth up his wares with indignation when the chapman biddeth an unworthy price.

[2.] It must be a thorough resistance of all sin, 'take the little foxes,' dash 'Babylon's brats against the stones.' Lesser sticks set the great ones on fire. The devil cannot hope to prevail for great things presently. At first it is, 'Hath God said?' and then, 'Ye shall not

surely die.' The approaches of Satan to the soul are gradual, he
asketh a little, it is no great matter. Consider the evil of a temptation is better kept out than gotten out. Many think to stop after they
have yielded a little; but when the stone at the top of a hill begins
to roll downward, it is hard to stay it, and you cannot say how far you
shall go. 'I'll yield but once,' saith a deceived heart; 'I'll yield but
a little, and never yield again.' The devil will carry thee further and
further, till he hath not left any tenderness in thy conscience. Some
that thought to venture but a shilling, by the witchery of gaming
have played away all; so some have sinned away all principles of
conscience.

[3.] It must not be for a while, but continued; not only to stand
out against the first assault, but a long siege. What Satan cannot
gain by argument he seeketh to gain by importunity; but 'resist him,
stedfast in the faith,' as his instrument spake to Joseph, 'day by day,'
Gen. xxxix. 10. Our thoughts by time are more reconciled to evil.
Now we must keep up our zeal to the last. To yield at last is to lose
the glory of the conflict. Therefore rate away the importunate suitor,
as Christ doth.

2. Arguments to persuade it.

[1.] Because he cannot overcome you without your own consent.
The wicked are 'taken captive by him at his will and pleasure,'
2 Tim. ii. 26, because they yield themselves to his temptations; like
the young man, Prov. vii. 22, 'He goeth after her straightway, as an
ox goeth to the slaughter, and as a fool to the correction of the stocks.'
There is a consent, or, at least, there is not a powerful dissent.
Satan's power lieth not in a constraining efficacy, but persuasive
allurement.

[2.] The sweetness of victory will recompense the trouble of resistance. It is much more pleasing to deny a temptation than to yield
to it; the pleasure of sin is short-lived, but the pleasure of self-denial
is eternal.

[3.] Grace, the more it is tried and exercised, the more it is evidenced to be right and sincere: Rom. v. 3–5, 'Knowing that tribulation worketh patience, and patience experience, and experience hope,
and hope maketh not ashamed, because the love of God is shed abroad
in our hearts, by the Holy Ghost, which is given to us.' It is a comfortable thing to know that we are of the truth, and to be able to
assure our hearts before God.

[4.] Grace is strengthened when it hath stood out against a trial; as
a tree shaken with fierce winds is more fruitful, its roots being
loosened. Satan is a loser and you a gainer by temptations wherein
you have approved your fidelity to God; as a man holdeth a stick the
faster when another seeketh to wrest it out of his hands.

[5.] The more we resist Satan, the greater will our reward be: 2
Tim. iv. 7, 8, 'I have fought a good fight, I have finished my course,
I have kept the faith; henceforth there is laid up for me a crown of
righteousness.' The danger of the battle will increase the joy of the
victory, as the dangers of the way make home the sweeter. There will
a time come when he that is now a soldier will be a conqueror: Rom.
xvi. 20, 'The God of peace shall bruise Satan under your feet shortly.'

[6.] Where Satan gets possession, after he seemeth to be cast out, he returneth with the more violence, and tyranniseth the more : Mat. xii. 45, ' Then goeth he and taketh with himself seven other spirits more wicked than himself, and they enter in, and dwell there ; and the last state of that man is worse than the first.'

[7.] The Lord's grace is promised to him that resisteth. God keepeth us from the evil one, but it is by our watchfulness and resistance ; his power maketh it effectual. We are to strive against sin and keep ourselves, and God keepeth us by making our keeping effectual.

3. What are the graces that enable us in this resistance? I answer, the three fundamental graces, faith, hope, and love, so the spiritual armour is represented : 1 Thes. v. 8, ' But let us, who are of the day, be sober, putting on the breastplate of faith and love, and for an helmet the hope of salvation.'

[1.] A strong faith : 1 Pet. v. 9, ' Whom resist, stedfast in the faith.' This is, in the general, a sound belief of eternity, or a deep sense of the world to come : when we believe the gospel with an assent so strong as constantly to adhere to the duties prescribed, and to venture all upon the hopes offered therein.

[2.] A fervent love, arising out of the sense of our obligations to God, that we do with all readiness of mind set ourselves to do his will, levelling and directing our actions to his glory. ' Love is strong as death, and many waters cannot quench love, neither can the floods drown it,' Cant. viii. 6, 7. This love will neither be bribed nor frightened from Christ.

[3.] A lively hope, that doth so long and wait for glory to come, that present things do not greatly move us, either delights : 1 Pet. i. 8, ' Whom having not seen ye love, in whom, though now ye see him not, yet believing, ye rejoice with joy unspeakable and full of glory ;' or the terrors of sense : Rom. viii. 18, ' For I reckon that the sufferings of this life are not worthy to be compared with the glory that shall be revealed in us.'

Doct. 3. That those that come out of eminent conflicts are usually delivered by God in a glorious manner.

Christ was a pattern of this : ' The devil leaveth him, and behold angels came and ministered unto him.' When God delivered his people, after a long captivity, he delivered them with glory, and some kind of triumph, when he turned the Egyptian captivity : ' They borrowed of the Egyptians jewels of silver and jewels of gold and raiment. And the Lord gave the people favour in the sight of the Egyptians, so that they lent unto them such things as they required ; and they spoiled the Egyptians,' Exod. xii. 35, 36. So, in the Babylonian captivity, Cyrus chargeth his subjects, in the place where the Jews remain, to furnish them with all things necessary for their journey : Ezek. i. 4, ' And whosoever remaineth in any place, where he sojourneth, let the men of his place help him with silver, and with gold, and with goods, and with beasts, besides the freewill-offering for the house of God, that is in Jerusalem.' So, in a private instance : Job xlii. 10, 11, ' And the Lord turned the captivity of Job, when he prayed for his friends : also the Lord gave Job twice as much as he had before. Then came there unto him all his brethren, and all his sisters, and all they that had been of his acquaintance before, and did eat bread with him in his house, and they bemoaned him, and comforted him over all the evil that the Lord had brought upon him; every man also gave him a piece of money, and every one an earring of gold.' It is said, ' The Lord turned the captivity of Job,' because he had been delivered to Satan's power till the Lord set him at liberty again, and then all his friends had compassion on him, even those that had despised him before relieved him. So Isa. lxi. 7, ' For your shame you shall have double, and for confusion they shall rejoice in their portion; therefore in their land they shall possess the double, everlasting joy shall be unto them.' They should have large and eminent honour, double honour for their shame, such a reparation would God make them for all the troubles and damages they had sustained. So, in an ordinary providence, God raiseth up comforters to his servants after all the injuries done them by Satan's instruments. And so also in spirituals; the grief and trouble that cometh by temptation is recompensed with more abundant consolation after the conquest and victory; and God delighteth to put special marks of favour upon his people that have been faithful in an hour of trial. Now God doth this:—

1. To show the world the advantage of godliness, and close adhering to him in an hour of temptation: Ps. cxix. 56, ' This I had, because I kept thy precepts.' And Ps. lviii. 11, ' So that a man shall say, Verily there is a reward for the righteous, verily he is a God that judgeth in the earth.'

2. To check our diffidence and murmurings under trouble. Within a while and God's children will see they have no cause to quarrel with God, or repent that they were in trouble. For sometimes God giveth not only a comfortable but a glorious issue. There is nothing lost by waiting on providence; though we abide the blows of Satan for a while, yet abide them; God is, it may be, preparing the greater mercy for you: Isa. xxv. 9, ' And it shall be said in that day, Lo, this is our God; we have waited for him, and he will save us: this is the Lord; we have waited for him, we will be glad and rejoice in his salvation.' Afflictions are sharp in their season, but the end is glorious.

Use. Do not always reckon upon temporal felicity, refer that to God, but do as Jesus, who, in his sharp trials, Heb. xii. 2, 3, ' For the joy that was set before him, endured the cross, despising the shame, and is set down at the right hand of the throne of God.' There is a sure crown of life: James i. 12, ' Blessed is the man that endureth temptation, for when he is tried, he shall receive the crown of life, which the Lord hath promised to them that love him.' That is enough to content a Christian, the eternal reward is sure. In this world he shall receive with persecution an hundred-fold, but in the world to come eternal life: Mark x. 29, 30, ' There is no man that hath left house, or brethren, or sisters, or father, or mother, or wife, or children, or lands, for my sake and the gospel's, but he shall receive an hundred-fold now in this time, houses, and brethren, and sisters, and mothers, and children, and lands, with persecutions, and in the world to come eternal life.'

Doct. 4. That God maketh use of the ministry of angels in supporting and comforting his afflicted servants.

He did so to Christ, he doth so to the people of Christ. Partly for the defence and comfort of the godly : Ps. xxxiv. 7, ' The angel of the Lord encampeth round about them that fear him, and delivereth them ;' Heb. i. 14, ' Are they not all ministering spirits, sent forth to minister to them who shall be the heirs of salvation ?' Their ministry is now invisible, but yet certain. And partly also for the terror of their enemies. When David had said, ' The Lord hath chosen the hill of Sion to dwell in,' Ps. lxviii. 16, he adds, ver. 17, ' The chariots of God are twenty thousand, even thousands of angels;' implying that no kingdom in the world hath such defence, and such potent and numerous armies as the church hath, and the kingdom of Christ. God hath fixed his residence there, and the angels serve him, and attend upon him ; and he will be no less terrible to his foes in Sion, that oppose the gospel, than he showed himself in Sinai, when he gave the law. Where the king is there his attendants are ; so where Christ is the courtiers of heaven take up their station. Now Christ is with his church to the end of the world, therefore these thousands of angels are there, ready to be employed by him. Now we may be sure of this ministry.

1. They delight in the preaching of the gospel, and the explication of the mysteries of godliness: 1 Pet. i. 12, ' Which things the angels desire to look into ;' Eph. iii. 10, ' To the end that now, unto the principalities and powers in heavenly places, might be known by the church the manifold wisdom of God.'

2. They delight in the holy conversation of the godly, as they are offended with all impurity, filthiness, and ungodliness. If good men be offended at the sins of the wicked, as ' Lot's righteous soul was vexed from day to day with their ungodly deeds,' 2 Pet. ii. 8, much more are these holy spirits, especially when all things are irregularly carried in the worship of God : 1 Cor. xi. 10, ' For this cause ought the woman to have power on her head, because of the angels;' 1 Tim. v. 21, ' I charge thee before God, and the Lord Jesus Christ, and the elect angels, that thou observe these things, without preferring one before another, doing nothing by partiality.'

3. They fight against the devil, and defend the godly in their extreme dangers. When the devil cometh into the church of God, like a wolf into the flock, they oppose and resist him. Therefore there is said to be war in heaven, that is, in the church, between Michael and his angels, and the devil and his angels: Rev. xii. 7, ' And there was war in heaven, Michael and his angels fought against the dragon, and the dragon fought and his angels.' In the highest heaven there is no war. In short, the angels and believers make one church, under one head, Christ ; and at length shall both live together in the same place.

Why doth God make use of the ministry of angels ? and how far ?

1. To manifest unto them the greatness and glory of his work in the recovering mankind, that their delight in the love and wisdom of God may be increased. All holy creatures delight in any manifestation of God, the angels more especially : 1 Pet. i. 12, ' Which things the angels desire to look into ;' Eph. iii. 11, ' To the intent that now, unto the principalities and powers in heavenly places, may be known by the church the manifold wisdom of God.' Though they themselves be not the parties interested, the spectators, not the guests; yet they

are delighted in the glory of God, and are kindly affectionated to the salvation of lost men ; and that they may have a nearer view of this mystery, God gratifieth them by sending them often to attend upon the dispensation of the gospel, and to assist in it so far as is meet for creatures. They are present in our assemblies : see 1 Cor. xi. 10, 1 Tim. v. 21. They see who is negligent in his office, who hindereth the preaching of the gospel ; they observe what is the success of it, and when it obtaineth its effect: Luke xv. 7, ' There shall be joy in heaven over one sinner that repenteth.' They are hereby more excited to praise and glorify God, and are careful to vouchsafe their attendance about the meanest that believe in him : Ps. xci. 11, 12, 'He shall give his angels charge over thee, to keep thee in all thy ways. They shall bear thee up in their hands, lest thou dash thy foot against a stone.'

2. To maintain a society and communion between all the parts of the family of God. When God gathered together the things in heaven and in earth, he brought all into subjection and dependence upon one common head, Jesus Christ: Eph. i. 10, ' That in the dispensation of the fulness of times, he might gather together in one all things in Christ, both which are in heaven, and which are on earth, even in him.' Men by adoption, angels by transition, are taken into the family of Christ. Now there is some intercourse between the several parts thereof. Our goodness extendeth not to them, but is confined to the saints on earth, in whom should be our delight ; yet their help may be useful to us, they being such excellent and glorious creatures ; but we are forbidden to invoke them or trust in them. God doth employ them in the affairs of his people. Their help is not the fruit of our trust in them, but their obedience to God ; and it is seen in frustrating the endeavours of Satan and his instruments, and other services wherein Christ employeth them. God showed this to Jacob in the vision of the ladder, which stood upon earth, and the top reached to heaven—a figure of the providence of God, especially in and about the gospel: John i. 51, ' Hereafter you shall see the heaven open, and the angels of God ascending and descending upon the Son of man ;' to carry on the work of the gospel, and to promote the glory and interest of Christ's kingdom in the world. Thus far in the general we may be confident of.

3. To preserve his people from many dangers and casualties, which fall not within the foresight of man, God employeth ' the watchers,' as they are called in the Book of Daniel, chap. iv. 13, 17, for he is tender of his people, and doth all things by proper means. Now the angels having a larger foresight than we, they are appointed to be guardians. This they do according to God's pleasure, preventing many dangers, which we could by no means foresee. They observe the devil in all his walks, and God useth them to prevent his sudden surprisals of his people, as instances are many.

4. Because they are witnesses of the obedience and fidelity of Christ's disciples, and, so far as God permitteth, they cannot but assist them in their conflicts. Thus Paul, 1 Cor. iv. 9 : ' We are made a spectacle unto the world, and to angels and to men.' Now the angels, that are witnesses to their combats and sufferings, cannot but make report to God : Mat. xviii. 10, ' Take heed that ye despise not one of

these little ones, for I say unto you, that in heaven their angels do always behold the face of my Father which is in heaven.' The angels which are appointed by God to be their guardians have their continual recourses, and returns to God's glorious presence. Now, being so high in God's favour, and having continual access to make their requests and complaints known to him, they will not be silent in the behalf of their fellow-servants, that either the trial may be lessened, or grace sufficient may be given to them.

5. They do not only keep off hurt, but there are many blessings and benefits that we are partakers of by their ministry. As the angel of the Lord delivered Peter out of prison : Acts xii. 7, ' And behold the angel of the Lord came upon him, and a light shined in the prison; and he smote Peter on the side, and raised him up, saying, Arise up quickly; and his chains fell off from his hands,' &c. But he doth not give thanks to the angel, but to God; ver. 11, ' Now I know of a surety that the Lord hath sent his angel, and hath delivered me,' &c. He directeth it to God, not to the creature. The angels do us many favours; all the thanks we do them is that we do not offend them by our sins against God ; other gratitude they expect not.

6. Their last office is at death and judgment. In death, to convey our souls to Christ : Luke xvi. 22, 'And it came to pass that the beggar died, and was carried by the angels into Abraham's bosom ;' that so we may enjoy our rest in heaven. In the last day they will gather the bodies of Christ's redeemed ones from all parts of the world, after they have been resolved into dust, and mingled with the dust of other men, that every saint may have his own body again, wherein he hath obeyed and glorified God : Mat. xxiv. 31, 'And he shall send his angels with a great sound of a trumpet, and they shall gather together his elect from the four winds, from one end of heaven to the other.' That is, from all parts and quarters of the world, that their souls may return to their old beloved habitations, and then both in body and in soul they may be for ever with the Lord.

Use. Now this is a great comfort to the church and people of God, when the powers and principalities on earth are employed against them, to consider what powers and principalities attend upon Christ. We serve such a master as hath authority over the holy angels, to employ them at his pleasure ; and in their darkest condition his people feel the benefit of it. As the angel of the Lord appeared to Paul in a dreadful storm: Acts xxvii. 23, 24, 'There stood by me this night the angel of the Lord, whose I am, and whom I serve, saying, Fear not, Paul,' &c. So to Christ in his agonies : Luke xxii. 43, ' There appeared an angel to him from heaven strengthening him.' So against Satan, the good angels are ready to comfort us, as the evil angels are ready to trouble and tempt us. Let us then look to God, at whose direction they are sent to help and comfort us.

Doct. 5. If God taketh away ordinary helps from us, he can supply us by means extraordinary, as he did Christ's hunger by the ministry of angels. Therefore till God's power be wasted there is no room for despair. We must not limit the Holy One of Israel to our ways and means, as they did : Ps. lxxviii. 41, 'They turned back, and tempted God, and limited the Holy One of Israel.'

THE TRANSFIGURATION OF CHRIST.

SERMON I.

*And after six days Jesus taketh Peter, James, and John his brother,
and bringeth them into an high mountain apart.*—MAT. XVII.
1; with,

*It came to pass about an eight days after these sayings, he took Peter,
and John, and James, and went up into a mountain to pray.*—
LUKE IX. 28.

I MEAN to handle the transfiguration of Christ, which was:—

1. A solemn confirmation of his person and office.

2. A pledge of that glorious estate which is reserved for us in
heaven.

1. It was a confirmation of his person and office, as appeareth
Mat. xvii. 5, 'This is my beloved Son, in whom I am well pleased;
hear ye him.' So Peter, who was one present, urgeth it, 2 Pet. i.
16–18, 'We have not followed cunningly-devised fables when we
made known unto you the power and coming of our Lord Jesus
Christ, but were eye-witnesses of his majesty. For he received from
God the Father honour and glory, when there came such a voice to
him from the excellent glory, This is my beloved Son, in whom I
am well pleased. And this voice which came from heaven we heard
when we were with him in the holy mount.' And John also: John i.
14, 'We beheld his glory, as the glory of the only-begotten of the
Father.' They were eye and ear witnesses, and therefore could affirm
the certainty of this doctrine.

2. It is a pledge of our glorious estate; for Christ's body was
adorned with heavenly glory, and he had spoken, chap. xvi. 27, of his
coming in the glory of the Father; and now he gives his disciples a
pledge and earnest of it.

In this introduction four things are observable:—

1. The time : *after six days.*

2. The persons whom he takes with him : *Peter, James, and John.*

3. The place he brings them to : *into an high mountain apart.*

4. The preparative action : *he went up into a mountain to pray.*

First, The time. The evangelist Luke saith, 'about an eight days ; '
Matthew and Mark, 'after six days.' The reconciliation is easy.
Matthew and Mark spake of the space of time between the day of
prediction, and the day of transfiguration exclusively ; Luke includeth
them both. The Jews called that flux of time between one Sabbath
and another, eight days, including not only the intervening week, but
both the Sabbaths. According to their custom Luke speaketh ;
Matthew of the time between.

Secondly, The persons chosen to attend him in this action: ' Peter,
James, and John.'

1. Why *three ?*

2. Why *those* three ?

1. Why three ? So great an action as this was needed valuable
testimony ; for the law saith, ' In the mouth of two or three witnesses
everything shall be established,' Deut. xvii. 6. Now Christ would
go to the utmost of the law, and would have, not two only, but three
witnesses, as the apostle speaks of three witnesses in heaven and three
on earth, 1 John v. 7, 8 ; so here are three and three—three from
heaven, God the Father, Moses, and Elias ; and three from earth,
Peter, James, and John.

2. Why those three ? Many give divers reasons. Peter had led the
way to the rest in that notable confession of Christ, Mat. xvi. 16, and is
conceived to have some primacy for the orderly beginning of actions
in the college of the apostles. James was the first apostle who shed
his blood for Christ, Acts xii. 2 ; and John was the most long-lived of
them all, and so could the longer give testimony of those things which
he heard and saw, till the church was well gathered and settled.
Others give other reasons. But to leave conjectures, it is certain
that these had many singular favours afforded them above the rest of
the twelve, as appeareth partly in this, that Christ changed their names,
calling Peter, Cephas, or a stone ; and the other two Boanerges, sons
of thunder, which was a token that Christ loved these more than the
rest. Yea, among these, John was his bosom favourite, and therefore
called often ' the disciple whom Jesus loved,' partly because he was in
the whole course of his life more intimate with these than with the
rest of the disciples. You shall see when he raised Jairus's daughter
from death to life, Luke viii. 51, he suffered nobody to go in but
Peter, James, and John, and the father and mother of the maiden.
So these very persons were those who in Mount Olivet were conscious
to his agonies : Mat. xxvi. 27, ' He took with him Peter and the two
sons of Zebedee, and began to be sorrowful and very heavy.' Now
these who were to be conscious to his agonies are first in Mount Tabor
beholders of his great majesty and glory, for their better encouragement and preparation for his and their own sufferings.

Thirdly, The place : ' He bringeth them into an high mountain
apart.' This mountain is supposed to be Tabor, though not named by
the evangelists—a fit place both for height and secrecy, both which
were necessary to the double action that was to be performed there,
either his transfiguration or prayer.

1. To his transfiguration height and secrecy were necessary.

[1.] Height : This work required not only a mountain, but a high mountain, for his transfiguration was a middle state between the infirmity of his flesh and the glory that he now possesseth. So the top of a very high mountain was chosen; it is as a middle place between heaven, the habitation of God, and earth, the habitation of men. Besides, since Moses and Elias were to appear in this action, and that with bodies above the state of those natural bodies which we have here below, it was more agreeable this should be done in a mountain than in the lower parts of the earth; yea, moreover, they were so nearer to heaven, to which they went back again.

[2.] Secrecy was necessary to his transfiguration, for Christ was about a business which he would not have presently to come abroad, and therefore it was to be confined to the knowledge of a few, who were to be called up from the rest into an high mountain: ver. 9, Jesus 'charged them that they should tell the vision to no man till the Son of man was risen from the dead;' and what was done before many will hardly be concealed. The due time for the general and public manifestation of the divine glory was not yet come, therefore he would not have it unseasonably divulged. And hereby he teacheth us modesty. Christ was crucified in the city before all, but transfigured in the mountain only before a few.

2. The other action, of prayer, doth very well agree with height and secrecy.

[1.] For height: Though God heareth us everywhere, wheresoever we 'lift up pure hands, without wrath and doubting,' yet a mountain is not altogether disagreeable to this duty. It is good to be as near heaven as we can. I am sure it is good to get up the heart there. We have a freer prospect of heaven from a mountain, and may look up to those blessed regions where our God is; therefore Christ often chose a mountain to pray in, not only now, but at other times: Mat. xiv. 23. Certainly when we pray we should turn our backs upon all earthly things, and have our hearts and minds carried up to him to whom our prayers are directed, and that place where he dwelleth.

[2] Secrecy is necessary for this duty, partly to avoid ostentation: Mat. vi. 6, 'When thou prayest, enter into thy closet, and shut thy doors.' Public prayer must be performed before others, but not private, for fear of hypocrisy; so also to increase fervency. Secret prayers are usually most ardent. *Ille dolet verè qui sine teste dolet.* 'My soul shall weep sore in secret places,' Jer. xiii. 17. And Peter went out and wept bitterly,' Mat. xxvi. 75. And Jacob wrestled with God alone, Gen. xxxii. 24. Frequency of objects draws away the mind, obstructeth our affections, abates the vehemency of our zeal, fills us with carnal thoughts; therefore Christ retireth himself and his three disciples, that being separated from all distractions, they might attend the prayer and the vision without interruption.

Fourthly, The preparative action. In Luke it is, 'He went into a mountain to pray.' Christ had two ends; he told his disciples the one, but concealeth the other. He spake only of prayer, the more to hide the thing from the rest of the apostles, which would soon be evident enough to those whom he took along with him. Now this telleth us that every weighty business should be begun with prayer. When we go about the performance of weighty and serious duties, we should withdraw ourselves from all occasions which may hinder us and distract us therein, as our Lord, being to give himself to prayer, goeth apart into a mountain.

In this introduction I shall only take notice of two things :—

1. The choice of his company.

2. His preparative action : he prayed, and whilst he prayed he was transfigured.

1. Of the choice of his company : he took Peter, James, and John. That Christ doth not use all his servants alike familiarly in everything, partly because he had his liberty ; for in matters of free favour it is not acceptance of persons to pass by some and admit others—no, not in the most necessary spiritual dispensations : Mat. xi. 27, 'All things are delivered to me of my Father, and no man knoweth the Son but the Father, and he to whomsoever the Father will reveal him.' The plea of the Lord of the vineyard will ever hold firm and valid : Mat. xx. 15, ' Is it not lawful for me to do what I will with my own ?' But this is a thing of another nature. The dispensing of his arbitrary respects, acceptance of persons in judgment, is a violation of justice, but not in matters of free favour, partly because he would consecrate and hallow spiritual friendship, and commend it to us by his own example ; and, therefore, though he loved all his disciples, yet he chose out some for intimacy and special converse. These were ἐκλέκτων ἐκλεκτότεροι, the flower of the apostles, either because, of their suitableness, he had a special inclination to them, or, for their sincerity and eminency in grace, he delighted in them more than in the rest. *Sicut se habet simpliciter ad simpliciter, ita magis, ad magis :* if I love all that are godly, I love those most who are most godly. Now as Christ consecrated holy friendship in his own person, so was it exemplified in his disciples, for I find a great friendship between two of these mentioned in the text, John and Peter. You find them mostly together : John xx. 2–4, Mary Magdalene runneth and cometh to Peter, and to the other disciple whom Jesus loved ; Peter went forth and the other disciple, and came to the sepulchre. So Acts iii. 1, ' Now Peter and John went up together into the temple at the hour of prayer :' John xxi. 7, 'The disciple whom Jesus loved said unto Peter, It is the Lord ;' and John xxi. 21, 22, ' Peter, seeing the disciple whom Jesus loved, said, Lord, and what shall this man do ?' as willing to know the future state of his friend. So Acts viii. 14, Peter and John go to Samaria to confirm the disciples. See John xviii. 15, ' And Simon Peter followed Jesus, and so did another disciple, and that other disciple was known unto the high priest,' meaning himself. So that in these and other places you still find Peter and John together as very near and fast friends : they always keep together, possibly for spiritual assistance ; for Peter was of an hot temper, John the disciple of love ; Peter hasty and of a military valour, John all for lenity and peace. Well, then, though we ought to seek peace with all men as much as is possible, Rom. xii. 18, and there should be special concord and communion with all Christians—Φιλαδελφία riseth higher than Αγάπη, 2 Pet. i. 7— yet friendship and inward conversation should only be with a few,

such as may be helps to us in godliness, and may promote our mutual
good, temporal and spiritual. So did Christ, who had twelve disciples, single out three of them for greatest intimacy; and so did
Peter, who, though he had eleven colleagues, and held concord with
all, yet his intimate friendship was with John, the disciple whom
Jesus loved. It is good to hold friendship with those who are
beloved of God, and one who, by his love and lenity, might cool his
heats and abate his hasty fervours, which were so natural to him.

Now, having so fair an occasion, I shall treat of spiritual friendship, for an heavenly, faithful friend is one of the greatest treasures
upon earth. A friend is valuable in secular matters, much more a
spiritual friend: Prov. xxvii. 17, ' As iron sharpeneth iron, so doth
the countenance of a man his friend,'—that is, when he is dull his
friend setteth an edge upon him.

[1.] Friendship is necessary for every one that would live in the
world, because man is ζῶον πολιτικὸν, a sociable creature. Man was
not made to live alone, but in company with others for mutual
society and friendship; and they that fly all company and live to
and by themselves are counted inhuman: Eccles. iv. 9–12, 'Two
are better than one, for if they fall, the one will lift up his fellow;
but woe to him that is alone when he falleth, for he hath not another
to lift him up. Again, if two lie together, they have heat; but
how can one be warm if he lie alone? And if one prevail against
him, two shall withstand him.' Thus far Solomon. The Egyptians
in their hieroglyphics expressed the unprofitableness of a solitary
man by a single millstone, which alone grindeth no meal, but with its
fellow is very serviceable for that purpose. The Lord appointed
mankind to live in society, that they might be mutually helpful to one
another. Surely God never made them to live in deserts; the wild
beasts love to go alone, but the tame in flocks and herds. The
Lord doth give variety of gifts to the sons of men; to all some, but
to none all, that one might stand in need of another, and make use of
one another; and the subordination of one gift to another is the
great means of upholding the world. Man is weak and insufficient
to himself, and wanting the help of others, needeth society, and is
inclined to it by the bent of his nature.

[2.] Though man affecteth society, yet in our company we must
use choice, and the good must converse with the good, for these reasons:—

(1.) Partly because like doth best sort with like. Friendship is
founded in suitableness and maintained by it—*eadem velle et nolle*,
to will and nill the same things, breedeth an harmony of minds; the
godly will have special love to the godly, and they that fear God will
be companions of them that fear him, Ps. cxix. 63; they must needs
be more dear and precious to them than others, as a wicked man easily
smelleth out a fit companion for him: Ps. l. 18, 'When thou sawest
a thief, then thou consentedst with him, and hast been partaker with
adulterers.' Like will to like; every man showeth his temper in his
company. The fowls of heaven flock together according to their several
kinds; ye shall not see doves flocking with the ravens, nor diverse
kinds intermixed. Men that delight in excess of drink choose company

suitable to their brutish humour; those that delight in gaming choose such as make no conscience of their time, or have no care of their souls. That which every one is taken withal he loveth to do with his friends, therefore they that love God delight in those that love him, those that are most apt to stir them up to the remembrance of everlasting things and the preparation necessary: so they are of singular use to us.

(2.) If they be not like to us, intimacy and converse will make us like to them. Every man is wrought upon by his company; we imitate those whom we love and with whom we frequently converse: Prov. xiii. 20, 'He that walketh with wise men shall be wise, but a companion of fools shall be destroyed.' As a man that walketh in the sun is tanned insensibly, so, if we are not aware, we adopt their manners and customs, and get a tincture from them, especially in evil; for we are more susceptible of evil than of good—as the sound get a sickness from the diseased sooner than the sick get health from the sound. Or in the types of the law: that which was clean, by touching the unclean became unclean, but the unclean were not purified by touching the clean: Prov. xxii. 24, 25, 'Make no friendship with an angry man, and with a furious man thou shalt not go, lest thou learn his ways, and get a snare to thy soul.' A man would think that of all sins wrath and anger should not be propagated by converse, the motions and furies of it being so uncomely and indecent to any beholder; yet secretly a liking of the person breedeth a liking of the sin, and a man is habituated into such a frame of spirit as they have whom he hath chosen for his companions. Now this should be regarded by us, because we are sooner made evil by evil company than good by good company; therefore how careful should we be to converse with such as may go before us as examples of godliness, and provoke us by their strictness, heavenly-mindedness, mortification, and self-denial, to more love to God, zeal for his glory, and care of our own salvation. Especially doth this concern the young, who, by the weakness of their judgment or the vehemency of their affections and want of experience, may easily be drawn into a snare.

(3.) Because our love to God should put us upon loving his people and making them our intimates; for religion influenceth all things— our relations, common employments, friendship, and converse: 1 John v. 1, 'Every one that loveth him that begat, loveth him also that is begotten of him.' The new nature inclineth to both: there is an inward propension and inclination needing no outward provocation and allurements: 1 Thes. iv. 9, 'As touching brotherly love, ye need not that I write unto you, for you yourselves are taught of God to love one another.' God's teaching is by effectual impression or inclining the heart. It is a smart question that of the prophet, 2 Chron. xix. 2, 'Shouldest thou hate the godly, and love those that hate the Lord?' Surely a gracious heart cannot take them into his bosom: he loveth all with a love of good will, as seeking their good, but not with a love of complacency, as delighting in them. Our neighbour must be loved as ourselves—our natural or carnal neighbour as our natural self, with a love of benevolence, and our spiritual neighbour as our spiritual self, with a love of complacency. We have hated our sinful neighbour as we hate ourselves; much more as to love of benevolence—we must neither hate ourselves, our neighbour, nor our enemy. But it is complacency we are speaking of, and so 'the wicked is an abomination to the righteous,' Prov. xxix. 27. The hatred of displacency is opposite to the love of complacency, as the hatred of enmity to the love of benevolence. We cannot enter into a confederacy and intimate kindness with them.

(4.) Because that love which is built upon holiness is the most durable and lasting.   There is a confederacy in evil, as between drunkards with drunkards, and robbers with robbers: Prov. i. 14, ' Cast in thy lot amongst us, let us all have one common purse.' Or when men conspire against the truth and interest of Christ in the world ; as Gebal and Ammon and Amalek leagued themselves against God's people, divided in interests but united in hatred ; as the Pharisees and Herodians agreed together to tempt Christ ; and Herod and Pilate, though otherwise no very good friends, agreed to mock him.   This is *unitas contra unitatem*, as Austin ; or *consortium factionis,* a bond of iniquity. Now this friendship is soon dissolved, for these men, though they agree in evil, yet have contrary lusts and interests ; and besides, partners in evil are usually objects reviving guilt ; their very presence upbraids the consciences of one another with the remembrance of their past sins ; and sin, though it be sweet in the committing, yet it is hateful and bitter in the remembrance of it.   Again, there is a civil friendship built on natural pleasure and profit.   Certainly men are at liberty to choose their company as their interests and course of employments leads them.   This may be a society for trade or civil respect ; it cannot be a true and proper friendship, for riches, which are so frail and slippery, can never make a firm tie and bond of hearts and minds : Prov. xiv. 20, 'The poor is hated even of his own neighbour, but the rich hath many friends ;' Prov. xix. 6, ' Many will entreat the favour of a prince, and every man is a friend to him that giveth gifts : all the brethren of the poor do hate him,' &c.   And as it is a fluid, so it is a base and sordid friendship that is built upon riches, for that concerneth the estate rather than the soul.   Well, then, religious friendship, which is built upon virtue and grace, and is called ' the unity of the spirit,' Eph. iv. 3, is the most firm bond of all.   Sinful societies are soon dissolved, and the profane, though they seem to hold together, yet upon every cross word may fall out and break ; and civil friendship, which is only built upon pleasures and profit, standeth upon a brittle foundation.   Certainly the good and the holy are not so changeable as the bad and the carnal.   Besides, that friendship which is built upon honesty and godliness, is *amicitia per se*, the other is *amicitia per accidens.* It cometh from constitution of soul and likeness of spirits, and the good we seek may be possessed without envy ; the friends do not straiten and intrench upon one another.   Again, there is a virtuous friendship, which consists in a harmony of minds, or an agreement in some common studies. This is more noble, and more like true friendship than society for trade and temporal interests ; but yet this friendship is not so durable, for at last it must be broken off by death ; but the godly are everlasting companions.   Besides, self-love and envy are more apt to invade other friendships ; but the godly, if they be true to the laws of spiritual friendship, they seek the good of one another as much as their own, and rejoice in the graces of one another as much as in their own.

[3.] Though we owe this religious friendship to all that fear God, yet some few may be chosen for our intimacy and spiritual solace. We owe it in some respects to all that fear God, and must dispense the general acts of friendship to them : Acts iv. 32, ' The multitude of them that believed were of one heart and of one soul.' And Christian love is called σύνδεσμος τῆς τελείοτητος, 'the bond of perfectness,' Col. iii. 14, because it is the band by which holy and Christian societies, called churches, are bound together and preserved ; otherwise, like a besom unbound, they fall all to pieces. But yet this doth not hinder but that some may be chosen for our intimacy. Christ, that denied himself to many of the commodities of human life, would not live without special friends, and would enjoy this virtuous solace ; and in David and Jonathan we have an instance of it : 1 Sam. xviii. 1, ' And the soul of Jonathan was knit to the soul of David.' Certainly too many cannot perform the acts of intimate friendship to us, nor we to them. The love being like a river dispersed into several channels, must needs be shallower and weaker ; therefore our choice friends must be but few : *inter binos et bonos* was the old rule, though it need not be so straitly confined.

[4.] In the choice of these few friends we must use caution. (1.) Such as are near to us, with whom we have frequent and familiar converse, and perform a mutual interchange of all offices of love : Prov. xviii. 24, 'A man that hath friends must show himself friendly, and there is a friend which sticketh closer than a brother.' Consanguinity and affinity is not so near a tie as this friendship. (2.) Not only near, but those who are holy, prudent, and good : Prov. xiii. 20, 'He that walketh with the wise shall be wise, but a companion of fools shall be destroyed.' (3.) Such as are most likely to be faithful : Job vi. 15, 16, ' My brethren have dealt deceitfully with me as a brook, and as the stream of brooks they pass away '—pools in winter, when less need of water, but dried up in summer, when water in those parched countries was a great commodity. So many seem to be great friends, heighten our expectation ; but in our necessities and straits leave us destitute. ' Ye see me cast down and are afraid,' saith Job, ' as if I should be a burden to you.' Dearest friends may disappoint us ; their affection wants an inward principle ; it is a winter brook, and not a spring. Therefore, since the heart of man is so deceitful, and not only deceitful, but though sincere for the present, very changeable ; and this is so important an interest of human life, and the vexation of a disappointment in a bosom friend is so grievous, and involveth us in many inconveniences, natural and spiritual ; for Solomon telleth us, Prov. xxv. 19, ' Confidence in an unfaithful friend in time of trouble, is like a broken tooth, and a foot out of joint.' When we think to eat with the broken tooth, or to walk with the foot out of joint, we are put to grievous pain and torment ; therefore we should go to God, and pray him to direct us in the choice of intimate friends. David sadly regrets a disappointment in a friend : Ps. lv. 12–15, ' For it was not an enemy that reproached me ; then I could have borne it : nor was it he that hated me that did magnify himself against me; then I would have hid myself from him: but it was thou, a man mine equal, my guide, and mine acquaintance,' &c. A deceitful friend may become the greatest foe, and we resent their ingratitude more than the injuries of others, when they abuse their trust and the familiarity they had with us. The worst that a professed enemy can do is not so grievous as the treachery of a professed friend. This is more piercing, less to be avoided; therefore, whom we have used most familiarly and freely, loved as our soul and life, from such we expect the same firm and hearty friendship. Therefore it concerneth us to seek to God that we may have a godly wise man with whom we may be free in all cases of mind or conscience, and to whom we may freely open ourselves, and be strengthened in the service of God. It is a great part of our contentment and happiness, therefore, that we may not be deceived in our choice. Let us go to God who knoweth hearts, and God hath a great hand in this: Ps. lxxxviii. 8, 'Thou hast put away my acquaintance from me; thou hast made me an abomination to them.' By the providence of God they left him as a man whose condition they were afraid to look upon. And again, ver. 9, 'Lover and friend hast thou put far from me; they stand aloof from me as an execrable thing.' He owneth providence in it.

[5.] When friends be thus chosen, there must be a faithful discharge of the duties of friendship, both in counsels and reproofs; for the godly use this friendship chiefly for spiritual ends.

(1.) In counsel, for Solomon telleth us, Prov. xxii. 9, 'As ointment and perfume rejoice the heart, so doth the sweetness of a man's friend by hearty counsel.' As sweet pefumes are a reviving, so to be supported in good resolutions, or directed and guided in our way to heaven by a faithful friend, is very cheering and comfortable. And we read, 1 Sam. xxiii. 16, 17, that 'Jonathan went to David, and strengthened his hand in God.' Whereas, on the contrary, a carnal friend is the greatest bane that may be, who doth strengthen us in evil; an instance whereof we have in Jonadab, the son of Shimeah, 2 Sam. xiii. 3, 4, and 'Amnon had a friend whose name was Jonadab, and Jonadab was a subtile man;' and he gave him counsel how he should surprise his sister, to defile her, and satisfy his incestuous lust. Such a friend is really and truly our greatest foe. He was a friend to his vice, but a foe to his person and soul; whereas a true friend, whose friendship is grounded on godliness, will be a foe to our sins, by wholesome admonition and rebukes, and a friend to our soul's salvation.

(2.) Reproofs: that is also a part of friendship: Prov. xxvii. 6, 'Faithful are the wounds of a friend, but the kisses of an enemy are deceitful.' A faithful friend's wounds are a more sincere testimony than an enemy's kisses, and so afterwards they will be interpreted: Prov. xxviii. 23, 'He that rebuketh a man, afterwards shall find more favour than he that flattereth with his tongue.' For this we must trust God, though for the present we displease our friends. So Lev. xix. 17, 'Thou shalt not hate thy brother in thy heart by suffering sin upon him.' It is kindness to his soul to reprove him. In the general, holy friendship must be improved to the use of edifying: Rom. i. 11, 12, 'I long to see you, to impart some spiritual gift unto you, that I may be comforted together with you by the mutual faith of you and me.'

[6.] After the best care is used, you must remember that our friends are but an outward help, which God can continue or withdraw at his pleasure; and that our chief help, comfort, and counsel cometh of God. So it was with Christ: John xvi. 32, 'Behold the hour is come that ye shall be parted every man to his own, and shall leave me alone; and yet I am not alone, because the Father is with me.' Christ was forsaken of his disciples, but not forsaken of his Father. So Paul, 2 Tim. i. 16, 'At my first answer, no man stood with me, but all men forsook me;' Ps. xli. 9, 'My familiar friend, in whom I trusted, hath lifted up his heel against me.' Those that have been acquainted with the secrets of your soul may not only grow strange to you, but betray you; therefore, do not over-value any earthly friend. Man will be man still, that God may be God, all in all unto his people: and when we are deserted of men, we must learn to trust in God, who never faileth us, fail who will: Ps. xxvii. 10, 'When my father and mother forsake me, then the Lord will take me up;' and cxlii. 4, 5, 'I looked on my right hand and beheld, and no man would know me: refuge failed me, no man cared for my soul. I cried unto thee, O Lord; I said, Thou art my refuge and portion in the land of the living.' We are left alone for God to help us. The defectiveness of all worldly friends shows us more of the goodness of God.

2. The preparative action: he went up into a mountain to pray, and whilst he prayed he was transfigured.

[1.] In that he prayed, it teacheth us to hallow all our actions by prayer. We do not bid ourselves God speed, unless we re-commend our affairs to God; whatsoever assurance we have of the blessing, yet we must pray: Jer. xxix. 10–12, 'For thus saith the Lord, After seventy years be accomplished at Babylon, I will visit you, and perform my good word towards you, in causing you to return to this place, &c. Then shall ye call upon me, and ye shall go and pray unto me, and I will hearken unto you;' Ezek. xxxvi. 37, 'I will for this be inquired of by the house of Israel to do it for them.' Therefore we should be daily in the practice of this duty, and not look upon it as a work that may well be spared. If Christ, who as to his divine nature was equal with God, surely we should often come and prostrate ourselves before him in this act of holy adoration. Christ had right and title to all, all was his due, yet he was much in prayer. How dare we go about any business without his leave, counsel, and blessing; and usurp any of his blessings without begging them by prayer?

[2.] While he prayed he was transfigured, Luke ix. 29; which teacheth us two things:—

(1.) That we have the highest communications from God in prayer, for then Christ's shape was altered. By prayer the soul hath the most familiar converse with God that possibly it can have, and also by the means of this duty God hath most familiar converse with us. In our prayers to God we have experience of the operations of the Spirit: Rom. viii. 26, 'Likewise the Spirit also helpeth our infirmities; for we know not what we should pray for as we ought; but the Spirit

itself helpeth us with groanings which cannot be uttered ;' Jude 20,
' But ye, beloved, building up yourselves on your most holy faith,
praying in the Holy Ghost ;' and in God's answering our prayer we
have experience of the comforts of the Spirit, and those spiritual
solaces which he secretly giveth to his people.   Hannah, when she had
prayed, went away, and ' her countenance was no more sad,' 1 Sam.
i. 18.   In praying we put forth the groans of the spirit ; in the answer
God gives the joys of the spirit : Ps. xxxiv. 5, ' They looked unto him
and were lightened, and their faces were not ashamed.'

(2.) That we should pray so as that the heart may be raised
and lifted up unto God, and in some sort made like God.   When
Christ prayed to God, he is made partaker of the divine glory, as
Moses also, by conversing with God, his face shined, Exod. xxxiv.
29, 30.   This was extraordinary ; but sure the oftener we converse
with God the more holy and heavenly should we grow, more like him
in spirit, be changed into the glory of the Lord spiritually ; and so
we are, if we be instant and earnest in prayer.   If we have communion with God, there will be some assimilation to God.

Use.   It reproveth our remiss, feeble, benumbed souls.   There is no
life in prayer, no working up the heart to God and heaven ; either
our prayers are formal and cursory—James v. 16, δέησις ἐνεργουμένη
—or our prayers are doctrinal, instructive rather than warning.[1]   We
get lightly over duties, but we should get life by prayer.   This duty
is not to inform the judgment, but to raise the affections, that they
be all in a flame ; or else we content ourselves with a dull narrative,
without getting up the heart to a sight of God and heaven ; or are
seldom in praises or adoration of the excellences of God.

SERMON II.

And he was transfigured before them ; and his face did shine as the sun,
and his raiment was white as the light.—Mat. XVII. 2 ; with,
And, as he prayed, the fashion of his countenance was altered, and his
raiment was white and glistering.—Luke IX. 29.

In both these texts, compared together, you may observe two things :—
    1. The circumstance of time : during prayer.
    2. The transfiguration itself.
    [1.] More generally propounded, *he was transfigured before them.*
    [2.] More particularly explained by the change of his face and
raiment.   The form of any man is most seen in his face.   There was
a glorious shining brightness.   Luke saith, ' The fashion of his countenance was altered ;' Matthew, that ' His face did shine as the sun.'
And in the glorious description of God in the prophet Habakkuk,
it is said, chap. iii. 2, ' And his brightness was as the light.'   For his
garments, Luke saith, ' His raiment was white and glistering ;' Mark,
chap. ix. 3, ' White as the snow, so as no fuller on earth could whiten
them ;' but Matthew, ' white as the light,' which carrieth it higher.

---

[1] Qu., ' warming ?'—ED.

The works of nature exceed those of art. The transfiguration that was plainly to be seen in his face was accomplished also in other parts of his body. All his body was clothed with majesty, so as it could not be obscured and hidden by his garments.

Now, first I shall speak of the circumstances of time, and then of the transfiguration itself.

I. Of the time: ' and as he prayed.' Now what Christ prayed for is not specified. (1.) If he asked common blessings, and prayed only in order to his usual solace and converse with God, it showed the success of vehemency in prayer. Christ prayed at such a rate as that he was transfigured and changed into the likeness of God in prayer. (2.) If He asked to be transfigured for the confirmation of his disciples, it showeth God's readiness to answer fervent and earnest prayers.

1. Of the first consideration. If Christ's prayer were of ordinary import, it teacheth us that we should pray so that the heart may be raised and lifted unto God in prayer, and in some sort made like unto God. Let us state this matter aright.

[1.] It must be granted that this shining of Christ's countenance as the sun, while he prayed, was extraordinary, and a dispensation peculiar to the Son of God. So also was the shining of Moses's face while he conversed with God in the mount, Exod. xxxiv. 29, 30. And for ordinary Christians to expect the like is to put a snare upon themselves, for these things are proper only to the end for which God appointed them.

[2.] This must be also considered, that the eminent and extraordinary passions and affections in the soul do discover themselves in the body, especially in the face; for it is said of Stephen, that when he was heightened into a great zeal for Christ, Acts vi. 15, that ' All that sat in the council, looking stedfastly upon him, saw his face as it had been the face of an angel.' Angels have not bodies or faces, but they often assume bodies, and then they appear with a glorious and bright countenance, as the angel of the Lord that appeared at the sepulchre : Mark xxviii. 3, ' His countenance was like lightning, and his raiment white as snow.' Now such a glory and gladness did God put upon the countenance of his servant Stephen, that he looked like an angel. Something extraordinary there might be in the case, but yet there was an ordinary reason for it. Stephen's mind was filled with such an incredible solace in the sense of God's love, that he showed no troubledness, but a mind so unconcerned and freed from all fear and sorrow, as if he had been among the angels of God in full glory, and not among his enemies, who sought his blood ; and so may God raise the hearts of his people sometimes, as if they had put their heads above the clouds, and were in the midst of the glory of the world to come among his blessed ones. If that were extraordinary, Solomon tells us, Eccles. viii. 1, that ' a man's wisdom maketh his face to shine,' as it gives him readiness and tranquillity of mind, and cheerfulness of countenance. Guilt and shame cast down the countenance, but righteousness and wisdom embolden it, more particularly in prayer. As our confidence and joy in God is increased, it bewrayeth itself in the countenance : Ps. xxxiv. 15, ' They looked unto him and were lightened, and their faces were not ashamed.'

They are revived and encouraged, and come away from the throne of grace other manner of persons than they came to it.

[3.] That some kind of transformation is wrought by prayer, appeareth by these considerations :—

(1.) That as God is glorious in himself, so he maketh him that cometh to him partaker of his glory. For certainly all communion with God breedeth some assimilation and likeness unto God. It is clear in heavenly glory, when we see him as he is, we shall be like him, 1 John iii. 2; and it is clear also in our communion with him in the Spirit; for the apostle telleth us, that by ' Beholding the glory of the Lord as in a glass, we are changed into the same image, from glory to glory, even as by the Spirit of the Lord,' 2 Cor. iii. 18. Not only doth vision or immediate intuition produce this effect, but also spiritual specular vision, or a sight of God in the ordinances, produces a divine and God-like nature, inclining us to hate sin and love righteousness. The more we are above with God, the more we are like him. We see it in ordinary converse: a man is as the company that he keepeth. ' He that walketh with wise men shall be wise,' saith Solomon, ' but a companion of fools shall be destroyed,' Prov. xiii. 20. Now it is not imaginable that a man should converse often with God fervently, seriously, and not be more like him. He that liveth in a mill, the dust will stick upon his clothes. Man receiveth an insensible taint from his company. He that liveth in a shop of perfumes, often handleth them, is conversant among them, carrieth away somewhat of the fragrancy of these good ointments ; so by conversing with God we are made like him.

(2.) Nearer we cannot come to God, while we dwell in flesh, than by lifting up the heart to him in fervent prayer. This is the intimate converse and familiarity of a loving soul with God; therefore it is called a lifting up the heart to God. He will not come down to us, therefore we lift up the heart to him : Lam. iii. 41, ' Let us lift up our hearts with our hands to God in the heavens.' So Ps. xxv. 1, ' Unto thee, O Lord, do I lift up my soul;' and Ps. lxxxvi. 4, ' Rejoice the soul of thy servant, for unto thee do I lift up my soul;' so Ps. cxliii. 8, ' Cause me to know the way wherein I should walk, for I lift up my soul unto thee.' All these places show that there can be no sincerity and seriousness in this duty, unless there be this ascension of the soul to God; it is an act of spiritual friendship, therefore called an ' acquainting ourselves with God,' Job xxii. 21. Now as acquaintance is kept up by frequent visits, so prayer is called a giving God a visit : Isa. xxvi. 16, ' In their trouble they have visited thee.' Well, then, here is the greatest intimacy we have with God. In the word, God speaks to us by a proxy and ambassador—another speaketh for him. In the Lord's Supper we are feasted at his cost, and remember him ; but we are not admitted into his immediate presence, as those that are feasted by the king in another room than he dineth in. But prayer goeth up to God, and speaketh to himself immediately ; and therefore this way of commerce must needs bring in much of God to the soul.

(3.) In fervent prayer we have a double advantage—we get a sight of God, and exercise strong love to God ; and both conduce to make us like God.

(1st.) We get a sight of God, for in it (if it be seriously performed) we turn our back upon all other things, that we may look to God as sitting upon the throne, governing all things by his power for his glory. By faith we see the invisible one, Heb. xi. 27. Surely if we do not see God before the eye of our faith when we pray to him, we worship an idol—not the true and living God, who is, and is a rewarder of them that diligently seek him. Our hearts should be shut up against the thoughts of any other thing, and confined only to the object to whom we direct our worship. I reason thus: If a Christian foreseeth the Lord before him in all his ways, and keepeth always as in his eye and presence, surely he should set the Lord before him in his worship and in his prayers, Ps. xvi. 8. A good Christian doth always keep as in God's eye and presence, much more when he calleth upon his name. Now every sight of God doth more affect and change the heart. As none but the pure in heart see God, so none see God but are most pure in heart. There is a self-purifying in moral things; purity of heart maketh way for the sight of God, Mark v. 8. So the sight of God maketh way for the purity of heart: 3 John 11, ' He that doth evil hath not seen God.' A serious sight of God certainly worketh some change in us.

(2dly.) In prayer, a strong love to God is acted, for it is the expression of our delight in him: Job xxvii. 10, ' Will he delight himself in the Almighty? Will he always call upon God?' Now we are changed into the likeness of him in whom we delight in. Love transformeth and changeth us into the nature of what is loved. There is the difference between the mind and the will: the mind draweth things to itself, but the will followeth the things it chooseth, and is drawn by them as the wax receiveth the impression of the seal. Carnal objects make us carnal, and earthly things earthly; and heavenly things heavenly, and the love of God godly: Ps. cxv. 8, ' They that make them are like unto them, so are all they that put their trust in them,' stupid and senseless as idols: it secretly stamps the heart with what we like, and esteem, and admire.

[4.] There are agents in prayer to help us to improve this advantage.
(1.) The human spirit.
(2.) The new nature; and,
(3.) The Spirit of God.
(1.) The human spirit, or our natural faculty, so that, by our understandings, we may work upon our wills and affections: surely God maketh use of this, for the Holy Ghost doth not work upon a man as upon a block; and we are to rouse up ourselves, and to attend upon this work with the greatest seriousness imaginable. The prophet complains, Isa. lxiv. 7, ' There is none that calleth upon thy name, that stirreth up himself to take hold of thee.' Without this it is but dead and cold work, and if there be no more than this, it is but dry literal work: not that fervent effectual prayer which will change the heart, δέησις ἐνεργουμένη, James v. 16. The ἐνεργούμενοι were those that were inspired and possessed by a spirit; therefore it must be a prayer that not only hath understanding and will in it, but spirit and life in it. However, we are to put forth our utmost endeavour, and raise the natural spirit as far as we can.

(2.) The second agent is the new nature, which inclineth us to God as our chief good and last end. This also must be taken in, for the Holy Ghost doth not blow as to a dead coal ; the new nature is made up of faith, hope and love, and all these must be acted in prayer : faith, or the firm belief of God's being, and providence, and covenant ; ' For how shall they call on him in whom they have not believed?' Rom. x. 14. Then love to God, or the desire of the fruition of him in heavenly glory, praying in the Holy Ghost : ' Keep yourselves in the love of God,' Jude 20, 21. If I do not love God, and desire to enjoy him, and delight in as much of God as I can get here, certainly there will be no life in prayer, or no ravishment and transport of soul, no spirit of desire animating our requests, and no spiritual solace and delight in our converse with God. Hope is also necessary to fervent praying, for a man coldly asketh for what he doth not hope for. Hope respecteth both means and end—supplies of grace by the way, and our final fruition of God in glory. This is called trust in scripture, and is the great ground and encouragement of prayer: Ps. lxii. 8, ' Trust in the Lord at all times ; pour out your souls before him.' Prayer is the act of a trusting soul. Now these graces quicken our natural faculties, as they elevate and raise our hearts and minds to God and heaven.

(3.) The third agent in prayer is the Holy Spirit. He is sometimes said to pray in us, Rom. viii. 26 ; sometimes we are said to pray in him, Jude 20. The divine Spirit exciteth those graces in us which incline us to God ; he raiseth our minds in the vision and sight of God. ' In thy light shall we see light,' Ps. xxxvi. 9 ; and he raiseth our hearts to a desire after and delight in God, for all that spiritual solace and joy is called ' joy in the Holy Ghost ; ' for both unutterable groans and unspeakable joys are of his working : Rom. viii. 26, ' The Spirit itself maketh intercession for us with groanings which cannot be uttered ; ' compared with 1 Pet. i. 8, ' In whom, though ye see him not, yet believing, ye rejoice with joy unspeakable and full of glory.' Well, then, these work a kind of an ecstasy. If you would pray so as to be transported, transformed in prayer, something you must do as reasonable creatures, something as new creatures, and the Spirit influenceth all, and causeth the soul to follow hard after God. We must put forth our utmost endeavour, stir up the gift of God in us ; and though we cannot command the influences of the Spirit, yet he is never wanting to a serious soul as to necessary help. Pray thus, and you will find, as the help of the Spirit in prayer, so the comforts of the Spirit as the success of prayer.

[5.] As there is daily and constant prayer in which we must ever bewray a seriousness and sincerity for these daily supplies of grace, so there are extraordinary occasions, because of some great business, conflict, or temptation : in those the heart and mind must be more than ordinarily raised and stirred. In every prayer of Christ there was not a transfiguration ; and we read of our Lord Jesus, that in his agonies he prayed, ἐκτενέστερον, more earnestly than at other times, Luke xxii. 44 ; and upon eminent occasions, as the necessities of the saints are greater, so their acts of prayer are more earnest. On these weighty occasions many Christians are wholly swallowed up with the thoughts of God, and carried beyond themselves by their high love to God, and earnest desires of the spiritual blessings they stand in need of, so that they seem to be rapt into heaven in their admiration of God and delight in him.

APPLICATION.

Use. To reprove our feeble, remiss, and benumbed requests. There is no life in our prayers, no working up of the heart to God and heaven, no flames of love, no transports of soul by the vision and sight of faith, no holy and ardent desires after God, or spiritual solace and delight in him.

Reasons—1. We pray cursorily, and go about prayer as a customary task for fashion's sake; we come with a few cold devotions morning and evening, and so 'God is near in our mouths, and far from our reins,' Jer. xii. 2. Oh, take heed of this! Nothing breeds slightness and hardness of heart so much as perfunctory praying. The rule is, 'Continue instant in prayer,' Rom. xii. 12. And it is said of the saints that they 'Served God instantly night and day,' ἐν ἐκτενείᾳ, Acts xxvi. 7, that they might come to the blessed hope, with the united service of all their powers and faculties.

2. Our prayers are doctrinal and instructive, rather than affectionate and warming. We get light by other duties, but we should get life by prayer. This duty is not to inform the judgment, but to raise the affections, that they may be all flame. Other duties are feeding duties, but this is a spending duty, an egression of the soul after God: Ps. lxiii. 8, 'My soul followeth hard after thee.' A man may better spend two hours in hearing than half an hour in praying, if the heart be employed in it as it ought to be, in the sight of God, and an earnest desire after him. The prayers in scripture are all supplications or doxologies; there is no excursion into doctrines and instructions.

3. Else we are lamenting sin, and spend the time in confessing sin, which also hath its use in the seasons thereof; but are seldom in praises or adorations of the excellences of God, and the wonderful mysteries of his love in our redemption by Jesus Christ. Yet it is said, Ps. xxii. 3, 'O Lord, that inhabitest the praises of Israel.' These are the things that do most ravish the heart, and raise it in the contemplation of that glorious God to whom we speak; and fill us with the ecstasies of love, that we may be more like him—holy, wise, and good, as he is holy, wise, and good.

4. We think a dry narrative to be enough; that is, the fruit of a human spirit, or a mere product of memory and invention is a sufficient prayer, without acting faith, hope, or love in it, or those spiritual and heavenly desires which are the life of prayer: Ps. x. 17, 'Lord, thou hast heard the desire of the humble, thou wilt prepare their heart, thou wilt cause thine ear to hear.' The ardency of humble addresses is God's own gift, and he will never reject and despise those requests that, by his own Spirit and appointment, are direct and brought to him.

But what if I have not those strong and earnest desires? I answer, Yet keep not off from prayer: for,

[1.] Good desires must be asked of God, for it is said, he prepareth the heart.

[2.] Such desires as we have must be expressed, and that is the way to increase them, and to quicken us more. A sincere heart, that would serve God with his best, findeth more in a duty than he could expect, and by praying gets more of the fervency and ardours of praying: as a bell may be long a-raising, but when it is up, it jangleth not as it did at first.

[3.] Those cold affections which we have are killed by disuse and turning away from God; therefore go to him to get thy heart warmed.

2. Of the second consideration. If he prayed for this transfiguration, observe:—

That God often answereth his people in the very time while they are praying: Isa. lviii. 9, 'When they call I will answer, and when they cry he shall say, Here I am.' This hath been the course of God's dealing with the prayer-makers all along: Abel, Gen. iv. 4, 'God had respect to;' it is ἐνεπύρισεν, set his offering on fire. Daniel prayeth, and saith he, Dan. ix. 21, 'While I was speaking in prayer, the angel Gabriel was sent unto me;' and he said, 'At the beginning of thy supplications the commandment came forth.' While many of the disciples were gathered together praying, God sent Peter to them, Acts xii. 12, 13. While Cornelius was in the act of prayer, 'At the ninth hour of the day,' which was the hour of prayer, 'he saw in a vision the angel of God,' Acts x. 3–9. While Peter went up to the house-top to pray, then he had the heavenly vision. So when Paul was in prayer, Ananias was sent to him: Acts ix. 11, 'Behold he prayeth;' and then God taketh care of him. So Acts iv. 31, 'When they had prayed, the house was shaken, and they were all filled with the Holy Ghost.' Thus God delighteth to honour his own ordinance, and to reward the waiting soul, that is frequent and constant in this way of waiting upon God, which should encourage us to be more frequent and serious in this work. You shall see how, in the very act of prayer, God hath—(1.) averted judgments; (2.) bestowed mercies and favours.

[1.] He hath put a stop to judgments: Ps. xcix. 6–8, 'Moses and Aaron among the priests, and Samuel among them that call upon his name: they called upon the Lord, and he answered them; he spake unto them in the cloudy pillar; they kept his testimonies and the ordinance that he gave them. Thou answeredst them, O Lord our God; thou wast a God that forgavest them, though thou tookest vengeance of their inventions.' The drift of the Psalmist in this place is to show, by eminent instances of holy men that were most notable for prayer, how they have stopped judgments when they began to be executed. Moses, at his prayer God was propitiated, after the provocation of the golden calf; for it is said, Exod. xxxii. 11, 'Moses besought the Lord his God;' ver. 14, 'The Lord repented of the evil which he thought to do.' The second, Aaron's making an atonement for the people, whereby the plague was staid: Num. xvi. 46, 'Take a censer quickly, for wrath is begun;' and ver. 48, presently the plague was stayed. Upon Samuel's prayer the Philistines were discomfited when they were overrunning Israel, 1 Sam. vii. 5, with ver. 9, 10. With every one of these God was pleased to talk and commune as a friend. Such honour was God pleased to put on these his faithful servants; and when the people had provoked God, and God's wrath was already gone out against them for their crying sins, their prayers were so effectual as to divert the plagues and obtain remission.

[2.] So powerful, also, are they for obtaining blessings: Elijah (James v. 17, 18), though 'a man of like passions with us,' yet he could lock heaven and open it at his pleasure; 1 Kings xviii. 42, 45, the rain came as soon as Elijah put himself into a zealous posture to obtain it. Often success hath overtaken the prayer, and the blessing has been gotten before the supplication hath been ended. Isaac went out to meet with God, to meditate or pray, and he espied Rebecca afar off. Isa. lxv. 24, 'Before they call I will answer, and whilst they are yet speaking I will hear.' Oh, therefore, let us not entertain hard thoughts of God, as if he did not regard our suits and requests, and prayer were a lost labour.

II. I come now to the transfiguration itself, as it is here propounded and explained.

Doct. That one necessary and solemn act of Christ's mediation and manifestation to the world was his transfiguration before competent witnesses.

This was one solemn act, and part of Christ's manifestation to the world, for we have the record of it here; and it was necessary, for Christ doth nothing in vain. And here are competent witnesses,— three persons of eminent holiness, before whom all this was done, and they were eye-witnesses of his majesty, and ear-witnesses of the oracle which they heard from heaven, or the voice from the excellent glory.

I shall open:—

First, The nature of this transfiguration.

Secondly, The ends of it.

First, The nature of this transfiguration. It was a glorious alteration in the appearance and qualities of his body, not a substantial alteration in the substance of it. It was not a change wrought in the essential form and substance of Christ's body, but only the outward form was changed, being more full of glory and majesty than it used to be or appeared to be.

Two things are to be handled:—

1. How it differed from his body at another time, whilst he conversed here on earth.

2. How this change differed from the state of his body as it is now in glory.

1. How his body, now transfigured, differed from his body at other times during his conversing with men. Though the fulness of the Godhead dwelt in him always, yet the state of his body was disposed so as might best serve for the decency of human conversation; as the sun in a rainy, cloudy day is not seen, but now, as it might, discover his divine nature, it would break out in vigour and strength.

[1.] It was not a change or alteration of the substance of the body, as if it were turned into a spiritual substance. No; it remained still a true human, mortal body, with the same nature and properties it had before, only it became bright and glorious.

[2.] As the substance of the body was not changed, so the natural shape and features were not changed, otherwise how could it be known to be Christ? The shape and features were the same, only a new and wonderful splendour put upon them.

[3.] This new and wonderful splendour was not in imagination and appearance only, but real and sensible. If it had been in imagination, show, and appearance, it would make Christ like those deceivers who would dazzle the eyes of beholders with a false appearance, as magical impostors, or those apish imitators of divine glory; as Herod Agrippa, of whom we read, Acts xii. 21–23, how he appeared in royal state and made an oration, and they said, 'The voice of a God, and not of a man.' Josephus telleth us the manner, how he sat in the sun with glistering garments of cloth of silver, and when the sunbeams did beat upon it, the people cried him up as κρείττονα τῆς θνητῆς φύσεως, as something higher and more excellent than a mortal creature. No; this was not a phantastical representation, but a real impression of divine glory on the body of Christ.

[4.] Although this appeared in the face chiefly, as the most conspicuous part of the body,—the text saith his face did shine as the sun,—yet more or less the other parts of his body were clothed with majesty and glory, and thence was the splendour derived to his garments.

2. How his body transfigured differed from his glorified body. This must be stated also, for Christ, by his transfiguration, was not admitted into the fulness of the state of glory, but only giveth some glimpse and resemblance of it. These two estates agree in the general nature, but some clarity, glory, and majesty is put upon Christ's glorified body that was not now. But the difference is:—

[1.] Partly in the degree and measure; the clarity and majesty of Christ's glorified body is greater and more perfect. Here is a representation, some delineation, but not a full exhibition of His heavenly glory.

[2.] Partly in continuance and permanency. This change was not perpetual, but to endure for a short time only, for it ceased before they came down from the mount.

[3.] The subject or seat of this glory differed, the body of Christ being then corruptible and mortal, but now incorruptible and immortal. If Christ's body had been immortal and impassible, then Christ could not die.

[4.] Here are garments, and a glorified body shall have no other garments than the robes of immortality and glory in heaven. Christ shall be clothed with light as with a garment.

Secondly, The ends of it. By this transfiguration God would show:—
1. What Christ was.
2. What he should be; and also,
3. What we shall be.

1. What Christ was. The dignity of his person and office. That he was the eternal Son of God, and the mediator of the new covenant; the great prophet whom God would raise up to his people.

[1.] The dignity of His person was seen, for the transfiguration was a ray of the divine glory. It was not the addition of any glory to Christ which he had not before, but a manifestation of the glory which he had, though obscured under the veil of our flesh; for the fulness of the Godhead dwelt in him bodily, Col. ii. 9, 'And we beheld his glory, as the glory of the only-begotten Son of God,' John i. 14. But it is said, 2 Pet. i. 17, that he received from God the same honour and glory. This is spoken of him as mediator; the glory of the Son of God incarnate was so obscured, for our sakes, that he needed this solemn act to represent him to the world.

[2.] His office: the great prophet of the church, 'Hear ye him.' A greater prophet than Moses. Moses saw the face of God, but he was in the bosom of God. Moses, his face shone, but not as Christ's, for it could be hidden by a veil; Christ darts his glory through his garments. Moses, his shining was terrible; Christ's was comfortable —the apostles were loath to lose the sight of it.

2. To show what Christ should be; for this was a pledge with what glory he should come in his kingdom, Mat. xvi. 27 : it prefigured the glory of his second coming. Thus, for the confirmation of their faith, Christ would give his disciples a glimpse of his glory; he knew they would be sorely assaulted and shaken by the ignominy of his cross. But what is all this to us? We see not his glory.

[1.] What was once done and sufficiently attested needs not to be repeated ; but it is a great satisfaction to us that we have a glorious head and chief ; when we suffer for him we need not be ashamed of our sufferings. The apostles urge this concerning us as well as them.

[2.] The immediate manifestations of him who dwelleth in light inaccessible would undo us while we are in our mortal bodies. Blessed be God that he hath chosen fit means to reveal himself to us, that we may behold the glory of the Lord in a glass, 2 Cor. iii. 18, by the ministry of the word and other ordinances. The Israelites were sensible how little they could endure him who is, as it were, all sun, and all light, and all fire: Exod. xx. 18, 19, 'Let not God speak to us, lest we die.' Elijah wrapt his face in a mantle when God appeared unto him, 1 Kings xix. 13; when Christ appeared to Paul from heaven he trembled and was astonished, and was three days without sight, as you may see, Acts ix. 9. There was a special reason why an apostle should see him in person.

[3.] We shall see this glory when fit for it : John xvii. 24, 'Father, I will that they whom thou hast given me may be with me where I am, that they may behold my glory which thou hast given me.' The queen of Sheba took a long journey to behold the glory of Solomon, that was but a temporal, fading, and earthly glory. Now much more transcendent is the glory of Christ's body in heaven ; this we shall see to all eternity.

3. To show what we shall be ; for Christ is the pattern, *primum in unoquoque genere*, &c.

[1.] It showeth the possibility of our having a glorified body. When the Lord is pleased to let forth and communicate his glory, he is able to adorn and beautify our earthly and obscure bodies. The body of man in its composition hath a great mixture of earth, which is dark and obscure. Now God can make this clod of earth to shine as the star or sun for brightness: Phil. iii. 21, ' Who shall change our vile body, that it may be fashioned like unto his glorious body, according to the working whereby he is able to subdue all things to himself.' We are apt to say, How can it be ? If we consider the infinite and absolute power of God, and this instance of Christ, it will make it more reconcilable to your thoughts, and this hard point will be of easier digestion to your faith.

[2.] The certainty of it, as well as the possibility; for Christ assumed our body, not for passion only, but for glorification, that therein he might be an instance and pattern to us. For if the head be glorious, so will the members also. How base soever the people of God seem to be in this world, yet in the life to come they shall be wonderfully glorious : Mark xiii. 43, 'The righteous shall shine as the sun in the kingdom of their father.' So Col. iii. 3, 4, 'Now our life is hidden with Christ, but when he who is our life shall appear, we shall appear with him in glory;' 1 John iii. 2, 'When he shall appear we shall be like him, for we shall see him as he is;' 2 Thes. i. 10, 'Christ shall be glorified in his saints, and admired in all them that believe.' All these places show we shall be partakers of this glory.

[3.] The manner. Glorification taketh not away the substance and natural properties of the body, for there is a glorious transfiguration, but no abolition of the substance of Christ's body ; it was the same body of Christ before and after transfiguration. Glory freeth us from natural infirmities, but it doth not strip us of natural properties. Christ hath showed in his own body what he can or will perform in ours—these same bodies, but otherwise adorned, τοῦτο τὸ σῶμα τῆς ταπεινώσεως: and 'with these eyes shall I see God,' Job xix. 26, 27: Τοῦτο τὸ φθαρτὸν, 'This corruptible must put on incorruption, and this mortal must put on immortality,' 1 Cor. xv. 53.

Use 1. Be transformed that you may be transfigured : 'Be ye transformed by the renewing of your minds,' Rom. xii. 2. The change must begin in the soul (2 Cor. iii. 18), and thence it is conveyed to the body. The lustre of grace maketh way for the splendour of glory: Prov. iv. 18, 'The path of the just is as the shining light, which shineth more and more to the perfect day.' The way of the wicked is an increasing darkness—ignorance, sin, outer darkness.

2. Be contented to be like Christ in reproaches, disgraces, and neglect in the world, that you may be like him in glory. Bear the reproach of Christ: Heb. xiii. 13, 'Let us go forth therefore unto him without the camp, bearing his reproach;' Heb. xi. 26, 'Esteeming the reproach of Christ greater riches than the treasures of Egypt.' Prefer it before all earthly honour : Acts v. 41, 'And they departed from the council, rejoicing that they were counted worthy to suffer shame for his name;' and 2 Sam. vi. 22, 'I will yet be more vile and base in my own sight.' Your Lord is a glorious Lord, and he can put glory upon you.

3. To wean our hearts from all human and earthly glory. What is a glorious house to the palace of heaven, glorious garments to the robes of immortality ? The glory of Christ should put out the glory of these petty stars that shine in the world, as the sun puts out the fire. We have higher things to mind; it is not for eagles to catch flies, or princes to embrace the dunghill.

4. Since this glory is for the body, do not debase the body, to make it an instrument of sin: 1 Thes. iv. 4, 'Possess your vessels in sanctification and honour.' Do not offend God to gratify the body, as they do, Rom. xiv. 13, 'who make provision for the flesh to fulfil the lusts

thereof.' Do not spare the body to do God service: Acts xxvi. 7, ' Unto which promise our twelve tribes, instantly serving God day and night, hope for to come; for which hope's sake, King Agrippa, I am accused of the Jews:' 2 Cor. vii. 1, ' Having therefore these promises, dearly beloved, let us cleanse ourselves from all filthiness of the flesh and spirit, perfecting holiness in the fear of God.'

SERMON III.

And behold there appeared unto him Moses and Elias talking with him.—MAT. XVII. 3; with,
And behold there talked with him two men, Moses and Elias, who appeared in glory, and spake of his decease which he should accomplish at Jerusalem.—LUKE IX. 30, 31.

HAVING spoken of Christ's transfiguration, we come now to speak of those special accidents and adjuncts which happened at the time of his transfiguration. Here are two mentioned:—

1. The extraordinary apparition of Moses and Elias.
2. Their conference with our Saviour.

In the first:—

1. The persons who appeared: Moses and Elias.
2. The manner of their appearing. Luke saith, ' They appeared in glory.' Since the scripture affixeth a *behold*, or note of attention, wherever this history is mentioned, it will not be unprofitable for us to consider it a little.

First, Who appeared: Moses and Elias. These were there in person, as well as Christ was there in person; for it is not a vision, but a thing really done and transacted. Christ would have but two, being to give us a glimpse only, not the full lustre and splendour of his glory and majesty, as he will at the last day, when he shall come in the glory of the Father, and all his holy angels with him.

But why these two?

1. With respect to the gospel or new law which he was to set up, it is for the confirmation thereof that Moses and Elias appear talking with him, showing the harmony and agreement between them, and the subordination of their dispensation to Christ and salvation by him. Moses was the person by whom the law was given, and Elias was a principal prophet. The law is represented by Moses, and the prophets by Elias. Both did frequently foretell and prefigure the death and resurrection of Christ, and all the scripture which was then written was usually called by this term, law and prophets: Acts xxiv. 14, ' Believing all things that are written in the law and the prophets;' and Mat. xi. 13, ' For all the law and the prophets prophesied until John;' Luke xvi. 24, ' They have Moses and the prophets, let them hear them;' so Acts xxvi. 22, ' I witness no other things than those which Moses and the prophets say should come to pass;' so Mark

vii. 11, 'Whatsoever ye would that men should do to you, do you the same to them, for this is the law and the prophets.' Well, then, the books of the Old Testament are frequently and solemnly thus called law and prophets; the Messiah was spoken of and foretold in both, and the godly before his coming waited for him as such. One place I had almost forgotten: Rom. iii. 21, 'The righteousness of God without the law is manifested, being witnessed by the law and the prophets.' Which showeth that not only the person of Christ was set forth, but also his institution and gospel dispensation. Well, to manifest this consent, here is law and prophets, Moses and Elias friendly conferring with Christ, or rather attending upon him, as servants upon their Lord. Christ and Moses, Christ and the prophets, are not at variance, as the Jews suppose, but here is a fair agreement betwixt them.

2. With respect to the persons themselves, there are many special reasons. These had been the most faithful and laborious servants of the Lord, and public eminent instruments of his glory: Moses a giver of the law, and Elias a restorer of the law; Moses faithful in all the house of God, and Elias zealous for the glory of God. Both had ventured their lives: Moses by encountering Pharaoh, and Elias Ahab. Both had seen the glory of God in Mount Horeb, and spake with God also: Moses, Exod. xxxiii. 11, 'He saw the Lord face to face, and spake with him as a man doth with his friend;' and Elias, 1 Kings xix. Both had fasted forty days, as Christ also did; therefore conveniently were these chosen.

3. With respect to our profit and instruction, Christ would not choose two angels for this service, but two men. Here the business was not to see glorified spirits, but glorified bodies; therefore the angels, having no bodies of their own, and must appear in assumed bodies, if in any, are not fit; therefore two men that had bodies wherein they might appear.

But you will say, If two men must appear in glorified bodies, why not Enoch rather than Moses, who was translated into heaven, and remaineth there with a glorified body as well as Elias?

Ans. Enoch had no public charge; Enoch lived before the legal dispensation. These both belonged to it, and were chief in it, of great authority among the Jews. Enoch hath an honourable testimony in the word of God, but had no public office and charge in the church, which the other two had, and managed with great fidelity. By the appearance of Moses the whole legal economy is supposed to appear in his person, and by the appearance of Elias the prophetical ministry, which was a kind of chancery to the law, is supposed to appear also. Both do, as it were, deliver over to Christ their whole dispensation, and lay it down at his feet, as the magistrates that are to go out of office solemnly resign the ensigns of their authority to him that succeedeth; and also they come both to reverence the majesty of their supreme Lord. In short, it is for our comfort that one that died, and one alive in glory, should come to show that Christ is Lord of quick and dead, Rom. xiv. 9. Moses was dead, Elias translated: these two come, the one to give a pledge of the glory of the world to come, the other of the resurrection of the dead, which is the way and introduction to it;

and both these persons come to attend and adore our Saviour and do homage to him.

Secondly, They appeared in glory, that is, in a corporeal shape, shining with brightness and glory as Christ's body did, bating only for the degree and proportion, that there might be a difference between the Lord and his servants. Now, whether they appeared in bodies formed and assumed for the present purpose, and to be laid down again, as we do our garments, or in their own proper bodies, is often disputed by interpreters, upon this occasion. That they appeared in bodies is certain, for bodily acts and properties are ascribed to them—as their talking with Christ, their being seen by the apostles; for a spirit cannot be seen. If in bodies, why not their own? It is as easy to the Lord to cause them to appear in their own bodies as in a body assumed for this special purpose and service; and they were known by the disciples to be Moses and Elias, not by the external lineaments, for they never saw them in person before, but either were made known to them by some internal revelation, or by Christ's words, or by some words of Moses and Elias themselves; but which way soever they knew them, certain it is they knew them, and took them to be Moses and Elias, therefore Moses and Elias they were, both as to soul and body. The apostles that were admitted to this transfiguration were not to be deceived by a false appearance, for they were admitted to be confirmed in the truth of Christ's person and office, that by what they saw they might confirm others. How would it weaken the testimony if what they saw appearing before them in glory were not the bodies of Moses and Elias, but only other bodies assumed! Concerning Elias the matter is without difficulty, for since he saw not death, but was translated both body and soul into heaven, why should he lay down his own body and take another to come and serve Christ upon this occasion? Cause sufficient there was why he should come from the blessedness of heaven to Mount Tabor; no cause why he should lay aside his own proper body. It is no loss nor trouble, but advantage, to blessed and heavenly creatures to be serviceable to their Redeemer's glory, though it be to come out of the other into this world. But concerning Moses the matter is more doubtful. We read that he died in Mount Nebo, and his body was buried by God in the plains of Moab, so that his grave was known to no man unto this day, Deut. xxxiv. 5, 6. Some think it was preserved from putrefaction by the extraordinary power of God, that he might resume it at this time. The Jews say that God sucked out Moses's soul from his body with a kiss, and afterwards restored it again, and so he liveth in immortality; but he that looketh for divinity among the Jewish rabbins will much sooner find a ridiculous fable than any sound doctrine. Suffice it to us that he was really dead and buried, and his body mouldered into dust as our bodies are, and now, on this special occasion, raised out of the dust; but after this, whether it were laid down in dust again or carried into heaven, it is not for us to determine: it may be either, according to the analogy of the Christian faith. If his body returned to corruption again, surely it is a great honour that it was raised up for this special use: I say it was a great joy to these prophets to see all their predictions fulfilled in Christ. If we say it entered into glory, what inconvenience was there if God would indulge him this peculiar prerogative, to be raised from the dead and enjoy blessedness both in soul and body before the last day ? He granted it to Enoch and Elias, and those who came out of their graves after Christ's death, Mat. xxvii. 53 : the great harvest is at the last day, but some first-fruits before.

Secondly, Their conference with our Saviour: they 'talked with him,' saith Matthew ; they 'spake of his decease which he should accomplish at Jerusalem,' saith Luke. They talked with Christ, not with the apostles. Here is an apparition to them, but no parley and intercourse between them and the glorified saints. The saints that are glorified are out of the sphere of commerce of the living; nay, it is a question whether they heard at all what was said to Christ; but of that in the next verse.

Here observe three things:—

1. What they spake of Christ's death.

2. The notion by which his death is set forth : it is ἔξοδος.

3. The necessity of undergoing it, in the word πληρεῖν, ' which he *should accomplish* at Jerusalem.'

1. What they spake of none could divine, unless it had been told us, and the evangelist Luke telleth us that it was of his death. This argument was chosen :—

[1.] Because it was at hand. The next solemn mediatory action after this was his death and bloody sufferings. After he was transfigured in the mount he went down to suffer at Jerusalem.

[2.] This was an offence to the apostles, that their master should die : Mat. xvi. 22, 23, ' Then Peter took him, and began to rebuke him, saying, Be it far from thee, Lord ; this shall not be unto thee.'

[3.] This was the Jews' stumbling-block : 1 Cor. i. 23, ' We preach Christ crucified, to the Jews a stumbling-block.'

[4.] This was prefigured in the rites of the law, foretold in the writings of the prophets. In the figures of the law it was represented : Heb. ix. 22, ' And almost all things are by the law purged with blood, and without the shedding of blood there is no remission ;' especially the apostle urgeth the entering of the high priest with blood to the mercy-seat, ver. 23, 24. All the legal sacrifices were slain, and their blood brought before the Lord. So the predictions of the prophets: Isa. liii. 10, ' Yet it pleased the Lord to bruise him ; he hath put him to grief, when thou shalt make thy soul an offering for sin,' &c.; and Dan. ix. 26, ' The Messias shall be cut off, but not for himself.' In short, that Christ should die for the sins of the world, was the great thing represented in the law and prophets. Rabbi Simeon and Rabbi Hadersim out of Daniel, that after Messias had preached half seven years he shall be slain.

[5.] It was necessary that by death he should come to his glory, of which now some glimpse and foretaste was given to him: Luke xxiv. 46, ' Thus it is written, and thus it behoved Christ to suffer, and rise from the dead the third day'—that is, with respect to the predictions ; ver. 44, ' All those things which were written in the law of Moses, and the prophets, and the book of Psalms, concerning me may be fulfilled ;' and again, Luke xxiv. 25, 26, ' Oh fools, and slow of heart to

believe all that the prophets have spoken! ought not Christ to have
suffered these things, and to have entered into his glory?'

[6.] The redemption of the church by Christ is the talk and discourse we shall have in heaven; the angels and glorified spirits are
blessing and praising him for this: Rev. v. 9, 'Thou art worthy, for
thou wert slain, and hast redeemed us to God by thy blood.' The
angels, ver. 12, 'Worthy is the lamb that was slain to receive power,
and riches, and wisdom, and strength, and glory, and honour, and
blessing.' The redeemed church, and glorified saints and angels, have
all one song, and one praise—the honour of the Lamb that was slain.

[7.] It is an instructive pattern to us, that Christ, in the midst of
his transfiguration, and the glory which was then put upon him, forgot
not his death. In the greatest advancements we should think of our
dissolution. If Christ in all his glory discoursed of his death, surely
it more becometh us, as necessary for us to prevent the surfeit of
worldly pleasures, we should think of the change that is coming; for
'Surely every man at his best estate is vanity,' Ps. xxxix. 5. In some
places they were wont to present a death's head at their solemn feasts.
Merry days will not always last, death will soon put an end to the vain
pleasures we enjoy here, and the most shining glory will be burnt out
to a snuff.

2. The notion by which his death is expressed: his decease, ἔξοδον,
which signifies the going out of this life into another, which is to be
noted :—

[1.] In respect unto Christ his death was ἔξοδος, for he went out of
this mortal life into glory, and so it implieth both his suffering death
and also his resurrection: Acts ii. 24, 'God hath raised him up,
having loosed the pains of death, because it was impossible he should
be holden of it.' The grave was like a woman ready to be delivered;
it suffered throes till this blessed burden was egested.

[2.] With respect to us. Peter calls his death ἔξοδον: 2 Pet. i. 15,
'I will endeavour that ye may be able after my decease.' The death
of the godly is a going out but from sin and sorrow to glory and immortality, as Israel's going out of Egypt (whence the second Book of
Moses is called Exodus) was no destruction and cessation of their
being, but a going out of the house of bondage into liberty. Paul
saith, 'I desire to be dissolved,' ἀναλῦσαι, Phil. i. 23—a setting sail
for the other world. In scripture language the body is the house, the
soul is the inhabitant: 2 Cor. v. 1, 'We know that if our earthly
house of this tabernacle were dissolved, we have a building of God,
an house not made with hands, eternal in the heavens.' The soul
dwelleth in the body as a man in a house, and death is but a
departure out of one house into another—not an extinction, but a going
from house to house.

3. The necessity of undergoing it, in the word πληρεῖν. This word
accomplish noteth three things :—

[1.] His mediatorial duty, with a respect to God's ordination and
decree declared in the prophecies of the Old Testament, which when
they are fulfilled are said to be accomplished. Whatsoever Christ
did in the work of redemption was with respect to God's will and
eternal decree: Acts iv. 28, 'To do whatsoever thy hand and counsel

determined before to be done.' Now this was the more binding,
being it was a declared counsel in the prophecies and figures of the
Old Testament, therefore Christ cried out at his death, John xix. 30,
'It is finished,' or accomplished—meaning principally that the prophecies, and figures, and types which prefigured his death were all
now accomplished.

[2.] His voluntary submission, 'which he should accomplish,' noteth
his active and voluntary concurrence. It is an active word, not
passive, not to be fulfilled upon him, but by him; for though his death
in regard of his enemies was violent and enforced, yet he voluntarily
underwent it for our sakes ; no man could have taken his life from
him unless he had laid it down, John x. 18; it was not forced upon
him, but he yielded to it by a voluntary dispensation. As to men, it
was an act of violence ; but as to his Father, it was an act of obedience ; as to us, an act of love. On Christ's part his enemies could not
have touched him against his will, as indeed they cannot also one
hair of our heads but as God permitteth.

[3.] That it was the eminent act of his humiliation, for this cause
he assumed human nature. His humiliation began at his birth,
continued in his life, and was accomplished in dying : all was nothing
without this, for less could not serve the turn than the death of the
Son of God. Then all sufferings were undergone which were necessary to take away sin ; therefore there is a consummation or perfection
attributed to the death of Christ : Heb. x. 14, 'By one offering he
hath perfected for ever them that are sanctified.' There is done enough
to expiate sin, to open a way to heaven and happiness. This accom-
plisheth all that is necessary by way of merit and satisfaction.

Now what shall we learn from hence, for surely such solemn actions
of Christ were not in vain?

I. A notable argument to confirm the Christian faith, namely, the
consent between the law and the prophets and Christ ; for Moses
and Elias are all Christ's ministers and servants, agreeing in one
with him, and therefore appear at his transfiguration, where he is
proclaimed to be the beloved Son of God, and the great doctor of the
church, whom all are bound to hear under pain of damnation.

I will prove two things :—

First, The necessity of this appearance, both to the Jews and us
Gentiles.

1. To the Jews in that age; for there were three opinions concerning Christ. Some had a blasphemous opinion of him, as if he
were an imposter, and called him Samaritan and devil. So the chief
priests and Pharisees, Mat. xxvii. 63, 'We remember that that deceiver said, while he was yet alive, After three days I will rise again ;'
and Mat. xii. 24, 'This fellow doth not cast out devils, but by
Beelzebub the prince of the devils.' Generally they looked upon him
as an enemy to Moses : John ix. 29, 'We know that God spake to
Moses ; as for this fellow, we know not whence he is.' Others had a
more moderate opinion, who were alarmed by his miracles, and convinced by his holiness : Mark vi. 14–16, 'Some said it is Elias, others
said it is a prophet, Jeremias, or one of the prophets ; but Herod said
it is John whom I beheaded, who is risen from the dead, and there-

fore mighty works do show forth themselves in him.' Herod's conscience could not digest John's murder, therefore he twice saith it is John, it must needs be John. The third opinion was that of the disciples, 'Thou art the Christ, the Son of the living God,' John vi. 69. Now, to set all at rights, to confute the blasphemous Jews, to rectify the moderate Jews, to confirm the disciples, here come Moses and Elias to justify him. They would not have owned him if a blasphemer and imposter, nor have come from heaven to honour him and do him homage if he had been an ordinary prophet; therefore they appear in glory, and talk with him of his death.

2. With respect to the modern Jews, and us Gentiles, this apparition was necessary to confirm us in the faith both of Christ's person and office; that he was the great teacher sent from heaven to make known the way of salvation to lapsed mankind; and Moses and Elias must be hereafter silent. Now the great prophet and doctor of the church is brought forth; and no other revelation or dispensation is to be expected or regarded, now he is brought forth. There is need that this should be sufficiently evidenced, partly because Christ had the law of Moses to repeal, which was well known to the Jews to be God's own law, else they and every true subject of God might refuse to obey him: partly because he had a new law to promulgate, even the law of faith and gospel ordinances, and so must manifest his authority before they can be received and submitted unto with that firm assent and consent which is necessary: partly because he himself was to be received and entertained as the Redeemer of the world, who had expiated our sins by his decease at Jerusalem, which was a new work, yet man's salvation lay upon it. And his death there was clouded with many prejudices; for they put him to death as a false prophet, guilty of blasphemy and sedition. Therefore it needed to be made manifest that such a man of sorrows, reckoned among transgressors, was the Saviour and Redeemer of the world.

Secondly, The sufficiency of this evidence. For if Moses and Elias appear in glory to countenance this dispensation, and declare their hearty concurrence and consent, there is no reason Jew or Gentile should scruple it. If Moses the lawgiver, and Elias, so zealous for the law, consent, why should the Jews refuse the gospel so agreeable to their dispensation, or the Gentiles question a doctrine so long ago manifested to the church by God, long before Christ and his apostles were in being? Those that lived in so many different ages could not lay their heads together to cheat the world with an untruth. There is a double argument may be drawn hence :—

1. The matter of fact. Moses and Elias did appear to witness their consent. Now this dependeth upon the testimony of the apostles present, whose testimony was by other means ratified and made valuable: 2 Pet. i. 16–18, 'For we have not followed cunningly-devised fables, when we made known unto you the coming of our Lord Jesus Christ, but were eye-witnesses of his majesty. For he received from God the Father honour and glory, when there came such a voice to him from the excellent glory, This is my beloved Son, in whom I am well pleased. And this voice which came from heaven we heard when we were with him in the holy mount.'

2. Their consent in doctrine, which is obvious in all their writings. The apostles related nothing concerning Christ but what Moses and the prophets had foretold, and what was history in the New Testament was prophecy in the Old, either as to the person of Christ, or as to his kingdom—the duties and privileges thereof : John v. 39, 'Search the scriptures, for in them ye think ye have eternal life, and they are they that testify of me.' So ver. 45–47, 'Do not think that I will accuse you to the Father ; there is one that accuseth you, even Moses, in whom ye trust. For had ye believed Moses, ye would have believed me, for he wrote of me. But if ye believe not his writings, how will ye believe my words ?' The Old Testament beareth witness of Christ's person, natures, offices, birth, life, sufferings, and the glory that should ensue : 2 Pet. i. 19–21, 'We have also a more sure word of prophecy, whereunto ye do well that ye take heed, as to a light that shineth in a dark place, till the day dawn, and the day-star arise in your hearts. Knowing this first, that no prophecy of the scripture is of any private interpretation. For the prophecy came not in old time by the will of men, but holy men of God spake as they were moved by the Holy Ghost.' The apostles taught the same things the prophets had written, only applied them to Jesus of Nazareth, whom they had crucified, that they might know that he was Lord and Christ. The heathens take notice that at that time when Christ appeared, there was *Vetus et constans fama* (Sueton.) ; *Ex antiquis sacerdotum libris* (Tacitus)—that their King, Messiah, should come.

Use 1. For confutation of the Jews, and to show their obstinacy in not receiving Christ as the Messiah. God had told Moses, Deut. xviii. 18, 'I will raise them up a prophet from among their brethren like unto thee ; and will put my words into his mouth, and he shall speak unto them all that I shall command him ; and whosoever will not hearken unto him, I will require it of him ;' which cannot be understood of any other prophet but Christ the Messiah ; for it is said, Deut. xxxiv. 10, 11, 'There arose not a prophet in Israel like unto Moses, who knew the Lord face to face, in all the miracles and wonders which the Lord sent him to do.' But the Messias doth match and overmatch him. He was a man as Moses was ; for the promise was made on that occasion, 'Let me hear the voice of the Lord God no more, nor see this great fire, that we die not.' Saith God, 'They have well spoken : I will raise up a prophet like unto thee from among their brethren.' He must be a lawgiver as Moses, but of a more perfect law ; he must be such an one as should see God face to face ; he is of a divine nature, approved to the world by miracles, signs, and wonders. As Moses was, so Christ. Moses divided the sea as dry land, Christ walked upon it ; Moses healed the bitter waters that were sick, Christ raised the dead. All the prejudice is, that he changed the law of Moses into the rites and institutes of the Christian religion. *Ans.* That was necessary, the substance being once come, that the shadows and ceremonies should be abolished ; and besides, these were proper and peculiar to one nation in the world, namely, Judea ; the exercise permitted but in one only place of that country, namely, Jerusalem, whither they were all to repair three times each year. But the Messiah's law was to be common to all men—serves for all countries, times, places, persons, for he was to be the light of the

Gentiles, as well as the glory of his people Israel.   How should nations
so far distant from Jerusalem repair thrice every year ? or a woman
dwelling in England or America repair thither for purification after
every childbirth ? Lev. xii.   When Moses delivered the law to
them: Deut. xviii. 15, ' The Lord thy God will raise thee up a prophet like unto me, unto him shalt thou hearken.'   And the prophets,
when they prophesy of his law : Isa. ii. 3, ' The law shall go forth out
of Zion, and the word of God from Jerusalem.'   Moses's law was published from Sinai, not from Sion ; but the preaching of the gospel
began at Jerusalem, and from thence was spread over all the world.
Again it is said, Isa. xlii. 4, ' The isles shall wait for his law ;' that is,
the maritime countries.   I pursue it no farther now.

2. To us Christians.   Our religion is true: oh, let us be true in the
profession of it ; otherwise it will little help us in the day of our accounts : 2 Thes. i. 8, ' Taking vengeance on them that know not God,
and that obey not the gospel of our Lord Jesus Christ.'   You stand
upon the vantage-ground, but are not taller in stature than heathens
and Jews.   Disciples in name, not in deed : John viii. 31, ' If ye continue in my words, then are ye my disciples indeed:'   Christians of
letter, not of the spirit.   Oh, reverence Christ, if Moses and Elias did
him homage.   When we have found truth, let us look after life ; and
having owned the true religion, express the power of it.

II. The next thing we learn is the necessity and value of Christ's
death.   For Moses and Elias insist upon ' his decease at Jerusalem ;
which quite contradicteth the Jewish deceit, and establisheth the
Christian hope.   The death of Christ for our redemption is the great
article of the Christian faith, the thing foretold and prefigured by law
and prophets, Luke xxiv. 44 ; and the ground of our comfort and
peace : Isa. liii. 4, 5, ' Surely he hath borne our griefs, and carried our
sorrows ; yet we did esteem him stricken, smitten of God, and afflicted.
But he was wounded for our transgressions, he was bruised for our
iniquities: the chastisement of our peace was upon him ; and with his
stripes we are healed.'

Let us consider :—

1. The notions by which Christ's death is set forth.

2. The necessity of it.

First, The notions by which Christ's death is set forth.   Two solemn
ones : a ransom, and a mediatorial sacrifice.

1. A ransom, λύτρον ἀντὶ πολλῶν, Mat. xx. 28 ; ἀντίλυτρον, 1 Tim.
ii. 6, ' Who gave himself a ransom for all.'   A ransom is a price
given to a judge, or one that hath power of life and death, for to
save the life of one capitally guilty, or by law bound to suffer
death, or some other evil and punishment.   This was our case: God
was the supreme judge, before whose tribunal man standeth guilty,
and liable to death ; but Christ interposed that we might be spared,
Job xxxiii. 24, ' Deliver him from going down to the pit, for I
have found a ransom.'   There is a price or recompense given in
our stead.

2. A mediatorial sacrifice: Isa. liii. 3, ' When thou shalt make his
soul an offering for sin ;' Eph. v. 2, Christ ' hath loved us, and hath
given himself for us, an offering and a sacrifice to God for a sweet-
smelling savour.'   He hath undertook the expiation of our sins, and

the propitiating of God. God's provoked justice would not acquit the controversy it had against us till it were appeased by a proper sacrifice : 1 John ii. 2, ' He is the propitiation for our sins.'

Secondly, The necessity of it.

1. The sins and guilty fears of mankind needeth such a remedy. We are naturally sensible that the punishment of death is deserved and due to us by the law of God : Rom. i. 32, ' They which commit such things are worthy of death.' Now these fears are not easily appeased : Micah vi. 6, 7, ' Wherewith shall I come before the Lord, and bow myself before the high God ? Shall I come before him with burnt-offerings, with calves of a year old ? Will the Lord be pleased with thousands of rams, or with ten thousands of rivers of oil ? Shall I give my first-born for my transgression, the fruit of my body for the sin of my soul ? ' Christ came and died to free us from them, that we might serve God cheerfully : Heb. ii. 14, 15, ' Forasmuch, then, as the children are partakers of flesh and blood, he also himself took part of the same, that through death he might destroy him that had the power of death, that is the devil ;' Heb. ix. 14, ' How much more shall the blood of Christ, who through the eternal Spirit offered himself without spot to God, purge your consciences from dead works, to serve the living God ? '

2. The glory of God requires it :—

[1.] To declare his justice : Rom. iii. 25, 26, ' Whom God hath set forth to be a propitiation through faith in his blood, to declare his righteousness for the remission of sins that are past, through the forbearance of God : to declare, I say, at this time his righteousness ; that he might be just, and the justifier of him which believeth in Jesus.' If God will pardon sin, there must be a fit means to keep up the honour of his justice, and the authority of his law ; for sin is not a wrong done to a private party offended, but a disobedience to authority, and disturbeth the order of government.

[2.] To declare his holiness, that he is a pure and holy God, hating sin. This was demonstrated in the sufferings of Christ, and the dear rate at which it was expiated ; for if this was done in the green tree, what shall be done in the dry ?

Use 1. Oh, then, be affected with this great mystery, the death which the Son of God accomplished at Jerusalem ; look upon it under a double notion. With respect to his Father's command, it was an act of obedience, carried on with such humility, patience, self-denial, resignation of himself to God, charity, pity, as the like cannot be done by man or angel : Rom. v. 19, ' By the obedience of one many were made righteous ;' Phil. ii. 8, ' He humbled himself, and became obedient to death, even the death of the cross.' This commendeth obedience to us. It was an act of love : Gal. ii. 20, ' Who loved me, and gave himself for me ;' Rev. i. 5, ' To him that loved us, and washed us from our sins in his blood.' He thought no price too dear for our salvation. Let us love him, again, who loved us first : 1 John iv. 19, ' We love him, because he first loved us ; ' and be contented to suffer with him and for him, that we may enter into his glory : Rom. viii. 17, ' If so be that we suffer with him, that we may be also glorified together,' if he call us thereunto.

2. Feel the virtue of it in heart and conscience. In heart : by our dying to sin, then we are planted into the likeness of his death, Rom. vi. 5. 'They that are Christ's have crucified the flesh, with the affections and lusts thereof,' Gal. v. 24 ; 'Who his own self bare our sins in his body on the tree, that we, being dead to sin, should live unto righteousness.' Then glory in it : Gal vi. 14, 'God forbid that I should glory, save in the cross of our Lord Jesus Christ, by whom the world is crucified to me, and I unto the world.' In conscience : 1 John v. 10, ' He that believeth in the Son of God hath the witness in himself,' &c. ; Heb. xii. 24, ' And to Jesus, the mediator of the new covenant, and to the blood of sprinkling, that speaketh better things than the blood of Abel '—doth it appease our guilty fears, and purge our consciences from the stain and guilt of sin.

III. The state of future glory and felicity.

1. The dead in the Lord are not perished, but live for ever with God in heaven ; for here they appear long after their departure hence : Luke xx. 38, ' He is not the God of the dead, but of the living ; for all live unto him.' They all live to God. Though they are gone out of the sphere of our commerce, they have another life with God. Now fix this in your hearts, for many carry it so as if there were no immortality or life to come : we do not vanish into the air when we die. Moses is somewhere, and Elias somewhere, in the hand of God, and can appear when God will have them.

2. The saints appeared in a true, and in their own bodies, to establish the faith of the resurrection ; their bodies were reserved for this use. One of them was already in glory in soul and body, the other now raised out of the dust after many years' burial. And why cannot God gather up our dust again and enliven it, that we may accompany Christ at his coming?

3. This instance showeth also the degrees of glory. All the saints have their portion in bliss, but not a just equality. Moses and Elias appeared in glory, not Enoch ; nor were any of the rest admitted to this solemnity. Here were three choice disciples, when the rest stood at a remote distance ; so two glorified saints, but the rest not admitted to this honour, but stood waiting for his glorious ascension. There is difference on earth in the worldly state—some have greater riches, honours, and dignity than others ; difference in the church, both in gifts and graces ; yea, a difference in hell—some have a hotter, others a cooler punishment. So in heaven, according to eminency in holiness and faithfulness with God; otherwise there would not be a suitableness in God's dispensations.

4. The perfect subjection of the glorified spirits to the will of God, either to remain in the vision of God, or to be employed in the service of their Redeemer. We should think that a self-denial which they count an happiness, to come from heaven to Mount Tabor ; they take up or lay down a body as God pleaseth. Heaven is a state not only of perfect happiness, but of exact conformity to God.

5. We shall have the company of the blessed saints in heaven. The disciples here did not only enjoy the company and sight of Christ, but the company and sight of Moses and Elias, being glorified saints. So in the heavenly life : Mat. viii. 11, it is made a part of our blessed-

ness in the kingdom of God to ' sit down with Abraham, Isaac, and Jacob ;' and Heb. xii. 23, ' Ye are come to the general assembly and church of the first-born, which are written in heaven, and to God the judge of all, and to the spirits of just men made perfect.' Here we are joined to them by faith and hope ; there by sight and fellowship. The company of wicked men is now grievous and tedious to us, Ezek. ii. 6 ; but we shall have better company hereafter. Here we often part with our choicest friends and acquaintance, but there we shall meet and never part more. It is not to be imagined but that we shall have the comfort of our glorified fellow-creatures. The body hath its objects and felicity fit for a body.

6. The saints shall know one another, as the disciples knew Moses and Elias, though not by countenance, having never seen them before, but by revelation. Christ told them who they were, and we who have known before our old acquaintance shall know them again. Memory is not abolished, but perfected ; we shall make one body, one society. Now we shall not converse as strangers; Abraham knew Lazarus, Luke xvi. 25. Ministers, 1 Thes. ii. 19, ' What is our hope, or joy, or crown of rejoicing ? Are not even ye in the presence of our Lord Jesus Christ at his coming ?' Christ's argument, Luke xvi. 9, ' Make to yourselves friends of the mammon of unrighteousness, that when ye fail they may receive you into everlasting habitations.' Angels know not only themselves, but all the elect now ; how else do they minister about them ? They know the least believer : Mat. xviii. 10, ' Take heed that ye offend not one of these little ones, for I say unto you that in heaven their angels do always behold the face of my Father which is in heaven.' And they are at length to gather them from the four winds: Mat. xiii. 41, ' The Son of man shall send forth his angels, and they shall gather out of his kingdom all things that do offend.'

7. The conference of the blessed saints. We shall be with them, speak to them, hear them speak to us, though not after an earthly manner. We have now bodies, and so tongues and lips, which are the instruments of speech ; ears, which are the instruments of hearing. Now these would seem vain and to no purpose if there were no use of speech and hearing. It was a blessed thing for Peter, James, and John to stand by and hear the conference between Christ, Moses, and Elias: 1 Kings x. 8, ' Happy are thy men, happy are these thy servants, which stand continually before thee, and hear thy wisdom.' Much more may it be said here.

Use. Well, then, Christian religion is true, Christ's death necessary, eternal life certain. Oh let our time, and hearts, and care be taken up about these great and glorious things ; meditate on them, seek after them. First begin with the sureness of Christian doctrine, that you may lay a good foundation; that Christ is the teacher of the church, who hath ' brought life and immortality to light through the gospel,' 2 Tim. i. 10 ; then penitently sue out your pardon, in the name of Christ, depending on the merit of his death ; and make this eternal life and happiness your choice, and the scope of your life and conversation : 2 Cor. iv. 18, ' While we look not at the things which are seen, but at the things which are not seen : for the things which are seen are temporal ; but the things which are not seen are eternal.'

SERMON IV.

Then answered Peter, and said unto Jesus, Lord, it is good for us to
be here : if thou wilt, let us make here three tabernacles ; one for
thee, and one for Moses, and one for Elias.—MAT. XVII. 4 ;
with,

But Peter and they that were with him were heavy with sleep : and
when they were awake, they saw his glory, and the two men that
stood with him.   And it came to pass, as they departed from him,
Peter said unto Jesus, Master, it is good for us to be here: and
let us make three tabernacles ; one for thee, and one for Moses,
and one for Elias : not knowing what he said.—LUKE IX. 32, 33.

WE are upon the adjuncts of Christ's transfiguration.

The first was the appearance of Moses and Elias talking with him.

The second is the entertainment which the apostles gave to this
glorious dispensation, or their behaviour under it.   Three things are
observable :—

1. Their posture for some while : *and Peter and they that were with*
him were heavy with sleep.

2. Peter's motion when they were awake : *let us build here three*
tabernacles.

3. The censure of it : *not knowing what he said.*

First, Their posture after the transfiguration was begun : ' And
Peter and they that were with him were heavy with sleep.'   This sleep
might arise either from a common natural cause, or from a special cause
peculiar to this dispensation.

1. A common natural cause, being tired with labour in ascending
the mountain, for it was ὑψηλὸς λίαν, ' exceeding high.'   Or it was
with watching, for they tarried there all night, and Christ continued
long in prayer, and possibly being a little withdrawn from them, as in
his agonies, he was transfigured before them.

2. The special cause of this sleep was the extraordinary apparition,
as the prophets often were in a deep sleep and trance when they saw
the like : Dan. viii. 18, ' As the angel Gabriel was speaking to me, I
fell into a deep sleep, with my face towards the ground.'   Again, Dan.
x. 9, ' When I heard his voice, then was I in a deep sleep.'   So the
prophet Zechariah, in the midst of his visions : Zech. iv. 1, ' The
angel of the Lord wakened me as one in a deep sleep.'   Any eminent
passion causeth sleep, and they were astonished so with these visions
and representations, that nature fainted under them, and they fell into
a sleep ; so the apostles seeing Christ, in the midst of fervent prayers,
transfigured before them.

Now, whether it came from the one cause or from the other, we must
conclude this sleep was a weakness on their parts, but directed and
overruled by God for just and wise reasons.

1. It was a weakness and infirmity on their part, for questionless
they were to attend with all vigilancy to this manifestation of our
Saviour's glory, and observe the passages of it.   Why else did he take
them into the mountain apart, but as witnesses of it, as they were to

watch in his agonies? So in his transfiguration. It was a fault then: Mat. xxvi. 40, 'When he cometh he findeth them asleep. What! could you not watch with me one hour?' But the best men are clogged with human infirmities, in the most glorious manifestations of God to them.

2. The providence of God is to be observed in this sleep. That which came to pass through their fault was ordered by God's providence; for if they had been awake, they had heard all the discourse that passed between Christ and the two great prophets, which neither their present condition nor the state of the time did permit. Christ had told them that he should suffer an ignominious death, which they did not thoroughly understand; nor could they reconcile it with the present thoughts which they had of the Messiah; nor was it fit for them to hear all, how the death of Christ was foretold in the prophecies, prefigured in the sacrifices, shadowed out in all the rest of the types of the law, and sung of in the book of Psalms, to satisfy the justice of God, and open a way for his mercy and the gift of the Holy Spirit. Christ would not have the great work of his dying hindered, and these things they were not to learn from Moses and Elias, but he would teach them himself after the resurrection: Luke xxiv. 44–46, 'These are the words that I spake unto you, while I was yet with you, that all things must be fulfilled which were written in the law of Moses, and in the prophets, and in the psalms, concerning me. Then opened he their eyes that they might understand the scriptures, and said unto them, Thus it is written, and thus it behoved Christ to suffer, and to rise from the dead the third day.' And the full knowledge of them was reserved till the pouring out of the Spirit on the day of Pentecost. If they had heard them now, they would have begotten scruples and troublesome thoughts in their minds, and hindered the present service.

Observe hence our weakness during the time we are environed with mortality, that we cannot bear up long under spiritual duties; either our hearts are soon overcharged with wonder and astonishment, or else we yield to natural infirmities. However, let it be a warning to us against sleepiness in the worship of God. It is true the best may be surprised with it, as here Christ's disciples. Yet it was a sin in them to be asleep when Christ was at prayers, and it is a sin God hath severely punished; witness Eutychus: Acts xx. 9, 'And there sat in the window a young man named Eutychus, being fallen into a deep sleep: and as Paul was long preaching, he sunk down with sleep, and fell down from the third loft, and was taken up dead.' Mark, though the sermon continued till midnight, and it was a youth that slept, yet he fell down as dead. It was a small sin—a sin of infirmity—a boy's sin; yet God would leave this warning. I do not animadvert too severely upon this infirmity, only give you caution. Christ praying all night on Mount Tabor, this weakness prevailed on these choice apostles, and elsewhere during the time of Christ's agonies. Yet we are to strive against it, and be sure it may be said of us as of them: Mark xxvi. 41, 'The spirit is willing, but the flesh is weak.' Make conscience of avoiding this sin; do not compose yourselves to sleep; do not come to these duties spent with labours and worldly cares, nor clogged with excess of meat or drink, nor having defrauded ourselves of necessary refreshing by sleep, by vain pleasures the night before.

Secondly, Their carriage when they were awake. When they awaked, they saw his glory, and the two men that stood with them; they saw Christ transfigured before they fell asleep, but I think they saw not Moses and Elias before, but now saw them, that they might give testimony of it to the church, not by common fame and hearsay, but as eye-witnesses; and they knew Moses and Elias either by information from Christ, or some secret instinct and revelation of the Spirit, or as hearing some part of the discourse, they heard enough to show what they were, or what the general matter of their discourse was. But that which is most remarkable is Peter's motion and proposal, 'It came to pass, as they departed from him'—just as they were parting—'Peter said, Lord, it is good for us to be here: let us make three tabernacles; one for thee, one for Moses, and one for Elias.' He mentioned no distinct tabernacle for himself and fellow-disciples, because they would be with Christ, attending on their master in his tent.

The motion in the general is rash, sudden, and unadvised; but being made by a good man, though under a passion, there is something good and something bad in it.

1. That which was good in it is, he yet retaineth his reverence.

[1.] That he submitteth his proposal to the judgment of his Lord and Master, wherein he expresseth his reverence of Christ—'Lord, if thou wilt.' He desireth a continuance of this dispensation, leaveth it to his consent, acknowledging herein his wisdom and authority.

[2.] It showeth the valuableness and felicity of conversing with Christ and the glorified saints; for when but two of them appear in glory, talking with Christ, Peter said it is good to be here, to continue and abide in this place together with thyself, Moses, and Elias. What a blessed dignity is this! The glory of heaven is so ravishing and satisfactory to the soul, that the soul can rest in the least glimpse and degree of it! If a glimpse, what is the fulness? If the splendour of his humanity not yet glorified be so great, what is the glory of his Godhead? If a sight of these things at a distance, what is the participation when the glory shall be revealed in us, or we shall appear with him in glory? If Moses and Elias, what is the company of all the saints and angels? If it be thus at Mount Tabor, what will it be in heaven, when all the world is renewed and refined, and the church gathered together in one great assembly?

[3.] The nature of a state of glory, and how easily it maketh us to forget all things here below. Peter had a family, and household affairs to mind; for we read in the Gospel that his wife's mother was sick and cured by Christ: Mat. viii. 14. He had friends, and a brother called Andrew, who was one of the disciples of Christ, left below in the valley: John i. 40. Nay he forgot his own present condition of life, which could not long brook his remaining in that mountain, without the supply of food, and other necessaries. Now all this showeth that when we are translated to heaven, we shall be so ravished with that kind of life we shall have there, as that all sense and memory of things that we have left behind shall cease, as Peter being ravished with this sight and spectacle, thinketh not of kindred, friends, or household, or any kind of worldly comfort, but saith only, it is good to be here ; so that it teacheth us that the delights of the other world make us forget all our concernments here below : all shall be forgotten and swallowed up in that heavenly delight we shall have there.

2. That which was evil in it.

[1.] That he mistook the nature of the present dispensation. This was to be a representation, not a fruition, to be transient and moment-ary ; for confirmation, not possession ; rather a *viaticum*, a bit by the way, than a feast. It was good and commendable to be affected with joy and delight in the presence and company of Christ, and Moses, and Elias, but it was not to be rested in as their full reward.

[2.] If this request had taken place, the work of our redemption had been hindered. What had become of Christ's death and passion, which he should accomplish at Jerusalem ? All our happiness dependeth on that, and if God should give way to our carnal desires, what mischief would ensue ! If Christ had hearkened to him, he would not have gone up to Jerusalem to suffer, nor would any man living have dared to lay hands upon him while he continued in this glory and majesty.

[3.] This request was injurious to Moses and Elias, that they should utterly forsake their heavenly mansions for an abode on earth, and therefore to desire their continuance there was to desire their loss. They were a little time to appear on earth with Christ, and then to return to their blessedness, or to the enjoyment of the sight of God in the third heavens.

[4.] It was injurious to Christ. To hope to learn something from Moses and Elias which Christ could not teach them, and to equal them with his Lord and Master, in building tabernacles for all three alike and without difference, was some lessening of his respect to Christ. If they were to learn anything from them, they were to consult the books, not the persons : Luke xvi. 29, ' They have Moses and the prophets ; let them hear them.' And the desires of extraordinary means argueth a contempt of ordinary.

[5.] It was an error to imagine that tabernacles were necessary for Moses and Elias, who now appeared in such heavenly glory in the mount. They needed not earthly houses and tents to dwell in, to defend them from the injuries of the weather, neither had they such present conveniencies to prepare them.

Thirdly, The censure of the Holy Ghost : Luke saith, ' not know-ing what he said.' In Mark, chap ix. 6, ' He wist not what to say ; for they were sore afraid.' They were words of a man in a rapture, or surprised with great astonishment. There were two affections, dazzled with the majesty of this glory, and transported with joy. There was also a great fright. Usually, τὰ λύπηρα φοβερὰ, such things as bring a hurt, occasion fear, and also things of excellent glory ; such as surpass our present meanness ; as here the change of Christ's person, and the glorious appearance of the great prophets, so long since separated from the commerce of mankind.

Observe, before we proceed, the inconvenience of great and excessive passions : they make us speak we know not what. Peter is an instance in scripture. Let us keep to him. You see him surprised with a great passion of fear, when at Christ's command a great draught of fish came to hand in an unlikely time: Luke v. 8, 9, 'Depart from me; for I am a sinful man, O Lord. For he was astonished, and all that were with him, at the draught of fishes that they had taken.' You find him at other times transported with a passion of excessive reverence or humility: John xiii. 8, 'Lord, thou shalt never wash my feet.' With a passion of love, or pity to his Master: 'Lord, let it be far from thee; this shall not be unto thee,' when his Master had foretold his death: Mat. xvi. 22, in case of contempt of Christ. Here with a passion of joy or ravishment, or transport of soul, 'Lord, it is good for us to be here.' Now all these passions were religiously exercised; but it is dangerous when religion, which should bridle and govern our passions, is made the matter and fuel of them. Passionate joy, or passionate fear, passionate reverence, or passionate zeal, and anger, may easily transport us to some uncomely action or motion; for though in all these there was religion at top, yet sin at the bottom; and, therefore, you see how much it concerneth us to moderate and reduce ourselves to a due temper; for passion causeth us to do things without and against reason; yea, to speak and do we know not what; and when religious matters overheat our affections, we may err exceedingly.

Now, having opened this part of the history, let us observe something that conduceth to our practical instruction.

Doct. 1. That the state and condition of the glorified saints is a most delightful state and condition.

For when Peter had but a glimpse of it in the transfiguration of Christ, it seemed so ravishing and transporting, that here would he abide and stay by it; so was he affected with joy in the company and presence of Christ, and Moses and Elias appearing with him, that all his natural comforts and relations were forgotten. This would compensate all. If once we be gotten into this blessed estate, we shall never desire to come out of it, and part with it. This which the disciples had was but a little glimpse and taste of the life to come. This must needs be so; it is called joy: Mat. xxv. 21, 'Enter thou into the joy of thy Lord;' and fulness of joy: Ps. xvi. 11, 'In thy presence there is fulness of joy; at thy right hand there are pleasures for evermore.' No better estate can be expected. The soul is at rest, as having obtained its end. And it is also proved by the privileges and benefits the saints shall enjoy in the world to come.

1. A freedom from all evil, which here are matter of grief to us. And

2. The fruition of all good, which may any way bring joy, and delight, and contentment.

1. There is a freedom from all evil. There is a twofold evil, either of sin or punishment. In heaven there is neither sin nor misery.

[1.] To begin with sin, that is the worst evil, because it maketh us hateful to God, and grieveth the saints most: Rom. vii. 24, 'Oh wretched man that I am! who shall deliver me from the body of this death?' If any man had cause to complain of afflictions, Paul much more, being often imprisoned, whipped, stoned; but his lusts troubled him more than scourges; and his captivity to the law of sin more than prisons. God's children are most weary of the world, because they are sinning here whilst others are glorifying of God, and enjoying God and the company of his blessed ones. Now in heaven there is no sin : Eph. v. 27, there is neither spot nor blemish, nor wrinkle on the face of the glorified saints. Their faces were once as black as yours, but now they are washed in the Lamb's blood and fully cleansed; now with much ado we mortify sin, but then it is nullified. But if we subdue the power of sin, we do not get rid of the being of it, but then we are rid of all at once—of all sin, and temptation to sin. There was a serpent, a tempter in Paradise, but there is none in heaven ; the devil is shut out, and the old man is left in the grave never to rise more.

[2.] There is not the least evil of affliction: Rev. xxi. 4, ' All tears shall be wiped away from their eyes.' Whatsoever is painful and burdensome to nature, is a fruit of sin, a brand and mark of our rebellion against God. Therefore, when sin is done away, affliction, which is the fruit of it, is done away also. In hell there is evil, and only evil ; in heaven, happiness, and only happiness. Here our wounds are healed, but the scars remain—something to put us in mind that we have sin yet dwelling in us ; but there all the effects of it cease—there is neither death, nor sorrow, nor crying, nor any more pain.

2. They shall enjoy all good things, which shall bring joy and comfort to them. In blessedness there is a confluence of all good ; our joys are full and eternal.

[1.] There is the immediate sight and presence of God and Jesus Christ, who shall be all in all to them : 1 Cor. xiii. 12, ' Now we see through a glass, darkly ; but then face to face : now I know in part ; then shall I know as also I am known.' And John xvii. 24, ' Father, I will that they also whom thou hast given me be with me where I am ; that they may behold my glory, which thou hast given me : for thou lovedst me before the foundation of the world.' We are brought into the presence of him who is blessedness itself.

[2.] The society of all the blessed angels and saints glorified : Mat. viii. 11, ' Many shall come from the east and west, and shall sit down with Abraham, and Isaac, and Jacob, in the kingdom of heaven.'

[3.] The perfection of all heavenly gifts both in soul and body.

(1.) In soul : that is the heaven of heaven : 1 John iii. 2, ' Now are we the sons of God ; but it doth not yet appear what we shall be : but this we know, that when he shall appear we shall be like him, for we shall see him as he is ;' Ps. xvii. 15, ' When I awake I shall be satisfied with thy image and likeness.' By knowing we come to love, and by loving God we know him. There is vision, assimilation, satisfaction. The object is efficacious, the intimation vigorous and clear, the subject prepared for the impression.

(2.) In body : Phil. iii. 21, ' Who shall change our vile body, that it may be fashioned like unto his glorious body.' The body shall be endued with all glorious qualities, as brightness, strength, agility. It is a body wholly impassible and incorruptible, fit for the operations of a glorified soul, and with it shall for ever remain, a glorious temple of the Holy Ghost; therefore it is good to be here.

Use 1. Let this draw forth our love to such a blessed estate, which is so full of delight and contentment, and wean us from these things which are most pleasing in the world.

1. The best estate in the world is but vanity, altogether vanity, Ps. xxxix. 5, mingled with some grievances. Wealth hath its incident cares, and honour its tortures, and all pleasures here are but bitter sweets; there is a worm that feedeth on our gourd, and will in time wither it. At last death cometh, and then the lust of the world is gone: 1 John ii. 17, ' The world passeth away, and the lust thereof.' The godly themselves have but a mixed estate, because of remaining infirmities, they live here in a vale of tears and snares, and sin doth not gasp its last till death removeth us from this sinful flesh, and puts us into the sight of God himself. Wherefore the saints are groaning and longing for the parting day, when putting off the flesh we shall put off sin, and come and dwell with God for ever.

2. None are translated into heaven but such whose hearts are there first: 2 Cor. v. 2, ' In this we groan, earnestly desiring to be clothed upon with our house which is from heaven;' Phil. i. 23, ' I desire to be dissolved and to be with Christ;' Rom. viii. 23, ' We that have the first-fruits of the Spirit groan within ourselves, waiting for the adoption, the redemption of our bodies.' A Christian waiteth and longeth for a purer state of bliss and immortality. The first-fruits show what the harvest will be, and a taste what the feast will prove; though they are thankful for this refreshing by the way, yet they are longing to be at home—cannot be contented without it.

3. The excellency of this estate requireth it: if it be not worth your desires and best affections, it is little worth. Christ procured it for us by a life of labours and sorrows, and the pangs of a bitter, cursed death; and when all this is done shall not we desire it and look after it?—that is foul ingratitude. Oh then let your hearts be upon it; desire must go before delight.

Use 2. To move us to labour for it, and seek it in the first place, and to get it assured that we have a part in this blessed and joyful condition: Mat. vi. 33, ' Seek ye first the kingdom of God, and the righteousness thereof;' Luke xiii. 24, ' Strive to enter in at the strait gate;' so 2 Pet. i. 10, ' Give diligence to make your calling and election sure.' What profit is it to know that there is such a blessed and joyful estate, if we have no interest in it? Heaven is worth our pains, and will bear all the cost we can lay out upon it. So the children of God thought: Acts xxvi. 7, ' Unto which promise our twelve tribes, instantly serving God day and night, hope to come.' If we do not desire it, we do not believe it; if we do not labour for it, we do not desire it.

Use 3. Let us comfort ourselves with the hopes of this blessed and joyful condition.

1. Against all the miseries and afflictions of this present life. These are necessary; we would sleep too quietly in the world if we did not sometimes meet with thorns in our beds; we should be so pleased with our entertainment in the way as we should forget home. But God awakeneth us out of our drowsy fits by sharp afflictions, as if he said, ' Arise, depart hence, this is not your rest,' Micah ii. 10. While we wallow in sensual comforts our hearts say, it is good being here.

2. When there is a joyful and blessed condition beyond them, it is some comfort in this shipwreck of man's felicity that we can see banks and shores, a landing-place where we may be safe and enjoy our repose. 'To you that are troubled rest with us, when the Lord Jesus Christ shall be revealed from heaven with his mighty angels,' 2 Thes. i. 7. Here our days are sorrow and our travail grief, but there is our repose.

3. That our joy and contentment is so infinitely above our sorrow and trouble, 2 Cor. iv. 7, so that in all the troubles and sorrows of this life, we may look beyond them and through them to the joy and comfort of the life to come. This joy is set before us in the promises of the gospel: Heb. xii. 2, Christ, 'for the joy that was set before him, endured the cross,' &c., and Heb. vi. 18, 'Who have fled for refuge to lay hold on the hope set before us,' we see it by faith, though not by sense.

Doct. 2. That one of the diseases of mankind is that we catch. at felicity, without considering the way that leadeth to it.

Peter seeing and apprehending this estate to be an estate of happiness and glory, doth not consider what he must first do and first suffer before he could come to converse with Christ and the glorified saints. Our Saviour had lately told him that he must deny himself, and take up his cross and follow him; but Peter overlooketh all this, and saith, 'It is good to be here.' He would be glorified before he was abased and had suffered all the afflictions foretold, and would have his wages before he had done his work. Every one would enjoy Christ's glory and happiness, but we do not like his yoke—are loth to submit to his cross. If we would enjoy happiness with Christ and the glorified saints, we must be humbled with them and suffer with them first. But we would triumph before we had fought any battle, and receive the crown before we have run our race, and reap in joy before we have sowed in tears, or performed that necessary work that God requires at our hands.

Now the reasons of it are these :—

1. Because by nature we love our own ease and contentment : Gen. xlix. 15, 'He saw that rest was good.' We are loth to undergo the cross, and desirous to enjoy happiness and glory before and without afflictions; but this is an untimely and preposterous desire, proceeding from self-love. God hath appointed another order, that the cross should go before the crown: Rom. viii. 17, 'If so be that we suffer with him, that we may be glorified together.'

2. From the libertinism and yokelessness of our natures, and that spirit of unsubjection which is so natural to us : Rom. viii. 7, 'The carnal mind is enmity against God; for it is not subject to the law of God, neither indeed can be ;' Ps. ii. 3, 'Let us break their bands asunder, and cast away their cords from us.' Duties are more displeasing to the flesh than happiness, and we like pardon and life more than we like strictness, purity, and that watching and striving, and waiting, and exercising ourselves unto godliness which the scripture calleth for.

Use. To press us to get this disease cured, and our hearts reconciled to our duty as well as to our happiness. These considerations may be a help to you.

1. God is a governor as well as a benefactor, and must be respected in both relations ; and therefore we must not only desire and wait for his benefits, but submit to his government. His government is seen in his laws and providence. In his laws he appoints our duty, in his providence he appoints our trials ; to refuse either is to question his sovereignty: Ps. xii. 4, 'Who have said, With our tongue will we prevail: our lips are our own : who is lord over us ?' Exod. v. 2, 'And Pharaoh said, Who is the Lord, that I should obey his voice to let Israel go ? I know not the Lord, neither will I let Israel go ;' so also not to submit to his trials. Therefore now, if we love God as a benefactor, we must be subject to him as our true and proper sovereign, who will bring us to heaven in what way he pleaseth.

2. The terms and means appointed conduce to mortify our love to the false happiness, for one great part of religion is to draw off our hearts from the vain pleasures and honours of the world, the other part is to carry us on in the pursuit of the true happiness—a recess from the world and an access to God, mortification and vivification. We shall sit down with present things if we abandon ourselves to our sensual inclinations, Luke xvi. 25, so that our desires of the true happiness will be feeble and easily controlled if we submit not to the means.

3. The care and due observance of the means showeth the value and respect to the true happiness. If we do not labour for it and suffer for it, we do not value it according to its worth. There is a simple, naked estimation, and a practical esteem. Naked approbation, Rom. ii. 18, 'And knowest his will, and approvest the things that are excellent, being instructed out of the law.' The practical esteem is a self-denying obedience, Rom. ii. 7, 'To them who by patient continuance in well-doing seek for glory,' &c. Then they respect means and end together, and submit to the one to obtain the other. If the wicked are said to despise eternal happiness, it is not simply as happiness, nor as eternal, for they that love themselves would be happy, and everlastingly happy ; but it is in conjunction with the means, as the Israelities despised the pleasant land, and murmured in their tents: Ps. cvi. 24, 'Yea, they despised the pleasant land ; and they believed not his word ; but murmured in their tents, and hearkened not to the voice of the Lord.' The land was a good, fertile land, but afar off, and because of giants and walled towns, and so not thought worthy the pains and difficulties to be undergone. Heaven is a good place, but out of indulgence to the ease of the flesh we dislike difficulties and strictness of holy walking.

4. The difficulty of salvation lies not in a respect to the end but the means, and therefore the trial of our sincerity must rather be looked for there. There is some difficulty about the end, to convince men of an unseen felicity ; but that may be done in part by reason, but savingly and thoroughly by the Spirit of revelation : Eph. i. 18, 'The eyes of your understandings being enlightened; that ye may know what is the hope of his calling, and what the riches of the glory of his inheritance in the saints.' But man is sooner convinced than converted, than drawn off from worldly vanities, that he may seek after this happiness ; and usually we have a quicker ear for offers of

happiness than precepts of duty and obedience.   Balaam, Num. xxiii. 10, ' Oh that I could die the death of the righteous, and that my latter end were like his !'   John vi. 34, 'Evermore give us this bread' of life ; but a true Christian, 'If by any means I may attain to the resurrection of the dead,' Phil. iii. 11.

5. The necessity of this self-denying resignation of ourselves to God, to bring us to heaven in his own way, is necessary.   That we may begin with God : Luke xiv. 26, ' If any man come to me, and hate not father, and mother, and wife, and children, and brethren, and sisters, yea, and his own life also, he cannot be my disciple.'   And also that we may be true to him, and go on with him, and be fortified against all the difficulties we meet with in the way to heaven : Heb. xi. 35, ' Others were tortured, not accepting deliverance ; that they might obtain a better resurrection.'   ' But none of these things move us,' Acts xx. 24 : Mat. xx. 22, ' Are ye able to drink of the cup that I shall drink of, and to be baptized with the baptism that I am baptized with ? '

6. There is such an inseparable connexion between the end and means, that God will not give us the one without the other.   If we believe, mortify, wait, suffer, then shall we reign with him—otherwise not.

Doct. 3. Much evil would ensue if we had our desires in all those things that we think good for us.

Peter said, ' It is good for us to be here ;' but, alas ! how ill would it have been for the world if Christ had abode still in the mount. Peter's instance showeth us two things :—

1. That we are apt to consult with our own profit rather than public good.   The world needed him, he had great business to do in the valley ; but he would be in the mount.   It is our nature, if it be well with ourselves, to forget others.   Peter little minded his fellow-apostles, the redemption of the world, the conversion of nations, &c.

2. How much we are out when we judge by present sense and the judgment of flesh.   We consult with the ease of the flesh, and so desire rest more than pains and labour ; what pleaseth rather than what profiteth.   Peter saith, ' It is good to be here,' but he must labour first, suffer first, before he entereth into glory.

Well, then, let us learn by what measure to determine good or evil.

1. Good is not to be determined by our fancies and conceits, but by the wisdom of God ; for he knoweth what is better for us than we do for ourselves, and the divine choices are to be preferred before our foolish fancies ; and what he sendeth and permitteth to fall out is better for us than anything else.   Could we be persuaded of this, how would we be prepared for a cheerful entertainment of all that is, or can, or shall come, upon us.   God is wiser than we, and loves us better than we do ourselves.   The child is not to be governed by his own fancy, but his father's discretion, nor the sick man by his own appetite, but the skill of the physician.   It is expedient God should displease his people, for their advantage : John xvi. 6, 7, ' Because I have said these things unto you, sorrow hath filled your heart.   Nevertheless I tell you the truth : it is expedient for you that I go away.'

We are too much addicted to our own conceits : Christ's dealing is expedient and useful, when yet it is very unsatisfactory to us. He is to be judge of what is good for us, his going or tarrying, and not we ourselves. We are short-sighted creatures, distempered with passions ; our requests many times are but ravings, we ask of God we know not what, as the two brethren, Mat. xx. 22, we pray ourselves into a mischief and a snare, and it were the greatest misery if God would carve out our condition according to our own fancies and desires.

2. That good is to be determined with respect to the chief good and true happiness. Now what is our chief happiness, but the enjoyment of God ? Our happiness doth not consist in outward comforts, riches, health, honour, civil liberty ; or comfortable relations, as husband, wife, children ; but our relation to and acceptance with God. Other things are but additional appendages to our happiness : Mat. vi. 33, προστεθήσεται, ' they shall be added to you.' Therefore poverty is good, afflictions are good ; they take nothing from our essential, solid happiness, rather help us in the enjoyment of it, as it increaseth grace and holiness, and so we enjoy God more. Surely that is good that sets us nearer to God, and that evil that separateth us from him. Therefore sin is evil because it makes an estrangement between us and God : Isa. lix. 2, ' Your iniquities have separated between you and your God, and your sins have hid his face from you.' But affliction is good, because many times it makes us the more earnestly to seek after him : Hosea v. 16, ' In their affliction they will seek me early.' Therefore every condition is good or evil, as it sets us farther off or draweth us nearer to God ; that is good that tendeth to make us better, more like unto God, capable of communion with him, and conduceth to our everlasting happiness. So it is good that man ' bear the yoke from his youth,' that he be trained up under the cross, in a constant obedience to God, and subjection to him, and so be fitted to entertain communion with him. If afflictions conduce to this end they are good, for then they help us to enjoy the chief good.

3. That good is not always the good of the flesh, or the good of outward prosperity ; and, therefore, certainly the good of our condition is not to be determined by the interest of the flesh, but the welfare of our souls. If God should bestow upon us so much of the good of the outward and animal life as we desire, we could not be said to be in a good condition : if he should deny us good spiritual, we should lose the one half of the blessings of the covenant by doting upon and falling in love with the rest. The flesh is importunate to be pleased, but God will not serve our carnal appetites. We are more concerned as a soul than as a body : Heb. xii. 10, ' He verily chasteneth us for our profit, that we might be partakers of his holiness.' Certain it is God will chasten us for our profit. What do we call profit ? the good things of this world, the great mammon which so many worship ? If we call it so, God will not ; he meaneth to impart some spiritual and divine benefit, which is a participation of his own holiness. And truly the people of God, if they be in their right temper, value themselves, not by their outward enjoyments, but by their inward improvement of graces : 2 Cor. iv. 16, ' For this cause we faint not ; but though our outward man perish, yet the inward man is renewed day by day.' A discern-

ing Christian puts more value upon holiness wrought by affliction than upon all his comforts ; so that though affliction be evil in itself, it is good as sanctified.

4. A particular good must give way to a general good, and our personal benefit to the advancement of Christ's kingdom and the glory of God. The advancement of Christ's kingdom, or the good of the church, must be preferred before our personal benefit or contentment. Paul could want the glory of heaven for a while, if his continuance in the flesh were needful for the saints : Phil. i. 24, ' To abide in the flesh is more needful for you.' We must not so desire good to ourselves as to hinder the good of others. All elements will act contrary to their particular nature, for the conservation of the universe, so for the glory of God. That may be good for the glory of God which is not good for our personal contentment and ease. Now the glory of God is our greatest interest ; if it be for the glory of God that I should be in pain, bereft of my comfort, my sanctified subjection to the will of God must say it is good : John xii. 27, 28. Here you must have the innocent inclination of Christ's human nature, ' Father, save me from this hour ;' and the overruling sense of his duty, or the obligation of his office, ' but for this cause came I to this hour.' We are often tossed between inclination of nature and conscience of duty ; but in a gracious heart the sense of our duty and the desire of glorifying God should prevail above the desire of our own comforts, ease, safety, and welfare. Nature would be rid of trouble, but grace submits all our interests to God's honour, which should be dearer to us than anything else.

5. This good is not to be determined by the judgment of sense, but by the judgment of faith ; not by present feeling, but future profit. That which is not good may be a means to good. Affliction for the present is not pleasant to natural sense ; nor for the present is the fruit evident to spiritual sense ; but it is good, because in the issue it turneth to good : Rom. viii. 28, ' All things work together for good to them that love God,' &c. While God is striking, we feel the grief and the cross is tedious ; but when we see the end, we acknowledge it is good to be afflicted : Heb. xii. 11, ' No affliction for the present seems joyous, but grievous ; nevertheless afterwards it yields the peaceable fruits of righteousness to them that are exercised therein.' A good, present, is the cause of joy ; and an evil, present, is the cause of sorrow. But there are two *termini diminuentes*, terms of abatement, πρὸς τὸ παρὸν, and δοκεῖ, present sense, and the conceits of the sufferer. When we are but newly under the affliction, we feel the smart, but do not presently find the benefit ; but within a while, especially in the review, it is good for me. It is matter of faith under the affliction, it is matter of sense afterwards. God's physic must have time to work. That which is not good may be good ; though it be not good in its nature, it may be good in its use ; and though for the present we see it not, we shall see it. Therefore good is not to be determined by feeling, but by faith. The rod is a sore thing for the present, but the bitter root will yield sweet fruit. If we come to a person under the cross, and ask him, What ! is it good to feel the lashes of God's correcting hand ? to be kept poor, sickly, exercised with losses and reproaches, to part with friends and relations, to lose a

beloved child ? he would be apt to answer, No. But this poor creature, after he hath been exercised, and mortified, and gotten some renewed evidences of God's favour ; ask him, then, Is it good to be afflicted ? Oh yes, I had been vain, neglectful of God, wanted such an experience of the Lord's grace. Faith should determine the case when we feel it not.

Well, then, let us learn to distinguish between what is really best for us and what we judge to be best. Other diet is more wholesome for our souls than that which our sickly appetite craveth. It is best many times when we are weakest, worst when strongest : all things are good as they help on a blessed eternity : so sharp afflictions are good. That part of the world that is governed by sense will never yield to this. You cannot convince a covetous man that the loss of an estate is good ; or a worldly, rich man that poverty is good ; or an ambitious man that it is good to be despised and contemned ; or a sensual, voluptuous man that it is good to be in pains, that the body be afflicted for the good of the soul : they will never believe you. But those that measure all things by eternity, they know that poverty makes way for the true riches, and ignominy for the true glory, want for fulness of pleasures, and misery mortifies sin.

SERMON V.

While he yet spake, behold, a bright cloud overshadowed them : and behold, a voice out of the cloud, which said, This is my beloved Son, in whom I am well pleased ; hear ye him.—MAT. XVII. 5.

IN this branch of the story two things are remarkable, and there is a *behold* prefixed before either of them to excite our attention. First, they see a bright cloud, and then they hear a voice out of the cloud.

First, Of the cloud : *and while he yet spake, behold, a bright cloud overshadowed them.* It was not a dark cloud, as upon Mount Sinai, when God gave the law, but a bright one, yet not so bright and lightsome but that it was mixed with some obscurity. It was no natural and ordinary cloud, such as are commonly engendered in the air above us, but extraordinary and supernatural, created by God for this occasion. The use of it was double.

1. To convey Moses and Elias out of their sight when this conference was ended. Therefore some expound that which is said, Luke ix. 34, ' They feared as they entered into the cloud,' after this manner, the disciples feared when they saw Moses and Elias entering into the cloud—that is, involved and covered in it. It is said of Jesus Christ himself, when he ascended into heaven, Acts i. 9, ' A cloud received him out of their sight.'

2. To be a token of the extraordinary presence of God, whose voice immediately came out of the cloud, as also to veil the glory thereof, which was best done by a cloud, a thing of a middle nature between terrestrial and celestial bodies. When Solomon builded the temple the Lord showed his special presence there by filling the house with

a cloud, 1 Kings viii. 10. This way of apparition God useth to moderate the splendour of his excellent glory. We are not able to behold God as he is, and must not pry into his glory ; there is a cloud and veil upon it.

Secondly, They heard a voice: *and behold, a voice out of the cloud which said, This is my beloved Son in whom I am well pleased; hear ye him.*

1. Observe, That there was a voice distinctly and audibly heard. Though God did sensibly now manifest his presence in the mount with Christ, and did audibly speak to them, yet he did not appear in any distinct form and shape, either of man or any other living creature, but all was done by a voice out of the cloud ; so Deut. iv. 12, ' Ye heard the voice of the words, but saw no similitude,' and ver. 15, 'Take good heed to yourselves, for ye saw no similitude in the day that the Lord spake to you in Horeb, lest ye corrupt yourselves, and make to you any graven image.' The similitude of any figure, &c. The voice of God may with less danger come to us than any sight or representation of him.

2. The matter, or what this voice said: *This is my beloved Son ; hear ye him.* By this voice there is :—

[1.] A testimony given to Christ.

[2.] A command to hear him ; or,

(1.) The dignity of Christ. He is the beloved Son of God, in whom he is well pleased.

(2.) A suitable respect bespoken for him.

The words are few, but yet contain the sum of the whole gospel, and they are spoken, not by a man, nor by an angel, but by the Lord himself, and therefore they should be entertained with the more reverence. The apostle Peter, who was one of the parties present, could never forget this testimony of the Father concerning his Son Jesus Christ: 2 Pet. i. 17, ' He received from the Father honour and glory, when there came such a voice to him from the excellent glory, This is my beloved Son, in whom I am well pleased ;' and besides, what Christ speaketh of another voice from heaven is true of this : John xii. 30, ' This voice came not because of me, but for your sakes,' not so much to encourage him in his suffering as to our edification and instruction. All the testimonies given unto Christ from heaven tended to point him out to sinners as the true Messiah, approved and accepted of God; therefore these words should ever be in our minds, especially when we draw nigh to God in solemn duties.

I shall begin with the dignity, honour, and glory of Christ, solemnly declared from heaven. There are three things in it :—

1. The relation between him and the Father : he is a *Son.*

2. The dearness of that relation : his *beloved Son.*

3. The complacential satisfaction which he taketh in him, and the price of our redemption paid by him : *in whom I am well pleased.*

Doct. That it is the main and principal point of the gospel, and of great necessity to be known and believed to salvation, that Jesus Christ is the beloved Son of God, in whom he is well pleased.

1. I shall open this testimony given to Christ.

2. Speak of the importance and weight of it.

I. Of the testimony given to Christ.

1. Let me open the term that expresseth his filiation, that he is God's Son. Christ is the Son of God properly so called, a Son only-begotten : John iii. 16, ' God so loved the world that he gave his only-begotten Son ;' eternally begotten, Prov. viii. 22, 23, ' I was set up from everlasting, the Lord possessed me in the beginning of his way, before his works of old.' A Son co-equal with his Father, John v. 18. The Jews sought to kill him because he said God was his Father, making himself equal with God, πατέρα ἴδιον ἔλεγε τὸν Θεὸν, his own proper Father. So co-essential, of the same substance with his Father, John i. 1, ' In the beginning was the Word, and the Word was with God, and the Word was God.' Now thus is he the Son of God.

Why is it mentioned there ?—

[1.] To show the special dignity of Christ above all others. He is the Son of God : Christians are the sons of God, but in a different manner—he by nature, we by adoption. Though God have many sons by creation and adoption, yet Christ is his Son in a peculiar and proper way, by eternal generation, and communication of the same essence, ὁ υἱὸς ἀγαπητὸς, that Son, that beloved Son; so a Son as none else is ; the Son of God, properly so called.

[2.] To distinguish him from Moses and the prophets. From Moses, Heb. iii. 5, 6, ' Moses verily was faithful in all his house as a servant, but Christ as a Son over his own house, whose house we are,' &c. ; so from the rest of the prophets: Heb. i. 1, 2, ' God at sundry times, and in divers manners, spake in times past unto the fathers by the prophets, but hath in these last days spoken to us by his Son, whom he hath appointed heir of all things, by whom also he made the world.' This is the great doctor of the church ; now as to meekness above Moses, as to zeal above Elias, as to familiarity and communion he was with God and was God.

[3.] To show the old prophecies were fulfilled, which foretold the union of the two natures in his person, the predictions concerning one whose name should be Immanuel, God with us, and who should save and redeem the church, Isa. vii. 14 ; and of a child that should be ' the mighty God, the everlasting Father,' Isa. ix. 6. This the prophets foretold, that he should be God, and the Son of God : Micah v. 2, ' His going forth is from everlasting,' though born at Bethlehem ; so the bud of the Lord and the fruit of the earth, Isa. iv. 2. The man God's fellow, Zech. xiii. 7 ; and in many other places the union of the two natures is asserted.

2. He is the beloved Son.

[1.] That God loved Christ. Christ is the object of his Father's love, both as the second person and as mediator. As the second person of the Trinity—two things are wont to attract love, nearness and likeness, they are both here. Nearness, he was in the bosom of the Father: John i. 18, ' The only-begotten Son, which is in the bosom of the Father, he hath declared him.' Likeness is another loadstone of affliction:[1] Heb. i. 3, He is ' the brightness of his glory, and the express image of his person.' Such as the Father is so is Christ.

---

* Qu., ' affection ' ?—ED.

[2.] As mediator, so God loveth him on the account of his obedience: John x. 17, 'Therefore doth my Father love me, because I lay down my life for the sheep;' John iii. 35, the Father hath loved him and put all things into his hand. The Father approved Christ's undertaking for sinners, delighted in it as an excellent way of glorifying his name, and recovering poor creatures out of their lost condition; and rested satisfied, and was pleased with his death, as a sufficient ransom for poor souls. Well, then, God loved him so as to trust the souls of all mankind in his hands, and to appoint him to be the great mediator, to end all differences between him and us; and the more he doth in pursuance of his office, the more beloved he is and acceptable to God.

[3.] The testimony of his love to him as mediator; for his unspeakable rejoicing in him, as second person in the Trinity, we are not competent judges of. It is described: Prov. viii. 30, ' I was daily his delight, rejoicing always before him.' The mutual complacency which the divine persons take in one another is there set forth; God delighted in Christ, and Christ in God. But in the second love as mediator, God expressed his love to him in two things: the gift of the Spirit, and the glory of his human nature.

(1.) The gift of the Spirit: John iii. 34, ' God giveth not the Spirit in measure to him, for the Father loveth the Son, and hath put all things into his hands.' This was the great expression of his love to Christ as mediator, not to make him a visible monarch of the world, but by the gift of his Spirit to be head of the church.

(2.) The other expression of his love to him as mediator was the gift of everlasting glory: John xvii. 24, ' Father, I will that those whom thou hast given me should be where I am, and behold my glory, for thou hast loved me before the foundation of the world.' God's love to Christ, as mediator, was manifested in exalting him to glory, and this everlasting. These are the great expresses of God's love to Christ, as God incarnate, or appearing in our nature.

Why is it put here?—

[1.] To show the end for which Christ came; to represent the amiableness of God—that he is love, 1 John iv. 8, and hath love for his children. Christ is the pattern of all, for he is first beloved, and the great instance and demonstration of God's love to the world.

[2.] To intimate the redundancy of this love; it overfloweth to us, for Christ being beloved, we are beloved also: Eph. i. 6, ' He hath made us accepted in the beloved,' to the praise of his glorious grace. It is an overflowing love; he is loved, and all that have an interest in him are loved. There is a twofold love in God—the love of benevolence and complacency. The elect from all eternity are loved by God with a love of benevolence, whereby he willed good unto them, and decrees to bestow good upon them; but the love of complacency and delight is that love whereby God accepteth us, delighteth in us, when he hath made us lovely as his own children, reconciled them by the death of Christ, renewed them by the Spirit of Christ, and furnished them with all the graces which make us acceptable to him, and precious in his sight.

[3.] To show the kind and manner of the expressing of his love to

his redeemed ones. Christ prayed : John xvii. 23, 'That the world
may know that thou hast loved them as thou hast loved me.' And
ver. 26 : ' That the love wherewith thou hast loved me may be in
them,' that is, by the gift of the Spirit and everlasting glory. Though
Christ was the beloved Son, yet his state was but mean and despicable in the world ; ' he was afflicted,' ' a man of sorrows,' pursued to
the death, even a shameful, painful, accursed death ; yet all this while
he was full of the Holy Ghost, of his graces, comforts, and afterwards
received to glory ; and so will he love us. At this rate and tenor, his
love bindeth him not to give us worldly greatness, but if we have the
Spirit, and may be welcomed to heaven at the last, we have that which
is the true discovery of God's love. So he manifested his love to the
only-begotten Son, and therefore the adopted children should be contented with this love, if by the Spirit they may be enabled to continue with patience in well-doing, till they receive eternal glory and
happiness.

3. The next thing is ἐν ᾧ εὐδόκησα, ' in whom I am well pleased.'
This is to be interpreted of Christ as mediator, or God incarnate ; for
this was twice spoken—at Christ's baptism, Mat. iii. 17, and now at
his transfiguration. Both imply his mediatorship ; for his baptism
had the notion of a dedication ; he did then present himself to God as
a mediator for us, to be the servant of his decree, as we in baptism
dedicate ourselves to fulfil the precepts which belong to us, and as we
are concerned to promote his glory in the world. Christ presented himself as a mediator, that is, as a prophet to acquaint us with the way of
salvation, as a priest to pay a perfect ransom for us, as a king to give
us all things, and defend and maintain all those who submit to his
government till their glory be perfected, and they attain unto their
final estate of bliss and happiness. Now, then, God from heaven
declared himself well pleased ; and now, again, when Christ had
made some progress in the work, confirmeth it for the assurance of
the world.

This, then, must be interpreted :—

[1.] As to Christ.

[2.] As to those who have benefit by him and interest in him.

[1.] As to Christ. He was well pleased ; partly, as to the design—
the reparation of lost mankind ; partly, as to the terms by which it
should be brought about ; partly, as to the execution and management of it by Christ.

(1.) As to the design. God was well pleased that lapsed mankind
should be restored. At the first, God was pleased with his creation,
Exod. xxxi. 17. ' On the seventh day he rested, and was refreshed ;'
that is, recreated in the view of his works, as the effects of his wisdom,
power, and goodness. And Ps. civ. 31, ' The Lord shall rejoice in his
works.' The Lord saw all to be good in the beginning and working,
not to be repented of. This was God's rest and Sabbath, to take
delight in his works. When he looked on it altogether, behold it was
exceeding good ; but afterwards man, the ungrateful part of the creation, though the masterpiece of it in this visible and lower world, fell
from God his creator, and preferred the creature before him, to his
loss and ruin ; then God was so far displeased that he had reason to

wish the destruction of mankind. It is said, Gen. vi. 6, that ' it repented God that he had made man ; ' that is, he was displeased with us, estranged from us, no more contented with us than a man is in what he repenteth of. For, properly, God cannot repent ; but this is an expression to show how odious we were grown to him : Ps. xiv. 2, 3, ' The Lord looked down from heaven upon the children of men, to see if there were any that did understand, and did seek after God. They are all gone aside, they are all together become filthy : there is none that doeth good, no, not one.' Alas ! there is a lamentable appearance of mankind to God's sight, now nothing good to be found in them ; an universal defection, both in piety and humanity. But then Christ undertook the reparation of mankind, and the design was pleasing to God, that he might not lose the glory of his creation, and all flesh be utterly destroyed : Col. i. 19, 20, ' It pleased the Father that in him should all fulness dwell ; and, having made peace through the blood of his cross, by him to reconcile all things unto himself.' The restoring of fallen man to friendship with God, and all things tending to it, were highly pleasing to God, namely, that Jesus Christ, the second person in the Trinity, should become a mediator ; for that end he had a great affection and liking to this thing : εὐδόκησε, it is the same word used here, the thing is highly pleasing to God, that the breach should be made up ; that man, who had lost the image, favour, and fellowship with God, should be again restored, by renewing his heart, reconciling his person, and admitting him again into communion with God, who was so justly provoked by him. God stood in no need of our friendship, nor could any loss come to him by our hatred and enmity ; only it pleased the Father to take this way : Isa. liii. 10, for ' it pleased the Lord to bruise him ; he hath put him to grief : when thou shalt make his soul an offering for sin, he shall see his seed, he shall prolong his days, and the pleasure of the Lord shall prosper in his hand.'

(2.) He is pleased with the terms. God, who is the supreme governor of the world, and the offended party, stood upon these terms, that the honour of his governing justice should be secured, and the repentance and reformation of man carried on. Strictly these must be done, or else man must lie under his eternal displeasure ; if one be done and not the other, no reconciliation can ensue. Now that God is highly pleased with the satisfaction and compensation made to his governing justice : Heb. x. 6, 7, ' In burnt-offerings and sacrifices for sin thou hast no pleasure. Then said I, Lo, I come to do thy will, O God ; ' ver. 10, ' By the which will we are sanctified through the offering of the body of Christ once for all.' God rejected all other sacrifices, but was fully satisfied with this, as enough to expiate the sin of man. Christ delighted to give it, and God delighted to accept of it. He paid a perfect ransom for us, besides or above which he craved no more, but rested fully content in it. For the other, the renovation of man's nature, to put him into a capacity to serve and please God, for God would not admit us to privileges without change of heart and disposition : Acts v. 31, ' God exalted him to be a prince and saviour, to give repentance and remission of sins.' In short, God is so satisfied with these terms, that (1.) He seeketh no further amends for all their wrongs: Rom. iii. 25, ' Whom God hath set forth to be a propitiation through faith in his blood, to declare his righteousness for the remission of sins that are past;' (2.) No further price for what they need: 1 Pet. i. 18, 19, ' Ye are not redeemed with corruptible things, as silver and gold, but with the precious blood of Christ, as of a lamb without spot and blemish.' The repentance of a sinner is pleasing to him, there is joy in heaven : Luke xv. 7, ' Joy in the presence of the angels over one sinner that is converted.' A feast was made at the return of the prodigal : ' As I live, saith the Lord, I have no pleasure in the death of a sinner.' Our conversion is more pleasing to God than our destruction.

(3.) He is pleased with the execution and management of it by Christ. He carried himself in the office of the mediator according to what was enjoined him : John viii. 29, ' I do always the things that please him.' John v. 30, ' I can of myself do nothing ; as I hear I judge, and my judgment is just ; because I seek not my will, but the will of the Father which sent me.' And did finish all that was necessary for the redemption of the elect before he died : John xix. 30, ' When Jesus had received the vinegar, he said, It is finished : and he bowed his head, and gave up the ghost.' Evidences of this are his resurrection from the dead : Acts v. 30, 31, ' The God of our fathers raised up Jesus, whom ye slew and hanged on a tree. Him hath God exalted with his right hand to be a Prince and a Saviour, to give repentance to Israel, and remission of sins.' Heb. xiii. 20, ' The God of peace brought again the Lord Jesus from the dead, through the blood of the everlasting covenant.' As pacified in Christ, ' received into glory,' 1 Tim. iii. 16. Certainly God is well pleased, since he hath given not only a discharge, but a reward. The gift of the Spirit, for renewing the heart of man, which is the great pledge of God's being satisfied : John vii. 39, ' This he spake of the Spirit, which they that believe on him should receive, for the Holy Ghost was not yet given, because that Jesus was not yet glorified ;' a sure evidence that our ransom is paid: Acts v. 32, ' And we are his witnesses of these things, and so is the Holy Ghost, which he hath given to them that obey him.' A sacrifice of infinite value and esteem.

[2.] That he is well pleased with us who have an interest in him. In our natural estate we are all displeasing unto God. Whatever we are in the purpose of his decree, we must look upon ourselves as we are in the sentence of his law ; so ' Children of wrath,' Eph. ii. 3 : ' Enemies by our minds in evil works,' Col. i. 21 : ' Estranged from the womb,' Ps. lviii. 3 ; so that all of us were cut off from the favour of God, obnoxious to his wrath ; this is our miserable condition by nature, that we were no way pleasing to him, ' for without faith it is impossible to please God,' Heb. xi. 6. A sinner as a sinner can do nothing acceptable ; indeed, God having found a ransom, is *placabilis*, but not *placatus*, not actually reconciled to us till we are in Christ ; and he is *placandus antequam placendus*, to be appeased before he can be pleased ; he is not actually reconciled till we are in Christ.

(2.) Awakened sinners are not easily satisfied, so as to look upon themselves as pleasing unto God ; for the conscience of sin is not easily laid aside, nor is the stain soon got out. And though the grant be passed in heaven, yet we have not the sense of it in our own hearts ; for it is the blood of Christ can only do it : Heb. ix. 14, ' How much more shall the blood of Christ, who through the eternal Spirit offered himself without spot to God, purge your conscience from dead works to serve the living God ? ' The carnal offer thousands of rams, and rivers of oil, and ' the fruit of the body for the sin of their soul,' Micah vi. 6, 7. They would give anything for a sufficient sin-offering ; yea, the renewed and pardoned have not so firm a peace as to be able always to look upon themselves in a state of well-pleasing, therefore often beg that God would dissipate the clouds and cause the light of his countenance to break forth upon them : Ps. lxxx. 19, ' Turn us, O Lord God of hosts ; cause thy face to shine, and we shall be saved.' So that when there is a grant of pardon, and peace, and access to God, we have not always the sense.

(3.) Yet the ground is laid. As soon as we have an interest in Christ, God is well pleased with us ; if you consent to his mediation, and take him in his three offices, as a prophet, priest, and king. As a prophet, hear him ; the business is put out of all question, that God will love you because he loved Christ. When you depend on him as a priest, you have reconciliation and access to God : Rom. v. 1, 2, ' Therefore being justified by faith, we have peace with God through our Lord Jesus Christ : by whom also we have access by faith into the grace wherein we stand.' When you subject yourselves to him as a king, Col. i. 13, ' He hath translated us into the kingdom of his dear Son.' Christ is dear to God, and to him all the subjects of his kingdom are dear also. So that if you will be more explicit in your duty, you may be more explicit in your comforts ; if you will receive his doctrine, so as it may have authority over your hearts ; if in the anguish of your souls you will depend on the merit of his sacrifice, and give up your-selves to live in a constant obedience to his laws ; you will find him to be a dear Son indeed, one very acceptable with God, for you also will be accepted with him, for his sake.

II. Concerning the weight and importance of this truth.

1. It is propounded as the foundation upon which God will build his church : Mat. xvi. 16–18, ' And Simon Peter answered and said, Thou art Christ, the Son of the living God. And Jesus answered and said unto him, Blessed art thou, Simon Barjona, for flesh and blood hath not revealed it unto thee, but my Father which is in heaven. And I say unto thee, that thou art Peter, and upon this rock will I build my church : and the gates of hell shall not prevail against it.'

2. It is the question put to those that would enter upon Christianity : Acts viii. 37, ' If thou believest with all thy heart, thou mayest : and he answered and said, I believe that Jesus is the Son of God.' When they were serious in the profession, that was enough : 1 John v. 1, ' Whosoever believeth that Jesus is the Christ is born of God.'

3. This engaged the hearts of the disciples to tarry with him when others murmured at his doctrine. He that cleaveth to this profession carrieth himself accordingly, whatever temptations he hath to the con-trary : we believe and are sure that thou art that Christ, the Son of the living God.

4. For this end the scriptures were written : ' These things are writ-

ten, that ye might believe that Jesus is the Christ, the Son of God; and
that believing ye might have life through his name,' John xx. 31.
By obedience to his laws, dependence on his promises.

5. This is the ground of submission to Christ in all his offices, why
we should hear him as a prophet in this place (which I shall more
fully make manifest in the next sermon), why we should depend on
him as a priest, for the virtue of his oblation and intercession : ' If
God spared not his own Son, but delivered him up for us all, how
shall he not with him also freely give us all things ? ' Rom. viii. 32.
1 John iv. 10, ' Herein is love, not that we loved God, but he loved
us, and sent his Son to be the propitiation for our sins.' 1 John ii. 1,
' If any man sin, we have an advocate with the Father, Jesus Christ
the righteous.' The blood of Christ is of high esteem and infinite
value, both as to merit and satisfaction, to purchase all manner of
blessings for us, and to satisfy God's provoked justice for our sins.
And if the Father be so well pleased with him, what can he not obtain
at his hands ? which is an encouragement in our prayers and supplications. So for our improvement of his kingly office, which respects
duties and privileges; our duty with respect to the kingly office is
subjection: Ps. ii. 12, ' Kiss the Son lest he be angry, and you perish
in the midway.' Because Christ Jesus is the Son of God, he should
be submitted unto and embraced with the heartiest love and subjection ; for to kiss, is a sign of religious adoration, Hosea xiii. 2 ; as
they kissed the calves, and offer homage and hearty subjection ; as
Samuel kissed Saul, because God had anointed him to be king over
his people, 1 Sam. x. 1. So for privileges ; he is God co-equal, co-
eternal with his Father, able to protect all those that apply themselves
to him, till he bring them to eternal glory and happiness; and, therefore, it is said, 1 John v. 5, ' Who is he that overcometh the world,
but he that believeth that Jesus is the Son of God ? ' That is the
fortifying truth ; this both cautioneth us against all the delights and
snares, and supports us against all the terrors and fears of the world.
If we have the Son of God for our prophet, priest, and king, we ought
to carry ourselves with greater reverence, trust, and subjection.

Use 1. Believe it, lay up this truth in your hearts by a firm and
sound belief. There are in faith three things—assent, acceptance, dependence. The matter in hand calleth for all these.

[1.] A firm assent ; for here we have the testimony of God concerning his Son. The apostle tells us, that ' he that believeth not hath
made God a liar,' because he believeth not the testimony of God concerning his Son,' 1 John v. 10. The great testimony is this, that we
have in hand that Jesus is his beloved Son, with whom he is well
pleased ; that he will give pardon and life to all that hearken to him,
embrace his person, receive his doctrine, believe his promises, fear his
threats, obey his precepts, the strictest of them. Oh ! labour to work
it into your hearts that indeed it is so. In matters of fact we receive
the testimony of men, two or three credible men ; why not in matters
of faith ?—the testimony of God evidenced to us by this solemn action,
an account of which we have from ear-witnesses and eye-witnesses,
who were men that hazarded their all for the delivery of this truth,
and yet referred us to the surer word of prophecy, 1 Pet. i. 19. He

was owned as a Son: Ps. ii. 7, ' Thou art my Son: this day have I begotten thee.' As a beloved Son, in whom God is well pleased : Isa. xlii. 1, ' Behold my servant whom I uphold, my elect in whom my soul delighteth.' If you be not wanting to yourselves, you may have this witness in your hearts : 1 John v. 10, ' He that believeth on the Son of God hath the witness in himself.' Oh ! let us not give the flat lie to God. Rouse up this languid faith. Is this true, or is it a cunningly devised fable ?

[2.] Faith is an acceptance of Christ, or an entering into a covenant with God by him. You must have the Son : 1 John v. 12, ' He that hath the Son hath life.' John i. 12, ' As many as received him, to them gave he power to become the sons of God, even to them which believe on his name.' Receiving, respects God's offer. God gives Christ, and we receive what God giveth,—to what end ? Why, he giveth him as king, priest, and prophet, to dwell in our hearts by faith, to rule us and guide us by his word and Spirit, and maintain God's interest in us against the devil, the world, and the flesh, till we come to everlasting glory.

[3.] Dependence. He is able to save to the uttermost all that come to God by him ; therefore on him alone should we depend for all things necessary to salvation. Two things persuade this dependence :—

(1.) That nothing can be done without Christ : Acts iv. 12, ' Neither is there salvation in any other : for there is none other name under heaven given among men whereby we must be saved.' Nothing can be done without Christ that may be effectual to our recovery, either for the paying of our ransom, or for the changing of our hearts. Alas ! what could we do to please God, or profit our own souls ? The work would cease for ever if it should lie upon our hands.

(2.) That he can do what he pleaseth for the good of his redeemed ones : John xvii. 2, ' As thou hast given power over all flesh, that he should give eternal life to as many as thou hast given him.' All that Christ did for our salvation did highly content and please the Father ; he is satisfied with him ; he can make us lovely in his sight : Eph. i. 6, ' To the praise of the glory of his grace, wherein he hath made us accepted in the beloved.' And will now joy in his people, Isa. lxv. 19, and rest in his love, Zeph. iii. 17. Well, then, let us believe ; faith is a ratifying God's testimony concerning his Son ; we believe what God hath said, that Christ is his Son ; we receive him as he is freely offered, and subscribe to this declaration. The Father saith from heaven, ' This is my beloved Son, in whom I am well pleased ; hear him.' So penitent believers must answer back again, This is our beloved Redeemer, in whom we are well pleased ; let the Father hear him. He hath somewhat to say to the Father as well as to us ; his doctrine concerneth us, but his intercession is made to God.

Use 2. Entertain it with thankfulness. That such a remedy should be provided for us argueth the unspeakable love of God : 1 John iv. 9, ' In this was manifested the love of God to us, because that God sent his only-begotten Son into the world, that we might live by him.' That God should bestow his Son upon us to procure our salvation. God tried Abraham's love in sacrificing his son, but manifested his love to us in sending his own Son ; ' He spared him not, but delivered

him up for us all.' Now that such a remedy and ransom is found out
for us, it should leave an impression of God's love on our hearts, that
we may love him again who first loved us, 1 John iv. 19. Think
nothing too dear for God, who thought no rate too dear to purchase
our life and peace. As our salvation was precious to him, let his
glory be dear to us; only let me tell you, this love must not be confined to a bare act of our reason, but you must pray to God to shed
abroad this love in your hearts by the Holy Spirit, Rom. v. 5, that so
you may study to love and please God, prize Christ and his precious
benefits above all things in the world, and live to him who died for
you, that you may feel the constraining efficacy and force of love.

SERMON VI.

This is my beloved Son, in whom I am well-pleased; hear ye him.—
MAT. XVII. 5.

I. THE design and intent of this scripture is to set forth the Lord
Jesus as the great mediator, as appeareth—

1. From the occasions upon which this voice came from heaven.
At his baptism, which was Christ's dedication of himself to the work
of a redeemer and saviour; and now at his transfiguration, to distinguish him from Moses and the other prophets, and publicly to
instal him in the mediatory office.

2. The matter of the words show his fitness for this office, for here
you have:—

[1.] His dignity: not a servant, but a Son: Heb. iii. 5, 6, 'Moses
verily was faithful in all his house, as a servant, but Christ as a Son
over his own house.' Now the old prophecies foretold the union of
the two natures in his person, and necessary it was that our mediator
should be God-man. There is a congruity between his person and
office, one fit to be familiar with man, and naturally interested in his
concerns, and yet so high and near the Father as may put a sufficient
value upon his actions, and so meet to mediate with God for us.

[2.] The dearness between God and him: 'My beloved Son.'
Christ is the object of his Father's love, both as the second person in
the Trinity and mediator. The one is the ground of the other, for
because he loved him he intrusted him with souls: John iii. 35,
'The Father hath loved him, and put all things into his hands'—the
elect and all things else, all power that conduceth to their salvation.
Afterwards loved him as mediator: John x. 17, 'Therefore doth my
Father love me, because I lay down my life, that I might take it again.'
Now such a beloved Son is fittest to mediate for us, and to come
upon a design of love, to demonstrate God's great love to wretched
sinners, and to be a pledge of that love which God will bestow upon
us who are altogether so unworthy of it.

[3.] His acceptableness to God, who is well pleased with the design,
the terms, the management of it.

II. This work of mediator Christ executeth by three offices, of king, priest, prophet. For he is head and lord of the renewed state; a priest to offer a sacrifice for sin, which, having once offered, he for ever represents in heaven ; he was also to be teacher of mankind, to acquaint us with the way of salvation. These offices are often alluded unto in scripture: Rev. i. 5, 'The faithful witness, the first-begotten from the dead, the prince of the kings of the earth ;' so Heb. i. 2, 3, 'God hath spoken to us by his Son, he having by himself purged our sins, sat down on the right hand of the majesty on high.' The effect of them is more briefly described : John xiv. 6, 'I am the way, the truth, and the life.' The way was opened by his passion, and is kept open by his intercession. Truth as a prophet. Life we have from him, as prince of life, or head of the renewed estate. So the effects : 1 Cor. i. 30, ' But of him are ye in Christ Jesus, who of God is made unto us wisdom and righteousness, sanctification and redemption.' Wisdom as a prophet to cure our ignorance and folly ; righteousness and sanctification as a priest ; redemption as the king and captain of our salvation. The same benefits which he purchaseth as a king, he bestoweth as a priest, revealeth as a prophet. These three offices were typed out by the first-born, who were heads of families, and also prophets and priests.

That though all the three offices be employed, yet the prophetical office is more explicitly mentioned, partly as suiting with the present occasion, which is to demonstrate that Christ hath sufficient authority to repeal the law of Moses, which the prophets were to explain, confirm, and maintain till his coming. But now Moses and Elias appear in person to certify their consent, and God his approbation, from heaven, to that new law of grace which Christ should set up ; partly because it is not necessary that in every place all the offices should be mentioned; sometimes but one, as where Christ is called either king, priest, or prophet ; sometimes two together, Heb. iii. 1, prophetical, sacerdotal : ' Consider the apostle and high priest of our profession, Christ Jesus ;' sometimes his prophetical and kingly, Isa. lv. 4, ' Behold I have given him for a witness to the people, and for a leader and commander to the people:' partly because if Christ be received in this one office he will be received in all the rest ; for as a prophet he hath revealed that doctrine which establisheth his kingly and priestly office, for he hath revealed all things necessary to salvation, and therefore his own sacrifice and regal power. Lastly, some think all expressly mentioned here. Thus Christ is God's beloved Son, and therefore the heir of all things, and lord and king, in whom he is well pleased—that is, pacified and satisfied with his offering as a priest, or appeased by his complete sacrifice. Hear him as the great prophet and doctor of the Church.

This premised, I come now to observe :—

Doct. That Christ is appointed by God the Father to be the great prophet and teacher, whose voice alone must be heard in the Church.

I. That Christ is the great prophet and teacher of the Church appeareth :—

1. By the titles given to him. He is compared with Moses the

great lawgiver among the Jews : 'The Lord thy God will raise up unto thee a prophet from the midst of you like unto me, unto him shall ye hearken,' Deut. xviii. 15. He was to be like a Moses, but greater than Moses. A lawgiver as he, a man as he, one that saw God face to face as he, a mediator as he ; but far other in all respects —a better law, a more glorious person, a more blessed mediator, working greater miracles than ever did Moses. So he is called our rabbi or master : Mark xxiii. 8, 'One is your master, even Christ, and ye are brethren.' The supreme authority, the original right is in Christ. We are not leaders and teachers, but fellow disciples ; so Heb. iii. 1, 'Consider the apostle and high priest of our profession, Jesus Christ.' Again, he is called the angel or messenger of the covenant, Mal. iii. 1. Christ with a great condescension took upon him the office of his Father's ambassador to the church, to promote the covenant of recon-ciliation between God and man, and make offers of it in preaching the gospel ; and he it is that doth by his Spirit persuade the elect, and doth make his covenant sure to them. Once more, he is called 'Amen, the faithful and true witness,' Rev. iii. 14. There can be no prejudice against his testimony ; he can never deceive nor be deceived ; it is so, it will be so, as he hath said, *Amen* is his name.

2. By the properties of his office : he hath three things to qualify him for this high office :—

[1.] Absolute supreme authority : and therefore we must hear him and hearken to him. This is usually made the ground and reason of the gospel invitation, to invite sinners to submit themselves to seek after God in this way : as Mat. xi. 27, 28, 'All things are delivered unto me of my Father : and no man knoweth the Son, but the Father ; neither knoweth any man the Father, save the Son, and he to whomsoever the Son will reveal him. Come unto me, all ye that are weary and heavy laden,' &c. There is no true knowledge of God but by Christ and the gospel revelation which he hath established, therefore here we must seek rest for our souls : so John iii. 35, 36, 'The Father loveth the Son, and hath put all things into his hands. He that believeth on the Son hath everlasting life : and he that believeth not the Son hath not seen life, but the wrath of God abideth on him.' First, his mediatorial authority is acknowledged ; and then faith and obedience to the gospel is called for, for to the sentence of the Son of God we must stand or fall. So when Christ instituted and sent abroad his messengers to invite the world to the obedience of the gospel : Mat. xxviii. 18–20, ' All power is given to me both in heaven and in earth. Go ye, therefore, and teach all nations, baptizing them in the name of the Father, and of the Son, and of the Holy Ghost ; teaching them to observe all things whatsoever I have commanded you.' He hath absolute and supreme authority to gather his church, to appoint ministers and ordinances, to bestow the Spirit, to open and close heaven and hell as he pleaseth, to dispose of all affairs in the world for the furtherance of the gospel, and to enjoin the whole world obedience to his commands, and to embrace his doctrine.

[2.] All manner of sufficiency and power of God to execute this office: John iii. 34, ' For he whom God hath sent speaketh the words of God, for God giveth not the Spirit by measure to him.' The former prophets had the Spirit in a limited measure bestowed on them by God, for such particular purposes as best pleased him; therefore all their prophecies begin, Thus saith the Lord, as having for every particular message and errand new revelation. But on Christ the Spirit descended once for all, and commanded the belief of all and obedience to all that he should say. Therefore it is said, Col. ii. 3, 'In him are all the treasures of wisdom and knowledge.' He is ignorant of none of those things which are to be known and practised in order to our eternal salvation; they are deposited with him to be dispensed to us.

[3.] There is in him a powerful efficacy. As he hath absolute authority to teach in his own name, and fulness of sufficiency to make known the mind of God to us; so he hath power to make his doctrine effectual. As when he dealt with his disciples, after he had opened the scriptures, he 'opened their understandings,' Luke xxiv. 25; so he 'opened the heart of Lydia,' Acts xvi. 14. He can teach so as to draw, John vi. 44, 45. He can excite the drowsy mind, change and turn the rebellious will, cure the distempered affections, make us to be what he persuadeth us to be. There is no such teacher as Christ, who doth not only give us our lesson, but an heart to learn; therefore to him we must submit, hear nothing against him, but all from him.

II. About hearing him, that must be explained also.

First, What it is to hear; it being our great duty, and the respect bespoken for him. In the hearing of words there are three things considerable—the sound that cometh to the ear, the understanding of the sense and meaning, and the assent or consent of the mind. Of the first the beasts are capable, for they have ears to hear the sound of words uttered. The second is common to all men, for they can sense such intelligible words as they hear. The third belongeth to disciples, who are swayed by their Master's authority. So that, *Hear him*, is not to hear as beasts, nor barely to hear as men, but to hear as disciples; to believe him, to obey him; to believe his doctrines and promises, and to obey his precepts. For his authority is absolute, and what he doth say, doth warrant our faith, and command our practice and obedience. I gather this partly from the word 'hear,' which not only signifies attention and belief, but obedience: as 1 Sam. xv. 22, 'To obey is better than sacrifice, and to hearken than the fat of rams,' where to *obey* and *hearken* are put as words of the same import and signification. Partly from the matter of Christ's revelation; he hath revealed not only doctrines to inform the mind, but precepts to reform the heart and practice. If we assent to the doctrine, but do not obey the precepts, we do not hear him. Therefore to hear him is to yield obedience to what he shall teach you; and when Christ cometh to take an account of the entertainment of the gospel, 'he shall come in flaming fire, taking vengeance on them that know not God, and that obey not the gospel of our Lord Jesus Christ.' Partly too from the intimate connexion there is between his prophetical and regal office. Christ is so a prophet, that he is also a sovereign; and doth not only give us counsel and direction, but a law, which we are to observe under the highest penalties. If the gospel were an arbitrary direction, which we might observe or not observe, without any great danger to ourselves, surely it were folly to despise good counsel; but it hath the force of a new law from the great king and lawgiver of the world, therefore it must not only be believed but obeyed: Heb. v. 8, He that is the chief prophet of the church is also the king of saints. Partly also from the near connexion that is between faith and obedience. The matter which we believe is of a practical concernment, and doth not require only a simple faith, or bare belief, which were enough in points merely speculative, but a ready obedience. It is said, Rom. xvi. 26, ' The mysteries of the gospel are made manifest to all nations for the obedience of faith.' They are not matters of speculation and talk, but practice; and blessedness is pronounced on such as hear them and keep them: Luke xi. 28, ' Blessed are they that hear the word of God and keep it.' Many hear and talk, hear and stuff their minds with notions, but they do not frame themselves to the practice of what they hear. Many question not Christ's authority, but yet they do not regard his doctrine. Now, faith doth not only silence our doubts, but quicken our affections and enliven our practice.

Secondly, How can we now hear Christ, since he is removed into the heaven of heavens, and doth not speak to us in person?

Ans. Surely it doth not only concern the believers of that age, who conversed with Christ in the days of his flesh, but it is the general duty of all Christians to hear Christ; for during the whole gospel dispensation, God speaketh to us by his Son, Heb. i. 2: the revelation is settled, and not delivered by parcels, as it was to the ordinary prophets. Now we hear Christ in the scriptures: Heb. ii. 3, 4, ' How shall we escape if we neglect so great salvation? which was first spoken by the Lord, and afterwards confirmed to us by them that heard him.' He began to speak and to declare the gospel both before and after his resurrection; and they that heard him were especially the apostles, who, being induced by the Holy Ghost, declared it first to the Jews, and then to the Gentiles, to whom it was continued by divers signs and wonders, as to the apostles, and to extraordinary messengers. Christ saith, Luke x. 16, ' He that heareth you heareth me; and he that despiseth you despiseth me; and he that despiseth me despiseth him that sent me.' The despising of the messenger is the despising him that sendeth the message. A man's apostle is himself, is a Jewish proverb. As to ordinary ministers he saith, ' Lo, I am with you to the end of the world,' Mat. xxviii. 20; they are taken into part of the apostolical commission and blessings; they preach in Christ's name, and we, as in his stead, pray you to be reconciled, 2 Cor. v. 20; so that it is his voice and his message; he affordeth his presence and assistance unto the world's end. If you receive it with faith and obedience, you are in a course and way which will bring you to everlasting blessedness; but if you stand out obstinately against his message, you are in the way to everlasting misery, for refusing God's methods for your redemption.

Thirdly, The properties of this hearing or submission to our great prophet.

1. There must be a resolute consent or resignation of ourselves to his teaching and instruction. All particular duties are included in the general. First, we own Christ in his offices, before we perform

the duties which each of those offices calleth for at our hands and from us—before we depend on him as a priest, or obey him as a king. As we receive him with thankfulness and love as our dearest Saviour, and with reverence and a consent of subjection as a sovereign lord, so also with a consent of resolution to follow his directions as our prophet and teacher, being convinced that he is sent from God to show us the way of life and happiness: John vi. 63, 'Lord, to whom shall we go? thou hast the words of eternal life.' His doctrine showeth that there is such a thing, how it was purchased, which way it may be had, by God's offer, and the terms prescribed. Before we take any particular direction from Christ about this or that duty, we must first consent in the general that he shall be our teacher and prophet. A particular consent to Christ in this relation is as necessary as to any of the rest.

2. This resignation of our souls to Christ as a teacher, as it must be resolute, so it must be unbounded and without reserves. We must submit absolutely to all that he propoundeth, though some mysteries be above our reason, some precepts against the interest and inclination of the flesh, some promises seem to be against hope, or contrary to natural probabilities. There are some mysteries in the Christian religion, though not against reason, yet above natural reason. Now we must believe them upon Christ's word, *captivantes omnem intellectum in obsequium Christi*: 2 Cor. x. 5, 'Bringing into captivity every thought into the obedience of Christ.' All our disputings and reasonings against the Christian doctrine must be captivated by a submission to the authority of our teacher and prophet. A disciple is to be a learner, not a caviller; and some principles are not to be chewed, but swallowed as pills on the credit of the physician, when it appeareth on other grounds that Christ is the great teacher sent from God. And as there are mysteries above our reason, so there be duties against the interest and inclination of the flesh. Many of Christ's precepts are displeasing to corrupt nature—to deny ourselves, to take up the cross, to mortify our appetites and passions, to cut off right hands, and to pluck out right eyes; that none shall be saved that are not regenerate and holy; that non-condemnation is the privilege of those that walk not after the flesh but after the Spirit; that if we live after the flesh we shall die; that we must not seek great things for ourselves; that we must hate father and mother, and our own life, if we will be Christ's disciples. Flesh and blood can hardly down with these things—that there shall be such an exact day of account, such eternal torments in the other world; yet if this be revealed by our great prophet, as reason must not be heard against Christ, so the flesh must not be heard against Christ, nor the world heard against Christ; so if some of our hopes exceed the probability of natural causes: Rom. iv. 18, he 'against hope believed in hope,' as the resurrection of the body. We must believe and obey him in what he offereth and commandeth, notwithstanding the contradiction of our carnal minds and hearts, in what is hard to be believed and practised, as well as in what is easy.

3. It must be speedy as to the great solemn acts of submission. Do not delay to hear him: Heb. iii. 7, 'To-day, if you will hear his voice, harden not your hearts.' Christ must not be put off with dilatory shifts;

if we refuse to hear to-day, Christ may refuse to speak to-morrow. The Father hath his time of waiting, the Son of his gospel-offers, the Spirit of his earnest motions: it is dangerous to slip our day ; therefore, if you will hear him, hear him now ! Hear him betimes ; the season falleth under the precept as well as the duty : ' Now, while it is called to-day.'

4. Your consent to hear him must be real, practical, and obedien-tial, verified in the whole tenor and course of your lives and actions ; for Christ will not be flattered with empty titles. ' Why call ye me lord and master, and do not the things which I say ?' Luke vi. 46. If you pretend to hear his word, you must do it also, for you do not hear to please your minds with knowing, but that you may make it your seri-ous care and business to serve, love, and please God. Many study Christianity to form their opinions rather than reform their hearts and practice. The great use of knowledge and faith is to behold the love of God in the face of Jesus Christ, that our own love may be quickened and increased to him again. If it serve only to regulate opinions, it is but dead speculation, not a living faith. A naked be-lief is but the sight of a feast,—it is the gracious soul doth eat and digest it ; when our faith is turned into love and obedience, that is the true faith.

III. The reasons why this prophet must be heard.

1. Consider whose voice it is who speaketh—the only beloved Son of God, or God himself—and surely when he speaketh he must be heard : Heb. xii. 25, ' See that ye refuse not him that speaketh. For if they escaped not who refused him that spake from earth, much more shall not we escape, if we turn away from him that speaketh from heaven.' It is Christ doth speak, and God by him, commanding us to repent and believe the gospel ; now to refuse him is a high contempt. God, when he gave the law, he spake on earth ; but when he spake by Christ, he spake from heaven ; for Christ came from heaven to acquaint us with the mind of God, and having done it, is returned to heaven again, from whence he sent down his Spirit on the apostles, who revealed his gospel to the world. This was a mystery hidden in the bosom of God, and brought to us thence by his only-begotten Son. Surely, with all humble submission, we should attend unto and obey his word : Ps. ciii. 20, ' Bless the Lord, ye his angels, that excel in strength, that do his commandments, hearkening to the voice of his word.'

2. The matter which he speaketh and we hear—the doctrine of the gospel ; it is the most sweet, excellent, and comfortable doctrine that can be heard, or understood by the heart of man : Prov. viii. 6, ' Hear,' saith Wisdom, ' for I will speak of excellent things : and the opening of my lips shall be of right things.' This is the brightest light that ever shone from heaven, the profoundest wisdom, the greatest love and mercy that ever was or can be shown to sinful wretches, of the highest concernment to man ; because his everlasting state lieth upon it, a state of everlasting woe or weal.

Three things I shall take notice of :—

[1.] The way of reconciliation with God manifested and discovered out of his intimate love to us. Man had fallen from the love of God to the creature, and was conscious to himself of having displeased his

Maker, and so lay under the fears of his vindictive justice. Now God by Christ declareth his love to the offender in the fullest and most astonishing way, reconciling himself to him, and showeth his readiness to forgive and save him: 1 Tim. i. 15, ' This is a faithful saying, and worthy of all acceptation, that Jesus Christ came into the world to save sinners: of whom I am chief ;' and, 2 Cor. v. 19, ' God was in Christ reconciling the world to himself.' Oh, what should be more welcome to the creature than this news of this pardoning covenant founded in the blood of Christ !

[2.] Our duty exactly stated, with convenient motives to enforce it. Not only the comfort of man is provided for, but also our subjection to God, and that upon the freest and most comfortable terms, that we should serve him in love, and glorify and please him, that we may be happy in his love to us ; for the sum of religion is to love him, and keep his commandments : John xiv. 21, 23, ' He that keepeth my commandments, he it is that loveth me : and if any man love me, he will keep my words.' To love him is our work, and to be beloved of him is our happiness ; and ver. 24 : ' He that loveth me not keepeth not my sayings : and the word which you hear is not mine, but the Father's which sent me.' The gospel is the very word of God, both the Father's and the Son's ; it is an act of loving, serving, and pleasing God ; for this is the word Christ preached, that we love God, and Christ loveth us again.

[3.] A prospect of eternal happiness : 2 Tim. i. 10, ' He hath brought life and immortality to light through the gospel.' This is news, but darkly revealed before, and without this man knew not how to satisfy all his capacities and desires, but was like Leviathan in a little pool. Nay, we have not only a prospect of it, but the offer of it as a reward appointed, if we will be sincere in our faith, love, and obedience : 1 John ii. 25, ' This is the promise that he hath promised us, even eternal life.' Everlasting joy and blessedness is propounded to us ; Oh, then, hear him, if this be that he speaketh of.

3. The danger of not hearing this prophet.

[1.] For the present : to continue to slight and contemn the gospel is the mark that you are in a carnal, perishing condition : 2 Cor. iv. 3, ' If our gospel is hid, it is hid to them that are lost ;' John x. 3, ' My sheep hear my voice ;' and ver. 16, ' Other sheep are there which are not of this fold, and they shall hear my voice.' Christ's sheep, whether Jew or Gentile, they have all the same character, they all hear his voice ; and ver. 27, ' My sheep hear my voice, and I know them, and they follow me.' They distinguish his voice, own his voice, obey his voice. So John viii. 47, ' Whosoever is of God heareth God's words ; ye therefore hear them not, because ye are not of God ;' so that you lose all this comfort if ye do not hear the voice of Christ and his faithful servants.

[2.] For the future : Deut. xviii. 19, ' Whosoever will not hearken to the words which that prophet shall speak in my name, I will require it of him ;' that is, he must look to answer it another day. Peter rendereth it : Acts iii. 23, ' Whosoever will not hearken to that prophet shall be destroyed among the people.' It is not a bodily punishment, but eternal torment : John iii. 36, ' The wrath of God abideth on

him;' Mark xvi. 16, 'He that believeth not shall be damned.' Thus
you see how dangerous it is to refuse this prophet.

Use 1. Of conviction to the carnal Christian for not submitting to
Christ's authority.   All Christians do it in pretence, but few that
do it in reality.   Doth his word come to you not only in word but in
power?

[1.] Do you seriously come to him that you may have pardon and
life.   When Christ had proved that he was the Son of God, the great
prophet of the church, by the testimony of John, the testimony of his
works, the testimony of his Father, and the testimony of the scriptures: John v. 40, 'And ye will not come unto me that ye may have
life;'—though John, his works, the Father, the scriptures, will prove
him to be what he was, the Messias, the Saviour and Redeemer of the
world, yet they would not come to him, nor believe, but wilfully rejected him, and their own blessedness.   What the Jews did wilfully,
carnal Christians do lazily; they prize his name and slight his office,
do not come to him to be taught, sanctified, and drawn to God.

[2.] Do you respect the word of the gospel, entertain it with reverence and delight, as the voice of the great prophet?   Do you meditate on it, digest it as the seed of the new life, as the rule of your
actions, as the charter of your hopes?   A good man is described to be
one that ' delighteth in the law of the Lord, and meditateth therein
day and night,' Ps. i. 2; and, again, Ps. cxix. 97, 'Oh, how I love
thy law! it is my meditation all the day long.'   But, alas! few are
of this temper: Hosea viii. 12, 'I have written to them the great
things of thy law, but they were counted as a strange thing, they contemned the word of God,' as if its directions were of little importance, or did not concern them.   Most men live like strangers to the
word of God, little conversant in it, as there were no great hazard in
breaking it.

[3.] Do you mingle it with faith in the hearing, that it may profit
you, Heb. iv. 2, and feel the power of it for your good?   But rather you
shun it—run from it: John iii. 20, ' They that do evil hate the light,
and will not come to the light, lest their deeds should be reproved.'
The word is a torment rather than a comfort to you; you are afraid it
will be found too true.

[4.] Do you receive it as the word of God?   1 Thes. ii. 13.   It may
be you do not contradict the divine authority in the scriptures, but do
you soundly believe them, and know the certainty of those things
wherein you are instructed?   Luke i. 4.   Have you done anything to
prove the supreme truth that Jesus is a teacher sent from God?   Most
men's faith is so weak and slight, because it is taken hand-over-head,
there is no deepness of earth, Mark xiii. 6.   You have some light
sense of religion, but slight impressions are soon defaced, and truths
easily taken up are as soon quitted; the more we search into the grounds
of things the more we believe, Acts xvii. 11.   The Bereans ' searched
the scriptures whether those things were so or no.'

[5.] Doth it come to you as the Mediator's word?—' not in word only
but in power,' 1 Thes. i. 5.   There is a convincing power in the
word: Acts ii. 37, ' When they heard these things, they were pricked
in the heart, and said to Peter and the rest of the apostles, Men and

brethren, what shall we do ? ' Many have not felt this power, but they fear it: John iii. 20, ' Every one that doeth evil hateth the light, neither cometh to the light, lest his deeds should be reproved.' A converting power when it becometh the seed of a new life : 1 Pet. i. 23, ' Being born again, not of corruptible seed, but of incorruptible, by the word of God, which liveth and abideth for ever.' A comforting power, giving the heirs of promise strong consolation, Heb. vi. 18. Do you find anything of this in your hearts ? is it engrafted in your souls ? James i. 21, ' Receive with meekness the engrafted word, which is able to save your souls.'

[6.] Do you hear him universally ? It is said of the great prophet, Acts iii. 22, ' Him shall ye hear in all things that he shall say unto you.' Many will hear him in the offers of pardon, but not in the pre-cepts of duty : you must take his whole covenant, the promises for your happiness, the duty for your work.

[7.] Do you hear him so as to prefer God and Christ and the life to come above all the sensual pleasures and vain delights and worldly happiness which you enjoy here ? Religion is obstructed, not soundly received, if your hearts be not taken off from these things : Luke viii. 14, ' That which fell among thorns are they, which, when they have heard, go forth, and are choked with cares and riches and pleasures of this life, and bring no fruit to perfection.' He is not a scholar of Christ who is not more devoted to the love and obedience of God than any sensual satisfaction here below—unless you can renounce the devil, the world, and the flesh, and give up yourselves to Christ, to be taught, sanctified, and saved, and brought home to God, to enjoy him in ever-lasting glory, and taught how to deny ungodliness and worldly lusts, Titus ii. 12.

Use 2. Advice to weak Christians :—

[1.] To excite themselves to obedience by this *hear him*, when dead and lifeless. Many times the heart is dull and needeth quickening. Conscience groweth sleepy and needeth awakening—you are too bold in sinning, cold and careless in spiritual and heavenly things. Now the first means to quicken us is Christ's divine authority : 2 Pet. i. 16, ' For we have not followed cunningly-devised fables, when we made known unto you the power and coming of our Lord Jesus Christ, but were eye-witnesses of his majesty, when there came such a voice to him from the excellent glory, This is my beloved Son, in whom I am well pleased.' When you are customary in prayer and hearing,—It is Christ's will ; I must do it as I will answer it to him another day.

[2.] When you do renounce some beloved lust or pleasing sin, urge your hearts with Christ's authority. Remember who telleth you of cutting off your right hand, and plucking out your right eye. How can I look the Mediator in the face, if I should wilfully break any of his laws, prefer the satisfaction of a base lust before the mercies and hopes offered me by Jesus Christ.

[3.] In deep distresses, when you are apt to question the comfort of the promises. It is hard to keep the rejoicing of hope, without regard-ing whose word and promise it is : Heb. iii. 6, ' Whose house are ye, if ye hold fast the confidence and the rejoicing of hope firm unto the end.'

SERMON VII.

*And when the disciples heard it, they fell on their faces, and were sore
afraid. And Jesus came and touched them, and said, Arise, be
not afraid. And when they had lift up their eyes, they saw no
man save Jesus only.*—MAT. XVII. 6-8.

IN this part of the history are three things :—

    I. The disciples' fear and astonishment, ver. 6.

    II. Their comfortable and gracious recovery by Christ, ver. 7.

    III. The event and issue of all, ver. 8.

    I. Their astonishment: *They fell on their faces, and were sore
afraid.* Their falling on their faces was not out of worship and reverence, but consternation, as those John xviii. 6, ' As soon as he said to
them I am he, they went backward and fell to the ground.' The
causes of their fear must be inquired into. These were holy men, the
flower of Christ's disciples ; they were men in an holy action—(for
Belshazzar in his cups to tremble were no news)—they were not in the
presence of an angry God, it was a gospel-voice that they heard :
' This is my beloved Son, in whom I am well pleased ; hear ye him.'
They had not a full dispensation of his glory, but only a glimpse of it,
and that·under a cloud and revealed in mercy ; yet they were sore
afraid. Upon any visions and apparitions of the divine majesty, God's
servants fell to the earth : Ezek. i. 28, ' When I saw the appearance
of the likeness of the glory of God, I fell on my face.' Paul, when
Christ appeared to him from heaven, he fell to the earth, Acts ix. 4 :
Rev. i. 17, ' When I saw him, I fell at his feet as dead.' Abraham
was cast into great horror, Gen. xv. 12, when God appeared solemnly
to enter into covenant with him. So Isa. vi. 5, ' Then said I, Woe is
me ! for I am undone.' So Daniel x. 8, 9, ' When I saw this great
vision, there was no strength in me : for my comeliness was turned
into corruption, and I retained no strength. Yet heard I the voice of
his words : then was I in a deep sleep upon my face, and my face was
towards the ground.'

    Now I shall give—(1.) The special reasons why the manifestation and
appearance of God to his great prophets did breed this astonishment
and fear ; (2.) What general note and observation may be concluded
hence for our profit.

    1. The special reasons why these manifestations and appearances of
God to his great prophets do breed this astonishment and fear—they
are two :—

    [1.] To humble them to whom he vouchsafed so great a favour.
To humble them lest the glory of these heavenly visions should too
much puff them up. Therefore there was ever some weakness discovered in those that did receive them. Jacob wrestled with God,
but came off halting and maimed, though he prevailed, Gen. xxxii. 31.
When he came off from seeing God face to face, he halted on his
thigh. Paul was rapt into the third heaven, yet presently buffeted
with a messenger of Satan, lest he should be lifted up with the abundance of revelations, 2 Cor. xii. 7. Corruption remaineth in us, and

we are not able to bear these favours which God manifesteth to his choice servants, and therefore there is something to humble them in the dispensation, and to keep them from being puffed up with pride, something that is a balance to the great honour wherewith God hath honoured them.

[2.] All those that received visions from him to teach his people, God would season them by leaving a stamp and impression of his excellency upon them. This was the preparation of the prophets, and a preparation of the disciples to fit them for the work of the gospel. A due representation of God's glory and excellent majesty doth qualify them for their duty; they are fittest to carry God's message and describe him to others who are thus qualified and prepared, and have some reverence and awe of God impressed upon their own hearts, and have felt the power of his great majesty : 2 Cor. v. 16, ' Knowing the terrors of the Lord, we persuade men.'

The general conclusion and observation which we may draw from thence is this :—

Doct. That God is of such glorious excellency and majesty, that we are not able to bear any emissions or extraordinary representations thereof in this state of frailty.

1. I will prove that God is a great God and of glorious majesty.

2. Give you the reasons why we are not able to bear the extraordinary manifestations thereof in this state of frailty.

1. That God is a God of great majesty, and ought to be reverenced by all that have to do with him. The point being a matter of sense, and evident by natural light, needeth not to be proved so much as improved.

[1.] Scripture representeth him as such : Dan. ix. 4, he is called 'the great and dreadful God ;' so Deut. vii. 21, 'A mighty God and terrible ;' and Nahum i. 5, ' A great and terrible God is he ;' and, again, Job xxxvii. 22, ' With God is terrible majesty.'

[2.] This eminently shineth forth both in his works of creation and providence. (1.) Creation, in the stupendous fabric of the heavens : Jer. xxxii. 17–19, ' Ah Lord God ! behold, thou hast made the heaven and the earth by thy great power and outstretched arm, and there is nothing too hard for thee,' &c. In that mighty collection of waters in the sea : we cannot look upon that vast expansion of the firmament, that huge body of waters in the sea, without some religious horror. What is the God that made all this ? Jer. v. 22, ' Fear ye not me ? saith the Lord : will ye not tremble at my presence, which have placed the sand for a bound to the sea by a perpetual decree, that it cannot pass it ; and though the waves thereof toss themselves, yet can they not prevail ; though they roar, yet can they not pass over it ? ' (2.) Providence, whether in his way of mercy or judgment. Mercy : what a majestic description of God is there, Ps. l. 1–5, yet there his presence in his church is described. The drift of the psalm is, to set forth God's power and majesty when he comes to call the Gentiles, and to set up the evangelical way of his worship, when the light of the gospel shall shine forth from Sion : Ps. lxv. 5, ' By terrible things in righteousness wilt thou answer us, O God, thou God of our salvation.' Though God is a God of salvation, yet the way of his delivering them

carrieth majesty and terror with it. So his works of judgment : Ps.
cxix. 120, ' My flesh trembleth for fear of thee ; and I am afraid of
thy judgments, when the wicked of the earth are put away like dross.'
A lion trembleth to see a dog beaten before him, and it is imputed as
a fault to the wicked that they do not take notice of it : Isa. xxvi. 10,
' They will not behold the majesty of God.'

[3.] His greatness and majesty is such that we cannot comprehend
it : Job xxxvi. 26, ' Behold, God is great, and we know him not, nor
can the number of his years be searched out.' The greatness of God
cannot be known, but only by way of negation, that he hath none of
those infirmities which may lessen his being in our thoughts; or by
way of comparison, that he is above all, God is greater than man,
Jer. xxxvi. 12.

[4.] So great that he is fain to put a covering on, to interpose the
clouds between us and him, for we are not able to bear his glorious
and majestic presence : Job xxvi. 9, ' He holdeth back the face of his
throne, and spreadeth his cloud upon it.'   What would become of us
if he should discover all his glory ? This is his condescension to
the lower world to appear under a veil, and cover his throne with
clouds.

But though we do not know his full majesty, yet there is enough
discovered both to faith, reason, and sense, that God is great and
glorious, both in himself and in all his works.   Scripture declareth it
to faith, and reason will soon subscribe to so evident a truth, that he
that made and sustaineth all things must needs be a great God.
What other conceptions can we form of him when we look to the
heaven and this earth which he sustaineth by his great power, and he
declareth himself to sense by his daily providence to be a God of great
majesty.

The proof of it needeth not so much to be spoke to as the improvement of it, which we are called upon for everywhere.

(1.) It is a mercy that, being so great, he taketh notice of us : Ps.
viii. 3, 4, ' When I consider thy heavens, the work of thy fingers, the
moon and the stars, which thou hast ordained ; what is man, that
thou art mindful of him, and the son of man, that thou visitest him ? '
When we consider how the majesty of God shineth forth in the
heavenly bodies, and those many glorious creatures God hath made
besides us, we may wonder that God should esteem of man, and take
care of man, and be so solicitous about man's welfare, who was formed
at first out of so vile materials as the dust of the earth, and is still
of so very frail, infirm, and mortal condition, and hath carried himself so unthankfully to God, that he should take care of him above his
whole creation : Ps. cxiii. 6, 7, ' The Lord our God dwelleth on high,
who humbleth himself to behold the things in heaven and earth.'
That the great God of such glorious majesty should take notice of
worms, and behold us not only by visiting, over-seeing, and governing
the affairs of this lower world, but should condescend to this low
estate of ours in taking our flesh, whose excellency and majesty is so
great that he might despise the angels, of whom he hath no need ;
but to stoop so low towards men is matter of wonder, praise, and
adoration.

(2.) We should be humble in our conversing with him, considering what he is and we are : Job xlii. 5, 6, ' I have heard of thee with the hearing of the ear, now mine eye seeth thee, therefore I abhor myself in dust and ashes.' This should keep his children in a holy awe. Oh ! how low should we lie before this great God : Gen. xviii. 27, 'Who am I, that am but dust and ashes, that I should speak unto God?'

(3.) That we must not please ourselves with the performance of ordinary service to him, but we should raise it to an eminent degree of worship and adoration : Ps. xlviii. 1, ' Great is the Lord, and greatly to be praised in the city of our God ; ' and Ps. cxlv. 3, 'Great is the Lord, and greatly to be praised.' Alas ! the best we do is much beneath God. What low thoughts had Solomon of his stately temple 2 Chron. ii. 6, ' Who is able to build him an house, seeing the heaven of heavens is not able to contain him ? who am I that I should build him an house ? ' Thus should we see that our best resolutions and performances come much short of the excellency and greatness of God. All formality and lifeless service proceedeth from hence, that we have not due and raised thoughts of his majesty and being : Mal. i. 14, ' I am a great king, saith the Lord of hosts.' The greatness of God calleth for other service than usually we give to him—he gets nothing from us that is perfect. But surely we should not put him off with our refuse, but spend the best of our strength, time, parts, and affections, in his service. Superficial dealing in it argueth mean thoughts of God, it is a lessening of his majesty.

(4.) We serve a great master, and so may expect great things from him. He discovereth himself unto his people according to the greatness and majesty of his being : Ps. cxxvi. 2, 3, ' The Lord hath done great things for them, yea, the Lord hath done great things for us whereof we are glad.' Kings or princes do not give pence or brass farthings, but bestow gifts becoming their magnificence. The heathens were forced to acknowledge it, and the people of God do willingly acknowledge it. So Joel ii. 21, ' Fear not, O land, be glad and rejoice, for the Lord will do great things.' Be the mercies never so rare, the way never so difficult, God is able to accomplish them.

(5.) This should banish the fear of man, as to any danger can come from them to us, or to any attempts against God : Mat. x. 28, ' Fear not them which kill the body, but are not able to kill the soul; but rather fear him who is able to destroy both body and soul in hell fire.' They may threaten great things to us, but God threateneth greater. See Exod. xviii. 11, ' Now I know that God is greater than all gods, for in the thing wherein they dealt proudly God was above them.' There is a greater being we have to depend upon.

(6.) Because God is of such majesty and greatness, we should quarrel at none of his dealings, for he is too high to be questioned by the creature, and his counsels are carried on in such a way as we cannot judge of them, no more than a worm can judge of the affairs of a man ; he is great in counsel, and wonderful in working.

(7.) This should keep his children in an holy awe : Heb. xii. 28, 29, ' Let us have grace whereby we may serve God acceptably with reverence and godly fear, for our God is a consuming fire.' When we come in the holy assemblies : Gen. xxviii. 17, ' How dreadful is this place!' In our general course we must not slight his frowns nor despise his favours, all comes from a great God; nor behave ourselves irreverently in his presence, but still walk as those that have to do with a great and glorious God.

2. That in this present state we are not able to bear any extra-ordinary manifestation of his greatness and majesty.

[1.] Because of his glory, which would consume and swallow us up. This was a voice 'from the excellent glory,' 2 Pet. i. 17. Now if this excellent glory by the vail of the firmament were not obscured, man were not able to bear it: Job xxxvii. 20, 'If man speak, he shall be swallowed up:' 1 Tim. vi. 16, 'He dwelleth in light which no man can approach unto, whom no man hath seen, nor can see,' till we are received to heaven. Thus it is, his glory would kill us, his voice confound us. There is a mighty disproportion between mortal creatures and the infinite majesty of God; the brightness of his glory soon burdeneth and over-burdeneth the infirmity of the best creatures.

[2.] Because of our weakness.

(1.) Natural. We faint when we meet with anything extraordi-nary, and therefore no wonder if we are astonished with the near approach of the excellent majesty of God, and made unfit for any action of body or mind. If we cannot look on the sun, how can we see God? our felicity in heaven would be our misery on earth. This wine is too strong for old bottles.

(2.) Sinful infirmity, consciousness of guilt is in it also, and our disconformity to God through sin: Isa. vi. 5, 6, 'Woe is me, for I am undone; I am a man of unclean lips, and I dwell in the midst of a people of unclean lips, and mine eyes have seen the king, the Lord of hosts.' So Peter: Luke v. 8, 'Depart from me, for I am a sinful man.' This raiseth a fear in us upon every eminent approach or dis-covery of God's glory. Before the fall, God and Adam were friends; he would have endured God to speak to him; yet after the fall, the appearance of God became terrible. When he heareth his voice, he is afraid, and hideth himself; and something of this fear sticketh to the best of his people, and when God is eminently near it is dis-covered; for persons that have sin in them, to be near to so holy and glorious a majesty, that is a part of the reason of this fear and trouble. Well, then, both these causes go together, the representation of the majesty of God, and the sense of our own frailty and weakness.

Use. Is to press us to two things:—

1. To press us to an holy awe and reverence when we come near to God.

2. To take heed that our fear of God do not degenerate into a slavish fear.

First, To press us to an holy awe and reverence of God, when we draw nigh unto him. Surely we should in all our worship have such thoughts of God as may leave a stamp of humility and some im-pressions of the majesty and excellency of God upon us; and we should fall upon our faces, though not in a way of consternation, yet in a way of adoration. And because usually we bewray much slight-ness and irreverence in our converse with God and approaches to him, I shall press it a little.

1. I will show how the scriptures in the general do call for this holy awe of the majesty of God in all our worship : Ps. cxi. 9, ' Holy and reverend is his name,' and therefore never to be used by us but in an awful and serious manner : Ps. xcvi. 4, ' The Lord is great, and greatly to be praised ; he is to be feared above all gods.' Whether we pray, or whether we praise God, still the heart must be deeply possessed with a sense of his excellency ; and we must admire him above all created or imaginable greatness whatsoever, and so mingle reverence with our most delightful addresses to him. Again, Ps. lxxxix. 17, ' God is greatly to be feared in the assembly of his saints, and to be had in reverence of all that are round about him.' Holy angels and sanctified men, who of all creatures have nearest access to God, should most adore and reverence him, because they are best acquainted with him, and have the clearest sight of him that mortal creatures are capable of. The angels are an assembly of holy ones, that always behold his face, therefore always lauding and glorifying God. So God is said to be terrible in his holy place, Ps. lxviii. 35, whether heaven or the church. Indeed, the awful carriage of his people in his worship should be one means to convince of the excellency and majesty of God, 1 Cor. xiv. 25. The apostle showeth there that an unbeliever, coming into the Christian assemblies when they are managed with gravity and awe, is ' convinced and judged, and will fall down on his face and worship God, and say, God is in you of a truth ;' that is, seeing their humility, brokenness of heart, hearing their praises and admirations of God, and seeing their orderliness and composedness of spirit ; whereas rudeness, slightness, and irreverence doth pollute and stain the glory of God in their minds.

2. Other addresses will not become faith and love.

[1.] Faith, for whosoever cometh to God must fix this principle in his mind, 'that God is,' Heb. xi. 6. We do not worship God aright if we do not worship him as believers ; and if we worship him as believers, we will worship him with reverence and godly fear. Faith giveth us not only a thought of God, but some kind of sight of God, and sight will leave an impression upon the heart of reverence and seriousness. Surely a sight or believing thought of God should be able to do anything upon the soul. It is the great work of faith ' to see him that is invisible,' Heb. xi. 27. We should in our whole conversation live as in his sight, and live as those that remember God standeth by and seeth all that we are about : but especially in our worship—we then set ourselves as before the Lord. Pray as to our Father that seeth what we do : Mat. vi. 6, ' Pray to thy Father, which is in secret ; and thy Father which seeth in secret will reward thee openly.' Hear as before the Lord : Acts x. 33, ' We are all here present before God, to hear all things that are commanded thee of God ;' then the soul should turn the back upon all other things, that the mind may be taken up with nothing but God.

[2.] No other worship will become love. Worship is an act of love and delight. Now love is seen in admiring the excellencies of that glorious being whom we love, and ascribing all to him, as being deeply affected with his goodness : Rev. iv. 10, ' The four and twenty elders fall down before him that sat on the throne, and worship him that liveth for ever and ever, and cast their crowns before the throne, saying, Thou art worthy, O Lord, to receive glory, honour, and power; for thou hast created all things, and for thy pleasure they are and were created.' They fell down, not out of astonishment, but reverence, and cast their crowns before the throne. Whatever honour they have, they had it from God, and are content to lay it at his feet, from whom they have life, and being, and all things. They have such an high esteem of God that before him they cannot be too vile. They are unworthy to wear any crown in God's presence, and are content that their honour be a footstool to advance and extol his glory. Certainly those that are heartily affected to God will go about his worship, as with cheerfulness, so with humility and reverence.

Secondly, To take heed that our humility and reverence do not degenerate into servile fear and discouragement. It is apt to do so even in the best of God's people. We can hardly keep the middle between the extremes; our faith is apt to degenerate into presumption, and our humility into despondency of spirit, and our fear into discouragement and distrust. So hard a matter is it to ' serve the Lord with fear, and to rejoice with trembling,' Ps. ii. 11, or to walk in the fear of God, and in the comforts of the Holy Ghost.

Therefore, to avoid this consternation, do two things :—

1. Consider how amiable God hath represented himself in Jesus Christ, and how near he is come to us; and within the reach of our commerce there is ' a new and living way through the veil of his flesh,' Heb. x. 20. So that, though our God be a consuming fire, yet there is a screen between us and this fire; though if he should draw away the veil, a glimpse of his glory would kill us, yet this glory being veiled, we may have ' access with confidence,' Eph. iii. 12. There are naturally in our hearts fears, estrangedness, and backwardness from God. But now God is incarnate, and hath been manifested in our flesh, we may have more familiar thoughts of him, and they are made more sweet and acceptable to us.

2. Get your own peace with God made and confirmed to you more and more : Rom. v. 1, 2, ' Being justified by faith, we have peace with God, through Jesus Christ our Lord.' So Eph. ii. 18, he ' preached peace to you which were afar off, and to them that are nigh, for through him we both have an access by one Spirit to the Father.' See the breach made up between you and God, and be very tender of putting it to hazards any more. God, that is a consuming fire to guilty souls, is a Sun of righteousness to the upright. When we are accepted in the Beloved, those thoughts of God which guilt will make amazing and terrible, will be through peace comfortable and refreshing.

II. Their comfortable and gracious recovery by Christ, ver. 7, ' And Jesus came and touched them, and said, Arise, be not afraid.' He relieveth and helpeth them by three things:—(1.) His approach; (2.) His touch; (3.) His word.

1. His approach. He came to them, you must understand, having laid aside his glory which he had in the transfiguration, that he might more familiarly converse with them, and without prejudice. Because of their weakness and infirmity he layeth aside his majesty, and re-

assumeth the habit of his humiliation ; as Moses did put a veil upon his face, that the people might endure his sight and presence. God's appearing at first may be terrible ; but the issue is sweet and comfortable : a still, calm voice followed the earthquake, wind, and fire, 1 Kings xix. And God doth good to his people after he hath humbled them and proved them, Deut. viii. 16. Here, when the apostles lay like dead men, Christ came and put new life and strength into them. He came out of love and pity to them, that nothing more grievous might happen to them, either loss of life or senses. He would not let them perish in these amazements.

2. His touch. He touched them. Christ's touch is powerful, and a means of application. Usually thus Christ conveyed and applied his power : Mat. viii. 3, He touched the leper and cleansed him. Mat. viii. 15, He touched Peter's wife's mother and cured her of a fever. So Mat. ix. 19, He touched the two blind men and they received their sight ; and in many other places. So this touching of the apostles was to apply his power, and to recover them out of their trance.

3. His speech : ' And said, Arise, and be not afraid.' The glorious voice of the Father affrights them, and the gracious voice of the Son reviveth and refresheth them. He comforts those whom the terrors of the Almighty had cast down. He doth not chide them for their fear or little faith, as he doth at other times ; he considered the greatness of the cause, their natural infirmity, the governing of which was not in their power, and the terribleness and suddenness left no time for deliberation ; therefore he doth not chide them, but encourageth them. The like was done in other cases, as to Ezekiel in his trance : Ezek. ii. 1, 'Son of man, arise, stand on thy feet, and I will speak to thee.' So too the apostle John : Rev. i. 17, 18, ' When I saw him, I lay at his feet as dead. And he laid his right hand upon me, saying, Fear not ; I am the first and the last.' So here, be not afraid. We must reverence Christ, but not be scared at him. Such a fear as may stand with our duty is required, but not that which disableth us for it, or discourageth us in it ; that is no more pleasing to God than security.

[1.] Observe Christ's tender care over his disciples in their faintings and discouragements.

(1.) That he comforteth and reviveth his disciples. Christ alone can help us, and confirm us against our fears ; the disciples did not stir, but lay prostrate upon their faces, till he came and touched them, and said, ' Arise, be not afraid.' In all the troubles and perplexities of his people, he will be owned as the causer and curer of them : Hosea vi. 1, ' Come, let us return unto the Lord : for he hath torn, and he will heal us, he hath smitten, and he will bind us up.' So Job v. 18, ' He maketh sore and bindeth up, he woundeth and his hands make whole.' As all our troubles and perplexities are from his hands, so must the healing be. If he make the wound, all the world cannot find a plaster to heal it ; and no wound given by himself is above his own cure ; and he woundeth not as an enemy, but as a chirurgeon, not with a sword, but a lancet. All other means are blasted till we come to him.

(2.) That he is exceeding ready, and hath great pity and tenderness towards them. As appeareth by laying aside his glory, and coming to the disciples, when they came not to him ; and speedily, that he might not leave them long in the trance, lest worse effects should follow. And is he not like affected to all his people in their perplexities and troubles ? Yes, verily. See Isa. lvii. 16, 'I will not contend for ever, nor will I be always wroth : for the spirit should fail before, me, and the souls which I have made.' He speaketh as if he were afraid lest man's spirit should fail, being long overwhelmed with terror and trouble. So the apostle, 2 Cor. ii. 7, ' Comfort him, lest he be swallowed up with overmuch sorrow.' The Lord Christ is full of bowels and compassions, pitieth his people in their infirmities, fears, and troubles.

[2.] The manner and way which he taketh is considerable also—by touch and speech. The touch noteth the application of his power ; and in his speech he saith, 'Arise, be not afraid.' Christ doth not love to confound, but comfort, his servants, and therefore taketh this double course, by secret power enlivening and strengthening their hearts : Ps. cxxxviii. 3, ' I cried unto the Lord, and thou answeredst me, and strengthenedst me with strength in my soul ;' that is, God did secretly support him and strengthen him under the trouble. He doth it also by a word ; therefore we read of God's speaking peace to his people : Ps. lxxxv. 8, ' I will hear what God will say, for he will speak peace to his people and his saints.' Besides an inward strengthening, there is a necessity of a word from Christ's own mouth ere we can cast off our discouragements. Besides his touching or his laying his right hand upon us, there is need of his word to us.

Use. It teacheth us what to do when we have serious thoughts of appearing before God. For the case in hand is about those that were affrighted and disquieted with divine visions, which was occasioned by natural frailty, and partly by a sense of sin. Now all of us must shortly come into God's presence, but who can dwell with devouring burnings ? If your thoughts be serious, you will find that it is no slight thing to appear before God, who is our creator and our judge, and who is an holy and glorious God, to whom we have carried it very unthankfully and undutifully. Now who can relieve you in these perplexed thoughts but the Lord Jesus Christ ? Get a word from him that your iniquity is taken away, and your sin purged, Isa. vi. 7; and wait on him till he settleth your souls in the peace and hope of the gospel, Isa. lvii. 14 ; and then you are relieved in your agonies of conscience; stand up, be not afraid: the gospel is a sovereign plaster, but his hand must make it stick.

III. The event and issue of all, ver. 8, ' And when they had lift up their eyes, they saw no man save Jesus only.' This intimateth two things :—

1. That this testimony from heaven did only concern Jesus Christ, for Moses and Elias vanish out of sight, and Jesus is left alone, as the person in whom God is well pleased, and all the church must hear him. When they are withdrawn, Christ remaineth as Lord and head of the church, and so it showeth the ceasing of Moses's law, and the continuance and authority of the law of Christ. The apostle telleth us, ' When that which is perfect is come, that which is in part shall

be done away.' They only prophesied, prefigured Christ to come, but now, upon the exhibition, the legal ordinances vanished.

2. That God manifesteth himself, for time, measure, and degree, as he himself seeth fit for our good; for the vision is removed when the intent of it is obtained.   Here the spiritual banquet doth not always last; heaven is a perpetual feast, but we must not look upon earth to be feasted always with spiritual suavities.   There is no permanency, but perpetual vicissitudes, in our enjoyments within time; we have clear and cloudy days in the world, a feast, a desertion : Cant. v. 1, 2, ' I am come into my garden, my sister, my spouse; I have gathered my myrrh with my spice; I have eaten my honeycomb with my honey; I have drunk my wine with my milk: eat, O friends; drink, yea, drink abundantly, O beloved.   I sleep, but my heart waketh ; it is the voice of my beloved that knocketh, saying, Open to me, my sister, my love, my dove, my undefiled ; for my head is filled with dew, and my locks with the drops of the night.'   And ver. 6, ' I opened to my beloved; but my beloved hath withdrawn himself and was gone.'   After the greatest manifestations of Christ's love, there may be a withdrawing ; we cannot bear perpetual comforts, and God reserveth them for a better time, when we are more prepared for them.   There must be day and night in this world, and winter and summer ; but in heaven it is all day, there is a perpetual sunshine, never clouded nor overcast.

CHRIST'S ETERNAL EXISTENCE

AND

THE DIGNITY OF HIS PERSON

ASSERTED AND PROVED,

IN OPPOSITION TO THE DOCTRINE OF THE
SOCINIANS.

TO THE CHRISTIAN READER.

HERE are presented to thy view some of the further profitable and pious labours of that eminent divine, Dr Manton (now with God), who though, like a tree full of fruit, he has already yielded much fruit, yet still more and more falls from him. Since his much to be lamented death, two very large volumes (with some lesser) of his sermons have been published, which give a clear discovery to the world of his great abilities for, and great diligence in, the office and work of the minis-try. Now this small piece succeeds, which, in comparison of the former, is but a poor stripling,—but as ' the shaking of an olive tree, as the gleaning grapes when the vintage is over.' Yet let it not be rejected or slighted upon that account ; for though it is not so bulky as they, yet, according to its proportion, it is of equal value, and shows the same head and heart which they do.

My pen (upon this opportunity) would fain be launching forth into the commendation of the worthy author, but I will not suffer it, con-sidering how little he needs that from any, and how much he is above it as from me. Neither will I suffer it to run out in the commending of these sermons ; for I hope, to impartial and judicious readers, they will commend themselves (the best way of commending). I only recommend them, as judging them worthy of the perusal of all who are desirous of a fuller knowledge of our Lord Jesus.

For he is the grand subject treated of in them. His person, offices, works, blessings, are here described, asserted, vindicated, and improved. Our redemption by his blood ; his being the image of the invisible God, the first-born of every creature ; his creating and sustaining all things ; his headship over the church, pre-existence before all created beings ; his being the first-born from the dead, the union of the two natures in his person ; his reconciling of sinners to God through the blood of his cross,—these are the heads insisted upon in these sermons (the author following the apostle, Col. i. 14–20).

And are not these great points, of a very sublime nature, containing the very vitals of gospel revelation ? Can ministers preach, print too much of them ? Can private Christians hear, read, meditate too much of them ? Oh, they are the τὰ βάθη, ' the deep things of God,' in which is manifested the πολυποίκιλος σοφία, ' the manifold wisdom of God,' which ' the angels desire to look into,' which are the wonder and astonishment of heaven, which put such a transcendent excellency upon the knowledge of Christ. Should we not, therefore, thankfully receive and diligently peruse all discourses that may clear up our light in and about these profound mysteries? I hope the consideration hereof will make these sermons acceptable to many gracious souls. They all hanging upon this string, and pointing to this argument (of what Christ is, has done, suffered, and procured for believers), they are not unfitly put together, and printed by themselves, in this small volume.

Several of the points mentioned are controversial; for a long track of time there has been hot disputes about them. What volumes *pro* and *con* have been written, both by ancient and modern divines, about them! But our reverend author does not so much concern himself in what is polemical and controversial, but chose rather in a plainer way (as best suiting with sermon-work) to assert and prove the truth by scriptural testimonies and arguments: and that he has done to the full.

Reader, whoever thou art into whose hands these sermons shall come, let me assure thee they are the genuine work of the person whose name they bear. They were copied out from, and according to, his own notes, by one who I am sure would be as exact therein as possibly he could. But how earnestly could I wish, if God had not seen it good to order it otherwise, that the author himself might have lived to have reviewed and polished them; for what hand so fit to polish the stone as that which cuts it? But now what is amiss must be left to the understanding reader to discover, and to the candid reader to pardon.

Christian, I commit thee to God; may he bless thee, and all the labours of his faithful servants (whether living or dead), to the promoting of thy spiritual and eternal good. Which he ardently desires, who is,—

Thine to serve thee in our Lord Jesus,

THO. JACOMB.

REDEMPTION BY CHRIST.

SERMON I.

In whom we have redemption through his blood, even the forgiveness of sins.—COL. I. 14.

THE apostle, in the former verse, had spoken of our slavery and bondage to Satan, from which Christ came to deliver us; now, because sin is the cause of it, he cometh to speak of our redemption from sin: 'In whom we have redemption through his blood, even the forgiveness of sins.' Here is—

    I. The author.

    II. The benefit.

    III. The price.

The point is this:—

Doct. That one principal part of our redemption by Christ is remission of sins. Here I shall show you:—

    1. What remission of sins is.

    2. The nature of redemption.

    3. That remission of sins is a part, and a principal part of it.

First, What remission of sins is. Both terms must be explained—what sin is, and what is the forgiveness of sin.

For the *first*, sin is a violation of the law of the eternal and living God: 1 John iii. 4, 'Whosoever committeth sin, transgresseth also the law, for sin is the transgression of the law.' God is the lawgiver, who hath given a righteous law to his subjects, under the dreadful penalty of a curse. In his law there are two things—the precept and the sanction. The precept is the rule of our duty, which showeth what we must do, or not do. The sanction or penalty showeth what God will do, or might justly do, if he should deal with us according to the merit of our actions. Accordingly, in sin, there is the fault and the guilt.

[1.] The fault: that man, who is God's subject, and so many ways obliged to him by his benefits, instead of keeping this law, should break it upon light terms, and swerve from the rule of his duty, being carried away by his own ill-disposed will and base lusts. It is a great and heinous offence, for which he becometh obnoxious to the judgment of God.

[2.] The guilt: which is a liableness to punishment, and that not ordinary punishment, but the vengeance of the eternal God, who every moment may break in upon us. Where there is sin, there will be guilt; and where there is guilt, there will be punishment, unless we be pardoned, and God looseneth the chains wherewith we be bound.

Secondly, Forgiveness of sin is a dissolving the obligation to punishment, or a freedom, in God's way and method, from all the sad and woful consequences of sin. Understand it rightly.

[1.] It is not a disannulling the act, as it is a natural action; such a fact we did, or omitted to do; *factum, infactum fieri nequit*—that which is done, cannot be undone. And, therefore, though it be said, Jer. l. 20, 'The iniquity of Jacob shall be sought after, and the sins of Judah, and they shall not be found; for I will pardon them whom I reserve;' yet that must not be understood as if God would abolish the action, and make it as if it had never been, for that is impossible. But he would pass by, and overlook it as to punishment.

[2.] Nor is it abolished as a faulty or criminal action, contrary to the law of God. The sins we have committed are sins still, such actions as the law condemneth. Forgiveness is not the making of a fault to be no fault. An accused person may be vindicated as innocent, but if he be pardoned, he is pardoned as an offender. He is not reputed as one that never culpably omitted any duty, or committed any sin, but his fault is forgiven upon such terms as our offended governor pleaseth 'I will be merciful to their unrighteousness, and forgive all their sins,' Heb. viii. 12. They are pardoned as sins.

[3.] Nor is the merit of the sinful act lessened; in itself it deserveth condemnation to punishment. *Merito operis*, it is in itself damnable, but *quoad eventum*: Rom. viii. 1, 'There is no condemnation to them that are in Christ Jesus,' &c.; because the grace of the gospel dischargeth us from it. We must still own ourselves deserving the wrath of God, which maketh for our constant humiliation and admiration of grace; so that he that is pardoned still deserveth punishment.

[4.] It remaineth, therefore, that forgiveness of sin is a dissolving the obligation to punishment, or passing by the fault, so as it shall not rise up in judgment against us to our confusion or destruction: the fault is the sinner's act, the punishment the judge's, which he may forbear on certain terms stated in the law of grace. He passeth by the fault so far, that it shall not be a ground of punishment to us. I prove it :—

(1.) From the nature of the thing ; for there is such a relation between the fault and the guilt, the sin and the punishment, that the one cannot be without the other. There can be no punishment without a preceding fault and crime. Therefore, if the judge will not impute the fault, there must needs be an immunity from punishment, for the cause being taken away, the effect ceaseth, and the sin committed by us is the meritorious cause of punishment. If God will cover that, and overlook it, then forgiveness is a dissolving the obligation to punishment.

(2.) From the common rule of speaking used among men, for surely the scripture speaketh intelligibly. Now in the common way of speaking, he cannot be said to forgive or remit a fault that exacteth the whole punishment of it. How can a magistrate be said to forgive

an offender, when the offender beareth the punishment which the law
determineth ? And what do men pray for to God, when they pray
for the forgiveness of sins, but that they may be exempted from the
punishment which they have deserved ?

(3.) It would seem to impeach the justice and mercy of God, if he
should exact the punishment where he hath pardoned the offence.
His justice, to flatter men with hopes of remitting the debt, where he
requireth the payment ; his mercy, in making such fair offers of
reconciliation, when still liable to his vindictive justice. There may be
indeed effects of his fatherly anger, but not of his vindictive wrath.

(4.) The phrases, and way of speaking in scripture, by which forgiveness of sin is set forth, show God doth blot out our sins : Ps.
li. 2, ' Wash me thoroughly from my iniquity, and cleanse me from
my sin.' And cover them : Ps. xxxii. 1, ' Blessed is he whose transgression is forgiven, whose sin is covered.' To cast them behind his
back : Isa. xxxviii. 17, ' Thou hast cast all my sins behind thy back.'
And cast them into the bottom of the sea : Micah vii. 19, ' Thou wilt
cast all their sins into the depths of the sea.' To remember them no
more : Jer. xxxi. 34, ' I will forgive their iniquity, and I will remember their sin no more.' By such emphatical metaphors doth it express
God's free and full forgiveness, if we seriously enter into his peace ;
and do clearly show, that if God punisheth sins, he doth remember
them ; if he avenge them, he imputeth them ; if they are brought into
the judgment against us, they are not covered ; if he searcheth after
them, he doth not cast them behind his back ; if he bringeth them
into light, he doth not cast them into the depths of the sea ; much
more if he punish us for them.

Secondly, The nature of redemption.

What is redemption by the blood of Christ ?

In opening it to you, I shall prove six things :—

1. A captivity or bondage.

2. That from thence we are freed by a ransom, or price paid.

3. That none but Christ was fit to give this ransom.

4. That nothing performed by Christ was sufficient till he laid
down his life.

5. That thence there is a liberty resulting to us.

6. That we do not actually partake of the benefit of this ransom
till we be in Christ.

[1.] Our being redeemed supposeth a captivity and bondage. All
men in their unrenewed estate are slaves to sin and Satan, and subject
to the wrath of God. That we are slaves to sin appeareth by scripture and experience : Titus iii. 3, ' Serving divers lusts and pleasures ;'
John viii. 34, ' Whosoever committeth sin, is the servant of sin.' Men
imagine a life spent in vanity and pleasure to be a very good life ; it
were so, if liberty were to be determined by doing what we list, rather
than what we ought. But since it is not, experience showeth that
they are convinced of their brutish satisfactions as mean and base, yet
they cannot leave them, for that true and solid happiness offered by
Christ. Now as they are under sin, so they are under Satan, ' who
worketh in the children of disobedience,' Eph. ii. 2 ; and hath a great
power over wicked men in the world, who fall to his share, as the

executioner of God's curse, and are taken captive by him at his will and pleasure, 2 Tim. ii. 26. This is the woful captivity and servitude of carnal men, that they fall as a ready prey into the mouth of the roaring lion. Now, for this they are liable to the curse and wrath of God; therefore called ' children of wrath, even as others,' Eph. ii. 3 ; that is, obnoxious to his righteous displeasure and punishment. Thus were we lost in ourselves under sin, Satan, and the wrath of God, from which we could no way free ourselves ; and if grace had not opened a way for us to escape, what should we have done ?

[2.] To recover us, there was a price to be paid by way of ransom to God. We are not delivered from this bondage by prayer or entreaty, nor by strong hand or mere force, nor yet by the sole condescension and pity of the injured party, without seeking reparation of the wrong done, but by the payment of a sufficient price, and just satisfaction to provoked justice. This price was not paid indeed to Satan, who detaineth souls in slavery as a rigid usurping tyrant or merciless jailor (from him indeed we are delivered by force), but the price was paid to God. Man had not sinned against Satan, but against God, to whom it belongeth to condemn or absolve. And God being satisfied, Satan hath no power over us, but is put out of office, as the executioner hath nothing to do when the judge and law is satisfied. Now, that redemption implieth the paying of a price is clear, because the word importeth it, and the scripture often uses this metaphor : Mat. xx. 28, ' The Son of man came not to be ministered unto, but to minister, and to give his life a ransom for many ;' 1 Tim. ii. 6, ' Who gave himself a ransom for all, to be testified in due time.' Redemption in the general is a recovery out of our lost estate. God could have saved men by the grace of confirmation, but he chose rather by the grace of redemption. This recovery was not by a forcible rescue, but by a ransom. Christ, in recovering his people out of their lost estate, is sometimes set forth as a lamb, sometimes as a lion. In dealing with God, we consider him as the lamb slain, Rev. v. 5, 6 : in dealing with Satan, and the enemies of our salvation, he doth as a lion recover the prey. But why was a ransom necessary ? Because God had made a former covenant, which was not to be quit and wholly made void but upon valuable consideration, lest his justice, wisdom, holiness, veracity, authority should fall to the ground.

(1.) The honour of his governing justice was to be secured and freed from any blemish, that the awe of God might be kept up in the world : Rom. iii. 5, 6, and Gen. xviii. 25, ' That be far from thee, to do after this manner, to slay the righteous with the wicked ; and that the righteous should be as the wicked, that be far from thee : shall not the judge of all the earth do right ?' If God should absolutely pardon without satisfaction equivalent for the wrong done, how should God else be known and reverenced as the just and holy governor of the world ? Therefore Rom. iii. 25, 26, it is said, ' Whom God hath set forth to be a propitiation through faith in his blood, to declare his righteousness for the remission of sins that are past, through the forbearance of God ; to declare, I say, at this time his righteousness; that he might be just, and the justifier of him which believeth in Jesus.'

(2.) His wisdom. The law was not given by God in jest, but in the greatest earnest that ever law was given.   Now, if the law should be recalled without any more ado, the lawgiver would run the hazard of levity, mutability, and imprudence in constituting so solemn a transaction to no purpose.   Paul was troubled when forced to retract his word, 2 Cor. i. 17, 18 ; that his word should be yea to-day, and nay to-morrow.   Therefore, when God had said, Thus I will govern the world, he was not to part with the law upon light terms.

(3.) His holy nature would not permit it.   There needed some way to be found out,· to signify his purest holiness, his hatred and detestation of sin, and that it should not be pardoned without some marks of his displeasure.   His soul hates the wicked, and the righteous God loveth righteousness, Ps. xi. 6.

(4.) His authority.   It would be a derogation from the authority of his law, if it might be broken, and there be no more ado about it. Now, that all the world might know that it is a dangerous thing to transgress his laws, and might hear and fear, and do no more presumptuously, God appointed this course, that the penalty of his law should be executed upon our surety, when he undertook our reconciliation with God, Gal. iv. 4.

(5.) The veracity and truth of God.   It bindeth the truth of God, which sinners are apt to question : Gen. iii. 5, ' Hath God said ?' and Deut. xxix. 19, 20.   We look upon the threatenings of the law as a vain scarecrow ; therefore, for the terror and warning of sinners for the future, God would not release his wrath, nor release us from the power of sin and Satan, which was the consequent of it, without a price and valuable compensation.

[3.] None was fit to give this ransom but Jesus Christ, who was God-man.   He was man to undertake it in our name, and God to perform it in his own strength ; a man that he might be made under the law, and humbled even to the death of the cross for our sakes ; and all this was elevated beyond the worth of created actions and sufferings by the divine nature which was in him, which perfumed his humanity, and all done by it and in it.   This put the stamp upon the metal, and made it current coin, imposed an infinite value upon his finite obedience and sufferings.   By taking human nature a price was put into his hands to lay down for us : Heb. x. 15, and his divine nature made it sufficient and responsible, for it was the blood of God: Acts xx. 28, ' Feed the church of God, which he hath purchased with his own blood ;' and Heb. ix. 13, ' For if the blood of bulls and goats, and the ashes of an heifer, sprinkling the unclean, sanctifieth to the purifying of the flesh, how much more shall the blood of Christ, who through the Spirit offered himself without spot to God, purge your conscience from dead works to serve the living God ?'   It was that flesh and blood which was assumed into the unity of his person—as a slip or branch grafted into a stock is the branch of the stock, and the fruit of it is the fruit of the stock.   A naked creature without this union could not have satisfied the justice of God for us.   This made his blood a precious blood, and his obedience a precious obedience. In short, God-man, the Son of God and the son of Adam, was he that redeemed us.   So, in short, there were different parties to be dealt with before the fruit of redemption could be obtained : God, satan, man.

God was an enemy that could not be overcome, but must be reconciled ; Satan was a usurper, and was to be vanquished with a strong hand ; man was unable and unwilling to look after the fruits of redemption, and our obstinacy and unbelief could only be overcome by the Spirit of Christ.

[4.] Nothing performed by Christ could be a sufficient ransom for this end, unless he had crowned all his other actions and sufferings by laying down his life, and undergoing a bloody and violent death. This was the completing and crowning act.   Partly to answer the types of the law, wherein no remission was represented without a bloody sacrifice ; partly from the nature of the thing, and the fulness of the satisfaction required until all that was finished, John viii. 20. Death was that which was threatened to sin, death was that which was feared by the sinner.   Many ignorant people will say the least drop of Christ's blood was enough to save a thousand worlds.   If so, his circumcision had been enough without his death.   But Christ is not glorified but lessened by such expressions.   Surely his death was necessary, or God would never have appointed it ; his bloody death suited with God's design.   God's design was to carry on our recovery in such a way as might make sin more hateful, and obedience more acceptable to us.

(1.) Sin more hateful by his agonies, blood, shame, death ; no less remedy would serve the turn, to procure the pardon and destruction of it : Rom. viii. 3, 'By sin he condemned sin in the flesh ;' that is, by a sin-offering.   God showed a great example of his wrath against all sin by punishing sin in the flesh of Christ. His design was for ever to leave a brand upon it, and to furnish us with a powerful mortifying argument against it, by the sin-offering and ransom for souls. Surely it is no small matter for which the Son of God must die ! At Golgotha, sin was seen in its own colours—there he showed how much he hateth it, and loveth purity.

(2.) To commend obedience.   Christ's suffering death for the sin of man at the command of his Father was the noblest piece of service and the highest degree of obedience that ever could be performed to God—beyond anything that can be done by men or angels. There was in it so much love to God, pity to man, so much self-denial, so much humility and patience, and so much resignation of himself to God, who appointed him to be the redeemer and surety of man, to do this office for him, as cannot be paralleled.   The great thing in it was obedience : Rom. v. 14, ' By the obedience of one shall many be made righteous ;' so Phil. ii. 7, God was not delighted in mere blood, but in blood offered in obedience.   All his former actions, together with his death and sufferings, make but one entire act of eminent obedience ; but his painful and cursed death, so willingly and readily undergone, was the crowning act.   The formal reason of the merit was that Christ came to fulfil the will of God, ' by which will we are sanctified,' Heb. x. 10, therefore his death was necessary.

[5.] From this ransom and act of obedience there is a liberty resulting unto us, for the redeemed are let go when the ransom is paid. Now this liberty is a freedom from sin, that we may become the servants of God : Rom. vi. 22, ' Being made free from sin, ye became servants of righteousness.'   Christ came not to free us from the duty

of the law, but the penalty and curse thereof. To free us from the
duty of the law is to promote the devil's interest. No; he freed us
from the wrath of God that we may serve him cheerfully, to establish
God's interest upon surer and more comfortable terms, to restore us
to God's favour and service: to God's favour, by the pardon of sin; to
his service by writing his laws on our hearts and minds. Sometimes
our redemption from the curse is spoken of: Gal. iii. 13, 'Christ
hath redeemed us from the curse of the law, being made a curse for
us.' Sometimes our redemption from sin: Titus ii. 14, 'Who gave
himself for us, that he might redeem us from all iniquity;' and so
by consequence from the power of the devil, which is built on the curse
of the law and reign of sin. Satan's power over us doth flow from the
sentence of the condemnation pronounced by the law against sinners, and
consists in that dominion sin hath obtained over them. If the curse
of the law be disannulled, and the power of sin broken, he is spoiled of
his power: Col. ii. 14, 15, 'Blotting out the handwriting of ordinances
that was against us, which was contrary to us, and took it out of the
way, nailing it to his cross; and having spoiled principalities and
powers, he made a show of them openly, triumphing over them.'

[6.] That we are not partakers of this liberty, nor of the benefit of this ransom, till we are in him, and united to him by faith, for
the text saith, 'In whom we have redemption by his blood.' Certainly
we must be turned from Satan to God before we are capable of receiving the forgiveness of sins, Acts xxvi. 18. We do not actually
partake of the privileges of Christ's kingdom till we be first his subjects: 'Who hath delivered us from the power of Satan, and hath translated us into the kingdom of his dear Son: in whom we have redemption
through his blood, the forgiveness of sins.' Christ and his people are
an opposite state to the devil and his instruments. While we are under
the opposite power we belong not to Christ, and the privileges of his
kingdom belong not to us; but as soon as we are translated and put into
another estate, then we have the first privilege, 'remission of sins.'
Look, as in the fall there was sin before guilt, so in our reparation there
must be conversion, renovation, or repentance before remission. We are
first effectually called or sanctified, and then justified and glorified.
Man's recovery to God is in the same method in which he fell from him.
It is first brought about by a new nature, and communication of life
from Christ. He regenerateth that he may pardon, and he pardoneth
that he may further sanctify and make us everlastingly happy.

Thirdly, That remission of sins is a part, and a principal part of
redemption.

1. How is it a part or fruit of redemption?

I answer—Redemption is taken either for the impetration or application.

[1.] The impetration or laying down the price, that was done by
Christ upon the cross. So it is said, Heb. ix. 12, 'Christ by his own
blood obtained eternal redemption for us.' Then was God propitiated,
the deadly blow given to the kingdom and power of the devil, and the
merit and ransom interposed, by the virtue of which we are pardoned.
The obtained redemption and remission of sins is a fruit flowing from
it, and depending upon it as an effect upon the cause.

[2.] The scripture considers redemption in its application. Besides laying down the price, there is an actual deliverance and freedom by virtue of that price. This is either begun or complete. The complete redemption, or freedom from sin and misery, is that which the godly shall enjoy at the last day: Rom. viii. 23, 'We which have the first-fruits of the Spirit, even we ourselves groan within ourselves, waiting for the adoption, to wit, the redemption of our body;' Eph. iv. 30, 'Grieve not the Holy Spirit of God, whereby ye are sealed unto the day of redemption;' Eph. i. 14, 'In whom also, after ye believed, ye were sealed with that Spirit of promise, which is the earnest of our inheritance, until the redemption of the purchased possession.' The inchoate or begun deliverance is that measure of deliverance which believers enjoy now by faith, which consists of two parts—justification and sanctification. Sanctification: 1 Pet. i. 18, Titus ii. 14, 'Who gave himself for us, that he might redeem us from all iniquity, and purify unto himself a peculiar people, zealous of good works;' when we are free from the power and weight of sin. Justification, so it is in the text, and Eph. i. 7; when sin is freely pardoned, and our debt cancelled, and we are delivered from evil and wrath to come.

2. As it is a part, so it is a principal part. This will appear if you consider the evil we are freed from.

[1.] The power of the devil is destroyed. All the advantage which he hath against us is as we are sinners, guilty sinners before God. For we are put into his hands when we have forfeited the protection of our righteous Lord, but forgiveness of sins gives us a release from him, Acts xxvi. 18. When Christ came to procure it he destroyed the devil's power; when we are converted we are interested in the privilege.

[2.] The reign of sin is broken, or sanctifying grace is inseparable from pardoning grace; yea, I will venture to say, that the gift of the sanctifying Spirit is a part of our pardon executed and applied; for a part of the punishment of sin was spiritual death, or the loss of God's image: Col. ii. 13, 'He hath quickened you together with Christ, having forgiven all your trespasses.' When God pardoneth he sanctifieth and createth us anew, that we may be fit for his service, so that we are renewed by the Spirit, as well as recovered out of the snares of the devil.

[3.] We are eased of tormenting fears in a great measure. Man can have no firm peace and comfort in his own soul while sin remaineth upon him. Our case is dangerous, whether we be sensible of it or no, because our condition is not to be valued by our sense and feeling, but by the sentence of the law of God, which we have broken and violated. If there be any difference in the case, the more insensible we are, the more miserable. The generality of men indeed are senseless and careless, put far away the evil day from them, and so make light work of reconciling themselves to God. But are they the more safe for this? No; if they will dance about the brink of hell, and go merrily to their execution, it argues not their safety, but their stupidness. The thought of danger is put off when the thing itself is not put away, but if they be serious they cannot be without trouble: Rom. i. 32, 'Knowing the judgment of God, they conclude that they that do such things are worthy of death.' The very light of nature will revive many unquiet thoughts within them. The justice of the supreme Governor of the world will still be dreadful to them, whose law they have broken, and whose wrath they have justly deserved. They may lull the soul asleep by the stupifying potion of carnal delights, and while conscience is asleep please themselves with stolen waters, and bread eaten in secret, which is soon disturbed by a few serious and sober thoughts of the world to come. God is offended, and what peace can they have ?

[4.] Death is unstinged. That is the usual time when convictions grow to the height, and the stings of an awakened conscience begin to be felt, 1 Cor. xv. 56. Then the thoughts of death and judgment to come are very terrible to them, and men begin to see what it is to bear their own sins, and how happy they are who are sure of a pardon.

[5.] The obligation to eternal punishment ceases. Pardon is dissolving and loosing that obligation. Now the punishment is exceeding great; hell and damnation are no vain scarecrows. Eternity makes everything truly great, the *pœna damni*, an everlasting separation from the comfortable presence of the Lord: Mat. xxv. 41, 'Go, ye cursed;' Luke xiii. 27, 'Depart, ye workers of iniquity.' When God turned Adam out of paradise his case was very sad, but God took care of him in his exile, made him coats of skin, gave him a day of patience, afterwards promised the seed of the woman, who should recover the lapsed estate of mankind, intimated hopes of a better paradise. That estate, therefore, is nothing comparable to this, for now man is stripped of all his comforts, sent into an endless state of misery, whence there is no hopes of ever changing his condition. So for the *pœna sensus*, the pain: Mark ix. 44, 'Where their worm never dieth, and their fire is never quenched.' The worm is the worm of conscience reflecting on past folly and disobedience. See here a man may run away from the rebukes of conscience by many shifts—sleeping, sporting, distracting his mind with a clatter of business ; but there not a thought free, but is always thinking of slighted means, abused mercies, wasted time, the offences done to a merciful God, and the curse wherein they have involved themselves ; the fire is the wrath of God, or these unknown pains that shall be inflicted on body and soul, which must needs be great when we fall into the hands of the living God. If a little mitigation, a drop to cool your tongue be thought a great matter, oh ! what a blessedness is it to be freed from so great an evil. Perhaps you coldly entertain the offer of a pardon now, but then to be freed from wrath to come—oh, blessed Jesus ! 1 Thes. i. 10.

II. The good depending on it: Luke i. 77, ' To give us the knowledge of salvation by the remission of sins.' Eternal life dependeth on it, for you are not capable of enjoying God till his wrath be appeased. As all evil was introduced by sin, so all happiness by pardon. This is an initial blessing, which maketh way for the rest.

Use, of exhortation : To persuade you to seek after this benefit. All of us once needed it, and the best of us, till we are wholly freed from sin, still need it.

1. We all of us once needed it; for we are not only criminal persons liable to condemnation, but actually condemned in the sentence of God's law: John iii. 18, 'He that believeth not is condemned already.' Now, should not a condemned man make means to be pardoned? and should not we accept of God's terms, especially when there is but the slender thread of a frail life between us and execution? He that securely continues in his sins, despiseth both the curse of the law and the grace of the gospel. Oh, consider! nothing but a pardon will serve the turn—not forbearance on God's part, nor forgetfulness on yours.

[1.] Not forbearance of the punishment on God's part. God may be angry with us while he doth not actually strike, as the psalmist saith: Ps. vii. 11–13, ' God is angry with the wicked every day; if he turn not he will whet his sword. He hath bent his bow and will make it ready.' God, who is a righteous judge, will not dispense with the offences of wicked men, by which he is continually affronted and provoked. Though in the day of his patience he doth for a while spare, yet he is ready to deal with them *comminus*, hand to hand, for he is sharpening his sword; *eminus*, at a distance, for he is bending his bow. The arrow is upon the string, and how soon he may let it fly we cannot tell. We are never safe till we turn to him, and enter into his peace, and so the obligation to punishment be dissolved.

[2.] On our part, our senseless forgetfulness will do us no good. Carnal men mind not things which relate to God, or the happiness of their immortal souls; but they are not happy that feel least troubles, but they that have least cause. A benumbed conscience cannot challenge this blessedness. They put off the thoughts of that which God hath neither forgiven nor covered; and so do but skin the wound till it festers and rankles into a dangerous sore. Our best course is to see we be justified and pardoned.

2. The best of us still need it: partly because though we be justified, and our state be changed, yet renewed sins need a new pardon. We are still sinning against God—either we are omitting good, or committing evil. What will we do if we be not forgiven? Renewed sins call for renewed repentance. We do not need another Redeemer, or another covenant, or another conversion; yet we do need renewed pardon, partly because our final sentence of pardon is not yet passed, nor shall be passed till the last judgment: Acts iii. 19, 'Repent ye, therefore, and be converted, that your sins may be blotted out, when the times of refreshing shall come from the presence of the Lord.' We are now pardoned and justified constitutively by the tenor of the new covenant, and there by description. The sincerity of our faith and repentance is not presently evident; it is possible, but difficult, to know that we are sincere penitent believers; but at last, when our pardon is actually pronounced by our judge's mouth, sitting on the throne, then all is clear, evident, plain, and open. And partly because daily infirmities call for daily repentance. We do not carry ourselves with that gravity and watchfulness, but that we need to cry for pardon every day.

SERMON II.

Who is the image of the invisible God, the first-born of every creature.—
Col. I. 15.

The apostle having mentioned our redemption, doth now fall upon a description of the Redeemer. He is set forth by two things:—

First, His internal relation to God.

Secondly, By his external relation to the creature.

Doct. It is a great part of a believer's work to have a deep sense of the Redeemer's excellency imprinted upon his mind and heart.

Here I shall show:—

I. How it is set forth in this verse.

II. Why this should be much upon our minds and hearts.

I. How it is set forth in this scripture:—

1. That he is ' the image of the invisible God.'

2. 'The first-born of every creature.'

For the first expression there I shall consider :—

1. What belongs to an image.

2. In what respects Christ is the image of God.

3. How he differeth from other persons.

1. What belongeth to an image, and that all this is in Christ. In an image there are two things—impression and representation. Both are in Christ. There is a divine impression upon him, and he doth represent God to us.

[1.] For impression, there is:—

(1.) Likeness; for an image must be like him whom it representeth. An artificial image of God, or such as may be made by us, is forbidden upon this account: Isa. xl. 18, ' To whom, then, will ye liken God ? or what likeness will ye compare unto him ? ' What is there among all the creatures that can be like such an infinite and almighty essence ? or by what visible shape or figure would they represent or resemble God ?

(2.) Deduction and derivation. The image is taken from him whom it is intended to represent. It is not some casual similitude between two men that have no reference or dependence one upon another; but such as is between a father and his only-begotten son; as it is said of Adam, Gen. v. 1, ' He begat a son in his own image;' and so it is verified in Christ because of his eternal generation. Like him, because begotten of him.

(3.) There is not a likeness in a few things, but a complete and exact likeness ; so Christ, as the second person, is called, Heb. i. 3, ' The express image of his person.' There is not only likeness, but equality. God cannot make a creature equal to himself, nor beget a son unequal to himself.

[2.] Representation ; for an image it serveth to make known and declare that thing whose image it is. If light produce light, the light produced doth represent the light and glory producing ; and the more perfect and immediate the production is, the more perfect is the resemblance ; a lively expression of the pattern and exemplar. And this is the reason why the word *invisible* is added, because God, who in his own nature is invisible, and incomprehensible to man, revealeth himself so far as is necessary to salvation to us by Christ. Visible things are known by their visible images, with more delight, but not with more accuracy. The image is not necessary to know the thing ; but here it is otherwise. We cannot know God but by Christ: John i. 18, ' No man hath seen God at any time; the only-begotten Son, which is in the bosom of the Father, he hath declared him.' God is invisible, and incomprehensible by any but Jesus Christ, who being his only Son, and one in essence with the Father, he doth perfectly know him, and reveal unto mankind all that they know of him. Thus you see what belongs to an image.

2. In what respects Christ is the image of God.

[1.] In respect of his eternal generation. So Christ is ' the express image of his person '—not substance, but subsistence. We do not say that milk is like milk, nor one egg like another, because they are of the same substance ; so Christ is not said to be of the same substance, but of the same subsistence. He is, indeed, of the same substance with him whom he doth resemble, but the image is with respect to the subsistence; so he resembleth the Father fully and perfectly. There is no perfection in the Father but the same is in the Son also. He is eternal, omnipotent, infinite in wisdom, goodness, and power.

[2.] As God incarnate, or manifested in our flesh ; so the perfections of the Godhead shine forth in the man Christ Jesus, in his person, word, and works.

(1.) In his person. They that had a discerning eye might see something divine in Christ : John i. 14, 'We beheld his glory, as the glory of the only-begotten of the Father.' There is the *as* of similitude, and the *as* of congruity ; as if a mean man taketh state upon him, we say he behaveth himself *as* a king, but if we say the same of a king indeed, we mean he behaveth himself king-like, that is, becoming the majesty of his high calling. So we beheld his glory *as*, &c., that is, such a glory as was suitable and becoming God's only Son. So Christ was angry with his disciples because they were too importunate to see the Father, though they saw him ordinarily, conversing with him : John xiv. 7, ' If ye had known me ye should have known my Father also, and from henceforth ye know him and have seen him.' The Father is no otherwise to be known but as he hath revealed himself in Christ ; and having seen and known Christ, who was his image, they might both see and know him ; and when Philip saith ' Show us the Father and it sufficeth us '—this will convince us all without further argument—Christ answereth, ver. 9, ' He that hath seen me hath seen the Father.' They might see the Father's infinite power acting in him, his wisdom teaching by him, his goodness in the whole strain of his life ; so that in Christ becoming man, God doth in and by him represent all his own attributes and properties, his wisdom, goodness, and power.

(2.) In his word ; where God is revealed to us savingly, so as we may be brought into communion with him, so it is said, ' lest the light of the glorious gospel of Christ, who is the image of God, should shine unto them,' 2 Cor. iv. 4. As God shineth forth in Christ, so doth Christ shine forth in the gospel. There we have the record of his doctrine,

miracles, and the end for which he came into the world ; and this is
the great instrument by which the virtue and power of God is conveyed to us, for the changing of our hearts and lives : 2 Cor. iii. 18,
' Beholding the glory of the Lord as in a glass, we are changed into
his image and likeness, from glory to glory.'   Some sight of God we
must have, or else we cannot be like him : the knowledge or sight of
God with mortal or bodily eyes is impossible ; the external manifestations and representations in the creature is imperfect, and sufficeth
rather for conviction than conversion, or to leave us without excuse,
than to save the soul, Rom. xii. 1 (they have not the excuse of fault-
less ignorance).   To know him in the law, or covenant of works, doth
but work wrath, Rom. iv. 15, or revive in us a stinging sense of our
hopeless condition.   To know him in person, or to see his glorious
works, or hear his glorious words, was a privilege vouchsafed but to
few, and to many that made no good use of it ; therefore there is only
reserved his word to bring us into communion with God, or the
glass of the gospel to represent the glory of the Lord, that we may be
changed into his likeness from glory to glory ; there the knowledge
of God is held out powerfully in order to our salvation.

(3.) His works—all which in their whole tenure and contexture
showed him to be God-man.   If at any time there appeared any evidence of human weakness, lest the world should be offended and
stumble thereat, he did at the same time give out some notable demon-
strations of his divine power. When he lay in a manger at his birth, a
star appeared, and angels proclaimed his birth to the shepherds ;
when he was swaddled as an infant, the wise men came and worshipped
him ; when he was in danger of suffering shipwreck, he commanded
the winds and the waves, and they obeyed him ; when he was tempted
by Satan, he was ministered unto by the angels, Mat. iv. 11 ; when
they demanded tribute for the temple, a fish brought it to him, Mat.
xvii. 26 ; when he was deceived in the fig-tree (which was an infirmity of human ignorance), he suddenly blasted it, discovering the
glory of a divine power ; when he hung dying on the cross, the
rocks were rent, the graves opened, the sun darkened, and all nature
put into a rout.   Though he humbled himself to purchase our mercies,
yet he assured our faith by some emissions and breakings forth of his
divine power. Well, then, though it be our duty to seek and find out
God's track and foot-print in the whole creation, and to observe the
impressions of his wisdom, goodness, and power, in all the saints ;
especially this is our duty to admire his image in Jesus Christ, for in
his humanity the perfections of the Godhead shine forth in the highest
lustre.   Whatever perfection we conceive to be in his person, word, or
works, the same may we conclude to be in the Father also.   Did the
winds and seas obey Christ ? the whole creation is at the beck of
God.   Did Christ show himself to be the wisdom, goodness and power
of God ? surely God is infinitely wise. Was Christ holy and undefiled ?
surely so is God—light in whom is no darkness at all. Was Christ
loving, pitiful, and compassionate, not abhorring the most vile and
miserable, whether in soul or body, that came to him for relief ? surely
God is love, and he will not be strange to those that seek him in Christ.

3. How he differeth from other persons ; for the saints also are

made after the image of God: Col. iii. 10, 'And have put on the new man, which is renewed in knowledge after the image of him that created him;' Eph. iv. 24, 'And that ye put on the new man, which after God is created in righteousness and true holiness.' I answer,—There is a great difference between the image of God in man and the image of God in Christ.

[1.] Man resembleth God but imperfectly. Man was made, and is now made, after the image of God, but with much abatement of this high perfection which is in Christ, for he hath all the substantial perfection which his Father hath. In other creatures there is some resemblance, but no equality: other creatures are made like God, but he is begotten like God.

[2.] It is derivative from Christ. God would recover man out of his lapsed estate by setting up a pattern of holiness in our nature: Rom. viii. 29, ' Whom he did foreknow he also did predestinate to be conformed to the image of his Son, that he might be the first-born among many brethren.' None was fit to restore this image of God that was lost, but God incarnate, for thereby the glory of God was again visible in our nature. God is a pure spirit, and we are creatures, that have indeed an immortal soul, but it dwelleth in flesh; therefore to make us like God, ' the Word was made flesh,' that he might represent the perfections of God to us, and commend holiness by his own example.

Secondly, The next thing ascribed to Christ is that he is ' the first-born of every creature :' that is, born of God before any creature had a being, or begotten of the Father of his own proper essence, and equal with him before anything was created and brought forth out of nothing. But here the adversaries of the eternal Godhead of Christ triumph, and say, The first-born of the creatures is a creature, one of the same kind. I answer—If we grant this that they allege, they gain nothing, for Christ had two natures—he was God-man. As God, he is the Creator, and not a creature; for the apostle proveth that ' by him all things were made:' but as man, so he is indeed a creature. This double consideration must not be forgotten: Rom. i. 3, 4. Our Lord Jesus Christ was ' made of the seed of David according to the flesh, but declared to be the Son of God, with power according to the Spirit;' therefore we must distinguish between Christ and Christ, what he is according to the Spirit, and what he is according to the flesh.

2. I answer—That metaphors must be taken in the sense in which they are intended. Now what is the apostle's intention in giving Christ the appellation of the first-born?

Four things are implied by this metaphor :—

[1.] Identity of nature.
[2.] Likeness of original.
[3.] Antiquity.
[4.] Dignity.

Nothing else can be insinuated into the mind of man by such a form of speech but identity and sameness of nature between the brethren, which is true as to Christ's humanity: Heb. ii. 14, ' Forasmuch then as the children are partakers of flesh and blood, he also took part of the same ;' or else sameness of stock, which is true also, for tne same reason : Heb. ii. 11, ' For both he that sanctifieth and they who are sanctified are all of one ; for which cause he is not ashamed to call them brethren ;' or priority of time, for the first-born is before all the rest ; or else dignity, authority, and pre-eminence. Now, which of these doth the apostle intend ? The two last—the pre-existence of Christ before anything was made, as appeareth by this reason, ver. 16, ' For by him all things were made, whether they be in heaven or in earth ;' and also his dignity and authority above them, as appeareth by the frequent use of the word. For the first-born in families had authority over the rest. When Jacob had got the birthright, this was a part of Isaac's blessing : Gen. xxvii. 29, ' Let people serve thee, and nations bow down to thee : be lord over thy brethren, and let thy mother's sons bow down to thee.' Sovereignty was implied in the birthright, so David is called ' the first-born of the kings of the earth,' Ps. lxxxix. 27, as the most glorious amongst them. So here nothing else is intended but that Christ is in time and dignity before all creatures.

Thirdly, Though Christ be called the first-born of every creature, it doth not imply that he is to be reckoned as one of them, or accounted a creature. It is true, when it is said, Rom. viii. 29, that ' he is the first-born among many brethren,' it implieth that he is head of the renewed estate, that he and all new creatures are of the same kind— allowing him the dignity of his rank and degree ; for God is his God, and their God his Father and their Father. But here it is not the first-born amongst the creatures, but the first-born of every creature. And for further confirmation, here is not identity of nature, for he is not at all of the same nature with the angels—those principalities and thrones, dominions and powers, spoken of in the next verse—nor issued of the same stock with any of them. Mark, he is called the first-born, not first created, which must be understood of his divine nature and eternal generation of the Father before all creatures. The creatures are not begotten and born of God, but made by him. So Christ is *primogenitus*—that is, *unigenitus*, the first-born, that only-begotten. In the following verse he is brought in, not as a creature, but the creator of all things. The first-born is not the cause of the rest of the children. Peter was the first-born, yet may be a brother to James and John, but not a father to them. Now all the rest of the creatures are created and produced by him ; he is not reckoned among them as one of them—he is the image of the invisible God.

II. Why this excellency of our Redeemer should be so deeply impressed upon our minds and hearts ? For many reasons.

1. This is needful to show his sufficiency to redeem the world. The party offended is God, who is of infinite majesty ; the favour to be purchased is the everlasting fruition of God ; and the sentence to be reversed is the sentence of everlasting punishment. Therefore there needed some valuable satisfaction to be given to reconcile these things to our thoughts ; that we may be confident that we shall have redemption by his blood, even the remission of sins. There are three things that commend the value of Christ's sacrifice—the dignity of his person, the greatness of his sufferings, and the merit of his obedience. But

the two latter without the former will little quiet the heart of scrupulous men. His sufferings were great, but temporary and finite—the
merit of his obedience much ; but how shall the virtue of it reach all
the world ? And if he be but a mere creature, he hath done what he
ought to do. I confess a fourth thing may be added—God's institution, which availeth to the end for which God hath appointed it; but
the scripture insists most on the first—the dignity of his person—which
putteth a value on his sacrifice: Acts xx. 18; Heb. ix. 13, 14; at least
there is an intrinsic worth. This answers all objections. His sufferings
were temporary and finite ; but it is the blood of God,—he hath offered
up himself through the eternal Spirit.

2. To work upon our love, that Christ may have the chief room in
our hearts. There is no such argument to work upon our love as that
God over all, blessed for ever, should come to relieve man in such a
condescending way : 1 John iii. 16, ' Hereby we perceive the love
which God hath to us, in that he laid down his life for us: ' that very
person that died for us was God. There was power discovered in the
creation, when God made us like himself out of the dust of the ground ;
but love in our redemption, when he made himself like us. The person that was to work out our deliverance was the eternal Son of God.
That God that owes nothing to man, and was so much offended by
man, and that stood in no need of man, having infinite happiness and
contentment in himself, that he should come and die for us ! Hereby
perceive we the love of God. When we consider what Christ is, we
shall most admire what he hath done for us.

Thirdly, That we may give Christ his due honour ; for God will
have all men to honour the Son as they honour the Father, John v.
23, he being equal in power and glory. The setting forth of his glory
is a rent due to him from all creatures. We are to praise him both
in word and deed, in mind, and heart, and practice, which we can
never do unless we understand the dignity of his person. We are apt
to have low thoughts of Christ, therefore we should often revive the
considerations that may represent his worth and excellency.

Fourthly, That we may place all hope of salvation in him, and may
make use of him to the ends which he came to accomplish. We can
hardly consider the work of redemption but some base thoughts arise
in our minds, nor entertain this mystery, with due respect to the truth,
and greatness, and admirableness of it, without raising our thoughts to
the consideration of the dignity of the person who is to accomplish it :
Heb. iii. 1, ' Therefore, brethren, consider the Lord Jesus, the great
high priest and apostle of our profession.'

Fifthly, That we may the better understand two things :—

1. The humiliation of the Son of God.

2. The way how we may recover the lost image of God.

1. The humiliation of the Son of God. Certainly, he that came to
redeem us was the brightness of his Father's glory and the express
image of his person. Now, how did he humble himself ? Was he
not still the image of God in our nature ? Yes, but the divine glory
and majesty was hidden under the veil of our flesh : little of it did
appear, and that only to those who narrowly did observe him ; the
brightness of his glory did not conspicuously shine forth. Was this

all ? No ; his dignity was lessened ; there was *capitis diminutio*, the lessening of a man's estate or condition,—as of a man degraded from the senatorian order to the degree of knight, thence to the plebeian. Thus was the eternal Son of God lessened, less than God, as mediator : John xiv. 28, ' My Father is greater than I.' As God incarnate he took an office designed to him by God, and obeyed him in all things. They were one in essence, John x. 30 ; yet with respect to his office to save souls, he was lessened. Nay, not only less than God, but lesser than the angels : Heb. ii. 7, ' He was made a little lower than the angels.' Not born so, but made so. Man is inferior to an angel as a man in the rank and order of beings ; the angels die not : therefore his incarnation and liableness to death is a great lessening of his dignity ; so not in respect of office only, but human nature assumed.

2. It showeth us how the image of God may be recovered ; if we be changed into the likeness of Christ, for he is the image of God. His merit should not only be precious to us, but his example. It is a great advantage not only to have a rule but an example ; because man is so prone to imitate, that an example in our nature maketh it the more operative. His excuse is ready at hand : we are flesh and blood— what would you have us do ? Therefore Christ came incarnate to be an example of holiness. He had the interests of flesh and blood to mind as well as we ; and so would show that a holy life is possible to those that are renewed by his grace. He obeyed God in our nature ; therefore in the same nature we may obey, please, and glorify God, though still in a self-denying manner. The foundation of it is laid in the new birth. The Spirit that formed Christ out of the substance of the Virgin, the same Spirit is ready to form Christ in you. He maketh new creatures ; so that there is not only Christ's example, but Christ's power.

Use 1. Then let the excellency and dignity of Christ's person be more upon your minds and hearts ; think often of those two notions in the text—that he is the image of the invisible God, that therein you may be like him. You cannot be the image of God so as he was, but you must be in your measure. ' The fulness of the Godhead dwelt in him bodily,' but you must be ' partakers of the divine nature.' He showed himself to be the Son of God by his works, when the Jews said he blasphemed when he said he was the Son of God : John x. 27, ' If I do not the works of my Father, believe me not.' He allowed them to doubt of them, if he did not those works which were proper to one sent from God. Certainly this is the glory of man, to be the image of God ; there is no greater perfection than to live in the nearest resemblance to his Creator. Christ is more excellent, because he hath more of the image of God upon him.

2. Consider, again, that he is Lord of the whole creation, and there-fore called ' the first-born of every creature.' Well, then, we should be subject to him, and with greater diligence apply ourselves to the obedience of his holy laws, and use the means appointed by him to obtain the blessedness offered to us. There is in us a natural senti-ment of the authority of God, and we have a dread upon our hearts if we do what he hath forbidden ; but we have not so deep a sense of the authority of Christ, and play fast and loose with religion, as fancy

and humour and interest lead us. Now, from this argument, you see
we should honour the Son as we honour the Father, and be as tender
of his institutions as we are of the commandments evident by natural
light ; for he is not only the messenger of God, but his express image,
and the first-born of every creature. Not to believe him, and obey
him, and love him, is to sin, not only against our duty, but our remedy
and the law of our recovery.

SERMON III.

*For by him were all things created, that are in heaven, and that are
in earth, visible and invisible, whether they be thrones, or dominions, or principalities, or powers: all things were created by him,
and for him.*—COL. I. 16.

THE apostle had told us in the former verse that Jesus Christ is the
first-born of every creature. The Arians thence concluded that he
himself was created out of nothing in order of time before the world.
But it is not ' the first created of any creature,' but ' the first-born,'
which noteth a precedency, not only in point of antiquity, but dignity ;
and is as much as to say, Lord of every creature. For the first-born
was the lord of the rest, and the title may be given either relatively or
comparatively.

1. Relatively ; when the rest are of the same stock, or have the
relation of brethren to him that hath the pre-eminence. So it is given
to Christ with respect to new creatures: Rom. viii. 29, ' That he
might be the first-born among many brethren.'

2. Comparatively only ; when several persons or things be compared, though there be no relation between them. So David is called
' the first-born of the kings of the earth,' Ps. lxxxix. 27—that is,
superior in dignity and honour. So here it is taken not relatively, for
so Christ is *primogenitus*, the first-born, that he is also *unigenitus*,
the only-begotten. None went before, or come after him, that are so
begotten of God. What he asserteth in that verse, he now proveth
by the creation of all things, in ver. 16, and the conservation of all
things, ver. 17. We are now upon the first proof. Surely he that
created all things is supreme lord of all things, or hath the right of
the first-born over them. Two ways is Christ said to have a right to
the creatures : as God, and as mediator. His right as God is natural
and perpetual; his right as mediator is by grant and donation. It is
a power acquired and obtained. His natural right is antecedent to his
actual susception of the office of mediator ; for it comes to him by
creation. He made all, and it is fit that he should be sovereign and
lord of all. But the other power and sovereignty is granted to him as
a part of his reward and recompense for the sorrows of his humiliation : Phil. ii. 9, 10, ' Wherefore God also hath highly exalted him,
and given him a name above every name ; that at the name of Jesus
every knee should bow, of things in heaven, and things in earth, and
things under the earth.' The apostle speaks not of this latter now,

but of the former—his right as the only-begotten Son of God : he is the first-born, that is, Lord of the whole creation.   And good reason, ' for by him were all things created that are in heaven, and that are in earth,' &c.   In the words, the creation of the world is ascribed to Christ.   Take notice—

1. Of the object of this creation.
2. Christ's efficiency about it.

1. The object of creation is spoken collectively and distributively.

[1.] Collectively : ' By him were all things created.'

[2.] Distributively: They are many ways distinguished.

(1.) By their place : ' Things in heaven, and things in earth.'

(2.) By their nature : ' Things visible and invisible.'

(3.) By their dignity and office : ' Thrones, dominions, principalities, and powers'—words often used in scripture to signify the angels, whether good or bad.   The good angels: Eph. i. 21, 'Far above all principality and power, and might and dominion;' Eph. iii. 10, ' That unto principalities and powers in heavenly places might be known by the church the manifold wisdom of God.'   Sometimes this term is given to the bad angels: ' We wrestle not against flesh and blood, but against principalities and powers,' Eph. vi. 12 ; and Rom. viii. 38, ' Nor angels, nor principalities, nor powers.'   So that the meaning is, the angelical creatures, together with their degree and dignity, as well among themselves as over the lower world; of what rank and degree soever they are, they are all created by him.   He insisteth more on them than on the other branches, because some cried up the dignity of the angels, to the lessening of the honour and office of Christ, and because they were the noblest and most powerful creatures.   And if the most glorious creatures were created by him, surely all others had their being and life from him.   Well, then, there is a gradation notable in setting forth the object of the creation.   Christ made not only things in earth but things in heaven ; not only the visible things of heaven, the sun, moon, and stars, but the invisible, the angels—not the lower sort of angels only, but the most noble and the most potent —thrones, dominions, principalities, and powers.

2. Christ's efficiency about them ; in these words, they were ' created by him, and for him.'

[1.] *By him ;* as an equal co-operating cause, or co-worker with God the Father: John v. 19, 'Whatsoever things the Father doeth, those doeth the Son likewise.'   To bring a thing out of nothing belongeth unto God.   The distance of the terms is infinite ; so must the agent be.   Creation is an act of divine power.

[2.] They are *for him :* they are *by him* as their first cause ; they are *for him* as their last end.   God is often represented in scripture as first and last : Isa. xli. 4, 'I the Lord, the first and the last, I am he ;' Isa. xliv. 6, ' I am the first and the last; there is no God besides me ;' so Isa. xlviii. 2, ' I am the first ; I am also the last.' Now all this is repeated and applied to Christ: Rev. i. 17, ' He said unto me, Fear not; I am the first and the last; I have the keys of death and hell;' Rev. ii. 8, ' These things saith the first and the last, which was dead, and is alive;' Rev. xxii. 13, 'I am Alpha and Omega, the beginning and the end, the first and the last.'   Now these expressions do imply his eternal power and Godhead. He hath been before all things were made, and shall be when all things in the world are ended. He is the first being from whom all things are, and the last end to whom all things are to be referred. He is the efficient and final cause of all the creatures.

Doct. That all creatures, angels not excepted, owe their very being to Christ, the Son of God, our blessed and glorious Redeemer.

I shall take the method offered in the text, and show you:—

First, That all things were created by him.

Secondly, Why the creation of angels is so particularly mentioned and insisted upon.

Thirdly, That all things were created for him.

First, For creation by him. This is often asserted in scripture: John i. 3, 'All things were made by him, and without him was not anything made that was made.' John begins his Gospel with the dignity of Christ's person; and how doth he set it forth? By the creation of the world by the eternal Word. And what he saith is an answer to these questions—When was the Word? 'In the beginning;' Where was the Word? 'With God;' What was the Word? He 'was God;' What did he then do? 'All things were made by him;' What! all without exception? Yes, 'Without him nothing was made that was made,' be it never so small, never so great. From the highest angel to the smallest worm, they had all their being from him. Two things are to be explained:—

1. How he made all things.

2. When he made the angels.

1. How he made all things. Freely, and of his own will: Rev. iv. 11, 'Thou art worthy, O Lord, to receive honour, and glory, and power: for thou hast created all things, and for thy pleasure they are and were created.' They use three words to set forth the honour that is due to Christ for creating the world: glory, because of his excellencies discovered; honour, which is the ascription or acknowledgment of those excellencies; and power, because 'the invisible things of his Godhead and power are seen by the things that are made,' Rom. i. 20. For in the creating of the world he exercised his omnipotency. And this they do, not to express their affection, but his own due desert: 'Thou art worthy, O Lord.' The reason they give is, because he hath created all things for his own pleasure, or according to his own will—not out of necessity. There was no tie upon him to make them, but only he of his good pleasure thought fit to do so. He might have done it in another manner, or at another time, or in another order. There is nothing in the world that hath a necessary connexion with the divine essence, so as, if God be, that must be; nothing external cometh from God by necessity of nature, but all is done according to the counsel of his own will. Some thought all created things did come forth from the Creator by way of emanation, as rivers flow out of their fountain; but there is no stream floweth out of any fountain but it was before a part of that fountain while it was in it. But that cannot be said of any creature in respect of God, that it was any part of God before it came out from him. Others say the creatures came out from God by way of representation, as an image in the glass from

him that passeth by or looketh on it; but before the world was made
there was no such glass to represent God.   Others would express it
thus—that the world cometh out from God as a shadow from the body.
But yet this will not fit the turn neither: for the shadow doth not
come out from the body, but follows it, because of the deprivation of
light from the interposition of another body.   Others say—all cometh
from God as a footprint, or track in clay or sand, from one that passeth
over it; but there was nothing on which God, by passing, might
make such an impression.   Whatever good intention they might have by
setting forth the creation by these expressions, yet you see they are
not proper and accurate.   These expressions may have their use to
raise man's understanding to contemplate the excellency and majesty
of the Creator; for they all show his incomparable excellency and
perfection, together with the vanity, nothingness, or smallness of the
creature if compared with him, as great a bulk as it beareth in our
eye.   They are but as a ray from the sun, a stream from the fountain,
or a drop to the ocean; an image in the glass, or a shadow to the substance; or like a footprint of a man in the clay or sand; and so
are but certain signs leading up to the thing signified, or letters and
syllables out of which we may spell God—as the streams lead us to
the fountain, the image to the man, the shadow to the body, or the
track to the foot that made it.   But the scripture, leaving those comparisons, showeth us that the world came out from the Creator as the
workmanship from the artificer, the building from the architect, Heb.
xi. 10.   Now every artificer and builder worketh merely out of the
counsel of his own will.   And herein they resemble God; but only
what they do with great labour, God doth with the beck of his own
will and word: Ps. xxxiii. 6, ' By the word of the Lord the heavens
were made, and all the host of them by the breath of his mouth.'   A
bare word of his immediately created all the world, the heavens
and earth, and all that is in them.

2. When did he make the angels ? for in the history of Moses there
seemeth to be a great silence of it.

I answer—We read, Gen. i. 1, that in the beginning—that is,
when God did first set himself to create—that then he created the
heaven and the earth; but we read again in the 20th verse, ' That in
six days the Lord made heaven and earth, and the sea, and all that
in them is.'   I argue, that if within that compass of time, the Lord
made heaven and earth, and all things that are in them, angels are
included in that number, being the inhabitants of heaven, as men and
beasts are of the earth, and fishes of the sea; as here, by things in
heaven, the apostle principally understands the angels, and by things
on earth, men.   Therefore, as things on earth were not made but
after the earth, so things in heaven were not created but after the
heavens were created.   The heavens were not created till the second
day, nor perfected and fitted till the fourth.   Therefore, as God did
furnish the earth with plants and beasts before men, so did he adorn
the heaven with stars before he filled it with angels; for he first framed
the house and adorned it before he brought in the inhabitants.   Therefore, probably they were made the fourth day.   If this seemeth too
short a time before the fall of the apostate angels, you must remember

how soon man degenerated.   Some think he did not sleep in innocency, quoting that Ps. xlix. 12, ' Man being in honour abides
not, but is like the beasts that perish.'   The word signifies a night's
lodging in an inn—shall not lodge or stay a night.   Others make
his fall on the next day, the Sabbath, for at the end of the sixth
day all was good, very good.   The angels fell from their first state
as soon as they were created—so short and uncertain is all created
glory.

Secondly, All things were created for him—that is, for the honour
of the Son, as well as for the honour of the Father and the Holy
Ghost.   Now this is necessary to be thought of by us, because there is
a justice in the case that we should return and employ all in his
service from whom we have received all, even though it be with the
denial of our nearest and dearest interest.   He is worthy of this glory
and honour from us, and that we should trust upon him as a faithful
Creator in the midst of all dangers.

1. I will prove that the greatest glory the creature is capable of is
to serve the will and set forth the praise of its Creator, for everything
that attaineth not its end is vain.   What matter is it whether I be a
dog, or a man, a beast, or an angel, if I serve not the end for which I
was made ?   And that is not the personal and particular benefit of any
creature, but the glory of the Creator, for God made all things for
himself, Prov. xvi. 4 ; whether he made beasts, or man, or angels, it
was still with a respect to his own glory and service.   God is independent and self-sufficient of himself and for himself.   Self-seeking in
the creature is monstrous and incongruous.   It is as absurd and un-
beseeming to seek its own glory as to attribute to itself its own being :
Rom. xi. 36, ' Of him, and through him, and to him are all things.'
God's glory is the end of our being and doing, for being and doing
are both from him, and therefore for him alone.   Above all, it concerneth man to consider this: who can glorify God not only objectively
by the impressions of God upon him, and passively, as God will over-
rule all his actions to his own glory, but actively, as he is the mouth
of the creation—not only to honour God himself, but to give him the
praise which resulteth from all his works.   It was well said of a
heathen, *Si essem luscinia*—if I were a nightingale I would sing as
a nightingale ; *Si alauda*—if I were a lark I would pere as a lark.
When I am a man what should I do but know, love, and praise God
without ceasing, and glorify my Creator ?   Things are unprofitable
or misplaced when they do not seek or serve their end ; therefore for
what use are we meet, who are so unmeet for our proper end ?   Like
the wood of the vine that is good for nothing, not so much as to make
a pin whereon to hang anything, Ezek. xv. 2—good for nothing but
to be cast into the fire unless it be fruitful.   What are we good for if
we be not serviceable to the ends for which we were created ?

2. The design of God was that the whole creation should be put
in subjection to the Word incarnate—not only this lower world, wherein
man is concerned, but the upper world also.   Our Redeemer, who hath
bought us, hath an interest in all things that may concern us, that they
may be disposed of to his own glory and our good and advantage.
All are at the making and at the disposal of our Lord Jesus Christ.

Therefore it is said, Heb. ii. 10, 'For whom are all things, and by whom are all things.' God that frameth all things ordereth all things to their proper end. His works are many, and some are more excellent and glorious than others; and one of the chief of them is the salvation of man by Jesus Christ. Therefore all things are subordinated thereunto, to the glory of the Mediator by whom this is accomplished: 1 Cor. viii. 6, 'But to us there is but one God, the Father, of whom are all things, and we in him; and one Lord Jesus Christ, by whom are all things, and we by him.'

Secondly, Why the creation of angels is so particularly and expressly mentioned? I answer—For three reasons:—

1. To show the glory and majesty of the Redeemer. The angels are said to 'excel in strength,' Ps. ciii. 20, and elsewhere they are called 'mighty angels.' This potency they have from their Creator, who giveth power and strength to all his creatures as it pleases him. Their strength may be conceived by that instance, that one angel in a night slew one hundred and eighty-five thousand in Sennacherib's camp. Now, these potent creatures are infinitely inferior to our Redeemer, by whom and for whom they were made. Though they are the most excellent of all the creatures, yet they are his subjects and ministers, at his beck and command, both by the law of their creation, as Christ is God, and also by the Father's donation, as he is Mediator and God incarnate: 1 Pet. iii. 25, 'He is set down on the right hand of God; angels, authorities, and powers being made subject to him.' And again, Eph. i. 21, 'He hath set him far above all principality, and power, and might, and dominion, and every name that is named, not only in this world, but in that which is to come.' They have a great name, but Christ hath 'a more excellent name than they,' Heb. i. 4, for they are all bound to worship him, ver. 6, and serve him, for he employeth them for the defence and comfort of the meanest of his people. They are subject not only to God, but to Christ, or God incarnate. Look, as it is the glory of earthly kings to command mighty and powerful subjects—('Are not my princes altogether kings?' Isa. x. 8, that so many princes held under him as their sovereign and served him as their commander; and when God speaks of the Assyrian he calleth him 'a king of princes,' Hosea viii. 10, namely, as he had many kings subject and tributary to him)—so is this the majesty of our Redeemer, that he hath these powerful creatures, the mighty angels, in his train and retinue. These heavenly hosts make up a part of that army which is commanded by the Captain of our salvation.

2. This is mentioned to obviate the errors of that age. Both the Jews and the Gentiles had a high opinion of spirits and angels, as God's ministers and messengers; for he doth not always immediately administer the affairs of mankind. Now, as they were right in the main as to their service, so they added much of curiosity and superstition to the doctrine of angels, and by their vain speculations infected the minds of many in the Christian church, who were but newly come out from among them, insomuch that they fell to the worshipping of angels as mediators to God; as the apostle intimateth, Col. ii. 18. Now, because this was to the disparagement of Christ, the apostles did set themselves to check this curiosity of dogmatising about angels, and

the superstition or idolatry of angel-worship thence growing apace.
Now this they did by asserting the dignity of Christ's person and
office. As Paul, Col. ii., and the author to the Hebrews, chapters
i., ii., iii., 'Hath in these last days spoken unto us by his Son, whom
he hath appointed heir of all things, by whom also he made the worlds,
who being the brightness of his glory, and the express image of his
person, and upholding all things by the word of his power, when he
had by himself purged our sins, sat down on the right hand of the
Majesty on high.' It is true, Christ was sent from heaven as the angels
are, and he came in a despicable way of appearance to promote our
salvation and recovery, as they assumed bodies suitable to their message; yet his superiority and pre-eminence above the angels is clear and
manifest. He was not only equal to them, but far above them, Heb.
i. 3. Seven things are observable in that verse :—

(1.) Christ came as the eternal Son of God : ' He hath spoken unto
us *by his Son.*' When he cometh to the angels, he saith, they are
servants and ministering spirits. For a short while he ministered in the
form of a servant in the days of his flesh—they continue to be so from
the beginning to the end of the world.

(2.) He was *heir of all things*—that is, Lord of the whole creation—
they only principalities and powers, for certain ends, to such persons
and places, over which Christ sets them.

(3.) He was the Creator of the world. ' By whom also he *made the
worlds,*' saith the apostle. They are noble and divine creatures indeed,
but the work of Christ's hands.

(4.) He is ' the brightness of his Father's glory, and the express
image of his person '—that is, the essential image of God ; they only
have some strictures of the divine majesty.

(5.) The 'upholding all things by the word of his power'—that
is, the conserving cause of all that life and being that is in the creature.
The angels live in a continual dependence upon Christ as their creator,
and without his supporting influence, would be soon annihilated.

(6.) By himself he ' purged our sins.' He was sent into the world
for that great and glorious work of mediation, which none of them was
worthy to undertake, none able to go through withal, but himself
alone. They are sent about the ordinary concernments of the saints,
or the particular affairs of the world : he is the author of the whole
work of redemption and salvation, and they but subordinate assistants
in the particular promotion of it.

(7.) He ' sat down on the right hand of the Majesty on high ; they
are spirits near the throne of God, ever in his presence, attending on
him like princes. God never made any of them universal and eternal
king, for he set Christ at his right hand, not the angels. To sit at
God's right hand, is not only to be blessed and happy in enjoying
those pleasures which are there for evermore, not only to be advanced
to the highest place of dignity and honour next to God, but to be
invested with a supreme and universal power above all men and
angels. Take these, or any one of these, and he is above the angels,
though they be the most noble and excellent creatures that ever God
made.

3. Because Christ hath a ministry and service to do by them. He

makes use of them partly to exercise their obedience, without which
they forsake the law of their creation and swerve from the end for
which they were made: Ps. ciii. 20, 'They do his commandments,
hearkening to the voice of his word.' They do whatsoever he commandeth them, with all readiness and speed imaginable, and therein
they are an example to us: Mat. vi. 10, 'Thy will be done in earth,
as it is in heaven.' They are our fellow-servants now in the work,
hereafter in the recompense, when we are admitted into one society,
under one common head and Lord, Heb. xii. 27, who shall for ever
rejoice in the contemplation of God's infinite excellencies. Well, then,
if these excellent creatures, so great in power, be always so ready and
watchful to do the will of God, and count it their honour to assist in
so glorious a work as the saving of souls, or do any other business he
sendeth them about, how should we, that hope to be like the angels
in happiness, be like them in obedience also!

2. Because the church's safety dependeth upon it. We stand in
need of this ministry of angels. The service of the angels is protection to the people of God—vengeance on their enemies.

(1.) For protection. Christ hath the heavenly host at his command,
and sendeth them forth for the good of his people: Ps. lxviii. 17,
'The chariots of the Lord are twenty thousand, even thousands of
angels: the Lord is among them in Sinai in the holy place.' Mark,
that thousands of angels are his chariots, conveying him from heaven
to earth, and from earth to heaven; and mark, the Lord is among
them—that is, God incarnate—for he presently speaketh of his ascending up on high. 'Thou hast ascended up on high, and led captivity
captive; thou hast received gifts for men,' ver. 18. Among them in
his holy place—that is, in heaven. It is added, as in Mount Sinai—
that is, as at the giving of the law. They were then there, and still
attend on the propagation of the gospel. For more particular cases,
see Heb. i. 14, 'Are they not all ministering spirits, sent forth to
minister for them who shall be heirs of salvation?' So Ps. xxxiv.
7, 'The angel of the Lord encampeth round about them that fear him,
and delivereth them.' All that obediently serve and wait on God
have the promise of this protection.

(2.) The other part of this ministry and service is to restrain and
destroy the devil and his instruments. The scripture often speaks of
God's executing judgments by the angels. Their influence doth not
always personally appear, yet it is great and powerful. Though the
powers and authorities on earth, and their messengers and forces, be
often employed against the saints, yet the Captain of our salvation is in
heaven, and all the mighty angels are subject to him, and at his disposal. By this means the prophet Elisha confirmed himself and his
servant, when the king of Syria sent chariots and horses, a great host,
to attack him in Dothan: 2 King vi. 14, 15, 'And when his servant
saw it early in the morning, he said, Alas, my master! what shall we
do?' The prophet answered, ver. 16, 'They that be with us are
more than they that be against us.' And then, ver. 17, he prayed,
'Lord, open his eyes that he may see; and the Lord opened his eyes,
and behold the mountain was full of chariots and horses of fire, round
about Elisha.' These fiery horses and chariots were nothing else but

the angels of God.   Here is force against force, chariots against chariots, horse against horse, if we could open the eye of faith and shut that of sense.   We read, Acts xii. 23, that an angel smote Herod in the midst of his pride and persecution : the angel of the Lord smote him.

Use 1. Let us more deeply be possessed with the majesty of our Redeemer.   He is the Creator of all things, of angels as well as men, and so more excellent than all the men in the world, whether they excel in power or holiness, which the psalmist expresseth thus : ' Fairer than the children of men,' Ps. xlv. 29.   But also, then, the most excellent and glorious angels ; he is their creator as well as ours, head of principalities and powers, as well as of poor worms here upon earth. Surely the representing and apprehending of Christ in his glorious majesty is a point of great consequence.

1. Partly to give us matter for praise and admiration, that we may not have mean thoughts of his person and office.   He is a most glorious Lord and King, that holdeth the most powerful creatures in subjection to himself.   If Christians did know and consider how much of true religion consists in admiring and praising their Redeemer, they would more busy their minds in this work.

2. Partly to strengthen our trust, and to fortify us against all fears and discouragements in our service.   When we think of the great Creator of heaven and earth, and all things visible and invisible, angels, men, principalities, &c., surely the brightness of all creature glory should wax dim in our eyes: ' Our God is able to deliver us,' Dan. iii. 18, and will, as he did by his angel.   This was that which fortified Stephen: Acts v. 55, 56, ' He saw Jesus standing at the right hand of God.'   It is easy for him who made all things out of nothing to help us.   See Ps. cxxi. 2, ' My help standeth in the name of the Lord, who made heaven and earth.'   The Almighty Creator, ruler, and governor of the world, what cannot he do ?   As long as I see those glorious monuments of his power standing, I will not distrust he can afford me seasonable help by his holy angels, through the intercession of his Son, who hath assumed my nature.

3. Partly to bind our duty.   All creatures were made by him and for him ; therefore we should give up ourselves to him, and say with Paul, Acts xxvii. 23, ' His I am, and him I serve.'   His by creation and redemption, therefore everything we have and do ought to have a respect to his glory and service.   There is a variety of creatures in the world, of different kinds and different excellencies.   In the whole and every kind there is somewhat of the glory of God and Christ set forth. Now this should strike our hearts—Shall we only, who are the persons most obliged, be a disgrace to our Lord, both Creator and Redeemer, when the good angels are so ready to attend him at his beck and command, and that in the meanest services and ministries ?   Shall poor worms make bold with his laws, slight his doctrine, despise his benefits ?   Heb. ii. 2, 3, ' If the word spoken by angels was steadfast, and every transgression and disobedience received a just recompense of reward, how shall we escape if we neglect so great salvation ? '

4. And lastly, to make us more reverent in our approaches to him ; for he sits in the assembly of the gods, the holy angels are round

about him : Ps. cxxxviii. 1, ' Before the gods will I sing praise to
thee '—that is, in the presence of the holy angels: 1 Cor. x. 10 ;
Eccles. v. 6, ' Suffer not thy mouth to cause thy flesh to sin, neither
say thou before the angel that it was an error.' The angels in heaven
observe our behaviour in God's worship—what vows we make to God,
what promises of obedience. But, above all, there is our glorious Redeemer himself : Heb. xii. 28, 29, with what reverence and godly fear
should we approach his holy presence !

Use 2. Is to quicken us to thankfulness for our redemption ; that
our creator is our Redeemer. None of the angels did humble himself
as Christ did do, to do so great a piece of service, and yet he is far
above them. There is a congruity in it, that we should be restored
by him by whom we were made ; but he made the angels as well as
men, but he did not restore them. No ; they were not so much as in
a condition of forbearance and respite ; he assumed not their nature,
he created all things, but he redeemed mankind. His delights were
with the sons of men ; he assumed our nature, and for a while ' was
made a little lower than the angels,' Heb. ii. 9. We cannot sufficiently
bless God for the honour done to our nature in the person of Christ,
for it is God incarnate that is made head of angels, principalities, and
powers—God in our nature, whom all the angels are called upon to
adore and worship. The devil sought to dishonour God, as if he were
envious of man's happiness : Gen. iii. 5, ' God doth know that in the
day ye eat thereof ye shall be as gods.' And he sought to depress
the nature of man, which in innocency stood so near to God. Now, that
his human nature should be set so far above the angelical, in the
person of Christ, and be admitted to dwell with God in a personal
union, this calleth for our highest love and thankfulness.

Use 3. Is an encouragement to come to Christ for sanctifying
and renewing grace. I have three arguments :—

1. The person to whom we come. To whom should we come but
to our Creator, God infinitely good, wise, and powerful ? The creation
showeth him good, and whatever is good in the creatures is wholly
derived from his goodness. It is but like the odour of the sweet ointments, or the perfume that he leaveth behind him where he hath been,
James i. 19. He is infinitely wise. When he created and settled the
world, he did not jumble things in a chaos and confusion, but settled
them in a most perfect order and proportion, which may be seen,
not only in the fabric of the world, but in the disposition of the parts
of man's body, yea, or in any gnat or fly. Now cannot he put our
disordered souls in frame again ? If the fear of God be true wisdom,
to whom should we seek for it but from the wise God ? His infinite
power is seen also in the creation, in raising all things out of nothing.
And if a divine power be necessary to our conversion, to whom should
we go but to him who calleth the things that are not as though they
were ? Rom. iv. 17; ' According as his divine power hath given unto
us all things that pertain unto life and godliness,' 2 Pet. i. 7.

2. From the work itself, which is a new creation, which carrieth
much resemblance with the old : Eph. ii. 10, ' For we are his workmanship, created in Christ Jesus unto good works ;' 2 Cor. iv. 6,
' For God, who commanded the light to shine out of darkness, hath

shined into our hearts, to give the light of the knowledge of the glory
of God in the face of Jesus Christ.' It is such an effect as comes from
a being of infinite power, wisdom, and goodness, that man may be in
a capacity to love, please, and serve God. What was lost in Adam
can only be recovered by Christ.

3. From the relation of the party that seeketh it: Ps. cxix. 73,
'Thine hands have made me and fashioned me; give me understanding, that I may learn thy commandments.' We go to him as his own
creatures. This plea hath great force because of God's goodness to
all his creatures. (1.) Not only the angels, but every worm and fly had
their being from Christ; there is a great variety of living things in
the world, but they are all fed from the common fountain; therefore
we may comfortably come to him for life and quickening, John i. 4.
We need not be discouraged by our baseness and vileness, for the
basest worm had what it hath from him. (2.) That Christ, as Creator,
beareth such affection to man as the work of his hands: 'Is it good
unto thee that thou shouldst despise the work of thy hands?' Job x.
3. Artificers, when they have made an excellent work, are very chary
of it, and will not destroy it and break it in pieces: Job xiv. 15,
'Thou wilt have a desire to the work of thine hands.' As creatures
beg relief and help; if you cannot plead the covenant of Abraham, plead
the covenant of Noah. (3.) God forsakes none of the fallen creatures
but those that forsake him first: 2 Chron. xv. 2, 'The Lord is with
you while you be with him, and if ye seek him he will be found of
you, but if ye forsake him he will forsake you;' 1 Chron. xxviii. 9,
'If thou seek him he will be found of thee, but if thou forsake him he
will cast thee off for ever.' (4.) Especially will Christ be good to man
seeking after him for grace, that we may serve and obey him. For he
is no Pharaoh, to require brick and give no straw. Creating grace
laid the debt upon us, and his redeeming grace provideth the power
and help, that we may discharge it. Now, when we acknowledge the
debt and confess our impotency to pay it, and our willingness to
return to our duty, will Christ fail us? A conscience of our duty
is a great matter, but a desire of grace to perform it is more. Therefore, come as creatures earnestly desiring to do their Creator's will, and
to promote his glory. God will not refuse the soul that lieth so submissively at his feet.

SERMON IV.

And he is before all things, and by him all things consist.—
COL. I. 17.

THE apostle had asserted the dignity of Christ's person by ascribing
the work of creation to him: now the work of conservation and providence. By the same divine power by which Christ made all things
he doth preserve and sustain all things.

In this verse two things are ascribed to Christ :—

First, His precedency in point of time, or his antiquity before all creatures : *and he is before all things*—that is, he had an eternal being before anything that now is created.

Secondly, His sustaining all things by his almighty power : *and by him all things do consist.* All creatures owe their continuance and preservation to him.

The first point is his precedency and pre-existence before all creatures whatsoever.

Doct. That Jesus Christ had a being before any of the creatures were made.

1. That he had a being long before he was born of the Virgin, for he was in the time of the patriarchs, as John viii. 48, ' Before Abraham was, I am ;' to say nothing of that godlike way of speaking—I am ; not I was, but I am ; that which I now plead for is, that he was before Abraham. The words are occasioned by Christ saying that Abraham saw his day and was glad, which the Jews understood not of a prophetical but of a real vision, and therefore objected the impossibility that he was not yet fifty years old, and how could he see Abraham, or Abraham see him ? Christ doth not answer to their ill interpretation, but showeth that their very objection contained no absurdity if taken in their own sense, for he was not only in the time of Abraham, but long before, and so affirmeth more than that objection required. The Jews thought it absurd that Christ should be in the time of Abraham, but Christ affirmeth more, and that with a strong asseveration. He was not only by the constitution of God, but really existing before Abraham, for the predestination not only of Christ but of Abraham, and all the elect, was before the foundation of the world. If, in respect of special prediction, mark then what must follow. Then Cyrus must be in the time of Isaiah, Josiah must be in the time of Jeroboam, the calling of the Gentiles must be in the time of Moses, for they prophesied of these things.

2. That he had a being at the time of the creation, that is also clear; for it is said, 'In the beginning was the Word,' John i. 1—that is, when Christ set himself to create all things. The word *beginning*, signifies many things, but chiefly the beginning of all time, especially when it is put absolutely, without any limitation to the matter in hand. So John viii. 44, ' The devil was a murderer from the beginning '— that is, almost as soon as created ; Mat. xix. 4, ' He that made them at the beginning, made them male and female.' So Heb. i. 10, 'And thou in the beginning hast laid the foundations of the earth;' and in many other places. Therefore Christ had a being when the world and all creatures were made, visible and invisible. So Prov. viii. 22– 31, ' The Lord possessed me in the beginning of his way, before his works of old. I was set up from everlasting, from the beginning, or ever the earth was. When there were no depths, I was brought forth ; when there were no fountains abounding with water. Before the mountains were settled, before the hills was I brought forth : while as yet he had not made the earth, nor the fields, nor the highest part of the dust of the world. When he prepared the heavens, I was there: when he set a compass upon the face of the depth : when he established the clouds above : when he strengthened the fountains of the deep : when he gave to the sea his decree, that the waters should not

pass his commandment: when he appointed the foundations of the earth: then I was by him, as one brought up with him : and I was daily his delight, rejoicing always before him ; rejoicing in the habitable parts of his earth; and my delights were with the sons of men.' There the Wisdom of God, or the eternal Word, describeth the antiquity of his person. All the question is, what this Wisdom is that is there spoken of?

(1.) It is not human, but divine; for the Wisdom there spoken of was before the world was.

(2.) Whatever it be, it is not a divine attribute, but a divine person; for those things which are there ascribed to Wisdom cannot properly belong to an attribute, to be begotten, brought forth, ver. 23, 24. to have the affections of love, ver. 27, delight, ver. 31. All along the expressions agree only to a person. That Wisdom which inviteth sinners, promises the Spirit, threatens eternal destruction to those which hearken not to him, commendeth not the laws of Moses, but requireth obedience to his own laws—what can this Wisdom be but a person? If the intent were only to express that God is wise, what strange expressions would these be! To what purpose were it to give us notice that he was wise from the beginning, if there were no other mystery in it?

(3.) This person was Christ, who is the Wisdom of God, 1 Cor. i. 24; 'And in whom are hid all the treasures of wisdom and knowledge,' Col. ii. 3.

3. Thirdly, That Christ was before the world was, from all eternity: Micah v. 2, 'His goings forth are from everlasting.' The prophet there speaketh of his birth at Bethlehem, and his eternal generation, and distinguishes the one from the other: 'But thou, Bethlehem Ephrata, though thou be little among the thousands of Judah, yet out of thee shall he come forth unto me that is to be ruler in Israel ; whose goings forth have been from of old, from everlasting ;' or from the days of eternity. This last clause is added lest any should look upon this ruler as only man, and beginning to be at his incarnation. He that was born at Bethlehem was also true God, begotten of the Father from all eternity.

4. Fourthly, That Christ was God subsisting in the divine nature. I shall bring two places to prove that. The first, Phil. ii. 6, 'Who being in the form of God, thought it not robbery to be equal with God, but emptied himself, and made himself of no reputation.' He was first in the form of God, before he appeared in the form of a servant. The form of God is his divine glory and blessedness, every way equal to God ; the form of a servant is either his coming in the similitude of sinful flesh, or his subjecting himself to the curse of the law, or his humble and mean condition while he lived among men. It consists in one of these, or in all three. Now before he submitted to this, he existed in the form of God—that is, was clothed with divine majesty, and in all things equal with God the Father : his being and existence which he then had was truly divine. The form of God is the very divine essence, as clothed with glory and majesty ; this did justly and naturally belong to him, and was not usurped by him. The other place is Christ's prayer: John xvii. 5, 'And now, O Father, glorify

thou me with thy own self, with the glory which I had with thee before the world was.' God is said to glorify any person when he giveth him glorious qualities and powers; or by revealing and manifesting those glorious qualities which he hath; or when he doth receive him and treat him agreeably to his glory. The meaning of Christ's prayer, then, must be of one or other of all these senses. When he prayeth that the Father would glorify him with that glory that he had with him before the world was, if you take it in the first sense, he desireth that God would bestow upon him as Mediator, or God incarnate, a glory suitable to that glory he had with him from all eternity; if in the second sense, he desireth his glory may be revealed, or become conspicuous in his human nature; if in the third, that God would receive him honourably and agreeably to that glory: which sense is the chiefest, for it containeth the other two. The meaning, then, in short, is, that he might be received to the full enjoyment of that glory which he had before the world was. Christ was from all eternity the glorious God. This glory of his Godhead, by his humiliation was not diminished and lessened, but obscured and hidden; and therefore prayeth that he may be received by the Father, and openly declared to the world to be the Son of God; or that the glory of his Godhead might shine forth in the person of Christ, God-man. Well, then, before any creature was, Christ had a divine glory. How had it he? The enemies of this truth say, By decree or designation, not by possession. But that cannot be: he that is not, hath nothing. If he had not a divine being, how could he have divine glory before the world? None can say Paul was an apostle of Christ before the world was, because he was appointed or designed to this work; yea, none can say he had faith and brotherly love when he was yet an unbeliever and persecutor; yet it pleased God to separate him from his mother's womb, and predestinated him to have these things. Again, then, all true believers may thus pray to God, ' Glorify me with,' &c., for they are thereunto appointed. But this is absurd. Besides, if he had it then, how could he want it now? The decree is the same. It remaineth, then, that Christ had a being and substance in the Godhead before any of the creatures were made.

Use 1. This serveth for the confutation of those atheists that say, Christ took upon him the appellation of a god to make his doctrine more authentic and effectual. They confess the morals of Christianity are most excellent for the establishment of piety and honesty, but, men's inclination carrying them more powerfully to vice than virtue, this doctrine would not be received with any reverence if it came recommended to them by a mere man, and therefore Christ assumed the glorious appellation of the Son of God, or pretended to be God— a blasphemy very derogatory both to the honour of Christ and Christianity, and quite contrary to the drift of the scriptures, both of the Old and New Testament. The Messiah promised in the Old Testament was to be God, all the prophets agree in that. Jesus Christ proved himself to be God by his word and works, and the apostles still assert it. Could they that lived in so many several ages as the prophets and apostles did, lay their heads together and have intelligence one with another to convey this imposture to the world? Surely, if Christ be the Messiah promised in the Old Testament, as clearly he is, then he

is God, for that describeth him to be such; and if Christ usurped
this honour, how did God so highly favour him with such extraordinary graces, by inspiring him with the knowledge of the best
religion in the world, to authorise him with miracles, to raise him
from the dead? And must this religion, that condemneth all frauds,
and doing evil that good may come of it, be supported by a lie? Or
cannot God govern the world without countenancing such a deceit?
Or is it possible that such holy persons as our Lord Jesus and his
apostles were, could be guilty of such an imposture? Did they do
this by command of God? No, surely; for God, which is the God of
truth, would not command them to teach a lie, or to make use of one.
He hath power enough to cause the truth to be embraced by some
other means; and a greater injury cannot be done him than to go
about to gratify him with what he hateth; much less would God have
commanded a mere man to call himself his eternal Son, and God equal
to him, which is a blasphemy and sacrilege as well as a lie—the
greatest of the kind, for mortal man to take upon himself to be the
eternal God. If it were not by his express commandment, would he
suffer such an attempt to go unpunished? Would he witness from
heaven, 'This is my beloved Son in whom I am well pleased'?
Would he have raised him from the dead, and so engaged the world
to believe in him and adore him? Acts xvii. 31.

2. If Christ were before all things, let us prefer him above all
things. This consideration is of great use to draw off our hearts from
all created things, and to lessen our respects to worldly vanities, that
they may be more earnestly fixed on what is eternal and glorious. He
that was before the world was will be when the world shall be no
more. Christ is from everlasting to everlasting, Ps. xc. 2. To him
should we look, after him should we seek: he is first and last, the
beginning and ending. It is for an everlasting blessedness, for the
enjoyment of an eternal God, that our souls were made. He that was
from the beginning, and will be when all things shall have an end, it
is he that should take up our minds and thoughts. How can we have
room for so many thoughts about fading glories, when we have an
eternal God and Christ to think of? What light can we see in a
candle when the sun shineth in his full strength? All things in the
world serve only for a season, and then wither; and that season is but
a short one. You glory in your riches and pre-eminence now, but
how long will you do so? To-day that house and lands is thine, but
thou canst not say it will be thine to-morrow. But a believer can say,
'My God, my Christ, is mine to-day, and will be mine to all eternity.'
Death taketh all from us—honours and riches, and strength, and life;
but it cannot take God and Christ from us. They are ours, and everlastingly ours.

Secondly, We come now to the second point—his sustaining all
things by his almighty power: 'and by him all things consist.'

Doct. 2. That as Christ made all things, so he doth sustain them
in being and working.

Let me explain this, how the creatures are preserved by Christ.

1. This is to be understood not only meritoriously as a moral cause,
but efficiently as a natural cause of the creature's sustentation: for the

apostle doth not consider here so much what Christ doth as a Mediator, as what he doth as God. It is true Christ, as Mediator, hath reprieved the world from that ruin which might come upon it for man's sin; but here his merit is not considered, but his power: Heb. i. 3, 'He upholdeth all things by the word of his power.' The weight of the whole creation lieth upon his hands. As Daniel telleth Belshazzar, that his breath and his ways were in the hand of God, Dan. v. 23, so is the being, life, and operation of all the creatures. If he should withdraw his withholding hand, they would quickly return to their first nothing; which showeth the great power of our Redeemer. Moses complaineth, Num. xi. 11, 12, 'Thou hast laid the burden of all this people upon me. Have I conceived this people? have I begotten them, that thou shouldst say unto me, Carry them in thy bosom?' But Christ hath the care and charge of all the world, not to rule them only, but to sustain them. A king or a governor hath a moral rule over his subjects, but Christ giveth them being and existence, and doth preserve and keep them in their present state and condition from dissolution.

2. Not only indirectly, but directly. Indirectly, Christ may be said to sustain and preserve the creatures, as he keepeth off evil, or removeth those things that may be destructive to them: as he preserveth a town that repelleth their enemies. But directly, he preserveth them as he continueth his providential influence: Acts xvii. 28, 'For in him we live, and move, and have our being;' as the root feedeth the fruit, or the breath of the musician maintains the sound: Ps. civ. 29, 'Thou takest away thy breath, and they die, and return to their dust.' Life, and all the joys and comforts of it, every minute depend upon God. It is by his providential influence and supportation we subsist. The greatest creature cannot preserve itself by its power and greatness, and the least is not neglected; both would sink into nothing without this continued influence.

3. He doth this not only mediately, by means appointed, but immediately, as his efficacy pierceth through all. God preserveth the creatures by means, for he giveth them those supplies which are proper for them: as to man, food and raiment; for other creatures, what may relieve them; and the wise dispensing these supplies, without any care and solicitude of the creatures, is a notable part of his providence. But here we consider his intimate presence with all things, by which he upholdeth their beings; which all the means of the world cannot do without him. God doth as it were hold the creatures in his own hand, that it may not sink into its old nothing, as a man holdeth a weighty thing. This is supposed to be alluded unto, Job vi. 9, 'Let him loose his hand and cut me off.' If he doth but loose his almighty grasp, all the creatures fall down.

4. Christ doth this so as that he doth not overturn their nature; he worketh by natural and necessary causes necessarily, with voluntary causes voluntarily. He that enlighteneth the world by the sun, causes man to discourse and reason; the sun would not shine if Christ were not the light of it, nor man discourse if he did not continue the faculty: John i. 4, 'In him was life, and this life was the light of man.' It is man seeth, man heareth, man talketh, man acteth, but yet 'the seeing eye, and hearing ear, is of the Lord,' Prov.

xx. 12. As God hath made both, so he sustaineth both in their operation and exercise. All that we do naturally and spiritually we have
from Christ.

5. He is not the bare instrument of God in sustaining the creature, but as a co-equal agent. As he made the world, and with the
Father created all things, so he doth support and order all things.
It is as well the work of the Son as of the Father, for he is God, equal
with him in glory and power: John v. 17, 'My Father worketh
hitherto, and I work.' And he hath a command of all the creatures,
that they can do nothing without him, how much soever they attempt
to do against him.

Secondly, Let me give you the reasons of this, why all things must
subsist by him.

1. Because preservation is but a kind of continued creation, or a
continuance of the being which God hath caused. God's will in
creation maketh a thing to be, his will in preservation maketh it continue to be. The same omnipotency and efficacy of God is necessary
to sustain our beings as at first to create them. Therefore, it is said,
Ps. civ. 2, ' Thou stretchest out the heavens like a curtain,' which
noteth a continued act. God erected them at first, and still sustaineth
them by his secret power in this posture ; so that, with respect to God,
it is the same action to conserve as to create. That the creature may
have a being, the influence of God is necessary to produce it ; that the
creature may continue its being, it is necessary that God should not
break off that influence, or forsake the creature so made ; for the being
of the creature doth so wholly depend on the will of God, that it cannot subsist without him. Nothing can be without the will of God,
which is the cause both of the being and existence of all creatures.
Therefore their being cannot be continued unless God will ; therefore
it belongeth to the same power to make anything out of nothing,
and to keep anything that is made from returning to its first
nothing.

2. It is impossible to cut off the dependence of the creature upon
the first cause, for no creature hath a self-sufficiency to maintain and
support itself. Things of art may subsist without the artificer, as a
carpenter maketh a house, and then leaveth it to stand of itself, the
shipwright maketh a ship, and then leaveth it to the pilot to guide it ;
but all things of nature depend upon God that made them, because
they have their whole being from him, matter, and form, which he
continueth no longer than he pleaseth, whether they be things in earth,
or things in heaven, visible or invisible. No impression of the agent
remaineth in the effect when his action ceaseth ; when the effect
wholly dependeth on the cause, as when the air is enlightened which
receiveth light from the sun, but when the sun is gone the light
ceases : so when God withdraws the creature vanishes, for they have
no other being than God is pleased to bestow upon them.

3. If it were not so, many absurdities would follow ; as, for instance—

[1.] If things do subsist by themselves, then they would always be ;
for nothing would destroy itself.

[2.] Then the creature would be independent, and whether God will
or no they would conserve their being ; and then how should God

govern the world? Therefore it undeniably followeth, 'Thou hast made all things, and thou preservest them all.'

4. It would destroy all worship, and our piety and respect to God would be cold and languid. The service we owe to God is reducible to these four heads :—

[1.] Adoration of his excellent nature above all other things.

[2.] Affiance in his goodness, with expectation of relief from him.

[3.] Thankfulness for his benefits.

[4.] Obedience to his precepts and commands.

Now, unless we acknowledge his intimate presence with and pre-servation of all things, these necessary duties will either be quite abolished, or degenerate into a vain and needless superstition.

[1.] The adoration we owe to his excellent nature, above all other things in the universe. Alas! we see how little reverence and respect we have for the great potentates of the earth, whose fame we hear of indeed, but are not concerned in their favour or frowns, or have no dependence on them at all. The least justice of peace or constable in our neighbourhood is more to us than all these mighty foreign princes, with whom we have nothing to do but only to hear and read the reports of their greatness, when we have no other business to divert us. So cold and careless would be our respect to God if we did not depend on him every moment, and were neither concerned in his wrath nor love. Those practical atheists that were settled on their lees, and lived in a secure neglect of God, they fostered it by this presumption— 'Tush! he will neither do good nor evil,' Zeph. i. 13. Fine things may be told us of the excellency of his nature, but what is that to us? He hath so shut up himself within the curtain of the heavens, that he takes no notice or care of things here below. How soon would such a conceit dispirit all religion, and take away the life and vigour of it! But if you would plant a reverence and due veneration of God, you must do it by this principle, ' In his hands is the soul of every living thing, and the breath of all mankind.' No creature can subsist with-out him for a moment. Now this respect is due not only to God the Father, but our Lord Jesus Christ.

[2.] As to trust and dependence on his goodness for relief in all our straits and necessities. This is the grand principle that keepeth up an acknowledgment of God in the world, by prayers and supplica-tions : Ps. lxii. 8, 'Trust in the Lord at all times ; ye people, pour out your heart before him.' When you retire your souls from all secular confidences, and repose all your trust in him, you will be instant in prayer, and earnestly beg his relief ; you see all things sub-sist by him, and it is in vain to expect any real assistance from the creature, but what God will communicate to us by it. Now, if it be not so, but the creatures could stand of themselves, and live of them-selves, this would blast all devotion, and prayer be withered and dried up at the root ; humbling ourselves to God in our straits and neces-sities would look like dejection or poorness of spirit, whining to no purpose.

[3.] For thankfulness for benefits received, which is the great means to knit the hearts of men to God, and the bellows which bloweth up the fire of love and religion in our hearts. How can we ascribe our deliverances to God, if he hath not a hand in all things? But when we acknowledge his sustaining and governing power, we see God in the face of the creature, and every benefit we receive representeth his goodness to us. But, alas! they have no thought or care of praise and thanksgiving that think not themselves obliged to God for the least hair of their heads. God is banished out of their sight, because they look for all from the creature. But they cannot enough praise and bless God, who is the strength of their lives, and the length of their days. They acknowledge that every good gift cometh from him, that he heareth their prayers, relieveth their necessities, continues their lives to them every moment; therefore God is all in all with them, but to others he is a shadow or nothing. His memory is kept up in the world by his benefits, Acts xiv. 17.

[4.] For obedience and service to him. Certainly dependence begets allegiance and observance. We are obsequious to those from whom we expect our dole and portion: Ps. cxxxi. 2, 'As the eyes of servants look to the hand of their masters, and the eyes of a maiden unto the hands of her mistress, so do our eyes wait on the Lord our God.' The masters gave the men-servants their portion and allowance; and the mistress to the maid-servants: they looked for all from their hands, and therefore to them they performed their service; so do the people of God. What reverence do we owe to him who is our Creator and preserver, as well as Redeemer! As he made all things, so he supporteth all things. Did we see God in us and in all things round about us, these thoughts would be more frequent in us, and we will still be considering what we shall render unto the Lord for all his benefits towards us. But obedience soon languisheth where men think they subsist of themselves without God: Ps. lv. 19, 'Because they have no changes, therefore they fear not God.' They are not interrupted in their sinful course, and therefore have no reverence and respect to God.

Use 1. This doth strengthen our dependence and reliance on our blessed Redeemer. By him all things do subsist, therefore he can hear all prayers, relieve us in all our straits, supply us in all wants, preserve us in all dangers. All nations are in his hands, our whole life is in his keeping, and upheld by his intimate presence with us; our days cannot be longer nor shorter than he pleaseth. If he were absent from us, he might forget us or neglect us; but he is within us, and round about us in the effects of his power and goodness. Since he is so near us, why should we doubt of his particular care and providence? All nations are in his hands, the lives and hearts of friends and enemies, therefore our eyes should be upon him: Ps. xvi. 8, 'I have set the Lord always before me, he is at my right hand, I shall not be moved.' We set the Lord before us both in point of reverence and dependence —for fear and trust agree in their common nature—and so it may note our care to please him, or our trust and quietness in him. All means are nothing to us, can do nothing for us without him.

2. It teaches us a lesson of humility. We depend on him every moment, can do nothing without him, either in a way of nature or grace; not in a way of nature, for God hath not left us to stand by ourselves on the first foundation of our creation. The creatures are not

capable of subsistence without dependence on the first cause, but merely live and act by his power : ' In him we live and move and have our being:' Ps. civ. 29, ' Thou takest away their breath and they die, and return to their dust.' The withdrawing his concurrence and supportation is the cause of all our misery. When he sees fit, all the creatures soon return to the elements of which they are compounded ; all the strokes and judgments which light upon them are dispensed according to his pleasure. In a way of grace we are nothing, can do nothing without him, John xv. 5. He must have all the praise, Luke xvi. 14, 1 Cor. xv. 10, Gal. ii. 20. The more perfections we have, the more prone we are to fall if he sustain us not : witness the fallen angels, and Adam in innocency.

3. It teaches us a lesson of reverence and obedience. If God be so near, let us observe him, and take notice of his presence. He knoweth what he doth when he sustaineth such a creature as thou art. This thought should continually affect us—that God is with us, still by us, not only without us, but within us, preserving our life, upholding our being. It should be a check to our sluggishness, and mispense of time—Doth God now continue me ? to what end and purpose ? If God were absent or gone, it were more justifiable to loiter or indulge the ease of the flesh ; but to spend my time vainly and foolishly, which he continueth for service, what have we to say ?

SERMON V.

And he is the head of the body, the church : who is the beginning, the first-born from the dead ; that in all things he might have the pre-eminence.—Col. I. 18.

The context is spent in representing the dignity and excellency of Christ. He is set forth by three things :—

1. By the excellency of the benefits we have by him—the greatest the fallen creature is capable of for the present, ver. 14.

2. By the excellency of his person ; so he is set forth as the eternal and only-begotten Son of God, ver. 15, and proved by his being the Creator and preserver of all things. The Creator, ver. 16 ; the preserver, ver. 17. Now the apostle cometh to the third thing.

3. The excellency of his office. This is done in the text ; where, observe, that next after the Son of God there is nothing more venerable and august than Christ's being head of the church. And again, that Christ hath another title to us than that of Creator : he is Redeemer also. The same God that created us by his power hath redeemed us by his mercy. By the one he drew us out of nothing, by the other he recovered us out of sin. Therefore, after he had declared what Christ is to the world and the church too, he showeth what Christ is particularly to the church. He hath a superiority over angels and all creatures, but he is our head : Eph. i. 22, ' He hath put all things under his feet,

and gave him to be head over all things to the church.' Christ is the sovereign of the world, but, by a special relation to his people, ' he is the head of the body, the church : who is the beginning, the first-born from the dead,' &c.

In which words observe :—

1. The titles which are given to Christ with respect to the church : he is *the head, the beginning, the first-born from the dead.*

2. The consequence of it : *that in all things he might have the pre-eminence.*

1. The titles ascribed to Christ. They are three :—

[1.] The first is ' the head of the body, the church '—where observe two correlatives, the *head* and the *body* ; the head is Christ, the body is the church. The head is the most eminent part of the body, the noblest both as to nature, and place, or situation. As to nature, the head is the most illustrious throne of the soul, as being the seat not only of the nerves and senses, but of the memory and understanding. In place, as nearest heaven, the very situation doth in a manner oblige the other parts to respect it. These things agree to Christ, who, as to his essence, is infinitely of much more worth than the church, as being the only-begotten Son of God. As to office, in him there is a fulness of perfection to perform the office of a head to such a crazy and necessitous body as the church is. All the treasures of wisdom and knowledge are in our head for the use of the body, Col. ii. 3 ; and he is also the fountain of life and grace to every particular member, John i. 16. And, for place, he reigneth in heaven with his Father, and from thence he vieweth all the necessities of the body, and sendeth forth such influences of grace as are needful to every particular member.

For the other correlative—the church is the body. By the church is meant the church mystical, or all such as are called out of the world to be a peculiar people unto God. Now, these considered collectively or together, they are a body ; but singly and separately, every believer is a member of that body : 1 Cor. xii. 29, ' Now ye are the body of Christ, and members in particular.' All the parts and members joined together are a spiritual body, but the several persons are members of that body. Yea, though there be many particular churches, yet they are not many bodies, but one body, so it is said, 1 Cor. xii. 12, ' As the body is one, and hath many members, and all the members of that body, being many, are one body, so also is Christ.' He is the head, and the many and divers members of the universal Christian church are but one body. The universal invisible church of real believers is one mystical body knit by faith to Christ, their head, and by love among themselves. And the visible universal church is one politic body, conjoined with Christ their head, and among themselves, by an external entering into covenant with God, and the serious profession of all saving truths. They have all the same king and head, the same laws—the word of God—the same sacraments of admission and nutrition, which visibly, at least, they subject themselves unto, and have a grant of the same common privileges in the gospel. But of this more anon.

[2.] The next title is ἀρχὴ, *the beginning.* I understand it that he is the root and the beginning of the renewed estate. The same degree which Christ hath in the order of nature, he hath in the order of grace also : he is the beginning both of creation, so also of redemption: he is *origo mundi melioris*, still the beginning and ending of the new creature as well as the old, Rev. i. 8.   He is called, in short, *the beginning*, with respect to the life of grace ; as in the next title, ' the first-born from the dead,' with respect to the life of glory.

[3.] The third title is, *the first-born from the dead*.   He had before called him the first-born of every creature, now the first-born from the dead: Rev. i. 5, ' The first-begotten from the dead,' because those that arise from the dead are, as it were, new-born ; whence also the resurrection from the dead is called a regeneration, Mat. xix. 20 : and St Paul referreth that prophecy, Ps. ii. 7, ' Thou art my Son ; this day have I begotten thee,' in Acts xiii. 33, to the resurrection of Christ.   Things are said to be when they are manifested to be : compare Rom. i. 4, ' Declared to be the Son of God with power, according to the Spirit of holiness, by the resurrection from the dead.'   He was declared to be the true, and everlasting Son of, God, and head of the church : so the adoption of believers shall appear by their resurrection: Rom. viii. 19, ' The earnest expectation of the creature waiteth for the manifestation of the sons of God ;' ver. 23, ' We ourselves groan within ourselves, waiting for the adoption, to wit, the redemption of the body.'

2. The sequel and consequent of these things : *that in all things he might have the pre-eminence*—that is, as well in the spiritual estate of the church as in the creation and natural estate of the world : Rom. viii. 29, ' That he might be the first-born among many brethren.'

I begin with the first.

Doct. 1. That this is the honour appropriate and peculiar to Jesus Christ, to be head of the church.

1. Here I shall show what the church is to which Christ is an head.

2. How is he an head to this body.

3. The reasons why this body must have such an head.

1. What the church is.   A society of men called out of the world by God's effectual grace, according to the purpose of his election, and united to Christ by faith and the participation of his Spirit, and to one another by the band of charity—that after remission of sins obtained in this world, together with regenerating grace, they may at length be brought to eternal life.   Let us a little open this description.   By effectual calling God worketh faith, which uniteth us to Christ, and that effectual calling is the fruit of election ; and the effect of this union is remission of sins, and the necessary consequence of this communion is salvation or eternal life.   This society of men is called a church in the text.   The word *church* is taken in divers acceptations.

First, and most properly, it signifies those whom I have now described, the universal collection of all and every one of those who, according to the good pleasure of God, are, or may be, called out of a state of sin into a state of grace, to obtain eternal glory by our Lord Jesus Christ.   This is the church of the first-born whose names are written in heaven, Heb. xii. 22—that chosen generation, that royal priesthood, that holy nation, that peculiar people, whom to show forth his praises God hath called out of darkness into his marvellous light, 1 Pet. ii. 9. This church, most generally and properly taken, is the kingdom of God, the body and spouse of Christ: Cant. vi. 9, 'My dove, my undefiled one, is but one.' This is that one fold under one shepherd, John x. 16. And it was prophesied of Christ that he should die to gather together in one the children of God that were scattered abroad, John xi. 52.

Secondly, Of this universal church there are two parts—one of travellers, the other of comprehensors, or the church militant and triumphant; they both belong to God's family: Eph. iii. 15, 'Of whom the whole family, whether in heaven or earth, is named ;' so Col. i. 10. That part of the family which is in heaven triumpheth with God there—that which is in earth is yet warring against sin, Satan, and the world.

Thirdly, This part, which is the military, comes in the second place to be called by the name of the universal church, because, being scattered and dispersed throughout the whole world, it comprehendeth all and every one that belongeth to Christ's flock, which are found in several folds : known to God they are, and to themselves, and do indeed belong to Christ's body and his kingdom. This is often and not undeservedly called the invisible church, because, so far as it is the church of God, their reality and sincerity is rather believed by faith than seen by the eyes of the body. This church, this kingdom of God, though it be yet in this world, yet it is not of the world, neither doth it come with observation, for the faithful have this kingdom of God within them, Luke xvii. 20. The world knows them not, other believers know them not, but God knoweth those that are his, 2 Tim. ii. 19.

Fourthly, The universal visible church. While they are in the way, and in the midst of their conflicts, it is possible many hypocrites may take up the profession, as in the great house are many vessels, some to honour, some to dishonour. From these ariseth an external promiscuous multitude, who also are called the catholic church, for the sake and with respect to those holy ones among them who truly belong to Christ's mystical body. We read often the kingdom is like to a net wherein are good and bad fishes, Mat. xiii. ; to a thrashing-floor wherein is chaff and wheat ; to a field wherein groweth good corn and also tares, Mat. xiii. 24, 25. Now all these ways is the universal church taken.

Fifthly, There are particular churches wherein the ordinances and means of grace are dispensed, as the church of Corinth, Cenchrea, Galatia, Greek, Roman. None of these particular churches contain all believers or the elect of God, that out of them or any of them there should be no salvation. Again, the universal church may remain in the world total and entire, though these particular churches, one or other of them, may successively be destroyed, as it hath often fallen out. And it is a great sin so to cry up a particular church as to exclude all the rest from saving communion with Christ ; and for any one particular church to arrogate power over the others, they being but members.

This church is called a body in two respects :—

(1.) In regard of the union of all the parts.

(2.) Dependence upon one and the same head.

(1.) With respect to union, as in man all the members make but one body, quickened by the same soul, so in the mystical body of Christ all the parts make up but one body, animated by the same vital principle, which is the Spirit of Christ, and are joined together by certain bonds and ligaments—faith and love; and all is covered with the same skin—the profession of the faith of Christ. Look, what the soul is in man, the form in the subject, life in the body, and proportion in the building ; that in the universal church of God is the union and communion of the several and single parts, with the head among themselves. Take away the soul from man, the form from the subject, life from the body, proportion and conjunction from the parts of the building, and what will man be but a carcase, and the building but ruin and confusion ? So take away union and communion from the universal church, then Jerusalem will become a Babel, and Bethel a Bethaven, and for life there will be death, and for salvation eternal destruction. How else shall all that come out from one, return again to one, and all and every one have all things in one, that at length they may acquiesce in the enjoyment of one—that is God—as their chiefest good ? Alas ! without this union with the head, and among themselves in necessary things, what can they expect but wrath and the curse, and everlasting destruction ?

(2.) With respect to dependence on one head: Rom. xii. 5, ' We, being many, are one body in Christ, and every one members of one another'—that is, all things make up one body, of which Christ is the head, and are fellow-members in respect of one another. As necessary and as desirable as it is to be united to God, to life and glory everlasting, so necessary and desirable it is to depend upon Christ, the head ; for no man, after the entrance of sin, can return to God, or enjoy God, without Christ the mediator: John xiv. 6, ' I am the way, the truth, and the life ; no man cometh to the Father but by me,' Acts iv. 12 ; ' There is no other name under heaven by which we can be saved, but only Jesus Christ,' 1 Cor. iii. 11 ; ' Other foundation can no man lay, but that which is laid, Jesus Christ,' 1 John v. 12 ; ' He that hath the Son hath life, and he that hath not the Son hath not life.' God proclaimed from heaven, Mat. iii. 17, ' This is my beloved Son, in whom I am well pleased.' He being one God with the Father and the Spirit, of the same substance and essence, he only can procure merit, and effect our union with God. He first assumed our nature, and united it to his own person, and so became one flesh with us : but then all those that belong to that nature, if they believe in him, and enter into his covenant, are not only literally one flesh, but mystically one body, and so also one Spirit, 1 Cor. vi. 17—that is, by the bond of the Spirit he hath brought them into the state and relation of a body to himself. To gather up all : Man's return to God is necessary to his blessedness, that he may be inseparably conjoined to him as his chiefest good. To this purpose the Son of God assumed our nature in the unity of his person, and thereby bringeth about the union of the church with himself as our head, and our communion with one another in faith and charity, if we desire to be blessed, and so is according to Christ's prayer: John xvii. 21,

' That they may be all one, as thou, Father, art in me and I in thee, that they also may be one in us ;' ver. 23, ' I in them and thou in me, that they may be made perfect in one.' So that as ' there is one God, and one mediator between God and man,' and one church united to Christ as his body, to this church we must every one of us be united if we mean to be saved, and in the church with Christ, and by Christ with God ; therefore out of this mystical body there is no salvation.

2. How is Christ a head to this body ? This must be explained by answering two questions :—

[1.] What are the parts of his headship ?

[2.] According to what nature doth this office belong to him—divine or human ?

[1.] The parts and branches of this headship. He is our head with respect to government and sovereignty ; and in regard of causality and influence ; he governeth, he quickeneth.

(1.) It implies his authority to govern, as is manifest by Eph. v. 22, 23, ' Wives, submit yourselves to your own husbands as unto the Lord, for the husband is the head of the wife, even as Christ is the head of the church.' So that to be the church's head implies superiority or right to govern.

(2.) For the other notion, in regard of influence, that is evident in scripture also : Col. ii. 19, ' Not holding the head, from which all the body by joints and bands having nourishment ministered, and knit together, increases with the increase of God.' The head is the root from whence the vital faculty is diffused to all the members. We use to say *Homo est arbor inversa*, a tree turned upside down ; if this be so, the head is the root of this tree. So doth life flow from Christ to the church ; the Spirit is from him either to begin the union or to continue the influence. But let us speak of these branches apart.

(1st.) His authority and power to govern. His excellency gives him fitness, but his office right to rule and govern the church. When he sent abroad his officers and ambassadors to proselyte the world in his name, he pleadeth his right : Mat. xxviii. 18, ' All power is given to me both in heaven and in earth.' Now the acts which belong to Christ as a governor may be reduced to these heads:—

First, To make laws that shall universally bind all his people.

Secondly, To institute ordinances for worship.

Thirdly, To appoint officers.

Fourthly, To maintain them in the exercise of these things.

First, The first power that belongeth to a governing head is legislation or making laws. Now Christ's headship and empire being *novum jus imperii*, a new right which he hath as mediator for the recovery of lapsed mankind, his law is accordingly. It is *lex remedians*, a law of grace, which is given us in the gospel of our salvation. The sum of his own proper remedial laws are faith in our Lord Jesus Christ, and repentance towards God, Acts xx. 21. Without repentance our case is not compassionable, without faith we do not own our Redeemer, by whom we have so great a benefit : yet because this new right of empire is accumulative, not privative, beneficial to us, indeed, but not destructive of our duty to God ; therefore the whole law of God, as purely moral, hath still a binding force upon the conscience, as it is explained in the word of God. Now to these laws of Christ none can add, none diminish, and therefore Christ will take an account of our fidelity at the last day, 2 Thes. i. 8.

Secondly, He hath instituted ordinances for the continual exercise and regulation of our worship and the government of his people, that they may be kept in the due acknowledgment and obedience to him, such as the preaching of the word, sacraments, and the exercise of some government. Now all the rules and statutes which Christ hath made for the ordering of his people must be kept pure until his coming. His institutions do best preserve his honour in the world. Great charges are left: 1 Tim. v. 21, ' I charge thee before God and our Lord Jesus Christ, and his elect angels, that thou observe these things;' where he speaketh of ecclesiastical censures and disciplines; he conjureth him by all that is sacred and holy, that it be rightly used: 1 Tim. vi. 14, ' Keep this commandment without spot and unrebukable unto the appearing of Jesus Christ.' The doctrines are so determined by Christ that they cannot be changed, the worship not corrupted, the discipline not abused, to serve partial humours and private or worldly interests.

Thirdly, God hath appointed officers, who have all their ministries and services under Christ and for Christ: Eph. iv. 11, ' He gave some apostles, some prophets, and some evangelists, and some pastors and teachers, for the perfecting of the saints, for the work of the ministry, for the edifying of the body of Christ.' Mark there, he doth not describe all the officers, for the deacon is not mentioned, but only such as labour in the word and sacraments; and observe, he mentioneth ordinary and extraordinary—apostles to write scripture, prophets to attest it, pastors and teachers to explain and apply it. And mark, *Christ gave some ;* it is his prerogative, as head of the church, to appoint the several sorts of offices and officers. He gave them at first, and will raise up some still, according as the exigence of the times requireth it. The end why, ' to perfect the saints'—that is, to help them on to their final perfection—' and for the work of the ministry.' All offices under Christ are a ministry, not a power ; and imply service, not lordship or domination over the flock of Christ. Lastly, the great end is to prepare and fit men more and more to become true members of Christ's mystical body.

Fourthly, To maintain and defend his people in the exercise of these things, to preserve the verity of doctrine and purity of worship. Alas! many times, where neither worship nor government is corrupted, yet the church may be in danger to be dissipated by the violence of persecutions. Now, therefore, it is a part of Christ's office, as head of the church, to maintain verity of doctrine, purity of worship, and a lawful order of government, for all which he hath plenty of spirit. The papists think this cannot be without some universal visible head to supply Christ's office in his absence ; and so are like the Israelites: Exod. xxxi. 1, ' Make us gods that shall go before us.' They would have a visible head that should supply Christ's room in his absence— an external, infallible head. But that is a vain conceit ; for since the pope hath his residence in Rome, and cannot perform these functions but by the intervention of ordaining pastors, why should it be more difficult for Christ in heaven to govern the church than for the pope in Rome—when he sitteth at the right hand of God till he hath made his foes his footstool ?   Is he less powerful to govern the church, and to preserve and defend his people against the violence of those that would root out the memorial of religion in the world ?   Who is more powerful than Jesus Christ, who hath all judgment put into his hands ? John v. 22.

(2d.) In regard of influence : So Christ is an head to the church as he giveth us his Spirit.   That Spirit which gives life to believers is often called Christ's Spirit : Gal. iv. 6, 'God hath sent forth the Spirit of his Son into your hearts.' It is purchased by his merit, Titus iii. 6 ; conveyed to us by his power : John xv. 26, ' I will send the Comforter from the Father.'   The communication is by his ordinances. The word : 2 Cor. iii. 18, ' Beholding as in a glass the glory of the Lord, we are changed into the same image from glory to glory, even as by the Spirit of the Lord.'   Sacraments : 1 Cor. xii. 13, ' For by one Spirit are we all baptized into one body, whether we be Jews or Gentiles, whether we be bond or free : and have all been made to drink into one Spirit.'   To promote the religion which he hath established : John xvi. 13, 14, ' When the Spirit of truth is come, he will guide you into all truth : for he shall not speak of himself, but whatsoever he shall hear that he shall speak : and he will show you things to come.   He shall glorify me : for he shall receive of mine, and shall show it unto you.'   He comes to us as his members, and by influence from him, as in the natural body the animal spirits are from the head, are by the members conveyed to all the parts of the body.   So Christ in this spiritual union worketh in us a quickening Spirit : Eph. iv. 15, 16, ' We grow up to him in all things, which is the head, even Christ : from whom the whole body joined together maketh increase,' &c.   The Spirit is not given to any one believer, but derivatively from Christ to us.   First, it is given to Christ, as mediator, and to us only by virtue of our union with him.   He is in Christ as radically inherent, but in us operatively, to accomplish certain effects ; or he dwelleth in our head by way of radiation, in us by way of influence and operation.

[2.] According to what nature doth this office belong to Christ— divine or human ?

I answer—Both ; for it belongeth to him as God incarnate.

(1.) He must be man, that there may be a conformity of nature between the head and the rest of the members ; therefore Christ and the church have one common nature between them : he was man as we are men—' bone of our bone, and flesh of our flesh,' Eph. v. 30. We read of a monstrous image that was represented to Nebuchadnezzar in a dream, where the head was gold, the breast and arms of silver, the belly and thighs of brass, and the legs and feet part of iron and part of clay, Dan. ii. ; all the parts of a different nature. In every regular body there is a proportion and conformity.   So it is in the mystical body of Christ—' because the brethren took part of flesh and blood, he also took part of the same.'   The Godhead, which was at such a distance from us, is brought down in the person of Christ in our nature, that it might be nearer at hand, and within the reach of our commerce ; and we might have more encouragement to expect pity and relief from him.

(2.) God he also must be. None was fit to be head of the church but God, whether you respect government or influence.

First, For government : to attend all cases, to hear all prayers, to supply all wants, defend us against all enemies, to require an absolute and total submission to his laws, ordinances, and institutions, so as we may venture our eternal interests upon his word : Ps. xlv. 11, ' He is thy God, worship thou him.'

Secondly, For influence : none else hath power to convey the Spirit, and to become a vital principle to us, for that is proper to God to have life in himself, and to communicate it to others : 1 Tim. vi. 13, ' I charge thee in the sight of God, who quickeneth all things,' &c. Whatever men may think of the life of grace, yet surely as to the life of glory he is the only life-making Spirit, 1 Cor. xv. 45. Now this honour is not given to the angels, much less is it due to any man, nor can it be imagined by him, for none can influence the heart of man but God.

3. The reasons why this body must have such a head.

[1.] Every society must be under some government, without which they would soon dissolve and come to nothing. Much more the church, which, because of its manifold necessities, and the high ends unto which it is designed, more needs it than any other society.

[2.] The privileges are so great, which are these : pardon of sins, and sanctifying grace, and at length eternal glory.

(1.) Pardon of sins. By this union with him, ' he is made sin for us, that we might be made the righteousness of God in him,' 2 Cor. v. 21. A sacrifice for sin, that we might be justified and accepted with God.

(2.) Sanctifying grace by the communication of his Spirit. We not only agree with him in the same common human nature, but the same holy nature may be in us that was in Christ, Heb. ii. 11. We are doubly akin, *ratione incarnationis suæ, et regenerationis nostræ.*

(3.) At length eternal glory followeth. For what is the condition of the head, that is also the condition of the members. First Christ, then they that are Christ's. And also Christ is set up as a pattern, to which the church must be conformed, Rom. viii. 29. Bating the preeminence due to the head, we are to be glorious as he is glorious.

[3.] The duties are far above bare human power and strength ; therefore we need the influence of our head, John xv. 5. To obey God, to believe in his name, to deny ourselves in what is most dear and precious to us in the world, to be fortified against all temptations, are duties not so easily done as said.

[4.] We have so foully miscarried already that he will no more trust his honour in our hands, but hath put the whole treasure of grace into the hands of Christ for our use, John i. 16. So John iii. 35, 36, ' The Father hath put all things into his hands. He that believes on the Son hath everlasting life : and he that believes not the Son hath not seen life.' God would not leave us to ourselves to live apart from him, but hath put all things that belong to our happiness into his hands, that, being united to him, virtue might be communicated to us, even all the gifts and graces of the Spirit. They are not intrusted with us, but with him ; and we shall have no more of pardon, grace, and glory, but what we have in and from the Son of God.

Use 1. Is information, to show how much we are bound to God for putting this honour upon us, that Christ should be our head. Christ is over the angels in point of superiority and government, but not properly said to be an head to them, in that strict notion which implies relation to the church. As to influence, he is not a head to them. You will say they are confirmed by him ; but the mediation of Christ presupposes the fall of Adam, for Christ had not been mediator if Adam had never fallen. Now, if Christ should come to confirm angels, if this had not been, is groundless ; besides, Christ merited for those that have benefit by him, and the consummate act of his merit is his death. But where is it said that he died for angels ?

Use 2. It informs us of the shameless usurpation abetted by the papists, who call the pope head of the church. None can be a head of the church to whom the church is not a body ; but it would be strange to say the church is the pope's body. None can be a governing head of the church but he who is a mediatorial head of vital influence. The papists, indeed, distinguish these things—ascribe the one to the pope, the other to Christ ; but the scripture allows not this writ of partition. None can be the one but he must also be the other. But they say he is a ministerial head ; but a ministerial universal head that shall give law to other churches and Christian societies, and if they depend not on him, shall be excluded from the privileges of a Christian church. This is, as to matter of right, sacrilege ; for this honour is too great for any man, and Christ hath appointed no such head, and therefore it is a manifest usurpation of his royal prerogative without his leave and consent. And, as to matter of fact, it is impossible—the church being scattered throughout all parts of the world, which can have no commerce with such an head in matters essential to its government and edification. They that first instituted such an universal head, besides that they had no authority or commission so to do, were extremely imprudent, and perverters of Christianity. Therefore let us consider how it came up at first, and how it hath been exercised. It came up at first for the prevention of schisms and divisions among Christians. They thought fit the church should be divided into certain dioceses, according to the secular divisions of the empire, which at first were thirteen in number, under the names of patriarchs and bishops of the first see, who should join in common care and counsel for the good of the Christian commonwealth. Among these, some who, in regard of the cities wherein they resided, were more eminent than the rest, and began to encroach upon the others' jurisdiction, till at length they were reduced to four. The bishop of Rome, being the imperial city, had the precedency, not of authority *super reliquos,* but of place and order *inter reliquos.* It was *potestas honoraria,* a difference or authority by courtesy, afterwards *ordinaria,* an ordinary power ; then what was *de facto* given was afterwards challenged *de jure.*

2. Let us consider how this power hath been exercised to the introduction of idolatry, and divers corruptions and superstitions, to the

destruction of kingdoms, the blood of the martyrs, and tumults and confusions too long to relate.

Use 3. To persuade you to accept Christ as your head. We are to preach him as Lord, 2 Cor. iv. 5 ; you are to receive him as Lord, Col. ii. 6 ; our consent is necessary. God hath appointed him, and the church appointeth him—God by authority, the church by consent. We voluntarily acknowledge his dignity, and submit unto him, both with a consent of dependence and subjection. Some God draweth to Christ and gives them to him, and him to them, John vi. 44. All that live within hearing have means to seek this grace, and if they so do, they shall not lose their labour. God sets not men about unprofitable work : mind but the duties of the baptismal covenant, and the business is at an end, Acts ii. 39.

Use 4. To put us upon self-reflection. If Christ be your head—

1. You must stand under a correspondent relation to Christ ; be members of his mystical body, which is done by faith and repentance.

2. None can be a true member of Christ's body who doth not receive vital influence from him, Rom. viii. 9. It is not enough to be members of some visible church ; they that are united to him have life, there is an influence of common gifts according to the part we sustain in the body. A common Christian hath common graces, those gifts of the Spirit which God gives not to the heathen world ; as knowledge of the mysteries of godliness, ability of utterance about heavenly things, Heb. vi. 4.

3. If Christ be our head, we must make conscience of the duties which this relation bindeth us unto ; as obedience and self-denial.

[1.] Obedience to his laws and the motions of his Spirit. His laws, Luke vi. 46, ' Why call you me Lord, Lord, and do not the things which I say ? ' The motions of his Spirit : Rom. viii. 14, ' As many as are led by the Spirit of God, they are the sons of God.'

[2.] Self-denial. Christ spared not his natural body to promote the good of his mystical body ; he exposed his life for our salvation, we should hazard all for his glory. Nature teaches us to lift up the hands to save the head.

4. There must be suitableness and imitation : 1 John ii. 6, ' He that abideth in him, ought to walk as he walketh.'

5. If you be planted into this mystical body, you will make conscience of love and tenderness.

Use 5. Let us triumph in this head, depend on him. There are two arguments—his ability and his sympathy.

1. His ability. He can give us life, strength, health : Eph. iii. 16, ' That he would grant you according to the riches of his glory to be strengthened with might by his Spirit in the inner man :' Col. i. 11, ' Strengthened with all might, according to his glorious power, unto all patience and long-suffering with joyfulness.'

2. His sympathy. He is touched with the feeling of our infirmities : Heb. iv. 15, ' We have not an high-priest, which cannot be touched with the feeling of our infirmities ; but was in all points tempted like as we are, yet without sin.' The head is concerned for the members.

SERMON VI.

Who is the beginning, the first-born from the dead.—COL. I. 18.

I COME now to consider the first particular title which is given to Christ.

There are two other titles given to Christ—the one respects the state of grace, the other the state of glory. And,

First, With respect to the state of grace, he is called ἀρχή, the beginning—that is, *Origo mundi melioris*, the beginning of the new creature as well as the old; for the same place and dignity which Christ hath in the order of nature he hath in the order of grace also. Therefore he is called 'the beginning of the creation of God,' Rev. iii. 14. The word ἀρχή is not taken there passively, as if it were the first thing that was created, but actively, that he giveth a being and beginning to all things that are created, and by the creation of God is meant the new creation. So that the point is—

Doct. That Jesus Christ is the author and beginning of the new creation.

I shall briefly explain this, and pass to the next branch. Christ is the beginning two ways:—

I. In a way of order and dignity.

II. In a way of causality.

I. In a way of order, as first and chief of the renewed state. This is many ways set forth in scripture. Two things I shall take notice of:—

1. That he is the builder of the church.

2. The lord and governor of it.

1. As founder and builder of the church: Mat. xvi. 18, 'Thou art Peter, and upon this rock will I build my church.' Christ challenges it to himself as his own peculiar prerogative to build the church. More fully, the apostle, Heb. iii. 3–5, 'For this man was counted worthy of more glory than Moses, inasmuch as he that builded the house hath more honour than the house; for every house is built by some man, but he that buildeth all things is God. And again, Moses was faithful in all his house as a servant, but Christ as a Son over his own house.' The scope of the apostle is to prove that Christ must have the pre-eminence above all others that have been employed in and about God's house. Moses was one of the chief of that sort, that had greater familiarity with God than others, and intrusted by him in very great and weighty matters; yet Christ was not only equal to Moses, but far above him. He proveth it by a comparison taken from a builder and an house, and from a lord of the house and a servant in the house; but Christ is the builder of the house, and Moses but a part of the house. Christ is the Lord, and Moses but the servant, therefore Christ is more excellent and worthy of greater honour. One of the noblest works of God is the church of the first-born; none could build, frame, and constitute this but the Son of God coming down in our flesh, and so recovering the lost world into an holy society which might be dedicated to God. For the materials of this house are men

sinful and guilty. Neither men nor angels could raise them up into an holy temple to God; none but the eternal Word or the Son of God incarnate: 'he that buildeth all things is God'—τα πάντα, all these things, the things treated of; he doth not speak of the first creation, but the second, the restoring of the lapsed world to God.

2. The other honour is that Christ is Lord of the new creation, as well as the founder and builder of it; for the world to come is put in subjection to him, not to the angels, Heb. ii. 7. By the world to come is not meant the state of glory, but the state of the church under the times of the gospel. It is made subject to God the Redeemer; it is solely and immediately in his power, and under his authority, and cast into a dependence upon him.

II. In a way of causality. So he is the beginning, either as a moral or efficient cause.

1. As a moral meritorious cause. We are renewed by God's creating power, but through the intervening mediation of Christ, or God's creating power is put forth with respect to his merit. The life of grace is purchased by his death: 1 John iv. 9, 'God sent his only-begotten Son into the world, that we might live by him.' Here *spiritually*, hereafter *eternally*. For life is opposite to death incurred by sin. We were dead legally, as sentenced to death by the law; and spiritually, as disabled for the service of our Creator. And how by him? That he speaketh of ver. 10—by his being a propitiation. We were in the state of death when the doors of mercy were first opened to us, under the guilt and power of sin; but we live when the guilt of sin is pardoned, and the power of sin broken. But this life we have not without Christ being a propitiation for our sins, or doing that which was necessary, whereby God without impeachment of honour might show himself placable and propitious to mankind.

2. As an efficient cause; by the efficacy of his Spirit, who worketh in us as members of Christ's mystical body. Wherefore it is said, 2 Cor. v. 17, 'If any man be in Christ, he is a new creature;' and Eph. ii. 10, 'We are his workmanship, created in Christ Jesus unto good works.' Whatever grace we have cometh from God through Christ as Mediator, and from him we have it by virtue of our union with him. It is first applied by the converting grace, and then continually supplied by the confirming grace of the Spirit. The influence we have from him as our head is life and likeness.

[1.] Life: Gal. ii. 20, 'I am crucified with Christ, nevertheless I live; yet not I, but Christ liveth in me; and the life which I now live in the flesh,' &c. Christ is the beginning of the new life, therefore he is called the prince, or author of life. All life is derived from the head to the body, so we derive life from Christ: John vi. 57, 'As I live by the Father, so he that eateth me shall live by me.' We derive life from Christ, as he from the Father.

[2.] Likeness: Gal. iv. 19, 'My little children, of whom I travail in birth till Christ be formed in you,' and 2 Cor. iii. 18. It is for the honour of Christ that his image and superscription should be upon his members, to distinguish them from others. In short, as to life, he is the root: John xv. 1, 2, 'I am the true vine, and,' &c. As to likeness, he is the pattern: Rom. viii. 29, 'Whom he did foreknow, he also did predestinate, to be conformed to the image of his Son, that he might be the first-born among many brethren.'

Secondly, The reasons of this.

1. It is for the honour of the Son of God that he should be head of the new world. In the kingdom of Christ all things are new. There is a new covenant, which is the gospel; a new paradise, not that where Adam enjoyed God among the beasts and trees of the garden, but where the blessed enjoy God amongst the angels. A new ministry, not the family of Aaron, or tribe of Levi, but the ministry of reconcilation, whom God hath qualified and fitted to be dispensers of these holy mysteries. New ordinances; we serve God not in the oldness of the letter, but the newness of the Spirit; new members, or new creatures, that are made partakers of the benefits, therefore also a new head, or a second Adam, that must be the beginning of this new creation, and that is the Lord Jesus Christ, who is made a quickening spirit to all his members: 1 Cor. xv. 45, 'The first Adam was made a living soul, the second a quickening spirit.' Adam communicated natural life to his posterity, but from Christ we have the Spirit.

2. It is suited to our lost estate. We were in a state of apostasy and defection from God, averse from all good, prone to all evil. Now that we might have a new being and life, the Son of God came in our nature to rectify the disordered creation. The scripture representeth man as blind in his mind, perverse in his will, rebellious in his affections, having no sound part left in him to mend the rest; therefore we must be changed. But by whom? who shall make us of unclean to become pure and holy? Not one amongst all the bare natural sons of men, Job xiv. 4. Of carnal to become spiritual? We must be new made and new born: John iii. 6, 'That which is born of the flesh is flesh, and that which is born of the Spirit is Spirit;' that we may mind the things of the Spirit, and not of the flesh. Of worldly to become heavenly? 'He that formeth us for this very thing is God,' 2 Cor. v. 5. He that is the framer and maker of all things; a God of infinite wisdom, power, and love, he frameth and createth us anew.

Use 1. To show us the necessity of regeneration.

Use 2. The excellence of it.

1. The necessity. We must have another beginning than we had as bare creatures: it is one thing to make us men, another to make us saints or Christians. We have understanding, will, affections, and senses as men, but we have these sanctified as Christians. The world thinketh Christianity puts strange names upon ordinary things; but is it an ordinary thing to row against the stream of flesh and blood, and to raise men to those inclinations and affections to which nature is an utter stranger—to have a divine nature put into us? 2 Pet. i. 4. The necessity is more bound upon us if we look upon ourselves not only as men but Christians; for whosoever is in Christ is a new creature. Some are in Christ by external profession, *de jure*; they are bound to be new creatures, that they may not dishonour their head. Others by real internal union. They not only ought to be, but *de facto* are, new creatures, because they are made partakers of his Spirit,

and by that Spirit are renewed and sanctified. Little can they make out their recovery to God, and interest in Christ, who are not sensible of any change wrought in them, who have the old thoughts, the old discourses, the old passions, and the old affections, and their old conversations still; the same deadness to holy things, the same proneness to please the flesh, the same carelessness to please or honour God; and the drift and bent of their lives is as much for the world, and as little for God and heaven as before.

2. The excellency of regeneration or renewing grace. What a benefit it is, it appeareth in two things:—

1. That it is the fruit of reconciling grace: 2 Cor. v. 18, 'All things are of God, who hath reconciled us to himself by Jesus Christ, and hath given to us the ministry of reconciliation.' God gives grace only as the God of peace, as pacified by the death of Christ. The Holy Spirit is the gift of his love, and the fruit of this peace and reconciliation which Christ made for us. Our Lord Jesus Christ merited this grace by the value of his sacrifice and bloody sufferings, Titus iii. 5, 6.

2. It is applied to us by the almighty power of his Spirit. Christ is first the ransom for, then the fountain of life to, our souls; and so the honour of our entire and whole recovery is to be ascribed only to our Redeemer, who, as he satisfied the justice of God for our sins, so he also purchased a power to change our hearts; and he purchased this power into his own hands, not into another's, and therefore doth accomplish it by his Spirit, 2 Cor. iii. 18. We should often think what a foundation God hath laid for the dispensation of his grace, and how he would demonstrate his infinite love in giving us his Son to be a propitiation for us, and at the same time showeth forth his infinite power in renewing and changing the heart of man, and all to bring us back to him, to make us capable of serving and pleasing him.

I come now to the other title, which respects the life of glory: 'The first-born from the dead.' The same appellation almost is given to Christ when he is called, Rev. i. 5, 'The first-begotten from the dead.' The reason of both is, because those that arise from the dead are, as it were, new born, and, therefore, the resurrection from the dead is called a regeneration, Mat. xix. 28. And as to Christ in particular, the grave, when he was in it, is represented as being under the pains and throes of a woman in travail: Acts ii. 24, λύσας τὰς ὠδῖνας τοῦ θανάτου, 'God having loosed the pains of death, for it was not possible that he should be holden of it;' but which is not only a metaphor, but a higher mystery. St Paul referreth that prophecy, Ps. ii. 7, 'Thou art my Son, this day have I begotten thee,' in Acts xiii. 33, to the resurrection of Christ: 'God hath raised up Jesus from the dead; as it is also written, Thou art my Son, this day have I begotten thee.' Things are said to be done when they are manifested to be done. Compare Rom. i. 4, 'Declared to be the Son of God with power, according to the spirit of holiness, by the resurrection from the dead.' So the adoption of believers shall appear by their resurrection: Rom. viii. 19, 'The earnest expectation of the creature waiteth for the manifestation of the sons of God;' ver. 23, 'And not only they, but ourselves also, which have the first-fruits of the Spirit, even we ourselves groan within ourselves, waiting for the adoption, to wit, the redemption of our body;'

1 John iii. 2, 'It doth not yet appear what we shall be, but we know that when he shall appear we shall be like him, for we shall see him as he is.' This for the title of 'First-born from the dead.'

Doct. That Christ's rising from the dead is the evidence and assurance of a Christian's happy resurrection.

1. Let me open the terms.

2. Vindicate the notion.

3. Show you how this is an evidence and assurance to all good Christians of their happy and joyful resurrection.

1. For the terms. He is here called 'The first-born from the dead.' If the grave was as the womb to him, and his resurrection as a birth, then Christ was in a manner born when he rose again. Only he hath the precedency—he is the first-born, he rises first, and surely others will follow after him. So we read, Acts xxvi. 23, 'That he should be the first-born that should rise from the dead;' as he saith elsewhere, 'First Christ, then they that are Christ's.' Christ hath the primacy of order and the principality of influence. So again he is said to be 'the first-fruits of them that slept,' 1 Cor. xv. 20. As in the consecrating of the first-fruits the whole harvest is also consecrated, so Christ by rising himself raises all others with him to eternal glory and happiness. And so his resurrection is a certain proof that others shall have a resurrection also.

2. Let us vindicate the notion here used by the apostle. How was he the first-born, the first-fruits, the first raised from the dead? Two objections lie against it:—

[1.] That many were raised from the dead before Christ.

[2.] Concerning the resurrection of the wicked. They are not parts of his mystical body, and in respect of them how could Christ rise as the first-born and the first-fruits?

1. For the first objection, how was Christ the first, since many were raised before him? As the widow of Sarepta's son, who was raised to life by Elijah, 1 Kings xvii.; the Shunammite's son by Elisha, 2 Kings iv.; a dead man by the touch of Elisha's bones, 2 Kings xiii. 21. Our Saviour in his lifetime raised the widow of Nain's only son, Luke vii. 15; Jairus's daughter, Luke viii. 55; Lazarus, John xi. 44; some others at his death, Mat. xxvii. 52. How was he then the first? I answer—

[1.] We must distinguish of a proper and an improper resurrection. Christ was the first-born from the dead, because he arose from the dead by a proper resurrection, which is to arise again to a life immortal; others were raised again to a mortal estate, and so the great disease was rather removed than cured. Christ's resurrection is a resurrection to immortality, not to die any more; as the apostle saith, 'Death hath no more power over him.' They only returned to their natural life, they were raised from the dead, but still mortal; but 'he whom God raised again shall see no corruption,' Acts xiii. 34.

[2.] Others are raised by the power and virtue of his resurrection, but he hath risen again by his own power, John x. 18, 'I have power to lay down my life, and power to take it up again.' Raising the dead is a work of divine power, for it belongs to him to restore life who gave it at first. Therefore Christ is said not only to be raised again, but to rise from the dead: Rom. iv. 25, 'He died for our offences, and rose again for our justification,' as the sun sets and rises by his own motion.

[3.] All those that rose again before Christ, arose only by special dispensation, to lay down their bodies once more when God should see fit, and rose only as private and single persons; but Christ rose as a public person. His resurrection is the cause and pattern of ours, for head and members do not rise by a different power; he rose again to show the virtue that should quicken our mortal bodies, and raise them at length.

2. The second objection is concerning the raising of the wicked. Christ cannot be the first-born or the first-fruits to them, they belong not to his mystical body. The first-born implieth a relation to the rest of the family; and offering of the first-fruits did not sanctify the tares, the cockle, or the darnel, or the weeds that grow amongst the corn, but only the corn itself. I answer—

[1.] Certain it is that the wicked shall rise again, there is no question of that, Acts xxiv. 15. I believe a resurrection of the dead, both of the just and the unjust, all that have lived, whether they have done good or evil: Mat. v. 45, 'He makes his sun to rise on the evil and the good, and sendeth rain on the just and on the unjust;' and it is said, John v. 28, 29, 'All that are in their graves shall hear his voice, and shall come forth, they that have done good to the resurrection of life, and they that have done evil to the resurrection of damnation.' Both must rise, that both may receive a full recompense according to their several ways; and though it be said, Ps. i. 5, 'The ungodly shall not stand in the judgment, nor sinners in the congregation of the righteous,' it doth not infringe this truth. The sense is, those unhappy miscreants shall not be able to abide the trial, as being self-condemned. To stand in the judgment is to make a bold defence. And whereas it is said, also, they shall not stand in the congregation of the righteous, you must know that at the day of doom there is a congregation or a gathering together of all men, then a segregation, a separating the sheep from the goats, then an aggregation—'He shall set the sheep on his right hand and the goats on his left '—so that they make up two distinct bodies, one of the good, which is there called the congregation of the righteous, the other of the wicked, who are to be judged by Christ as a just and righteous judge, assisted with his holy angels, and the great assembly and council of saints. Not one of the sinners shall remain in the company of the righteous, nor appear in their society.

[2.] The wicked are raised *ex officio judicis,* not *beneficio mediatoris;* they are raised by Christ as a judge, but not by him as a Redeemer. The one sort are raised by the power of his vindicative justice, the other by the Holy Ghost by virtue of his covenant: Rom. viii. 11, 'He shall quicken your mortal bodies by his Spirit that dwelleth in you.' The one by Christ's power from without, put forth by him as judge of dead and living; the other by an inward quickening influence that flows from him as their proper head. When the reaper gathers the wheat into his barn, the tares are bound in bundles and cast into unquenchable fire, Mat. xiii. 30.

[3.] The wicked are forced to appear, and cannot shift that dreadful tribunal, the other go joyfully forth to meet the bridegroom; and when the sentence of condemnation shall be executed upon the one, the other by virtue of Christ's life and resurrection shall enter into the possession of a blessed and eternal life, wherein they shall enjoy God and Christ, and the company of saints and angels, and sing hallelujahs for ever and ever.

Thirdly, How is this an evidence and assurance to all good Christians of their happy and glorious resurrection?

1. The resurrection of Christ doth prove that there shall be a resurrection.

2. That to the faithful it shall be a blessed and glorious resurrection.

1. There shall be a resurrection: it is necessary to prove that; partly because it is the foundation of all godliness. If there were not another life after this, there were some ground for that saying of the atheists, ' Let us eat and drink, for to-morrow we shall die,' 2 Cor. xv. 32. If there be no future estate nor being after this life, let us enjoy the good things of the world whilst we can, for within a little while death cometh, and then there is an end of all. These atheistical discourses and temptations to sensuality were more justifiable if men were annihilated by death. No! the soul is immortal, and the body shall rise again, and come into the judgment; and unless we live holily, a terrible judgment it will be to us. Partly because we cannot easily believe that the same body shall be placed in heaven which we see committed to the grave to rot there. Of all articles of religion this is most difficultly assented unto. Now there is relief for us in this business in hand: ' Christ is the first-born from the dead.' There were many *prœludia resurrectionis*, foretokens and pledges of the resurrection given to the old world, in the translation of Enoch, the rapture of Elijah, the reviving of these few dead ones which I spake of before; but the great and public evidence that is given for the assurance of the world is Christ's rising from the grave. This makes our resurrection: —

[1.] Possible.

[2.] Easy.

[3.] Certain and necessary.

[1.] Possible. The least that we can gather from it is this, that it is not impossible for dead men to rise; for that which hath been may be. We have the proof and instance of it in Christ; see how the apostle reasoneth: 1 Cor. xv. 13, ' If there be no resurrection from the dead, then Christ is not risen, and then our whole faith falleth to the ground.' For all religion is bottomed on the resurrection of Christ; if therefore Christ be risen, why should it seem an incredible thing to us that others should be raised also?

[2.] It is easy. For by rising from the dead he hath conquered death and gotten the victory of it, 1 Cor. xv. 57. A separation there will be of the soul from the body, but it is not such as shall last for ever. The victory over sin is the victory over death, and the conquest of sin makes death an entrance into immortality. The scriptures often speak of Christ destroying the power of death: Heb. ii. 14,

'That through death he might destroy him that had the power of death.' The devil's design was, by tempting men to sin, to keep them for ever under the power of death, but Christ came to rescue men from that power by a resurrection from death to life. Again it is said, ' He hath abolished death, and brought life and immortality to light in the gospel.' He hath voided the power of death by taking a course for the destruction of sin, and made a clear revelation of that life and immortality which was not so certainly known before. We look to the natural impossibilities, how what is turned to dust may be raised again, because we do not consider the power of God ; but the moral impossibility is the greater, for 'the sting of death is sin, and the strength of sin is the law ;' that which makes sin able to do us hurt is the guilt of sin, otherwise it would be but as a calm sleep; and this guilt is bound upon us by the law of the righteous God, which threateneth eternal death to the sinner. Now get free from sin, and it is easy to believe the conquest of death. I will prove two things— that Christ's resurrection shows both his victory over sin, and his victory over death.

[1.] His victory over sin. That he hath perfectly satisfied for sin, and appeased the wrath of God, who is willing to be reconciled with all those that come to the faith and obedience of the gospel, which could not be if Christ had remained under the power of death ; for the apostle saith, 1 Cor. xv. 17, 'If Christ had not risen, ye are yet in your sins '—that is, God is not pacified, there is no sufficient means of atonement or foundation laid for our reconciliation with him. But his resurrection declareth that he is fully satisfied with the ransom paid for sinners by Jesus Christ, for it was in effect the releasing of our surety out of prison ; so it is said, Rom. iv. 15, 'He was delivered for our offences, and raised up for our justification.' He died to ex-piate and do away sin, and his resurrection showeth it was a sufficient ransom, and therefore he can apply the virtue of it to us.

[2.] His victory over death. For he got out of it, which not only shows there is a possibility for a man by the power of God to be raised from death to life, but a facility ; as a second Adam he brought re-surrection into the world—there were two Adams, the one man brought death, and another brought resurrection into the world. The sentence of death is gone out against all the children of Adam as such, and the regenerate believers that are recovered by Christ shall be raised to im-mortal life : he hath gotten out of the power of death, so shall we.

[3.] Certain and necessary. For several reasons.

First, Our relation to Christ, he is the head of the body. Now the head will not live gloriously in heaven and leave his members behind him under the power of death. Believers are called the fulness of him that filleth all things, Eph. i. 23. Head and members make up one perfect man, or mystical body, which is called the fulness of Christ, Eph. iv. 13. Otherwise it would be a maimed Christ, or a head without a body, and therefore we should not doubt but he will raise us up with him.

Secondly, The charge and office of Christ, which he will attend upon and see that it be carefully performed : John vi. 39, 'This is the Father's will which hath sent me, that of all which he hath given me I should lose nothing, but raise it up again at the last day;' as *none* so *nothing;* in the prophet's expression concerning the good shepherd, not so much as a leg or a piece of an ear, that he should be careful to preserve every one who belongs to his charge, and whatever befalls them here, he is to see them forthcoming at the last day, and to give a particular account of them to God. Now certainly Christ will be very careful to fulfil his charge and make good his office.

Thirdly, There is the mercy of God through the merits of Christ towards his faithful ones who have hazarded their bodies and their bodily interests for his sake : 1 Thes. iv. 14, 'If we believe that Jesus died and rose again, even those also which sleep in Jesus will God bring with him.' Upon the belief of Christ's death and resurrection depends also the raising of their bodies that die for the testimony of Christ, or by occasion of faith in Christ, and that so certainly and speedily, that they that die not at all shall at the day of judgment have no advantage of those that have lain in the grave so many years, the raising of the one being in the same twinkling of an eye with the change of the other, for the apostle saith, they that are alive shall not prevent them that are asleep. So 2 Cor. iv. 14, ' Knowing that he that raised up the Lord Jesus, shall raise us up also with Jesus, and present us with you.' He gives it as the reason why he had the same spirit of faith with David, who in his sore afflictions professed his confidence in God, because he believed he spake. So they do profess the faith of Christ, though imminent death and danger is always represented to them as before their eyes. Because they steadfastly believed that God would raise them to a glorious estate through Christ, therefore did they openly proclaim what they did believe concerning him. To the same purpose to confirm Timothy against all danger of death: 1 Tim. vi. 13, ' I give thee charge in the sight of God, who quickeneth all things'—that is, as thou believest that God is able and will raise thee from the dead, that thou hold out constantly unto the death, and do not shrink for persecution.

2. It proveth that to the faithful it shall be a blessed and a glorious resurrection.

[1.] Because Christ's resurrection is not only a cause but a pattern of ours ; there is not only a communion between the head and members in the mystical body, but a conformity. The members were appointed to be conformed to their head, as in obedience and sufferings, so in happiness and glory ; here in the one, hereafter in the other : Rom. viii. 29, ' He hath predestinated us to be conformed to the image of his Son.' As Christ was raised from the dead, so we shall be raised from the dead. God ' raised him from the dead, and gave him glory and honour, that your faith and hope might be in God,' 1 Pet. i. 21. So God will raise us from the dead and put glory and honour upon us. There is indeed a glory put upon Christ far surpassing the glory of all created things ; but our glory is like his for quality and kind, though not for quantity, degree, and measure, as to those prerogatives and privileges which his body in his exaltation is endowed withal. Such a glory it is that Christ shall be admired in his saints ; the world shall stand gazing at what he means to do.

[2.] By the grant of God. They have a right and title to this glorious estate; being admitted into his family, they may hereafter expect to be admitted into his presence. The Holy Spirit abideth in them as an earnest, till it be accomplished: Eph. i. 14, ‘Ye were sealed with that holy Spirit of promise, which is the earnest of our inheritance, until the redemption of the purchased possession.’ The Spirit of holiness marketh and distinguisheth them as heirs of promise from all others. The mark or seal is the impression of Christ’s image on the soul; this seal becomes an earnest or part of payment, which is a security or assurance to us that more will follow, a fuller conformity to Christ in the glorious estate; and this earnest doth continue till the redemption of the purchased possession; the purchased possession is the church, and their redemption is their final deliverance, Eph. iv. 30, when their bodies are redeemed from the bands of the grave. See Rom. viii. 28.

Use 1. Is to persuade you to the belief of two grand articles of faith—the resurrection of Christ, and your own resurrection.

1. The resurrection of Christ. The raising of Christ from the dead is the great prop and foundation of our faith: 1 Cor. xv. 14, ‘If Christ be not risen, then is our preaching vain, and your faith also is vain.’ All the apostles’ preaching was built upon this supposition, that Christ died and rose again. Partly because this is the great evidence of the truth of the Christian religion; for hereby Christ was evidenced to be what he gave out himself to be, the eternal Son of God, and the Saviour of the world, ‘whereof he hath given assurance to all men, in that he raised him from the dead,’ Acts xxiii. 31, that is the ground of faith and assurance. So Acts xiii. 33, ‘God hath raised Jesus from the dead, for it is written, Thou art my Son,’ &c. Partly to show that he is in a capacity to convey life to others, both spiritual and eternal; which, if he had remained under the state of death, could not be. The life of believers is derived from the life of Christ: John xiv. 19, ‘Because I live,’ &c. If he had been holden of death, he had neither been a fountain of grace nor glory to us: 1 Pet. i. 3, ‘He hath begotten us unto a lively hope by the resurrection of Christ from the dead.’ Partly because the raising of Christ is the pledge of God’s omnipotency, which is our relief in all difficult cases; the power which raised Christ exceedeth all contrary powers, Eph. i. 20, 21. Now the resurrection of Christ, besides the veritableness of the report manifested by the circumstances, when a great stone was rolled at the mouth of the sepulchre, a guard of soldiers set to watch against all fraud and impostures, yet he brake through; his frequent apparitions to the apostles, yea, to five hundred disciples at once, 1 Cor. xv. 6, a great part of which were alive to testify the truth of it for some competent space of time; his pouring out of the Spirit; the apostles witnessing the truth of it in the teeth of opposition; his appearing from heaven to Paul; the prophecies of the Old Testament foretelling of it; the miracles wrought to confirm it; the holiness of the persons who were employed as chosen witnesses; their unconcernedness in all temporal interests; their hazarding of all; their success. It would make a volume to give you the evidences.

2. Your own resurrection, what may facilitate our belief and hope of it?

[1.] Consider it is a work of omnipotency. We are apt to say, How can it be, that when our bodies are turned into dust, and that dust mingled with other dust, and hath undergone many transmutations, that every one shall have his own body and flesh again? Why, consider the infinite and absolute power of God, and this will make it more reconcilable to your thoughts, and this hard point will be of easier digestion to your faith. To an infinite power there is no difficulty at all: Phil. iii. 21, 'According to the working whereby he is able to subdue all things to himself.' He appeals to God's power, how much God's power out-works our thoughts; for he were not infinite if he might be comprehended. We are not fit judges of the extent of his power; many things are marvellous in our eyes which are not so to his, Zech. viii. 6. Therefore we must not confine God to the limits of created beings or our finite understandings. Alas! our cockleshell cannot empty an ocean: we do no more know what God can do than a worm knoweth a man. He that made the world out of nothing, cannot he raise the dead? He that brought such multitudes of creatures out of the dark chaos, hath he forgotten what is become of our dust? He that gave life and being to that which before was not, cannot he raise the dead? He that turned Moses' rod into a serpent, and from a serpent into a rod again, cannot he raise us out of dust into men, and turn us from men into dust, and from the same dust raise us up into the same men and women again?

[2.] We have a relief from the justice of God. All will grant that God is, and that God is a rewarder of good and bad. Now in this life he doth not dispense these rewards. Many times here instruments of public good are made a sacrifice to public hatred, and wicked men have the world at will; therefore there is a judgment when this life is ended; and if there be a judgment, men must be capable to receive reward and punishment. You will say, so they are by having an immortal soul; ay! but the soul is not all of a man, the body is a part: it hath had its share in the work, and therefore it is most equal to conceive it shall have its share in the reward and punishment. It is the body which is gratified by the pleasure of sin for a season, the body which hath endured the trouble and pain of faithful obedience unto Christ, therefore there shall be a resurrection of just and unjust, that men may receive according to what they have done in the body. God made the whole man, therefore glorifies and punishes the whole man. The apostle urgeth this as to the godly, 1 Cor. xv. 29,

[3.] God's unchangeable covenant love, which inclines him to seek the dust of his confederates. God hath taken a believer into covenant with himself, body and soul; therefore Christ proveth the resurrection from God's covenant title, Mat. xxii. 31. To be a God is certainly to be a benefactor, Gen. xxv. 26; not 'Blessed be Shem,' but 'Blessed be the Lord God of Shem.' And to be a benefactor, becoming an infinite eternal power. If he had not eternal glory to bestow upon us, he would not justify his covenant title, Heb. xi. 16. To whom God is a benefactor, he is a benefactor not to one part only, but to their whole persons. Their bodies had the mark of his covenant upon them, their dust is in covenant with him, and wherever it is dispersed, he will look after it. Their death and rotting in the grave doth not make void his interest, nor cause his care and affection towards them to cease.

[4.] We have relief also from the redemption of Christ, which extendeth to the bodies of the saints, as it is often interpreted in scripture; as where Christ speaks of his Father's charge—this was a special article in the eternal covenant : John vi. 39, 40, ' This is the will of my Father, that of all that he hath given me I should lose nothing, but raise it up at the last day.' Christ hath engaged himself to this; he is the guardian of the grave, as Rispah kept the dead bodies of Saul's sons, 2 Sam. xxi. 10. Christ hath the keys of death and hell; he hath a charge of the elect to the very day of their resurrection that he may make a good account of them, and may not lose so much as their dust, but gather it up again. What shall I say? When the intention of his death is spoken of : 1 Thes. v. 10, ' That whether we wake or sleep, we should live together with him;' that is, whether dead or alive; for they that are dead in the Lord, are said to be fallen asleep. Whether we live or die, we should live a spiritual life here, and eternal life in glory hereafter. So where the obligation : 1 Cor. vi. 20, ' Ye are bought with a price.' There would be no consequence if Christ had not purchased the body as well as the soul, and Christ will not lose one jot of his purchase; if he expect duty from the body, you may expect glory for the body; so redemption is particularly applied to the body: Rom. viii. 23, ' Waiting for the adoption, the redemption of our bodies.' Then is Christ's redemption full, when the body is exempted from all the penalties induced by sin.

[5.] The honour which is put upon the bodies of the saints.

(1.) They are members of Christ : 1 Cor. vi. 15, ' Know ye not that your bodies are members of Christ ? shall I then take the members of Christ and make them members of an harlot ? God forbid.' No members of Christ can for ever remain under death, but shall certainly be raised up again. When a godly man dieth, the union between soul and body is dissolved, but not the union between him and Christ, as Christ's own natural body in the grave was not separated from his person, and the hypostatical union was not dissolved;—it was the Lord of glory which was crucified, and the Lord of glory which was laid in the grave,—so the mystical union is not dissolved between Christ and his people, who are his mystical body, when they are dead.

(2.) They are temples of the Holy Ghost; therefore if they be destroyed they shall be built up again : 1 Cor. vi. 19, ' Know ye not that your bodies are temples of the Holy Ghost ? ' As Christ redeemed not the soul only, but the whole man, so the Spirit in Christ's name takes possession both of body and soul; the body is cleansed and sanctified by the Spirit, as well as the soul ; and therefore it is quickened by the Spirit: Rom. viii. 11, ' If the Spirit of him that raised Jesus from the dead dwell in you, he shall also quicken your mortal bodies by his Spirit which dwelleth in you.' The Holy Ghost will not leave his mansion or dwelling-place; the dust of believers belongs to them who were once his temple. So it is a pledge of the resurrection. Now therefore labour with yourselves, think often of it.

SERMON VII.

For it pleased the Father that in him should all fulness dwell.—
COL. I. 19 ; with,
For in him dwelleth all the fulness of the Godhead bodily.—
Chap. II. 9.

THESE words are produced to prove that there is no defect in the
evangelical doctrine, and therefore there needeth no addition to it
from the rudiments of men.   That there is no defect, he proveth from
the author of it, Jesus Christ, who was not only man, but God ; and
beyond the will of God we need not look.   If God will come from
heaven to teach us the way thither, surely his teaching is sufficient, his
doctrine containeth all things necessary to salvation.   This is the
argument of these words, ' For in him dwelleth all the fulness of the
Godhead bodily.'

In which words, observe three things :—

First, The house: *in Him.*

Secondly, The inhabitant : *all the fulness of the Godhead.*

Thirdly, The manner of dwelling : in the word *bodily.*

First, the house, or place of residence : ' in Him.'   In the man Christ
Jesus, or in that human nature in which he carried on the business of
our salvation ; as despicable and abject as it was in the eyes of men, yet
it was the temple and seat of the Godhead.

Secondly, The inhabitant : ' the fulness of the Godhead ;' not a
portion of God only, or his gifts and graces (as we are made partakers
of the divine nature, 1 Pet. i. 4.), but the whole Godhead.

Thirdly, The manner, σωματικῶς, ' bodily.'   The word may relate—

1. To the shadows and figures of the law, and so it signifieth
essentially, substantially.   God dwelt in the tabernacle, temple, or ark
of the covenant, συμβολικῶς, because of the figures of his presence.
In Christ, σωματικῶς, bodily, as his human nature was the true tabernacle or temple in which he resideth.   Christ calls his human nature
a temple, John ii. 19.   Or else,

2. With respect to the intimacy and closeness of the union.   So
σωματικῶς may be rendered *personally;* for body is often put for a
person.   The two natures were so united in him, that he is one Christ.

Doct. That Jesus Christ is true God and true man in one person.

I shall prove the point :—

1. By testimonies of scripture.

2. By types.

3. By reasons taken from Christ's office.

1. By testimonies of scripture.   I shall pass by those that speak of
the reality of either nature apart, and only allege those that speak of
both together.   Now these do either belong to the Old Testament or
the New.   I begin with the former, the testimonies of the Old Testament, because this union of the two natures in the person of Christ is
indeed a mystery, but such as was foretold long before it came to pass ;
and many of the places wherein it was foretold were so understood by

the ancient Jews.   The controversy between them and Christians was not whether the Messiah were to be both God and man—they agreed in that—but whether this was fulfilled, or might be applied to Jesus of Nazareth.   But the latter Jews, finding themselves not able to stand to the issue of that plea, say that we attribute many things to Jesus of Nazareth which were not foretold of the Messiah to come, as namely, that he should be God-man in one person; therefore it is necessary that this should be proved, that the Old Testament aboundeth with predictions of this kind.   Let us begin with the first promise touching the Messiah, which was made to Adam after his fall, for the restoring of mankind : Gen. iii. 15, ' The seed of the woman shall bruise the serpent's head.'   That is to say, one of her seed, to be born in time, should conquer the devil, death, and sin.   Now, when he is called the ' seed of the woman' it is apparent he must be man, and made of a woman.   And when it is said that ' he shall break the serpent's head,' who can do this but only God ?   It is a work of divine omnipotency, for Satan hath much more power than any bare man.   Therefore it is said, Rom. xvi. 20, ' The God of peace shall bruise Satan under your feet shortly.'   Come we next to the promise made to Abraham, Gen. xii. 3, ' In thee shall all the families of the earth be blessed.' *In thee*, that is, in thy seed, as it is often explained: Gen. xxii. 18, ' In thy seed shall all the nations of the earth be blessed.'   This seed was Christ, the Messiah to come.   Now he was to be God-man : he was to be man, for he is the seed of Abraham ; God, because that blessedness is remission of sins, or justification.   For it is said, Gal. iii. 8, ' The scripture, foreseeing that God would justify the heathen through faith, preached before the gospel unto Abraham, saying, In thee shall all nations of the earth be blessed.'   Regeneration and the renovation of our natures is also included in it, as a part of this blessing : Acts iii. 25, 26, ' Ye are children of the prophets, and of the covenant which God made with our fathers, saying unto Abraham, In thy seed shall all the kindreds of the earth be blessed.   Therefore unto you first God, having raised up his Son Jesus, sent him to bless you, in turning away every one of you from his iniquities.'   There is also redemption from the curse of the law, and the gift of eternal life included in it.   Now all these are works proper to God alone.   Let us come to the promise made to David : 2 Sam. vii. 12, 13, ' I will set up thy seed after thee, and I will establish the throne of thy kingdom for ever.'   It is spoken in the type of Solomon, but in the mystery of Christ, who is true man as David's seed, and true God, for his kingdom is everlasting.   And so David interpreteth it : Ps. xlv. 6, ' Thy throne, O God, is for ever and ever.'   The kingdom of the Messiah is never to have an end.   And the apostle affirmeth expressly that those words are spoken to Christ the Son of God, Heb. i. 7.   Let me next allege Job's confession of faith, which was very ancient : Job xix. 25, 26, ' I know that my Redeemer liveth, and that he shall stand at the latter day upon the earth ; and though after my skin worms destroy this body, yet in my flesh I shall see God.'   His Redeemer was true man, as appeareth by his title *Goel;* and because he shall stand on the earth, and be seen by his bodily eyes ; true God, for he calleth him so : ' I shall see God.'   Go we on in the scriptures: Isa. iv. 2, Christ is prophesied of: 'In that day the branch of the Lord shall be beautiful, and glorious, and the fruit of the earth shall be excellent and comely.' When he is called 'the branch of the Lord,' his Godhead is signified; when he is called 'the fruit of the earth,' his manhood. So again, Isa. vii. 14, 'A virgin shall conceive and bear a son, and thou shalt call his name Immanuel'—that is to say, 'God with us;' which can agree to none but to him that is God and man. So that this mystery of God incarnate was not hid from the church of the Old Testament, for his very name did import God with us, or God in our nature reconciling us to himself. So Isa. ix. 6, 'To us a child is born, to us a son is given, and the government shall be upon his shoulders, and his name shall be called The Wonderful, Counsellor, the mighty God, the everlasting Father, the Prince of Peace.' Who can interpret these speeches and attributes but of one who is God-man? How could he else be a child and yet the everlasting Father—born of a virgin, and yet the mighty God? So Isa. xi. 1, with the 4th verse, 'A rod out of the stem of Jesse, and a branch out of his roots:' therefore man; and ver. 4, 'He shall smite the earth with the rod of his mouth, and with the breath of his lips shall he slay the wicked:' therefore God. So Isa. liii. 8, 'He shall be taken from prison and judgment:' therefore man; yet 'who shall declare his generation?' therefore God. So Jer. xxiii. 5, 6, 'A branch raised unto David from his dead stock:' therefore man: yet 'the Lord, or Jehovah our righteousness;' therefore God. Shall I urge that speech whereby Jesus did silence divers of the learned pharisees? Ps. cx. 1, 'The Lord said to my Lord, Sit thou on my right hand, until I make thy foes thy footstool.' He was born in the mean estate of human flesh and King David's seed, and yet David's Lord; which he could not be if he were not God himself, the King of kings, and Lord of lords. Well, then, he was David's son as man, but David's Lord as he was God. And so do many of the ancient Jewish rabbins interpret this place. So again, Micah v. 2, 'Thou Bethlehem Ephratah, though thou be little among the thousands of Judah, yet out of thee shall he come forth unto me that is to be ruler in Israel; whose goings forth have been from old, from everlasting.' He is born in Bethlehem, yet his goings forth are from everlasting. He came out of Bethlehem, and therefore man; his goings forth are from everlasting, and therefore God. So Zech. xii. 10, 'I will pour out the spirit of grace and supplication, and they shall look upon me whom they have pierced.' He is God, because he giveth the Spirit of grace; man, because he is pierced or crucified. So Zech. xiii. 7, 'Against the man, my fellow.' A man he was, but God's companion, his only-begotten Son, and co-essential with himself, and so God.

Secondly, Come we now to the New Testament, in which this mystery is more plainly and fully demonstrated. There often the Son of Man is plainly asserted to be also the Son of God. Thomas calleth him his Lord, his God, John xx. 28. We are told that the Word was made flesh, John i. 14; that God purchased the church with his own blood, Acts xx. 28, which can be understood of no other but Christ, by whose blood we are redeemed, and who, being incarnate, hath blood to shed for us. But God, as a pure spirit, hath not flesh and blood and bones as we have: so Rom. i. 3, 4, 'Jesus Christ

was made of the seed of David, according to the flesh, but declared to
be the Son of God with power, according to the spirit of holiness,' &c.
In respect of his divine subsistence, he was begotten, not made; in
regard of his human nature, made, not begotten. True man, as David
was, and true God, as the Spirit and divine nature is. Again, Rom.
ix. 5, 'Whose are the Father's, and of whom as concerning the flesh,
Christ came, who is over all, God blessed for ever.' Than which
nothing can be said more express as to that nature which is most apt
to be questioned; for surely he that is God over all cannot be said to
be a mere creature. The Jews confessed him to be man, and one of
their blood, and Paul asserteth him to be God over all; they accounted
him to be accursed, and Paul asserteth him to be blessed for ever;
they thought him inferior to the patriarchs of whom he descended;
and Paul over all. So that no word is used in vain; and when he
saith 'according to the flesh,' he insinuateth another nature in him to
be considered by us. The next place is 1 Cor. ii. 8, 'They crucified
the Lord of glory.' He was crucified—there his human nature is
acknowledged; but in respect of the divine nature he is called 'the
Lord of glory:' as in the 24th Psalm, the Lord or King of glory is
Jehovah Sabaoth, 'the Lord of hosts.' Go we further: Phil. ii. 6, 7,
'Who being in the form of God, thought it not robbery to be equal
with God, but made himself of no reputation, and took upon him the
form of a servant, and was made in the likeness of men.' By *the
form of God* is meant not only the divine majesty and glory, but also the
divine essence itself—for without it there can be no true divine majesty
and glory. Now this he kept hidden under his human nature, letting
only some small rays sometimes to shine forth in his miracles. But
that which was most sensible and conspicuous in him was a true
human nature in a low and contemptible estate. Again, 1 Tim. iii.
16, 'Great is the mystery of godliness, God manifested in our flesh'—
that is, the eternal Son of God became man, and assumed the human
nature into the unity of his person. Once more: 1 Pet. iii. 18, 'He
was put to death in the flesh, but quickened in the Spirit'—that is,
died according to his human nature, but by his divine nature raised
from the dead. It is not meant of his soul. Quickened signifies not
one remaining alive, but made alive—that power belongeth to God.

Secondly, By types. Those that come to hand are these :—

1. Melchisedec : Gen. xiv. 18, 'Melchisedec, King of Salem, brought
forth bread and wine to Abraham.' Which type is interpreted by the
apostle, Heb. vii. 2, 3, 'First being by interpretation King of
righteousness, and after that also King of peace; without father
and without mother; having neither beginning of days nor end of life,
but made like unto the Son of God, abideth a priest continually.'
What Melchisedec was is needless to dispute. The apostle considereth
him only as he is represented in the story of Moses, who maketh no
mention of his father or mother, birth or death. Certainly he was a
very man; but as he standeth in scripture there is no mention of
father or mother, beginning or end, what he was, or of whom he came.
So is Christ as God without mother, as man without father; as God
without beginning, as God-man without ending of life.

2. Another type of him was Jacob's ladder, the top of which

reached heaven, and the bottom reached earth, Gen. xxviii. 12 ; and
the angels of God were ascending and descending upon it. This
ladder represented Christ the Son of man, upon whom the angels of
God ascend and descend, John i. 51. The bottom, which reached the
earth, represented Christ's human nature and conversing with men ;
the top, which reached heaven, his heavenly and divine nature ; and
in both his mediation with God for men. *Ascende per hominem, et
perveniens ad Deum.* Christ reaches to heaven in his divine original ;
to earth in his manhood, and him the angels serve. By his dwelling
in our nature, this commerce between earth and heaven is brought about.

The third type is the fiery cloudy pillar : Exod. xiii. 21, ' And the
Lord went before them in the day in a pillar of a cloud ; and by night
in a pillar of fire, to give them light ; to go by day and night.' This
figured Christ's guidance and protection of his church travelling
through this world to his heavenly rest. The cloud signified his
humanity, the fire his divinity. There were two different substances,
the fire and the cloud, yet but one pillar. So there are two different
natures in Christ, his divinity shining as fire, his humanity darkening
as a cloud, yet but one person. That pillar departed not from them
all the while they travelled in the wilderness ; so, while the church's
pilgrimage lasteth, Christ will conduct us, and comfort and shelter us
by his presence. His mediatory conduct ceaseth not.

The fourth type is the tabernacle, wherein God dwelt symbolically,
as in Christ bodily. There God sat on the mercy-seat, which is called
ἱλαστήριον, Heb. ix. 5. So Christ : Rom. iii. 25, ' A propitiation.'
He there dwelt between the cherubims, and did exhibit himself graciously to his people, as now he doth to us by Christ. The next shall
be of the scape-goat on the day of expiation, Lev. xvi. 10. One goat
was to be slain, the other kept alive. The slain goat signified τὴν
σάρκα, τὸ παθητόν, his flesh, or human nature suffering ; the live
goat, τὸ ἀναθὲς τῆς Θεότητος, his immortal deity, or as the apostle
expresseth it, 2 Cor. xiii. 4, That Christ was to be ' crucified through
weakness,' yet to ' live by the power of God ; ' or as we heard before,
1 Pet. iii. 18, ' Put to death in the flesh, and quickened by the Spirit.'
Because these two things could not be shadowed by any one beast,
which the priest having killed, could not make alive again ; and it
was not fit that God should work miracles about types, therefore he
appointed two, that in the slain beast his death might be represented,
in the live beast his immortality. The like mystery was represented
also in the two birds for the cleansing of the leper, Lev. xiv. 6, 7.

Thirdly, I prove it by reasons taken from his office, which may
be considered in the general ; and so it is expressed by one word,
Mediator ; or in particular, according to the several functions of it, expressed by the terms of King, Priest, and Prophet ; or with respect to the
persons that are to be considered and concerned in Christ's mediation.

1. His office considered in the general : so he is called, ' Jesus the
mediator of the New Testament,' Heb. xii. 24. It was agreeable that
μεσίτης, a mediator, should be μεσῆ, a middle person, of the same
essence with both parties, and that his operative mediation should
presuppose his substantial mediation ; that, being God-man in the same
person, he should make an atonement between God and man. Sin hath

made such a breach and distance between us and God, that it raiseth our fears, and causeth backwardness to draw nigh unto him, and so hindereth our love and confidence in him. How can we depend upon one so far above us, and out of the reach of our commerce? Therefore a mediator is necessary, one that will pity us, and is more near and dear to God than we are. One in whom God doth condescend to man, and by whom man may be encouraged to ascend to God. Now, who is so fit for this as Jesus Christ, ' God manifested in our flesh'? The two natures met together in his person, and so God is nearer to man than he was before in the pure deity; for he is come down to us in our flesh, and hath assumed it into the unity of his person; and man is nearer to God, for our nature dwelleth with him so closely united, that we may have more familiar thoughts of God, and a confidence that he will look after us, and concern himself in our affairs, and show us his grace and favour, for surely he will not hide himself from his own flesh, Isa. lviii. 7. This wonderfully reconcileth the heart of man to God, and maketh our thoughts of him more comfortable, and doth encourage us to free access to God.

2. Come we now to the particular offices by which he performeth the work of a mediator, and they all show the necessity of both natures: these offices and functions are those of prophet, priest, and king.

[1.] Our mediator hath a prophetical office belonging to his administration, that he may be made wisdom to us, and therefore he must be both God and man. God, that he may not only teach us outwardly, as an ordinary messenger or minister, but inwardly, putting his law into our minds, and writing it upon our hearts: Heb. viii. 10, and 2 Cor. iii. 3, ' Ye are manifestly declared to be the epistle of Christ ministered by us, written not with ink, but with the Spirit of the living God; not in tables of stone, but in the fleshly tables of the heart.' Men may be the instruments, but Christ is the author of this grace, and therefore he must be God. To convince men's understandings of their duty, and to incline their hearts to perform it, requireth no less than a divine power. If such an infinite virtue be necessary to cure the blindness of the body; how much more to cure the natural blindness and darkness of the mind! A man he must also be; for the great prophet of the church was to be raised up among his brethren like unto Moses, Deut. xviii. 15. Till such an one came into the world, they were to hear Moses; but then they were to hearken to him. He that was to come was to be a lawgiver as Moses was, but of a far more absolute and perfect law—a lawgiver that must match and overmatch Moses every way. He was to be a man as Moses was in respect of our infirmities, such an one as Moses was whom the Lord had known face to face; but of a far more divine nature, and approved to the world by miracles, signs, and wonders, as Moses was. Again, it was prophesied of him that, as the great prophet of the world, he should be anointed, that he might come and preach the gospel to the poor, Isa. lxii. 1; which could not be if he had spoken from heaven in thunder, and not as a man conversed with men. Again, he was to approve himself as one who had grace poured into his lips, Ps. xlv. 2; that all might wonder at the gracious speeches that came from his mouth, as they did at Christ's. In short, that Wisdom of the Father, which was wont to assume some visible shape for a time, when he would instruct the patriarchs concerning his will, that he might hide his majesty and put a veil upon his glory, was now to assume our nature into the unity of his person, not a temporary and vanishing appearance; that 'God who at sundry times and in divers manners spake in time past unto the fathers by the prophets, might in these last days speak to us by his Son,' Heb. i. 1, 2. Then God delivered his will by parcels, now by him he would settle the whole frame of the gospel.

[2.] Jesus Christ, as he is the apostle of our profession, so also he is the high priest, Heb. iii. 1, and so must be both God and man. Man, that he might be made sin for us; God, that we might be made the righteousness of God in him, 2. Cor. v. 21. Man, to undertake our redemption; God, to perform it. Man, that he might suffer; God, that he might satisfy by suffering and make our atonement full—we are purchased by the blood of God. Man, that he might have a sacrifice to offer; God, that the offering might be of an infinite price and value, Heb. ix. 14. Man, that he might have a life to lay down for us; God, that the power of laying it down and taking it up again might be in his own hands: John x. 17, 18, ' I lay down my life, that I may take it again. No man taketh it from me, but I lay it down of myself. I have power to lay it down, and I have power to take it again.' This was fit that his suffering should be a pure voluntary act, required, indeed, by God, but not enforced by man. He had a liberty, at his own pleasure, as to anything men could do, and thereby commendeth his love to sinners. What shall I say? He was man that he might die; he was God that by death he might destroy him that had the power of death. He was man, that by his death he might ratify the new covenant; God, that he might convey to the heirs of promise these precious legacies of pardon and life. Man, that he might be a merciful high priest, touched with the feeling of our infirmities; God, that we, coming boldly to the throne of grace, might find mercy and grace to help in every time of need, Heb. iv. 15, 16.

[3.] His kingly office. He that was to be King of kings and Lord of lords needed to be both God and man. God, that he might cast out the prince of this world, and having rescued his church from the power of darkness, might govern it by his word and Spirit, and finally present it to himself a glorious church, without spot or wrinkle, or any such thing. Man he needed to be for his own glory, ' that he might be the first-born among many brethren,'—and head and members might suit, and be all of a piece,—and for our consolation, that we might be heirs of God and joint-heirs with Christ, Rom. viii. 17, —and for the greater terror and ignominy of Satan, that the seed of the woman might break the serpent's head. In short, God, that he might govern and influence a people so scattered abroad upon the face of the earth, and raise them up at the last day; man, that our nature (the dignity of which was so envied by Satan) might be exalted at the right hand of Majesty, and placed so near God, far above the angelical.

Thirdly, With respect to the persons who are to be considered and concerned in Christ's mediation: God, to whom we are redeemed; Satan, from whom we are redeemed; and we ourselves who are the redeemed of the Lord. And you shall see, with respect to God, with respect to Satan, with respect to ourselves, our Mediator ought to be both God and man.

1. God he need to be. With respect to God, that he may be appeased by a valuable compensation given to his justice. No mere man could satisfy the justice of God, appease his wrath, procure his favour; therefore our surety needed to be God to do this. And with respect to Satan, that he might be overcome. Now none can bind the strong one and take away his goods but he that is stronger than he, Luke xi. 21. Now no mere man is a match for Satan; the conqueror of the devil must be God, that by strong hand he may deliver us from his tyranny. And with respect to man, that he may be saved. Not only because of the two former respects must he be God, but also there is a special reason in the cause—the two former respects evince it; for unless God be appeased, man cannot be reconciled, and unless the devil be overcome, man cannot be delivered. If a God be needful for that, man cannot be saved unless our Redeemer be God; but there is a special reason, because of our own obstinacy and rebellion, which is only overcome by the divine power. It is necessary man should be converted and changed, as well as God satisfied and Satan overcome. Now who can convert himself or change his own heart? That work would cease for ever unless God did undertake it by his all-conquering Spirit. Therefore our Mediator must be God, to renew and cleanse our hearts, and by his divine power to give us a divine nature.

2. Man also he ought to be with respect to these three parties:—With respect to God, that the satisfaction might be tendered in the nature which had sinned, that ' as by man came death, by man also might come the resurrection from the dead,' 1 Cor. xv. 21, 22; that ' as in Adam all die, so by Christ shall all be made alive.' So with respect to the devil, that he might be overcome in the nature that was foiled by his temptations. And with respect to us, that ' he that sanctifieth and they that are sanctified, might be of one,' Heb. ii. 11. The priest that wrought the expiation, and the people for whom it was wrought, were of one stock; the right of redeeming belonged to the next kinsman. Christ is our *Goel* who redeemed us, not only *jure proprietatis*, as his creatures—to God as God—but *jure propinquitatis*, as his kinsmen. So as man we are of kin to him, as he came in our nature, and as he sanctifieth; doubly akin, not only by virtue of his incarnation but our regeneration, as he was made of a woman, and we born of God. These are the reasons.

Use. Let me press you to admire this mystery of godliness. The man Christ Jesus in whom the fulness of the Godhead dwelt bodily. The life and strength of our faith depends upon it, for as he is true man, flesh of our flesh, and bone of our bone, he will not be strange to us, and as he is God, he is able to help us.

Two things I will press you to:—

1. Consider what a fit object he is for your faith to close with.

2. Own him as your Lord and your God.

First, To raise your trust and confidence, consider what a fit object he is for your faith, how he is qualified for all his offices of prophet, priest, and king.

1. As your prophet, consider how necessary it was that God dwelling in man's nature should set afoot the gospel. Partly because whenever you come seriously to consider this matter, this thought will arise in you, that this blessed gospel could not be without repealing the law of Moses, given with such solemnity by God himself, and it was not fit it should be abrogated by any but him who was far above Moses, to wit, by the Son of God himself, not any fellow-servant equal to Moses. The apostle telleth us that Moses was faithful in God's house as a servant, but Christ as a Son over his own house, Heb. iii. 5, 6. The servant must give place when the Son and Lord himself cometh. But rather take it from what Moses foretold himself : Deut. xviii. 18, 19, 'I will raise them up a prophet from among their brethren like unto thee, and I will put my words into his mouth, and he shall speak unto them all that I command him ; and it shall come to pass, that he that will not hearken to my word which he shall speak in my name, I will require it of him.' Now these words cannot be verified in any other prophet after Moses until Christ, for that of these prophets there arose none in Israel like unto Moses, Deut. xxxiv. 10. They had no authority to be lawgivers as Moses had, but were all bound to the observation of his law till Christ should come, whom Moses calleth a prophet like unto himself, that is a law-maker, exhorting all men to hear and obey him. None of the prophets did take upon them that privilege ; they must let that alone till the Messiah should come, whose office it is to change the law given upon Mount Sinai, and instead thereof to propagate or promulgate a new law to begin at Zion : Isa. ii. 3, 'The law shall go forth of Zion, and the word of the Lord from Jerusalem.' And in another place, 'The isles shall wait for his law,' Isa. xlii. 4. Well, now, this is a mighty confirmation of our religion, and bindeth both our faith and obedience to consider Christ's authority, that a greater than Moses is here. Partly because it concerneth us to receive the gospel as an eternal doctrine that shall never be changed, for it is called an everlasting covenant; and nothing conduceth to that so much as to consider that it is promulgated by the eternal God himself, by him ' in whom the fulness of the Godhead dwelleth bodily.' Partly because the gospel, if we would profit by it, is to be received by all believers, not only as an everlasting covenant, but as certain, perfect, and saving. Now if the fulness of the Godhead dwelt in him who gave this covenant, we cannot deny either the certainty or the perfection, or the savingness of it ; for if we receive it from him who is truth itself, we cannot be deceived. It is certain if he taught us in person ; surely all his works are perfect. Subordinate ministers may mingle their weaknesses with their doctrine ; if we have it from a Saviour, surely it is a doctrine that bringeth salvation.

2. Consider what a fit object here is for your faith. As Christ is a priest, so his great business is to reconcile us to God in the body of his flesh through death, who once were strangers and enemies, Col. i. 21. Consider how fit he was for this ; God and man were first united in his person, before they were united in one covenant. If you consider the fruits of his redemption and reconciliation ; the evil from whence we were to be delivered, the good that was to be procured, Christ is every way a commodious Mediator for us as God-man. If you consider the

evil from whence we are delivered, he was man, that the chastisement of our peace might be put upon his shoulders ; God, that by his stripes we might be healed, Isa. liii. 5.   Or, if you consider the good to be procured, he doth it as God-man.   He was a man, that as by the disobedience of one many were made sinners, so by the obedience of one many might be made righteous ; God, that as sin reigned unto death, so grace might reign through righteousness unto eternal life, by Jesus Christ our Lord, Rom. v. 19, 21.   As he is God, his merit is full ; as he is man, we are partakers of the benefit of it.

3. Consider how fit an object he is for our faith as king.   For as the fulness of the Godhead dwelt in him bodily, he is the greatest and most glorious person that ever was in the world, infinitely superior above all power that is named in this world, or in the world to come. The man who is our shepherd is fellow to the Lord of hosts.   The thought of Immanuel maketh the prophet startle, and break out into a triumph when Sennacherib brake in with his forces like a deluge in the land of Judah : ' They fill thy land, O Immanuel,' Isa. viii. 8.   Then ver. 9, 10, 'Associate yourselves, and ye shall be broken in pieces ; gird yourselves, and ye shall be broken in pieces; take counsel together, it shall come to nought ; speak the word, it shall not stand : for God is with us.'   Or because of Immanuel.   Surely Christ is the foundation of the church's happiness, and may afford us comfort in the most calamitous condition ; we are in his hands, under his pastoral care and protection : John x. 28, 'I give unto them eternal life, and they shall never perish, neither shall any pluck them out of my hand.'   Neither man nor devil can break off totally and finally their union with him. In short, he that assumed our nature to himself, will communicate himself to us.   All union is in order to communion—here is a commodious and a blessed Saviour represented unto you.

Secondly, Own him as your Lord and your God.   This was the profession of Thomas's faith : John xx. 28, ' My Lord and my God.' I shall insist on that scripture.   In the history there are these remarkables :—

1. Thomas, his absence from an assembly of the disciples, when Christ had manifested himself to them, ver. 24.   Being absent, he not only missed the good news which many[1] brought, but also the comfortable sight of Christ, and was thereby left in doubts and snares.

2. When these things were told him he betrays his incredulity, ver. 25.   When they told him, ' he said unto them, Except I see in his hands the print of the nails, and put my finger into the print of the nails, and thrust my hand into his side, I will not believe.'   This unbelief was overruled by God's providence for the honour of Christ.   His incredulity was an occasion to manifest the certainty of Christ's resurrection.   If credulous men, or those hasty of belief, had only seen Christ, their report had been liable to suspicion.   Solomon maketh it one of his proverbs, ' The simple believeth every word.'   Here is one that had sturdy and pertinacious doubts, yet brought at last to yield.   However, this is an instance of the proneness of our hearts to unbelief, especially if we have not the objects of faith under the view of the senses, and how apt we are to give laws to heaven, and require our terms of God.

[1] Query, ' Mary ' ? —Ed.

3. Christ's condescension in two things :—

[1.] In appearing again, ver. 26, on the first day of the next week, to show how ready he is to honour and bless his own day, and to give satisfaction to poor doubting souls by coming again to them ; and it was well Thomas was there at this time.

[2.] In giving Thomas the satisfaction of sense : ver. 27, 'Reach hither thy finger, and behold my hands, and reach hither thy hand, and thrust it into my side.' With what mildness doth our Lord treat him, though under such a distemper. Unbelief is so hateful to Christ, that he is very careful to have it removed, and in condescension grants what was his fault to seek.

4. The next thing is Thomas his faith : ver. 28, ' And he answered and said, My Lord, and my God.' He presumeth not to touch Christ, but contents himself only to see him, and having seen him, makes a good confession, ὁ κύριος μου, ὁ Θεὸς μου.

[1.] Observe the two titles given to Christ : *God* and *Lord*. He is God, the fountain of all our happiness, and Lord, as he hath a dominion over us, to guide and dispose of us at his own pleasure.

[2.] Observe the appropriation or personal application to himself. *my* God and *my* Lord.

Hence we may observe :—

1. That God leaveth some to themselves for a while, that themselves and others may be more confirmed afterwards. Thomas his faith was as it were dead and buried in his heart, and now, upon the sight of Christ, quickened and revived. We must not judge of men by a fit of temptation, but stay till they come to themselves again. Who would have thought that out of an obstinate incredulity so great a faith should spring up suddenly ?

2. We may observe Thomas, that is with much ado awakened, makes a fairer confession than all the rest. They call him their Lord, but he his Lord and God.

3. We may observe, again, that true believing with the heart is joined with confession of the mouth : Ps. cxvi. 10, ' I believed, therefore have I spoken.'

4. Hence you may take notice of the reality of the two natures in the unity of Christ's person, for he is both *Deus and Dominus*. But how cometh he to acknowledge Christ's Godhead ? He did not feel the divinity of Christ in hands, or side, or feet. *Videbat tangebatque hominem, et confitebatur Deum, quem non videbat neque tangebat,* saith Austin. Herein his faith was beyond sense, he felt the manhood and acknowledgeth the deity.

5. Hence we may observe, that those that are rightly conversant about Christ and the mysteries of his death and resurrection, should take Christ for their Lord and their God. Thomas saith, ' My Lord and my God,' and his confession should be the common confession of all the faithful. I shall quit the three first, and insist only on the two last. I therefore begin with the fourth observation.

Fourthly, Hence you see the reality of the two natures in the unity of Christ's person. The name of God is joined with the title of Lord ; therefore the name of God belongeth to him no less than the title of Lord. Thomas, when he saith my Lord, he seemeth not to have

satisfied himself till he had added this other name and title, my God:
now this importeth the reality of his divine nature, for these three
reasons:—

1. Those things which are proper to God cannot, ought not, to be
transferred to a mere creature; but this title of *my God* is a covenant
title, and so often used in scripture, and therefore Christ was God.

2. To whom truly and properly the names and titles of things do
belong, to him that which is signified by those names and titles doth
belong also; for otherwise this would destroy all certainty of speech.
You cannot speak or write, unless words signify what in vulgar use
they are applied unto; there could be no reasoning *a signo ad rem
significatam*, from the sign to the thing signified. If I should call a
brute a man, or a creature God, how can we understand what is spoken
or written? The argument is the more cogent, because a name is an
implicit contracted definition, as a definition is a name explained and
dilated. As when I say a man is a reasonable creature, so a God is
one that hath power over all, blessed for ever.

3. The greater any person is, the more danger there is of giving him
titles that do not belong to him; for that is to place him in an honour
to which he hath greater pretensions than others, but no right; especially doth this hold good in religion—it is true in civils. To give
one next the king, the title of king, would awaken the jealousy of
princes, and breed much inconvenience. But especially doth this hold
good in religion, where God is so jealous of giving his glory to another,
Isa. xlii. 8. Therefore the greater the dignity of Christ was above
all other creatures, the more caution was necessary that the name of
God might not be ascribed to him, if he were only mere man, and it
did not properly agree to him; for the more dangerous the error,
the more cautiously should we abstain from it.

4. Consider the person by whom this title was given; by a godly
man. No godly man would call an idol, or a magistrate, or a teacher,
or a king, or an angel, or any created thing above an angel, his Lord
and his God. But this was done by Thomas, one bred up in the
religion taught by Moses and the prophets; and the chief point of
that religion was, that God is but one: Deut. vi. 4, ' Hear, O Israel,
the Lord our God is one Lord.' This was one of the sentences written
on the fringes of their garments, and it is quoted by Christ, whose
disciple Thomas also was, Mark xii. 29, and explained by a learned
scribe which came to him: Mark xii. 32, ' Well, master, thou hast
said the truth, for there is but one God, and there is none other but
him.' Now, Thomas knowing this, and the first commandment, ' Thou
shalt have no other gods before me,' if he were not persuaded of it,
would he say to Christ, ' My Lord and my God'?

5. The person to whom he spake it: ' He said to him;' not to the
Father, but to Jesus of Nazareth: ' My Lord and my God.' Surely
as the saints would not derogate from God, so Christ would not
arrogate what was proper to his Father. Therefore as his disciples
would have been tender of giving it to him, so he would have refused
this honour, being so holy, if it had not been his due. But Christ
reproved not, but rather approved this confession of faith; therefore
it was right and sound. Christ had said to him, ' Be not faithless, but

believing,' and then Thomas saith, ' My Lord and my God.' ' And
Jesus saith to him, Thomas, because thou hast seen me, thou hast
believed; blessed are they that have not seen, and yet have believed.'
There is no rebuke for ascribing too much to him.

6. The conjunction of the divine and human nature is so necessary
to all Christ's functions and offices, that less would not have been
sufficient than to say, ' My Lord, my God.' The functions and offices
of Christ are three—to be a prophet, priest, and king.

[1.] To be a prophet, Mat. xxiii. 10, ' One is your master, even
Christ.' Now to be our master and teacher, it is necessary that he
should have the human nature and divine conjoined. The human
nature, that he might teach men by word of mouth, familiarly and
sweetly conversing with men ; and also by his example, for he perfectly teacheth that teacheth both ways, by word and deed. And it is
a mighty condescension, that God would come down, and submit to
the same laws we are to live by. His divine nature was also necessary,
that he might be the best of teachers ; for who is such a teacher as
God ? and that he might teach us in the best way, and that is, when
God, taking the nature of man, doth vouchsafe to men his familiar
converse, ea ting and drinking and walking with them, offering himself to be seen and heard by them ; as he of old taught Abraham,
Gen. xviii., accepting his entertainment ; nothing more profitable, or
honourable to men can be thought of. In Christ's prophetical office,
four things are to be considered :—

(1.) What he taught.

(2.) How he taught.

(3.) By what arguments he confirmed his doctrine.

(4.) How he received it from the Father.

(1.) What he taught. Christ preached, but chiefly himself ; he revealed and showed forth God, but by revealing and showing forth himself, John xiv. 9 ; he called men, but to himself ; he commanded men
to believe, but in himself, John xiv. 1 ; he promised eternal life, which
he would give, but to men believing in himself ; he offered salvation
to miserable sinners, but to be had by himself ; he wrought a fear of
judgment to come, but to be exercised by himself ; he offered remission
of sins, but to those that believed in himself ; he promised the resurrection of the dead, which he by his own power and authority would
bring to pass. Now who could do all this but God ? A mere man, if
faithful and holy, would have turned off men from himself to God :
2 Cor. iv. 5, ' For we preach not ourselves, but Christ Jesus the Lord,
and ourselves your servants for Jesus' sake.' They designed no
honour to themselves, but only to Christ ; they were loth to transfer
any part of this glory to themselves ; so would Christ if he had not
been God. Therefore what should his disciples say, but ' My Lord,
my God ' ?

(2.) How he taught. There is a twofold way of teaching—one
human, by the mouth, and sound of words striking the ear ; the other
divine, opening and affecting the heart. Christ used both ways. As
the human nature was necessary to the one, so the divine to the other.
As the organs of speaking cannot be without the human nature, so
the other way of teaching cannot be without a divine power. When

the disciples came to Christ, ' Lord, increase our faith,' Luke xvii. 5,
he did not answer, as Jacob did to Rachel (when she said, ' Give me
children or I die'), ' Am I in the place of God?' Christ after his
resurrection did not only open the scriptures, as was said before, but,
Luke xxiv. 45, ' He opened their understandings, that they might
understand the scriptures.' And he opened the heart of Lydia, Acts
xvi. 14; and poured the Holy Spirit on the apostles on the day of
Pentecost, Acts ii. ; and by the same efficacy teacheth the church,
wherever it is scattered.

(3.) If you consider by what arguments he confirmed his doctrine.
By many, and the greatest miracles, not done by the power of another,
but his own ; and he required men to believe it : Mat. ix. 28, ' Believe
ye that I am able to do this?' Whence had he the power to know
the thoughts of men, to cure all sorts of diseases in a moment, to open
the eyes of the blind, to raise the dead, to dispossess devils, but from
that divine nature which was in him ? Was it in his body and flesh ?
then it was finite, and in some sort material. Was it in his soul,
understanding, will, or phantasy, or sensitive appetite ? How could it
work on other men's bodies ? Therefore it was from his divine nature :
' My Lord, my God.'

(4.) How he received this doctrine from the Father. Did God ever
speak to him, or appear to him? Is there any time, or manner, or
speech noted by the evangelists when God made this revelation ?
None at all. If he were a mere creature, or nothing but a man, surely
that should have been done. He revealed the most intimate counsels
and decrees of God, as perfectly knowing them; but when or how
they were revealed to him by his Father is not said, which, if he had
been mere man, would have conduced to the authority of his message
and revelation. But all this needed not, he being a divine person, of
the same essence with his Father. Therefore, ' My Lord, my God.'

[2.] His priestly office. The human nature was necessary for that,
for the reasons alleged by the apostle, Heb. ii. 14, 17. And also the
divine nature, that there might be a priest as well as a sacrifice.
There had been no sacrifice if he had not been man, and no priest, if
he had not been God, to offer up himself through the eternal Spirit,
Heb. ix. 14. The sacrifice must suffer, the priest act ; and besides,
he could not enter into the heavenly sanctuary to present himself
before God for us, Heb. ix. 24. Then the heavenly sanctuary and
tabernacle need first to be made before he entered. For as the earthly
priest made the earthly tabernacle before he ministered in it, so the
true priest was to make the heavenly tabernacle, as the author to the
Hebrews saith in many places. But to leave that ; the priest was to
expiate sins by the offering of a sacrifice instead of the sinner. So
Christ was to satisfy the justice of God for sinners by his mediatory
sacrifice. Now this he could not do unless he had been God as well
as man. The dignity of his person did put a value upon his sufferings. Without this, how shall we pacify conscience, representing to us
the evil of sin, and the dreadfulness of God's wrath, and the exact
justice of the judge of all the world, Rom. iii. 25, 26 ; especially when
these apprehensions are awakened in us by the curse of the law and
the stinging sense of God's threatenings, which are so absolute, uni-

versal, and every way true and evident, unless we know a sufficient satisfaction hath been made for us ? If you think the promises of the gospel are enough, alas ! when the threatenings of the law are so just, and built upon such evident reason, the soul is exposed to doubtfulness. And if the threatenings of the law seem altogether in vain, the promises of the gospel will seem less firm and valid. The truth and honour of God's government must one way or other be kept up, and that will not be unless there be a fair passage from covenant to covenant, and that the former be not repealed or relaxed but upon valuable consideration, as it is when our mediator and surety beareth our sorrows and griefs, and satisfieth for us. But now, if he were mere man, it would not have that esteem and value as to be sufficient for so many men, and so many sins as are committed against an holy God. Therefore he needeth to be God also.

[3.] His kingly office. How can that be exercised without an infinite power ? Because by our king and judge, all our enemies are to be overcome ; the world, sin, death, and the devil. And what is necessary to do this every man may soon understand. And as an infinite power is necessary, so an infinite knowledge ; that all things in heaven and earth may be naked and open to him, and that he search the heart, and try the reins : and then, that he may subject all things to himself, raise all the dead to life, govern and protect the faithful in all the parts of the world ; that he may be present with them, in every age and place, to help and relieve them. In short, to do all things both in heaven and in earth, that fall within the compass of his office. Now what is a divine and infinite power, if this be not ? What can the Father do which the Son cannot do also ? yea, what doth the Father do which the Son doth not likewise ? John v. 19. Is there any work which the one doth that the other cannot do ? Besides, there needeth infinite authority and majesty, therefore the king of the church must be infinite. But how is he infinite, if he hath only a finite nature, such as a mere creature hath ? Or how could his finite nature, without change and conversion into another nature, be made infinite ? For without doubt that nature is infinite which hath an infinite power of understanding, willing, and acting. Well, then, Christ cannot be truly owned, unless he be owned as Lord and God.

Fifthly, Those that are rightly conversant about Christ, and the mysteries of his death and resurrection, should take Christ for their Lord and their God. Every one of them should say, My God, on whom I depend ; my Lord, to whose use I resign myself. I shall—

1. Explain in what sense these words may and ought to be used.

2. Give you the reasons why it becomes Christians to be able to say, ' My Lord, my God.'

1. In what sense these words may and ought to be used, ' My Lord, and my God.' There are two things considerable in those words :—

[1.] An appropriation or a claim, and challenge of interest in him.

[2.] A resignation or dedication of ourselves to his use and service.

Both are implied in these titles, ' My Lord, my God.' Christ was his God or benefactor, and also his Lord and Master. However that be in the mutual stipulation of the covenant, it is evident: Cant. ii. 16, 'I am my beloved's, and my beloved is mine.' There is the appropriation of faith, and the resignation of obedience: Ezek. xxxvi. 28, 'Ye shall be my people, and I will be your God;' Zech. xiii. 9, 'I will say, It is my people, and they shall say, The Lord is my God.'

(1.) The one is the fruit and effect of the other. God saith, 'I am thy God;' and the soul answereth, 'I am thy servant.' As when Christ said, 'Mary,' she presently said, 'Rabboni.' God awakeneth us by the offer of himself and all his grace to do us good, and then we devote ourselves to his service, and profess subjection to him. If he will be our God, we may well allow him a dominion and lordship over us, to rule us at his pleasure. We choose him, because he chooseth us, for all God's works leave their impression upon our hearts—he cometh with terms of peace, and we with profession of duty. God loveth first, and most, and purest, and therefore his love is the cause of all.

(2.) The one is the evidence of the other. If God be yours, you are his. He is yours by gift of himself to you, and you are his by gift of yourselves to him. The covenant bindeth mutually. Many will be ready to apply, and call God their God, that do not dedicate and devote themselves to God. If you be not the Lord's, the Lord is not yours. He refuseth their claim that say, Hosea viii. 2, 'Israel shall cry unto me, My God, we know thee. Israel hath cast off the thing that is good.' In their distress they pleaded their interest in the covenant, but God would not allow the claim, because they denied obedience.

(3.) The one is more sensible and known to us than the other. A believer cannot always say God is mine, but he will always say, I am his: Ps. cxix. 94, 'I am thine, save me.' I am thine, and will be thine, only thine, wholly thine, and always thine. Appropriation hath more of a privilege in it, resignation is only a duty. We have leave and allowance to say God is my God, but we cannot always say it without doubt and hesitancy, because our interest is not always alike evident and clear. When you cannot say, My God, yet be sure to say, My Lord. We know God to be ours by giving up ourselves to be his. His choice and election of us is a secret till it be evidenced by our choice of him for our God and portion—our act is more sensible to the conscience. Be more full and serious in the resignation of yourselves to him, and in time that will show you your interest in God.

(4.) God's propriety in us by contract and resignation speaketh comfort, as well as our propriety and interest in God. You are his own, and therefore he will provide for you and care for you: 1 Tim. v. 8, 'If any provide not for his own, he hath denied the faith, and is worse than an infidel.' Interest doth strangely endear things to us. 'The world will love its own,' John v. 19; and will not God love his own, and Christ love his own? John xiii. 1. You may trust him, and depend upon him, and serve him cheerfully, for you are his own. So that if we had no interest in God established by the covenant, if God had not said to us, I am yours, yet our becoming his would make it com-

fortable.   For every one taketh himself to be bound to love his own,
provide for his own, and to defend his own, and do good to his own.
Indeed, God is ours, as well as we are his; but our being his draweth
along with it much comfort and blessing.   But to speak of these
apart :—

(1st.) The appropriation or claim of interest is a sweet thing.   If God
be your God, why should you be troubled? Ps. xvi. 5, 6, 'The Lord
is the portion of my inheritance, and of my cup.   Thou maintainest
my lot.   The lines are fallen unto me in pleasant places, yea, I have a
goodly heritage.'   You have a right to God himself, and may lay
claim to all that he hath for your comfort and use.   His attributes
yours, his providences yours, his promises yours, what may not you
promise yourselves from him ?   Support under all troubles, relief in
all necessities.   You may take hold of his covenant, Isa. lvi. 4, and
lay claim to all the privileges of it.   It is all yours.

(2nd.) This dedication, this resignation of ourselves to God's use, to
be at his disposing without reservation or power of revocation, is often
spoken of in scripture : Isa. xliv. 5, 'One shall say, I am the Lord's,
another shall call himself by the name of Jacob, and another shall
subscribe with his hand to the Lord, and surname himself by the
name of Israel.'   The meaning is, to give up their names to God, to
be entered into his muster-roll, and to be listed in his service : Rom.
vi. 13, 'Yield up yourselves to God, as those that are alive from the
dead.'   It is the immediate fruit of grace and new life infused in us.
A natural man liveth to himself, to please himself, and give satisfaction to his own lusts.   Grace is a new being and life, that inclines
us to live and act for God.   As soon as this life is begotten in us by
the power of his Spirit, our hearts are inclined towards God, and you
devote yourselves to serve and please him.   As your work and business was before to serve the devil, the world, and the flesh, so now to
please, serve, and glorify God.

Secondly, The reasons why it becometh Christians to be able to
say, 'My Lord, my God.'

1. Because our interest in him is the ground of our comfort and
confidence.   It is not comfortable to us that there is a God, and that
there is a Lord, that may be terrible to us.   The devils believe, and
the damned spirits feel there is a God and there is a Lord ; but their
thoughts of God is a part of their misery and torment, James ii. 19.
The more they think of God, the more their horror is increased; to
own a God, and not to see him as ours, the remembrance of it will
be troublesome to us: 1 Sam. xxx. 6, 'David comforted himself in
the Lord his God.'   There was the comfort, that he had a God to go
to when all was lost, and that God was his God.   So Hab. iii. 18, 'I
will rejoice in the Lord, I will joy in the God of my salvation.'   If
God be our God, we have more in him than trouble can take from
us.   So Luke i. 47, 'My spirit hath rejoiced in God my Saviour.'
When you make particular application to yourselves, it breeds strong
comfort.

2. Because nothing strikes upon the heart with such an efficacy, as
what nearly concerns us affects us most.   The love of Christ to
sinners in general doth not affect us so much as when it is shed

abroad in our own hearts by the Spirit: Gal. ii. 20, ' He loved me, and gave himself for me ; ' that draws out our hearts to God again, and is a quickening motive to stir us up to the life of love and faith.   So Eph. i. 13, ' In whom ye trusted, after ye heard the word of truth, the gospel of your salvation.'   It is not sufficient to know that the gospel is a doctrine of salvation to others only, but to find it a doctrine of salvation to themselves in particular, that they may apply the promises to their own heart.   A Christian is affected most with things according as he is concerned in them himself.   It bindeth our obedience the more firmly when we know that we are particularly engaged to God, and have chosen him for our God and our Lord.

3. Because without a real personal entering into covenant, the covenant doth us no good ; unless every one of us do choose God for our God and Lord, and particularly own him.   Every man must give his hand to the Lord, and personally engage for himself.   It is not enough that Christ engage for us in being our surety, but we must take a bond upon ourselves.   Something Christ did for us and in our name, he interposed as the surety of a better testament, Heb. vii. 22. Something must be done personally by us before we can have benefit by it.   You must give up yourselves to the Lord.   It is not enough that the church engage for us, but every man must engage his own heart to draw nigh to God : Jer. xxx. 21, ' Who is he that engageth his heart to draw nigh to me ? '   It is not enough that our parents did engage for us, Deut. xxix. 10–12.   They did in the name of their little ones avouch God to be their God, as we devote, dedicate, and engage our children to God in baptism ; but no man can savingly transact this work for another.   We ratify the covenant in our own persons, 2 Cor. ix. 13, by a professed subjection to the gospel of Christ. This is a work cannot be done by a proxy, or assignees ; unless we personally enter into covenant with God for ourselves, our dedication by our parents will not profit us, we shall be as children of the Æthiopians unto God, Amos ix. 7; though children of the covenant, all this will not serve—these are visible external privileges.   But there is something required of our persons, every one must say for himself, ' My Lord, and my God.'   And this must not only be done in words, and by some visible external rites that may signify so much.   As for instance, coming to the Lord's Supper, that is the new testament in Christ's blood, Luke xxii. 20.   It is *interpretative*—a sealing the new covenant between Christ and us.   God giveth, and you take the elements as a pledge and token that God and you are agreed.   That he will give you himself, his Christ, and all his benefits ; and you will walk before him in newness of life.   Now to rest in the ceremony, and neglect the substance, is but a mockery of God.   As many rend the bond yet prize the seal, care much for the sacrament, that never care for the duty it bindeth them unto.   If your hearts be hearty and well with God, you come now personally to enter into covenant with him ; but this business must not be done only externally, but internally also.   It is a business done between God and our souls, though no outward witnesses be conscious to it.   God cometh speaking to us by his Spirit in this transaction : Ps. xxxv. 3, ' Say unto my soul, I am thy salvation.'   And we speak to God, Lam. iii. 24, ' The Lord

is my portion, saith my soul.' There is *verbum mentis*, as well as *verbum oris*. This covenant is carried on in soul language: Ps. xvi. 21, ' O my soul, thou hast said unto the Lord, Thou art my Lord.' So Ps. xxvii. 8, ' When thou saidst, Seek ye my face, my heart said, Thy face, Lord, will I seek.' The Lord offereth or representeth himself as our Lord, and we profess ourselves to be the Lord's. No eye seeth, or ear heareth what passeth between God and the soul. Now, without this personal inward covenanting, all the privileges of the covenant will do us no good. And this personal inward covenanting amounts to full as much as ' My Lord, my God.' Therefore it concerneth every one of us to see whether we have thus particularly owned Christ; if there have been any treaty between God and our souls ; and whether it came to any conclusion, and particular soul engagement ; that you could thus own Christ, not only as God and Lord, but as *your* God and *your* Lord.

SERMON VIII.

And having made peace by the blood of his cross, to reconcile all things to himself; by him, I say, whether they be things in earth, or things in heaven.—COL. I. 20.

IN these words observe:—

First, What Christ was to do.

Secondly, The manner how he did it; or,

First, The end for which he was appointed. To be our Mediator and Redeemer, and accordingly promised and sent into the world to reconcile all things to God, ' Whether they be things in heaven, or things in earth.'

Secondly, The means by which he accomplished it: ' Having made peace by the blood of his cross;' that is, by his bloody sacrifice on the cross, thereby answering the sacrifices of atonement under the law. In the first branch take notice of :—

1. The benefit : *reconciliation with God.*

2. The person procuring it: *by him;* and it is repeated again, *I say, by him.*

3. The persons to whom this benefit is intended, expressed—

[1.] Collectively, πάντα, *all things.*

[2.] Distributively : *whether they be things in earth or things in heaven.*

As they are collectively expressed, it teaches us that grace is revealed and offered in the most comprehensive expressions, that none may be excluded, or have just cause to exclude themselves. As it is distributively expressed, the latter clause is of a dubious interpretation. Some ' by things on earth,' understand men, but by ' things in heaven ' the angels. Surely not the fallen angels, for they are not in heaven, neither was Christ sent to reconcile them, nor relieve them in their misery and reduce them to God, Heb. ii. 16, οὐκ ἐπιλαμβάνεται τῶν ἀγγέλων. What then shall we understand by 'things in heaven'? Some think the holy angels, others the glorified saints. (1.) Those that assert the first argue thus: that the angels are properly inhabitants of heaven, and so fitly called things in heaven; and they are enemies to men whilst they are ungodly, idolatrous, and rebels to God (as good subjects hold with their prince, and have common friends and enemies with him), but are reconciled to them as soon as they partake of the benefits of Christ's death, as we are told of 'joy in heaven among the angels of God, at the conversion of one sinner,' Luke xv. 10. Now if there be so much joy over one sinner repenting, how much more when many sinners are snatched out of the jaws of hell? They make the sense to be thus : before, for the sins of men, they were alienated from them, but then reconciled. But this scripture speaks not of the reconciliation of angels and men, but the reconciliation of all things to God; for so it is expressly in the text, to reconcile all things to himself. Now the good angels cannot be said to be reconciled to God, for there was never a breach between them, *Se nunquam cum matre in gratiam rediisse.* (2.) Therefore, I interpret it of the glorified saints. See the like expression, Eph. i. 10, ' To gather together in one all things to Christ which are in heaven and in earth.' And more clearly, Eph. iii. 15, 'Of whom the whole family in heaven and earth is named.' Meaning thereby the faithful who are already in heaven, and those who are now remaining upon earth. This is a comfortable note, and teaches us :—

1. That the apostle Paul knew no purgatory, or third place for souls after death.

2. That the saints departed are now in heaven as to their souls, and gathered to the rest of the spirits of just men made perfect.

3. The souls now in heaven once needed the merit of Christ, even as we do. None come thither but they were first reconciled to God. By him their peace was made, and they obtained remission of sins by the blood of his cross, as ye do. In short, all that go to heaven go thither by the mediation, sacrifice, and meritorious righteousness of the same Redeemer.

Doct. One great benefit we have by Christ is peace and reconciliation with God. Here I shall show :—

1. What this reconciliation is.
2. How it was obtained.
3. What assurance we have that it is obtained.
4. How and upon what terms it is applied to us.

1. What this reconciliation is.

I answer : It is not an original peace, but a returning to amity after some foregoing breach. Now the breach by sin consisted in two things —an aversion of the creature from God, and an aversion of God from the creature. So before peace and reconciliation can be made, two things must be removed—God's wrath, and our sinful nature : God must be pacified, and man converted. God's wrath is appeased by the blood of Christ, and our natures are changed and healed by the Spirit of grace. First, God's wrath is appeased, and then the Spirit is bestowed upon us; for while God is angry and offended, no saving benefit can be expected from him. This text speaks not how he took away our enmity, but how he appeased God for us, not so much of the application as the impetration of this benefit. The application is spoken of ver. 21, how it is applied to us, but here the apostle more directly speaks of the impetration, how it was procured and obtained for us— namely, by Christ's satisfying God's justice for that wrong which caused the breach, or the dying of the Son of God for a sinful world. Now this hath an influence on God's pardon and our conversion, for by virtue of this reconciliation we are justified and pardoned. Therefore, we are said to be justified by his blood, Rom. viii. 9, that is, the price is paid by Christ and accepted by God. There needeth nothing more to be done on the Mediator's part. By virtue of the same peace made we are also sanctified and converted unto God, 2 Cor. v. 18. The gift of the sanctifying Spirit is given us as the fruit of Christ's death.

2. How it was obtained—by the blood of his cross he made peace. This implieth death, and such a death as in appearance was accursed ; for the death of the cross is the vilest and most cruel death : Gal. iii. 13, ' Christ hath redeemed us from the curse of the law, being made accursed for us : for it is written, Cursed is every one that hangeth on a tree.' Now we must see the reasons of this course or way of reconciling the world, that we may not mistake God's design, nor be possessed with any imaginations which are derogatory to God's honour—as, suppose, if we should hence conceit that God is all wrath and justice, unwilling of himself to be reconciled to man, or that he delighteth in blood, and is hardly drawn to give out grace. Oh, no ! these are false misprisions and misrepresentations of God. Therefore let us a little inquire into the reasons why God took this way to reconcile all things to himself, and ordained Christ to bear the chastisement of our peace. I answer : That the justice of God might be eminently demonstrated, the lawgiver vindicated, and the breach that was made in the frame of government repaired ; and God manifested to be a hater of sin, and yet the sinner saved from destruction ; and that the love of God might be eminently and conspicuously discerned ; and our peace the better secured. As let us a little see these things more particularly. I begin—

[1.] With the holiness of God's nature, who is of purer eyes than to behold iniquity, Hab. i. 13,—that is, so as to approve of it, or altogether connive at it, so as to let it go without punishment or mark of his displeasure ; therefore some way must be found out to signify his purest holiness, and his hatred and detestation of sin, and that it should not be pardoned without some testimony of his displeasure against it. We are told God hateth the workers of iniquity, Ps. v. 5, and the righteous Lord loveth righteousness, Ps. xi. 7 ; and, therefore, when God was to grant his universal pardon he would not do it without this propitiatory atonement.

[2.] The honour of his governing justice was to be secured, and freed from any blemish, that the awe of God might be kept up in the world. In the mystery of our redemption we must not look upon God only as *pars læsa*, the wronged party ; but as *rector mundi*. God was to carry himself as the governor of the world. Now there is a difference between a private person and a governor—private persons may pass by offences as they please, but a governor must do right, and what conduces to the public good. There is a twofold notion that we have of public right, *justum est quod fieri debet*, and *justum est quod fieri potest.* That which ought to be done, or we are unjust; as for instance, to punish the righteous equally with the wicked, that Abraham pleadeth, Gen. xviii. 25, 'That be far from thee, to do after this manner, to slay the righteous with the wicked, and that the righteous should be as the wicked, that be far from thee. Shall not the judge of all the earth do right?' Not that Abraham mindeth God of his office, but he was confidently assured of the nature of God that he could not do otherwise. But now there is *justum quod fieri potest,* which if it be done, or if it be not done, the party is not unjust. The first part of justice is paying of debts; the second, exacting or requiring of debts. Now the Judge of the world doth all things wisely and righteously. The question is, therefore, whether God, passing by the offences of the world without any satisfaction required, doth deal justly? As a free Lord he may make what laws he pleases; but as a just Judge, with respect to the ends of government, he doth that which is for public good. The right of passing by a wrong, and the right of releasing a punishment, are different things; because punishment is a common interest, and is referred to a common good to preserve order and government, and for example to the future. The government of the world required it that God should stand on the satisfaction of Christ, and the submission of the sinner, that he may be owned and reverenced as the just and holy governor of the world. A valuable compensation is insisted on for this end: Rom. ii. 25, 26, 'Whom God hath set forth to be a propitiation through faith in his blood, to declare his righteousness for the remission of sins that are past, through the forbearance of God. To declare, I say, at this time his righteousness, that he might be just, and the justifier of him which believeth in Jesus.'

[3.] To keep up the authority of his law. God had made a former covenant, which was not to be quitted and wholly made void but upon valuable consideration; therefore if it be broken, and no more ado made about it, all respect and obedience to God would fall to the ground. The law may be considered either as to the precept or sanction. The authority of the precept is kept up by Christ's submission to the law, and living by the same rules we are bound to live by, and performing all manner of obedience to God; for it behoved him to fulfil all righteousness, Mat. iii. 15, being set up as a pattern of holiness in our nature, to which we are to be conformed. But that which is most considerable in this case is the sanction or penalty. If this should be relaxed, and no satisfaction required, it might leave upon God the blemish of levity, mutability, and inconstancy. The law was not given in jest, but in the greatest earnest that ever law was given; and so solemn a transaction was not constituted to no purpose, therefore God will not part with the law upon light terms: Gal. iv. 4, 5, 'When the fulness of time was come, God sent forth his Son made of a woman, made under the law, to redeem them that were under the law.' That men may know that it is a dangerous thing to transgress his law, and that they may fear and do no more presumptuously; partly that it might not foster in us hopes of impunity, which are very natural to us, Gen. iii. 5. The devil seeks to weaken the truth of God's threatenings, Deut. xxix. 19, 20. We are apt to look upon the threatenings of the law as a vain scarecrow ; therefore, for the terror and warning of sinners for the future, God would not release us from the punishment till our surety undertook our reconciliation with God by bearing the chastisement of our peace.

[4.] Christ's death was necessary to make sin odious, and obedience more acceptable to us.

(1.) Sin more odious or hateful—no other remedy would serve the turn to procure the pardon and destruction of it than the bloody death of the cross, Rom. viii. 3. Surely it is no small thing for which the Son of God must die. When you read or hear of Christ's sufferings, you should never think an extenuating and favourable thought of it more.

(2.) To commend obedience : for Christ's suffering death at the command of his Father was the noblest piece of service, and highest act of obedience that ever could or can be performed unto God. It is beyond anything that can be done by men or angels. There was in it so much love to man, so much self-denial, humility, and patience, so much resignation of himself to God, who had appointed him to be our Redeemer, that it cannot be paralleled. The great and most remarkable thing in Christ's death was obedience : Rom. v. 18 ; Phil. ii. 7, 8. God delighteth not in mere blood, but blood offered in obedience as the best way to impress upon man a sense of his duty, and to teach him to serve and please God at the dearest rate.

[5.] This death commendeth the love of God to us, for it is the great demonstration of it. Many draw a quite contrary conclusion, as if he were with much ado brought to have mercy on us ; but they forget that he is first and chief in the design : 2 Cor. v. 19, 'God was in Christ reconciling the world unto himself.' Christ came from heaven to declare to us the greatness of God's love. God thought nothing too dear for us—not the Son of his love, nor his death, ignominy, and shame : Rom. v. 8, God commendeth his love in that while we were yet sinners Christ died for us. When we had alienated our hearts from God, refused his service, and could expect nothing but the rigour of his law and vindictive justice, then he spared not his own Son to bring about this reconciliation for us.

[6.] As God is pacified, so it gives us hopes our business lieth not with a God offended, but with a God reconciled. If we had not to do with a pacified God, who could lift up his face to him, or think a comfortable thought of him ? But this gives us hope : Rom. v. 10, 'For if when we were enemies we were reconciled to God by the death of his Son, much more, being reconciled, we shall be saved by his life.' We were enemies by sin in us, which God hateth, and declareth his wrath against it in the law. Then by the satisfaction wrought by Christ we were restored to his favour, so far that free and easy conditions were procured in the gospel, and his Spirit is offered to prepare and fit us for a life of glory. We have heard what Christ hath done.

Thirdly, What assurance have we that this peace is obtained ?

Consciences are not easily settled, therefore some visible evidences are necessary that God is pacified. I shall name three or four:—

1. Christ's resurrection and ascension into glory. This shows that God was propitiated, and hath accepted the ransom that was given for souls. We read, Rom. iv. 25, that he died for our offences, and rose again for our justification. His dying noteth his satisfaction, his rising again the acceptance of it. God by raising him up from the dead showed that he had received the death of his Son as a sufficient ransom for our sins—for he died in the quality of a surety, and in that quality was raised up again. By his death he made the payment; by his resurrection the satisfaction of it was witnessed to the world—for then our surety was let out of prison: Isa. liii. 8, ' He shall be taken from prison and from judgment.' In his death he was in effect a prisoner, under the arrest of divine vengeance; but when he rose again he was discharged. Therefore there is great weight laid upon it as to our acquittance: Rom. viii. 34, ' Yea, rather, that is risen again, who is even at the right hand of God.' There is some special thing in his resurrection comparatively above his death which hath influence on our justification—that is, it was a visible evidence given to the world that enough was done for the expiation of sins, and to assure us of our deliverance if we be capable; and his ascension into glory doth further witness it. He being exalted to the greatest dignity, is able to defend and protect his people, and hath the advantage of interceding with his Father for the supply of all our wants.

2. The grant of the new covenant—which is therefore called the covenant of his peace: Isa. liv. 10, ' The covenant of my peace shall not be removed;' Ezek. xxxvii. 26, ' I will make a covenant of peace with them.' It is so called not only because thereby this peace and reconciliation is offered to us, but the terms are stated, and the conditions required are far more equitable, gracious, and commodious for us than the terms of the law covenant. Man, as a sinful creature, is obnoxious to God's wrath for the violation of the law of nature, and so might perish without remedy, and no impeachment to God's goodness can happen thereby. But when God will give bounds to his sovereignty over him, and enter into terms of covenant with him, and give him a bottom to stand upon, whereon to expect good things from him, upon the account of his faithfulness and righteousness—this is a condescension; and so far condescended in the first covenant, that after that man hath cast away the mercies of his creation, and his capacity to fulfil that covenant, this was mere mercy and grace. That God would enter into a second covenant, it is not from any mutableness in God, but from the merit and satisfaction of a Redeemer. Surely there must be some great and important cause to change, alter, and abrogate a covenant so solemnly made and established—to lay aside one covenant, and to enter into another, especially since the former was so holy, righteous, and equal, fit for God to give, and us, in the state we then were in, to receive. Now, what was the important reason? Christ came to salve God's honour in the first covenant, and to secure the ends of his government. Though a second covenant should be set up, the blood of his cross hath made this covenant everlasting, Heb. xiii. 20, and upon gracious terms doth convey great and precious privileges to us.

Thirdly, The pouring out of the Spirit, which certainly was the fruit and effect of Christ's death, and also an evidence of the worth and value of it. The apostle telleth us that Christ was 'made a curse for us, that the blessing of Abraham might come upon the Gentiles by faith in Jesus Christ.' And what blessing was that? The gift of the Spirit, Gal. v. 13, 14. And in another place, when he interpreteth the types of the law, he telleth us that the fathers ' did all eat of the same spiritual meat that we do, and did all drink of the same spiritual drink, for they drank of the rock that followed them, and that rock was Christ.' If the rock was Christ, the water that gushed out of the rock was the Spirit, often compared to waters in scripture, John iv. 14, vii. 38, 39 ; and the rock yielded not this water till it was smitten with the rod of Moses—a figure of the curses of the law. Christ was stricken and smitten of God, and so procured the Spirit for us : John vii. 39, ' The Holy Ghost was not yet given, for Jesus was not yet glorified ; that is, had not finished his passion, and the acceptance of it was not yet attested to the world, till he was advanced at the right hand of God, and then this effect declared it. The Spirit was given before, but more sparingly, because it was given upon trust, and with respect to the satisfaction that was afterwards to be made and accepted. And then it was witnessed to the world by a more copious and plentiful effusion of the Spirit. Therefore it is said : Acts ii. 33, ' Therefore Jesus being by the right hand of God exalted, and having received of the Father the promise of the Holy Ghost, he hath shed forth this, which ye now see and hear.' The merit and value of the sacrifice is thus visibly attested, therefore this is one of the witnesses : Acts v. 30-32, ' The God of our fathers raised up Jesus, whom ye slew and hanged on a tree. Him hath God exalted with his right hand to be a prince and a Saviour, for to give repentance to Israel, and remission of sins. And we are his witnesses of these things ; and so is also the Holy Ghost, whom God hath given to them that obey him.' And what was the evidence given to the church in general, is the evidence given also to every particular believer.

Fourthly, Some have obtained the effects and fruits of Christ's death ; this peace begun here hath been perfected in heaven. The text saith, ' He hath reconciled all things to himself, whether they be things in heaven, or things in earth.' Here many are pardoned and accepted with God, and have the comfort of it in their own souls. Others are gone home to God, and have the full of this peace. All were by nature children of wrath, under the curse as well as others. Now, if some in all generations have enjoyed the love, favour, and friendship of God in this world, and upon their departure out of it have entered into glory upon this account, it is evident that Christ is accepted to the ends for which God sent him—thus Abraham, the father of the faithful, and all the blessed souls who are gathered into his bosom, and are alive with God in heaven. Certain it is they were all sinners by nature, for there is no difference between any of the children of men, and yet God admits them into his peace. Was it a personal privilege peculiar to them only ? No ; the apostle tells us, Rom. iv. 23, ' It was not written for his sake alone ;' and Paul obtained mercy ' for them that should hereafter believe on Christ for life everlasting,'

1 Tim. i. 16.   Therefore all penitent believers may be assured that this sacrifice is sufficient, and will avail for their acceptance with God. We take it for a good token of a healing water when we see the crutches of cripples that had been cured.   All the blessed saints in heaven are witness to a sincere soul—they all obtained this blessed condition through the blood of his cross reconciling them to God. There is none in glory but had his pardon sealed through the blood of Christ.

4. How and upon what terms is it applied to us? for we have considered hitherto only how Christ hath made peace or made the atonement.   Yet if we receive not the atonement we may perish for ever for all that; besides the work done on the cross by Christ alone, there is a work to be done in our hearts; the work of making peace is sufficiently done by Christ, there needeth nothing to be added to it, no other ransom, nor sacrifice, nor propitiation.   Christ hath so fully satisfied divine justice, that he hath obtained the new covenant; but we are not actually admitted into this peace till we have personally accepted the covenant.   Now here it sticketh.   God hath been in Christ reconciling the world unto himself, there was the foundation laid; but, therefore, we pray you to be reconciled, 2 Cor. v. 20.   There is our title, claim, actual right, security.   But how do we receive this atonement? or how are we interested in it?   The conditions and terms are gracious, such as the nature of the business calleth for.   As to our entrance into this peace, no more is required but faith and repentance.   The gospel is offered to all; but the penitent believer, as being only capable, is possessed of it.

1. Faith is required; that we believe what the Son of God hath done and purchased for us: Rom. v. 1, ' Being justified by faith, we have peace with God through our Lord Jesus Christ.'   If we sincerely embrace the gospel, we are reconciled to God and accepted with him. The faith that justifieth is partly an assent to the truth of the Christian religion, especially the fundamental truth that Jesus is the Son of God and Saviour of the world; and partly an acceptance of Christ as God offers him, a serious, thankful, broken-hearted acceptance of Christ as your Lord and Saviour: serious, because of the weight of the business; broken-hearted, because of the condition of the person accepting, a self-condemning sinner, or one that hath an awakening sense of his sin and misery.   Thankful, because reconciliation with God and fruition of them in glory is so great a benefit: and you take him as Lord; for every knee must bow to Christ, he is a Saviour by merit and efficacy.   By his meritorious righteousness you obtain all benefits; by the efficacy of his Spirit you perform all duties.   The last thing is trust and dependence, Eph. i. 13.   Trust is such an expectation of the benefits offered by Christ, that forsaking all other things you entirely give up yourselves to the conduct of his word and Spirit.

2. The next thing is repentance, which is a turning from sin to God.   We turn from sin by hatred, and we turn to God by love.   We turn from sin by hatred; hatred of sin is the ground of all mortification. There is a twofold hatred—of abomination and of enmity.   We turn to God by love, which is the great principle to incline us to God, and is

the bottom of vivification or living to God. Now all this is necessary to actual peace, for our refreshing begins in conversion, Acts iii. 19. There is no peace allowed to the wicked ; we must take Christ's yoke, or we shall find no rest for our souls, Mat. xi. 29. We are not reconciled to God till our enmity be broken and overcome : then, of enemies, we become friends ; of strangers, intimates—then we are reconciled. This, then, is required of you; only let me add this caution, what is at first vows and purposes must be afterwards deeds and practices; and having engaged yourselves to God, to live to him, to keep yourselves from sin, and to follow after holiness, this must be your business all the days of your lives, for so you continue your peace and interest in God : Gal. vi. 16, ' And as many as walk according to this rule, peace be on them, and mercy, and on the Israel of God.'

Use 1. To exhort you to enter into this peace, that you may be partakers of the fruit of Christ's blood, and the virtue of his cross may be effectual in you.

[1.] Let me reason, *a periculo*, from the danger. Consider what it is to be at odds with God, and how soon and how easily he can revenge his quarrel against you, and how miserable they will be for ever that are not found of him in a state of peace : Ps. vii. 11–13, ' God is angry with the wicked every day. If he turn not, he will whet his sword ; he hath bent his bow, and will make his arrows ready.' There the psalmist representeth God and man as in a state of hostility against each other. The wicked man affronts his holiness, questions his justice, slights his wrath, breaks his laws, wrongeth his people, and saith, Tush! I shall have peace though I add drunkenness to thirst. God for a while giveth time and warning ; but every moment can break in upon us, for he is able easily to deal with us, *comminus*, hand to hand, for he hath his sword ; *eminus*, at a distance, for he hath his bow. He is not only able to deal with them, but ready, for he is whetting his sword and hath bent his bow, the arrow is upon the string, though not as yet sent or shot out. What remedy, then, is there ? There is but one exception : ' if he turn not.' If he be not reduced and brought home to God by a timely repentance, he falleth into the hands of the living God. Now, no persons are in so dangerous an estate as those that have peace offered and despise it : Isa. xxvii. 4, ' Let him take hold of my strength ; ' when God is ready to strike. A man that is fallen into the power of his enemy will take hold of his arm. We are always in God's power, his vengeance may surprise us before we are aware. What is our business, but to be found of him in peace ?

[2.] *Ab utili*, from the happiness of being at peace with God. Your great work is over, and you have a world of benefit by it—you stop all danger at the fountain-head. When you are at peace with God, you are at peace with the creatures : Ezek. xxxiv. 25, ' I will make with them a covenant of peace, and will cause the evil beasts to cease out of the land. Danger might waylay us at every turn. Then for men : Prov. x. 17, ' When a man's ways please the Lord, he makes his enemies to be at peace with him.' Then peace in your own consciences : Rom. xv. 13, ' Now the God of hope fill you with joy and peace in believing.' To have a man's conscience settled on sound terms is a great mercy. Peace with the holy angels ; instead of being instruments of vengeance, they are ' ministering spirits,' Heb. i. 14. Lastly, Communion with God himself: Rom. v. 1, 2, ' Therefore being justified by faith, we have peace with God through our Lord Jesus Christ: by whom also we have access by faith,' &c.; Eph. ii. 17, 18, ' Preaching peace, by whom also we have access by one Spirit unto the Father.'

[3.] I reason from the confidence we may have of this benefit if we submit to godly terms.

1. God is willing to give it: ver. 19, ' It pleased the Father that in him all fulness should dwell.' There is God's authority and good pleasure in it. The first motive came from God, who received the wrong, not from him that gave it. God was in Christ, 2 Cor. v. 14. Among men, the inferior should seek to the superior, the party offending to the party offended, the weaker to the stronger, they that need the reconciliation, to him that needeth it not; but here all is contrary.

2. You may be confident of it upon another ground, the sufficiency of Christ to procure all fulness. The whole divine nature did inhabit and reside in the man Christ Jesus, and so he is completely fitted and furnished for this work. He hath paid a full price for this peace when he bare our sins and carried our sorrows; and by his Spirit he changes our hearts as well as pacifies the wrath of God. And then he preserveth this peace by his constant intercession, Heb. ii. 17, 18. Now, shall we doubt of it but that we may get it?

[1.] Let us take the way of entrance by faith and repentance. It concerns us much to see whether we be in peace or trouble: if in trouble, you see the cure; if in peace, the next question is, is it God's peace? That is had by the blood of Christ, the merit of which we must depend upon, and devote ourselves to God, break off our old league with sin, and bind ourselves with a bond to live unto God, to be the Lord's for evermore.

[2.] When this peace is made, be very tender of it, that no breach fall out between you and God: Ps. lxxxv. 8, ' He will speak peace to his people, and to his saints: but let not them turn again to folly.'

[3.] Let us be thankful to God for this fruit of Christ's death; it is an act of free and undeserved mercy, and to be imputed to nothing but his mere grace that God hath appointed such a way: ' It pleased the Father to bruise him,' Isa. liii. 9. That he sendeth ambassadors to publish it: Acts x. 36, ' The word which God sent unto the children of Israel, preaching peace by Jesus Christ (he is Lord of all): ' and that he appointeth a ministry. It is a great privilege in itself; for by this peace we have not only the beginnings but the increase of grace till all be perfected in heaven: Heb. xiii. 20, 21, ' Now the God of peace, that brought again from the dead our Lord Jesus, make you perfect in every good work to do his will, working in you that which is well pleasing in his sight.' 1 Thes. i. 23, ' The God of peace sanctify you, that you may be preserved blameless unto the coming of our Lord Jesus Christ.' This peace doth encourage us in all temptations from the devil: Rom. xvi. 20, ' The God of peace shall bruise Satan under your feet shortly.' From the world: Eph. vi. 15, ' Shod with the preparation of the gospel of peace.' Fears of the wrath of

God, and doubts about our eternal condition: Rom. xiv. 17, 'The kingdom of God is not meat and drink, but righteousness, peace, and joy in the Holy Ghost.' Here are three words—*comfort, peace,* and *joy.* These succeed one another as so many degrees: comfort is support under trouble, peace a ceasing from trouble, joy a lively sense of the love of God.

THE END OF VOL. I.